CONCEPTUALIZING
AND MEASURING
FATHER INVOLVEMENT

CONCEPTUALIZING AND MEASURING FATHER INVOLVEMENT

Edited by

Randal D. Day
Brigham Young University

Michael E. Lamb
National Institute of Child Health and Human Development

LEA
2004

LAWRENCE ERLBAUM ASSOCIATES, PUBLISHERS
Mahwah, New Jersey   London

Editor: Bill Webber
Editorial Assistant: Kristin Duch
Cover Designer: Kathryn Houghtaling Lacey
Textbook Production Manager: Paul Smolenski
Full Service Compositor: TechBooks
Text and Cover Printer: Sheridan Books, Inc.

This book was typeset in 10/12 pt. Times Roman, Bold, and Italic.
The heads were typeset in Americana, Americana Bold, and Americana Bold Italic

Copyright © 2004 by Lawrence Erlbaum Associates, Inc.
All rights reserved. No part of this book may be reproduced in
any form, by photostat, microfilm, retrieval system, or any
other means, without prior written permission of the publisher.

Lawrence Erlbaum Associates, Inc., Publishers
10 Industrial Avenue
Mahwah, New Jersey 07430
www.erlbaum.com

Library of Congress Cataloging-in-Publication Data

Conceptualizing and measuring father involvement / edited by
    Randal D. Day, Michael E. Lamb.
       p.   cm.
     "Result of an invited conference of scholars"—Introd.
     Includes bibliographical references.
     ISBN 0-8058-4359-0 (casebound : alk. paper)
     1. Fathers—Research—Congresses.   2. Father and child—Research—Congresses.
   3. Family—Research—Congresses.   4. Family assessment—Congresses.
   I. Day, Randal D., 1948–   II. Lamb, Michael E., 1953–

   HQ756.C66   2003
   306.874′2—dc21   2003001718

Books published by Lawrence Erlbaum Associates are printed on
acid-free paper, and their bindings are chosen for strength and
durability.

Printed in the United States of America
10 9 8 7 6 5 4 3 2 1

For my family that teaches, loves, cares, and believes in me.

Randal D. Day

Amen.

Michael E. Lamb

Contents

Foreword *ix*

Acknowledgments *xv*

Contributors *xvii*

1 Conceptualizing and Measuring Father Involvement: Pathways, Problems, and Progress   1
Randal D. Day and Michael E. Lamb

2 Assessing Father Involvement in Mexican-American Families   17
Ross D. Parke, Scott Coltrane, Sharon Borthwick-Duffy, Justina Powers, Michele Adams, William Fabricius, Sandford Braver, and Delia Saenz

3 Father Involvement in Britain: The Research and Policy Evidence   39
Lynda Clarke and Margaret O'Brien

4 Studying Fathering Trajectories: In-depth Interviewing and Sensitizing Concepts   61
William Marsiglio

5 A Narrative Approach to Paternal Identity: The Importance of Parental Identity: "Conjointness"   83
Joseph H. Pleck and Jeffrey L. Stueve

6 A Narrative Approach to Exploring Responsible Involvement of Fathers with Their Special-Needs Children   109
David C. Dollahite

7 Internal Reliability, Temporal Stability, and Correlates of Individual Differences in Paternal Involvement: A 15-Year Longitudinal Study in Sweden   129
Susan S. Chuang, Michael E. Lamb, and C. Philip Hwang

8 A Multimethod Study of Father Participation in Family-Based Programming   149
Stephen Gavazzi and Angie Schock

viii   CONTENTS

9 Fathering in a Beijing, Chinese Sample: Associations with Boys'
       and Girls' Negative Emotionality and Aggression   185
       Chongming Yang, Craig H. Hart, David A. Nelson, Christin L.
       Porter, Susanne F. Olsen, Clyde C. Robinson, and Shenghua Jin

10 Measuring Father Involvement in Divorced, Nonresident Fathers   217
       Kay Pasley and Sanford L. Braver

11 Early Father Involvement in Fragile Families   241
       Marcia J. Carlson and Sara S. McLanahan

12 Youth Ratings of Family Processes and Father Role Performance
       of Resident and Nonresident Fathers   273
       Randal D. Day and Alan Acock

13 Father Involvement and the Diversity of Family Context   293
       Kathleen Mullan Harris and Suzanne Ryan

14 Multiple Determinants of Father Involvement: An Exploratory
       Analysis Using the PSID-CDS Data Set   321
       Brent A. McBride, Sarah J. Schoppe, Moon-Ho Ho
       and Thomas R. Rane

15 Measuring Mother and Father Shared Caregiving: An
       Analysis Using the Panel Study of Income
       Dynamics–Child Development Supplement   341
       Allison Sidle Fuligni and Jeanne Brooks-Gunn

16 Violent Men, Bad Dads? Fathering Profiles of Men Involved
       in Intimate Partner Violence   359
       Greer Litton Fox and Michael L. Benson

17 Fathering Indicators for Practice and Evaluation: The Fathering
       Indicators Framework   385
       Vivian L. Gadsden, Jay Fagan, Aisha Ray, and James E. Davis

18 The DADS Initiative: Measuring Father Involvement
       in Large-Scale Surveys   417
       Natasha Cabrera, Kristin Moore, Jacinta Bronte-Tinkew, Tamara
       Halle, Jerry West, Jean Brooks-Gunn, Nancy Reichman, Julien
       Teitler, Kirsten Ellingsen, Christine W. Nord, and Kimberly Boller

Author Index   453
Subject Index   465

Foreword

In 1993, the National Institute of Child Health and Human Development (NICHD) formed the NICHD Family and Child Well-Being Research Network (Network). The Network was formed to address (1) the frustration within public policy circles that basic information relating to family and child well-being was filled with gaps and analyzed in an uneven manner and (2) the concern within the research community that family and child research was spread among a large number of disciplines so diverse in their research approaches that communication across fields was difficult. The Network was conceptualized as a systematic effort to both understand the relationship of family and child well-being from a multidisciplinary point of view and address public policy concerns in a comprehensive and responsive manner.

The members of the Network all identified father involvement and its effect on children as an area that needed interdisciplinary attention, and the Network initiated a fatherhood working group as one of its first collaborative topics. The Network tried to involve as many people as possible, and it reached out to Randy Day and Michael Lamb as part of its effort to stimulate research on the effects of father involvement on families and children. The Network activities regarding fatherhood attracted the attention of the public policy community, and in 1996 the federal government undertook a comprehensive evaluation of policy, practice, and information concerning fatherhood. It was my pleasure to cochair a committee that examined the status of our research and information about fathers and their effects on children and families. I was in a good position to participate in a very active research enterprise focused on the effects of father involvement at the same time that the entire government was engaged in an evaluation of how to improve our research base on fathers. In addition, the collective effort persuaded NICHD to take extraordinary steps to promote fatherhood research, and these efforts continue today.

The Network was designed to support research and research-related activities necessary to make research results accessible for public policy purposes. It engaged in research with the Federal Interagency Forum for Child and Family Statistics (Forum) and its component agencies to improve and balance the information base about families and children. In the process, it helped create a series of indicators about child and family well-being that has been designated by a

ix

Presidential Executive Order to be an official yardstick of child well-being. The Network also sponsored a number of papers and conferences that supported the federal fatherhood initiative, which, in turn, has greatly improved the information base regarding the family behavior of men. A by-product of the research program on fathers has been the planned or actual enhancement of several important data sets with respect to male behavior. In addition, it partnered with the Forum to create the fatherhood indicators project. The Network and Forum produced a report entitled, *Charting Parenthood: A Statistical Portrait of Fathers and Mothers in America*, which is available from one of the Network institutions, Child Trends, Inc. It is the first attempt to compare the status of mothers and fathers across a broad spectrum of statuses and behaviors.

This volume results from the interplay of scientific and public interest generated by the aforementioned activities. In this, I foreword, examine what we have learned about father involvement and what issues we must confront in order to make further progress. I also address why we held the conference that gave rise to the papers in this volume and why the search for better conceptualization and measurement must continue.

What is wrong with the way that we measured father involvement in the past? The short answer is that father involvement was never really measured at all. Across all fields of relevant science, family process was measured by mother–child interaction, family systems analysis, or some other global measure of family process. No attention was given to father–child interaction because there was no evidence that father involvement was important in explaining child well-being or development. We thought that the most important thing a father could do was to support the mother and that mothers could provide whatever information we needed about, that support. In addition, it was too difficult and too expensive to include fathers in research designs. As a result, we were left with a heritage that predicated research on family structure, in which fathers were noted primarily by their absence; on mother–child interaction, on which fathers had some vague indirect influence; or on a family system, in which fathers were studied but scant attention was paid to child well-being or development. We had plenty of information about mother-headed households and mother–child interaction and clinical information about individual participation in family systems and outcomes for families. We had relatively little information on father involvement with their children and the impact of that involvement on children. We had almost nothing on the influence of public policy related to fathering and its effect on children.

The conventional wisdom that father involvement did not matter to children did not survive honest scrutiny. The field came to realize that when we actually asked the question of what difference father involvement made to outcomes of interest in their children, fathers did indeed matter. However, such research was forced to use measurement schemes that were not really constructed to tackle the problem of father involvement. Nevertheless, when we could cobble together a construct on father involvement, it usually added something important to our understanding

FOREWORD   xi

about child well-being and development. For example, the National Center for Educational Statistics (NCES) commissioned an analysis of their educational data and found that an involved father contributed positively to his children's academic achievement even when controlling for the mother's contribution. This analysis came about because my good friend Jerry West at NCES complained to me that out workshops did not include many educational researchers. I pointed out that there was a dearth of activity among educational researchers on father involvement. Jerry took action to remedy the situation and his efforts produced compelling findings that fathers do matter in regard to their children's academic achievement no matter what their circumstances. Father involvement is now a recognized priority in educational research.

New research strategies were formulated to include father involvement in studies of child well-being and development. One strategy focused on asking identical questions of both mother and father regarding involvement with their children. This approach assumed that mothers and fathers were capable of involving themselves with their children in similar ways and that it was the relative emphasis that each parent placed on various activities that mattered to children. The strategy also implied that both parents would be respondents in a study. New studies such as the national evaluation of Early Head Start, the Fragile Families Study, and the early Childhood Longitudinal Study–Birth Cohort have been fielded using this strategy. To make this approach work, fatherhood had to be conceptualized and related to motherhood. Existing research paradigms had to be incorporated into each of these studies, and we resolved to optimize the research opportunities presented by these new studies by ensuring that there were as many fathering commonalities among these studies as possible. The Developing a Daddy Survey (DADS) project was launched to accomplish this task. A happy consequence of the DADS project is that the aforementioned projects used compatible instrumentation in the studies. During the foreseeable future we should be able to greatly expand our knowledge of the effects of public policy on father involvement and the resulting effects on children.

In spite of these encouraging new developments, a fundamental problem remains. We have based our understanding of parental effects on children on a mother–child interaction paradigm. We now include fathers in the paradigm, but we have really only enlarged the parental paradigm to make it symmetric with respect to mother and father. What we observed in the mother's behavior we now also look for in the the father's. Although this is a logical first step toward understanding father involvement and has the virtue of producing a symmetrical parenting template that is easy to administer in survey research, does this strategy really capture all the ways that fathers are involved with their children? Is it sufficient to take a well-understood template used to study mother–child interaction and broaden it to include father–child interaction in the same manner? For me, the answer is NO.

The NICHD Network has often debated this problem. I have come to several conclusions as a result of these spirited debates. First, it is probably a mistake to

think that fathers want to be surrogate moms. Modern, well-educated fathers may very well want to experience the rich interpersonal relationships with their children that mother's have traditionally enjoyed but they want these interactions on their own terms. Such fathers are still numerically small and men are just beginning to develop accepted behavioral patterns that would enable the desired interactions. Most men still aspire to traditional behavior patterns, and this is particularly true of low socioeconomic status minority fathers. Second, a traditional pattern of fathering involves a specialization of parenting behavior in the family system. A symmetrical expansion of the parental template will do a wonderful job of covering the mother-like behaviors, but it will likely miss father-specialty behaviors. Third, we do not really know if father-specialty behaviors exist or what they are. Folk wisdom would indicate that a father's role is to provide economic support, protect the family from outside threats, and prepare the child to assume adult roles in the world. I believe that the symmetrical parenting template misses some aspects of these roles especially in the protection and preparation domains. The conference on father involvement and measurement arose out of these concerns, and the papers in this volume address the task of finding the missing pieces of the fatherhood construct that would work for new age as well as traditional and minority fathers.

Where might we look for missing pieces to the father construct and do some of these missing pieces create a "symbolic involvement" effect? Consider the following situation. Picture a living room in an American household. In it, mother interacts with a toddler. She gives the child a toy and helps him play with it. She then instructs the child in putting the toy away and supervises the child's compliance making sure that the child does not hurt himself in the process. Then mother leaves the room and father enters. He sits in a chair and turns on the TV. He watches out of the corner of his eye while the child takes out multiple toys and plays with them. He does not intervene in the choice of toy but encourages the child to play and he does not give admonishments regarding safety. How would we characterize parental involvement in this situation? I think that the overwhelming tendency of researchers would be to characterize mother as highly involved and father as not. But can we really interpret this situation without knowing something about the family system underlying this situation? Moreover, can father's decision not to put as many limits on the child's behavior as mother did be a form of involvement? To characterize father's behavior as involved in a positive way, one might have to know that the parents have established a family system that puts father at a greater emotional distance than mother. Indeed, the lack of active supervision might be a symbolic form of interaction that might have enormous long-run implications for the child's development that are different than those attendant to mother's actions. Indeed the fact that father is sitting in the living room and is not away on business or living in another household might also constitute involvement of the sort not really captured in conventional research designs.

Let's assume that I have convinced you that there are missing pieces to the fatherhood construct. Let's also assume that you are convinced that part of the

FOREWORD

reason that the construct is wanting is because there is a discontinuity among social science research (with its preoccupation with family structure and decision mechanics), family science (with its preoccupation with family systems), and developmental psychology (with its preoccupation with dyadic behavior). Suppose that led you to ask the question: How do family structure and family systems orientation influence father involvement and its impact on children? Then you are driven to do as Randy Day and Michael Lamb have done and produce this volume.

The reader will find that the volume contains articles from many of the major influences on the Network and the federal fatherhood initiative. The scope of the discussion combines topics of interest to basic researchers and public policy analysts. This is as it should be because these considerations have motivated the rather considerable progress that the field has enjoyed over the last decade. All these ideas should be considered with the understanding that we all are trying to find pieces of the fatherhood construct that we believe have been overlooked and in so doing to connect the research fields that have failed so far to find ways of relating to each other. The discussions within the Network have often ended in frustration and disappointment. Much praise goes to Randy and Michael for organizing an attempt to search for new ways of performing fatherhood research.

—V. Jeffery Evans
National Institute of Child
Health and Human Development

Acknowledgments

This project stems from a series of workshops and publications sponsored by the National Institute of Child Health and Development (NICHD) working through the NICHD's Family and Child Well-Being Network. In particular, Natasha Cabrera and V. Jeffery Evans played significant roles in bringing this project to fruition. Additionally, we thank the National Center on Fathers and Families (NCOFF) for its support. NCOFF has been a key player in the development of the conference from which this collection of papers emerged. Also, we thank the Family Studies Center at Brigham Young University for funding assistance. Through the generous contributions of funds, staff, and encouragement from all three of these agencies, this project was made possible.

Contributors

Alan Acock
Department of Human Development
and Family Services
Oregon State University
Corvallis, OR

Michele Adams
Center for Family Studies
University of California, Riverside
Riverside, CA

Michael L. Benson
Division of Criminal Justice
University of Cincinnati
Cincinnati, OH

Kimberly Boller
Mathematica Policy Research, Inc.
Princeton, NJ

Sharon Borthwick-Duffy
Graduate School of Education
University of California, Riverside
Riverside, CA

Jacinta Bronte-Tinkew
Child Trends, Inc.
Washington, DC

Jeanne Brooks-Gunn
Child Development and Education
Teachers College
Columbia University

Marcia J. Carlson
Columbia University School of Social
Work
Columbia University
New York, NY

Lynda Clarke
London School of Hygiene and
Tropical Medicine
London, UK

Scott Coltrane
Deparment of Sociology
University of California, Riverside
Riverside, CA

James Davis
Department of Educational Leadership
and Policy Studies
Temple University
Philadelphia, PA

Randal D. Day
School of Family Life
Brigham Young University

David C. Dollahite
Marriage, Family & Human
Development Program
Brigham Young University
Provo, Utah

xvii

CONTRIBUTORS

Kirsten Ellingsen
WESTAT
Rockville, MD

V. Jeffery Evans
Demographic and Behavioral Sciences
  Branch, NICHD
Bethesda, MD

Jay Fagen
School of Social Work
Temple University
Philadelphia, PA

William Fabricisus
Arizona State University
Tempe, AZ

Greer Litton Fox
Department of Child and Family
  Studies
University of Tennessee
Knoxville, TN

Allison Sidle Fuligni
Center for Improving Child Care
  Quality
UCLA Graduate School of Education
  and Information Science
Los Angeles, CA

Vivian Gadsden
National Center on Fathers and
  Families
Graduate School of Education
University of Pennsylvania
Philadelphia, PA

Stephen M. Gavazzi
Ohio State University
Columbus, OH

Tamara Halle
Child Trends, Inc.
Washington, DC

Kathleen Mullan Harris
Department of Sociology
The University of North Carolina
Chapel Hill, NC

Craig H. Hart
School of Family Life
Brigham Young University
Provo, UT

Moon Ho-Ho
Department of Psychology
University of Illinois at
  Urbana/Champaign
Urbana, IL

Carl-Philip Hwang
Department of Psychology
University of Goteborg
Goteborg, Sweden

Shenghua Jin
Department of Psychology
Beijing Normal University
Beijing, China

Michael E. Lamb
Section on Social and Emotional
  Development
National Institute of Child Health and
  Human Development
Bethesda, MD

William Marsiglio
Department of Sociology
University of Florida
Gainsville, FL

CONTRIBUTORS

Brent A. McBride
Department of Human and
  Community Development
University of Illinois at
  Urbana/Champaign
Urbana, IL

Sara S. McLanahan
Woodrow Wilson School
Princeton University
Princeton, NJ

Kristin Moore
Child Trends, Inc.
Washington, DC

David A. Nelson
School of Family Life
Brigham Young University
Provo, UT

Christine W. Nord
WESTAT
Rockville, MD

Susanne F. Olsen
School of Family Life
Brigham Young University
Provo, UT

Ross D. Parke
University of California at Riverside
Riverside, CA

Kay Pasley
School of Human Environmental
  Sciences
University of North Carolina at
  Greensboro
Greensboro, NC

Joseph H. Pleck
Department of Human and Community
University of Illinois
Urbana, IL

Justina Powers
Center for Family Studies
University of California, Riverside
Riverside, CA

Thomas R. Rane
Department of Human Development
Washington State University
Pullman, WA

Aisha Ray
The Erickson Institute for Advanced
  Study in Child Development
Chicago, IL

Nancy Reichman
Columbia School of Social Work
Columbia University
New York, NY

Clyde C. Robinson
School of Family Life
Brigham Young University
Provo, UT

Suzanne Ryan
Department of Sociology and the
  Carolina Population Center
University of North Carolina at Chapel
  Hill
Chapel Hill, NC

Delia Saenz
Department of Clinical Psychology
Arizona State University
Tempe, AZ

Angie M. Schock.
Department of Family Environmental
  Sciences
California State University, Northridge
Northridge, CA

Sarah J. Schoppe
Department of Psychology
University of Illinois at
  Urbana/Champaign
Urbana, IL

Jeffyre L. Stueve
Family Studies Program
University of New Mexico
Albuquerque, NM

Julien Teitler
Columbia School of Social Work
Columbia University
New York, NY

Jerry West
Early Childhood Studies Program
National Center for Education
  Statistics
Washington, DC

Chongming Yang
Marriage, Family, and Human
  Development
School of Family Life
Brigham Young University
Provo, UT

CONCEPTUALIZING
AND MEASURING
FATHER INVOLVEMENT

1

Conceptualizing and Measuring Father Involvement: Pathways, Problems, and Progress

Randal D. Day
Brigham Young University

Michael E. Lamb
National Institute of Child Health and Human Development

This volume is the result of an invited conference of scholars studying father involvement (see Foreword) who were asked to reflect on the conceptualization and measurement of father involvement within the academic and policymaking communities. Our central motivation for organizing this workshop and the resulting volume was a belief that family scholars and policymakers could enhance their insight and impact, respectively, if they achieved greater conceptual clarity and developed more refined measures of men's roles in family life.

By design, we brought together a broad multidisciplinary group. Represented at the conference were scholars from the disciplines of child development, family studies, sociology, demography, psychology, anthropology, and economics. Researchers who examine extensive national data sets as well as those who analyze smaller but more intensive ethnographic data sets or employ observational data collection techniques were all encouraged to share their work and ideas. As a result, the chapters in this volume sharpen our collective focus while setting an agenda for future research on the important and changing roles of men in families.

CONCEPTUALIZING FATHERHOOD

A few organizing ideas frequently surfaced during the conference and subsequent writing process. Those ideas helped to structure and organize many of the chapters that follow and thus merit articulation at this point. Most importantly, it is clear that how we conceptualize and assess father involvement reflects historical and social trends which, in turn, shape men's beliefs about their family identities as well as other family members' beliefs and views about men's roles in family life. As a result, those beliefs that influence behavior within the family, as well as assessments of men's activities and attitudes about those activities, constitute something of a moving target. In other words, at least from a research viewpoint, understanding men in families involves a dynamic process in which research agendas need to change as the protean nature of family life changes.

Not only have the cultural definitions of manhood and fatherhood shifted historically, but so too have men's identities and their self-definitions of performance and fulfillment within their families changed over time (Pleck & Pleck, 1997). Furthermore, as we enter this new millennium, men's identities within their families seem generally less certain than ever before, and researchers and opinion makers are discussing and questioning the roles men play in families to an unprecedented extent. Much of this public discourse is driven by the growing awareness that men's involvement in their families can directly and indirectly affect the economic, physical, and psychological well-being of children. The authors of several chapters in this volume address the idea that family members (fathers in particular) create meaning within the context of their family activities. In several places, contributors focus on what it means to be involved, and how those meanings, morals, and ideals are transmitted from one generation to the next.

Most researchers, policymakers, and practitioners believe that when fathers are actively involved in family life (Doherty, 1997), family members are more likely to achieve their individual and family goals (Day, Gavazzi, & Acock, 2001). Although men can and do play special roles in family life, we do not subscribe to the notion that men's influence in family life is "essential" and irreplaceable *per se* (see Silverstein & Auerbach, 1999, for a discussion of this idea). Instead, the scholars represented in this volume align with those researchers and practitioners who suggest that men's behavior can powerfully affect the lives of others within the family units to which they belong. Within the subculture of the family, fathers play a key role in shaping the creation and communication of these practices and shared familial understandings. Therefore, we suggest that father involvement (like maternal involvement) is a compelling family process (Day et al., 2001) that helps us understand the inner workings of families and advances our insights about "relationship science" (Gottman, Levenson, & Woodin, 2002).

Several of the contributors also speak directly to the idea that broad political, economic, and social changes have effected significant changes in the inner life of family units and that the dynamics of *how* men interact with their spouses/partners,

1. PATHWAYS, PROBLEMS, AND PROGRESS 3

former spouses/partners, children, and other family members must be explored in our quest to understand family life. These forces include changes in political ideology, cultural trends, and economic functioning. For example, economic changes have influenced the ways in which families organize their daily lives and how they cope with short-term changes of fortune as they encounter times of economic plenty or restriction, whether of national or individual origin.

Additionally, shifts in economic fortunes have realigned the intersection of men's and women's roles. When families were locked into economic production as a means of survival, cooperation and interdependence were essential. As Americans continue to embrace economic and psychological independence, the interdependence and necessity for cooperation are no longer necessary.

Rather dramatic shifts in family structure that have occurred over the last several decades have also attracted the attention of researchers, policymakers, and contributors to this book. In particular, the high rates of divorce, remarriage, and births to single mothers have all significantly affected our ideas about men in families, their expressed and understood responsibilities, and even their access to children.

Many contributors are also concerned with the effects of international and national political climates on men and, consequently, on their families. Two examples of the impact of global political events on family life are the century of war we just experienced and the war on terrorism currently being waged following the events of September 11, 2001. Millions of men, in a multitude of countries, and for years at a time were (and are) temporarily (or permanently) separated from their families because of war, threat of war, or the aftermath of conflict. At the national level, political decisions, such as the government policies and rules attendant to various welfare initiatives, have moved men away from or toward other family members.

As the role and texture of men's lives change, federal and state governments have become more aware of the need to understand better what men do in their families. They have begun to realize the value of understanding how men contribute to family life because that contribution, in the final analysis, influences family economics and thus broad government policy. For example, policymakers know that it is critical to understand men's economic roles in the family if they are to reduce welfare dependency.

Men's ability and/or motivations to become and remain involved in family life, especially when children are involved, are often a function of economic conditions and cultural expectations. These conditions, expectations, and climates have shifted, changed, and oscillated dramatically during the last 350 years of American/Western history. For example, the shift from a self-sustaining, small-farm, agricultural economic structure to one that has evolved into first industrial, then technological, and now informational economic systems dramatically influenced the relationships among family members. In previous times, men wielded substantial economic power as they directed their resources to specific family members upon their death. In contemporary American society, by contrast, farm families struggle to encourage children to remain on the farm (Keating & Munro, 1989).

Such changes in economic well-being have shifted men's primary role from one of authority (i.e., control of land, resources, and production) to one of both economic support (in a more general way) and affection and emotional support (in a much more child-specific way) (Greven, 1970).

Any conceptualization and/or measurement of men in family life forces us to examine their power, control, and influence. By definition, power is linked to the control of resources, and most fathers have typically had such control (Mintz, 1998). The connection between financial and social capital as the basis of men's power within family life has received considerable attention (Furstenberg, 1998; Furstenberg & Hughes, 1995), and those connections are mentioned several times in the chapters that follow. Several authors observe that men create social capital within the family context, consider how that capital is or can be distributed, and evaluate whether family members are willing to receive transfers of social and financial capital from fathers.

The cultural redefinition of fatherhood has also forced researchers to measure how power is formed and ultimately employed in families when men are restrained from using physical force. Several contributors illuminate how men can and do choose to be powerful forces for good within their families. Clearly, the source of influence with regard to economic well-being has changed but not vanished.

Overall, contemporary perspectives on fatherhood clearly underscore that the roles that fathers play in the lives of their own, their partners', and their ex-partners' children as well as the lives of their partners and ex-partners are not only complexly multifaceted but also continuously shaped by a panoply of changing economic, ideological, sociological, and cultural factors and circumstances. The roles, their impact, and the factors that shape them are all explored in the chapters that follow.

CONCEPTUALIZING, MEASURING, AND ASSESSING FATHER INVOLVEMENT

Variations in men's contribution to family life were not systematically studied until the last half—and especially the last 25 years—of the twentieth century (Lamb, 1997). Within the most recent decade, however, this line of inquiry has blossomed and various researchers and practitioners have become interested in men's lives within families, particularly the intensity of their involvement. For example, researchers have sought to define and assess the extent of men's contributions to their families, whether and how the time that men and women spend in household duties and child care should or can be equalized, and how variations in men's family commitments affect women's ability to realize their personal potential in extrafamilial settings. Other researchers have searched for linkages between father involvement and child outcomes, while social commentators such as David Popenoe (1996) have begun to see the analysis of men's roles in families as a

1. PATHWAYS, PROBLEMS, AND PROGRESS

leverage point for specific agendas that are simultaneously ideological, political, and economic. The professional landscape today is dotted with scholars and commentators focused on men's lives, their interactions with women and children, and the distributive resource equality within the family and with clarion calls for more and better involvement with children. In this section, we briefly describe three of the most popular approaches to the study of father involvement and its impact.

The Binary Approach

Those who study men in families have taken a variety of approaches. At the end of World War II, for example, a few child psychologists began to wonder about the effects of men's long-term absence on the psychological well-being of their children. Lois Stolz (1954) authored a book entitled *Father Relations of War-Born Children* in which she described a study of families in which the fathers were armed participants in World War II and were thus absent during the first year (at least) following the birth of the target children. Stolz used interviews with the fathers and mothers as a starting point and coded the children's behavior during projective play evaluations. The responses of the father-absent children were compared with those of children in a control group, thereby providing an early example of the "binary" approach to the study of paternal influences in which conclusions about paternal roles and influences are determined by comparing the status of children raised with and without resident fathers (Lamb, 2000). Stolz' work represents an important conceptual starting point because it is one of the few early studies in which fathers were not blamed for their absence. The geopolitical climate justified their absence, although it was still considered a significant event in the children's lives.

Conceptually, Stolz' research approach was simple: She considered whether fathers (including stepfathers, adoptive fathers, or live-in partners) were present in the children's lives. In addition, with very few exceptions, what fathers did within the home was rarely examined. As Biller (1974) later declared, "In our society, men have been judged to be good fathers if they provide for their family economically, but the quality of father–child interactions has not been given enough attention" (p. 3). Indeed, Stolz was hesitant to speculate what fathers might contribute to their children's overall well-being: The positive contribution made by their presence was simply assumed. Stolz mentioned the benefits of role identification, bread-winning, and family stability, but she did not explore the mechanisms of influence.

The binary approach to research remained popular into the 1970s (Lamb, 2000), although the reasons for paternal absence changed over time from war-related service to divorce; policymakers and politicians began to express concern about the rise in teen problem behaviors in the late 1950s and early 1960s. Driven by psychoanalytic thinking, much of the research until the late 1970s reflected the notion that men's absence affected children's sex role development, parental attachments, and psychological adjustment. In one of the first books written about men in families,

6   DAY AND LAMB

for example, Biller (1974) proposed that "paternal deprivation, including patterns of inadequate fathering as well as father absence, is a highly significant factor in the development of serious psychological and social problems" (p. 1). Biller further argued that "paternal deprivation is a term that can be used to include various inadequacies in a child's experience with his father" (p. 5). This approach has been labeled the *deficit* model in father research (Hawkins & Dollahite, 1997) because it focused primarily on the negative effects of father absence. During this era, few if any researchers systematically examined the ways in which men positively contribute to their children's well-being.

Separation and Divorce

During the 1980s, many researchers began to explore how divorce (or any transition to fatherlessness) influences child well-being. As Lamb (1986, 1997, 2000) summarized, five problems can arise when men are absent from families. First, the absence of one parent creates a "staffing" problem because the work within a home (i.e., child care, housework, leisure activities) can be done more effectively when two parents are available to participate. Second, divorce and other types of father absence (such as incarceration) often produce economic distress. Third, economic distress and the other pressures of single parenthood often create added levels of depression and emotional stress for single parents. Fourth, children are affected psychologically by actual and/or perceived abandonment when parents exit the home. Last, a still growing body of evidence confirms that marital and post-divorce interparental conflict has a "cancerous" effect on children's well-being (Kelly, 2000; Stone, Buehler, & Barber, 2002).

Our understanding of the roles men play in the lives of their children took a conceptual leap forward during this period as researchers began to catalogue the processes that describe more accurately how father absence (and presence) affects family life and child development. Instead of asking only whether fathers were present or absent, researchers began to consider the many ways in which they might contribute or fail to contribute to their children's development and adjustment.

Fathers, Mothers, and Children

Almost simultaneously, researchers began studying interactions among fathers, mothers, and children in the late 1970s. Like the second generation of studies concerned with variably absent fathers, these studies involved recognition that fathers could be present in varying ways and degrees. Researchers thus focused on what activities fathers actually performed with their children and partners and began to document associations between the type and extent of involvement, on the one hand, and variations in children's characteristics and adjustment on the other. As a result, the father present–absent dichotomy became first an implicit continuum and then a variety of continua, as many of the chapters that follow make clear.

MEASUREMENT STRATEGIES

Researchers seeking to explore facets of father involvement and their diverse impacts on child development have exploited a variety of research strategies and data sets.

In the 1990s, many students of fatherhood began to exploit large longitudinal and nationally representative data sets. Among the more prominent was the National Longitudinal Survey of Youth-1979 (NLSY-79) which has, for more than 20 years, been tracking the work histories, economic fortunes, and fertility patterns of several thousand individuals who were teenagers in 1979. The inner workings of family life were not a prominent focus of the original data collection, but researchers (e.g., Averett, Gennetian, & Peters 2000) have been able to follow the economic conditions, child-care patterns, work histories, and even transfer payments to minor children reported by the participants.

In the National Survey of Family and Households (NSFH), another large data set, about 13,000 families were surveyed in 1988 and again in 1995. Additionally, children within the initial households were themselves interviewed in 1995. Importantly, the NSFH targeted many family process variables—including parenting practices, styles of communication, family routines, and family life practices—and has thus contributed substantially to our knowledge of men in families.

Other large-scale data sets that remain the basis for valuable research on men in families are the Fragile Families (see chap. 11), the NLSY-97 (chap. 12), the Early Childhood Longitudinal Study (chap. 18), and the National Survey of Adolescent Health (chap. 13). Additionally, recent attempts have been made to collect data from a large sample of families using the well-established Panel Study of Income Dynamics (PSID). The PSID Child Development Supplement (CDS) provides researchers with in-depth time diary accounts of both parents' and children's activities (see chap. 14 for a further description).

In light of the growing number and availability of appropriate data sets, we expect that increasing numbers of articles about men in family life will appear in prestigious journals as researchers tap these resources. In addition, increasing numbers of scholars have employed careful, small-scale research designs based on ethnographic and qualitative methods to answer important questions about men in families (for examples see chap. 4, 5, and 6). Such research designs draw upon decades of methodological expertise gained by psychologists, ethnographers, and child developmentalists and offer opportunities for the close examination of individual behavior and motivation as well as interpersonal interaction, which is not possible when investigators are dependent on responses to survey questions. By using a variety of research methods (both quantitative and qualitative) and designs (experimental, quasi-experimental, survey, observational, and interview) scholars are likely to give us the broadest view of what men do in families and of how children and other family members are influenced by the presence and behavior

8   DAY AND LAMB

of men. This view should become apparent as readers sample the complementary
contributions and approaches offered by contributors to this volume.

OVERVIEW OF CHAPTERS

In chapter 2, Parke and his colleagues introduce us to the study of the fathers in
the Latino community, focusing on themes and methods that characterize recently
initiated work in this area. For example, Parke and his colleagues highlight the
emphasis that Latino men place on family life (see also Marsiglio, chap. 4; Pleck
and Stueve, chap. 5; Dollahite, chap. 6) and suggest that when financial stability is
difficult to achieve (as it is for many Latino men), some fathers may have to choose
levels of involvement constrained by the need to work even though they consider
themselves highly involved in family life. In such circumstances, sterile measures
of father involvement may inadequately represent real life processes. Additionally,
Parke and his colleagues suggest that, contrary to popular stereotypes, Latino
men are not authoritarian and uninvolved in comparison with Euro-American and
African-American fathers. In fact, African-American and Latino fathers probably
monitor their children more than Euro-American fathers do when family situations
are similar and appropriate statistical controls are employed. As Parke and his
colleagues explain, of course, it is important to be careful when generalizing
about Latino fathers, just as it is dangerous to make assertions about fathers in
general. Certainly, Cuban-American families who emigrated following the Cuban
Revolution nearly a half century ago struggle with different issues than do Mexican-
American families who have recently moved from central Mexico.

Chapter 3 takes us out of the United States and into the realm of research
emerging in the United Kingdom. Clarke and O'Brien show that definitions of father involvement, research about those issues, and attendant public policies about
men in general are affected simultaneously by cultural definitions of men in families, politicized governmental agendas, and the interests of individual researchers
attracted to this topical arena.

Clarke and O'Brien remind us how ideological shifts can affect the tenor and
direction of research on fathers. In the mid-1990s, for example, policy analysts
laid the blame for many social problems at the door of fathers (especially absent
fathers and "irresponsible younger fathers"). By contrast, recent changes in policy perspectives have turned the attention of British researchers and policymakers
toward the creation of initiatives that support men in their attempts to be responsible fathers or father figures. Clarke and O'Brien analyze carefully how father
involvement is being framed and constructed in contemporary research and policy
initiatives. Key issues that surface in these data collection efforts are the interpretation and representation of missing data, the under-identification of fathers and
of father–child relationships, and the measurement of parent–child relationships.
As in the United States, researchers in the United Kingdom have begun to collect

1. PATHWAYS, PROBLEMS, AND PROGRESS

time-use data; Clarke and O'Brien suggest that cross-national projects in which parental time use is assessed in a variety of cultures might be highly informative.

Clarke and O'Brien also describe how a group of researchers has begun conducting small-scale studies that highlight the highly textured content of men's roles in families and emphasize the many cultural contexts in which fathers function today. These diverse study groups include Caribbean, Asian (Indian, Pakistani, and Bangladeshi), and Muslim families. As in the United States, researchers in the United Kingdom are also beginning to recognize the value of studying inter- and intrafamily relationships. Indeed, many contributors to this volume note that many researchers now emphasize the importance of understanding interpersonal dynamics and intrafamily life. However, in contrast to U.S. researchers, British scholars and commentators place less emphasis on gender equity and on fathers' influences on young children.

Thereafter, Marsiglio (chap. 4) summarizes the tripartite nature of men's role as fathers or father figures—self-as-father, father–child relations, and coparent—using a qualitative approach to lead readers through the life histories of men and to convey, in their own words, the ways in which men make sense of their lives. By identifying a series of sensitizing concepts, Marsiglio captures the subjective experiences of men as they become and experience being fathers, reminding us that an understanding of men's involvement in family life lies in the deep meaning that men place on the process of "doing fathering." With the sensitizing constructs in mind, readers are coached to remember the mix of contexts, motivations, and trajectories that men experience. Marsiglio illustrates how information and constructs gained from small-scale and/or qualitative research can inform large-scale data collection efforts. Too often, survey researchers pay little attention to the ways in which the richness of men's private lives affects their behavior and relationships.

In a similar vein, Pleck and Stueve (chap. 5) exemplify how thoughtful theory construction can foster more precise measures of men's activities within their families. Like Marsiglio, Pleck and Stueve assert that one must understand the "self-meanings" of activities in order to understand what men do. By attending to the stories men tell about their roles and role performance, we can begin to understand motivations, choices, and the nature of fathers' images or idealized valuations of themselves. Drawing from the rich history of symbolic interaction theory, these authors show how the constructs of role identity can be used to create clear and practical measurement strategies. Pleck and Stueve show how one can collect parental narratives reflecting meaningful experiences and then code them in ways that elucidate how men and women construct their parental roles. In particular, fathers construct their parental identities within the context of coparental relationships much more often than mothers do. By analyzing use of the "we" voice in parent stories, Pleck and Stueve also found that mothers use this voice more when they perform fewer parenting tasks and work longer hours, whereas men are more likely to use the "we" voice when they perform more parenting tasks and work less. Pleck and Stueve integrate these findings into a broader family

systems perspective and show how voice provides a window into the boundaries and definitions of family subsystems.

Qualitative approaches are also illustrated by Dollahite (chap. 6), who shows how men can and do influence their families when children have serious disabilities or illnesses. By exploring the stories of men facing family crises, Dollahite illustrates the diverse pathways to responsible fathering and increased paternal involvement. As he points out, the literature on children with disabilities has focused primarily on the challenges faced by mothers (though see Lamb & Laumann-Billings, 1997) and thus while his study has limited generalizability (because it involves a selected sample of highly religious families), it does underscore the ways in which men can become involved with their children in times of great need. Methodologically, this chapter provides valuable suggestions about the ways in which scholars can gather and interpret narrative stories from family members.

In chapter 7, Lamb, Chuang, and Hwang provide unique insight into men's contributions to family life over time by drawing on data from an intensive qualitative study. There are very few research projects in which men's contributions are chronicled over time, and some previous reports suggest that unusually involved fathers gradually disengage from their children over time. In their longitudinal study of Swedish fathers, Lamb and his colleagues found that the amount of time men spent with their children generally decreased over the course of the study and that mothers consistently assumed more responsibility for child care than fathers did. Lamb and his associates attempted, with varying degrees of success, to measure several types of involvement, reasoning that conceptual distinctions between interaction/accessibility and responsibility demand measurement strategies that differentiate among these constructs. Their report underscores how poorly we may still be measuring many important constructs.

Drawing on another intensive small-scale study, Gavazzi and Schock (chap. 8) show how our conceptualization of father involvement can affect the design of intervention programs for adjudicated youth. They also examine the reasons given by fathers to explain why they chose to participate in family-based programs and illustrate methodological issues that arise in the course of multimethod research on paternal participation in such intervention programs.

Yang and his colleagues turn our attention in chapter 9 to patterns of parenting and fathering in Asian families, asking whether men's experiences are radically different (because of cultural mandates and social mores) in Beijing, China, and the United States. In particular, Yang et al. focus on the complexities of Asian parenting and the indigenous meanings of parental control in specific Asian and Western cultures, pointing to recent debates centered on whether coercive parenting has similar meanings for mainland Chinese and North American children and their parents (e.g., Grusec, 2002; Lau & Yeung, 1996). To further explore whether similar patterns of parenting are associated with similar behavioral outcomes in diverse cultures, they designed their research to assess whether coercive fathering in mainland China is associated with adolescent aggression in the same way that

1. PATHWAYS, PROBLEMS, AND PROGRESS   11

it is in other cultural contexts. Surprisingly, perhaps, many of the associations documented in the United States were also evident in Yang et al.'s Chinese sample.

In chapter 10, Pasley and Braver examine the ways in which father involvement has been conceptualized and measured when divorced fathers do not live with their children. As they note, some researchers fail to recognize and address the consequences of the structural changes caused by divorce and ignore the gendered perspective that emphasizes deficits and can thus invalidate men's voices and experiences. Pasley and Braver also describe the varied ways that fathers are involved after divorce, the developmental correlates of decreased involvement over time, and the accuracy of maternal and paternal reports regarding the involvement of nonresident fathers. They note that reporter biases are common but seldom recognized.

Chapter 11 introduces us to the Fragile Families data set, which was used to examine five measures of involvement by unmarried fathers around the time of a new child's birth. Carlson and McLanahan briefly review the relevant literature on measuring father involvement in at-risk cultures. They then present descriptive information about the characteristics of the fathers in the Fragile Families data set and show how their involvement was assessed. A multivariate analyses is presented that describes the specific characteristics that appear to be strongly linked to greater father involvement. Finally, these authors discuss particular methodological issues related to father involvement using the Fragile Families data.

Measurement issues take center stage in chapter 12, in which Day and Acock explore adolescent perceptions of family processes and of maternal and paternal role performance. They show how researchers can use existing national data sets, such as the National Longitudinal Survey of Youth-97, to assess important constructs such as these. Day and Acock examined variations in perceptions of fathers as a function of family status (i.e., biological vs. nonbiological), racial/ethnic group status, and gender and found, not surprisingly, that nonresident fathers reportless monitoring of their children than resident fathers do. Nonresident fathers, regardless of race, youth's gender, or family type were believed to know "nothing" or just "a little" about their youngsters' activities. Positive evaluations of the nonresident fathers' role performances were positively correlated with the adolescents' overall perceptions of family life, however. Interestingly, nonresident fathers were not rated more negatively than resident fathers or resident mothers.

Harris and Ryan (chap. 13) then introduce the National Longitudinal Study of Adolescent Health (Add Health) and use it to examine variations in father involvement according to the family context, noting that researchers typically confound biology with structure when examining father–child relationships. Taking the biological relationships between fathers and children as their starting point, Harris and Ryan analyze variations in father involvement for resident biological fathers, resident nonbiological fathers, and nonresident biological fathers. At the core of their argument is the idea that levels of father involvement vary depending on the family context, the behavior of various mother figures inside the home, and the presence

and relative involvement of resident nonbiological and nonresident biological fathers. Harris and Ryan take full advantage of the huge Add Health data set by closely examining youth living in the rare family settings that were over-sampled. Their demonstration of how greatly these factors affect father involvement contributes substantially to the burgeoning literature on father involvement.

McBride and his colleagues (chap. 14) likewise use a large national data set (the PSID–CDS) to address questions about the four factors that supposedly influence father involvement (Lamb, Pleck, Charnov, & Levine, 1987):

1. Motivation, or the extent to which fathers want to be involved with their children.
2. Skills and self confidence, or the actual physical skills needed to be effective care providers and perhaps more important, fathers' perceived competence in that regard.
3. Social supports and stresses, or the extent to which others in the social network, primarily mothers, support or resist increased involvement by fathers.
4. Institutional factors, or the degree to which workplace practices and policies (which often reflect broader societal expectations) serve to inhibit or facilitate increased involvement by fathers.

McBride and his colleagues investigate the interrelationships among the factors in this model and their cumulative influence on father involvement. Using data from the PSID–CDS, they report partial support for the Lamb et al. model and emphasize the need for a multidimensional analysis of father involvement in which researchers consider simultaneously how different aspects of each of the four factors outlined in the model are associated with different forms of paternal involvement.

Fuligini and Brooks-Gunn (chap. 15) also employed the PSID–CDS to explore the amount of time that parents (both mothers and fathers) spend with their children, especially when caring for them. By exploring father involvement within the context of its effects on mother involvement, they show how "shared caregiving" seems to operate in this large, nationally representative sample of American families and indicate that patterns of shared caregiving differ when specific domains of caregiving are measured. Although mothers and fathers spend more time eating meals with their children than in most other activities, for example, there are few other activities in which mothers, fathers, and children all participate for very long. Compared to mothers, fathers spend proportionally more time in activities like playing with children rather than in caring for their young children. Fuligini and Brooks-Gunn also argue that the father's contribution to parenting should be measured as a proportion of the total amount of time that children are engaged with either of their parents, rather than by the amount of time the father spends divided by the amount of time the mother spends with the children.

Switching focus from benevolent aspects of father involvement, Fox and Benson (chap. 16) examine and compare the attitudes and behaviors of fathers

1. PATHWAYS, PROBLEMS, AND PROGRESS

who have and have not abused their partners, drawing data from a large national data set, the NSFH. Fox and Benson test the important competing hypotheses that, on the one hand, "maritally violent men are indistinguishable from nonviolent men in their fathering, and on the other, that maritally violent men are notably different from nonviolent men when it comes to fathering." Support for both hypotheses was found. Fox and Benson explain that when the ordinary activities of family life were examined, violent and nonviolent fathers did not differ with respect to the amounts of time they spent with their children and there was little evidence that spouse/partner abuse increased the levels of abusive behaviors toward children. However, maritally violent fathers reported that their children had more behavior problems (ranging from school truancy to difficulties with police) and perceived children of all ages more negatively than did nonviolent fathers.

Gadsden and her colleagues (chap. 17) next provide a much-needed analysis of the ways in which intervention programs can evaluate their impact on father involvement using their Fathering Indicators Framework (FIF). Gadsden and her colleagues propose that the FIF can assist practitioners, researchers, and policymakers to evaluate their programs and help them develop a broader understanding of what men do in family life. Importantly, these authors describe the conceptual and methodological issues involved in developing a framework that can address the specific needs of diverse groups of fathers. Practitioners work primarily with men who have a multitude of needs and are often "out-of-touch" with their children, inexperienced as parents, struggling with personal development issues, and burdened by lack of the resources needed to improve the quality of their own lives and those of their children.

The final chapter in the volume was written by a large group of scholars, often referred to as the DADS group, who have sought to advance the measurement and conceptualization of what "good" fathers do or ought to do within their families. The overall goal of the DADS project is to increase the comparability of measures across surveys in order to generate better information about father involvement and serve as a guide for future research on father involvement. Cabrera and her colleagues remind us that previous approaches to the measurement of father involvement have been characterized by at least five limitations: (1) the use of mothers as proxies for fathers, (2) the often interchangeable use of generic fathering versus child-specific fathering, (3) the limited generalization of findings from middle-class, European-American groups to other cultural groups, (4) the validity of fathers' self-report data, and (5) the narrow or dichotomous (present/absent) definition of father involvement. These authors then discuss the methodological, design, and measurement issues that arise when studying father involvement and its impact on child development in three large national studies: The Early Head Start Father Studies (EHS), the Fragile Families Child Well-Being Study (Fragile Families), and the Early Childhood Longitudinal Study–Birth Cohort (ECLS–B).

CONCLUSION

Clearly, several themes repeatedly arise in the chapters that follow. First, as one becomes immersed in the fathering literature, it quickly becomes apparent that the label *father* covers a complicated and diverse group of men in families. In the future, careful researchers will learn to embrace the richness of this diversity instead of simply paying superficial homage to it. Within the vast array of family types (e.g., step-fathers, fathers in blended families of various kinds, divorced, custodial, noncustodial, biological, nonbiological, etc.) researchers must pay greater attention in the future to these important structural components of family life.

Second, very few attempts have been made to trace fatherhood trajectories over time. We actually know very little about developmental changes in men's roles, identities, and behavior in their families. Under the larger umbrella of a life-course perspective, we need to focus on the systematic transitions that begin with "becoming a father" and move toward "being a father."

Third, multiple methods are clearly necessary. Several chapters illustrate how informative research can be when multimethod approaches are employed. Likewise, many contributors demonstrate how small-scale, ethnographic research can inform investigators who use larger demographic data sets, and vice versa. We hope, by such examples, to further break down the intellectual barriers that inhibit meaningful dialogue among those representing a variety of disciplines and research approaches.

Fourth, researchers clearly benefit from exploring ways in which men and women behave differently, instead of rejecting out-of-hand the possibility that men's contribution to family life may have unique features.

Fifth, research on men needs to explore the potential dark side of fathering. Family violence, neglect, and the misuse of power unfortunately remain all-too-common features of family life.

Finally, several scholars have recently begun to examine the roles played by men in special circumstances, such as those in the military who are frequently absent, often not by choice. Additionally, more of our collective research attention needs to focus on the 600,000 men who are released from prison each year. It is our hope that this collection of essays will prompt more thoughtful attention to these issues.

REFERENCES

Averett, S. L., Gennetian, L. A., & Peters, H. E. (2000). Patterns and determinants of paternal child care during a child's first three years of life. *Marriage and Family Review, 29*(2–3), 115–136.

Biller, H. (1974). *Paternal deprivation.* Lexington, MA: Heath.

Day, R. D., Gavazzi, S., & Acock, A. (2001). Compelling family processes. In A. Thronton (Ed.), *The well-being of children and families: Research and data needs* (pp. 103–126). Ann Arbor, MI: University of Michigan Press.

Doherty, W. J. (1997). *The intentional family: How to build family ties in our modern world.* Reading, MA: Addison-Wesley.

1. PATHWAYS, PROBLEMS, AND PROGRESS

Furstenberg, F. F. (1998). Social capital and the role of fathers in the family. In A. Booth & A. C. Crouter (Eds.), *Men in families: When do they get involved? What difference does it make?* (pp. 295–301). Mahwah, NJ: Lawrence Erlbaum Associates.

Furstenberg, F. F., Jr, & Hughes, M. (1995). Social capital and successful development among at-risk youth. *Journal of Marriage and the Family, 57*(3), 580–592.

Gottman, J. M., Levenson, R., & Woodin, E. (2002). Facial expressions during marital conflict. *The Journal of Family Communication, 1*(1), 37–57.

Greven, P. J. (1970). *Four generations: Population, land, and family in colonial Massachusetts.* Ithaca, NY: Cornell University Press.

Grusec, J. E. (2002). Parental socialization and the acquisition of values. In M. H. Bornstein (Ed.), *Handbook of parenting, Vol. 5, Practical issues in parenting* (pp. 143–167). Mahwah, NJ: Lawrence Erlbaum Associates.

Hawkins, A. J., & Dollahite, D. C. (Eds.). (1997). *Generative fathering: Beyond the deficit perspective.* Thousand Oaks, CA: Sage.

Kelly, J. B. (2000). Children's adjustment in conflicted marriage and divorce: a decade review of research. *Journal of the American academy of child and adolescent Psychiatry,* United States; 39, 963–973.

Keating, N. C., & Munro, B. (1989). Transferring the family farm: Process and implications. *Family Relations, 38*(2), 215–219.

Lamb, M. E. (1986). The changing role of fathers. In M. E. Lamb (Ed.), *The fathers role: Applied perspectives* (pp. 3–27). New York: Wiley.

Lamb, M. E. (1997). Fathers and child development: An introductory overview and guide. In M. E. Lamb (Ed.), *The role of the father in child development* (Third ed., pp. 1–18; 309–313). New York: Wiley.

Lamb, M. E. (2000). The history of research on father involvement: An overview. *Marriage and Family Review, 29*(23), 23–42.

Lamb, M. E., & Laumann Billings, L. A. (1997). Fathers of children with special needs. In M. E. Lamb (Ed.), *The role of the father in child development* (Third ed., pp. 179–190; 356–360). New York: Wiley.

Lamb, M. E., Pleck, J., Charnov, E., & Levine, J. A. (1987). A biosocial perspective on paternal behavior and involvement. In J. B. Lancaster, J. Altmann, A. S. Rossi, & L. R. Sherrod (eds.) *Parenting across the lifespan: Biosocial Dimensions* (pp. 111–142). Hawthorne, NY: Aldine de Gruyter.

Lau, S. & Yeung, P. P. W. (1996). Understanding Chinese child development: The role of culture in socialization. In S. Lau (Ed.), *Growing up the Chinese way* (pp. 29–44). Hong Kong: Chinese University Press.

Marsiglio, W., Amato, P., Day, R. D., & Lamb, M. E. (2000). Scholarship on fatherhood in the 1990's and beyond. *Journal of Marriage and the Family, 62*(4), 1173–1191.

Mintz, S. (1998). From patriarchy to androgyny and other myths: Placing men's family roles in historical perspective. In A. Booth & A. C. Crouter (Eds.), *Men in families: When do they get involved? What makes a difference?* (pp. 3–30). Mahwah, NJ: Lawrence Erlbaum Associates.

Pleck, E. H., & Pleck, J. H. (1997). Fatherhood ideals in the United States: Historical dimension. In M. E. Lamb (Ed.). *The role of the father in child development* (Third ed., pp. 33–48; 314–318). New York. Wiley.

Popenoe, D. (1996). *Life without father.* New York: The Free Press.

Silverstein, L., & Auerbach, C. F. (1999). Deconstructing the essential father. *American Psychologist, 54*(6), 397–407.

Stolz, L. M. (1954). *Father relations of war-born children.* Stanford, CA: Stanford University Press.

Stone, G., Buehler, C., & Barber, B. K. (2002). Interparental conflict, parental psychological control, and youth problem behavior. In B. K. Barber (Ed.), *Intrusive parenting: How psychological control affects children and adolescents* (pp. 53–96). Washington, DC: American Psychological Association.

2

Assessing Father Involvement in Mexican-American Families

Ross D. Parke, Scott Coltrane, Sharon Borthwick-Duffy, Justina Powers, Michele Adams
University of California at Riverside

William Fabricius, Sanford Braver, and Delia Saenz
Arizona State University

Despite advances in our understanding of fatherhood, most social and behavioral science research is based on data from white, middle-class, European-American families. In this chapter, we argue for including Latino families in fatherhood studies and highlight some special issues in the assessment of Latino men's family involvement that have emerged from our recent research projects. Latino families face unique challenges and exhibit unique strengths, yet few social and behavioral scientists have addressed the assessment issues that are of particular importance to studies of this group. Unless researchers can gain access to Latino communities, build trust with key informants, and establish rapport with all family members, the validity of findings about Latino families will be limited. Until sampling and data collection techniques recognize the unique features of Latino subgroups, theoretical models and empirical findings will remain biased toward the experiences of the non-Latino white population. Latinos now constitute the largest ethnic minority group in the United States. We therefore encourage researchers to include Latino families in their studies and to become sensitive to the unique assessment issues that their inclusion necessitates.

In assessing family functioning and child development in Latino families, we found that it is important to focus on variables such as country of origin, immigration pattern, generational status, language usage, acculturation, education, and ethnic identity. Methods of assessing other variables that are commonly examined in family studies such as parent education, social networks, and economic standing must be examined and sometimes modified when studying Latinos. Wide variation in these social indicators among Latino families can have profound influences on the conclusions that researchers might reach. Rather than assuming that ethnic group membership per se influences family practices or child outcomes, we suggest that it is important to adopt research methods that allow for the complexity and variability of various social, individual, and family processes to emerge. Our ongoing research into the effects of economic stress on families in southern California and our nascent research on the meaning of fatherhood in different family types in Arizona and California have brought to light important commonalities and differences across Mexican-American and European-American families.

One of the major gaps in our knowledge about fathering is our lack of understanding of Latino families. This is an oversight of considerable importance since Latinos recently surpassed African Americans as the largest ethnic or racial minority group in the United States. The Hispanic/Latino population is a heterogeneous group of more than 35 million that includes all persons of Latin-American origin or descent (Massey, 1993; U.S. Census Bureau, 2001; Zinn & Wells, 2000). Latinos are distinguished by their country of origin, degree of acculturation, language, and location in the United States. The largest subgroup, representing nearly 60 percent of all U.S. Latinos, are Mexican American. Mexican Americans have a distinctive cultural heritage and a unique pattern of immigration compared to Puerto Rican, Salvadorian, Cuban, or other Latino groups (Leyendecker & Lamb, 1999). While these differences are important, several common themes appear to characterize many Latino fathers and families. Immigrant status, lower socioeconomic status, and a focus on the centrality of the family are themes common to most Latino groups in the United States. In this chapter, we address these themes using data from Mexican-American families residing in the southwestern United States and ask how they might influence our understanding of fatherhood. Our goal is not to provide a definitive summary of the status of father involvement in such families but to provide some guidelines for the assessment of Latino fathers' involvement and to report on some early illustrative findings from our ongoing research.

LATINO FATHERS AND FAMILISM

Mexican-American families are of particular interest to social scientists because of their longstanding emphases on child rearing and extended family bonds. Researchers have used the term familism to describe practices in this ethnic group that include high levels of family cohesion, cooperation, and reciprocity. For example,

2. MEXICAN-AMERICAN FAMILIES

Leyendecker and Lamb (1999, p. 251) define familism as "a deeply ingrained sense of being rooted in the family to which one is oriented and obligated," and McLoyd, Cauce, Takeuchi, & Wilson (2000, p. 289) refer to familism as a "strong value for family closeness and cohesion [that is] a distinguishing feature of Hispanic Cultures." Strong identification with family, community, and ethnic group encourages most Latinos to desire emotional and proximal closeness with immediate and extended family (Buriel, 1986; Cauce & Rodriguez, 2002; Vega, 1990). At the same time, it must be noted that research evidence on the extent, form, and effects of familism is often inconsistent or even contradictory (Zinn & Wells, 2000; Vega, 1990, 1995). Few researchers have examined how familism shapes the experience and practice of fatherhood in Latino families.

In various studies, Mexican Americans typically have been shown to exhibit higher levels of extended family support and contact when compared to other ethnic groups (Vélez-Ibáñez, 1996). An extended family network that lives in close proximity is thought to provide social, emotional, and instrumental assistance as family members share responsibilities, and it contributes to the healthy adjustment of children (Gonzales, Knight, Morgan-Lopez, Saenz, and Sirolli, 2002; Vega, 1990). Researchers have found that reliance on kinship networks can serve as an important survival strategy in poor Mexican-American neighborhoods, and such networks often provide cultural, emotional, and mental support for recent immigrants who are economically marginalized (Zinn & Wells, 2000; Keefe, 1984; Leyendecker & Lamb, 1999; Vélez-Ibáñez, 1996). Others have found that kinship networks also serve important functions for more affluent and educated Latinos (Buriel & DeMent, 1997).

Cooperation with others is another aspect of familism that is often described as a unique core value among Latinos, with researchers reporting that mutual obligation and reciprocity are strictly taught and reinforced in the family (Vega, 1995). Evidence of this value appears in studies in which Latino children exhibit higher rates of cooperation in peer interactions than European-American children (Knight & Kagan, 1977) and in observations of Mexican-American households in which parents emphasize interdependence in child socialization practices (Delgado-Gaitan, 1994). Although independence is stressed more in later generations, family cohesion and mutual interdependence remain central values as family and community members serve as "funds of knowledge" for each other (Vélez-Ibáñez, 1996).

Other core values related to familism concern status and role definitions in the Latino family, and these tend to shape attitudes toward fatherhood. In general, researchers suggest that Latino families tend to emphasize differences between the sexes and promote respect and obedience toward fathers, parents, and elders to a greater extent than non-Latinos (Vega, 1990). Several decades ago, ethnographers described Latino men as preoccupied with displays of manliness (machismo), which defended patriarchal and authoritarian family relations (e.g., Madsen, 1973). Some revisionist Latino scholars characterized these depictions as pejorative, suggesting instead that machismo can imply masculine respect, loyalty, responsibility,

20 PARKE ET AL.

and generosity (e.g., Mirandé, 1997). Patterns of respect and deference in Latino families are reflected and reproduced through extended-family rituals relating to birth (*compadrazgo*), marriage, and death (e.g., Keefe & Padilla, 1987). Some recent studies question how much family rituals continue to be a central integrating element for most Latinos' extended-family relationships (Williams, 1993), especially because extended-kinship networks may be declining among Latinos whose families have been in the United States for several generations (Roschelle, 1997). For example, first-generation immigrants are more likely to accept the husband's authority and to demand outward obedience from children, whereas subsequent generations are more likely to exhibit more variability in marital power dynamics (Zinn & Wells, 2000; Coltrane & Valdez, 1993; Zavella, 1987). Similarly, second-generation parents are more likely to invite their children's opinions than are first-generation Latino immigrants (Delgado-Gaitan, 1994).

To summarize, the concept of familism suggests a strong orientation and obligation to the family and a preference for the family over the individual. Most researchers find relatively high levels of familism among Latinos and some argue that this leads to a kinship structure that is qualitatively different from those of other groups. In contrast, other scholars suggest that the concept of familism is linked to deficit models of Mexican families and advocate more detailed measures so that we might better understand actual ideals and practices (Zinn & Wells, 2000; Mirandé, 1997; Vega, 1990). Although familism is deemed important, we suggest that researchers must carefully conceptualize and measure its separate demographic, structural, normative, and behavioral dimensions. Only then will we be able to specify how familism affects Latino fathers and families.

THE ECONOMIC STATUS
OF LATINO FAMILIES

Another essential theme that must be addressed in studying Latino fathers is their economic status. Compared to European-American groups, Latinos have experienced exceptionally low social mobility and little change in family income across generations (Chapa & Valencia, 1993; U.S. Census Bureau, 2000). Although most researchers have assumed that immigrants will be assimilated economically by working in entry-level jobs and advancing to better jobs, most Latinos have not followed this pattern (Zinn & Wells, 2000; Morales & Ong, 1993). In the 1990s, the average Latino family income in the United States was less than 60 percent of non-Latino family income, even though Latino men had consistently higher labor force participation rates than non-Latino men and despite the fact that Latinos entered the labor force in record numbers (Perez & Salazar, 1993; Zinn & Wells, 2000). Although second-generation Latinos fare better economically than the first generation, third generation and beyond remain largely stagnated in the lower economic strata.

2. MEXICAN-AMERICAN FAMILIES

21

Latinos, especially Mexican Americans, tend to be employed in the service sector and occupy jobs with low pay, limited benefits, few opportunities for advancement, and periodic instability (Ortiz, 1996; U.S. Census Bureau, 2000). Because of the low wages received by their parents in the late 1990s, 34% of Latino children under 18 were living in poverty, over three times the rate for non-Latinos (U.S. Census Bureau, 2000). And even though over two-thirds of Mexican-American children lived with two parents, they were still three times as likely to experience poverty as European-American children (Cauce & Rodriguez, 2001; Vega, 1995). The economic marginality faced by the majority of Latino fathers presents some unique methodological and analytical challenges for researchers. Above all, we recommend sampling from among various income levels and avoiding the tendency common in past research to attribute the effects of poverty to cultural or family practices.

Latino children experience heightened risk for a wide range of negative outcomes. The long-term academic success of Mexican-American students compared to non-Latino white students is characterized by major disparities in grade point averages, dropout rates, and post-secondary educational attainment (U.S. Census Bureau, 2000). Almost 40% of Mexican-Americans do not complete high school. Other indicators of problem behavior include alcohol and drug use, teen pregnancy, and delinquency—all are more prevalent among Latino youth than among European-American youth (Gonzalez, Knight, Morgan-Lopez, Saenz & Sirolli, 2002). Moreover, rates of depression and suicide are higher for Latino youth than for other ethnic groups, even when socioeconomic status is controlled (COSSMHO, 1999). We know relatively little about the potential contribution of fathering behavior to variations in the levels of these problems in Latino families.

ASSESSING FATHER INVOLVEMENT IN LATINO FAMILIES

Hawkins & Dollahite (1997, pp. 20–21) suggest that "fatherwork," including direct care, shared activities, monitoring, housework, and other sustained efforts on behalf of children, is likely to be the most important aspect of fathering for children, mothers, and the fathers themselves (see McBride, chap. 14, this volume). We also believe that it is important to focus on the meanings that fathers and other family members assign to the activities associated with fatherhood because these meanings can have profound consequences for the father's level of participation in family life (Palkovitz, 1997). When financial stability is hard to achieve, a father may be only minimally involved with his children on a daily basis but may nevertheless see himself as a "good father" because he works hard to make ends meet. According to family systems theory, the ideas of other family members about the meaning of fatherhood are also consequential for they shape patterns of parental

participation, interaction, and evaluation. We cannot simply assume that more father involvement is better for all families. As the emerging gatekeeping literature (e.g., Allen & Hawkins, 1999; Bietel & Parke, 1998) attests, too much father involvement can be interpreted as interference rather than helpfulness. For Latino families, it is critical that we understand more fully the norms, expectations, and beliefs that govern father involvement and the types of father–child activities that are considered culturally appropriate. When researchers assume that expectations will be similar (or different) across ethnic groups, faulty measurement and errors of inference often ensue. To guard against such assumptions and errors, we advocate using qualitative data gathering along with more standard measures yielding quantitative data. Techniques such as focus groups and narrative analyses are designed to ensure that questions are relevant to the experiences of the group under study. In addition, collecting information from multiple raters (fathers, mothers, children) about expectations, behaviors, and evaluations can provide a more complete picture of fathering and family practices. Finally, focusing on multiple meanings and adopting an interpretative perspective can also lead to a better understanding of how apparently similar levels of objective involvement yield different outcomes for fathers, mothers, and children.

In the remaining sections of the paper, we review three sets of issues: First, we outline briefly the current, albeit sparse, data on involvement of Latino fathers. Second, we outline several methodological considerations in the study of Latino fathers, and, finally, we present results from two recent efforts to explore subjective aspects of the fathering experience in Latino families. Our goal in presenting these preliminary findings is to underscore the value of including the father's perspective along with the perspectives of other family members on his participation and their general expectations of what constitutes good fathering.

What Do We Know About Father Involvement in Latino Families?

Several studies have examined this issue, and the results are relatively clear. In contrast to the expectations that Latino fathers are authoritarian and uninvolved, most reports in fact indicate that Latino fathers do not significantly differ from their non-Latino counterparts. For example, in a study by Hossain, Field, Malphus, Valle, and Pickens (1995), low-income Latino fathers of 4-month-old infants estimated that they spent about half as much time (1.8 hours) as mothers (3.6 hours) in basic caregiving activities (bedtime routines, physical care, feeding, soothing the infants). Comparisons between African-American and Latino low-income families suggest similar levels of parental involvement in both groups. Moreover, Hossain et al. (1995) also found that Latino and African-American fathers were just as involved with their infants as European-American fathers. Other studies reveal a similar pattern of involvement for Latino fathers with older children. As in the case of European-American families, Latino and African-American fathers spend more

2. MEXICAN-AMERICAN FAMILIES

time than mothers in play than in caregiving (Toth & Xu, 1999; Yeung, Sandberg, Davis-Kean, & Hofferth, 2001).

Fathers in African-American and Latino families are not, however, identical to their European-American counterparts. For example, both African-American and Latino fathers are more likely than European-American fathers to report that they monitor and supervise their children's activities, and they report more time with them in shared activities (Toth & Xu, 1999). Others find Mexican-American fathers to be similar to European-American fathers in their proportion of housework and child monitoring, but the former contribute more hours to these tasks and are more involved in activities with their children (Coltrane, Parke, & Adams, 2001). Latino fathers reportedly spend an hour more on weekends with a child than do European-American fathers (Yeung et al., 2001). Finally, some find that Latino fathers have a higher level of involvement in household and personal care activities than European-American fathers (Mirandé, 1997; Shelton & John, 1993; Yeung et al., 2001). Generally lacking, however, are estimates of the amount of time Latino fathers spend interacting with a specific child as opposed to being in the presence of several children in a family group setting.

In terms of determinants of involvement, some researchers have found that highly involved Latino fathers place a high value on obedience and compliance with family roles (Toth & Xu, 1999). Others, in contrast, have found that Latino fathers who hold nontraditional gender roles tend to be more involved with their children (Coltrane & Valdez, 1994). Recently, Coltrane, Parke, and Adams (2001) confirmed that nontraditional gender ideology was positively related to child supervision, monitoring, and higher levels of involvement in "feminine" activities with their children (e.g., shopping, reading, cooking) in both European- and Mexican-American families, though not necessarily in "masculine" activities (e.g., recreation, sports, outings). As in earlier work (see Parke, 1996, for a review), the nature of the marital relationship seems to be an important determinant of father involvement, and satisfaction with levels of involvement appears to be strongly related to the gender ideals and expectations of individual mothers and fathers. In other words, if family members want fathers to be more involved with their children, then his participation has positive effects on family functioning. If, on the other hand, family members feel that fathers changing diapers or doing laundry are an affront to the father's masculinity, then such practices can be detrimental to individual and family well-being.

The relation between family income and father involvement is a complex one. Higher income is often found to be a correlate of increased father involvement (Fagan, 1996, 1998) and probably reflects higher levels of education and social class. But the relative proportion of income contributed by husbands and wives needs to be considered as well. Coltrane et al. (2001) found that in European-American and Mexican-American families where wives earned a greater share of the family income, fathers were more involved in both housework and child supervision. In this case, the wives' increased power (from a higher relative income)

may lead to greater equity of roles between spouses. A further determinant of father involvement is economic stress; as this increases, father household and child responsibility increases. The increased involvement in this case may be due to the necessity of sharing family roles due to increased economic pressure, which may involve less flexible work schedules or longer maternal work hours to help ease the economic strain.

As this brief summary of knowledge about the involvement of Latino fathers shows, there is a clear challenge to the stereotypes of aloof and uninvolved Latino fathers (Mirandé, 1997). In fact, Latino fathers resemble European- and African-American fathers to a striking degree. What's more, most studies of family work that have included Latinos show similar patterns of association among variables whether the respondents are Latino or Anglo (Coltrane, 2000; Coltrane & Valdez, 1993; Golding, 1990; Herrera & Del Campo, 1995). At the same time, by restricting ourselves to "objective" and overt indices of involvement, much of the variation, which may be culture specific, may be inadvertently overlooked. As argued above, if serious progress is to be made in understanding Latino fathers' involvement, we need to expand the scope of our inquiry to focus on issues of interpretation and meaning in relation to the issue of involvement. This call for qualitative measures of dimensions of fathering that may not be captured by quantitative measures is consistent with a recurrent theme in the 1998 Federal Interagency Forum report, "Nurturing Fatherhood" (Marsiglio, Day, Evans, Lamb, Braver, & Peters, 1998; see also Marsiglio, Day, & Lamb, 2000). There is a need to discover what dimensions of fathering are symbolically important to children, to assess their perceptions of the quality of the father–child relationship on these dimensions, and to be able to assess similarities and differences between Mexican-American and European-American children and adolescents.

Methodological Considerations in Assessing Latino Father Involvement

As our brief review suggests, there is limited data upon which to base our understanding of Latino fathers. Part of the reason for this is the strong Euro-centric bias in previous studies of families and fathers (Parke & Buriel, 1998). In addition, a variety of methodological barriers have limited our understanding of Latino fathers, including issues of recruitment, retention, measurement of culturally relevant constructs, and coding and interpretation of data. In this section we briefly discuss each of these issues, drawing upon our experience in conducting a longitudinal study of Mexican-American families. Since 1997 an interdisciplinary team of researchers at the University of California, Riverside, has been following a group of Mexican-American families across a 4-year period to examine the impact of economic stress on family adaptation and children's well-being (NIH-MH 54154-01A2). Starting in 2000, we began collaborating with researchers from

2. MEXICAN-AMERICAN FAMILIES

Arizona State University to develop a study focused more specifically on the meaning of fatherhood and stepfatherhood in Mexican-American families (NIH-1R01MH64828-01). We draw on our experience with these two projects to suggest ways to address the methodological issues.

Asking the Right Questions and Choosing the Right Variables

Rather than relying solely on previous literature, it is particularly important at the beginning stages of a research project on understudied groups to let fathers share their unique views, attitudes, concerns, and experiences as fathers. Our insights about Latino fathering were gained in part by letting fathers "speak for themselves" in focus groups. As Morgan (1988) noted, focus groups rely on an emergent process of interaction among group members to produce data and insights and are particularly valuable at the early stages of a research project involving understudied groups. For example, finding out the extent to which shared parenting is valued by Latino fathers or identifying new variables such as the importance of "compadres" (godparents) in Latino families increases the validity of the research. Focus groups can also be useful in the scale-construction process; they can offer recommendations for working changes and identify culturally appropriate and inappropriate items (see Silverstein, 2002, and Hunter and Davis, 1994, for examples of the use of this approach with Latino and African-American fathers). Finally, focus groups help researchers understand cultural preferences in interviewing styles and the boundaries related to information respondents are willing to share with researchers.

An Example of the Focus Group Approach

In our pilot project on the effect of fathers and stepfathers on adolescent adaptation and functioning in Mexican American families, we conducted a series of focus groups. Focus groups included mother-only, father/stepfather-only, and child-only groups. Our groups included two family sets of English-speaking Mexican-American parents and one family set of Spanish-speaking Mexican-American parents. The children ranged in age from 8 to 17 years old, with most children aged 11 to 14. We asked the parents and stepparents a series of questions, including "What are good qualities about fathers? What are some good things that fathers say and do in families? Why are these important characteristics? How do these things contribute to child development?"

Our goal was to discover, before embarking on our project, major themes that are of concern to Mexican-American fathers and their families and issues that need to be addressed with this population. Several themes emerged from these focus groups relating to fathers and familism. First the fathers stressed the importance of

respect for parents and revealed how paternal authority was used to instill values of familism in children; an example follows:

> My wife was cooking dinner one day. My son came in and said "What are you cooking?" I don't remember what she said, but he said, 'I don't want any of that.' So, I told him to go sit on the curb out there. He sat there maybe 10 minutes. I called him and asked if any cars go by. He said 'Yes.' I asked 'Did anybody stop and feed you?' 'No.' 'Then you go inside and thank your mom for feeding you, and next time appreciate what you have.'

Another father invoked his deferential relationship with his own father to emphasize the importance of respect for parents and to lament how the younger generation lacked such respect:

> My father was a great man who always succeeded in his business and as an individual, and in every aspect he was a great friend. I had respect toward my father, and it is for this reason that I never smoked in front of him ... It never crossed my mind ... not because I was afraid of him, but rather out of respect. Nowadays both sons and daughters forget about their parents.

A second theme that emerged was the importance of religion to family life with several fathers commenting on its significance. For example, one father noted Catholicism's cross-generational role:

> I fall back to my Catholic upbringing and try to raise my kids with a spiritual background. If you don't give a prayer every once in a while, then your whole life is just shot. I teach them how to pray, how to give thanks once in a while.

Another father referred to his own childhood in suggesting that religion and family could be interchangeable:

> Religion has to be in the family. For me, when I was growing up, that's all I had. When everybody split, it was just me and my sister, and Sister Marion would come and check on us. When there is no one there, you have to teach your kids to depend on God, because I may not be there. Prayer helps you do a lot better.

A third theme that emerged from the focus groups was the centrality of father as a family provider. Mothers, fathers, and children mentioned that "breadwinning" was a key aspect of fathering. And several commented on how the economic marginality of Latino men presented unique challenges to their fatherhood:

> My husband switches jobs frequently. It is hard on the whole family; it is hard on the kids; it is hard on me. My daughter would probably say she wishes her dad had full time steady employment with health insurance. They see their aunts and uncles who

2. MEXICAN-AMERICAN FAMILIES   27

are in really different financial circumstances. They see us having to miss the family vacations. Or, we can't do this; we can't do that. Mom has to go to work. Dad doesn't have any vacation. I think my kids would probably say that employment/money is the most important thing.

What makes it difficult being a father is when you do not spend much time with your kids because of work. Every father always wants more for their families and wants a better life for them, but they have to work overtime to meet the needs. This, in fact, causes fathers not to spend much time with their kids. My children many times feel ignored or rejected by me. But, when I come home from work, I am very tired. My kids want to talk, but I say "Oh, I am too tired; tell me tomorrow."

As these quotes illustrate, focus groups are important in that they can help identify questions to be addressed in studies of Latino fathers. Our focus groups not only helped identify issues to investigate but also confirmed and raised questions about previous interpretations of findings and theories. The focus groups also contributed to the development of the narrative approach to studying fatherhood outlined later. Regardless of the data collection method, however, studies of Latino fathers must confront a range of issues having to do with recruitment, reporters, interviews, and management of data.

Recruitment Issues

Although trust is central in any recruitment attempt, establishing trust is especially important in the case of Latino families. Any minority group is likely to be skeptical about participation in a scientific study for a variety of reasons, including the past history of mistreatment of minorities as research participants. Also, Mexican-American families—many of whom are immigrants, some illegally— have a healthy wariness of official institutions and a distrust of individuals with whom no prior relationship has been established. In our UC Riverside economic stress project, recruitment success varied widely as a function of our recruitment method. Researchers typically use relatively impersonal strategies for contacting and enrolling participants in a sample, but such strategies are not likely to be successful with Mexican-American fathers and families. Use of mailed introductions to our study, followed by a phone call to the families by a Spanish-speaking staff member, resulted in a relatively low rate of recruitment into the study (approximately 10 percent).

In recognition of the importance of interpersonal trust for Mexican-American families (Keefe & Padilla, 1987), we enlisted the assistance of a familiar, trusted, bilingual individual (in most cases a secretary at the school attended by the recruited family's child), who made the initial phone call to the family to introduce the study goals and personnel. Then we followed up with a call from a bilingual member of our research team. Using this approach, we were able to successfully recruit 80% of eligible families—including fathers. Another issue involves recognizing

that wives in families, but especially Latino families, often serve as gatekeepers to father participation (Allen & Hawkins, 1999; Bietel & Parke, 1998). Our success rate is, in part, due to our use of the mother as a conduit to the father. When we were able to recruit fathers, the mother had often convinced him to participate.

A third issue is a careful presentation of the study focus and the potential benefits of participation. In our case, we cast our work as a study of how families of different ethnic backgrounds function, with the emphasis on using information to provide services that are better tailored to families. Especially in the case of Mexican-American families, who are more collectivistic than individualistic in their cultural orientation, the emphasis on the provision of guidelines to help the larger Mexican-American community is important.

A final issue is compensation. Because Latino family income tends to be low, sufficient payment for participation in research projects is an important issue. Compensating families generously for their time increases participation rates (R. Conger, personal communication, Jan. 20, 2001). In the late 1990s, our project paid Latino families $200 for two 3-hour visits, leading to enhanced participation rates and a greater representation of hard-to-recruit low-income families.

The Importance of Multiple Perspectives

While it is common to advocate the use of multiple reporters (Patterson, 1993) in any study of families, it is particularly critical in studies of Mexican-American families. As earlier work has documented, Latino families are more embedded in networks of extended-family members than Euro-American families (Vidal, 1988). For example, one father said, "My best memories of growing up as a kid was everyone, brothers and cousins, living in the same area. All my cousins were so close. Like a sports camp. We all got along. As a kid, all my relatives got along great, laughing and joking."

To understand fathering, it is critical to obtain the perspectives of multiple individuals belonging to the extended-family network. In addition, it is important to measure precisely how kin networks shape family roles and create normative understandings of fatherhood.

Retention Issues

The issue of retention is critical especially in longitudinal studies, so we use several strategies to permit us to keep track of our families and retain them as active participants. We use relatives as an alternative way of relocating families who have moved. We also keep families involved through a variety of strategies that personalize our contacts, such as birthday cards to family members, holiday cards, and periodic newsletters with information about our staff, brief feedback about our study findings, and some announcements about community events and services. To the extent practical, it is important to use the same staff members for families across subsequent testing points because, especially in Mexican-American families, the

2. MEXICAN-AMERICAN FAMILIES 29

trust and rapport established between staff and participants is particularly important for retaining participants across multiple years.

Management of Interviews

Treating research participants with respect is important in all cases; but in the case of Latino families, establishing rapport and trust is especially important to the collection of meaningful data. Only if fathers trust the interviewer will they give the kind of detailed, honest, and nonbiased responses that are so critical to obtaining high-quality data. Same-gender and same-ethnicity interviewers are vital in order to establish a meaningful rapport. Moreover, food creates a more relaxed assessment context; we always provide snacks and have, at times, served dinner as well. In view of the importance of food in Mexican-American families it is especially helpful to provide food as part of the data collection protocol (R. Buriel, personal communication, march 18, 2001). Also, providing child care at the research site or during home visits increased participation of families in the project (especially when caregivers spoke Spanish).

Scalar Equivalence

One of the major problems encountered in studies of ethnic groups is the establishment of scalar equivalence. As noted before, focus groups are helpful in ensuring the development of culturally meaningful scales, including the selection of salient items that carry similar interpretations across different ethnic groups. Translation and back translation is commonly used but critical in the process to ensure that meaning is retained in the translation process. In addition, a dual focus approach (Vazquez-Garcia, Erkut, Alarcon, Garcia Coll, Tropp & Vazquez Garcia, 1995) is being used, by which new concepts and items that arise in the course of the translation process are generated simultaneously in both languages. Work by Knight, Virdin, and Roosa (1994) provided models for establishing scalar equivalence of commonly used questionnaires for assessment of family functioning. Theoretical and statistical advances in scaling can be applied usefully to this issue of cross-group equivalency as well. Specifically, Flannery, Reise, & Widaman (1995) utilized item response theory (IRT) techniques to address the equivalence of scales across groups. The utility of this approach for establishing gender equivalence (Flannery et al., 1995) and cross-cultural equivalence (e.g., China vs. the United States) suggests that this strategy can be used to establish scalar equivalence across different ethnic groups within the U.S. culture as well. The application of IRT techniques to the study of Mexican-American fathers would be worthwhile.

Management of Data

In addition to the common precautions of providing carefully translated materials and using scales and measures of known scale equivalence, other issues must be addressed when studying Latino fathers, especially for collection of observational

data. There are several aspects to the issue. First, task selection is critical and care must be taken to choose an observation task of relevance to Latino families. We have had success with the use of family discussion tasks, in which families select topics about which they disagree (between wives and husbands or fathers and children), and with tasks that call for descriptions of activities that typically include a role for Latino fathers (e.g., barbeques, Sunday drives).

Second, in coding observational data, one encounters some of the same problems faced when designing an interview schedule or questionnaire. Coders should be of the same ethnic background as the videotaped participants. Codes must be tailored to capture the measures of the ethnic groups being studied. This requires coders to be conversant with the language as well as the nonverbal cues (facial and body) that are characteristic of the participants. In summary, this list of methodological concerns is provided in the hope that our experience with Latino fathers and families will serve as a guide for others who are venturing into this relatively uncharted research terrain.

A Narrative Approach to Studying the Meaning of Fatherhood

As a further illustration of the value of qualitative approaches in the study of fathers, we present results from piloting the use of story narratives to capture children's perceptions of their father's involvement and relationship. To explore this issue, we pilot tested an open-ended, narrative method in our joint UCR/ASU project. We asked European-American and Mexican-American children to tell us "the story" about their fathers and their relationships with them. In our pilot study of 20 seventh graders, we found that each child's narrative could be scored on the following dimensions:

> *Investment.* Reflects the child's evaluation of the time and energy the father invests in things they do together.
> *Emotional Quality of the Relationship.* Reflects the positive versus negative emotions the child feels toward the father.
> *Responsiveness.* Reflects the child's evaluation of the father's responsiveness to the child's requests or needs.

These dimensions represent two general aspects of the father–child relationship that are salient to children at this age: (1) what the father does to show the child how important he or she is to the father (Investment and Responsiveness) and (2) the quality of the child's emotional reaction to the father (Emotional Quality). The coding scheme we developed for the narratives (described in next paragraph) makes it possible to detect differences in fathering that are symbolically important to children and adolescents.

2. MEXICAN-AMERICAN FAMILIES 31

We asked children to describe their fathers and their relationships with them. The European- and Mexican-American seventh graders told us about what their fathers do (behaviors), their interpretation and evaluation of their fathers' behaviors, and their relationship with their fathers more generally (child meanings). We developed a two-stage coding scheme. In the *first stage*, we coded each statement as reflecting either (a) father behaviors or (b) child meanings. Child meaning statements included any of the following: reference to father's mental state, including his desires, thoughts, intentions, or emotions; causal statements about father's behavior, either what leads to it or what it leads to; evaluations of father's behavior, including words such as good, bad, nice, mean, cool, etc.; generalizations about father's behavior, including words such as always, never, most of the time, etc.; and finally, references to the child's own mental states about the relationship with father or father's behavior.

In the *second stage*, we coded each statement of child meaning into one of three dimensions, assigning each statement a score (on a three-point scale, "low" to "high" for Investment and Responsiveness; from "positive" through "neutral" to "negative" for Emotional Quality):

Investment. This reflects the child's evaluation of the time and energy the father invests in the child. It is reflected in the evaluation statements the child makes; e.g., "He is always working," "I never see him," "He does a lot with us."

Responsiveness. This reflects the child's evaluation of the father's responsiveness to the child's request or needs. References to helping the child or talking to the child are reflections of responsiveness; e.g., "He always listens to me," "He's always been there for us."

Emotional Quality. This reflects the child's evaluation of the emotional tone of the relationship; e.g., "He's nice to me," "He's nice but he can be mean," "He's very good to us."

In the *third stage*, we coded each father behavior and child meaning statement in terms of Perceived Focus. This captures whether the child described the father doing that behavior either with or for (a) himself (e.g., "He likes his job," "He can be hooked on TV"), (b) others ("He makes stuff for our friends," "He's nice to my friend"), (c) "us" in the sense of with or for the family (e.g., "He does a lot for us," "He's good to us though he scolds us"), or (d) "me" in the sense of with or for the child personally (e.g., "He listens to me," "We go on walks together").

Scoring and Reliability. In an initial assessment of reliability, two raters scored six transcribed narratives and assigned 82% of meaning statements to the same dimensions, gave 82% of statements the same rank, and agreed completely on 75% of the statements. A coder trained on the criteria for meanings versus behaviors coded six narratives and agreed with the authors 97.5% of the time

on whether each unit referred to father behavior or child meaning. Eighty-one percent of the units were child meanings. "Dimension importance" scores for each child were calculated as the number of meaning statements made on each dimension divided by the total number of statements. These proportions tell us which dimensions of fathering are given more importance in the narratives and can be used to determine whether differences exist between family structure, ethnicity, gender, and age groups.

The "valence" of each dimension for each child was calculated as the child's mean score across all meaning statements on each dimension. These scores can be used to predict various child outcome measures. For example, adolescents who feel that their fathers do not invest enough time and energy in them or respond adequately to their requests and needs and/or who feel negative emotions toward the father may be likely to develop greater mental health and behavioral problems. In our pilot data, we see a tendency for children with the highest valence scores on Emotional Quality and Responsiveness to have the highest scores on a scale measuring how much the adolescent felt he or she mattered to their father.

The "salience" of each dimension was calculated as the total number of meaning statements made on each dimension. An adolescent who has a low score, for example, on perceived investment by the fathers and for whom that dimension also has greater salience as evidenced by how much he or she talks about it in the narrative might be especially likely to develop behavioral problems. In other words, salience might moderate the effects of valence on child outcomes. We can test the main effects of valence and salience, and their interaction, on various dependent measures.

Similarly, perceived focus might moderate the effect of valence. For example, even though an adolescent might have a high score on perceived responsiveness and investment by the father, if the references to dad being responsive and investing time and energy are in terms of his focus not being on the adolescent but instead being on the family, that might signal difficulties. Reflecting what others have labeled familism, we noted a tendency for Mexican-American adolescents to describe their father's focus being on the family ("us") more than European-Americans. Regardless of ethnicity, adolescents who almost always saw the father's focus as not being on them personally tended to see themselves as mattering less to him. For example, one Mexican-American female adolescent said, "He's always keeping on his job. I never see him staying at home. When he has time he helps us. I love my dad. He's always been there for us. He always gives money for the house and buys clothes for us. He loves his family. He's always working, I never get to see him a lot." None of this girl's statements were coded as reflecting her father's perceived focus as being on her, in contrast to the following Mexican-American girl who shows a balance between "us" and "me":

Dad likes to work and clean the yard and help us in homework and help us in any way he can. He helps us, he doesn't leave us on our own. We have a good relationship but I can't talk to him the way I can talk to Mom. He treats us very well, both myself

2. MEXICAN-AMERICAN FAMILIES

and my brothers. Mostly he treats us all alike. I have a good time with him. When he is around we have a good time. Weekends are best because I get to spend time with him. He tells us what life is about. He would do anything for us. I get to express my feelings to him and he tells me his feelings.

The latter girl rated herself as mattering much more to her father than the former girl.

These narrative dimensions closely parallel the relationship dimensions that are important in attachment theory (Bowlby, 1969/1982). In attachment theory, the parent's ability to empathize with the child's emotions, to respond effectively to the child's signals especially when in distress, and to initiate satisfying social interactions are all identified as promoting secure child–parent relationships. Bowlby (1973) emphasized that these dimensions continued to be important in adolescence: "An unthinking confidence in the unfailing accessibility and support of attachment figures is the bedrock on which stable and self-reliant personalities are built" (p. 322). Although there is some recent evidence (Freeman, 1997) that adolescents tend to view their mothers as their primary attachment figures, the dimensions we have seen in the narratives seventh graders tell about their fathers show the importance of the attachment relationship with him as well. In the spontaneous comments they make in their narratives, they describe and evaluate him much more frequently as an attachment figure than for example, as simply a provider, teacher, disciplinarian, or role model (Freeman, 1997).

As in the focus group studies, this narrative approach permits an expansion of the range of involvement issues that can be assessed. In this case, the work illustrates that a child's perspective on fathering, including father involvement, has an interpretative component, which is often overlooked in quantitative approaches to this issue. By expanding our methodological toolbox to include qualitative as well as quantitative approaches, we will not only develop a richer understanding of Latino fathers but also perhaps expand our understanding of father involvement more generally.

Multiple Methods are Necessary to Understand Father Involvement

At the same time that we recommend that qualitative approaches are useful supplements to our quantitative methods, it is important to underscore that there are limitations to these qualitative techniques as well. For example, sampling issues can limit generalizability of findings from focus group or narrative studies just as they do for most other small-sample quantitative studies. And although focus groups and narrative approaches are well suited for capturing the interpretative and symbolic aspects of fatherhood, they are less well suited for exploration of the process aspects of our family and child development theories. Finally, issues of causality and direction of effects are not well served by most qualitative

approaches. As we have argued, qualitative approaches are particularly useful at the beginning of the research process during which variables are selected, study questions are refined, and the cultural equivalence of instruments is assessed.

Alternative strategies including surveys of nationally representative samples are necessary to enrich our profiles of involvement of Latino fathers and to track cross-time changes in patterns of father involvement as a result of economic shifts, immigration policies, and acculturative changes. The recent report by Yeung et. al. (2001) on the relative involvement of Latino and non-Latino fathers is a model for this kind of work. In recognition of the value of interdisciplinary approaches to the issue of father involvement, sociological surveys need to be combined with more microanalysis methods, such as observations—the central approach in the psychologist's methodological armature. Observational studies of the interaction patterns of fathers and partners and/or children have provided important insights into the nature of the affective and social processes that characterize these relationships (Lamb, 1997; Parke, 1996).

To correct for the representativeness bias associated with small-sample studies yet retain their advantages, there has been a movement toward multistage sampling. According to this strategy, a representative sample is surveyed, followed by intensive observation and/or interviewing of either the whole sample or a carefully selected subsample. As an example, consider the recent work of Hetherington, Reiss, and Plomin (1994). In their study of the effects of nonshared environments in stepfamilies, these investigators surveyed a nationally representative sample and subsequently observed and videotaped the family interaction patterns. Although expensive and time-intensive, this multimethod strategy goes a long way toward balancing representativeness and attention to process.

In addition, experimental studies should be undertaken for several reasons. Thus, although the goal is generally to increase paternal involvement in the interest of improving the life chances of children, another central but often neglected reason for experimental intervention is to provide a test of theoretical positions (McBride, 1991; Parke, Power, Tinsley, & Hymel, 1980). This serves as a reminder that intervention—often viewed as an applied concern—and theory testing—often viewed as a basic research theme—are quite compatible. In fact, one could argue that the intervention strategy most likely to yield the highest payoff in terms of efficacy is an approach that is theory based. Experimental interventions can assume a variety of forms and can be guided by the multilevel scheme outlined earlier. Individual interventions aimed at modifying fathering attitudes, beliefs, and behaviors is only one level of analysis. At the dyadic level, interventions targeting the marital couple or the spouse who is high in gatekeeping can provide a test of the importance of dyadic factors in shaping father involvement. Other types of experimental interventions involve targeting neither individuals nor dyads but focusing on links across contexts. These strategies include programs (Conners & Epstein, 1995) that provide opportunities for parents to become involved in the activities of child-center institutions (e.g., schools) by forming partnerships with other

2. MEXICAN-AMERICAN FAMILIES

fathers and mothers. Another target of such programs is to focus on how changes in the workplace such as flextime, leave, and reductions in job stress impact both fathering behavior and involvement (Levine & Pittinsky, 1997).

CONCLUSION

One goal of our chapter is to extend an invitation to the field to join in the examination of Latino fathers. As our review shows, our knowledge of Latino fathers involvement is still limited, although significant progress has been made over the last decade. We hope that our articulation of the methodological issues in the study of Latino fathers will serve as a helpful guide for other researchers and policy scholars in this area.

Finally, more attention needs to be given to the diversity within Latino populations. Although our focus has been on Mexican-American fathers, more work on Cuban, Puerto-Rican, and South and Central American fathers is needed before we are able to fully understand the similarities and differences among different types of Latino fathers. Similarly, future research should include sufficient attention to differences in education, income, language, generational status, family structure, and social networks to allow for more precise specification of conditions and processes leading to successful fathering. Only when we recognize diversity among Latino families will we be able to understand fully the intricate links between social conditions, cultural practices, and fatherhood ideals and behaviors. Recognition of this diversity is critical to appreciating the role of Latino fathers in their children's lives.

REFERENCES

Allen, S. H., & Hawkins, A. J. (1999). Maternal gatekeeping: Mothers' beliefs and behaviors that inhibit greater father involvement in family work. *Journal of Marriage and the Family, 61*, 199–212.

Bietel, A., & Parke, R. D. (1998). Maternal and paternal attitudes as determinants of father involvement. *Journal of Family Psychology, 12*, 268–288.

Bowlby, J. (1969/1982). *Attachment and loss. Vol. 1. Attachment.* New York: Basic Books.

Bowlby, J. (1973). *Attachment and loss. Vol. 2. Separation.* New York: Basic Books.

Buriel, R., & DeMent, T. (1997). Immigration and sociocultural changes in Mexican, Chinese, and Vietnamese American families. In A. Booth, A. C. Crouter, & N. Landale (Eds.), *Immigration and the family: Research and policy on U.S. immigrants.* Mahwah, NJ: Lawrence Erlbaum Associates.

Buriel, R. (1986). Latino value systems and their educational implications. Unpublished manuscript, Pomona College, Claremont, CA.

Cauce, A. M., & Rodriguez, M. D. (2002). Latino families: Myths and realities. In J. M. Contreras, K. A. Kerns, and A. M. Neal-Barnett (Eds.), *Latino children and families in the United States.* Westport, CT: Greenwood.

Chapa, J., & Valencia, R. R. (1993). Latino population growth, demographic characteristics, and educational stagnation: An examination of recent trends. *Hispanic Journal of Behavioral Science, 15*, 165–187.

Coltrane, S. (1996). *Family man: Fatherhood, housework and gender equity.* New York: Oxford University Press.

Coltrane, S. (2000). Research on household labor: Modeling and measuring the social embeddedness of routine family work. *Journal of Marriage and the Family, 62,* 1208–1233.

Coltrane, S., Parke, R. D., & Adams, M. (2001, April). Shared parenting in Mexican-American and European-American families. Paper presented at the Biennial meeting of the Society for Research in Child Development, Minneapolis, Minnesota.

Coltrane, S., & Valdez, E. (1993). Reluctant compliance: Work-family role allocation in dual earner Chicano families. In J. Hood (Ed.), *Men, work, and family* (pp. 151–174). Newbury Park, CA: Sage.

COSSMHO. (1999). *The State of Hispanic Girls.* Washington, DC: National Coalition of Hispanic Health and Human Services Organizations.

Conners, L. J., Epstein, J. L. (1995). Parent and School Partnerships. In M. Bornstein (Eds.), *Handbook of parenting,* (Vol. 4, pp. 437–450). Mahwah, NJ: Lawrence Erlbaum Associates.

Delgado-Gaitan, C. (1994). Socializing young children in Mexican-American families: An intergenerational perspective. In P. M. Greenfield & R. Cocking (Eds.), *Cross-cultural roots of minority child development,* (pp. 55–86). Hillsdale, NJ: Erlbaum.

Erkut, S., Alarcon, O., Garcia Coll, C., Tropp, L. R., Vazquez Garcia, H. A. (1999). The dual-focus approach to creating bilingual measures. *Journal of Cross-Cultural Psychology, 30,* 206–218.

Fagan, J. A. (1996). A preliminary study of low-income African American fathers' play interactions with their preschool-age children. *Journal of Black Psychology, 1,* 7–19.

Fagan, J. A (1998). Correlates of low-income African American and Puerto Rican fathers; Involvement with their children. *Journal of Black Psychology, 3,* 351–367.

Flannery, W. P., Reise, S. P., & Widaman, K. F. (1995). An item response theory analysis of the general and academic seeds of the Self-Description Questionnaire II. *Journal of Research in Personality, 25,* 168–188.

Freeman, H. (1997). Who can you turn to? Individual differences in late adolescent perceptions of parents and peers as attachment figures. Unpublished doctoral dissertation, University of Wisconsin-Madison.

Golding, J. M. (1990). Division of household labor, strain, and depressive symptoms among Mexican Americans and non-Hispanic Whites. *Psychology of Women Quarterly, 14,* 103–117.

Gonzales, N. A., Knight, G. P., Morgan-Lopez, A., Saenz, D. S., & Sirolli, A. (2002). Acculturation, enculturation and the mental health of Latino youths: An integration and critique of the literature. In J. M. Contreras, K. A. Kerns, & A. M. Neal-Barnett (Eds.), *Latino children and families in the United States,* (pp. 45–74). Westport, CT: Greenwood.

Hawkins, A. J. & Dollahite, D. C. (Eds.). (1997). *Generative fathering.* Thousand Oaks, CA: Sage.

Herrera, R. S., & Del Campo, M. (1995). Beyond the superwoman syndrome: Work satisfaction and family functioning among working-class, Mexican American women. *Hispanic Journal of Behavioral Sciences, 17,* 49–60.

Hetherington, E. M., Reiss, D., & Plomin, R. (1994). *Separate social worlds of siblings: The impact of nonshared environment on development.* Hillsdale, NJ: Lawrence Erlbaum Associates.

Hossain, Z., Field, T., Malphus, J., Valle, C., & Pickens, J. (1995). Fathers caregiving in low income African-American and Hispanic American families. Unpublished manuscript, University of Miami, Medical School.

Hunter, A. G. & Davis J. E. (1994). Hidden voices of black men: The meaning, structure and complexity of manhood. *Journal of Black Studies, 25,* 20–40.

Keefe, S. E., & Padilla, A. M. (1987). *Chicano ethnicity.* Albuquerque, NM: University of New Mexico Press.

Keefe, S. E. (1984). Real and ideal extended familism among Mexican-Americans and Anglo-Americans. *Human Organization, 43,* 65–70.

2. MEXICAN-AMERICAN FAMILIES 37

Knight, G. P., & Kagan, S., (1977). Acculturation of prosocial and competitive behaviors among second- and third-generation Mexican-American children. *Journal of Cross-Cultural Psychology, 8*, 273–284.

Knight, G. P., Virdin, L. M., & Roosa, M. (1994). Specialization and family correlates of mental health outcomes among Hispanic and Anglo American children. Consideration of cross-ethnic scalar equivalence. *Child Development, 65*, 212–224.

Lamb, M. E. (Ed.). (1997). *The role of the father in child development* (3rd ed.). New York: Wiley.

Levine, J. A., & Pittinsky, J. J. (1997). *Working fathers: New strategies for balancing work and family.* New York: Harcourt Brace.

Leyendecker, B., & Lamb, M. E. (1999). Latino families. In Lamb (Ed.), *Parenting and child development in "nontraditional" families*, (pp. 247–262). Mahwah, NJ: Lawrence Erlbaum Associates.

Madsen, W. (1973). *The Mexican-American of South Texas*, New York: Holt, Rinehart & Winston.

Marsiglio, W., Day, R., Evans, J., Lamb, M., Braver, S., & Peters, E. (1998). Report of the Working Group on Conceptualizing Male Parenting. *In Nurturing Fatherhood: Improving data and research on male fertility, family formation and fatherhood* (pp. 101–174). Washington DC: Federal interagency Forum on Child and Family Statistics.

Marsiglio, W., Day, R. D., & Lamb, M. E. (2000). Exploring fatherhood diversity: Implications for conceptualizing father involvement. *Marriage & Family Review, 29*, 269–293.

Massey, D. S. (1993). Latinos, poverty, and the underclass: A new agenda for research. *Hispanic Journal of Behavioral Sciences, 15*, 523–533.

McBride, B. A. (1991). Parental support programs and paternal stress: An exploratory study. *Early Childhood Research Quarterly, 6*, 137–149.

McLoyd, V. C., Cauce, A. M., Takeuchi, D., & Wilson, L. (2000). Marital processes and parental socialization in families of color: A decade review of research. *Journal of Marriage and the Family, 62*, 1070–1093.

Mirandé, A. (1997). Hombres et machos: Masculinity and Latino culture. Boulder, CO: Westview.

Morales, R. & Ong, P. M. (1993). The illusion of progress: Latinos in Los Angeles. In R. Morales & F. Bonilla (Eds.), *Latinos in a changing U. S. economy: Comparative perspectives on growing inequality*, (pp. 55–84). Newbury Park, CA: Sage.

Morgan D. L. (1988). *Focus groups as qualitative research.* Newbury Park, CA: Sage.

Ortiz, D. R. (1996). Descriptive study: High school students' problems, concerns, and ways of coping. *Dissertation Abstract International, Section A: Humanities & Social Sciences, 57*, 23–72.

Palkovitz, R. (1997). Reconstructing "involvement": Expanding conceptualizations of men's caring in contemporary families. In A. J. Hawkins & D. C. Dollahite (Eds.), *Generative fathering: Beyond deficit perspectives. Current issues in the family series* (Vol. 3., pp. 200–216). Thousand Oaks, CA: Sage.

Parke, R. D. (1996). *Fatherhood.* Cambridge: Harvard University Press.

Parke, R. D., Power, T. G., Tinsley B. R., & Hymel, S. (1980). Fathers at risk. A hospital based model of intervention. In D. B. Sawin, R. D. Hawkins, L. O. Walker, & J. H. Penticuff (Eds.), *Psychosocial risks in infant environment interaction* (pp. 174–189). New York: Brunner/Mazel.

Parke, R. D., & Buriel, R. (1998). Socialization in the family: Ecological and ethnic perspectives. In W. Damon (Editor-in-chief) & N. Eisenberg (Vol. Ed.), *Handbook of child psychology*, (Vol. 4, 5th ed., pp. 463–552). New York: Wiley.

Patterson, G. R. (1993). Orderly change in a stable world: The antisocial trait as chimera. *Journal of Consulting and Clinical Psychology, 61*, 911–919.

Perez, S., & Salazar, D. (1993). Economic, labor force, and social implications of Latino educational and population trends. *Hispanic Journal of Behavioral Sciences, 15*, 188–229.

Roschelle, A. (1997). *No more kin: Explaining race, class, and gender in family networks.* Thousand Oaks: Sage.

Shelton, B. A., & John, D. (1993). Does marital status make a difference? Housework among married and cohabiting men and women. *Journal of Family Issues, 14*, 401–420.

Silverstein, L. (2002). Fathers and families. In J. P. McHale and W. S. Grolnick (Eds.), *Retrospect and prospect in the psychological study of families* (pp. 35–64). Mahwah, NJ: Lawrence Erlbaum Associates.

Toth, J. F., Jr., & Xu, X. (1999). Ethnic and cultural diversity in fathers' involvement: A Racial/ethnic comparison of African American, Hispanic, and White fathers. *Youth & Society, 31*, 76–77.

U.S. Census Bureau. (2001). *The Hispanic Population: Census 2000 Brief.* Report prepared by Betsy Guzman, issued May 2001 (C2KBR01-3). Washington, DC: U.S. Government Printing Office.

U.S. Census Bureau. (2000). *The Hispanic Population in the United States: Population Characteristics, March 1999.* Current Population Reports P20-527. Washington, DC: U.S. Government Printing Office.

Vega, W. A. (1990). Hispanic families in the 1980s: A decade of research. *Journal of Marriage and the Family, 52*, 1015–1024.

Vega, W. A. (1995). The study of Latino families: A point of departure. In R. E. Zambrana (Ed.) *Understanding Latino families: Scholarship, policy, and practice* (pp. 3–17). Thousand Oaks, CA: Sage.

Vélez-Ibáñez, C. (1996). *Border visions.* Tucson: University of Arizona Press.

White, B. L., Kaban, B., Shapiro, B., & Attonucci, J. (1976). Competence and experience. In I. C. Uzgirls and F. Weizmann (Eds.), *The structuring of experience* (pp. 115–152). New York: Plenum.

Vidal, C. (1988). Godparenting among Hispanic Americans. *Child Welfare, 67*, 453–459.

Williams, N. (1993). Elderly Mexican American Men. In J. Hood (Ed.), *Men, Work and Family* (pp. 68–85). Newbury Park, CA: Sage.

Yeung, W. J., Sandberg, J. F., Davis-Kean, P. M., & Hofferth, S. L. (2001). Children's time with fathers in intact families. *Journal of Marriage & the Family, 63*, 136–154.

Zavella, P. (1987). *Women's work and Chicano families: Cannery workers of the Santa Clara Valley.* Ithaca: Cornell University Press.

Zinn, M. B., & Wells, B. (2000). Diversity within Latino families: New lessons for family social science. In D. H. Demo, K. R. Allen, & M. A. Fine (Eds.), *Handbook of family diversity* (pp. 252–273). New York: Oxford University Press.

3

Father Involvement in Britain: The Research and Policy Evidence

Lynda Clarke
London School of Hygiene and Tropical Medicine

Margaret O'Brien
University of East Anglia, England

In this chapter we examine the contemporary knowledge about father involvement in Britain and critically analyse how fatherhood has been explored by British family researchers since the initial wave of interest in the early 1980s. We are mainly concerned with assessing the research evidence, methodology, and theory formulation that has been conducted in Britain in contrast to the American evidence presented in the remainder of this volume. During the course of this exercise we identify research questions that remain unanswered and suggest fruitful directions for future study while noting specific problems to be anticipated by future investigators.

We begin by outlining the recent public policy interest in fatherhood in Britain, focusing on the impact of the Labor Government since 1997. We then review how British researchers have initiated this debate or reacted to it, the research questions that have been addressed, the theory development in this area, how data on fathers have been collected, and, in particular, how father involvement has been measured.

39

PUBLIC POLICY AND FATHERHOOD:
U.K. CONTEXT

What is striking about British policies affecting fathers to date is that they have been formulated in response to political decisions and have not been based on research evidence, which is in sharp contrast to American developments (Clarke & Roberts, 2002a). With the arrival of the Labor Government came the creation of Britain's first explicit national family policy (*Home office*, 1998b), which included some consideration of the place of fathers in family life. While the Government's current view on fatherhood is still unclear, in part reflecting the emphasis to date on the economic role of fathers within Government policy, its inclusion of fathers in public debate on the future of the family has stimulated further academic, policy, and practitioner enquiry. It is worth noting that the current focus in the United States, Britain, and Australia on fatherhood research and policy has taken a different emphasis to that across many European countries (Clarke & Roberts, 2002b). Despite an early interest in fatherhood in several Nordic countries, notably Sweden (Bjornberg, 1998), their primary concern has been with gender equity and the role of mothers in families. Fatherhood and father involvement has not been a dominant issue among mainstream European policymakers and family researchers, with certain notable exceptions (European Commission Network on Childcare, 1996; Fthenakis & Kalicki, 1999; Giovannini, 1998; Ministry of Social Affairs, 1993).

Interest in fatherhood research in Britain dates back to the late 1970s and early 1980s (Lewis, 1986; McKee & O'Brien, 1982), but it did not expand as quickly or as deeply as in the United States. At the same time there was an independent policy interest in fathers that was overwhelmingly created by the growth of single-parent households and the issue of the growing public expenditure on single-parent families. There was almost no analysis of the characteristics of absent fathers and their family circumstances before the controversial Child Support legislation of 1991was introduced (Bradshaw, Stimson, Skinner, & Williams, 1999). The ensuing protest, led mainly by separated and repartnered fathers, was perhaps due to this lack of groundwork and research interest. To date the story about the relationship between fathers and their children who are not coresident remains to be unraveled. Researchers are hampered by the methodological problems of accessing a representative sample of nonresident fathers to answer the important research questions. How many nonresident fathers have contact with their children, the frequency of contact, the quality of relationships, and whether these factors are important for each person's well-being are not known. Whether the relationship, characteristics, or circumstances of parents at the time of the child's birth or some prior or later factors are influential in shaping the "absent" father's role are not clear.

Another strand in the development of recent policy and academic theory development around father involvement and child development has been a concern with

3. BRITISH RESEARCH AND POLICY EVIDENCE   41

crime. Growing under the Conservative Government and continuing under the Labor Government has been a rising anxiety about crime and social disorder among
young people, especially young men. In the mid-1990s, some policy analysts were
laying the blame for social disorder at the door of fathers or at least at the absence
of effective fathers (Dennis & Erdos, 1993). These writers, in part influenced by
the American social commentator Charles Murray (1990), argued that groups of
young people were growing up completely unsocialized by fathers or male elders,
out of control in inner city neighborhoods with poor housing and education, and
with no work prospects. Despite some extreme interventions such as the Crime and
Disorder Bill (Home Office 1997), concern about the more general relationship
between fathers and their sons continues to be part of family policy discussion. In
a Home Office (1998a) seminar on boys, young men, and fathers, the Minister's
opening comments stressed that "probably the single most effective way of helping young men was by encouraging the involvement of their fathers in their lives"
(p. 3). However, little account has been taken of the limited evidence on young
and "vulnerable" fathers, which research funders are beginning to support (e.g.,
Quinton & Pollock, 2003; Speak, Cameron, & Gilroy, 1997).

A broader perspective on the place of fathers in families has recently emerged
as central to the research and policy debates (Burgess & Ruxton, 1996). The Government's family-policy agenda, framed by family support on the one hand and
child poverty reduction on the other, has many implications for the role of fathers
in families that have yet to be clarified (Featherstone, 2001). A platform has been
introduced of fiscal and social policy measures designed to both support families
(through support for child care and parenting) and decrease child poverty, primarily by encouraging parents, particularly poor parents, into employment. Several
practice and policy developments have been promoted including, significantly, a
funding stream to finance work on fatherhood mainly at a local level. Innovative
initiatives have included pump priming a new national organization, Fathers Direct, established in 1999 to directly support fathers and practitioners working with
fathers. In its inaugural year the organization distributed a fatherhood guide to all
new fathers and has since hosted a series of seminars, a Web site, and a magazine.
Research briefings and a plan to commission an audit of fathers in Britain are part
of Fathers Direct's future intentions. Also, most important is the Government's
formation of the National Family and Parenting Institute (NFPI), which is funded
with £2 million over 3 years to monitor and promote "good parenting." The NFPI's
overall brief is to act to improve knowledge and understanding about the role of
parents in British society, but it has no specific research brief.

The fact that Britain has the longest working hours for fathers in Europe has
often been cited as a major limiting influence on fathers' involvement with children
(Dex, 1999). Support for working fathers' parental responsibilities has received
some recent recognition at the macroeconomic level with the Labor Government's
acceptance of two European Union (EU) directives. In 1999 the Parental Leave directive for fathers to be able to take unpaid leave to cope with family responsibilities

was introduced, shortly followed by implementation of the EU Working Time Directive in 2000, which regulates the number of hours worked by employees. The results of a national consultation, announced in May 2001, indicate that from 2003 all new fathers will be entitled to 2 weeks paid paternity leave (to be taken within the first 2 months of the child's birth) (Department of Trade and Industry, 2000, 2001). The incorporation of the directives has highlighted the wider issue of fathers' nurturing role in families and men's "work–life balance" (Department for Education and Employment, 2000). Researchers are starting to evaluate the labor market changes on family life, including the role of fathers (Forth, Lissenburgh, Callender & Millward, 1997; O'Brien & Shemilt, 2003).

A policy shift to support fathers in general in both their child-caring and breadwinner functions appears to be emerging, although a preoccupation with "deadbeat" and "dead broke" dads remains, reflecting perhaps the diversity of fathers in contemporary Britain. Research evidence is beginning to be consulted by the policymakers, but there are many questions yet to be formulated, let alone answered. In summary, current British family policy on fatherhood occupies an intermediate position between the American "father involvement" agenda and the European "gender equity" agenda (Cabrera & Peters, 2000; Hantrais & Letablier, 1996; O'Brien, M. (in press)). The arrival of new administrations in both America and Britain during 2001 will inevitably produce further policy ideas and initiatives on fathers and family life.

CONCEPTUALIZING FATHER INVOLVEMENT

Although there have always been discreet studies of fatherhood in the social sciences in Britain, the range and extent of projects in the late 1970s and early 1980s signified a move away from a mother-centered focus. A new generation of social science researchers broadened the study of families to incorporate fathers (Beail & McQuire, 1982; Lewis, 1986; Lewis & O'Brien, 1987; McKee & O'Brien, 1982) and children (Clarke, 1992; James & Prout, 1990; Jenks, 1982).

The first wave of fatherhood research from psychologists and sociologists was primarily, although not exclusively, ethnographic and embedded in a "discovery" mode, with the intention of giving paternal accounts of family life a hearing and a center stage, a father-centered paradigm. Firsthand accounts of men's family life or life course transitions—for instance, becoming a father or caring for children alone—indicated that men could experience these events in an emotionally intense manner, showing behaviors that did not fit into the stereotype of the distant, disengaged father (Lewis, 1986). A common theme in this early work was to uncover more about the meaning of being a father—a search for the phenomenology of fatherhood, in much the same way as the endeavor of some contemporary American fatherhood scholarship (Marsiglio & Cohan, 2000). The legacy of this early work

3. BRITISH RESEARCH AND POLICY EVIDENCE 43

still remains but is now recast into a more robust methodological framework suggested by researchers at the time.

An important point was made early in the academic debate on fatherhood in Britain but is worth reemphasizing because it tends to be overlooked. In 1982, Martin Richards commented that "fathers should not be regarded merely as alternative mothers" (Richards, 1982, p. 57). British fatherhood researchers had concerns about what became known in the 1990s as the "deficit perspective" whereby a "mother template" was adopted for understanding the nature of fathering (Palkovitz, 1997).

Among contemporary family researchers in Britain there is a growing awareness of the importance of conceptualizing father involvement within a perspective that captures the inherent complexities and different levels of family life. Fathering does not take place in isolation but occurs in interaction with mothers and children in increasingly diverse sets of family alliances and household contexts. Accordingly future fatherhood researchers will need to develop measures that include multiple influences on father involvement and a wider perspective on what fathering in contemporary families may indeed encompass.

While this more holistic appreciation of fathering with its multiple dimensions and diversity of styles and relationships has played some part in recent British research on fatherhood, a concern with gender equity issues—how much time men contribute to housework and child care—has tended to dominate the research agenda. The focus on issues of equality and intimacy emerges from the legacy and continuing influence of feminism in British academic social science. The degree of male participation in domestic matters continues to be an important touchstone of gender equality. Increase in mothers' participation in the labor market throughout the 1990s, in particular the growth of full-time employment among mothers of young children, has heightened equity concerns (Brannen, Moss, Owen, & Wale, 1997). As Moss (2000, p. 172) has argued, for employed parents in the late 1990s, the prime working years have become a period when many are running around like "headless chickens, ... facing an ever increasing workload and considerable financial pressures, trying to fit too much into a finite day." Accordingly many British studies continue to rely on basic household division-of-labor indicators as key measures of father involvement alongside more crude measures of fathers' presence or absence in the household.

MEASURING FATHER INVOLVEMENT

National Surveys: Fertility Data

The tendency to use mothers as proxies for fathers' fertility has been strong within the United Kingdom in line with the historic mother-centerdness of family and child national statistics. For many years men's fertility was considered either

unacceptable to ask about or impossible to study and, as a result, such questions were not carried in surveys, in much the same way as questions to mothers about births outside marriage were avoided. However, it is important to note the numerous methodological problems associated with any study of fathers' fertility. The breakdown in parenting relationships and childbearing outside coresident unions create the potential for considerable underreporting of children, when men do not live with their children. Whether this misreporting is unwitting or deliberate, it still creates problems for estimating the demography of fatherhood that do not exist to the same extent for the demography of motherhood. There still remains the knotty problem of missing data, however, be it from underrepresentation of men with certain characteristics (for instance, fathers who were nonresident at birth) or from high nonresponse rates. A detailed evaluation of the quality of men's fertility information in survey and longitudinal data in both British and American studies by Rendall, Clarke, Peters, Ranjit, & Verropoulou (1999) revealed both survey underrepresentation and nonreporting of births. Incomplete recording of fertility by men in these surveys is between 11% and 17% of all births and between 35% and 50% of nonmarital births. Estimates of undercounting of men's births in the British Household Panel Study (BHPS) were 12% for all births, 36% for births outside marriage, and 39.5% for marital births for which the marital union had dissolved before the survey. For births overall, and particularly for nonintact marital births, underrepresentation rather than nonreporting appears to be the major contributor to the underreporting of fatherhood. Nonreporting is the major source of omission for nonmarital births. Any future study of fathers has to decide how to cope with fathers who will be missed, especially those who are not living with their children.

While underidentification of nonresident fathers will remain a problem, national data sets can provide important data on the demography of fatherhood. In the mid-1990s the first demographic analysis of fatherhood took place, using evidence from the BHPS as this was the first nationally representative survey in Britain to ask men about fertility histories (Burghes, Clarke, & Cronin, 1997). Further demographic analyses of fatherhood have been undertaken, including a comparison with American fathers and absent fathers (Clarke, Cooksey, & Verropoulou, 1999). These analyses found that young fatherhood was more common in the United States than in Britain, especially among Black men. In Britain, one-third (34%) of men had their first child before they were 25, but in the United States the comparative proportions were 41% of White fathers, 47% of Hispanic fathers, and 61% of Black fathers. Family breakdown was evident in the proportions of fathers who were not coresident with their children in both countries but this was higher in the United States, again being particularly high for Black American fathers. Only 54% of Black fathers were coresident with all of their children compared with 76% of Hispanic and 79% of White American fathers and 85% of British fathers. The risk factors for living apart from children were remarkably similar in both countries, namely being a young father and not married.

3. BRITISH RESEARCH AND POLICY EVIDENCE   45

Parenting and Child
Development Indicators

Large national data sets that include parenting and child development indicators
can also provide important resources for examining father involvement in families, as emphasized in the recent decade review of U.S. fatherhood scholarship
(Marsiglio, Amato, Day, & Lamb 2000). Within the British context, investigation
of father involvement has the potential to benefit from three unique national longitudinal birth cohort studies that have taken place over the last century: 1946 (the
National Study of Health and Development, NSHD), 1958 (the National Child
Development Study, NCDS), and 1970 (the 1970 British Cohort Study, BCS70).
However, to date fathers have not been a central topic of cohort research with two
notable exceptions: Ferri and Smith's study of fathers in the context of employment
and family life using the NCDS (Ferri, 1993; Ferri & Smith, 1996) and Osburn
and Morris's examination (1982) of paternal involvement of NSHD children at
5 years old.

Ferri and Smith (1996) focused on how mothers and fathers negotiated family-
employment commitments. They analyzed adult members of the cohort at 33 years
of age during the fifth sweep. Marked variations in the employment situations of
cohort mothers and fathers was found by the age of 33, although the majority—
59% of mothers and 53% of fathers—were in dual-earner households, primarily
where the mother worked part time, still the most typical pattern in the Britain when
dependent children are under 11 years old. The main measures of paternal involvement in this investigation, which followed, it could be argued, a maternal-template
model, were division-of-labor indicators of participation in basic child-care tasks
and in housework using survey questions. This showed that fathers' involvement in
the home has been increasing over time and that the gender gap in terms of average
time spent caring for children has narrowed. The analysis concentrated mainly on
differences between household types. When mothers worked, over a third cited
fathers as the main child-care provider, followed by grandparents or other kin. The
most egalitarian sharing of "general" child-care tasks (mainly cooking for children, bathing, and dressing) was found for dual-earner families where both parents
worked full time: Two-thirds of cohort mothers and three-quarters of cohort fathers
reported sharing these tasks. However, dual-earner fathers who worked more than
50 hours a week lowered their participation in child care.

The finding that dual-earner mothers and fathers also reported the highest levels
of stress among cohort parents is important for the current policy debate in Britain
on "work–home balance" and would benefit from future detailed examination.
The British father works an average of 47 hours per week, compared to the EU12
paternal average of 42.7 hours (Brannen et al., 1997); this average has increased
over the last decade, particularly among professionally employed fathers, but has
recently stabilized (O'Brien & Shemilt, 2003).

The employment context of fathers' lives was less salient at the time of the Osburn and Morris study (1982). They selected four dimensions of father involvement with 5-year-old children: looking after the child without the mother, putting the child to bed, collecting the child from the nursery, and reading to the child. Great variability in father involvement was found, resonating with later British studies (e.g., Lewis, 1986). For instance, fathers were roughly equally divided as to whether they had put their child to bed or not in the previous week. The investigators found some links between high father involvement and positive child outcomes at 5 years old. The benefits of father involvement were mainly in the cognitive domain (verbal IQ and a spatial motor task), although its impact on other dimensions of child behavior was less clear.

Further detailed analysis of father involvement, particularly in the context of mother and family factors, is necessary for comparison among all three cohort studies. It is encouraging that researchers are now beginning to use a wider range of father involvement measures embedded in the national cohorts to examine the impact of fathering on child outcomes. For instance, A. Buchanan and E. Flouri are using the NCDS cohort survey to measure father involvement from child or parent reports at child ages 7 and 11 and follow-up adolescent and adult outcomes.[1]

Similarly the very important new Millennium Cohort Study (MCS), which is gathering information on a sample of 15,000 babies born in Britain over a 12-month period, will be the first cohort study to gather data directly from fathers as well as mothers. As such, this study will become a crucial source of information on father involvement and its impact on children.[2]

NATIONAL SURVEYS

Time Use

A national survey data resource on father involvement in Britain is the Multinational Time-Use Study (MTUS) held at the University of Essex Economic and Social Research Council (ESRC) data archive. These useful time-budget studies combine quantitative and qualitative data with an update being carried out by the Office of National Statistics (ONS). The studies have been intensively analyzed over many years by Gershuny but with an emphasis on the gender division of

---

[1] The study is an ESRC project entitled "Father Involvement—outcomes in Adolescence and Adulthood." It will focus on four dimensions of child interaction with fathers: "Father reads to child," "outings with father," "father's role in managing the child," and "father's interest in child's education." Outcome measures include the following: in adolescence (age 16), psychological adjustment (Rutter Scale A), academic performance, personal relationships, welfare, and police involvement. In adulthood (age 33): psychological adjustment (Malaise Inventory), adult work history, personal relationships, welfare, and police involvement.

[2] H. Joshi, *ESRC Millennium Cohort Study*. Centre for Longitudinal Studies, Institute of Education, University of London (email: hj@cls.ioe.ac.uk).

3. BRITISH RESEARCH AND POLICY EVIDENCE 47

domestic and paid work rather than from a father-involvement perspective (Gershuny, 2001; Short, 2000). Gershuny (2001) has shown from international time-budget diary comparisons that British fathers are indicating similar trends in father child care as fathers in the United States; that is, men's involvement in child care has increased more than their contribution to other household work. There was increased child-care time spent by British fathers (and mothers) between the mid-1970s and end of the millennium, with increases especially sharp since 1985 and in particular for those fathers with children under age 5.

An important finding from this data set is the continuity of gender divisions in time spent on child care. Analysis of the 1995 ONS time-use survey has show that the average time men (whether they had children or not) spent on child care did not vary according to whether they worked or not (19 minutes per day if they worked and 18 minutes if they did not work) (Gersuny, 2001). By contrast, women spent 36 minutes per day if they worked compared with 1 hour, 23 minutes if they did not work. When put together with the tendency for fathers to earn an average of two-thirds of the family income, this pattern indicates that gender divisions in two-parent British households continue to look quite conventional.

There is great scope for further research on British fatherhood through the time-budget studies, which have been underutilized by family researchers. For example, potential exists for further secondary analysis of the ONS 1995 and 1999 time-use surveys where breakdown by parental status and employment status is available. Further analysis could include an examination of fathers' use of time in different occupational groups and different family contexts and would provide useful information on work–life balance issues.

Similarly the larger ONS U.K. Time-Use Survey 2000 covering 11,000 households will be a very important source of data on fathers' involvement in family life and paid work as it contains multiperson information collected at 10-minute intervals over a 24-hour period for a weekday and weekend.

However, reliance on "clock time," without contextual data on "process time" or the meaning of time use for family members, does not have the elements required to fully understand the nature of family-employment negotiations for mothers and fathers (Pleck & Steuve, 2001). For instance, perceptions of closeness may mean different things to men, women, and children and meanings change for any particular actor over time and in relation to changing circumstances. The meanings are negotiated between mothers and fathers and mediated, particularly by mothers. Mothers can be the "gatekeepers" to fathers' involvement and men often depend on the mother's interpretation of what is needed (Backett, 1982). In addition, father involvement can work in part because of the effect it has on the mother, and thus the satisfaction of the mother with the nature of the father's involvement is also an important factor (Lewis, Newson, & Newson, 1982). Awareness of maternal facilitation of father involvement and indeed paternal facilitation of maternal involvement is emerging as an important context in which to understand fatherhood in Britain, as in contemporary American family scholarship.

Attitudes to Parental Roles

National surveys also provide a useful resource for charting attitudes toward father involvement both cross-sectionally and over time. Attitudinal reports on beliefs about the roles of men and women in the family and workplace and on participation in basic child-care tasks have been and continue to be the core indicators of paternal participation in the main national and European data sets, particularly the British Social Attitudes Survey (BSAS), Eurobarometer, and European Social Survey Programme (linked to the International Social Survey Programme available at the ESRC data archives based at the University of Essex).

Some of these surveys allow change to be charted over time as well as across and between cohorts. Key questions have been centered on the development of the "new man": Are men becoming more involved in child care? Are men developing more egalitarian attitudes to gender issues? The short answer to both questions is yes but with many caveats as reported behavior and attitude appear to vary considerably across age/generation, socioeconomic group, family-employment configuration, and region. A theme in British research has been to highlight the discrepancy between attitudes and actions.

QUALITATIVE STUDIES

Mixed Method Community Studies

As noted before, one strength of British fatherhood research has been its ethnographic tradition spanning the disciplines of psychology and sociology and often embedding the research in a neighborhood or community context. Local case studies of a qualitative nature can illuminate the many ways in which British fathers have adapted and responded to wider family changes, as general processes rarely work themselves out in pure forms. In the British context there is a tradition of research charting the decline and transformation of working class families in which a consideration of the role of fathers in this transition has played some part, although that role is rarely a central focus (e.g., Dennis, Henriques, & Slaughter, 1956; Newson & Newson, 1963; Young & Willmott, 1957). Historic community studies such as Dennis et al.'s examination (1956) of a Yorkshire coalmining village and Young and Willmott's study (1957) of East London portray a complex tapestry of fathering activities rather than any homogeneous pattern among working class communities during the middle of the last century. They have also embraced father relations with children of a broader age band than found in many American studies.

Recent British community studies have looked more closely at fatherhood and have used a combination of methods, both quantitative and qualitative, in their studies of family life (McKee & Mauthner, 1999; O'Brien & Jones, 1995, 1996a; Warin, Solomon, Lewis, & Langford, 1999). For instance, O'Brien and Jones's study included a child survey, interview, and time use diary illuminating teenage children's perception of family life, particularly time-use with fathers and mothers.

3. BRITISH RESEARCH AND POLICY EVIDENCE   49

Based in a White, working class East London locality originally studied by Peter Willmott in the 1950s, the study was of 620 fourteen year olds of whom 20% kept daily diaries for 1 week. Interviews were also conducted with a subsample of fathers and mothers. Many of the fathers were in manual occupations, and manual work practices ("up from the tools," "hard graft") provided important metaphors for good fathering among parents, reflecting the hard physical labor of generations of men in this area (O'Brien & Jones, 1997).

The child generation of the study had a more modern view of fatherhood than their own fathers, expressing their ideal father as one, who takes on an active share in the life of his children as well as earning money to support a family (O'Brien & Jones, 1995). They valued his presence and wanted him to "be there", but their accounts did not include notions of working hard for the family. In the daily lives of children it seemed that relationships with fathers were less physically present and represented as less emotionally close than to relationships with mothers. Time-use data collected from the children in the O'Brien and Jones study (1996b, 1999) showed that they spent more time with their mothers than with their fathers on each day of the week, although differences were less marked on Sundays. In terms of father involvement indicators this time-use measure represents an overlap between two dimensions of Lamb and Pleck's father involvement construct, father accessibility (availability) and engagement (direct interaction) rather than responsibility (executive function) (Lamb, Pleck, Charnov, & Levine, 1987). According to children's diaries, when they were together with their fathers they often watched television or "did nothing," except on weekends when more talking and leisure activities were reported.

While the early U.K. qualitative fatherhood studies gathered data from only one respondent, Warin et al. (1999), in their recent study of fathers of teenagers in the North of England, attempted to extend indicators of father involvement by gaining accounts from all family participants. The study used a mix of methods including survey and interviews of 53 females and 42 males (not living in the same household) and of children aged 11–16 years drawn from a random survey of the electoral register reflecting the working class character of the locality. In this predominately working class area they also found that the idea of provider was central to expectations of fatherhood, particularly among the fathers themselves. Mothers were more likely to emphasize the emotional dimension of paternal involvement. The authors used the growth of consumerism among teenagers to explain the continued power of fathers' economic-provision role, suggesting that

> Fathers' relationships with their teenage children were frequently mediated through the provision of material goods, and this was intensified in families where fathers had low incomes (p. 19).

Teenagers were more likely to turn to their mothers than their fathers when they wanted to talk, as reported in the previous study, but interview data revealed that teenagers wanted to have their dad around "to be there." While fathers emerged as

50   CLARKE AND O'BRIEN

particularly important for play and sport, men were "hardly ever at the center of the family," instead they were watching watching from the sidelines. Within the study, three factors independently predicted high levels of father–child shared activities: when the respondent was male, when the target child was female, and when the target child was young. The authors interpreted these findings as fathers being more involved in chaperonage activity with daughters and the younger children of the sample. Interestingly, the study showed that fathering can take place in a range of settings including nondomestic ones, often overlooked by researchers, including hobby-related activities, mending bikes in the garage, or time together during car trips. This project highlights the need to move beyond the domestic scene in research on fatherhood. In the U.K. context, observational work at local football or rugby pitches during Saturdays and Sundays would reveal many fathers, and some mothers, showing high levels of parental commitment from another set of sidelines. The potential stresses on contemporary fathers to do it all, that is, to both provide and care for, are also apparent from this study.

Fathering Styles, Identities, and Child Outcomes

Relationships between parents and children continue to be one of the core interests of British developmental psychologists. During the 1990s more projects have been incorporating fathers into their research designs (e.g., Dunn, Davies, & O'Connor, 2000). Similarly, at a conceptual level, British psychologists and psychiatrists have been drawing together family systems ideas and psychodynamic theory on the father–child relationship (e.g., Kraemer, 1991, 1997) to offer further theoretical insights. The strength of psychological theory and research on fathers is that it uses detailed concepts and measures of fathering that can complement studies based on macrosocial and global units of analysis. As Parke (forthcoming; p. 54) recently argued, "It is likely that no single methodological strategy will suffice to understand the development of the father's role in the family."

One important prospective qualitative developmental study conducted by Steele, Steele, & Fonagy (1996) illustrates this category of research in Britain. This on-going study has followed a sample of mainly highly educated London-based mothers and fathers from before the birth of their first child, collecting observational and interview data on parent–child interactions and on parents' accounts of relationships in their own family of origin. Using an attachment theory approach, Steele et al. (1996) measured the quality of attachments between parents and their infants. The measures developed by attachment researchers, such as the in-depth Adult Attachment Interview schedule, have the potential to elucidate paternal states of mind. The range of observational measures used within this approach suggests that there may be domains where fathers and mothers interact in both similar and distinctive ways. This research will directly feed into the debate about whether gender patterns of parenting are more or less culturally scripted.

3. BRITISH RESEARCH AND POLICY EVIDENCE 51

The inclusion of fathers as well as mothers in developmental psychology research designs is beginning to highlight the interaction of mother and father influences on children's lives. For instance, Dunn et al. (2000) in their longitudinal study of parent–child relationships have shown that children are at risk or benefit from the life histories both parents bring to their parenting, summarized as the "double dose" impact. That is, positive and negative dimensions of fathers' and mothers' early lives can jointly influence their children's well-being. Affectionate relations between fathers and children are more common in families where fathers and mothers had fewer life course changes (e.g., relationship changes, negative life events). Negative influences on children are amplified when both parents experienced adverse life histories, leading the authors to argue that the quality of fathering as well as mothering mediates children's psychological outcomes.

There are several interesting new projects on father involvement in Britain that are taking a much more systemic and holistic approach to examining both father involvement and the relationship of father involvement to other family processes (Buchanan, Lewis, & Flouri, in progress[3]; Quinton & Pollock, 2003; Sylva, Stein, & Leach, 2000). For instance, Sylva et al. (2000) have commenced an important prospective study of the effects of different child care on children's development over the first 5 years, following a methodological framework of assessment similar to that of the U.S. NICHD Early Child Care Research Network team. Five types of parental and nonparental child care are being compared, and the project includes a study of a small subsample of fathers who are primary caregivers.

There has also been important psychological and sociological research on the complex issue of father identities. Within this field, the early British ethnographies of fathers have been built, developing a substantial body of literature on the social construction of masculinities (e.g., Collier, 1995; Hearn & Morgan, 1990; Morgan, 1992; Segal, 1990; Seidler, 1989) and more recently of fatherhood itself (Barker, 1994; Burgess, 1997; Dunne, 1999; Eadley & Wetherell, 1999; Henwood, 2001). A key theme in this work has been the active construction of paternal identities in contemporary culture. Reordering contact within the complex web of family relations in the aftermath of separation and divorce has been a key setting for studies of father identities (e.g., Simpson, Walker, & McCarthy, 1995; Trinder, Beck, & Connolly, 2001), as has the emergence of cohabitional parenting relationships between couples (Lewis, Papacosta, & Warin, 2001; Pickford, 1999).

For instance, the social psychological work of Eadley and Wetherell (1999), drawing on discourse theory and the study of rhetoric, analyzed group discussions to show how young men's talk about fatherhood and domestic life is constructed across different settings. They argue that young men are located within a set of competing cultural ideals of fatherhood, which create "ideological dilemmas." The

---

[3] A. Buchanan, J. Lewis, and E. Flouri. The study is a Joseph Rowntree Foundation project entitled "The Nature of Fathers' involvement: A study of Resident and non-resident Fathers with Secondary School Age Children."

52   CLARKE AND O'BRIEN

pressures of being the major breadwinner and the demands to also be involved as
a hands-on caregiver or "new dad" give rise to tension between competing ideals. This developing British strand of social psychological analysis of fatherhood
has links with the recent American work of Marsiglio, Hutchinson, and Cohan
(2000).

Supporting Fathers: Fathers in Transition and Trouble

The other significant type of qualitative research into fatherhood has examined
fathers and family services support with the intention of trying to understand how
health and social care organizations can become more father-sensitive and encourage father involvement with children (e.g., Collett, 2001; Featherstone, 2001;
Moss, 1995; Pringle, 1995; Ryan, 2000). It is well known that men and fathers are
less likely than women and mothers to seek help for individual health or family-
related problems (O'Brien, 1988). Similarly, family support services may be in-
sensitive to the needs of fathers. Ghate, Shaw, & Hazel (2000) recently found that
many workers at family centers felt uneasy about engaging fathers. Fathers also
expressed dissatisfaction with the activities offered at family centers, preferring
more active and practical activities including Do-it-yourself (DIY) and play.

Reviewing child-protection cases involving physically and sexually abusive
fathers, Ryan (2000) traced the problems that can emerge when professionals are
too mother-focused in their practitioner work. Most important, fathers may be lost
to the social care system and go on to make new relationships with mothers of
young children, potentially repeating previous patterns of abusive behavior. As
Featherstone (2001) has argued, professionals are still juggling with constructions
of father as risk and father as resource. Future research on fathers in trouble or in
transition should be extended to the study of fatherhood in missing populations,
for example homeless fathers and military and imprisoned fathers (c.f. Federal
Interagency Forum on Child and Family Statistics, 1998).

In terms of vulnerable low-income fathers another major new data set will
come on stream later in the decade. This data set will emerge from the National
Evaluation of Sure Start (NESS),[4] a national intervention similar to U.S. Headstart,
which is targeted to help families with children under the age of 4 in economically
deprived communities. (Lloyd, O'Brien and Lewis, 2003). NESS will compare
child outcomes in Sure Start and non-Sure Start communities and is designed to
focus on communities, families, and individual parents and children as units of
analysis. Linkage with the Millennium cohort is being built into the evaluation.
As with the MCS, the evaluation strategy is designed to incorporate multiple
perspectives on outcomes and multiple modes of assessment. Data on father contact
and involvement will be routinely collected.

---

[4] Study is underway at Birbeck College, University of London.

3. BRITISH RESEARCH AND POLICY EVIDENCE 53

Multiethnic Nature of British Families

Another notable gap in Britain's fatherhood research agenda is a body of research on minority ethnic fathers. Britain's minority ethnic communities are growing from a small base and high fertility levels among some groups, suggesting that "the Britain of the twenty-first century will be multi-ethnic" (Halsey, 2000, p. 18). However, the proportion of the population claiming to be from an ethnic minority is much lower (around 6%) than in the United States, and ethnic minority populations are highly clustered in the major cities. The major ethnic minorities are often grouped for analysis purposes into Afro-Caribbean, mainly from the former British protectorates in the West Indies, and Asian (Indian, Pakistani, and Bangladeshi), from the previous British Commonwealth. This categorization masks significant cultural and lifestyle differences because family organization and values governing minority ethnic households vary significantly both within and between groups (Berthoud, 2000). For instance, current family structures of the Asian British of South Asian descent (Bangladeshi and Pakistanis) on the one hand and the Black British of Caribbean descent on the other could hardly be more different from each other. Among South Asians, marriage rates are high and single-mother households relatively low. For Black British of Caribbean descent, marriage rates are low and the preponderance of single-mother families is marked, with a high tendency for fathers to be nonresident. To date there have been no systematic research studies of Black British fathers. Similarly, in research on British Asian families, fathers have been of marginal interest (Beishon, Modood, & Virdee, 1997). One important development that is provoking policy and research interest is the increase in mixed marriages and partnerships, especially between young Black men and White women. Individuals in mixed ethnic partnerships often have children at a young age, and it is thought they may be at higher risk of family breakdown than couples from the same ethnic group (Berthoud, 2000).

More research on fatherhood in a multiethnic and multifaith context is required. For instance, a recent study of Muslim families (2000) revealed the key role religion plays in the negotiation of tradition and change for many Muslim families in Britain. While some parents rely solely on rituals and teaching the *Qur'an*, others are critical of rote learning and symbolic rituals. Gender relations defined by traditional patriarchal laws and religious dictates have created a general impression of inflexibility and oppression that may not always be the case for individuals as they try to negotiate their everyday lives.

CONCLUSION

In Britain, research on fathers and fathering has not developed the same momentum as it has across the Atlantic. There are, however, important differences in the research questions that the British have addressed and the approach they have taken

that can prove instructive for American fatherhood researchers. One tendency has been the domination of a gender-equity perspective despite the early innovative research that suggested a more holistic appreciation of fathering with its multiple dimensions and diversity of styles and relationships. Also, British researchers have placed less emphasis on the study of fathers' effect on child development at young ages and more focus on fathers and older children.

Researchers in Britain must now acquire a firm basis of knowledge about the demography of fatherhood from which to develop further qualitative and quantitative studies of fathers' reproductive and family lives throughout the life course. Unlike the situation in America, British fatherhood researchers have not yet integrated developmental, ethnographic, and demographic approaches to the study of fathers.[5] Similarly, they must perform qualitative normative studies of fathers using sensitive father involvement indicators from multiple family members to redress the continuing tendency of using mothers as the rapporteurs of family life. The British tradition of qualitative inquiry into fatherhood needs to be updated and extended to normative studies of fathers through the life course as well as to incorporate sensitive populations of missing fathers.

Whereas fathers clearly matter in Britain, the fatherhood research base has a low critical mass. As described in this chapter, U.K. studies charting the impact of father involvement on outcomes for children are still small in number and limited by the inevitable methodological constraints. Many studies are cross-sectional and so cannot tease out clear associations, let alone attempt causal relationships. More longitudinal studies and secondary analysis of new and existing data sets are called for, especially those exploiting the rich data in the three existing national cohort surveys and the forthcoming, new Millennium cohort. Existing studies have rarely controlled for the quality of the mother–child relationship or family context, and this should be attempted in future research investigating the influence of fathers. Epidemiological data on fathers are routinely conflated with data on men. Analysis of men's lives by their parental status and fathers' health and well-being is urgently required in the United Kingdom.

Although national survey data continue to provide insight into the patterns of father involvement at the aggregate level, a fuller, more holistic appreciation of fathering has yet to be realized. The development of more comprehensive and sensitive British indicators will be influenced by the impressive range of American initiatives on measuring father involvement at the survey level currently in the field (e.g., Federal Interagency Forum on Child and Family Statistics, 1998), but this cross-Atlantic dialogue is only in its early stages. Clearly, to advance theory development and capture wider dimensions of male parenting, British researchers will have to continue to construct core indicators of father involvement beyond

---

[5] A multidisciplinary network to advance policy and research development on fatherhood in Britain is in place to work on these issues between 2001 and 2004. See *Fathers and Fatherhood: New Directions for Research and Policy* (ESRC funded) http://www.lshtm.ac.uk/cps.

3. BRITISH RESEARCH AND POLICY EVIDENCE 55

the narrow domestic division of labor. Moreover, researchers will have to adopt an inclusive approach to the constellation of father figures present in contemporary families, that is, to include data collection strategies for resident nonbiological fathers and nonresident biological fathers as well as resident biological fathers. However, whether measures identical to those used in the American context will be adopted in Europe remains to be seen, as clearly national and regional variations will inevitably generate different fatherhood dimensions for exploration.

In conclusion, while we are at the cusp of an expansion of interest in fathers in Britain, there is still confusion about the part men should or do play in contemporary families (Lewis, 2000; Matheson and Summerfield, 2001). Public policies and media attention continue to focus on the negative aspects of fathers or take a narrow economic view of fathering without making links to its subjective meanings. Nevertheless, a broader, more holistic perspective is developing in policy and academic circles alike. As indicated earlier in the chapter, governmental interest in fathers is buoyant and in transition. British researchers are well placed to contribute toward future research agendas on conceptualizing and measuring father involvement.

REFERENCES

Backett, K. C. (1982). *Mothers and fathers. A study of the Development and negotiation of parental behaviour.* New York: Macmillan.

Barker, R. W. (1994). *Lone fathers and masculinities.* Aldershot, England: Avebury.

Beail, N., & McGuire, J. (Eds.). (1982). *Fathers: Psychological perspectives.* London: Junction Books.

Beishon, S., Modood, T., & Virdee, S. (1997). *Ethnic minority families.* London: Policy Studies Institute.

Berthoud, R. (2000). *Family formation in multi-cultural Britain: Three patterns of diversity.* Institute for Social and Economic Research Working Paper 2000-34. Colchester, England: University of Essex.

Bjornberg, U. (1998). Family orientation among men: A process of change in Sweden. In E. Drew, R. Emerek, & E. Mahon (Eds.) *Women, Work and the Family in Europe.* (pp. 200–207). London: Routledge & Kegan Paul.

Bradshaw, J., Stimson, C., Skinner, C., & Williams, J. (1999). *Absent fathers?* London: Routledge, & Kegan Paul.

Brannen, J., Moss, P., Owen, C., & Wale, C. (1997). *Mothers, fathers and employment: Parents and the labor market in Britain 1984–1994.* London: Department for Education and Employment.

Burgess, A. (1997). *Fatherhood reclaimed.* London: Vermilion.

Burgess, A., & Ruxton, S. (1996). *Men and their children. Proposals for public policy.* London: IPPR.

Burghes, L., Clarke, L., & Cronin, N. (1997). *Fathers and fatherhood in Britain.* Occasional Paper 23. London: Family Policy Studies Centre.

Cabrera, N. J., & Peters, H. E. (2000). Public policies and father involvement. *Marriage and Family Review, 29,* 4, 295–314.

ChildCare Network. (1990). *Men as carers for children.* Brussels: European Commission.

Collett, P. (2001). Working with men in family centres. In L. McMahon & A. Ward (Eds.), *Therapeutic work in family centres.* London: Jessica Kinglsey Publishers.

Collier, R. (1995). *Masculinity, law and the family.* London: Routledge & Kegan Paul.

Clarke, L. (1992). Children's family circumstances recent trends in Great Britain. *European Journal of Population, 8*, 309–340.

Clarke, L., Cooksey, E. & Verropoulou, G. (1999). Fathers and absent fathers: Sociodemographic similarities in Britain and the United States. *Demography, 35*, 2, 217–228.

Clarke, L., & Roberts, C. (2002a). Fathers and grandparents: Research and policy in an international perspective. In A. Carling, S. Duncan, & R. Edwards (Eds.), *Analysing families: Morality and rationality in policy and practice* (pp. xxx) London: Routledge, & Kegan Paul.

Clarke, L., & Roberts, C. (Eds.). (2002b). *Fathers in the new Millennium project.* York, England: Joseph Rowntree Foundation.

Dennis, N., & Erdos, G. (1993). *Families without fatherhood.* London: Institute of Economic Affairs.

Dennis, N., Henriques, F., & Slaughter, C. (1956). *Coal is our life: An analysis of a Yorkshire mining community.* London: Tavistock.

Department for Education and Employment. (2000). *Work-life balance, changing patterns in a changing world.* London: Author.

Department of Trade and Industry. (2000). *Work and parents, competitiveness and choice*, a consultation paper. London: Author.

Department of Trade and Industry. (2001, May 8). *Press Release.*

Dex, S. (Ed.). (1999). *Families and the labour market: Trends, pressures and policies. Family and parenthood, policy and practice.* London: Joseph Rowntree Foundation, Family Policy Studies Centre.

Dunn, J., Davies, L., & O'Connor, T. (2000). Parents' and partners' life course and family experiences: Links with parent–child relationships in different family settings. *Journal of Child Psychology and Psychiatry, 41*, 955–968.

Dunne, G. (1999). *The different dimensions of gay fatherhood.* London: The Gender Institute.

Eadley, N., & Wetherell, M. (1999). Imagined futures: Young men's talk about fatherhood and domestic life. *British Journal of Social Psychology, 38*, 181–194.

European Commission Network in Childcare (1996). *The EC Childcare Network 1986–1996: A decade of achievement.* European Commission Network on Childcare & Other Measures to Reconcile Family Responsibilities.

Featherstone, B. (2001). Putting fathers on the child welfare agenda: A research review. *Journal of Child and Family Social Work, 6*, 2, 179–186.

Federal Interagency Forum on Child and Family Statistics. (1998). *Nurturing fatherhood: Improving data and research on male fertility, family formation and fatherhood.* Washington, DC: Author.

Ferri, E. (1993). *Life at 33: The fifth follow-up of the National Child Development Study.* London: National Children's Bureau.

Ferri, E., & Smith, E. (1996). *Parenting in the 1990s.* London: Family Policy Studies Centre.

Forth, J., Lissenburgh, S., Callender, C., & Millward, N. (1997). *Family friendly working arrangements in Britain.* DfEE Research Report No 16. London: Department for Education and Employment.

Fthenakis, W., & Kalicki, B. (1999, September). Subjective conceptions of fatherhood: An expanded approach. Paper presented at the IXth Conference on Developmental Psychology, Spetses, Greece.

Gershuny, J. (2001). *Changing times.* New York: Oxford University Press.

Ghate, D., Shaw, C., & Hazel, N. (2000). *Fathers and family centres; engaging fathers in preventative services.* York, England: Joseph Rowntree Foundation.

Giovannini, D. (1998). Are fathers changing? Comparing some different images on sharing of childcare and domestic work. In E. Drew, R. Emerek, & E. Mahon (Eds.), *Women, work and the family in Europe.* London: Routledge & Kegan Paul.

Halsey, A. J. (2000). *Social Trends.* London: Stationary Office.

Hantrais, L., & Letablier, M. T. (1996). *Families and family policies in Europe.* New York: Longman.

Haskey (1998). One-parent families and their dependent children. *Population Trends, 91*:14–21.

Hearn, J., & Morgan, D. (Eds.). (1990). *Men masculinity and social theory.* London: Unwin Hyman.

3. BRITISH RESEARCH AND POLICY EVIDENCE 57

Henwood, K. (2001). *Masculinities, identities and transition to fatherhood*. ESRC End of Grant Report. ESRC Web Site REGARD. url www.esrc.ac.uk

Home Office. (1998a, November 16). Boys, young men and fathers: A ministerial seminar. http:www.homeoffice.gov.uk/cpd/fmpu/boys.html.

Home Office. (1998b). *Supporting Families*. London: Author.

Husain, F. & O'Brien, M. (2000). Muslim communities in Europe: Reconstruction and transformation. *Current Sociology, 48*, 4, 1–13.

James, A., & Prout, A. (Ed.). (1990). *Constructing and reconstructing childhood*. London: Falmer Press.

Jenks, C. (1982). *The Sociology of Childhood*. London: Batsford.

Kraemer, S. (1991). The origins of fatherhood. *Family Process, 30,* 377-392.

Kraemer, S. (1997). What are fathers for? In C. Burck & B. Speed (Eds.), *Gender, Power and Relationships*. London: Routledge & Kegan Paul.

Lamb, M. E., Pleck, J. H., Charnov, E. L., & Levine, J. A. (1987). A biosocial perspective on paternal behaviour and involvement. In J. B. Lancaster, J. Altmann, A. Rossi, S. Rossi, & L. R. Sherrod (Eds.), *Parenting across the lifespan: Biosocial dimensions* (pp. 111–142). New York: Aldine de Gruyter.

Lewis, C. (1986). *Becoming a Father*. Buckingham, England: Open University Press.

Lewis, C. (2000). *A man's place is in the home: Fathers and families in the UK*. York, England: Joseph Rowntree Foundation.

Lewis, C., Newson, E., & Newson, J. (1982). Father participation through childhood. In N. Beail & J. McGuire (Eds.), *Fathers: Psychological perspectives*, (pp. 174–193). London: Junction Books.

Lewis, C., & O'Brien, M. (Eds.). (1987). *Reassessing fatherhood: New observations on fathers and the modern family*. London: Sage.

Lewis, C., Papacosta, A., & Warin, J. (2001). *Cohabitation, separation and fatherhood*. York, England: Joseph Rowntree Foundation.

Marsiglio, W., Amato, P., Day, R. D., & Lamb, M. E. (2000). Scholarship on fatherhood in the 1990s and beyond. *Journal of Marriage and the Family, 62,* 1173–1191.

Marsiglio, W., & Cohan, M. (2000). Contextualizing father involvement and paternal influence: Sociological and qualitative themes. *Marriage and Family Review, 29,* 2/3, 75–95.

Marsiglio, W., Hutchinson S., & Cohan, M. (2000). Envisioning fatherhood: A social psychological perspective on young men without kids. *Family Relations, 49,* 2, 133–142.

Matheson, J. and Summerfield, C. (eds.). (2001). *Social Focus on Men*. London: Satationary Office.

Mauthner, N., Maclean, C., & McKee, L. (forthcoming). My dad hangs out of helicopter doors and takes pictures of oil platforms': Children's accounts of parental work in the oil and gas industry. *Community, Work and Family*.

McKee, L., & O'Brien, M. (Eds.). (1982). *The father figure*. London: Tavistock.

McKee, L., & Mauthner, N. (1999). *Children, family, community and work: An ethnography of the oil and gas industry in Scotland*, ESRC Project, Department of Management, University of Aberdeen.

Ministry of Social Affairs. (1993). *Fathers in families of tomorrow*. EU Conference Report. Copenhagen: Author.

Morgan, D. (1992). *Discovering men*. London: Routledge & Kegan Paul.

Moss, P. (1995). *Fathers, nurseries and childcare, European Commission Network on Childcare*. London: Thomas Coram Research Unit.

Moss, P. (2000). Modest hopes or great expectations? In H. Wilkinson (Ed.), *Family business*. London: Demos.

Murray, C. (1990). *The emerging British underclass*. London: IEA Health and Welfare Unit.

Newson, E., & Newson, J. (1963). *Infant care in an urban community*. London: Allen & Unwin.

O'Brien, M. (in press). Social Science and Public Policy Perspective on Fatherhood in the European Union M. E. Lamb (ed.). *The Role of the Father in Child Development*, 4th Edition, New Jersey: Wiley.

O'Brien, M. (1988). Men and fathers in therapy. *Journal of Family Therapy, 10*, 109–123.

O'Brien, M., & Jones, D. (1995). Young people's attitudes to fatherhood. In P. Moss (Ed.), *Father figures* (pp. 27–39). Scotland: HMSO.

O'Brien, M. (1996). The Absence and Presence of Fathers: Accounts from Children's Diaries, in U. Bjornberg and A. K. Kollind (eds.). Men's Family Relations. Sweden: University of Goteborg.

O'Brien, M., & Jones, D. (1996a). Family and kinship in Barking and Dagenham. In T. Butler and M. Rustin (Eds.) *Rising in the East*. (pp. 23–39). Lawrence & Wishart.

O'Brien, M., & Jones, D. (1996b). The absence and presence of fathers: Accounts from children's diaries. In U. Bjornberg & A. K. Kollind (Eds.). *Men's family relations* (pp. xxx). Sweden: University of Goteborg.

O'Brien, M., & Jones, D. (1997). Young people, family life and education in Barking and Dagenham: Three case studies. *Journal of East London Studies, 1*, 97–117.

O'Brien, M., & Jones, D. (1999). Children, parental involvement and educational attainment: An English case study. *Cambridge Journal of Economics: Special Issue on the Family, 23*, 599–621.

O'Brien, M., & Shemilt, I. (2003). *Working Fathers: Earning and Caring* Manchester: Equal Opportunities Commission. www.eoc.org.uk/research

Osburn, A., & Morris, A. (1982). Fathers and child care. *Early Child Development and Care, 8*: 279–307.

Palkovitz, R. (1997). Reconstructing involvement: Expanding conceptualizations of men's caring in contemporary families. In A. J. Hawkins & D. C. Dollahite (Eds.), *Generative fathering: beyond deficit perspectives* (pp. 200–216). Thousand Oaks, CA: Sage.

Parke, R. D. (forthcoming). Fathers and families. In M. Bornstein (Ed.), *Handbook of parenting*, Hillsdale, NJ: Lawrence Erlbaum Associates.

Pleck, J. H., & Stueve, J. L. (2001). Time and paternal involvement. In K. Daly (Ed.). *Minding the time in family experience: Emerging perspectives and issues*. (pp. 205–226). Oxford, UK: Elsevier Science.

Pickford, R. (1999). *Fathers, marriage and the law*. London: Family Policy Studies Centre.

Pringle, K. (1995). *Men, masculinities and social welfare*. London: UCL Press.

Quinton, D., & Pollock, S. (2000). *The transition to fatherhood by young men: influences on commitment*. ESRC Web REGARD site. www.esrc.ac.uk

Rendall, M. S., Clarke, L., Peters, H. E., Ranjit, H., & Verropoulou, G. (1999). Incomplete reporting of men's fertility in the United States and Britain: A research note. *Demography, 36*, 1, 135–144.

Richards, M. (1982). How should we approach the study of fathers? In L. McKee & M. O'Brien. (Eds.), *The father figure* (pp. 57–71). London: Tavistock.

Ryan, M. (2000). *Working with fathers*, Department of Health Report. Oxford, England: Radcliffe.

Segal, L. (1990). *Slow motion: Changing masculinities, changing men*. London: Virago.

Seidler, V. (1989). *Rediscovering Masculinity*. London: Routledge & Kegan Paul.

Short, S. (2000, October). Time use data in the household satellite account. In *Economic Trends* (p. 536). London: Office of National Statistics.

Simpson, B., Walker, J., & McCarthy, P. (1995). *Being there: Fathers after divorce*. Newcastle: Relate Centre for Family Studies.

Speak, S., Cameron, S., & Gilroy, R. (1997). *Young single fathers: Participation in fatherhood–bridges and barriers*. London: Family Policy Studies Centre.

Stationary Office. (1997). *Crime and Disorder Bill*. London:

Stationary Office. (2000). *Social Trends*. London: Author.

Stationary Office. (2001). *Social Focus on Men*. London: Author.

Steele, H., Steele, M., & Fonagy, P. (1996). Associations among attachment classifications of mothers, fathers and their infants. *Child Development, 69*, 592–594.

3. BRITISH RESEARCH AND POLICY EVIDENCE 59

Sylva, K., Stein, A., & Leach, P. (2000). *Families, children and childcare project protocol.* University of Oxford, Department of Educational Studies, and The Leopold Muller Centre for Child and Family Mental Health, Royal Free and University College Medical School. www.edstud.ox.ac.uk/FELL/fed.html.

Trinder, L., Beck, M., & Connolly, J. (2001). *The contact project, first year report,* York, England: Joseph Rowntree Foundation.

Warin, J., Solomon, Y., Lewis, C., & Langford, W. (1999). *Fathers, work and family life.* London: Family Policy Studies Centre.

Young, M., & Willmott, P. (1957). *Family and kinship in East London.* London: Routledge & Kegan Paul.

4

Studying Fathering Trajectories: In-depth Interviewing and Sensitizing Concepts

William Marsiglio
University of Florida

INTRODUCTION

Qualitative researchers using in-depth interviewing can use diverse analytic frameworks to study the processes underlying father involvement as well as the way men describe and interpret their lives as fathers or prospective fathers (Lupton & Barclay, 1997; Riessman, 1993). Some of these frameworks can be distinguished from one another according to their epistemological assumptions. Traditional ethnographies and grounded theories, for example, treat first-person accounts as "realistic descriptions" that "mirror a world 'out there,'" a position consistent with the positivist tradition of survey methods. In contrast, narrative analysis is skeptical of realist assumptions, preferring instead to view participants' stories as being "constructed, creatively authored, rhetorical, replete with assumptions, and interpretive" (Riessman, 1993, pp. 4–5).

Research based on in-depth interviewing, irrespective of its epistemological assumptions, is well suited for studying the complex web of self-reflective and interpersonal processes associated with fathering. This style of research also captures the competing discourses men can use to describe their fathering practices and identities (Marsiglio & Cohan, 2000). Insights gleaned from in-depth interviewing and a life-story perspective can show more fully how men link "fragmentary

61

occurrences across temporal boundaries" and actively construct their personal histories as men who can create and "father" human life (Gergen & Gergen, 1997).

Men make sense of themselves and their experiences as fathers through the stories they tell (Sandelowski, 1991). Studies using some version of narrative analysis may reveal important insights by analyzing how and why men structure their complete stories as they do. For some purposes, analyses can generate useful insights by exploring the themes revealed in fragments of men's stories and their more limited self-reflections. Irrespective of the approach used, interpreters of men's qualitative accounts of fathering should recognize that "the terms by which the world is understood are social artifacts, products of historically situated interchanges among people" (Gergen, 1985, p. 267). By acknowledging that social ecologies (e.g., localized group activities, community norms, family social demography) provide opportunities for men to learn and construct identities and discourses about fathering, we can search for meaningful points of intersection between the various schools of symbolic interactionism that frame researchers' interpretations of men's own fathering accounts (Longmore, 1998).

Unlike survey methodologies, in-depth interviewing typically is based on an inductive and flexible approach where the content and strategy can change as the research project evolves (Creswell, 1998; Schwalbe & Wolkomir, 2002). Interviewers seek to facilitate storytelling that reveals the subjective processes underlying are feelings, thinking, and actions of individuals; or, from a narrative approach, how they "construct past events and actions in personal narratives to claim identities and construct lives" within a socially constructed interview context (Riesmann, 1993, p. 2). When these stories are shared in an interview setting, researchers can study the underlying social–psychological and narrative devices that men use to think and talk about their involvement, or potential involvement, with their children.

By focusing on men's stories and subjective realities about fatherhood, in-depth interviewing provides researchers opportunities to use sensitizing concepts. These loosely defined conceptual tools provide a basic orientation unencumbered by rigid *a priori* assumptions, to develop fresh theoretical insights from empirical observations (Blumer, 1969; Glaser, 1978; van den Hoonard, 1997).

My aim here, then, is to highlight how the use of in-depth interviewing, sensitizing concepts, and selective self-narrative themes can extend previous qualitative research on father involvement issues (e.g., Arendell, 1995; Cohen, 1993; Daly, 1993; Furstenberg, 1995; Gerson, 1993; Lupton & Barclay, 1997; Walzer, 1998). More specifically, I show how in-depth interviewing can be guided by an awareness of three overlapping, general types of fathering trajectories I label *self-as-father, father–child*, and *coparental*, with an emphasis on "responsibility" themes. I selectively draw upon my own qualitative research on the social psychology of young single men's procreative identities (Marsiglio & Hutchinson, 2002) to suggest how specific concepts may enhance the qualitative study of father involvement. I illustrate how these trajectories and sensitizing concepts can be used to frame research projects by suggesting a series of open-ended interview questions and probes.

4. INTERVIEWING AND SENSITIZING CONCEPTS   63

Though my research is based on realist assumptions, I stress the broad appeal of in-depth interviewing. Thus, the concepts I discuss may still prove useful for analyses that challenge positivist interpretations. After discussing the trajectories and sensitizing concepts, I highlight how several narrative themes may prove useful for interviewers and researchers as they probe for and interpret men's stories about fathering. Finally, I clarify why researchers should be mindful of how men may "do gender" while they're being interviewed about their experiences related to fatherhood.

BACKGROUND FOR STUDYING
FATHER INVOLVEMENT

Scholars have accentuated the value of applying a broader "fathering" time frame to men's experiences with creating and caring for children. For some purposes it makes theoretical sense to explore father involvement issues by folding them into a more expansive view of men as procreative beings (Levine & Pitt, 1995; Marsiglio, 1998; Marsiglio & Hutchinson, 2002). This approach highlights men's procreative identity and requires theorists to recognize more fully that men can venture into the expansive terrain of fatherhood prior to a child's birth and conception. Men can do so by envisioning aspects of fatherhood and engaging in anticipatory identity work and personal growth projects while making tentative or explicit plans to become fathers someday. They can also bond with their partners and the fetus during the pregnancy process (May, 1980).

Obviously, the visions men have of their potential children and fathering prior to conception or birth can be distinguished from fathers' behaviors that are directly or indirectly related to their living children. However, a full accounting of men's lives as fathers and their connection to their children should consider all forms of identity work they initiate in connection with their fathering experiences. This type of research will improve our understanding of men's transitions to becoming fathers (Cowan, 1988; Fox, Bruce, & Combs-Orme, 2000; LaRossa & LaRossa, 1989) and stepfathers (Marsiglio, in press). It may enhance our understanding of why men's prefatherhood perceptions vary from their domestic activities after they have a child (Cowan & Cowan, 1992). Moreover, it could help us refine our sense of the processes by which some men disengage totally or partially from being involved with their children. Just as men can be considered athletic as they train for a specific sporting event that has not yet occurred, so too men can be viewed as engaging in various cognitive, affective, and behavioral activities that can directly shape their identity as fathers and their involvement with prospective children. Similar activities may even take place for a period of time with fathers who are currently disengaged from their children (e.g., the previously abusive or alcoholic father who is attempting to reform his ways and reunite with his children).

It seems reasonable to exclude or treat differently those instances where men drift unknowingly into activities that ultimately will influence their style and degree of father involvement. But close attention should be given to men's visions of fathering that motivate them to develop human, financial, and social capital as part of their explicit plan to involve themselves with or contribute in specific ways to their children's well-being. A broad view of involvement recognizes that at least some of these processes are important expressions of men's responsible orientation toward or preparation for fathering, not simply antecedents of it.

In a related vein, more explicit attention has also been given to associating features of paternal influence such as breadwinning and social capital with images of father involvement (Amato, 1998; Christiansen & Palkovitz, 2000; Marsiglio & Cohan, 2000). The emphasis on breadwinning and social capital elevates the importance of an ecological model that embeds fathering within a larger social and often gendered context (Doherty, Kouneski, & Erikson, 1998). These forms of father involvement or paternal influence may be less direct, but important nonetheless.

To what extent the original paternal involvement formulation that emphasized engagement, accessibility, and responsibility (Lamb, Pleck, Charnov, & Levine, 1985, 1987; Pleck, Lamb, & Levine, 1985) was intended to tap each of the issues raised earlier is unclear (see chap. 1 for a description of the evolution of this debate). It seems safe to assume, however, that understanding the breadth and continuity/discontinuity of men's experiences as fathers can be enhanced by considering fathering issues in a manner that provides men an opportunity to weave together the various factors that have influenced how they are involved with their children. In addition to highlighting the typical cognitive, affective, and behavioral forms of engagement, accessibility, and responsibility, this perspective recognizes more explicitly the diverse instances where fathers' human, financial, and social capital contributions can influence children. These contributions appear to extend what was probably represented implicitly under the original "responsibility" label.

Regardless of what it is called, the area of father involvement and paternal influence that I focus on here is decidedly multidimensional, covering men's nurturance and provision of care; moral and ethical guidance; emotional, practical, and psychosocial support of female partners; economic provisioning; and forms of social capital (Marsiglio, Day, & Lamb, 2000; see also Bruce & Fox, 1997). In addition to these issues, I consider the mental and practical preparations for father involvement that men make prior to a child's birth, or in the case of stepfathers, efforts predating some defining moment when they embrace a stepfather or "father" identity.

GENERAL FATHERING TRAJECTORIES

One way to capture the qualitative complexity of men's life-course experiences and self-understandings as fathers is to highlight three different overlapping and dynamic trajectories associated with the social psychology of men's lives

4. INTERVIEWING AND SENSITIZING CONCEPTS 65

(Marsiglio & Hutchinson, 2002). Consistent with other social scientists' use of the trajectory concept, I use it to represent a course or path of experience as represented by the individuals themselves (Glaser, 1978; Glaser & Strauss, 1968). Trajectories imply a temporal element in that the experiences and processes that define them take place over time. However, my use of the "trajectory" metaphor should not be interpreted to mean that men move through a prescribed set of stages. Instead, it suggests that men's lives unfold in various ways along three distinct, yet often connected substantive paths. These paths represent life domains and, on occasion, may be accentuated by identifiable and significant events that reinforce or alter men's father-identity and perspective on fathering (McAdams, 1990; Strauss, 1969). Although is may be possible to discern patterns in how these paths unfold, the paths themselves are likely to be highly variable. The broad paths of interest here, marked by procreative and fathering subjectivities and behaviors, help define the micro context within which men construct their identities as fathers and "do fathering." Men's orientation or standing relative to these different paths can be assessed at any given point in time, including crucial transitional periods. Though particular trajectories may be irrelevant at times for individuals, some will become salient intermittently in response to men's changing life circumstances. The nexus between these paths represents an important site for research. Sample interview questions that would provide men opportunities to talk about fathering issues as they relate to these trajectories, and the sensitizing concepts described later, are presented in the Table 4.1.

Men can experience an individual or self-as-father trajectory as they engage themselves with the fathering domain. This trajectory encompasses men's fathering philosophy, intentions, and visions independent of any particular relationship they may have with a romantic partner or specific child. The nature and direction of this self-as-father trajectory can be influenced by processes associated with men's personal development and gendered experiences. From a social–psychological perspective, whatever types of thoughts and feelings men develop with regard to having children typically will originate from their initial awareness, usually during adolescence, that they are capable of impregnating a sex partner (Marsiglio & Hutchinson, 2002). Many boys may have a vague sense, prior to learning about their fecundity, that they will be fathers someday. Meanwhile, theorists of adult life interested in generativity issues underscore the developmental and motivational forces propelling some adult men to seek opportunities to nurture children (Hawkins & Dollahite, 1997; McAdams, 1990; Snarey, 1993).

Generally speaking, men's self-as-father trajectory can be seen as reflecting how men sometimes embrace fathering as an amorphous role or abstract image, not a concrete, interpersonal connection to a specific child. (See related discussion of "imago" as a "personified and idealized image of the self [that structures] a person's life story," McAdams, 1990, p. 191.) When men think about prospective fatherhood images, they do so in a general way, sometimes relying on their thoughts and feelings about their own fathers' previous and current involvement in their lives.

TABLE 4.1

Sample Questions for Sensitizing Concepts and Fathering Trajectories

Fathering Trajectories	Sample Questions
Self-as-father	**Q.** What does the thought of being a father mean to you? *Probe:* How important is it to you to be a father? A biological father? Why?
Father–child	**Q.** Describe how you are involved in your child's/children's life/lives? *Probe:* How does [involvement type] differ among your children?
Coparental	**Q.** Describe how your involvement with your child/children's mother(s) affects how you're involved in your child's/children's life/lives? *Probe:* Ways of making it easier, harder? Unique opportunities?
Sensitizing Concepts	
Procreative/paternal consciousness	**Q.** How do you think and feel about your physiological ability to create human life? **Q.** In what ways do you think about your child/children? *Probe:* How often? When? What activates it? Short-term, long-term? Problem-solving? To what extent does the child's mother play a role?
Fatherhood readiness	**Q.** Would you talk about the extent to which you feel ready to be (*examples*): (a) a father for the first time, (b) involved with a child who has (*name disability*), (c) involved with a stepchild. *Probe:* Would you describe: (a) any experience(s) you've had that prepared you for this, (b) things you have intentionally done to prepare yourself for this experience, (c) anything that you plan on doing to prepare yourself?
Child visions	**Q.** Would you describe any specific images or stories you've had while daydreaming about your future child (or child/children)? *Probe:* How did they come about? What prompted them? To what extent and how did your romantic partner play a role?
Fathering visions	**Q.** Would you describe any of the thoughts you've had about being a father someday? *Probe:* How do these thoughts relate to your own childhood? Your father/stepfather?
Character self-portrayals	**Q.** Would you describe the type of person you are and how this affects the way you're involved (*will be involved*) with your child/children? *Probe:* What specific personality features?
Fathering ideals	**Q.** Describe your image of the ideal father. *Probe:* How easy will it be for you to be this type of father? Why?
Comparative appraisals	**Q.** How would you judge the quality and level of your involvement with your child? *Probe:* Why? How did you come to feel this way? What types of standards or people do you compare yourself to?
Nuclear episodes/ turning points	**Q.** How has your involvement with your child/children changed over time? *Probe:* Would you describe any significant experiences that reinforced the way you focus on or interact with your child/children? The type and level of involvement? *Probe:* Would you describe any significant experiences that changed the way you focus on or interact with your child/children? The type and level of involvement?

4. INTERVIEWING AND SENSITIZING CONCEPTS 67

Once men become fathers, however, their personal images of fathering and the conversations they have with themselves about paternity and fatherhood concerns are likely to be deepened through personal experience. Their more abstract views will be interwoven with their experientially based sentiments for their specific children. Men's self-as-father trajectory will also be related to their experiences with their romantic partners (Peterson & Jenni, 2001). In the latter instance, the self-as-father trajectory is likely to become intertwined with the copartner trajectory (prior to a child's birth) that often evolves into a coparental trajectory after a child's birth.

One key feature of this self-as-father trajectory is that men will associate images of their future fathering roles with images of their "possible selves" (Markus & Nurius, 1986; Oyserman & Markus, 1990; Strauss & Goldberg, 1999). Men's perceptions of how they would like to think, feel, and behave as fathers will come into play. This type of trajectory does not necessarily end for men with the birth of their first child, but can evolve far beyond it. However, once men become fathers, their self-reflections about what type of father they would like to be are more likely to be connected with their own children, at least for the period of time in which they sustain an identity as a father and a commitment to these children (Fox & Bruce, 2001). Because many nonresident fathers' commitments to their children wane over time (Furstenberg & Cherlin, 1991), nonresident fathers (or previous stepfathers) may find themselves once again thinking about fathering in more abstract terms. The idea of becoming a father again, perhaps couched in the hopes of doing a better job the next time around, may influence some men's thinking. For other men, feelings of grief, remorse, anger, guilt, or discomfort about an earlier fathering experience may lead them to suppress their desire to imagine what it could be like to become a father again.

These experiences will shape how men think about, act upon, and articulate their orientation toward becoming and being a father. Some of the emotional, cognitive, and practical energy that men expend as part of this self-as-father trajectory can be viewed as being part of the responsibility domain of father involvement. Images of "possible selves" may motivate men to undertake self-improvement projects intended to increase their prospects of being a responsible father and family man. Meanwhile, men facing the prospects of stepfatherhood can visualize features of fathering typically associated with biological paternity and use these images to establish a point of reference and guide for self-evaluation.

The second and third trajectories are closely tied to men's parenting identity and their perceptions of "self-as-solo-parent" and "self-as-coparent" (Stueve & Pleck, 2001). The second trajectory involves men's relationships with their individual children. These father–child trajectories can include both biological and nonbiological children. In most cases, men develop and sustain some type of evolving relationship with individual children, although they may produce offspring with whom they never develop a father identity. In some instances, these father–child relationships may deteriorate to the point that men no longer play an active role

in their children's lives. With time, however, some fathers may rekindle their connection to and involvement with these children. They may also develop new relationships with other children.

When men are involved in multiple father–child relationships where they see themselves as a father or stepfather, they are likely to forge unique relationships to varying degrees with individual children (Marsiglio, in press). Nonetheless, in their minds, and in their stories and accounts, men may represent their fathering experiences in a summary fashion. In everyday life and interview settings (unless explicitly directed to do otherwise), they may consolidate their awareness of their child-specific fathering identities and activities. It seems reasonable to assume that men with children by different mothers *may* use the mothers as a reference point to compartmentalize the way they consider and represent their fathering experiences. Likewise, men may use the biological or step status of their children to group their subjective understandings of themselves as fathers.

Fathers can still develop and be aware of personalized bonds they have with individual children, a reality that may be both cause and consequence of the different ways they involve themselves in their children's lives. Having multiple children provides fathers unique opportunities to perceive, compare, and evaluate their father involvement. Much can be gained, then, by studying how fathers subjectively manage and verbally construct their sense of fathering based on their multiple father–child trajectories.

The third trajectory refers to men's involvements with the mother (or mothers) of their children. At its core, this coparental trajectory is about dyadic, coparental processes targeting biological or nonbiological children or both. Those men who have children with different mothers may experience multiple coparental trajectories that either intersect or coexist independently of one another. Fathers' interactions with mothers who serve as gatekeepers are essential to the coparental trajectory (Allen & Hawkins, 1999). Identity issues are associated with this coparental trajectory because fathers will have some sense of whether they are a coparent or more of a solo parent. The dyadic parenting processes that often emerge in fathers' lives, i.e., discussions about discipline, values, monitoring, financial support, etc., are intertwined with fathers' efforts to "do fathering" and involve themselves in their children's lives. One concrete measure of men's orientation in this regard is revealed in their narratives that are organized around the "parenting voice" ("I only" or "we joint" pronouns) that men use in describing meaningful parenting experiences to interviewers (Stueve & Pleck, 2001) and presumably to others outside of a research context.

To understand men's lives as fathers and to consider the nuances surrounding their involvement with their children, we must be sensitive to how these three trajectories overlap and influence one another at different times, including transitional periods. An approach that pays attention to the self-as-father, father–child, and coparental trajectories highlights the value of incorporating men's motivational interests into a larger discussion of father involvement. Even though motivation

4. INTERVIEWING AND SENSITIZING CONCEPTS   69

can be discussed as a separate factor related to fathers' involvement (Marsiglio, Day et al., 2000; Pleck et al., 1985; Pleck & Stueve, 2001), men's concerns about and efforts to achieve certain fathering ideals can be seen as a dimension of a broader view of father involvement that is independent of specific children.

From a methodological perspective this framework poses the intriguing challenge of how to study father involvement for fathers with multiple children, especially when some of these children have been born to different mothers. The conventional approach is to consider fathers' involvement with one target child, with one target mother, and often at one point in time. While qualitative interviews can obviously focus on one target child, the qualitative strategy can readily be adapted to consider the full range of subjective and interpersonal issues associated with men's multiple fathering relationships. A fruitful line of inquiry for father involvement research is to understand how fathers (and prospective fathers) weave together their self-as-father, father–child, and coparental trajectories through their self-narratives. For specific men, or categories of men sharing similar life circumstances, any of these trajectories may be more or less relevant (other trajectories also may emerge as significant) and different types of linkages may be featured.

SENSITIZING CONCEPTS

Sensitizing concepts are provisional conceptual tools used by qualitative researchers and are closely tied to the theoretical tradition of symbolic interactionism advanced by Blumer (1969). Essentially, these concepts highlight the unique properties that may be associated with a class of data—"father involvement" for this chapter. They offer researchers a general sense of reference and orientation without unduly restricting new paths for theoretical discovery. Thus, sensitizing concepts, by definition, are loosely defined and dynamic. In contrast, definitive concepts have more precise, rigid meanings. In the case of in-depth interviewing, sensitizing concepts provide researchers with preliminary insights about how to frame their questions and interpret their participants' replies. In other words, they enable scholars to locate an entry point for developing their line of inquiry while allowing them "to see those meanings that people attach to the world around them" (van den Hoonaard, 1997, p. 2). These concepts provide "a starting point in thinking about a class of data of which the social researcher has no definite idea and provides an initial guide to her research. Such concepts usually are provisional and may be dropped as more viable and definite concepts emerge in the course of her research."

Typically, sensitizing concepts emerge from a research process and are closely tied to research participants' thoughts and words, although they remain more abstract "second-order" concepts, one step removed from the data. Given the amount of scholarship that has addressed father involvement in recent decades, my use of "sensitizing" concepts is a bit more abstract and informed by previous research

than is usually the case in studies using sensitizing concepts. Nevertheless, scholars can use the sensitizing concepts I discuss to generate new theoretical insights about men as fathers.

With an eye on the three overlapping types of fathering trajectories presented above (self-as-father, father–child, and coparental), I selectively discuss eight sensitizing concepts I have worked with in recent years: procreative/paternal consciousness, fatherhood readiness, child visions, fathering visions, character portrayals, fathering ideals, comparative appraisals, and nuclear episodes/turning points. I refined these concepts while working on a project focusing on the social psychology of young men's procreative identities. My colleagues and I conducted in-depth interviews with a purposive sample of 52 main participants and a supplemental sample of 18 single men aged 16 to 30 years who volunteered for more focused interviews (see Marsiglio & Hutchinson, 2002, for a full description). One of the main objectives of our sampling strategy was to ensure diversity in men's procreative life experiences as well as their age, race/ethnicity, education, financial status, and relationship status. The sample was drawn from the north-central and northeast regions of Florida. Among the main sample of 52 men, 28 indicated they had no pregnancy or fertility experiences, 12 had partners who had aborted a pregnancy, 7 were involved with partners currently pregnant with their child, 4 had experienced a miscarriage, and 8 had biological children prior to the interview. Two men were interviewed twice, once while their partners were pregnant and then 1 to 2 months postpartum.

Procreative/Paternal Consciousness

Procreative consciousness is a broad concept I have used to consider the full range of thoughts and feelings that come into play because men are capable of thinking about their ability or inability to create human life (Marsiglio, 1998). The diverse thoughts and feelings associated with this experiential sense of self spring from men's sensitivity to environmental cues and personal histories. These stimuli trigger men to process everyday situations in a manner that makes them aware of issues related to the procreative realm. As my colleague and I have shown empirically (Marsiglio & Hutchinson, 2002), this type of consciousness can be expressed either as situational or global. Situational consciousness is activated because of the exigencies of an interaction episode that prompts men's awareness of their fecundity. Global consciousness refers to men's enduring awareness, disposition, or sentiment associated with their procreative identity that transcends a specific situation. Finally, men's procreative consciousness can exist largely independent of any particular relationship or it can be firmly connected to a romantic partner's interests.

Concerns such as these can inform and deepen assessments of men's paternal consciousness as it relates to father involvement, including their orientation toward being responsible for anticipating and meeting their children's needs. Researchers

4. INTERVIEWING AND SENSITIZING CONCEPTS

should examine men's everyday lives more systematically, including their more passive forms of consciousness where ideas and sentiments remain dormant but ready to be activated given the right set of circumstances. Having a certain type and degree of mindfulness enables men to foresee and plan for their children's needs. The processes associated with men's paternal consciousness are, therefore, interwoven with the way they frame their relationship to and responsibility for their children. These issues implicate a key question involving what Schutz (1970a, 1970b) referred to as "relevance structures": the cognitive representations of experience, encoded with meaning, that tend to prompt certain objects to come into a person's field of attention. Researchers may question to what extent and in what ways the relevance structures that prompt men to think about how they can manage their children's lives are connected to processes linking them to partners, most commonly the mothers of their children.

Fatherhood Readiness

My colleague and I have used the concept of fatherhood readiness to refer to men's impressions about how prepared they are to become fathers at this point in their lives. Our participants' narratives revealed men's tendency to depict their readiness by highlighting their concerns about either themselves, their partners, or their children. In some instances they consider how having a child would affect at least two of these parties. Their concerns involved thoughts about education, work opportunities, financial support for the child, depletion of leisure time, and whether they were emotionally mature enough to handle the demands of raising and caring for a child.

Fatherhood readiness is related to concerns about father involvement. This concept hints at where men are in terms of their self-as-father trajectory. The vast majority of men are aware by their mid-teens that they are capable of impregnating a sex partner. Many young men also think about how they would like to be involved with their child, views that frequently emphasize one-on-one play activities and financial responsibilities. Some young men are aware of the practical matters of fathering that involve managing children's lives, but most do not focus on the responsibility aspects of fathering other than financial support and many do not understand fully the costs associated with raising a child. Although much is made of men's sense of being ready for their first biological child, the fatherhood readiness concept can also capture men's thoughts about additional offspring or children not biologically related to them.

Men's sense of readiness can relate to a child's particular circumstances. For instance, when a child is born with disabilities (e.g., Down's syndrome, missing or dysfunctional limbs), it is possible to speak of the father's readiness to assume fathering responsibilities for a child with specific needs. This trajectory is illustrated by those men who attempt to learn as much as possible about their child's condition and develop strategies for adjusting to his or her special needs. This

theme can be extended to fathers who have children who develop a condition (e.g., mood disorder) or status (e.g., juvenile delinquent) that requires fathers to make a major adjustment in how they are involved with a child. This type of experience might more accurately be referred to as "fathering readiness."

Fatherhood or fathering readiness can be experienced alone or constructed with a partner. In some cases, men's awareness of their degree of readiness can prompt them to take steps to prepare themselves for being a father. One participant in my research spent considerable time retrieving and studying biblical passages that spoke to the issue of being a good husband and father. Other men might take it upon themselves to read voraciously about their child's mood disorder or attend family-based support programs designed to educate parents about their child's condition and treatment plan (Fristad, Gavazzi, & Soldano, 1998).

Child Visions

Most research on father involvement deals with fathers' demonstrable actions that directly involve their children and is generally related to child outcomes (Marsiglio, Amato, Day, & Lamb, 2000). My experience with listening to men talk about the visions they have of children who are not yet born, or even conceived, reinforces the recent plea to consider vigorously how men think about children (Hawkins & Palkovitz, 1999; Palkovitz, 1997; Walzer, 1998). While I have used the child visions concept to refer to men's fantasies about children not yet born, this concept is also related to the ways men think about their living children. Fathers may to some extent and in various ways sustain a mental map of their children's lives or focus on their children's short- versus long-term needs. Circumstances may prompt men to do mental work involving their children when they are not with them (e.g., problem solving). Research on these issues brings to light how important it is to understand the processes associated with whether men are mindful of their children in particular ways, and if they are, how men manage those thoughts and describe them to others. These processes, and men's accounts of them, are fundamentally shaped by the socially constructed, gendered realities of social and parental life (Marsiglio, in press; McMahon, 1995; Walzer, 1998).

In my recent work, I asked men to comment on whether they ever fantasized or thought about children they might someday father. Their responses indicated that when men report having mental images of potential children, their thoughts tend to focus on gender, personality, and physical appearance. Those who visualize their prospective children most often see them as young children or teenagers. Some men also have conversations with their partners that evoke images of children not yet born. How this type of preconception or prenatal imagining of children is related to fathers' more direct involvement with their children once they are born is an open question. For most types of involvement, the further in time one moves from when men had their initial visions, the weaker the connection will be between men's visions and actual involvement.

4. INTERVIEWING AND SENSITIZING CONCEPTS 73

Fathering Visions

Just as men may envision what their children might be like, they can also imagine themselves engaged in different aspects of fathering such as playing with their children or attending their school events. Child visions and fathering visions often occur together. These concepts deal with men's state of mind rather than their actual behavior with children. Although my work has focused on men's visions of fathering prior to their own fatherhood experiences, men can still envisage fathering after they have fathered a child. Those visions can focus on a living or future child. Men who have children when they are teenagers, for example, may go on to develop a new set of fathering visions 10 to 20 years later if they get involved with women who are interested in having their own children.

Men's fathering visions often reflect the way men think they would interact with their children. These visions sometimes reflect men's parenting philosophies and values. They also typically take into account how men perceive that their fathers interacted with or neglected them. In some respects, this mental imagining is a no-risk dress rehearsal for men. Men's visions may reflect how they want to orient themselves toward their children while also allowing them to project themselves into involvement fantasies that place them and their children at later life stages. Not surprisingly, this envisioning process among men who either have no children or have young children often focuses on the fun and emotional side of fathering. Consequently, men are less apt to daydream about their financial responsibilities and opportunities to build social capital. While breadwinning may be taken for granted and not featured prominently in men's fathering visions because it is an indirect form of paternal involvement, some men are eager to talk about their daydreams of spending money on their children to provide them with material goods and recreational opportunities.

Character Self-Portrayals

How men portray themselves sometimes provide a subtext for how they perceive and frame their fathering experiences. These characterizations may have a bearing on how they see themselves as fathers and evaluate their involvement with their children. Some self-portrayals directly highlight men's assessment of their fathering abilities whereas others are more general (e.g., free-spirit nomadic type, patient, easy-going, religious). When men without children talk about their fondness for children, they sometimes use this image of being a "child-loving" person as evidence that they want to be fathers and that they will be attentive to their children when they have them. Likewise, if they view themselves as reasonable, fair-minded, and cooperative individuals they may be inclined to depict their level and style of involvement with their children in a manner consistent with that image. Fathers not living with their children may infuse their stories with various self-portrayals as they try to explain the extent to which and how they are involved or

not involved in their children's lives. For example, incarcerated fathers or fathers addicted to drugs sometimes are reluctant to have their children come to see them because they fear that the stigma associated with their condition will damage their children's views of them (B. Nurse, 2002).

Fathering Ideals

When men begin to have fathering visions, they are often aware, at least in a rudimentary sense, of the standards they respect and aspire to achieve as fathers. These fathering ideals also provide opportunities to assess the quality and extent of their current involvement with their children. It may be the case, as Daly (1993) has shown, that fathers with young children are less likely to have a particular father in mind when they think about how they would like to parent. Instead, fathers may choose different features from various parental figures and construct their own basic ideal of what a father should be like. In addition to inquiring about fathers' real-life experiences with their children, interviewers should encourage men to talk about what types of preexisting images they have of the ideal father, how they arrived at them, how often they come to mind, and the ways these ideals affect their involvement with their children.

Comparative Appraisals

Because qualitative researchers are interested in the processes by which men come to understand the quality and quantity of their paternal effort or involvement, it is essential to ask men questions that enable them to evaluate their father involvement. In constructing a mental and verbal assessment of their type and level of father involvement, men may rely on a muddled assortment of parenting templates, standards, schema, and models to help them make sense of and characterize their involvement (Daly, 1993). Comparisons to a temporal self, specific others (e.g., the mother, one's own father, other fathers), or a generalized paternal image may all come into play at different times. As noted previously, fathers with multiple father–child relationships can also use these experiences as reference points to construct their accounts of their father involvement. Many of these experiences will be guided by the looking-glass self process whereby men respond to their perceptions of how they believe others see them (Cooley, 1902).

Nuclear Episodes/Turning Points

When studying fathers' involvement with their children, we should recognize that how they are involved, the extent of their involvement, and their perceptions about their involvement are all subject to change. Researchers using in-depth interviewing can explore how significant events and processes associated with men's lives are related to their accounts of their involvement with their children. McAdams (1990) writes of nuclear episodes as "key events or scenes that mark self-continuity

4. INTERVIEWING AND SENSITIZING CONCEPTS

and self-change." Those events that foster self-continuity reinforce men's preexisting perceptions about and level of father involvement. For example, a father who perceives that he spends a lot of time helping his daughter with her homework can have his self-image as an involved father reinforced in a dramatic way if the local newspaper publishes his daughter's essay for a "fathers day" contest in which she praises her "daddy" for the creative efforts he makes to teach her. Meanwhile, other situations that represent turning points fundamentally alter men's identity as fathers or their perspective on some aspect of life related to fathering, or both (Strauss, 1969). A father who overcomes a life-threatening illness may redefine the meaning of family and fatherhood while redirecting his energies to assume a more active role in his children's daily lives. My own research has considered some of the properties associated with turning points related to men's procreative identities (Marsiglio & Hutchinson, 2002). Similar efforts can be made to understand how turning points may affect fathers' involvement with their children. From a qualitative perspective, developing a deep understanding of fathers' involvement with their children and their interpretation of that involvement requires that we consider whether men have experienced nuclear episodes and turning points that have affected their lives as fathers.

SELF-NARRATIVES AND FATHERING TRAJECTORIES

Now that I have described the three fathering trajectories and eight selective sensitizing concepts, I briefly illustrate how a few self-narrative themes may be relevant to a qualitative understanding of father involvement and the intersections between the fathering trajectories. Other themes related to the nature and styles of storytelling are likely to be relevant to this discussion as well.

"Agency" and "communion," two motivational themes commonly found in individuals' life stories, are relevant to men's orientation toward father involvement issues, particularly fatherhood readiness (Bakan, 1966; McAdams, 1990). In this context, agency refers to men's desire to master the environment in a manner that enables them to achieve the type of fathering they envision. It conveys men's need for maintaining a sense of power, achievement, and control in their pursuit of becoming and being fathers. Communion, meanwhile, emphasizes the tendency for men to integrate themselves with an entity other than themselves (e.g., child, family, community) and to seek intimacy. This motive represents a "readiness for experiences of feeling close to and in communion with others, engaging in warm, friendly, and mutual interaction" (McAdams, 1990, p. 158). Men may weave one or both of these motives into their narratives about fathering before as well as after their children are born. If researchers are attentive to participants' use of such self-narrative strategies they may be able to question fathers in a manner that enriches

our understanding of how fathers orient themselves to certain types of involvement issues. These strategies may also give meaning to the potential intersections between men's self-as-father, father–child, and coparental trajectories. While there are surely instances where men can emphasize the communal motive when describing their father–child and coparental trajectories, this motive may also find its way into men's accounts that focus on themselves. Meanwhile, men may express the agency theme as they describe their desires and experiences in relation to any of the three trajectories. The agency theme may arise either in terms of men's sense of feeling in or out of control. The latter is likely to be most prominent when they feel as though their coparent is playing an unhealthy gatekeeping role that prevents them, in their minds, from interacting with their children in the way they would like.

When examining how men tell their stories about their involvement with their children, it is useful to consider what have been referred to as "stability," "progressive," and "regressive" narratives (Gergen & Gergen, 1997). A stability narrative, when applied to men's accounts of father involvement, would emphasize how particular aspects of involvement have remained consistent over a period of time. These aspects could include the type, quantity, or quality of involvement and may refer to specific domains of involvement or general involvement. The progressive and regressive narratives, on the other hand, reveal a dynamic trend in how men describe aspects of father involvement. Progressive narratives reflect an incremental movement along an evaluative dimension related to fathering. For example, fathers might speak of how they have continued to invest more time reading and learning about how to take care of their diabetic children during the past year. Meanwhile, regressive narratives would reflect men's description of some sort of decrement. Incarcerated fathers or those who have assumed time-consuming jobs may share thoughts about how they have spent far less time playing with their children. In some instances, a narrative may emphasize an entirely progressive trend; in other cases the trend may be depicted as entirely regressive. A relatively common situation may find men using both progressive and regressive narratives to describe their experiences. Men may use these narrative styles concurrently to describe particular situations with different children or different aspects of involvement. They may also draw upon these dynamic types of narratives to explain a series of sequential father involvement experiences.

INTERVIEWING FATHERS AS MEN

As researchers navigate the process of asking men questions and interpreting their replies about real and anticipated experiences as fathers, they should be mindful of Schwalbe and Wolkomir's (2002) admonitions and recommendations about interviewing men. In their words, "we cannot understand men's lives and experiences without paying attention to what men do to ensure that others perceive and treat them as men" (p. 218). They add that to maintain their masculine self

4. INTERVIEWING AND SENSITIZING CONCEPTS 77

within an interview setting, men may knowingly or unknowingly use impression-management techniques to display their rationality, autonomy, control, and sexual desirability. Unfortunately, little is known about how men think about and attempt to display this masculine self in relation to fathering, either within or outside an interview context. It seems safe to assume, however, that some men probably engage in a gendered form of impression management when they are asked to talk at length about fathering and coparenting issues. They may be most inclined to construct these displays when they talk about issues associated with responsibility, discipline, economic provisioning, and emotional displays.

The limited scope of this chapter does not permit an extensive discussion of Schwalbe and Wolkomir's detailed assessment of the key issues associated with flexible, intensive interviewing. The main problems interviewers need to be vigilant about are men's struggles to exhibit control within the interview; their efforts to avoid disclosing emotions to others; their tendency to exaggerate rationality, autonomy, and control; and their ploys to promote bonding between them and the interviewer—especially when the interviewer is male. Female interviewers may encounter their own set of problems associated with control when the fathers being interviewed perceive themselves as having experiences that are uniquely gendered, e.g., being nonresident fathers (Arendell, 1997).

The way men tell their stories about fathering is likely to be influenced by the manner and extent to which these interviewing problems surface during the course of an interview. Men's use of specific impression-management strategies may be linked at times to the way men orient themselves to different aspects of the three fathering trajectories. This may occur consciously or unconsciously. Speaking about fathering issues related to the self-as-father or father–child trajectories that imply an "emotional self" in the present may be more threatening than recalling stories that focus on emotions clearly experienced in the past. Additionally, as men talk about their coparental experiences they may attempt to bond with male interviewers if they suspect that particular interviewers are experienced in dealing with their own children's mothers. These participants will assume that the interviewers have access to a similar standpoint that would enable them to identify and empathize with the participants. Thus, they may use the ploy, "If you are a man who has to deal with your kid's mother, you must know what I mean." Another interviewing issue might involve men who attempt to maintain their masculine sense of self by exaggerating the amount of control they have over their children, their children's mother, or both. For example, some men may be reluctant to share an accurate history depicting their partners' extensive and disproportionate contribution to their children's financial support because it would threaten their traditional sense of how breadwinning defines masculinity.

Qualitative researchers, if they are sensitive to the possible ways that men can "do gender" during an in-depth interview, will be better equipped to improve the data men produce as they talk about their fathering experiences. Reviewing Schwalbe and Wolkomir's practical techniques for managing interviews with men

78   MARSIGLIO

should prepare researchers to conduct higher quality interviews with men about fathering.

CONCLUSION

Irrespective of the analytic framework, in-depth interviewing certainly provides researchers with the most effective means to capture the complex, multifaceted, and subjective aspects of fathers' involvement with their children. This type of inquiry is the most effective means to interpret the deep meanings and processes associated with men's lives as fathers. Qualitative researchers are therefore poised to explore the potentially wide-ranging and complex ways that men construct, negotiate, and experience their self-understandings as fathers over time.

To move forward, researchers must consider how in-depth interviewing techniques can be tailored to help men reflect and comment in the most meaningful manner on their past, present, and future lives as fathers. I suggest that the interview be framed to highlight the three separate trajectories of fathering (self-as-father, father–child, and coparental) as well as the ways they overlap. Eight sensitizing concepts have been particularly useful in my research on the social psychology of men's identities as persons who can create human life. These concepts have also guide my current research on the social psychology of stepfathering. The sensitizing concepts I introduced are not meant to be exhaustive. They merely underscore the value of identifying similar concepts for other projects; moreover, they represent possible leads for researchers who are interested in studying some aspect of father involvement through in-depth interviewing. Various sensitizing concepts will emerge out of other researchers' specialized projects. In presenting the sensitizing concepts, I suggested examples of probes I have used to get men to talk about their feelings, perceptions, and experiences related to fathering. As with the sensitizing concepts, the probes are meant to be suggestive. Thus, an important objective for the qualitative genre of research on fathering is to identify and refine sensitizing concepts and probes that can be useful in individual studies and across studies.

I integrated the trajectories and sensitizing concepts into my discussion for two main reasons. First, I wanted to encourage researchers to keep these ideas in mind when they make plans to launch their interview-based projects. Second, these ideas will be relevant to researchers when they modify their interview guides at various points during the course of their data collection. Given the dynamic nature of the qualitative in-depth interviewing process, it is important for researchers to evaluate their efforts repeatedly as their project unfolds. Encouraging fathers to assume the role of teacher as they interact with the interviewer is a vital part of this process. So, too, is sharing the fruits of this type of self-scrutiny with other scholars working in the field (e.g., Marsiglio & Hutchinson, 2002).

When it comes time to interpret men's stories about fathering there are various strategies for doing so. Those researchers who provide their participants the

4. INTERVIEWING AND SENSITIZING CONCEPTS 79

maximum amount of leeway in their storytelling may turn to various self-narrative themes as a way of making sense of their data. By way of example, I illustrated how the agency and communion motivational themes, along with the stability, progressive, and regressive self-narratives are worth considering when examining how fathers construct their stories about fathering. As researchers read their data, they should consider the circumstances that affect how and when these different narrative styles (as well as others) are used to describe expressions of fathering involving the self-as-father, father–child, and coparental trajectories. They should also study how contextual factors (e.g., children's age, gender, and personality; community, peer, and religious norms; fathers' social–demographic circumstances; financial resources; presence of another father figure) and interpersonal processes provide men with different standpoints, resources, and strategies to structure their accounts of father involvement.

I have stressed the value of using in-depth interviewing and sensitizing concepts to capture the complexity of men's lives as procreative beings and fathers, while framing a view of fatherhood that is based on three fathering trajectories. This approach will enable researchers to focus on men's inner worlds and personal stories about fathering. As researchers pose in-depth questions about fathering issues and interpret participants' replies, they should also be mindful of how men may use impression-management strategies to sustain their masculine self.

ACKNOWLEDGMENTS

I would like to thank Mark Cohan, Sally Hutchinson, and Suzanne Smith for their helpful comments on this chapter.

REFERENCES

Amato, P. (1998). More than money?: Men's contributions to their children's lives. In A. Booth & N. Crouter (Eds.), *Men in families: When do they get involved? What difference does it make?* (pp. 241–278). Mahwah, NJ: Lawrence Erlbaum Associates.

Allen, S. M., & Hawkins, A. J. (1999). Maternal gatekeeping: Mothers' beliefs and behavior that inhibit greater father involvement in family work. *Journal of Marriage and the Family, 61*, 199–212.

Arendell, T. (1995). *Fathers & Divorce*. Thousand Oaks, CA: Sage.

Arendell, T. (1997). Reflections on the researcher-researched relationship: A woman interviewing men. *Qualitative Sociology, 20*, 341–68.

Bakan, D. (1966). *The duality of human existence: Isolation and communion in Western man*. Boston: Beacon Press.

Blumer, H. (1969). *Symbolic interactionsim*. Englewood Cliffs, NJ: Prentice-Hall.

Bruce, C., & Fox, G. L. (1997, November). *Measuring parental involvement among low-income White and African American fathers*. Paper presented at the National Council on Family Relations, Arlington, VA.

Christiansen, S. L., & Palkovitz, R. (2000). Why the "good provider" role still matters: Providing as a form of paternal involvement. *Journal of Family Issues, 22*, 84–106.

Cohen, T. F. (1993). What do fathers provide? Reconsidering the economic and nurturant dimensions of men as parents. In J. C. Hood (Ed.), *Men, work, and family* (pp. 1–22). Thousand Oaks, CA: Sage.

Cooley, C. H. (1902). *Human nature and the social order.* New York: Scribner.

Cowan, P. A. (1988). Becoming a father: A time of change, an opportunity for development. In P. Bronstein & C. P. Cowan (Eds.), *Fatherhood today: Men's changing role in the family* (pp. 13–35). New York: Wiley.

Cowan, C. P., & Cowan, P. A. (1992). *When partners become parents: The big life change for couples.* New York: Basic Books.

Creswell, J. W. (1998). *Qualitative inquiry and research design: Choosing among five traditions.* Thousand Oaks, CA: Sage.

Daly, K. J. (1993). Reshaping fatherhood: Finding the models. *Journal of Family Issues, 14,* 510–530.

Doherty, W. J., Kouneski, E. F., & Erikson, M. F. (1998). Responsible fathering: An overview and conceptual framework. *Journal of Marriage and the Family, 60,* 277–292.

Fox, G. L., & Bruce, C. (2001). Conditional fatherhood: Identity theory and parental investment theory as alternative sources of explanation of fathering. *Journal of Marriage and Family, 63,* 394–403.

Fox, G. L., Bruce, C., & Combs-Orme, T. (2000). Parenting expectations and concerns of fathers and mothers of newborn infants. *Family Relations, 49,* 123–131.

Fristad, M. A., Gavazzi, S. M., & Soldano, K. W. (1998). Multi-family psychoeducation groups for childhood mood disorders: Program description and preliminary efficacy data. *Contemporary Family Therapy, 20(3):* 385–402.

Furstenberg, F. F., Jr. (1995). Fathering in the inner city: Paternal participation and public policy. In W. Marsiglio (Ed.), *Fatherhood: Contemporary theory, research, and social policy* (pp. 119–147). Thousand Oaks, CA: Sage.

Furstenberg, F. F., Jr. (1998). Social capital and the role of fathers in the family. In A. Booth & N. Crouter (Eds.), *Men in families: When do they get involved? What difference does it make?* (pp. 295–301). Mahwah, NJ: Lawrence Erlbaum Associates.

Furstenberg, F. F., Jr., & Cherlin, A. J. (1991). *Divided families: What happens to children when parents part.* Cambridge, MA: Harvard University Press.

Gergen, K. J. (1985). The social constructionist movement in modern psychology. *American Psychologist, 40,* 266–275.

Gergen, K. J., & Gergen, M. M. (1997). Narratives of the self. In L. P. Hinchman & S. K. Hinchman (Eds.), *Memory, identity, community* (pp. 161–184). Albany: State University of New York Press.

Gerson, K. (1993). *No man's land: Men's changing commitments to family and work.* New York: Basic Books.

Glaser, B. (1978). *Theoretical sensitivity.* Mill Valley, CA: Sociology Press.

Hawkins, A. J., & Dollahite, D. (1997). *Generative fathering: Beyond deficit perspectives.* Thousand Oaks, CA: Sage.

Hawkins, A. J., & Palkovitz, R. (1999). Beyond ticks and clicks: The need for more diverse and broader conceptualizations and measures of father involvement. *The Journal of Men's Studies, 8,* 11–32.

Lamb, M. E., Pleck, J. H., Charnov, E. L., & Levine, J. A. (1985). Paternal behavior in humans. *American Zoologist, 25,* 884–894.

Lamb, M. E., Pleck, J. H., Charnov, E. L., & Levine, J. A. (1987). A biosocial perspective on paternal behavior and involvement. In J. B., Lancaster, J. Altmann, A. S. Rossi, & L. R. Sherrod (Eds.), *Parenting across the lifespan: Biosocial dimensions* (pp. 111–142). Hawthorne, NY: Aldine.

LaRossa, R., & LaRossa, M. M. (1989). Babe care: Fathers vs. mothers. In B. J. Risman & P. Schwartz (Eds.), *Gender in intimate relationships: A microstructural approach.* Belmont, CA: Wadsworth.

Levine, J. A., & Pitt, E. W. (1995). *New expectations: Community strategies for responsible fatherhood.* New York: Families and Work Institute.

Longmore, M. A. (1998). Symbolic interactionism and the study of sexuality. *Journal of Sex Research, 35,* 44–57.

4. INTERVIEWING AND SENSITIZING CONCEPTS 81

Lupton, D., & Barclay, L. (1997). *Constructing fatherhood: Discourses and experiences.* Thousand Oaks, Sage.

Markus, H., & Nurius, P. (1986). Possible selves. *American Psychologist, 41,* 954–969.

Marsiglio, W. (1998). *Procreative man.* New York: New York University Press.

Marsiglio, W. (in press). *Stepdads: Stories of love, hope, and repair.* Boulder, Co: Rowman & Littlefield.

Marsiglio, W., Amato, P., Day, R. D., & Lamb, M. E. (2000). Scholarship on fatherhood in the 1990s and beyond. *Journal of Marriage and the Family, 62,* 1173–1191.

Marsiglio, W., & Cohan, M. (2000). Contextualizing father involvement and paternal influence: Sociological and qualitative themes. *Marriage & Family Review, 29,* 75–95.

Marsiglio, W., Day, R. D., & Lamb, M. E. (2000). Exploring fatherhood diversity: Implications for conceptualizing father involvement. *Marriage & Family Review, 29,* 269–293.

Marsiglio, W., & Hutchinson, S. (2002). *Sex, men, and babies: Stories of awareness and responsibility.* New York: New York University Press.

May, K. A. (1980). A typology of detachment/involvement styles adopted during pregnancy by first-time fathers. *Western Journal of Nursing Research, 2,* 445–453.

McAdams, D. (1990). Unity and purpose in human lives: The emergence of identity as a life story. In A. I. Rabin, R. A. Zucker, R. A. Emmons, & S. Frank (Eds.), *Studying persons and lives* (pp. 148–200). New York: Springer.

McMahon, M. (1995). *Engendering motherhood: Identity and self-transformation in women's lives.* New York: Guilford.

Nurse, A. M. (2002). *Fatherhood arrested: Parenting from within the juvenile justice system.* Nashville: Vanderbilt University Press.

Oyserman, D. & Markus, H. R. (1990). Possible selves and delinquency. *Journal of Personality and Social Psychology, 59,* 112–125.

Palkovitz, R. (1997). Reconstructing "involvement": Expanding conceptualizations of men's caring in contemporary families. In A. J. Hawkins & D. C. Dollahite (Eds.), *Generative fathering: Beyond deficit perspectives* (pp. 200–216). Thousand Oaks, CA: Sage.

Peterson, A., & Jenni, C. (2001). Men's experiences of making the decision to have their first child: A phenomenological analysis. Unpublished manuscript, Department of Educational Leadership and Counseling, University of Montana.

Pleck, J. H. (1997). Paternal involvement: Levels, sources, and consequences. In M. E. Lamb (Ed.), *The role of the father in child development* (3rd ed., pp. 123–167). New York: Wiley.

Pleck, J. H., & Stueve, J. L. (2001). Time and paternal involvement: In K. Daly (Ed.), *Minding the time in family experience: Emerging perspectives and issues.* (pp. 205–226). Oxford, UK: Elsevier Science.

Pleck, J. H., Lamb, M. E., & Levine, J. A. (1985). Epilog: Facilitating future change in men's family roles. In R. A. Lewis & M. Sussman (Ed.), *Men's changing roles in the family* (pp. 11–16). New York: Haworth Press.

Riessman, C. K. (1993). *Narrative analysis.* Qualitative Research Methods, vol 30. Newbury Park: Sage.

Sandelowski, M. (1991). Telling stories, narrative approaches in qualitative research. *Image, Journal of Nursing Scholarship, 23,* 161–166.

Schutz, A. (1970a). *On phenomenology and social relations.* Chicago: University of Chicago Press.

Schutz, A. (1970b). *Reflections on the problem of relevance.* New Haven, CT: Yale University Press.

Schwalbe, M. L. & Wolkomir, M. (2002). Interviewing men. In J. F. Gubrium & J. A. Holstein (Eds.), *Handbook of interview research: Context and method* (pp. 203–219). Thousand Oaks, CA: Sage.

Snarey, J. (1993). *How fathers care for the next generation.* Cambridge, MA: Harvard University Press.

Stueve, J. L. & Pleck, J. H. (2001). "Parenting voice": Solo parent identity and co-parent identity in married parents' narratives of meaningful parenting experiences. Journal of social and personal relationships, *18,* 691–708.

Strauss, A. (1969). Turning points in identity. *In Mirrors and Masks: Transformations of Identity* (pp. 92–100). New York: Macmillan.

Strauss, R. & Goldberg, W. A. (1999). Self and possible selves during the transition to fatherhood. *Journal of Family Psychology, 13*, 244–259.

van den Hoonaard, W. C. (1997). *Working with sensitizing concepts: Analytical field research.* Qualitative Research Methods, 41: Sage.

Walzer, S. (1998). *Thinking about the baby: Gender and transitions into parenthood.* Philadelphia: Temple University Press.

5

A Narrative Approach to Paternal Identity: The Importance of Parental Identity "Conjointness"

Joseph H. Pleck
University of Illinois

Jeffrey L. Stueve
University of New Mexico

INTRODUCTION

Prior research on paternal identity focuses on identity salience or commitment. Using an inductive approach, this study investigated paternal identity using fathers' narratives about meaningful experiences they have had or anticipate having with their child. In an exploratory study of 28 married couples ($N = 56$) with preschool children, the Parenting Narrative Interview (PNI) collected parents' stories about their experiences at five different points in time (Marker Experiences), and their stories about five different areas of parenting (Domain Experiences): caregiving, promoting development, breadwinning, arranging and planning, and relationship with the child. The construct of "parenting voice" emerged during analysis of these narratives, referring to whether parents described their experiences using the first-person singular *I* or plural *We*. Parenting voice is interpreted as reflecting the degree of "conjointness" in a father's or mother's parental identity, i.e., the balance between self-as-solo-parent and self-as-coparent. Parental identity conjointness did not differ between fathers and mothers across narrative time (Marker Experiences). Fathers' parental identities were more conjoint than mothers' for

four of five domains: caregiving, promoting development, arranging and planning, and relationship with the child. Use of the *We* voice in fathers' arranging and planning narratives was associated with both fathers' and mothers' reporting more play-companionship with their child. Mothers' use of the *We* voice in arranging and planning was associated with mothers doing fewer parenting tasks and working more hours, and with fathers doing more parenting tasks (caretaking, teaching, and arranging) and working fewer hours. These findings suggest that parental identity in the arranging and planning domain may function as an executive component of parental identity, associated with behavior in multiple domains.

Paternal Identity

Subsequent to the introduction of the construct of paternal involvement in the mid-1980s (Lamb, Pleck, Charnov, & Levine, 1985, 1987; Pleck, Lamb, & Levine, 1985), one of the areas of increasing interest in fatherhood research has been paternal identity (Marsiglio, 1998; Pleck, 1997). If one views father involvement as a purely behavioral construct, paternal identity can be considered as one of several major factors influencing fathers' behavior, as well as giving their behavior meaning. Alternatively, if one construes paternal involvement more broadly to include other dynamics and processes besides behavior, identity is clearly one of most important of these nonbehavioral components.

In this chapter we present an approach to understanding paternal identity employing fathers' narratives about meaningful experiences they have had or anticipate having as parents, and consider them in light of mothers' narratives. We first set forth the theoretical context for the narrative perspective on parental identity. Next, we describe how we operationalized the narrative approach in an initial study of married parents of preschool-age children, inviting parents to describe meaningful experiences they had had as parents in different domains of parenting (e.g., caregiving, promoting development) as well as at different points in time. Finally, we provide findings concerning one specific aspect of parents' narratives— whether parents describe their experiences in the first-person singular or plural *I* or *We*. We interpret mothers' and fathers' use of singular or plural parental voices as reflecting the degree of conjointness of their parental identity. We find that fathers' parental identity is relatively more coparental and less solo-parental than is mothers'. Finally, we present evidence that conjointness of parental identity in one particular domain of parenting—arranging and planning—is associated with parental behavior.

BACKGROUND

Role Identity

A variety of different theoretical and research traditions employ the construct of identity but construe it in rather different ways. Prior to the 1990s, most literature on parental identity framed the concept within a psychodynamic perspective

5. PATERNAL IDENTITY CONJOINTNESS 85

(e.g., Anthony & Benedek, 1970; Cath, Gurwitt, & Ross, 1982; Rubin, 1984), though not an Eriksonian one. This psychodynamic work on parental identity was generally conducted independently of, and had relatively little influence upon, the study of parenthood in human development and family studies.

When the family studies field began conceptualizing parental identity in the 1990s, it drew on the symbolic interactionist perspective. At the broadest level, this framework conceptualizes role identities as the "self-meanings" attached to a social position and its associated roles (LaRossa & Reitzes, 1993). However, the formulation of parental role identity (Ihinger-Tallman, Pasley, & Beuhler, 1993; McBride & Rane, 1997) drew on a more specific conceptualization of identity developed previously within symbolic interactionism by Stryker (1980, 1987) and Burke (Burke & Reitzes, 1991; Burke & Tully, 1977).

Full treatment of Stryker's and Burke's concepts of identity is beyond the scope of this chapter (see Ihinger-Tallman et al., 1993; McBride & Rane, 1997; Stryker & Burke, 2000), but we can make some summary observations. The primary dimension of variation in role identity on which both Stryker and Burke focused was its importance or intensity. Stryker termed this dimension identity salience, referring to the importance of a particular role and associated identity relative to others. Stryker further hypothesized that identity salience is associated with the individual's commitment to relationships linked to that identity, with these relationships potentially varying in quantity (extensivity) as well as quality (intensivity). By contrast, Burke used the term identity commitment to mean the more general dimension of importance or intensity of identity, referring to the individual's "commitment to a line of action." In Burke's "identity control" model, identity commitment is more specifically conceptualized as the degree to which discrepancies between individuals' identity standards and others' and their perception of their behavior lead to changes in behavior to reduce the discrepancy.

Applying the Stryker–Burke conception of identity to parenting dictates a particular kind of measurement strategy: Individuals give responses interpreted as reflecting how important parenting, or a particular aspect of parenting, is to them. For example, individuals may indicate their agreement or disagreement with statements about the importance of parenting in general, or about the value of fathers providing caregiving. Alternatively, respondents may be asked to divide a hypothetical pie chart into different areas representing the importance of parenting and other life roles to them. The general research expectation has been that identity should be linked to behavior, though perhaps more strongly in some contexts than others.

Parenting research using the Stryker–Burke approach has several important characteristics. First, it has concentrated primarily on parental identity in fathers, although recent studies are beginning to include mothers (Cast, 1998; Maurer, Pleck, & Rane, 2001). Second, this research has actually found few associations between measures of paternal identity and fathers' behavioral involvement (see review in Maurer et al., 2001). One source of these weak results may be the frequent assessment of identity at the relatively global level of "parent" or "father."

86   PLECK AND STUEVE

For example, one father may rate being a father as extremely important because being directly involved in caregiving is central to him. The same rating by another father may mean that being a good breadwinner is crucial. Because of this potential ambiguity, it is not surprising that rating being a father as important does not have clear behavioral correlates. Another source of the current weak results is that many factors may moderate the relationship between strength of identity and behavior, and thus clear associations should be expected only under certain conditions, a point emphasized by Ihinger-Tallman et al. (1993).

Further refinements in conceptualization and measurement will likely lead to stronger associations between paternal behavior and strength of paternal identity, or of specific types of paternal identity. In this chapter, however, we offer an alternative approach to paternal identity that addresses the more expansive meaning of identity in symbolic interactionism: identity not as the strength of the individual's commitment to a role, but identity as the broader meaning that the role has for the individual.

The Narrative Approach to Parental Identity

Our approach conceptualizes identity in a role as the "story" that one tells oneself and others about oneself in that role. There is an increasing use of narrative or story as a way of understanding human experience in diverse social science disciplines such as social psychology (Gergen & Gergen, 1987), personality psychology (Hermans, 1997; McAdams, 1988, 1990, 1993), developmental psychology (Mandler, 1984), and psycholinguistics (Bruner, 1986). The narrative approach is also emerging as a powerful tool in family therapy (Freedman & Combs, 1996). Indeed, the study of narratives is emerging as a social science field in its own right (Bamberg, 1997).

Particularly influential on our approach to narratives as a way of understanding parental identity is work by McAdams (1990, 1993; McAdams, Diamond, de St. Aubin, & Mansfield, 1997) and Gergen and Gergen (1987, 1997). McAdams is a leading advocate of the use of a "life story" narrative approach to study identity. Identity can "be viewed as an internalized and evolving life story, a way of telling the self, to the self and others, through a story or set of stories (complete with settings, scenes, characters, plots, and themes)" (McAdams et al., 1997, p. 678). Because identity can be understood as a life story, analyzing the components of the story gives us a way of understanding important aspects of identity.

McAdams (1990, 1993) distinguishes five story components: nuclear episodes, imagoes (or idealized role models), ideological settings, a generativity script (plans for how the story may continue), and thematic lines. Nuclear episodes, or important meaningful experiences, are of special significance as important indicators of identity. A nuclear episode can capture what a person sees as evidence of who they are. Interpretations (or reinterpretations) of these events can indicate continuity or change and may mark turning points in one's life story.

5. PATERNAL IDENTITY CONJOINTNESS 87

Gergen and Gergen (1987, 1997) identify another strength of examining identity as a self-narrative. They propose that individuals have the ability to reflexively reconstruct self-understanding, an ability expressed in self-narratives. One function of identity, then, is that it links past experiences and memories, as well as expected or hoped for events, to the present. It is through one's self-narrative that the past is interpreted and the future anticipated. In this way identity serves to give coherence to one's life.

The narrative approach has recently been used in the study of motherhood (McMahon, 1995) and fatherhood (Farrell, Rosenberg, & Rosenberg, 1993; Stueve & Pleck, 1998). McMahon was especially interested in mothers' "biographical self." She argued that it is important to consider that people appraise themselves (and others) in terms of the qualities, or "images of the self," they have, and how these may be evaluated independent of their occupying particular social locations. In a study of 59 single and partnered employed mothers of preschool children, McMahon used the term "moral transformation" to describe how the middle-class mothers in her study described their self-conception of their mothering. This transformation was experienced as a process of growth and development in their lives, and almost half the middle-class mothers experienced it as a sense of transcendent change in their relationships with the world, with life, or with humanity. Working-class mothers, less surprised by the work involved and their emotional responses to their children, were also transformed. But this self-transformation was more likely to be seen as a "moral reform" described in terms of "settling down" and having responsibilities. McMahon holds that the strong connectedness most mothers developed with their children represents how much the mothers' "sense of self...was generated and sustained through the social relationship of motherhood" (pp. 228–229).

Farrell, Rosenberg, and Rosenberg (1993) conducted a longitudinal study examining the self-narratives of the lives of fathers. In examining the narrative texts of 17 fathers at mid-life, they classified fathers' narratives into four types (romantic saga, comedy, tragedy, and ironic satire) presented in a model by Gergen and Gergen (1987). While men in their early 40s were somewhat more likely to have a romantic narrative (i.e., facing setbacks and then prevailing) men in their late 50s told stories that were more complex. Farrell et al. found that most narratives were often a mixture of these four types, both within and across work, marriage, and parenthood.

Stueve and Pleck (1998) used a modified "life story" approach to study paternal identity in 10 fathers of school-age children, in a precursor to the present study. Respondents were asked questions about their experience as fathers to elicit the five story elements specified by McAdams. Nuclear episodes were elicited by questions about "key events" in their fatherhood, positive or negative, with no further structuring of content. One clear finding from this study was that breadwinning was a central component of fathering from the men's perspective; its importance was sometimes reported explicitly, while other times its importance was highlighted

in the challenges they faced to provide. Breadwinning was also important because it often was perceived as conflicting with other domains of parenting. In addition, all fathers reported promoting their children's development (education was mentioned by all 10, six referred to college) and having good relationships with their children as parts of their fathering narratives. Another feature present in 4 of the 10 fathers' narratives was a life-changing "turning point" that reflected both strong negative and positive affects. This event was reported as changing their parenting experience in a dramatic way. For example, an African-American father who had spent an extended period hospitalized described the experience as follows:

> The surgery kind of changed my whole outline of life . . . It kind of made me realize that, you know, being a father, it just woke me up . . . opened my eyes. When you are down and out, sometimes you got to really realize, you know, that you try to do the right thing. Not like I used to, drink and, you know, write a check for money, for money they didn't have. That operation did it, just took a whole lot . . . It made a new approach on life for me. I went through a little crisis, but it made me a better father.

Developing a Narrative Assessment of Parental Identity

We had two key considerations in developing our particular strategy for collecting parental narratives. First, we wanted our instrument to collect parents' narratives about *meaningful experiences* they had or expected to have as parents. Among all the experiences that parents can potentially recall or construct in interaction with an interviewer, the subset of experiences that parents select as meaningful or important are most central to identity. These experiences correspond to McAdams' concept of nuclear episodes.

Second, we wanted our instrument to collect narratives about multiple experiences, with these experiences ranging across time as well as across different domains or areas within parenting. Multiple narratives from each individual are desirable, to give respondents the opportunity to describe a variety of experiences. Furthermore, prior narrative approaches to identity emphasized that narratives provide an occasion to interpret the past and anticipate the future, thus linking past, present, and future. Thus, we decided that individuals should be specifically prompted to describe past and future meaningful experiences. But in addition, we thought it important that respondents be asked about meaningful experiences in different domains or areas within parenting. Parenting includes many different kinds of activities. Prior measures assessing the importance of being a "parent" often did not recognize this multiplicity. Thus, our protocol provides activity framework for parents' narratives. However, the protocol elicits stories about different time periods in parenting before introducing this activity structure.

5. PATERNAL IDENTITY CONJOINTNESS

The overall objective of the narrative interview protocol developed in light of these considerations is to provide insight into the meaning that parenting has to respondents. It should be noted that many different aspects or dimensions of meaning can be derived from narratives collected with such a protocol, including ones that the researcher has not anticipated.

METHODS

Sample

We recruited parents of 2- to 5-year-old children enrolled in an on-campus laboratory preschool at a midwestern university. Both university and community families were represented. From the 96 families enrolled, the project recruited and conducted 45 to 90 minute qualitative interviews with both fathers and mothers from 30 couples, and with 6 mothers who were single parents or whose spouses or partners did not participate, yielding a participation rate of 37.5% (36 of 96 families). Analyses comparing families who participated with those who did not found that participating families included mothers with higher education than nonparticipating families, but they did not differ on other family or sociodemographic characteristics.

Findings reported here come from an analysis of both fathers and mothers in 28 couples. (Two interviews could not be transcribed.) Average age of the 28 fathers was 36.7 years ($SD = 6.2$), with a mean education level of 18.0 years ($SD = 2.2$). Average age of the 28 mothers was 35.3 years ($SD = 5.2$), with a mean education of 18.3 years ($SD = 1.9$). Average monthly income was \$4,846 for fathers ($SD = 5,028$; minimum \$0, maximum \$20,000) and \$1,673 for mothers ($SD = 2,117$; minimum \$0, maximum \$8,000).

If parents had more than one child (64.3%), they were asked to complete the instruments with respect to the oldest child in the preschool. Of the 28 target children, 13 (46.4%) were boys and 15 (53.6%) were girls. The children's average age was 4.3 years ($SD = 0.78$). Twenty-three were White (82.1%).

Procedures

Data were collected in a qualitative interview, the Parenting Narrative Interview (PNI), and with self-administered questionnaires. The PNI, described in more detail below, was conducted in parents' homes. Interviews were audiotape-recorded and subsequently transcribed. Summary notes were also kept during the interviews, which lasted 45 to 90 minutes. The Ethnograph software (Seidel, 1998) was used in the analysis of the transcripts. Following the interview, parents were given the option of completing the questionnaire during the remainder of the visit or mailing it in. Parents were instructed not to talk with their partners about the interviews until the questionnaire was completed.

90   PLECK AND STUEVE

Measures of Parents' Behavior

In addition to sociodemographic data, the questionnaire included closed-end measures of parents' behavior: parenting tasks, play-companionship, and breadwinning hours. The 17-item parenting tasks measure, which was adapted from Bruce and Fox's (1997) Paternal Involvement Inventory (PII), assessed the frequency of the parent's activities in three areas: caretaking (e.g., assisting or supervising the child in bathing or personal hygiene), teaching (e.g., teaching child athletic or other recreational skills or hobbies), and executive functions (e.g., making decisions that pertain to the child). Reliabilities for the scale were high (alpha = .85, fathers; .84, mothers).

The play-companionship scale consisted of three other items adapted from another subscale (socioemotional functions) of Bruce and Fox's (1997) PII. Items were "play together," "join your child in activities that he/she likes," and "spending time one-on-one with your child." This scale was used separately from the parenting tasks scale since exploratory analyses indicated that it had different associations with measures from the Parenting Narrative Interview. The scale has an alpha of .86 for fathers and .83 for mothers.

The breadwinning measure was the reported hours of paid employment. The specific question was, "If you are employed, approximately how many hours do you spend doing paid work each week?" For those not employed, hours were coded as zero.

The Parenting Narrative Interview (PNI)

The primary material from the PNI analyzed here consisted of parents' stories about their experiences at five different points in time (Marker Experiences), and their stories about five different areas of parenting (Domain Experiences). For parents with more than one child, the PNI focused on the parenting of a specific preschool child. As a warm-up, the interview began with questions about when the parent first started thinking about being a parent and about expectations he or she had. The interview then prompted parents for the first four of the five Marker Experiences. Parents were initially asked to share an experience related to becoming or deciding to become the parent of the targeted child (Becoming a Parent Experience). Next, participants were asked about an early parenting experience that was meaningful to them (Early Experience), and a more recent parenting experience (Recent Experience). Parents then had an opportunity to share any other important experience that came to mind (Other Important Experience).

Next, the interview transitioned to key events or experiences in five specific areas within parenting (Domain Experiences): caregiving, promoting development, breadwinning, arranging and planning, and relationship with the child. These domains were formulated following a review of prior conceptualizations of the specific components or domains within parenting (e.g., Bruce & Fox, 1997;

5. PATERNAL IDENTITY CONJOINTNESS

Palkovitz, 1997; Small & Eastman, 1991), and selected to be appropriate for parents of preschool children. After a brief introduction, parents were shown a card that listed the five domains with a brief description of each:

Caregiving: Things like feeding, bathing, dressing, cleaning cuts and scrapes, and putting a child to bed.

Development Promoting: Things that promote any type of development—language learning, music, sports, arts & crafts, school related, religious education, children's social groups.

Breadwinning: Things you do to earn money to support your family—a job, education or training for a job; might include decisions about taking or **not** taking a job.

Arranging and Planning: Things like making doctor and dentist appointments, arranging child care or transportation, and educational planning.

Your Relationship with Your Child: Things like how you get along with each other, things you enjoy or find frustrating about each other, how you feel about each other.

The caregiving and promoting development domains can be interpreted as aspects of the engagement component in Lamb et al.'s (1987) formulation of paternal involvement. The arranging and planning domain has some correspondence to the responsibility component of involvement. Relationship to the child is a qualitative dimension of parental behavior not included in Lamb et al.'s involvement concept. Breadwinning is also not included in the involvement construct but is considered a parental behavior here. Note that breadwinning is defined broadly.

After the last Domain Experience (relationship with child), parents shared an experience they anticipated in the future with their child: "As (child's) parent, is there any key event or experience that you anticipate in the future? Can you tell me your thoughts about this event or experience?" The question provided the fifth and last of the Marker Experiences.

THE EMERGENCE OF "PARENTING VOICE" IN PARENTS' NARRATIVES

In exploring the interviews to develop codes we became increasingly interested in what we call the "parenting voice" of the narratives. Participants at times referred only, or largely, to themselves as the parent but at other times included their partner. Furthermore, how partners were included in the parents' stories varied. Sometimes the partner was referred to so as to set the context for the story. Other times the participants described how the partners' parenting compared to or complemented their own. Finally, some of the stories were told as if both parents shared the same parenting experience.

We decided to make this aspect of our parents' narratives the focus of our analysis. We began to interpret these parenting voices as reflecting the degree of "conjointness" in a father's or mother's parental identity. Parents with coparental partners inevitably negotiate with their partners a balance between being individual parents and coparents. This balancing in the coparents' ongoing relationship is reflected in their individual parental identities as well. Thus, parental identity can be viewed as incorporating a balance between self-as-solo-parent and self-as-coparent. Observing how a parent uses the solo-parental or coparental voice across his or her 10 parenting stories potentially provides insight into this balance.

Parental identity conjointness, or the extent to which the parental self is a coparental self, is relevant to a widely accepted notion about fatherhood in the contemporary United States: that fathering is, in some global sense, "mediated" by mothers, in a way that mothering is not mediated by fathers. One empirical basis for this notion is evidence that mothers can act as gatekeepers who limit or regulate fathers' involvement (Allen & Hawkins, 1999; Beitel & Parke, 1998). Another piece of evidence is that when fathers' relationships with mothers are disrupted, as in divorce, fathers' relationships with their children by that mother frequently become attenuated (Furstenberg, 1990). If it is true that paternal identity is mediated by mothers more so than maternal identity is mediated by fathers, one would expect that in a sample of coupled parents, fathers would more often than mothers represent their partners as actors in their parenting narratives.

Other theoretical formulations in family studies also informed our concept of parental identity conjointness. A fundamental proposition of symbolic interactionism is that an individual's identities are developed through interactions with others, especially in close relationships (LaRossa & Reitzes, 1993). Thus, parental identity is developed, in part, through interactions with a coparent (as well as with the child and others). Marks (1986) extends the symbolic interactionist conception of identity further in his "three corners" model of the structure of the self-in-marriage. Marks distinguishes between the "interior me" and the "marital partner me" as different "selves" within a married individual. Marks also identifies a "third-corner me" (a self in which the individual and partner are connected to each other by being linked to a common external entity, e.g., an interest). The present study develops a conceptualization of the self-in-parenting that similarly distinguishes between a "solo-parent me" and a "coparent me."

In addition, we noted parallels between our concept of parental identity conjointness and Abidin and Brunner's (1995; Weissman & Cohen, 1985) concept of the "parental alliance," the degree to which individual parents perceive their coparent as supporting and valuing them and vice versa. The parental alliance includes dimensions such as valuing the partner's involvement, respecting the partner's parenting judgment, and desiring to communicate with each other. Also relevant is the cohesion dimension in Olson's (1993) Circumplex Model of Marital

5. PATERNAL IDENTITY CONJOINTNESS

and Family Systems, as applied to the coparental relationship. A central hypothesis of the Circumplex Model is that relationships characterized by intermediate levels of cohesion (termed connection and cohesion) rather than levels at either extreme (disengaged or enmeshed) are generally optimal for family functioning. In essence, the present research conceptualizes parental identity conjointness, expressed in parenting voice, as reflecting the dimension within individuals' parental identities corresponding to parental alliance and cohesion.

PARENTING VOICE CODING

To explore parenting voice more systematically, we developed a formal coding system. The texts of narratives in mothers' and fathers' 10 parenting experiences were first segmented into "units" to which codes could be applied. A unit was the participant's response to the question about a meaningful parenting experience and any follow-up questions about that experience.

Initially, two "parenting voices" were distinguished: *I* and *We*. (A few units were coded in the residual category *Child Only*.) The *I* voice refers to units in which there is either no reference to the parenting partner, or only a minor direct or indirect reference. *We* voice units have extended or multiple references to the parenting partner. Further distinctions observed within *I* and *We* units led to the development of *I Only* and *I Context* categories, and *We Complementary*, *We Compare*, and *We Joint* categories.

I Only units contain no reference to the parenting partner. The following is an example from a father's story about a meaningful breadwinning experience:

> Veronica [daughter] asked me if I have to go to work some days. "Yeah. I gotta go make money, you know. Somebody's gotta make money." And you know I said this a couple of times because she's asked about it a couple of times. And then she says "You know, Dad, when I get older I'm gonna get a job, and then you can stay home." [Laughs] All right! Sounds good. So she picked up on it that somebody's gotta work.

I Context units include a reference to the partner, but this reference only helps set the context of the experience. The following excerpt relates a White, adoptive father's expectations of a future meaningful experience. Because his wife is also White, it sets the context for what he anticipates he will experience:

> I'm preparing myself for the time when she [daughter] comes home and starts dealing with the race issue, you know. That's she's African American and we're White and, we're always trying to, you know, instill pride in her for her skin color and her cultural heritage and . . . [Pause] I guess I'm looking forward to that as sort of an event that's going to happen. Nothing's happened really yet that's been all that meaningful in that regard, so . . . It's only little things . . .

In *We Complementary* units, a parent describes herself or himself and the partner as having different parenting experiences or performing different parenting tasks, with the two seeming to fit together to make a positive contribution. A father describes his family's nighttime routine:

Umm. Well I mean [pause] yeah, I guess you know like every night I am the one who, we kind of trade off on giving baths and stuff like that and then the snack and all of that. But then Dawn has kind of, I mean we seem to have, Dawn takes care of brushing her teeth and having her go to the bathroom and stuff like that and then I come up and actually I am the one who puts her into bed.

We Compare units also describe different parenting experiences but emphasize comparisons in the amount of parenting each partner does (or does not do) rather than how the two parents' activities fit together. The following is an excerpt from a father's arranging and planning narrative:

I kind of see that this whole area of life for me and kids [goes] over to my wife. I'm terrible at arranging and planning. I can barely do it in my professional life. These examples, these are things my wife had taken over with my blessings. I'm just not very good at it.

Finally, the *We Joint* subcategory is used when a parent's narrative indicates little or no explicit differences between the parents' experience.

You see it's different because Anna is adopted. I guess what inspired us . . . We were trying to get pregnant for a couple of years and were still trying to get pregnant. One of Stephen's friends called and said, "My sister-in-law is pregnant and wants to give up the baby for adoption, are you guys interested?" And we're like "Wow!" because we had talked about adoption before we realized we were going to have problems.

After initial training, author Stueve and two female research assistants coded units using the five parenting voice categories (*I Only*, *I Context*, *We Joint*, *We Complementary*, *We Compare*), and the residual *Child Only* category. Stueve coded all units from the first four transcripts, and each assistant then independently coded a different subsample of units. The first assistant and Stueve matched on 123 out of 160 units. The second assistant and Stueve agreed on 126 out of 147 units. Thus, a total of 249 out of 307 (81.1%) of the units coded by the assistants matched parenting voice categories assigned by Stueve. Disagreements in the initial four transcripts were discussed and consensus reached. When there was not agreement, Stueve made final coding decisions. After the four initial transcripts, Stueve assigned the final code, taking assistants' coding into consideration.

PARENTAL IDENTITY CONJOINTNESS: HOW DO FATHERS AND MOTHERS COMPARE?

Table 5.1 presents the distribution of text units by parenting voice categories and parental gender, within types of experience. For example, the 28 fathers each provided five Marker Experiences, yielding a total of 140 text units for that column. The original *We Complementary* and *We Compare* codes had the smallest frequencies and were relatively similar conceptually. Thus, pooling them into a combined *We Distinct* category seemed justified, making the table easier to interpret.

The parenting voices used most frequently were *We Joint* and *I Only*, each accounting for about a third of all text units. Among the remaining third, *I Context* was most frequent, with *We Distinct* (pooling the *We Complementary* and *We Compare* codes) and *Child Only* employed relatively rarely.

Within Marker Experiences, gender differences in parenting voice were not significant, $\chi^2(3, N = 259) = 1.22$, ns. (Units coded *Child Only*, or where no experience was reported, were omitted from all χ^2 tests.) Further analyses (Stueve & Pleck, 2001) also found no gender differences for individual Marker Experiences. However, parenting voice usage varied according to *when* the experience occurred. The general pattern of differences was that for both genders, voice shifted from *We Joint* in the Becoming a Parent Experience to *I Context*, and especially *I Only*, in later experiences.

In Domain Experiences, significant differences in voice usage by gender were evident, $\chi^2(3, N = 278) = 14.18$, $p < .01$. Gender differences were especially pronounced in the use of *I Only* (23.6% for fathers, 36.4% for mothers) and

TABLE 5.1

Parenting Voices in Marker Experiences, Domain Experiences, and All Experiences, by Parent Gender

Parenting Voice	All Marker Experiences			All Domain Experiences			All Experiences		
	Total	Father	Mother	Total	Father	Mother	Total	Father	Mother
I only	33.6	34.3	32.9	30.0	23.6	36.4	31.8	28.9	34.6
I context	21.8	21.4	22.1	25.0	22.9	27.1	23.4	22.1	24.6
We distinct	1.4	0.7	2.1	10.0	15.7	4.3	5.7	8.2	3.2
We joint	35.7	34.3	37.1	34.3	37.1	31.4	35.0	35.7	34.3
Child only	5.0	5.7	4.3	0.7	0.7	0.7	2.9	3.2	2.5
Not given	2.5	3.6	1.4	0.0	0.0	0.0	1.3	1.8	0.7
N of text units	280	140	140	280	140	140	560	280	280

Note. Numbers are percentages of *N*.

96   PLECK AND STUEVE

We Distinct (15.7%, 4.3%) voices. The number of times a parent used either *We Distinct* or *We Joint* across the five Domain Experiences was also tabulated. Fathers employed a *We* voice 2.64 times ($SD = 1.42$), while mothers did so 1.79 times ($SD = 1.16$), $F(1, 27) = 6.10$, $p < .05$.

Analyses were then conducted separately for each domain (Table 5.2). These analyses indicated significant gender differences in mothers' and fathers' parenting voices in the caregiving domain, $\chi^2(3, N = 56) = 10.48$, $p < .05$, and in the arranging and planning domain, $\chi^2(3, N = 56) = 14.48$, $p < .01$.

Subsidiary analyses were conducted to collapse the voice categories in several different ways. When *I Only* was compared to a combined *I Context, We Distinct*, and *We Joint* pooled category, a difference in mothers' and fathers' use of parenting voice in the promoting development domain was found ($\chi^2 = 4.52$, df 1, $p < .05$). When *We Joint* was compared to a combined *I Only, I Context*, and *We Distinct* coding, gender differences were found in narratives of meaningful experiences concerning relationship with the child ($\chi^2 = 4.08$, df 1, $p < .05$). Finally, combined *I Only* and *I Context* voices were compared with combined *We Distinct* and *We Joint* voices. Mothers' and fathers' voices differed in arranging and planning narratives ($\chi^2 = 4.79$, df 1, $p < .05$). The general pattern is that for all domains except breadwinning, fathers more often use a *We* voice and less often use an *I* voice.

HOW IS PARENTAL IDENTITY CONJOINTNESS RELATED TO BEHAVIOR?

After finding that fathers' parental identity was more conjoint than mothers' in four of the five parenting domains, we next turned our attention to the relationship between parental identity conjointness and parents' behavior. According to symbolic interactionist theory, identity is both a cause and a consequence of behavior. That is, the self-meaning one has in a role guides one's behavior in that role; conversely, behavior and subsequent experience in a role affect self-meaning. However, it is not theoretically clear how the conjointness dimension of parental identity should be related to behavior. On the one hand, Stryker's (1980, 1987) concept of identity commitment (referring to the groundedness of an identity in relationships with others) might imply that conjoint parental identity is associated with high levels of parental behavior because conjointness reflects a direct representation of one's partner in one's identity. On the other hand, conjointness may represent a diffusion of one's sense of individual responsibility and thus be associated with less parental behavior. A parallel from a quite different research area is that condom use is less frequent among adolescent males who view responsibility for contraception as shared by both male and female compared to those who view responsibility for contraception as the male's alone (Pleck, Sonenstein, & Swain, 1988).

TABLE 5.2
Parenting Voices in Domain Experiences, by Parent Gender

Parenting Voice	Caregiving		Promoting Development		Breadwinning		Arranging and Planning		Relationship with Child	
	Father	Mother	Father	Mother	Father	Mother	Father	Mother	Father	Mother
I Only	21.4	39.3	14.3	39.3	28.6	28.6	10.7	28.6	42.9	46.4
I Context	28.6	17.9	14.3	10.7	28.6	42.9	14.3	25.0	28.6	39.3
We Distinct	25.0	0.0	3.6	3.6	3.6	7.1	39.3	0.0	7.1	10.7
We Joint	25.0	42.9	64.3	42.9	39.3	21.4	35.7	46.4	21.4	3.6
Child Only	0.0	0.0	3.6	3.6	0.0	0.0	0.0	0.0	0.0	0.0
N of Text Units	28	28	28	28	28	28	28	28	28	28

Note. Numbers are percentages of *N*.

PLECK AND STUEVE

It is possible that identity in a particular domain may have implications for behavior in other domains as well. In a qualitative study, Hood (1983) argued that whether a mother's employment led to a change in the division of family work depended on whether the couple defined the employed wife as a cobreadwinner. In effect, identity in the breadwinning domain served to organize behavior in other areas. In addition, Lamb et al.'s (1987) formulation of engagement, accessibility, and responsibility as three components of paternal involvement implies that responsibility is a more executive or administrative aspect of involvement, concerning the degree to which the father is accountable for arranging the performance of child-related care or tasks, or making sure that they are completed, as distinct from simply being the one who performs the tasks. Parents' narratives in the arranging and planning domain may in part reflect this executive aspect of parental identity. If so, identity conjointness in arranging and planning may be associated with behaviors in other parenting domains.

Correlational Analyses

Preliminary correlational analyses were conducted to explore the associations between parental identity conjointness in the five domains and self-reported behavior: parenting tasks, play-companionship, and breadwinning hours. In these analyses, parenting voice was dichotomized, with *We Distinct* and *We Joint* (= 1) compared to *I Only* and *I Context* (= 0). Although the four voice categories are ordered, there is no basis for assuming equal intervals between adjacent levels. A code of *Child Only* for a particular domain was treated as missing data.

The correlational analyses suggested that parental identity conjointness in the arranging and planning domain is significantly associated with parents' behavior. Among fathers, use of *We* voice in arranging and planning narratives is associated with greater play-companionship. Fathers' conjointness in arranging and planning narratives is also linked to mothers reporting higher levels of play-companionship. Among mothers, use of the *We* voice in the arranging and planning domain is associated with mothers' doing fewer parenting tasks and having more breadwinning hours. Mothers' arranging and planning conjointness was also associated with fathers' doing more parenting tasks and working fewer hours.

Regression Analyses

Multiple regression analyses were then conducted to test models predicting parenting tasks, play-companionship, and breadwinning hours from fathers' and mothers' use of the *We* voice in arranging and planning narratives. For parenting tasks and breadwinning hours, additional dependent variables were constructed representing fathers' proportion of the total reported by both parents. As background to these analyses, the bivariate correlation between mothers' and fathers' arranging and planning voice was $r = -.12$, ns. The mother–father correlations for parenting

5. PATERNAL IDENTITY CONJOINTNESS 99

tasks, play-companionship, and breadwinning hours were $r = .16, .35$, and $-.10$, all ns.

In each regression analysis, the target child's age and sex, parent's age and education, and partner's education were initially entered as control variables. For parental tasks and play-companionship, self's and partner's paid employment hours were also initially entered as controls. The models were then trimmed to exclude control variables whose association with the dependent variable was not significant at $p < .15$ or better. Partner's age was then added and evaluated as a potential control. This variable had not been included in the first block of potential controls because it was collinear with own age ($r = .52, p < .01$) and would have thus spuriously led both parental age variables to be dropped as potential controls. Partner's age was retained in the final regression models only if it was a significant predictor of the dependent variable at $p < .15$ or less. (Own and partner's education were unrelated, $r = .13$, ns.)

For parenting tasks (Table 5.3), mothers' use of the *We* voice in arranging and planning predicts mothers' performance of parenting tasks less frequently (beta $= -.57, p < .01$), fathers' performance of parenting tasks more frequently (beta $= .41, p < .05$), and fathers' performance of a higher proportion of parenting tasks (beta $= .70, p < .01$). Fathers' arranging and planning voice, however, has no independent association with parental task performance. The proportions of variance explained in the three models are relatively high (adjusted R-squares $= .13, .34$, and $.43$).

For play-companionship (Table 5.4), both parent's use of the *We* voice for arranging and planning has independent positive associations with fathers' behavior (father beta $= .50, p < .01$; mother beta $= .41, p < .05$) and with mothers' behavior (mother beta $= .47, p < .05$; father beta $= .39, p < .05$). Adjusted R-squares for these regressions are $.37$ and $.27$.

TABLE 5.3
Regressions Predicting Parenting Tasks and Proportion of Parenting Tasks

Model	B	SE B	Beta	Sig.
DV: Father parenting tasks[a]				
Father arranging and planning voice	.30	.20	.28	.154
Mother arranging and planning voice	.37	.17	.41	.043
DV: Mother parenting tasks[b]				
Mother arranging and planning voice	−.41	.12	−.57	.002
Father arranging and planning voice	.14	.14	.16	.338
DV: Father proportion of parenting tasks[c]				
Father arranging and planning voice	.013	.016	.12	.430
Mother arranging and planning voice	.061	.013	.70	.000

[a] Adjusted $R^2 = .13$, $F(2, 23) = 2.91$, $p = .075$.
[b] Adjusted $R^2 = .34$, $F(2, 23) = 7.41$, $p < .01$.
[c] Adjusted $R^2 = .43$, $F(2, 23) = 10.42$, $p < .01$.

TABLE 5.4
Regressions Predicting Play-Companionship

Model	B	SE B	Beta	Sig.
DV: Father play-companionship[a]				
Father arranging and planning voice	.63	.21	.50	.006
Mother arranging and planning voice	.41	.17	.41	.021
Father age	.13	.07	.28	.096
DV: Mother play-companionship[b]				
Mother arranging and planning voice	.48	.21	.47	.032
Father arranging and planning voice	.50	.23	.39	.041
Mother breadwinning hrs	−.02	.01	−.49	.030
Child sex (0, boy; 1, girl)	−.37	.20	−.36	.073
Father age	.14	.09	.31	.121

[a] Adjusted $R^2 = .20$, $F(3, 21) = 5.66$, $p < .01$.
[b] Adjusted $R^2 = .27$, $F(5, 19) = 2.77$, $p < .05$.

TABLE 5.5
Regressions Predicting Breadwinning Hours and Proportion of Breadwinning Hours

Model	B	SE B	Beta	Sig.
DV: Father breadwinning hours[a]				
Father arranging and planning voice	−.67	7.7	−.02	.931
Mother arranging and planning voice	−18.4	6.5	−.51	.010
DV: Mother Breadwinning Hours[b]				
Mother arranging and planning voice	13.9	6.7	.40	.051
Father arranging and planning voice	2.4	8.0	.06	.771
DV: Fathers proportion of breadwinning hours[c]				
Father arranging and planning voice	.09	.10	.13	.391
Mother arranging and planning voice	−.35	.08	−.62	.000
Mother age	−.10	.04	−.36	.021

[a] Adjusted $R^2 = .20$, $F(2, 23) = 4.04$, $p < .05$.
[b] Adjusted $R^2 = .08$, $F(2, 23) = 2.13$, n
[c] Adjusted $R^2 = .49$, $F(3, 22) = 8.83$, $p < .01$.

Finally, for work hours (Table 5.5), mothers' use of the *We* voice in arranging and planning narratives is positively associated with mothers' work hours (beta = .40, $p < .10$), negatively associated with fathers' work hours (beta = −.51, $p < .05$), and negatively associated with fathers' proportion of the couple's total work hours (beta = −.64, $p < .01$). Adjusted R-squares of .20, .08, and .47 are found.

Path Analysis

Mothers' *We* voice in arranging and planning was associated with both fathers' and mothers' parenting tasks and employment hours. Mother's *We* voice was associated with mothers having higher employment hours and lower levels of parenting tasks.

5. PATERNAL IDENTITY CONJOINTNESS 101

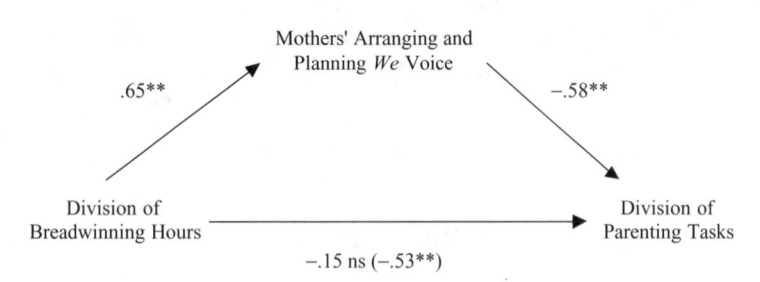

FIG. 5.1. Model testing mothers' arranging and planning *We* voice as a mediator in the relationship between mothers' proportion of breadwinning hours and proportion of parenting tasks. Note: Path coefficient in parentheses indicates the direct relationship between division of beadwinning hours and division of parenting tasks before controlling for the arranging and planning *We* voice. Coefficient from proportion of breadwinning hours to arranging and planning *We* voice is calculated from OLS regression, to be comparable to other coefficients. In logistic regression, $B = 6.60, SE = 2.32, p < .01$.

Conversely, mother's *We* voice was associated with fathers having lower employment hours and higher levels of parenting tasks. Much prior research has examined the link between maternal employment and couples' division of housework and childcare (Pleck, 1985). As noted earlier, Hood (1983) argued that whether a mother's employment led to a change in the division of family work depended on whether the couple defined the employed wife as a cobreadwinner. The regression results suggest the possibility that mothers' parental identity conjointness in arranging and planning may act as a mediator of the association between couples' division of breadwinning and their division of parenting tasks. Figure 5.1 presents a path analysis conducted to test this possibility (Baron & Kenny, 1986).

In this analysis couples' division of breadwinning and parental tasks were represented by mothers' proportion of each. The beta coefficient for the total effect of mothers' proportion of employment hours on their proportion of parenting tasks was $-.53, p < .01$, from a model in which mothers' proportion of employment hours was the only predictor. When mothers' arranging and planning voice was modeled as a hypothetical mediator of this association, the coefficient for the direct (unmediated) relationship between proportion of employment and proportion of parenting tasks dropped to $-.15, ns$. Further, both paths in the indirect (mediated) path between mothers' proportion of breadwinning hours and proportion of parental tasks were significant. For the path from mothers' proportion of breadwinning hours to arranging and planning voice, a dichotomous variable, logistic regression is appropriate ($B = 6.60, SE = 2.32, p < .01$). For the path diagram in Fig. 5.1, a beta coefficient using (OLS) regression was also calculated to produce

an effect parameter comparable to those used for the other two paths. These results support the notion that the relationship between parents' division of breadwinning and their division of parental tasks is largely mediated by mothers' arranging and planning parenting voice.

DISCUSSION

This qualitative study was conducted to explore how the analysis of fathers' narratives about their experiences as parents can contribute to the understanding of paternal identity. An inductive approach was used. Parents' narratives about their experiences varied in their parenting voice, that is, how the self and the partner were included or represented in the stories. In some narratives, a parent referred only to himself or herself, while other narratives included the partner in varying ways. This variation was interpreted as reflecting the degree of "conjointness" in a father's or mother's parental identity, the balance between self-as-solo-parent and self-as-coparent. Although this dimension of parental identity has not received much attention in recent research, it is consistent with symbolic interactionist theory, and with research on parental alliance and marital cohesion.

Gender Differences in Parental Identity Conjointness

A first conclusion suggested by this exploratory study is that compared to mothers, fathers construct their parental identity related to caregiving, promoting development, arranging and planning, and relationship with the child as relatively more coparental than mothers do, that is, more situated in the context of the relationship with the partner. However, there were no gender differences in parenting voice in breadwinning stories or in the parenting stories told about different points in time.

A possible interpretation is that parents' narratives in the Marker Experiences, where time but not content is specified, reflect identity at a more global or general "parent" level, whereas narratives in the Domain Experiences reflect parental identities at a more specific, activity-oriented level. If this is the case, fathers' and mothers' parental identities are similar in conjointness at the global level. Gender differences in parental identity conjointness become apparent, however, when identity related to more specific parental activities is investigated.

Arranging and Planning We Voice as Conjointness of "Executive" Parent Identity

Second, conjointness of parental identity specifically concerning the arranging and planning function of parenting is associated with parental behavior. Use of the We voice in fathers' arranging and planning narratives was associated with

5. PATERNAL IDENTITY CONJOINTNESS 103

both fathers' and mothers' reporting more play-companionship with their child. Mothers' use of the *We* voice in arranging and planning was associated with mothers doing fewer parenting tasks and working more hours, and with fathers doing more parenting tasks (caretaking, teaching, and arranging) and working fewer hours.

The associations observed between parental identity conjointness and behavioral involvement should not be interpreted causally. It is possible that the association between the two constructs is an artifact of their common association to a confounding external variable or variables. Several potentially confounding sociodemographic factors (child age and gender, parents' age and education) were ruled out in this analysis, but unmeasured confounding influences on both identity and involvement may nonetheless exist. Theoretically, the symbolic interactionist conceptual framework in which identity theory is grounded suggests that identity and behavioral involvement influence each other reciprocally. Thus, at this stage of research, it is appropriate to conclude only that, at least in this sample and with the present study's measures, certain distinctive configurations of associations between parental identity conjointness and parental behavior have been identified.

A tentative interpretation is that the component of parental identity reflected in parental reports of arranging and planning experiences functions in an "executive" fashion compared to the components of identity reflected in other domains. As precedent, family systems theory postulates an "executive function" organizing family systems (Broderick, 1993). The executive or orchestrating nature of the component of a parent's identity represented in narratives of arranging and planning is evidenced by the fact that only this component is associated with behavioral involvement. Furthermore, this parental identity component is associated with involvement across several behavioral areas. In essence, the relative representation of one's parental self and of one's partner in arranging and planning narratives may denote the extent to which the parental self, at a superordinate level, is a "self-as-sole-executive-parent" as compared to a "self-as-coexecutive-parent."

Mothers' executive-level parental identity conjointness appears to be centrally involved in both the balance between mothers' and fathers' employment hours and in the division of parental tasks being more balanced or skewed. A path analysis suggests that the relationship between the balance of parenting tasks and employment hours is largely mediated by mothers' executive-level parental identity conjointness. In couples in which fathers do relatively more breadwinning and mothers do relatively more parenting tasks, mothers' representation of their parenting responsibility in the executive domain as reflected in arranging and planning narratives is more often a representation of self-as-sole-executive-parent. In couples exhibiting the obverse pattern (mothers doing relatively more breadwinning and fathers doing relatively more parenting tasks), mothers' arranging and planning narratives more often represent a self-as-coexecutive-with-father. This interpretation can be viewed as a revision of Hood's (1983) earlier argument that whether mothers' employment leads to a change in the division of family work depends on whether the couple defines the employed wife as a cobreadwinner. In

the revised formulation, only mothers' definition of their identity is connected to the parental division of labor, and the specific aspect of mothers' identity at issue is as executive parent, not as breadwinner.

In addition, mothers' executive-level parental identity conjointness is also positively associated with fathers' and mothers' reporting more frequent play-companionship with their child. The association in fathers could be an artifact of the relationships already discussed because play-companionship is significantly associated with fathers' performing a higher proportion of parenting tasks. However, play is unrelated to the two other parenting measures in mothers, suggesting that the finding regarding mothers' play reflects an independent process. That is, mothers' perception of themselves as coparents at the executive level, distinct from its associations with breadwinning and parental tasks, is also connected to mothers' reports of more frequent play and companionship with their children.

With the arranging and planning *We* voice interpreted as reflecting whether a father's identity is as sole-executive-parent rather than as coexecutive-parent, only about a quarter of fathers in our sample demonstrated the former. Fathers' conjoint identity is positively associated with both fathers' and mothers' play-companionship. These associations appear to be independent of the relationships already discussed, since mothers' and fathers' arranging and planning *We* voices are unrelated, as are their levels of play-companionship. Thus, fathers' experiencing themselves as sole-executive-parent is linked to less enjoyable activity with the child for both themselves and their partners.

CONCLUSIONS AND FUTURE DIRECTIONS

Because this study was exploratory, and its sample small and selective, its conclusions cannot be generalized to broader populations of parents. Nonetheless, the narrative approach to fathers' and mothers' parenting experiences offers some promise in revealing dynamics of paternal identity that have not been identified or explored in prior research. One suggestive finding is that fathers more often than mothers construct that part of their parental identities related to specific activities as conjoint or as a "self-as-coparent." Another suggestive result is that parental identity conjointness related to arranging and planning may have an important relationship to parental behavior and may be interpreted as an "executive" component of parental identity.

Beyond these specific findings, however, the study has broader implications for how father identity is conceptualized and assessed. Most existing research stipulates a "generic" paternal identity that different men possess or manifest to varying degrees. Some research goes somewhat further by recognizing that paternal identity can take different forms defined according to more specific aspects of

5. PATERNAL IDENTITY CONJOINTNESS

parenting (e.g., caregiving, breadwinning). However, this latter research still tends to focus attention simply on the intensity with which fathers hold these differing paternal identities. While important, these approaches capture only a small part of the symbolic interactionist conception of identity as applied to fatherhood. Our study illustrates that when researchers use as a data source fathers' narratives instead of their responses to closed-ended questionnaire items or pie charts, other dimensions of paternal identity besides intensity—ones not anticipated by the researcher—may become evident. Emerging from our study are the concepts of parental identity conjointness and executive parental identity. Other dimensions of paternal identity await exploration. Our study suggests that narrative and other qualitative methodologies may have special value in eliciting them.

ACKNOWLEDGMENTS

The work reported here was supported by grants to Joseph Pleck from the Illinois Agricultural Experiment Station and the University of Illinois Foundation, and by grants to Jeffrey Stueve from the University of Illinois Graduate College and the University of New Mexico.

REFERENCES

Abidin, R. R., & Brunner, J. F. (1995). Development of a parenting alliance inventory. *Journal of Clinical Psychology, 24,* 31–40.

Allen, S., & Hawkins, A. (1999). Maternal gatekeeping: Mothers' beliefs and behaviors that inhibit greater father involvement in family work. *Journal of Marriage and the Family, 61,* 199–212.

Anthony, E. J., & Benedek, T. (Eds.). (1970). *Parenthood: Its psychology and psychopathology.* Boston: Little Brown.

Bamberg, M. (Ed.). (1997). *Narrative development: Six approaches.* Mahwah, NJ: Lawrence Erlbaum Associates.

Beitel, A. H., & Parke, R. D. (1998). Paternal involvement in infancy: The role of maternal and paternal attitudes. *Journal of Family Psychology, 12,* 268–288.

Broderick, C. (1993). *Understanding family process: Basics of family systems theory.* Newbury Park, CA: Sage.

Bruce, C., & Fox, G. L. (1997, November). *Measuring father involvement among lower White and African-American populations.* Presented at the National Council on Family Relations, Crystal City, VA.

Bruner, J. (1986). *Actual minds, possible worlds.* Cambridge, MA: Harvard University Press.

Burke, P. J., & Reitzes, D. C. (1991). An identity theory approach to commitment. *Social Psychology Quarterly, 54,* 239–251.

Burke, P. J., & Tully, J. C. (1977). The measurement of role identity. *Social Forces, 55,* 891–897.

Cast, A. D. (1998). *Parent identities and behavior: An Identity theory approach.* Unpublished doctoral dissertation, Washington State University, Pullman.

Cath, S. H., Gurwitt, A., & Ross, J. M. (Eds.). (1982). *Father and child: Developmental and clinical perspectives.* Boston: Little, Brown.

Farrell, M. P., Rosenberg, S. D., & Rosenberg, H. J. (1993). Changing texts of male identity from early to late middle age: On the emergent prominence of fatherhood. In J. Demick, K. Bursik, & R. DiBiase (Eds.), *Parental development* (pp. 203–224). Hillsdale, NJ: Lawrence Erlbaum Associates.

Freedman, J. M., & Combs, G. (1996). *Narrative therapy: The social construction of preferred realities.* New York: Norton.

Furstenberg, Frank, Jr. (1990). Divorce and the American family. *Annual Review of Sociology, 16,* 379–403.

Gergen, K. J., & Gergen M. M. (1997). Narratives of the self. In L. P. Hinchman & S. K. Hinchman (Ed.), *Memory, Identity, Community* (pp. 161–184). Albany: State University of New York Press.

Gergen M. M., & Gergen, K. J. (1987). The self in temporal perspective. In R. Abeles (Ed.), *Life span social psychology* (pp. 121–137). Hillsdale, NJ: Lawrence Erlbaum Associates.

Hermans, H. J. M. (1997). Self-narrative in the life course: A contextual approach. In M. Bamberg (Ed.), *Narrative development: Six approaches* (pp. 223–264). Mahwah, NJ: Lawrence Erlbaum Associates.

Hood, J. C. (1983). *Becoming a two-job family.* New York: Praeger.

Ihinger-Tallman, M., Pasley, K., & Beuhler, C. (1993). Developing a middle-range theory of father involvement postdivorce. *Journal of Family Issues, 14,* 550–571.

Lamb, M. E., Pleck, J. H., Charnov, E. L., & Levine, J. A. (1985). Paternal behavior in humans. *American Zoologist, 25,* 883–894.

Lamb, M. E., Pleck, J. H., Charnov, E. L., & Levine, J. A. (1987). A biosocial perspective on paternal behavior and involvement. In J. B. Lancaster, J. Altman, & A. Rossi (Eds.), *Parenting across the lifespan: Biosocial perspectives* (pp. 11–42). New York: Academic Press.

LaRossa, R., & Reitzes, D. C. (1993). Symbolic interactionism and family studies. In P. G. Boss, W. J. Doherty, R. LaRossa, W. R. Schumm, & S. K. Steinmetz (Eds.), *Sourcebook of family theories and methods: A contextual approach* (pp. 135–163). New York: Plenum Press.

Marks, S. R. (1986). *Three corners: Exploring marriage and the self.* Lexington, MA: Lexington Books.

Mandler, J. M. (1984). *Stories, scripts, and scenes: Aspects of schema theory.* Hillsdale, NJ: Lawrence Erlbaum Associates.

Marsiglio, W. (1998). *Procreative man.* New York: New York University Press.

Maurer, T. W., Pleck, J. H., & Rane, T. (2001). Parental identity and reflected-appraisals: Measurement and gender dynamics. *Journal of Marriage and Family, 63,* 309–321.

McAdams, D. (1988). *Power, intimacy and the life story: Personological inquiries into identity.* New York: Guilford.

McAdams, D. (1990). Unity and purpose in human lives: The emergence of identity as a life story. In A. I. Rabin, R. A. Zucker, R. A. Emmons, & S. Frank (Eds.), *Studying persons and lives* (pp. 148–200). New York: Springer.

McAdams, D. P. (1993). *The stories we live by: Personal myths and the making of the self.* New York: William Morrow & Co.

McAdams, D. P., Diamond, A., de St. Aubin, E., & Mansfield, E. (1997). Stories of commitment: The psychological construction of generative lives. *Journal of Personality and Social Psychology, 72,* 678–694.

McBride, B. A., & Rane, T. R. (1997). Role identity, role investments, and paternal involvement: Implications for parenting programs for men. *Early Childhood Research Quarterly, 12,* 173–197.

McMahon, M. (1995). *Engendering motherhood: Identity and self-transformation in women's lives.* New York: Guilford.

Olson, D. H. (1993). Circumplex Model of Marital and Family Systems: Assessing family functioning. In F. Walsh (Ed.), *Normal family processes* (2nd ed., pp. 104–137). New York: Guilford.

Palkovitz, R. (1997). Reconstructing "involvement": Expanding conceptualizations of men's caring in contemporary families. In A. J. Hawkins & D. C. Dollahite (Eds.), *Generative fathering: Beyond deficit perspectives* (pp. 200–216). Thousand Oaks, CA: Sage.

5. PATERNAL IDENTITY CONJOINTNESS 107

Pleck, J. H. (1985). *Working wives, working husbands*. Beverly Hills, CA: Sage.

Pleck, J. H., Lamb, M. E., & Levine, J. A. (1985). Epilog: Facilitating future change in men's family roles. *Marriage and Family Review, 9*(3–4), 11–16.

Pleck, J. H. (1997). Paternal involvement: Levels, sources, and consequences. In M. E. Lamb (Ed.), *The role of the father in child development* (3rd ed., pp. 123–167). New York: Wiley.

Pleck, J. H., Sonenstein, F. L., & Swain, S. O. (1988). Adolescent males' sexual behavior and contraceptive use: Implications for male responsibility. *Journal of Adolescent Research, 3*(3–4), 275–284.

Rubin, R. (1984). *Maternal identity and maternal experience*. New York: Springer.

Seidel, J. (1998). *The Ethnograph v5.0*. Thousand Oaks, CA: Sage.

Small, S. A., & Eastman, G. (1991). Rearing adolescents in contemporary society: A conceptual framework for understanding the responsibilities and needs of parents. *Family Relations, 40*, 455–462.

Stueve, J. L., & Pleck, J. H. (1998, November). Paternal identity in fathers of school-aged children: A "life story" perspective. Poster presented at the annual meeting of the National Council on Family Relations, Milwaukee, WI.

Stueve, J. L., & Pleck, J. H. (2001). "Parenting voices": Solo parent identity and co-parent identities in married parents' narratives of meaningful parenting experiences. *Journal of Social and Personal Relationships, 18*, 691–708.

Stryker, S. (1980). *Symbolic interactionism: A social structural version*. Menlo Park, CA: Benjamin/Cummings.

Stryker, S. (1987). Identity theory: Developments and extensions. In K. Yardley & T. Honess (Eds.), *Self and identity: Psychosocial perspectives*. New York: Wiley.

Stryker, S., & Burke, P. J. (2000). The past, present, and future of an identity theory. *Social Psychology Quarterly, 63*, 284–297.

Weissman, S. H., & Cohen, R. S. (1985). The parenting alliance and adolescence. *Adolescent Psychiatry, 12*, 24–45.

6

A Narrative Approach to Exploring Responsible Involvement of Fathers with Their Special-Needs Children

David C. Dollahite
Brigham Young University

This chapter briefly summarizes the main findings from research employing narrative methodologies on fathers of children with special needs conducted by me and my students (Brotherson & Dollahite, 1997; Dollahite, 2003; Dollahite, Marks, & Brotherson, 1998; Dollahite, Marks, & Olson, 2002; Marks & Dollahite, 2001; Olson, Dollahite, & White, 2002). This research is consistent with recent emphasis on narrative methods in the social sciences generally (Dollahite, Hawkins, & Brotherson, 1996; Josselson, & Lieblich, 1993; McAdams, 1993; Riessman, 1993; Sarbin, 1986) and with recent narrative studies of fathers of special-needs children (Brotherson, 1995) and fathers and religion (Latshaw, 1998; Marshall, Olsen, Allred, Mandleco, & Dyches, 1998; Palkovitz & Palm, 1998; Webb-Mitchell, 1993).

The findings reported here come from analyses of two main data sets consisting of Latter-day Saint (LDS, Mormon) fathers of children with a variety of serious disabilities and chronic illnesses. One sample consisted of 16 fathers of young children with special needs and the other sample, a follow-up study of the first, included 19 fathers with children of varying ages. The findings both confirm and extend some previous findings of research with fathers of special-needs children.

Beyond Paternal Pathology

Although there has been much understandable focus among policymakers on paternal pathologies (i.e., abusive fathers, fatherlessness, deadbeat dads), we must not forget that there are a great many fathers who are deeply committed to and highly involved with their children. We need to explore responsible, involved fathering as well as continue to understand paternal problems.

The research indicates that highly religious fathers tend to also be highly involved with their children and are less likely than nonreligious fathers to exhibit behaviors that harm children (see Marks & Dollahite, 2001; Dollahite, Marks, & Goodman, Forthcoming) and so a study of highly religious fathers can help illuminate responsible fathering (Dollahite, 1998). Religious communities seem to help fathers better provide the social or family capital (Dollahite & Rommel, 1993) that benefit their children.

In addition, we also know from a great deal of research that married fathers are likely to be more highly involved with their children than those fathers who are not married to the mothers of their children (Popenoe, 1996). Likewise, improving our understanding of the ways fathers work together with mothers to meet their children's needs is important. Thus, the study of married fathers is important.

Finally, we should acknowledge the many challenges that most fathers face and explore responsible fathering among fathers that face significant challenges. One of the many groups of fathers that face significant challenges are those with children having special needs (significant disabilities, chronic illness, or other significant challenges). The unique needs of these children usually call for greater degrees of responsible involvement from their parents as well as greater community and institutional support. Exploring the ways these fathers make both ordinary and extraordinary contributions to their children's well-being can help us define the boundaries of responsible, involved fathering.

Listening to Fathers Facing Unique Challenges

An important way to carefully explore responsible and involved fathering in challenging circumstances is to listen to the voices or hear the stories of these fathers themselves. There is much potential benefit to hearing fathers tell, in their own words, how they try to meet the needs of their children because they can articulate dimensions of involvement that may have been overlooked or underexplored in previous studies. A detailed exploration of the involvement of highly responsible and involved fathers has the potential to help us (a) better conceptualize father involvement, (b) improve the measurement of father involvement, and (c) provide policymakers, program developers, and scholars with much needed examples of "functional fathering."

6. SPECIAL-NEEDS CHILDREN

Special-Needs Fathers

Literature reviews of the research on special-needs fathers (Bristol & Gallagher, 1986; Hornby, 1994; Lamb & Laumann-Billings, 1997; Dollahite, Slife, & Hawkins, 1998; Olson, Dollahite, & White, 2002; Turbiville, 1994) indicate the following:

1. Most studies involving special-needs children have focused on mothers and relatively little research has been conducted with fathers.
2. Many of the findings in the literature on fathers are suspect because of flawed methods (i.e., interviewing mothers, relying on clinical impressions, lack of longitudinal data).
3. Until recently, fathers were often treated as relatively unimportant to the development of special-needs children by scholars and practitioners.
4. We know fairly little about what fathers actually do in their involvement with their children with disabilities.
5. There is great diversity of experience because of the variation in disabilities and fathering styles.
6. A disproportionate amount of the research has focused only on the negative aspects of the fathers' experience and less on the personal growth that occurs.
7. For many fathers, religious meanings and supports are (or become) significant to how they adapt to this challenge.
8. Fathers often respond creatively and often have a significant impact on their children with special needs.

Most research has focused on the negative aspects of fathers' experiences and less on the positive experiences and personal growth that also often occur (Dollahite, 2003). The findings from this literature support the idea that our answers are usually only as good as our questions and methods. The findings have not fully depicted the great strengths fathers bring to their work with their special children and the great joys and insights that emerge from this involvement. This is understandable in that until recently most studies of father involvement were undertaken from what Doherty (1991) called a deficit perspective and Hawkins and Dollahite (1997) labeled a role-inadequacy perspective. Moreover, many of the studies of families with challenging circumstances employed a stress and coping paradigm with its emphasis on difficulties rather than from a resiliency perspective.

This chapter focuses on major findings from qualitative (narrative) research I conducted with fathers of special-needs children. These findings not only confirm some of the previous findings but also provide additional information on the processes of involvement from personal narratives from the father. Because of the qualitative methodology and the unique nature of the sample (highly religious), these findings are not easily generalizable to the population of fathers of children with special needs. However, the rich descriptions of experiences and meanings

112   DOLLAHITE

provided by narrative methods allow scholars to become more aware of the range of experience of these fathers. And while not all fathers of special-needs children are as devoutly religious as the fathers in our samples, the research indicates that most fathers of such children wrestle with questions of meaning and that many try to find some strength and support in some type of spiritual or religious belief, practice, or community. Parenthetically, my professional experience in speaking with, interviewing, reading the writings of, and listening to hundreds of fathers from many backgrounds suggests that most of these fathers resonate with stories of a transcendent quality from whatever source they are shared.

The main findings that are illustrated with fathers' personal narratives include the following:

1. Significant insights are usually part of the experience of fathering a child with significant challenges and these insights are highly valued by the fathers.
2. Fathers and their special-needs children often share a unique and transcendent emotional bond that fathers find difficult to describe fully.
3. Fathers grow significantly through their involvement with their special children and their children have a profound influence on them and their lives.
4. Good fathering with special-needs children requires flexibility, innovation, and creativity—what Brotherson & Dollahite (1997) called *generative ingenuity*.
5. Fathers and mothers often provide what Olson et al. (2002) called relational complementarity in their care for special-needs children, and fathers believe their added and unique involvement matters.
6. Many fathers draw on faith, belief, prayer, spiritual experience, and social support from faith communities to help them.
7. The data support the major premises of the generative fathering perspective—that fathers feel a moral call to meet the needs of their children, they work hard to do so, and they bring strengths to this work.

After the presentation of these major findings I briefly discuss the potential value of qualitative (narrative) approaches alongside quantitative methods for understanding father involvement and informing programming and policy.

SAMPLES AND METHODS

Sample 1. This sample consisted of 16 married, middle-socioeconomic-status fathers of young children with special needs from central Utah. Most were involved in a support program for such families. The types of special needs in the children in this sample included mild intellectual and emotional limitations, serious emotional physical disabilities, and life-threatening chronic illnesses. Fathers were generally between 20 and 30 years old (mean 26) with between two and

6. SPECIAL-NEEDS CHILDREN 113

four children. The majority of the special-needs children were under age 3, but many of the families involved had older special-needs children as well. The sample was mainly Caucasian, with one African-American father and one native Chinese father. All participants were members of The Church of Jesus Christ of Latter-day Saints (Mormon or LDS).

Methods for Sample 1. Fathers' narratives were gathered through in-depth interviews of $1^1/_2$ to 2 hours in length. Interviews were conducted by two-person teams, usually a man and a woman. Questions were designed to elicit from fathers narratives that illustrated times when they felt closest to (and most distant from) their children, times when they felt they met (and did not meet) their children's needs, their most (and least) enjoyable experiences with children, and ways they tried to develop a good relationship with them. The questions asked were intended to draw out personal experiences, along with personal meanings of those experiences. No questions asked specifically about religious beliefs, practices, or experiences.

Sample 2. For this sample, again, all fathers were members of The Church of Jesus Christ of Latter-day Saints (LDS or Mormon). Of the 19 fathers, 18 were married and 1 was divorced; the married fathers were married to women who were also active in the LDS community. Of the 19 fathers, 17 were Caucasian, one was Pacific Islander, and one was Hispanic. Based on basic demographic information and place of residence, all fathers were of middle-socioeconomic status. The age range of the fathers was 25 to 49 years (mean = 34.8). The number of children in these families ranged from 1 to 6 (mean = 3.2), and each family had at least one child with special needs (four of the families had more than one child with special needs). The special needs of the children included a variety of moderate to severe physical and cognitive delays, serious chronic and terminal conditions, autism, Tourette's syndrome, Down syndrome, heart disease, severe scoliosis, deafness, and blindness. The age range of the children with special needs was 8 months to 16 years (mean = 4.5 years).

Methods for Sample 2. An agency that assisted families with special-needs children was contacted in a predominantly LDS community. To preserve confidentiality, the agency mailed out letters describing the project and requesting participation. Seventeen of the 19 fathers in the sample were contacted through this method. To broaden the age range of children and type of special needs, two other fathers were located through snowballing. Overall, a 26.5% response rate was obtained, which is reasonable for qualitative interviews of men (Marks & Dollahite, 2001).

The interview schedule consisted of 20 open-ended questions that were carefully constructed with sensitivity to the bodies of literature regarding (a) fathering, (b) fathering children with special needs, (c) fathering and religion, and (d) the

previous work of the authors. The first 12 questions addressed the contextual challenges of being the father of a special-needs child. The last 8 questions asked if religion was meaningful and influential to the father and his family and, if so, how. Questions designed to invite the sharing of personal stories, meanings, and interpretations relating to both contextual and religious questions were frequently asked. Interview times ranged from 50 minutes to 4 hours with a mean of 1.5 hours.

GENERATIVE CONCEPTUAL PERSPECTIVE OF RESPONSIBLE FATHERING

It is important to mention that my colleagues and I approach the study of responsible fathering in fathers of children with special needs from a generative perspective (Dollahite et al., 1997; Dollahite & Hawkins, 1998; Dollahite, et al., 1998; Hawkins & Dollahite, 1997). The generative approach assumes that (a) fathers face an ethical call from their child and communities to try to meet their child's needs, (b) fathers bring strengths to their "fatherwork" and they can and should care for their children in meaningful ways, and (c) responsible fathering emerges more from a father's deeply held values and beliefs than merely from responding to a socially imposed role. The generative fathering perspective emphasizes a father's moral obligation to work to meet the needs of his child. He does so by actively responding to the "call" for care and connection exerted by his child and by responding to his deepest feelings for and commitments to that child.

Thus, from a generative fathering perspective, responsible fathering is defined as active, responsive involvement with one's child, working to meet her/his varied needs. This definition centers on a father's responsiveness to the needs of his child and responsiveness to his own deeply held beliefs, rather than on his enacting a role obligation imposed by external cultural or societal ideologies. It is this feature of the generative fathering framework that gives it particular relevance to fathering children with special needs because these children exert an even greater call on their fathers' efforts and their needs call forth even greater moral work to seek to meet those needs (Dollahite, et al., 1998; Marks & Dollahite, 2001; Olson, Dollahite, & White, 2002).

In the research reported here, the data seem to support these general assumptions, although I have consciously and systematically tried to be open to data that may not support them. Where information to the contrary is not available in the data, these assumptions inform and implications for policy or practice are suggested.

Within each section, following a brief summary of the findings, the narratives are presented with only brief contextualizing introduction and little or no interpretive comment. Of course, names have been changed.

6. SPECIAL-NEEDS CHILDREN

Wrestling with Meaning:
Significant Insights

Significant insights are often part of the experience of fathering a child with challenges, and these insights are highly valued by the fathers. Wrestling with meaning
is an inherent part of raising a child with special needs, and finding new insight
into the challenges faced is both sought and valued.

Carl (a father of a child with autism):

> You don't know what you are going to run into. You don't know what great insights
> and blessings are going to come to you because you are devoting your life and your
> resources in a different direction than the one you anticipated. Your child may not
> go to college. They may never get married . . . but I am convinced that there is a plan
> for Marisa and we are a part of that plan and I don't want to thwart the purposes of
> God by denying her ability to achieve all that she can achieve, and being all that I
> can be.

Jack:

> There are always two sides and two views to everything. There is always a good and
> there is always a bad, and there is a happy and a sad . . . We could have been one of
> those that when this happened asked, "Why? It's not fair. Why did this happen to
> us?" The problem with that is there isn't an answer to the "Why?" You never know
> why it happens . . . you can never be satisfied and you can never get an answer. As
> hard as it might be to look at the positive, at least then there is something finite to
> the situations that you're in. There is something firm and something that you can
> grasp a hold of, something that can end your thought process at that time. I think
> that is important. I think that is why positive people have such an advantage over
> other people, because then they can take the next step. If you look at it the other way
> you can't take the next step because you are still trying to get the answer to the first
> question.

Charles:

> We did our best to make sure that we got through it well. We weren't going to say,
> "Why me?" and that is something I spent very little time on. . . I still wondered from
> time to time why she had to go through this, but I didn't spend any time being mad
> at God that we were chosen to go through this. I decided early on that we were going
> to tackle this with faith and determination, and we were going to make it. We were
> going to come out being in love with God and not hating Him.

Ethan:

> All of a sudden Bryce collapses in church and is back in the hospital. Back in the
> hospital again. I just said, "Why, hasn't he suffered enough?" I was so tired of
> watching Bryce suffer and there was not a thing I could do about it. What do I
> do? Take him home? [Laughs in frustration] Like that would really help. I had this
> emotion, I remember walking around the hospital with my wife and just sitting down
> and starting to sob. That's when she taught me a great lesson that "Heavenly Father

loves him more than you do and He's not going to do anything that Bryce can't handle so what's your problem?" She's really candid about those things. That was a great moment. There's been lots of moments like that.

Connection Through Care: Transcendent Bonds

Fathers and their special-needs children often share a unique and transcendent emotional bond that fathers find difficult to describe fully and which would be more difficult to fully assess without hearing fathers' personal descriptions of this bond.

Mel:

> When Stan was three months old. I laid him in the bottom of the tub and put in a washcloth so he wouldn't slide around. I put him in the bottom of the tub and slowly filled it with water until it was at his ear level, so that I knew if he turned one way or the other he could at least be safe. He didn't have very good motor movement at the time as a baby and was sort of jerky, but once he got into the water like that almost immediately his motor coordination began. I don't know how to explain it, but he started kicking and moving his arms, he brightened up and there was something almost transcendental about the movement of looking into his eyes while he was there in the water and he was making a moment of progression in his body. Somehow, he was on his own. It's very difficult to explain it, but you could see the water, his eyes, and the sky in all that one moment. It was just an important moment for me.... It may just be because you have moments when you look at people and there is a connection there which is inexplicable. I can't explain it. I looked into his eyes and said something. It was just a tie between father and child.

Matt:

> I look into her eyes. Autistic people in general never look at you, they will always look down. Early on Jennifer didn't make eye contact, but later on in life she started to make eye contact. For me, looking into her eyes is like looking into her soul. I see a lot, I read a lot, I sense a lot. This might be the primary method of communication between me and this little girl, by looking through her eyes. Sometimes I will just sit down with her in a chair, she will sit on my lap, and I will just look into her eyes. I feel I am gazing into eternity, it is enormously joyful for me to do that.

The following example illustrates the bond a father and son had during mid-adolescence, at a time when it was believed the end of the child's life was near due to serious heart problems.

Ethan:

> It was confirmed by doctors that Bryce's heart was shot. He was on IV's at home, kind of forcing the heart to pump ... the doctors gave him one to three months to live ... We spent a lot of time together talking ... 10–20 hours a week just talking ...

6. SPECIAL-NEEDS CHILDREN 117

he was failing noticeably. He weighed about 70 pounds, he was 14 years old . . . he was on oxygen. He couldn't bathe . . . he was too weak. He loved showers so I would prop him up in the shower. I could tell when we first started having to do this that he was kind of embarrassed. It was hard for me at first, I knew he was embarrassed. Those became really choice times [long pause, eyes fill with tears]. Sorry [pause], he was so submissive, in every way. He was so at peace with what was happening.

Adapting to Change: Generative Growth

Fathers grow significantly through their involvement with their special children and their children have a profound influence on them and their lives. For most, the diagnosis came early on, many times at birth, but for others it was a process of searching and learning of what special needs existed for the child.

Charles (his daughter Rachel suffered from Leukemia for 3 years and died at age 5):

We went to give blood at a stake blood drive, and our stake president was there giving blood. He'd given Rachel a couple of blessings. We had gone through the line and I was just happy because I'd just gotten a penicillin shot and they wouldn't take my blood. Sandra had given her blood and President Clyde [an LDS church leader] was there giving blood. Rachel went over and held his hand while he had that blood drawn because she knew what it was like to have needles poked in your skin and she felt for him. She couldn't do much but she could hold his hand and she did that. The impact that has on me just tells me that a little bit of loving concern for others goes a long way, not just in the life of either person in the interaction, but in the people who see that. It makes you want to go forth and do likewise.

Greg:

I think I'm a lot more conscientious about how I look at lots of people, look at other people in general. Because I recognize right now that he is not going to follow the path that I took intellectually; for me, and for my whole family. They all are well educated, intelligent, or intellect is very important, scholastics are very important. William isn't going to be a real scholar. . . . I have become much more sensitive to his worth as a person outside of his scholastic ability. And that has impacted the way I look . . . at people in general, how I judge people. There's worth there outside of their grade point average and education. He's got some great talents, some great gifts. It's just made me aware that, that I need to look at, to look at that and be aware of that in other people.

Many fathers described increased empathy, patience, tenderness, humility, and submissiveness, and felt they had put life in better perspective.

Larry:

I'm more thoughtful and patient, not that I'm perfect on all occasions, but I'm certainly more tender with the children in general.

Michael:

I've become more sensitive, more thoughtful, more empathic, you know as far as growing and changing and adapting.

Ethan:

Another significant thing that I've learned is that Bryce, as a person and as a situation, has served to kind of jerk me back to what's really important.

Meeting Demands through Generative Ingenuity

Good fathering with children with special needs requires flexibility, innovation, and creativity—what Brotherson & Dollahite (1997) called generative ingenuity. The stories told in this section highlight some of the ways fathers use their minds and energies to meet their children's needs.

Lewis:

I don't think [my child having spina bifida] changes anything for me personally. Obviously it's going to come into play later—I don't think that he's going to be a real hiker. But we'll find ways to deal with that. I don't think it's going to have a big effect.... He can still learn [to fish], too. You don't know me very well; I'd park in the stream if I have to. I've taken my dad out and he can't walk. I just say, "All right, you sit here in the truck." I drove up and parked in the stream, so he could fish. That was fun!

Curtis:

When he was a year old he was talking like any normal kid. He was starting to say words and then all of a sudden there was nothing. We tried and tried to get his ears cleared up with antibiotics, etc., and it didn't work. It was really kind of hard when you see other kids his age talking and communicating, and Matt would just sit there and do nothing. Physically he was fine. He could run and jump and throw.... I guess I'm kind of proud but I always wanted to be the best at what I did, and I thought, "Poor kid, he's got to go through school and he'll be behind." But then I decided he could catch up if we work with him, and so we've got to do it now and hold up our end of the deal. At first, it was kind of hard, but it doesn't bother me now.... I've seen him do [it] and how he can learn. He doesn't have a learning disability, he's just had a hard time hearing and now he's got to catch up.... Now, I've seen that it will work out.

Steven:

When I first got this diagnosis of autism, the hope, the high expectations, the assumed success that your child is going to have in life, just sort of all drained out of me. I mean the blood probably left my head, I probably turned white as a ghost or something when the realization hit me that here's this diagnosis—AUTISM. And it just sort of hits you like someone just swung a bat at you and knocked the wind

6. SPECIAL-NEEDS CHILDREN   119

right out of you. And so the first thing I would say [to a father in a similar situation] is this is not a death sentence. There is hope here. And it is not just false hope and stay positive for your child. Our child has made enormous gains by getting some very specific treatment for her and by taking an approach as a family, as a couple, as her parents, in dealing with her in certain ways, and helping her cope, and expanding her capabilities in other ways.... So there is always hope.... Quite frankly, as her father, I do whatever I can all the way around, making the best of the situation.

Relational Complementarity and Unique Strengths

Fathers and mothers often provide what Olson, et al. (2002) called relational complementarity and fathers believe their joint and unique involvement in caring for their children matters. Fathers often reported working with their child's mother to meet the needs of their child, drawing from each other's strengths and preferences. The fathers also reported that there were some aspects of caring for their child that they seemed to bring unique strengths to.

According to Olson, et al. (in press), "Fathers also related several experiences where they felt they were able to be uniquely involved in their child's life. This is consistent with literature [Bailey, Blasco, & Simeonsson, 1992; Beckman, 1991; Frey, Fewell, & Vadasy, 1989; Goldberg, et al., 1986] that has found fathers' experiences are often unique from mothers' experiences" (p. 57).

Matt:

When Jennifer was young she used to tantrum a lot, expressing her frustration and anger very physically. I used to pick her up and hold her close in an attempt to settle her down. Eventually I could wrap my arms around her and sit in a chair or something, partly to restrain her and partly to communicate to her the enormous love and caring I had for her. I am not sure if holding her is what calmed her, but it did. Laura couldn't do the same thing that I could do, maybe because of my size, but I always felt from a very young age, that we had a bit of a bond.

Derrick:

I don't know what the norm is for fathers [for nurturing their children]. I know what the stereotype is, at least in my mind, which is that the Mom gets up with the kids and rocks them while Dad is laying in bed and sleeping. Well, that has never happened in this family. I guess that I feel a little proud that I can do that and I actually do it, and it helps me in my relationship not only with that particular child but with the other kids.

Jake:

Whenever I come home, if my son's been having a bad day I just pick him up and take care of him. He doesn't always calm down, but I am the one that deals with it whenever I am home. We kind of joke about it, but he's my kid. I stay up all night

rocking him when he can't sleep; when he's screaming, having his night terrors, I just know him, I can just take care of him. I come home and he'll be screaming and I can pick him up and make him a sandwich and help him eat it and he'll calm down and go about his business, when he wouldn't eat before that. . . . Everybody knows he's my kid and I take care of him. [Knowing that he needs me like that] is a tremendous pressure and great at the same time.

Olson, et al. (2002) found that relational complementarity was based on each parent's strengths as opposed to gender norms and that those few cases in which the fathers related experiences where only they were able to meet their child's need usually involved situations where the father's physical strength was necessary.

Faith of the Fathers and Children

Research demonstrates that religion can provide great support for families with children with special needs (Bennett, Deluca, & Allen, 1995; Bishop, 1985; Marshall, et al., 2003; Marks & Dollahite, 2001; Maton & Wells, 1995; Pargament, 1997; Turbiville, 1994; Webb-Mitchell, 1993). These fathers also drew on their religious beliefs and faith communities to help them. Another source of help for these fathers came from "priesthood blessings" that usually took place soon after birth (in a naming ceremony) and at other times of need. Fathers also mentioned a connection between their religious involvement and a sense of responsibility to their children.

Monty:

They [the church members] have been there. They were helpful to me when my son was in the hospital. I could call on them and depend on them to pick me up if I needed a ride home [because my car was broken down]. They [also] helped us with meals. . . . It was great. It meant a lot to me. Here I had no transportation, my wife was at the hospital, and [we] could just call and rely on them.

Lucas:

We were kind of in a bind because we didn't have the money to rent an apartment over here [near the hospital and] I still needed to work [back home]. So my parents talked to [some old friends from the church here] and they invited us to come and stay with them. They were just great. They were like our parents. We stayed with them not only while Caleb was in the hospital, but when he first got out and we were looking for a place over here . . . It was such a huge help . . . to have that burden removed . . . so that we could be close to the hospital.

Michael:

We were relatively new members in our ward congregation and our bishop had learned of Alan's upcoming surgery. The bishop got up in church [laughs with emotion] and let the ward know that we have a good little guy in our ward who needs our prayers and faith right now, and needs our fasting and effort to request a blessing on his

6. SPECIAL-NEEDS CHILDREN 121

behalf. The ward just responded! Many church members told us of their fasting and prayer and their hope and wishes that he'd have a successful surgery, expressing their love and support for Alan and for our family.

The following narratives reflect the thoughts of many of the fathers who expressed that their religious commitments facilitated a greater sense of paternal responsibility and helped them to meet the challenging needs of their children.

Ryan:

When Luke was two he was extremely sick and I gave him a father's blessing, it was the best experience I have ever had. I knew at that time he was a perfect child, I have never forgotten that feeling. I recall wondering why I was chosen to have a perfect person in my house and hoping to live up to whatever was expected of me.

Lucas:

I think the best thing that the church has done for me and indirectly for Caleb is [that] it's allowed me to give him [priesthood] blessings. . . . I was there by myself [by his] incubator, and he was really having a hard time. They had a couple of nurses around him and they had his respirator in. He had some kind of infection that was filling up his lungs with secretions and he was having a really hard time breathing. [The respirator] was as high as the machine would go and he was still, I could just see in his eyes . . . there was that deer in the headlight panic look in his eyes. It was really hard for me because what can you do? They had the oxygen turned all the way up . . . [it was] a humbling thing for me, and anything I could do to help him I'll do. . . . I gave him a blessing. [It made] me want to be a better person so that if there is something that I can do for him, even if it is just giving a blessing, I can be worthy to do that. In that way it makes me a better person.

Chris:

[The doctors] kept working on [my daughter] trying to get her to breathe, and she was just lying there. They couldn't get her to breathe, and this went on and on. That's when I get hit with this mantle of fatherhood. [I] realize that she is new to this world, and her mom is lying on the table, has undergone major surgery, and you're the only person in the world she has. There's all the doctors, there's everyone around, but when she's in trouble, you're the one she's going to look to. You're the one that has to be there for her. I just had to start praying for her. . . . When she was in the most need it just hit me that it was up to me to pray for her. There was no one else on earth that could do that for her at that time. That was probably the most sacred [experience I've had].

Michael (a father whose son, age nine, was born with shortened forearms and missing fingers and an extreme case of scoliosis, told of his son's religious perspective on his challenges):

[Thinking about my son with special needs] I thought, "Well, what is the purpose of life?" And you know, to say it in a succinct way, life is not a beauty contest. Christ

never said, "Blessed are the physically most beautiful, for they shall inherit the kingdom of God." You know, if you read the beatitudes, they're pretty non-physical (laughingly), instead they have everything to do with the quality of our heart and our spirit. And Alan is an exceptionally extraordinary individual. Alan has this natural ability to elicit love from people. He elicits godly, goodwill from people in a real natural way. We've flown all over the country talking to physicians and everywhere he goes, people like him, they act in godly, kindly, unselfish, genuine ways around him. He brings this out of people. And Alan has an innate gift about that, and a real sensitivity about spiritual things.... One time Alan and I were alone in the kitchen and he just looked up at me and said, "You know dad, if I were born again, I would like to have hands like Kathleen, and like Benjamin." ... And I didn't say anything for just a moment, just a short pause, and then he said, ... "But this is just the challenge that Heavenly Father has given me for this life." And, he, paused again, and he goes, "So it's okay." But it wasn't a mournful okay, it was kind of a "this is alright"—almost like a little bit of a spunk, and possibly even enthusiasm in the tone, "This is alright, this is just my challenge."

Support for the Generative Framework

Overall, these in-depth interviews with 35 fathers of children with special needs provide evidence that the underlying assumptions of the "conceptual ethic" of generative fathering has some merit. These data provide a detailed picture of the ways these fathers feel a moral call to meet the needs of their children, work hard to do so, and bring significant strengths to their work. The following two narratives explicitly illustrate how many fathers thought of their fathering as the important work they are doing.

Ray shared a childhood recollection relating to his own father that strengthened Ray's commitment to his son and family in a way that he associated with his own religious beliefs. This narrative supports the generative fathering perspective on viewing fathering as work—or what Dollahite et al. (1997) called fatherwork:

Ray:

One of the things that I remember [from my childhood] is when we were working on the yard [at our] cabin in Minnesota. We children would get tired and leave and go and play, but my father would always stay until the job was done. It would always impress me that I would be playing with my friends, and then I would still see my dad working on the same job, until the job was done. It always impressed me and has carried throughout my life that that's what men do. They accomplish the job.... As far as the religious or spiritual things, I see from my father through his example that this is my job [being a good father]. I am to finish the job, so no matter what it takes or how long it is, you just stick to it and go to work, until the job is done. It is the father's responsibility, and the Church's teachings that ... you are responsible, that you are the support, that this is what you do.

Given the high rates of father abandonment among families with special-needs children (Fewell & Vadasy, 1986), this plan to "finish the job" is not insignificant.

6. SPECIAL-NEEDS CHILDREN

Charles (whose daughter Rachel suffered from leukemia for 3 years and died at age 5):

> I have just about spent my life caring for and nurturing Rachel, when I wasn't at work. Maybe the hospital is the part we like to forget but can't. When her pain got to the point that she couldn't go to the bathroom, I was the one that got to her bedpans for her. She would only let me do it; I was the one that did that. It wasn't a thing for Mom, and she didn't want anybody else in the room. She kicked everybody out of the room; nurses, Mom (Mom had to be outside the door), and I would get the bedpan as best as I could under her bottom without hurting her. Moving the sheets hurt her. It was not a good thing. But she let me do that for her, and I was able to take care of her needs, and it helped me that I was the only one she'd let do it . . . You wouldn't expect bedpan shuffling to be a wonderful memory, but it was. She trusted me to do my best job not to hurt her, an that was special to me that she let me do that.

Challenges of Dealing with Health and Education Systems

Some of the most difficult experiences for many fathers involved dealing with the health, educational, and insurance systems as a result of their child's disability or illness. Fortunately, most social agencies have responded to the frustrations many fathers expressed when they used to be treated as "second-class citizens" or unimportant to their child's development or well-being. However, it is still the case that feelings of frustration and loss can be exacerbated by a delivery system that sometimes excludes and disregards fathers while focusing on mothers and children (May, 1997).

USING NARRATIVE CREATIVELY TO UNDERSTAND AND ENCOURAGE FATHER INVOLVEMENT

I believe that both quantitative and qualitative methods can be useful at all stages of the research process and in all aspects of the challenging process of allowing research to inform programming and policy. That is, I believe both qualitative and quantitative methods together are most likely to provide the most complete information possible whether one is

- Exploring father involvement simply to understand it better,
- Measuring or assessing the quantity and/or quality of father involvement in different samples of fathers,
- Using research to inform the creation of a program to help increase father involvement,

- Using research to inform the formulation of public or corporate policy to increase father involvement, or
- Using research to evaluate an existing program or policy.

For the purposes of this paper, however, I will focus on two ways of using narrative (1) creating a "summary narrative" to facilitate validation of findings and potential quantitative application of narrative research and (2) testing and deriving conceptual frameworks from narrative—what I call linking story and theory.

Summary Narrative

One creative way to use narrative in research is to create a summary narrative that attempts to capture the essence of a given set of narratives and then ask respondents to indicate to what extent that summary narrative represents their experience. For example, Olson et al. (2002) utilize the concept of the summary narrative to test out the validity of their interpretations of fathers' narratives. Based on the findings from each of five fathers in the sample, a summary narrative was created and sent to each father with the request that he rate the narrative as to the congruence between the summary narrative and his lived experiences. The congruence was exceptionally high for four of the five fathers (5 on a 5-point scale) and moderately high for the other father (3.5). In addition, comments on the summary narrative were requested. The comments from the one father who saw his experience as being different to some extent allowed researchers to modify the summary narrative slightly to include that father's perspective. This revised summary narrative could then be used as part of a quantitative measure of other fathers' experiences with their special-needs children.

Linking Theory with Story

Qualitative data have the potential to provide rich, contextual information. Listening to people's ideas, opinions, concerns, dreams, goals, and personal theories can be very helpful in understanding them and others who share something in common with them. Narrative accounts are one kind of qualitative data focusing on stories told by the respondents. My own approach to narrative focuses on asking respondents to tell of actual events in lived experience along with some interpretative commentary about those stories. That is, I focus on their accounts of "what they actually did" more than other types of discourse. My theory is that reports of actual events are more likely to give helpful information than other types of discourse. I also try to have respondents tell me what that experience means to them. I then try to both test and formulate conceptual frameworks from those stories. Thus, my approach links theory with story (Dollahite, et al., 1996, 1998).

Many scholars with a narrative approach (e.g., Josselson & Lieblich, 1993; McAdams, 1993; Polkinghorne, 1988; Sarbin, 1986; Webb-Mitchell, 1993) argue

6. SPECIAL-NEEDS CHILDREN 125

that human beings "live in narrative" or make sense of their experiences through story. The idea is that people are uniquely skilled at creating meaning through attributions of cause and effect in the ongoing unfolding of events in their lives. These scholars would argue that if you want to really understand someone you must hear "their story" (their overall sense of who they are and why their life matters) as well as "their stories" or the prosaic and profound experiences they have had along with how they interpret these experiences and how they fit in their overall "story."

Thus, from a narrative perspective, a powerful way to test out the validity of ideas is to listen to people's stories and see how they correspond with those ideas. Of course, as scholars who employ grounded-theory approaches (Strauss & Corbin, 1990) will tell you, in-depth interviews that allow people to discuss their experiences (tell their story and stories) in a specific area of concern can be a rich source of material from which to formulate theory.

Application to Programming

One of the reasons I like to gather personal narratives from fathers is that these stories can be used in programming to help increase father involvement. A detailed discussion of this argument is available in Dollahite et al., 1996 and program evaluations of narrative methods of a fathering web site have been published. Suffice it to say that stories can appeal to people, inspire them, engage their cognitive, moral, affective, and spiritual selves, and give them a sense of the possible or a model for behavior. For an example of a narrative-based education program to encourage father involvement, see the FatherWork Web site at http://fatherwork.byu.edu.

ACKNOWLEDGMENTS

I express appreciation to the Family Studies Center and the Religious Studies Center at Brigham Young University for funding to support this research. My thanks also to Loren Marks and Michael Olson for assistance in gathering and coding data. I also express gratitude to Chris Porter for helpful comments on an earlier draft.

REFERENCES

Bailey, D. B., Blasco, P. M., & Simeonsson, R. J. (1992). Needs expressed by mothers and fathers of young children with disabilities. *American Journal on Mental Retardation, 97*, 1–10.

Beckman, P. J. (1991). Comparison of mothers' and fathers' perceptions of the effect of young children with and without disabilities. *American Journal on Mental Retardation, 95*, 585–595.

Bennett, T., Deluca, D. A., & Allen, R. W. (1995). Religion and children with disabilities. *Journal of Religion and Health, 34*, 301–312.

Bishop, L. C. (1985). Healing in the Loinonia: Therapeutic dynamics of church community. *Journal of Psychology and Theology, 13,* 12–20.

Bristol, M. M., & Gallagher, J. J. (1986). Research on fathers of young handicapped children. In J. J. Gallagher & P. M. Vietze (Eds.). *Families of handicapped persons: Research, programs, and policy issues* (pp. 81–100). Baltimore, MD: Brookes.

Brotherson, S. E. (1995). *Using fathers' narrative accounts to refine a conceptual model of generative fathering.* Unpublished master's thesis. Department of Family Sciences, Brigham Young University.

Brotherson, S. E., & Dollahite, D. C. (1997). Generative ingenuity in fatherwork with young children with special-needs. In A. J. Hawkins & D. C. Dollahite (Eds.). *Generative fathering: Beyond deficit perspectives* (pp. 89–104). Thousand Oaks, CA: Sage.

Doherty, W. J. (1991). Beyond reactivity and the deficit model of manhood: A commentary on articles by Napier, Pittman, and Gottman. *Journal of Marital and Family Therapy, 17,* 29–32.

Doherty, W. J., Kouneski, E. F., & Erickson, M. F. (1998). Responsible fathering: An overview and conceptual framework. *Journal of Marriage and the Family, 60,* 277–292.

Dollahite, D. C. (1998). Origins and highlights of the special issue on fathering, faith, and spirituality. *The Journal of Men's Studies, 7,* 1–2.

Dollahite, D. C. (2003). Fathering for eternity: Generative spirituality in Latter-day Saint fathers of children with special needs. *Review of Religious Research, 44,* 237–251.

Dollahite, D. C., & Hawkins, A. J. (1998). A conceptual ethic of generative fathering. *Journal of Men's Studies, 7,* 109–132.

Dollahite, D. C., Hawkins, A. J., & Brotherson, S. E. (1996). Narrative accounts, generative fathering, and family life education. *Marriage and Family Review, 24,* 349–368.

Dollahite, D. C., Marks, L. D., & Olson, M. M. (2002). Fathering, faith, and family therapy: Generative narrative therapy with religious fathers. *Journal of Family Psychotherapy, 13,* 263–294.

Dollahite, D. C., Marks, L. D., & Olson, M. M. (1998). Faithful fathering in trying times: Religious beliefs and practices of Latter-day Saint fathers of children with special needs. *Journal of Men's Studies, 7,* 71–93.

Dollahite, D. C., Hawkins, A. J., & Brotherson, S. E. (1997). Fatherwork: A conceptual ethic of fathering as generative work. In A. J. Hawkins & D. C. Dollahite (Eds.). *Generative fathering: Beyond deficit perspectives* (pp. 17–35). Thousand Oaks, CA: Sage.

Dollahite, D. C., & Rommel, J. I. (1993). Individual and relationship capital: Implications for theory and research on families. *Journal of Family and Economic Issues, 14,* 27–48.

Dollahite, D. C., Slife, B. D., & Hawkins, A. J. (1998). Family generativity and generative counseling: Helping families keep faith with the next generation. In D. P. McAdams & de St. Aubin (Eds.). *Generativity and adult development: How and why we care for the next generation,* (pp. 449–481). Washington, DC: American Psychological Association.

Dollahite, D. C. Marks, L. D., & Goodman, M. (forthcoming). Families and religious beliefs, practices, and communities: Linkages in a diverse and dynamic cultural context. In M. J. Coleman & L. H. Ganong (Eds.), *The handbook of contemporary families: Considering the past, contemplating the future.* Thousand Oaks, CA: Sage.

Fewell, R., & Vadasy, P. (1986). *Families of handicapped children.* Austin, TX: Pro-Ed.

Frey, K. S., Fewell, R. R., & Vadasy, P. F. (1989). Paternal adjustment and changes in child outcome among families of young handicapped children. *Topics in Early Childhood Special Education, 8,* 38–57.

Goldberg, S., Marcovitch, S., MacGregor, D., & Lojkasek, M. (1986). Family responses to developmentally delayed preschoolers: Etiology and the fathers' role. *American Journal of Mental Deficiency, 90,* 610–617.

Grant, T. R., Hawkins, A. J., & Dollahite, D. C. (2001). Web-based education and support for fathers: Remote but promising. In J. Fagan, & A. J. Hawkins (Eds.). *Clinical and educational interventions with fathers* (pp. 143–167). New York: Haworth.

6. SPECIAL-NEEDS CHILDREN 127

Hawkins, A. J., & Dollahite, D. C. (1997). *Generative fathering: Beyond deficit perspectives*. Thousand Oaks, CA: Sage.

Horn, W. F. (2001). Turning the hearts of the fathers: Faith-based approaches to promoting responsible fatherhood. In J. Fagan & A. J. Hawkins (Eds.). *Clinical and educational interventions for fathers*. Binghampton, NY: Haworth.

Hornby, G. (1994). Effects of children with disabilities on fathers: A review and analysis of the literature. *International Journal of Disability, Development, and Education, 41*, 171–184.

Josselson, R. J., & Lieblich, A. (1993). *The narrative study of lives* (Vol. 1). Newbury Park, CA: Sage.

Lamb, M. E, & Laumann-Billings, L. A. (1997). Fathers of children with special needs. In M. E. Lamb (Ed.). *The role of the father in child development* (3rd ed., pp. 179–190). New York: Wiley.

Lamb, M. E., & Meyer, D. J. (1991). Fathers of children with special needs. In M. Seligman (Ed.). *The family with a handicapped child* (2nd ed., pp. 151–179). Boston, MA: Allyn & Bacon.

Latshaw, J. S. (1998). The centrality of faith in father's role construction: The faithful father and the axis mundi paradigm. *The Journal of Men's Studies, 7*, 53–70.

Marks, L. D. (1999). *The meaning of religious belief, practice, and community for Latter-day Saint fathers of children with special needs*. Unpublished master's thesis, Brigham Young University.

Marks, L. D., & Dollahite, D. C. (2001). Religion, relationships, and responsible fathering in Latter-day Saint families of children with special needs. *Journal of Social and Personal Relationships, 18*(5), 625–650.

Marshall, E. S., Olsen, S. F., Mandleco, B. L., Dyches, T. T., Allred, K. W., & Sansom, N. (2003). "This is a spiritual experience": Perspectives of Latter-day Saint families living with a child with disabilities. *Qualitative Health Research, 13*, 57–76.

Maton, K. I., & Wells, E. A. (1995). Religion as a community resource for well-being: Prevention, healing, and empowerment pathways. *Journal of Social Issues, 51*, 177–193.

May, J. (1997). *Fathers of children with special needs: New Horizons*. Bethesda, MD: Association for the Care of Children's Health.

McAdams, D. P. (1993). *The stories we live by: Personal myths and the making of the self*. New York: Guilford.

Morris, S. N., Dollahite, D. C., & Hawkins, A. J. (1999). Virtual family life education: A qualitative study of father education on the World Wide Web. *Family Relations, 48*, 23–30.

Nock, S. J. (1998). *Marriage in men's lives*. New York: Oxford University Press.

Olson, M. M., Dollahite, D. C., & White, M. B. (2002). Involved fathering of children with special needs: Relationships and religion as resources. *Journal of Religion, Disability, & Health, 6*, 47–73.

Palkovitz, R., & Palm, G. (1998). Fatherhood and faith in formation: The developmental effects of fathering on religiosity, morals, and values. *The Journal of Men's Studies, 7*, 33–52.

Pargament, K. I. (1997). *The psychology of religion and coping: Theory, research, and practice*. New York: Guilford.

Polkinghorne, D. E. (1988). *Narrative knowing and the human sciences*. Albany: State University of New York Press.

Popenoe, D. (1996). *Life without father*. New York: The Free Press.

Riessman, C. K. (1993). *Narrative analysis: Qualitative research methods, Series #30*. Newbury Park, CA: Sage.

Sarbin, T. R. (1986). The narrative as a root metaphor for psychology. In T. R. Sarbin (Ed.), *Narrative psychology: The storied nature of human conduct* (pp. 3–21). New York: Praeger.

Strauss, A., & Corbin, J. (1990). *Basics of qualitative research: Grounded theory procedures and techniques*. Newbury Park, CA: Sage.

Turbiville, V. P. (1994). *Fathers, their children, and disability: Literature review*. Lawrence, KS: Beech Center on Families and Disability, University of Kansas.

Webb-Mitchell, B. (1993). Hope in despair: The importance of religious stories for families with children with disabilities. In J. L. Paul & R. J. Simeonsson (Eds.). *Children with special needs: Family, culture, and society* (2nd ed., pp. 97–110). New York: Harcourt Brace.

7

Internal Reliability, Temporal Stability, and Correlates of Individual Differences in Paternal Involvement: A 15-Year Longitudinal Study in Sweden

Susan S. Chuang, Michael E. Lamb
National Institute of Child Health and Human Development

C. Philip Hwang
Göteborg University Sweden

Over the last quarter century, researchers have paid increased attention to the roles that fathers play in their children's lives (Lamb, 1997). Scholars and social commentators have been especially concerned about day-to-day interactions with children and responsibility for child care, which we call paternal or father involvement in this chapter (Lamb, 2000). Secular increases in the rates of maternal employment have fostered widespread expectations that fathers should assume increased responsibility for their children's day-to-day care (Lamb, 1986; Pleck, 1997; Pleck & Pleck, 1997), and there is clear evidence of steady but small changes in this direction (Pleck, 1997). Several researchers have also shown that children benefit when their fathers are sensitively responsive and play active roles in childrearing (Amato & Gilbreth, 1999; Lamb, 1986, 1997; Pleck, 1997), although few studies have been longitudinal in nature. In addition, whereas many researchers now believe both that fathers play important roles in child development and that the extent

129

of paternal involvement is formatively significant, few have specifically focused on the stability of father involvement, convergence among the diverse measures that have been used, and factors that may affect fathers' involvement over time. These issues were examined in our ongoing longitudinal study of 144 Swedish families, recruited in 1982 when their first-born children averaged 16 months of age.

The few previous attempts to examine levels of paternal involvement over time yielded contradictory findings (see reviews by Pleck, 1997). For example, Lewis, Newson, and Newson (1982) reported that British mothers' reports of their husbands' participation in child care were consistently correlated over a 16-year period, especially when adjacent assessments were considered. By contrast, Russell (1982, 1983) found that many highly involved Australian fathers were not similarly involved 2 years later, although the "traditional" parents tended to maintain their division of responsibilities over the same period. Similarly, Radin (1982, 1988, 1994; Radin & Goldsmith, 1985) reported that more-involved American fathers of 3- to 6-year-old children tended to become less involved over a 4-year period, whereas fewer changes in paternal involvement were evident when mothers were primarily responsible for child care. Both Russell and Radin thus concluded that nontraditional divisions of family responsibility were much less stable over time than traditional arrangements were.

In an earlier report on the Swedish families studied here, Lamb, Hwang, Broberg, Bookstein, Hult, and Frodi (1988) examined mothers' and fathers' evaluations of their 16- and 28-month-old children's preferences, reports of the parents' relative responsibilities for child-related activities, and composite measures of the amounts of time the fathers spent with their children. Paternal involvement was somewhat stable from 16 to 28 months, with the fathers' levels of involvement predicted in part by whether the fathers took leave when their children were born. Hwang and Lamb (1997) subsequently reported modest but significantly stable levels of father involvement and responsibility over the first 8.5 years of the children's lives.

These studies thus yield contradictory evidence about the stability of father involvement, which may, in part, reflect differences in the ways that researchers have operationalized father involvement. Early estimates of the amounts of time that fathers spent with their children also varied widely, depending on which types of activities were examined as well as on the techniques used to gather and quantify the data (Lamb, Pleck, & Charnov, 1985, 1987). For example, time diaries tend to show that fathers spend less time with their children than do global estimates made by the parents, and consistency across studies is greater when father involvement is expressed as a proportion of maternal involvement rather than in absolute terms (Lamb et al., 1987; Pleck, 1997). According to Lamb et al. (1985, 1987; Pleck, Lamb, & Levine, 1985), more consistency is evident when researchers distinguish among three difference types of activities—engagement (including care and play), responsibility, and availability—in which parents can be involved. In the present study, we thus included many measures of involvement to

7. PATERNAL INVOLVEMENT IN SWEDEN   131

permit clearer insight into the associations and convergence among these different measures and to determine whether the individual and composite measures showed levels of paternal involvement to be stable over time.

In a short-term longitudinal study of Swedish couples before, during, and after the birth of their first children, Frodi, Lamb, Hwang, and Frodi (1982) examined the effects of major responsibility for child care on paternal behavior toward their children. In general, fathers who stayed home and fathers who continued to work did not behave differently, and their attitudes were also quite similar. Researchers have also examined the effects of maternal employment, noting that relative (but not absolute) levels of paternal involvement increased when mothers were employed (Baruch & Barnett, 1981; Goldscheider & Waite, 1991; Parke, 1996; Pleck, 1997). A more recent study by the National Institute of Child Health and Human Development (NICHD) Early Child Care Research Network (2000) reported that maternal employment did not fundamentally alter the fathers' levels of caregiving responsibilities although fathers were more involved when they worked fewer hours and mothers worked more hours. After a thorough literature review, Pleck (1997) concluded that a variety of factors such as maternal and paternal employment patterns affected levels of paternal involvement in complex ways; different factors may be important in different contexts or phases of the children's and fathers' lives (see also Parke, 1996).

Although researchers have identified several factors that may affect father involvement, most researchers have focused on one or two facets of father involvement and have seldom examined stability or change in levels of parental involvement. In the present study, by contrast, we explored the influence on various types of father involvement of various family characteristics and life circumstances that might influence father involvement—including maternal and paternal employment, paternal leave, birth of a new child, and type of child care—over a 15-year span.

METHODS

Participants

A total of 144 Swedish parents and their first-born children (74 boys, 70 girls) participated in our study. Families were recruited in 1982 from municipal records when their first-born children ranged in age from 11 to 24 months (mean age = 15.9 months, $SD = 2.9$ months). Only families in which the parents lived together were recruited into the study, which included families from varied sociodemographic backgrounds, representing the population of families with toddlers living in the Göteborg (Sweden) metropolitan region at the time. Approximately two thirds of the families contacted agreed to participate in the study. At recruitment, mothers and fathers averaged 29.5 and 31.5 years of age, respectively. Mothers' scores on the two-factor Hollingshead (1975) Index averaged 41.0, with fathers'

132   CHUANG, LAMB, AND HWANG

scores averaging 43.6. As might be expected, the number of participants declined over time: 136 families (68 boys) participated when the children were 2.3 years old (Phase II), 133 (68 boys) when the children were 3.3 years old (Phase III), 119 (60 boys) when the children reached 6.7 years of age (Phase IV), 116 (58 boys) when the children were 8.4 years of age (Phase V), and 108 (53 boys) when the children averaged 15.2 years of age (Phase VI); 104 families (51 boys) participated in all of the phases. The analyses reported here exclude families in which the parents divorced and the fathers ceased having substantial contact with their children. A total of 2, 2, 3, and 2 families were excluded for this reason from the analyses of data gathered in Phases II, III, IV, and V, respectively.

Procedure

In each phase, mothers and fathers were interviewed together and were also asked to complete a series of questionnaires individually. Parents were questioned each time about the amounts of time they spent interacting with their children, the division of child-care responsibilities and activities, their employment status (parental leave/student/unemployed or employed one-quarter, half, three-quarter, or full time), the amounts of time spent working on the weekend, whether fathers took paternal leave (more than 2 weeks), the birth of other children, and the type of child care used (home-care, family-based day care, day-care center).

Measures

Absolute Measures of Paternal Involvement. To assess the fathers' level of involvement with their children, a detailed diary recall method (Robinson, 1977) was employed when the children were 1.3, 2.3, 3.3, and 6.7 years old (Phases I to IV). Mothers and fathers together recalled the details of their last workday and their last nonworkday, focusing on the activities in which the children were involved. These interviews were recorded and the transcripts used to compute the number of minutes the fathers reportedly spent each day (1) providing care to, (2) playing with, (3) being accessible to (i.e., being within earshot when the child was awake, whether or not social interactions were actually taking place), and (4) being responsible for the child when the mother was not home. This diary recall method was not used when the children were 8 years old. Rather, parents simply estimated in Phase V the number of hours their children spent with (1) the father alone and (2) both parents during the previous week. No absolute measures of paternal involvement were obtained in Phase VI.

Parental Responsibility Questionnaire. The Parental Responsibility Questionnaire (PRQ; Lamb et al., 1988) was completed individually by the mothers and fathers in each of the six phases. In the first three phases, 6 of the 10 items were combined to form a composite measure of relative parental responsibility that was internally consistent on each occasion (alpha > .70). The items included taking

7. PATERNAL INVOLVEMENT IN SWEDEN

the child for preventative health care, taking the child to the doctor, buying clothes for the child, deciding whether the child needed new clothes, buying toys for the child, and making arrangements with babysitters. When the children were 7 years old (Phase IV), the same five items (except the item concerned with babysitting arrangements) were supplemented with seven new items: who took the child to day care/preschool, who the day care/preschool phoned if there was a problem, who stayed home with the sick child, who put the child to bed at night, who determined when the child needed to put on clean clothes, who played with the child, and who read to the child (alpha = .70).

When the children were 8 years old (Phase V), the PRQ questionnaire included the same items as Phase IV (except the item, who took the child to day care/preschool), as well as new items: who made babysitting arrangements, who took the child to the swimhall, cinema, theatre etc., and who told the child what he or she should not do (alpha = .76). When the children were 15 years old (Phase VI), the questionnaire included 11 age-appropriate items: who took the child for preventative health care, who bought clothes for the child, who drove the child to leisure-time activities, who told the child about rules and limits at home, who went to parent–teacher meetings at school, who helped the child do homework, who talked with the child in confidence about "delicate" matters, who went with the child to the movies, theatre, etc., who encouraged the child to behave more appropriately, who woke the child up in the morning, who reminded the child about homework, who washed the child's clothes, and who prepared the child's meals (alpha = .73).

In the first three phases, responses to the PRQ were provided using a scale to indicate whether (1) mother was almost always responsible, (2) mother was usually responsible, (3) parents were equally responsible, (4) father was usually responsible, and (5) father was almost always responsible. In Phases IV through VI, a seven-point scale was used: (1) always mother, (2) almost always mother, (3) more often mother, (4) either mother or father, (5) more often father, (6) almost always father, and (7) always father.

Mothers' and fathers' PRQ responses in each phase of assessment were highly correlated (mean r = .81), as previously reported by Hwang and Lamb (1997) for the first four phases, and thus their mean responses were used to create a single PRQ score in each phase.

RESULTS

Change Over Time in Mean Levels of Paternal Involvement and Responsibility

Diary-Based Accounts. A series of gender by type of day (weekday, weekend day) by phase (Phases I–IV) repeated-measures analysis of variance (ANOVAs), with the various types of father involvement as the dependent variables

TABLE 7.1

Diary-Based Measures of Paternal Involvement Over Time (Mean Hours/Day)

	Phase/Child's Mean Age in Years			
	I	*II*	*III*	*IV*
Measure	*1.3*	*2.3*	*3.3*	*6.7*
Play	1.71 (1.15)	1.51 (1.06)		
Care	0.83 (0.59)	0.58 (0.42)		
Play & care	2.55 (1.51)	2.08 (1.23)	1.69 (1.07)	0.95 (0.93)
Responsibility	1.31 (1.61)	1.31 (1.60)	1.35 (1.47)	1.54 (1.57)
Accessibility	5.26 (2.04)	5.47 (1.91)	6.10 (2.03)	6.35 (2.21)

Note. Standard deviations are in parentheses.

(i.e., accessibility, play, care, and sole responsibility), revealed significant main effects for phase on measures of accessibility ($F(3, 336) = 197.22$, $p < .001$) and play and care ($F(3, 333) = 62.35$, $p < .001$) as well as for play, ($F(1,130) = 39.99$, $p < .001$) over Phases I and II (see Table 7.1 for means). A series of posthoc t-tests revealed that fathers were more accessible to their children in Phases III and IV than in Phases I and II. The fathers' level of accessibility did not differ between Phases I and II and between Phases III and IV. Post-hoc analyses also showed that the amounts of time fathers spent playing with and caring for their children declined significantly from Phase II to Phase III, and from Phase III to Phase IV. The fathers also spent significantly less time playing with their children in Phase II than in Phase I (see Fig. 7.1).

The analyses also revealed significant main effects for type of day for play and care ($F(1,111) = 24.50$, $p < .001$) over four phases and more specifically for care

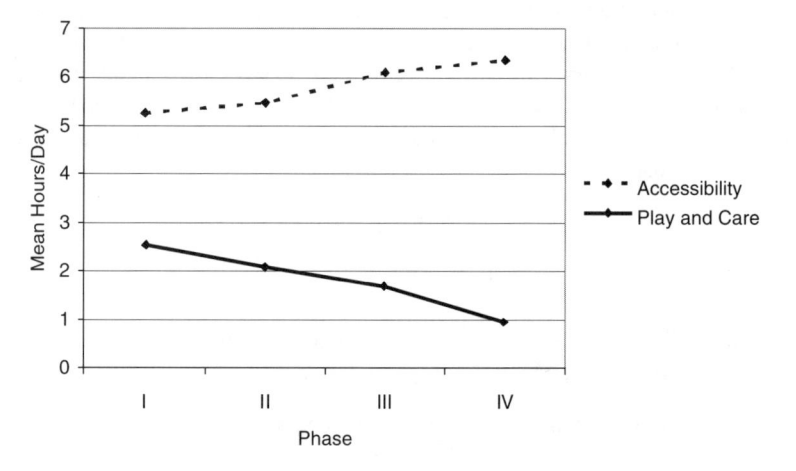

FIG. 7.1. The fathers' levels of accessibility and play and care over time.

7. PATERNAL INVOLVEMENT IN SWEDEN 135

$(F(1,130) = 17.81, p < .001)$ over Phases I and II. The fathers spent more time playing with and caring for their children on the weekends than on weekdays.

Overall, therefore, the fathers were increasingly accessible to their children as they got older whereas the amounts of time they spent playing with and caring for their children declined over time. The amounts of time that fathers' spent playing with and caring for their children were generally greater on the weekends than on the weekdays.

PRQ. In all phases, regardless of the children's gender, mothers assumed more responsibility for their children's care than fathers did. There was no indication that the fathers assumed higher levels of responsibility (relative to the mothers) as their children grew older.

Is Father Involvement a Single, Coherent Dimension?

Diary-Based Accounts. Bivariate correlations among the weekday measures revealed that in Phases I and II, the fathers who were more accessible to their children on weekdays also spent more time playing with ($r = .29$ and $.23$, respectively) and caring for their children ($r = .36$ and $.24$, respectively). The amounts of time the fathers spent playing with the children were also correlated with the amounts of time the fathers' spent caring for them on the weekdays ($r = .38$ and $.23$, respectively). Fathers' accessibility on weekdays was also significantly correlated with estimates of the amount of time fathers were solely responsible for their children's care while the mothers were not at home in the first four phases ($r = .36$, $.36$, $.34$, and $.30$, respectively). In addition, the amounts of weekday time fathers spent being solely responsible for their children were significantly correlated with the amounts of time they spent playing with ($r = .48$ and $.56$, respectively) and caring for ($r = .57$ and $.43$, respectively) their children in Phases I and II, and with the fathers' combined play and care time in Phases III and IV ($r = .52$ and $.47$, respectively).

With the exception of correlations with measures of accessibility, similar associations were evident when the weekend measures were examined. As on weekdays, the fathers who spent more time playing with their children also spent more time caring for them in Phases I and II ($r = .39$ and $.31$, respectively). The fathers who had more sole responsibility for their children in Phases I and II also spent more time playing with ($r = .32$ and $.18$, respectively) and caring for ($r = .47$ and $.35$, respectively) them and were also more involved in playing with and caring for their children in Phases III and IV ($r = .27$ and $.20$, respectively). By contrast, the more accessible fathers spent less time caring for ($r = -.24$ and $-.17$, respectively) and playing with ($r = -.35$ and $-.32$, respectively) their children in Phases I and II, and playing/caring for them in Phase III ($r = -.30$).

TABLE 7.2

Correlations Between the Scores on the Parental Responsibility
Questionnaire and the Diary-Based Measures

Phase	Diary Variable	Type of Day	r
I	Accessibility	Weekday	.24
I	Responsibility	Weekday	.35
I	Care	Weekday	.33
I	Care	Weekend	.21
II	Accessibility	Weekday	.19
II	Responsibility	Weekday	.27
III	Responsibility	Weekday	.28
III	Play and care	Weekday	.28
IV	Play and care	Weekday	.24

There were modest but significant correlations between measures of the fathers' weekday and weekend accessibility in Phases I ($r = .18$) and IV ($r = .24$). Weekday and weekend estimates of the amounts of time fathers spent playing with their children in Phase I ($r = .38$) and caring for ($r = .23$ and $.19$, respectively) their children in Phases I and II. In Phases III and IV, the fathers who were more accessible on the weekdays spent less time playing with and caring for their children on the weekends ($r = -.41$ and $-.21$, respectively).

In summary, measures of the amounts of time fathers spent playing with, caring for, being solely responsible for, and being accessible to their children on weekdays were associated with one another. Similar correlations were evident among measures of the fathers' weekend involvement, except that weekend accessibility was negatively correlated with measures of the fathers' weekend play and care time.

Diary-Based Accounts and the PRQ. As shown in Table 7.2, the fathers' levels of responsibility on the PRQ in Phases I and II were correlated with measures of their accessibility on weekdays. In Phases I to III, the fathers' PRQ scores were also correlated with the weekday estimates of the amounts of time that the fathers were solely responsible for child care while their partners were away. More responsible fathers, as defined by the PRQ responses, also spent more time caring for their toddlers on both weekdays and weekends in Phase I and spent more time interacting (play and caretaking combined) with their children on the weekdays in Phase III and on the weekends in Phase IV. In Phase V, however, the amounts of time that the children spent either with their fathers alone or with both of their parents were not systematically correlated with the PRQ scores. These results might reflect the change from a recall diary method for assessing involvement (Phases I to IV) to more global estimates of time expenditures (Phase V).

Overall, measures of the fathers' responsibility for various child-related activities, as indexed by the PRQ, tended to be associated with the various diary-based

7. PATERNAL INVOLVEMENT IN SWEDEN   137

measures of the amounts of time that they spent with their children on weekdays. Such findings speak to the convergent validity of the two strategies for assessing paternal responsibility.

Father Involvement Composites

Measures of internal reliability (Cronbach alphas) were computed to determine whether the diverse measures of father involvement could be combined to create composite measures of paternal involvement in each of the first five phases. In each of the first four phases, the inclusion of the diary-based measures of weekend involvement reduced the internal consistency of the composites. Modestly coherent composite measures of father involvement were evident, however, when standardized PRQ scores and weekday diary-based assessments were combined. In Phases I and II, composites comprising the standardized PRQ scores and the diary-based measures of weekday accessibility, play, care, and responsibility had alpha coefficients of .73 and .65, respectively. Excluding additional items did not increase internal reliability. In Phases III and IV, however, composite measures of father involvement were only reliable when weekday accessibility scores were excluded from the composites; the internal consistency coefficients for the resulting composites, comprising the PRQ, weekday play and care, and weekday responsibility scores, were both .62. A coherent composite measure of father involvement could not be created using the Phase V data. With this exception, the analyses thus suggested that the various measures of paternal involvement could generally be combined to create composite measures, although these composites were minimally reliable and typically excluded many of the possible component measures. These composites are identified in the following section as father involvement (FI) composites.

Domains of Father Involvement

Because the diary-based and PRQ scores could only be combined into composite measures of father involvement that were quite unreliable, we explored whether two or more different constructs (i.e., responsibility and accessibility) might in fact be confused in these composite measures.

Responsibility. PRQ scores, measures of the amounts of time that the fathers were solely responsible for child care on weekdays and weekend days, and measures of paternal/sick leave taken in Phases I, II, and III did not combine to yield coherent composites in any phase (alpha < .55). Thus, even when fathers were more likely to assume some forms of responsibility they did not necessarily assume similar levels of responsibility in other areas.

Accessibility and Engagement. Independent diary-based estimates of the amounts of time spent by fathers being accessible to, playing with, and caring for their children on weekdays in Phase I indeed combined into a single coherent index

(alpha = .74) but this was no more coherent than the broader index described earlier. In Phase II, however, the composite measure of weekday accessibility/engagement had a coefficient of internal reliability (alpha = .67) that was marginally higher than the broader index of paternal involvement described earlier (alpha = .65); but internally reliable composite measures of accessibility/engagement could not be created using data from Phases III and IV.

Overall, therefore, the broader composite measures of paternal involvement were at least as coherent, if not more reliable, than the composite measures of more specific constructs such as accessibility/engagement and responsibility.

Stability of the Individual and Composite Measures of Father Involvement Over Time

FI Composite Measures. Scores on the composite measures of father involvement were fairly stable across the first three phases. With the exception of a significant association between the Phase I and IV composites, however, the levels of involvement in the first three phases were unrelated to composites based on levels of involvement after school began (Phase IV) (see Table 7.3 for correlations).

Diary-Based Individual Measures. Levels of paternal accessibility to their children on weekdays were moderately stable across the first three phases (see Table 7.4 for correlations), but the levels of weekday accessibility in Phase IV were unrelated to earlier measures of the same construct. This lack of stability may reflect the length of time (4 years) between the third and fourth phases or the fact that the children's needs changed dramatically as they grew older and entered school. There was no significant stability over time in the levels of paternal accessibility on the weekends.

The amounts of time spent playing with and caring for children were not stable between Phases I and II, although weekday and weekend estimates in each phase

TABLE 7.3
Correlations Among Scores on the Composite Measure of Paternal Involvement Over Time

	Phase/Child's Mean Age in Years			
	I	*II*	*III*	*IV*
	1.3	*2.3*	*3.3*	*6.7*
I		23***	.28**	.16
II			.31***	.06
III				−.01
IV				

Note. **$p < .01$; ***$p < .001$.

7. PATERNAL INVOLVEMENT IN SWEDEN

TABLE 7.4

Correlations Among the Measures of Fathers' Weekday
Accessibility Over Time

| | Phase/Child's Mean Age in Years | | | |
| | I | II | III | IV |
	1.3	2.3	3.3	6.7
I		30**	.29**	.16
II			.25**	.06
III				.12
IV				

Note. **$p < .01$.

were significantly correlated for both play in Phase I ($r = .38$) and care ($r = .23$ and .19, respectively) times in Phases I and II. The total amounts of time fathers spent playing with and caring for their children were stable between Phases I and II on weekends ($r = .89$), but were otherwise unrelated to estimates in other phases.

Levels of sole responsibility for care of their children (mothers absent) were not stable over time (r ranged from $-.12$ to .19) and were not even consistent from weekday to weekend within phases, although fathers who took more sole responsibility on the weekends in Phase I were more likely to assume similar responsibilities in Phase III ($r = .23$).

Overall, therefore, with the exception of levels of accessibility in the first 3 years of life, diary-based measures of paternal involvement showed little stability over time.

PRQ Scores. The parents' PRQ scores in each of the six phases revealed that the fathers' relative responsibility for child-related activities was impressively stable over the 15-year time span studied (see Table 7.5 for correlations). Almost

TABLE 7.5

Correlations Among Scores on Parental Responsibility Questionnaire (PRQ) Over
a 15-Year Span

| | Phase/Child's Mean Age in Years | | | | | |
| | I | II | III | IV | V | VI |
	1.3	2.3	3.3	6.7	8.4	15.2
I		.62***	.61***	.34***	.40***	.31**
II			.71***	.21***	.26**	.19
III				.35***	.43***	.34***
IV					.69***	.42***
V						.38***
VI						

Note. **$p < .01$; ***$p < .001$.

all correlations were significant, with a predictable decline in the coefficients as the length of time between the pairs of assessments decreased.

Correlates of Father Involvement

We next examined correlations between the measures of father involvement and indices of family characteristics, including levels of maternal and paternal employment (unemployed/parental leave/student or employed one-quarter, half, three-quarter, or full time), the amounts of time fathers worked on the weekends, and whether fathers took paternity leaves (more than 2 weeks). The correlations tended to confirm the validity of the father involvement measures, although all associations were weaker than might be expected and many predictable associations were not significant.

In Phase I, maternal employment and paternity leave were associated with the scores on the FI composite and with levels of play and sole responsibility for children on the weekdays (see Table 7.6). The mothers' levels of employment were also associated with the amounts of time that the fathers spent caring for their children on the weekdays. The fathers' levels of responsibility for their children's activities (PRQ) were negatively associated with the fathers' levels of employment and positively associated with whether they took paternal leave. Fathers who worked longer hours were less likely to be solely responsible for their children on weekdays.

In Phase II (see Table 7.7), mothers' levels of employment were associated with the amounts of time fathers were solely responsible for their children. Fathers who worked longer hours were generally less involved with their children on the weekdays and were also less often solely responsible for and accessible to their children on the weekdays. The fathers who worked more hours on the weekend were more involved with their children, to the extent that they had more sole caretaking responsibilities on weekdays, although they spent less time caring for their children on weekdays and less time playing with their children on the weekends.

TABLE 7.6

Correlations Between Measures of Father Involvement and Family Characteristics in Phase I

	Measures of Father Involvement				
Family Characteristics	*FI[a] Composite*	*Weekday Care*	*Weekday Play*	*Weekday Responsibility*	*PRQ*
Maternal employment	.17*	.22**	.18*	.19*	
Paternal employment				−.19*	−.21**
Paternity leave	.19*	.17*		.23*	.30**

Note. $*p < .05; **p < .01$.

[a]FI = father involvement.

7. PATERNAL INVOLVEMENT IN SWEDEN

TABLE 7.7

Correlations Between Measures of Father Involvement and Family Characteristics
in Phase II

	Measures of Father Involvement					
Family Characteristics	FI[a] Composite	Weekend Care	Weekend Play	Weekday Respons[b]	Weekday Access[c]	Weekend Access[c]
Maternal employment				.23*		
Paternal employment	−.26**			−.29**	−.27**	
Weekend work	.20**	−.20**	−.26**	.22**		−.34**

Note. *$p < .05$; **$p < .01$.
[a] FI = father involvement.
[b] Respons = responsibility.
[c] Access = Accessibility.

Fathers who were more accessible on the weekends were also more likely to work less on weekends.

In Phase III (see Table 7.8), levels of both maternal and paternal employment were associated with father participation: Fathers were more involved, as assessed using the composite index, and were solely responsible for their children more often on weekdays when the mothers worked longer hours and when the fathers worked fewer hours. However, the amounts of time that the fathers were accessible to their children on weekdays declined as the fathers' work hours increased. Fathers who worked on weekends were also less accessible.

In Phase IV, no variables, including the extent of maternal or paternal employment or the birth of additional children, were associated with scores on any of the measures of father involvement.

In Phase V, the level of maternal employment was associated with the fathers' level of responsibility (PRQ scores; $r = −.26$), but measures of the amounts of time that fathers spent with their children were not significantly associated with any other family characteristics.

TABLE 7.8

Correlations Between Measures of Father Involvement and Family Characteristics
in Phase III

	Measures of Father Involvement			
Family Characteristics	FI[a] Composite	Weekday Responsibility	Weekday Accessibility	Weekend Accessibility
Maternal employment	.26**	.21*		
Paternal employment	−.19*		−.24*	
Weekend work				−.21*

Note. *$p < .05$; **$p < .01$.
[a] FI = father involvement.

Overall, therefore, the various measures of father involvement were related to such factors as the mothers' and fathers' employment, the amounts of time that the fathers spent working on the weekends, and whether they took paternal leave. These associations were not consistent from phase to phase, however; rather, the associations between the family characteristics and the measures of parental involvement varied depending on the age of the children and the type of day (weekday versus weekend day) studied.

Types of Child Care and Father Involvement

A series of ANOVAs revealed that, in general, father involvement—as assessed using the diary-based measures, scores on the PRQ, and the scores on the father involvement composite—did not vary significantly depending on the types of child care (home, family-based day care, and center care) received by the children in Phases I through IV, although the fathers were more accessible on the weekdays to children in exclusive home care than to center care children in Phases I ($F(2, 137) = 3.91$, $p < .05$) and II ($F(2, 130) = 4.38$, $p < .05$). In Phase IV, furthermore, the fathers of children cared for exclusively at home received higher PRQ scores than did fathers of children in the day-care center group ($F(2, 116) = 3.72$, $p < .05$).

DISCUSSION

In the present study, we examined the stability over time in the extent to which these Swedish fathers were involved in the care and socialization of their children as well as intercorrelations among diverse measures of paternal involvement over a 15-year span. Our findings revealed modest but significant patterns of association among measures of father involvement in the first four phases, with measures of weekday involvement combining to form a single, coherent composite measure in each of the first three phases. Correlations with various family characteristics tended to confirm the external validity of the individual and composite measures of father involvement.

Although fathers spend less time with older children (Barnett & Baruch, 1987; Marsiglio, 1991; McBride & Mills, 1993; Pleck, 1995, 1997), most researchers have examined fathers' roles at particular points in their children's lives rather than longitudinally (Easterbrooks & Goldberg, 1984; Radin, 1981). However, father involvement involves different types of activities at different ages (Lamb et al., 1985, 1987; Pleck et al., 1985), and it is unclear whether these types of involvement might have divergent trajectories over time. This increased the importance of studying changes over time in levels of paternal involvement.

We first examined changes over time using the parents' diary-based accounts of the time fathers spent with their children on specific workdays and nonworkdays

7. PATERNAL INVOLVEMENT IN SWEDEN
143

in each of the first four phases of assessment, when the children averaged 1.3, 2.3, 3.3, and 6.7 years of age. Analyses revealed that, as expected, fathers generally spent more time playing with and caring for their children on weekends than on weekdays. Similar findings were reported by McBride and Mills (1993) and Ishii-Kuntz (1994) in studies of 3- to 5- and 10- to 15-year-old children in the United States, respectively. The amounts of time these Swedish fathers spent playing with their 16-month-old toddlers significantly declined over the next year, although their levels of care and being solely responsible for their children did not change significantly. The total amounts of time spent in play and care by the fathers we studied declined over the first four phases. By contrast, the fathers' levels of accessibility to their children increased over time; this pattern had not been noticed previously (Pleck, 1997). In part, it likely reflects reductions over time in the amounts of time that children sleep but it may also reflect the Swedish fathers' beliefs that their children increasingly need them to be available as resources. O'Brien and Jones (1996) reported that British teenagers turned to their mothers when they wanted "to talk" but wanted their fathers to "be there" for them.

The present study also assessed the parents' relative responsibility for child-related activities using the Parental Responsibility Questionnaire (Lamb, et al., 1988). As in previous research, fathers and mothers tended to agree with one another regarding their relative responsibilities (Ahmeduzzaman & Roopnarine, 1992; Hwang & Lamb, 1997; Lamb et al., 1988; Levant, Slattery, & Loiselle, 1987; Roopnarine & Ahmeduzzaman, 1993; Smith & Morgan, 1994; Tulananda, Young, & Roopnarine, 1994). In all phases, mothers assumed more responsibility for their children's care than the fathers did (see also Leslie, Anderson, & Branson, 1991; McBride & Mills, 1993; Peterson & Gerson, 1992). As other scholars have noted, fathers may be capable of performing all forms of child care competently (e.g., Bhavnagri & Parke, 1991; Lamb, 1986, 1997; Marisiglio, Amato, Day, & Lamb, 2000), but they tend to view themselves primarily as "helpers" rather than as coequal parents (Coltrane, 1996), even in Sweden!

Although most researchers recognize that paternal involvement involves diverse types of activities—Lamb et al. (1985, 1987) distinguished among engagement, accessibility, and responsibility, for example—most researchers have looked at single facets of involvement and have not explored associations among different aspects of involvement. Such analyses were thus accorded special attention in the present study. When the children were 1, 2, 3, and 7 years of age (i.e., in the first four phases), measures of the various types of involvement on the weekdays were consistently intercorrelated. Specifically, fathers who were more accessible to their children spent more time playing with and caring for their children (the levels of play and care were associated in Phases I and II), and they also spent more time being solely responsible for their children's care. Similarly, fathers who spent more time taking care of their children by themselves also devoted more time to caring for and playing with them. Interestingly and unexpectedly, however, the

fathers who were more accessible on the weekends were less likely to spend time playing with and caring for their children in the first three phases.

Although a father's level of responsibility may be important to a child's well-being and development (Lamb, 1986), little research has focused on the dimensions of responsibility (Pleck & Stueve, 2001). Thus, the fathers' levels of relative responsibility for various child-related activities, as indexed on the PRQ, were assessed along with diary-based accounts of their sole responsibilities. The fathers' PRQ scores were associated with their levels of weekday involvement in play, care, and sole responsibility in Phases I through IV, although these intercorrelations were modest and not consistent in each phase. Moreover, the fathers' PRQ scores were only modestly associated with fathers' levels of weekday responsibilities in Phases I and II, suggesting that responsibility is not a unidimensional construct. Further research on the components of responsibility is clearly needed.

Not surprisingly, the diverse measures of weekday paternal involvement and the PRQ scores could be combined into single, statistically coherent composite measures of father involvement in each phase, although the Phase III and IV composites excluded the measures of weekday accessibility and the levels of internal reliability were quite modest. Scores on these composite measures of paternal involvement were stable over the first 3 years of the children's lives but became unstable after the children began school. Despite widespread agreement that accessibility and responsibility are quite different aspects of paternal involvement, measures of these dimensions did not combine into independent composite measures, although the measures of accessibility in Phases I and II were significantly correlated. The results of these analyses further underscore the importance of measurement construction efforts designed to distinguish empirically among conceptually distinct aspects of paternal involvement.

As noted earlier, few researchers have examined paternal involvement longitudinally. In earlier analyses of data obtained in this study, Lamb et al. (1988) reported temporal stability in levels of overall father involvement (computed by combining weekday and weekend diary measures) across the first years of the children's lives. Our findings similarly revealed that the composite paternal involvement scores were stable across the first three phases. The subsequent decline in stability may reflect changes in patterns of parent–child interactions after school began or the 4-year gap between Phases III and IV.

Closer examination of the time-diary measures revealed that scores on some measures were more stable over time than others. Specifically, measures of the amounts of time that the fathers were accessible to their children on weekdays were the most stable across the first three phases, whereas scores on the other measures were not very stable. Such findings further underscore the extent to which individual levels of involvement tend to vary quite substantially over time, with involved fathers becoming uninvolved and vice versa.

Correlations between measures of father involvement and family characteristics tended to confirm the validity of the father involvement measures, although

7. PATERNAL INVOLVEMENT IN SWEDEN 145

the correlates were nowhere near as strong and consistent as might have been expected. Levels of maternal employment were correlated with measures of father involvement at various phases. In Phase I, for example, mothers who worked more had husbands who were more involved with their toddlers and spent more time playing with, caring for, and being solely responsible for their toddlers on the weekdays. Maternal employment status was also correlated with measures of the fathers' overall involvement in Phase III. Estimates of the amounts of time that the fathers spent with their children were also associated with the mothers' work hours in Phase V. Such findings support Barnett and Baruch's (1988) claims that in middle-class American families, the number of hours mothers worked predicts the level of paternal involvement, although other researchers have reported that fathers have higher levels of child-care responsibilities when mothers are employed part time rather than full time (Barnett & Baruch, 1987, 1988; Presser, 1986, 1988, 1989).

Barnett and Baruch (1988) speculated that levels of paternal involvement would increase if the number of working hours decreased, and our findings are consistent with those speculations. In Phases II and III, the fathers who worked less were more involved with their children overall (FI composite) and were more accessible to their children on the weekdays and in Phase III, on the weekends. In Phase II, they also spent more time being solely responsible for their children on the weekdays. Contrary to previous findings (Nock & Kingston, 1988; Pleck & Staines, 1985; Staines & Pleck, 1983), fathers who worked more on the weekends were more involved on weekdays, as indexed by the FI composite, and had more sole responsibility for their children on weekdays. However, working on the weekend was negatively associated with caring for their children on weekdays and playing with them on the weekends.

Despite Sweden's generous parental-leave policies and the persistent efforts that have been made to encourage paternal involvement (see Hwang, 1987; Lamb & Levine, 1983; Steward, Yeatts, & Zottarelli, in press, for reviews), there were few signs that men who took more than 2 weeks of paternal leave were otherwise more involved in child care. When fathers took paternity leave following their children's birth (Phase I), their scores on the father involvement composite were higher because these men spent more time caring for and being solely responsible for their toddlers' child-care needs, and their PRQ scores were higher. Paternity leave was only associated with the level of weekday accessibility to their children in Phase II, however. Frodi et al. (1982) similarly reported no significant differences in the later responsibilities of fathers who worked and those who stayed home with their infants.

In summary, our results confirm that father involvement is multidimensional and that the stability of the individual dimensions vary over time. Although some correlations among the time-based measures and the PRQ were significant, many were not, and the measures within each phase did not consistently combine to yield coherent composite measures. On the other hand, scores on most of the measures

146 CHUANG, LAMB, AND HWANG

appeared valid, as indexed by significant correlations with family characteristics such as maternal and paternal employment levels and paternity leaves.

ACKNOWLEDGMENTS

The authors are grateful to Anders Broberg, Majt Frodi, Gunilla Hult, Thomas Tjus, and Anders Wellsmo for interviewing and observing the families.

REFERENCES

Ahmeduzzaman, M., E. & Roopnarine, J. L. (1992). Sociodemographic factors, functioning style, social support, and fathers' involvement with preschoolers in African-American families. *Journal of Marriage and the Family, 54*, 699–707.

Amato, P. A., & Gilbreth, J. G. (1999). Nonresident fathers and children's well-being: Media analysis. *Journal of Marriage and the Family, 61*, 15–73.

Bhavnagri, N. P., & Parke, R. D. (1991). Parents as direct facilitators of children's peer relationships: Effects of age of child and sex of parent. *Journal of Social & Personal Relationships, 8*, 423–440.

Barnett, R. C., & Baruch, G. K. (1987). Determinants of fathers' participation in family work. *Journal of Marriage and the Family, 49*, 29–40.

Barnett, R. C., & Baruch, G. K. (1988). Correlates of fathers' participation in family work. In P. Bronstein & C. P. Cowan (Eds.), *Fatherhood today: Men's changing role in the family* (pp. 66–78). New York: Wiley.

Baruch, G. K., & Barnett, R. C. (1981). Fathers' involvement in the care of their preschool children. *Sex Roles, 7*, 1043–1059.

Coltrane, S. (1996). *Family man.* New York: Oxford University Press.

Easterbrooks, M. A., & Goldberg, W. A. (1984). Toddler development in the family: Impact of father involvement and parenting characteristics. *Child Development, 55*, 740–752.

Frodi, A. M., Lamb, M. E., Hwang, C. P., & Frodi, M. (1982). Father–mother–child interaction in traditional and non-traditional Swedish families: A longitudinal study. *Alternative Lifestyles, 1*, 3–22.

Goldscheider, F. K., & Waite, L. J. (1991). *New families, no families: The transformation of the American home.* Berkley, CA: University of California Press.

Hollingstead, A. B. (1975). *The four factor index of social position.* Unpublished manuscript available from Department of Sociology, Yale University, New Haven, CT.

Hwang, C. P. (1987). The changing role of Swedish fathers. In M. E. Lamb (Ed.), *The father's role: Cross-cultural perspectives* (pp. 115–138). Hillsdale, NJ: Lawrence Erlbaum Associates.

Hwang, C. P., & Lamb, M. E. (1997). Father involvement in Sweden: A longitudinal study of its stability and correlates. *International Journal of Developmental Psychology, 21*, 621–632.

Ishii-Kuntz, M. (1994). Paternal involvement and perception toward fathers' roles: A comparison between Japan and the United States. *Journal of Family Issues,14*, 550–571.

Lamb, M. E. (Ed.). (1986). *The father's role: Applied perspectives.* New York: Wiley.

Lamb, M. E. (Ed.). (1997). *The role of the father in child development* (3rd ed.). New York: Wiley.

Lamb, M. E. (2000). The history of research on father involvement: An overview. *Marriage & Family Review, 29*, 23–42.

Lamb, M. E., Hwang, C.-P., Broberg, A., Bookstein, F. L., Hult, G., & Frodi, M. (1988). The determinants of paternal involvement in primiparous Swedish families. *International Journal of Behavioral Development, 11*, 433–449.

7. PATERNAL INVOLVEMENT IN SWEDEN

147

Lamb, M. E., & Levine, J. A. (1983). The Swedish parental insurance policy: An experiment in social engineering. In M. E. Lamb & A. Sagi (Eds.), *Fatherhood and family policy* (pp. 39–51). Hillsdale, NJ: Lawrence Erlbaum Associates.

Lamb, M. E., Pleck, & J. H., Charnov, E. L., (1985). Paternal behavior in humans. *American Zoologist, 25,* 883–894.

Lamb, M. E., Pleck, J. H., Charnov, E. L., & Levine, J. A. (1987). A biosocial perspective on paternal behavior and involvement. In J. B. Lancaster, J. Altman, & A. S. Rossi (Eds.), *Parenting across the lifespan: Biosocial perspectives* (pp. 11–42). New York: Academic Press.

Leslie, L. A., Anderson, E. A., & Branson, M. P. (1991). Responsibility for children: The role of gender and employment. *Journal of Family Issues, 12,* 197–210.

Levant, R. F., Slattery, S. C., & Loiselle, J. E. (1987). Fathers' involvement in housework and child care with school-aged daughters. *Family Relations, 36,* 152–157.

Lewis, C., Newson, F., & Newson, J. (1982). Father participation through childhood and its relation to career aspirations and delinquency. In N. Beail & J. McGuire (Eds.), *Fathers: Psychological perspectives* (pp. 171–193). London: Junction Books.

Marsiglio, W. (1991). Paternal engagement activities with minor children. *Journal of Marriage and the Family, 53,* 973–986.

Marsiglio, W., Amato, P. R., Day, R. D., & Lamb, M E. (2000). Scholarship in fatherhood in the 1990s and beyond. *Journal of Marriage and the Family, 62,* 1173–1191.

McBride, B. A., & Mills, G. (1993). A comparison of mother and father involvement on father involvement in child rearing. *Family Relations, 39,* 250–256.

NICHD Early Child Care Research Network (2000). Factors associated with fathers' caregiving activities and sensitivity with young children. *Journal of Family Psychology, 14,* 200–219.

Nock, S. L., & Kingston, P. W. (1988). Time with children: The impact of couples' work-time commitments. *Social Forces, 67,* 59–85.

O'Brien, M., & Jones, D. (1996). The absence and presence of fathers: Accounts from children's diaries. In U. Bjornberg & A. K. Kollind (Eds.), *Men's family relations,* (pp. xxx). Sweden: Göteborg University.

Parke, R. D. (1996). *Fatherhood.* Cambridge, MA: Harvard University Press.

Peterson, R. R., & Gerson, K. (1992). Determinants of responsibility for child care arrangements among dual-earner couples. *Journal of Marriage and the Family, 54,* 417–427.

Pleck, J. H. (1995). *Working wives, working husbands.* Beverly Hills, CA: Sage.

Pleck, J. H. (1997). Paternal involvement: Levels, sources, and consequences. In M. E. Lamb (Ed.), *The role of the father in child development* (3rd ed., pp. 66–103). New York: Wiley.

Pleck, J. H., Lamb, M. E., & Levine, J. A. (1985). Epilog: Facilitating future change in men's family roles. In R. A. Lewis & M. Sussman (Eds.), *Men's changing roles in the family* (pp. 11–16). New York: Haworth Press.

Pleck, J. H., & Pleck, J. H. (1997). Fatherhood ideals in the United States: Historical dimensions. In M. E. Lamb (Ed.), *The role of the father in child development* (3rd ed., pp. 33–48). New York: Wiley.

Pleck, J. H., & Staines, G. (1985). Work schedules and family life in two-earner couples. *Journal of Family Issues, 6,* 61–81.

Pleck, J. H., & Stueve, J. L. (2001). Time and paternal involvement. In K. Daly (Ed.), *Minding the time in family experience: Emerging perspectives and issues* (pp. 205–226). Oxford, UK: Elsevier Science.

Presser, H. B. (1986). Shift work among American women and child care. *Journal of Marriage and the Family, 48,* 551–563.

Presser, H. B. (1988). Shift work and child care among young dual-earner American parents. *Journal of Marriage and the Family, 50,* 133–148.

Presser, H. B. (1989). Can we make time for children? The economy, work schedules, and child care. *Demography, 26,* 523–543.

Radin, N. (1981). The role of the father in cognitive, academic, and intellectual development. In M. E. Lamb (Ed.), *The role of the father in child development* (pp. 379–428). New York: Wiley.

Radin, N. (1982). Primary caregiving and role-sharing fathers. In M. E. Lamb (Ed.), *Nontraditional families: Parenting and child development* (pp. 173–204). Hillsdale, NJ: Lawrence Erlbaum Associates.

Radin, N. (1988). Primary caregiving fathers of long duration. In P. Bronstein & C. P. Cowan (Eds.), *Fatherhood today: Men's changing role in the family* (pp. 127–143). New York: Wiley.

Radin, N. (1994). Primary-caregiver fathers in intact families. In A. E. Gottfried & A. W. Gottfried (Eds.), *Redefining families: Implications for children's development* (pp. 55–97). New York: Plenum.

Radin, N., & Goldsmith, R. (1985). Caregiving fathers of preschoolers: Four years later. *Merrill-Palmer Quarterly, 31,* 375–383.

Robinson, J. P. (1977). *How Americans use time: A socio-psychological analyses.* New York: Praeger.

Roopnarine, J. L., & Ahmeduzzaman, M. (1993). Puerto Rican fathers' involvement with their preschool-age children. *Hispanic Journal of Behavioral Science,* 96–107.

Russell, G. (1982). Shared-caregiving families: An Australian study. In M. E. Lamb (Ed.), *Nontraditional families: Parenting and child development* (pp. 139–171). Hillsdale, NJ: Lawrence Erlbaum Associates.

Russell, G. (1983). *The changing role of fathers?* Brisbane, Australia: University of Queensland Press.

Smith, H. L., & Morgan, S. P (1994). Children's closeness to father as reported by mothers, sons, and daughters: Evaluating subjective assessments with the Rasch Model. *Journal of Family Issues, 15,* 3–29.

Staines, G. L., Pleck, J. H. (1983). *The impact of work schedules on the family.* Ann Arbor, MI: Institute for Social Research.

Steward, R. R., Yeatts, D. E., & Zottarelli, L. K. (2002). Parental leave and father involvement in child care: Sweden and the United States. *Journal of Comparative Family Studies, 33,* 287—299.

Tulananda, O., Young, D. M., & Roopnarine, J. L. (1994). Thai and American fathers' involvement with preschool-age children. *Early Child Development and Care, 97,* 64–66.

8

A Multimethod Study of Father Participation in Family-Based Programming

Stephen Gavazzi
Ohio State University

Angie Schock
California State University, Northridge

PURPOSE OF THE CHAPTER

This chapter seeks to accomplish two major goals related to the overall purpose of this book. The first goal concerns the further reconceptualization of father involvement to include the topic of paternal participation in family-based programming. We believe that a greater understanding of the factors that predict whether fathers will participate in a family-based program will shed further light on how fathers more universally choose to become involved in various aspects of family life. The second goal of this chapter is the advancement of multimethod efforts to generate empirical information on fathers and families. The use of qualitative methods in conjunction with the gathering of quantitative data will help connect the specific voices of fathers to the information that can be inferred about fathers more generally in this area of inquiry.

From these efforts, the reader will be exposed to a variety of issues that are thought to impact the literature concerned with father participation in family-based programming. At the same time, the impact of the reported findings is believed to be more widespread, having the potential to influence the theoretical, empirical, and intervention-based work of the larger literature on fathers and families and beyond.

Although the emerging literature on fathers' participation in family-based programming has begun to examine the relationship between paternal participation rates and several family-specific, father-specific, and program-specific characteristics, research in this area remains limited and is considerably less developed than the existing data on mother characteristics and maternal participation in family programs (Lengua et al., 1992; Meyers, 1993). To a large extent, limitations in this area are due to the notion that fathers are more removed from family matters and hence less likely than mothers to become involved in various aspects of parenting their adolescents (Phares & Compas, 1992). However, current research may have neglected to consider certain unique factors contributing to fathers' decisions to become involved in family programming.

In this chapter, we attempt to reconceptualize the notion that fathers are less involved in family-based programs through both the identification of factors that are related to fathers' participation levels and the examination of reasons given by fathers as to how they choose to participate in family-based programming. In addition, we incorporate a multimethod approach to study fathers' participation in the program: A quantitative study was conducted to identify variables related to levels of paternal participation throughout the program; and a qualitative study was conducted to give a voice to fathers regarding the issues that contributed to their decision to participate in family-based programming.

More specifically, the first study examines the relationship among several family demographic variables, father characteristics, father's perceptions, adolescent-reported variables, and levels of paternal participation in a diversion program targeting court-involved adolescents and their families. This first study extends the current literature by focusing on fathers' differential levels of participation in an intervention program for at-risk adolescents. The second study employs a qualitative methodology to further investigate (a) specific factors contributing to the father's decision to be involved in the family-based diversion program and (b) reasons why fathers, in general, may be less likely than mothers to participate in family-based programming. This second study enhances our understanding of fathers' involvement in programming by allowing fathers to voice unique factors that influenced their decision to participate in a family-based program.

Additionally, the second study utilizes a purposeful sampling procedure to ensure perspectives from a diverse group of fathers from different ethnic backgrounds and family structures, obtains the father's perception of the severity of his adolescent's problem behaviors to supplement the adolescent's reports (in those cases in which the adolescent's reports are available, i.e., participating adolescents), and utilizes reports of the father's own past use of services to supplement the family's reported use of resources assessed in the first study. Finally, the chapter concludes with a discussion that outlines implications for future research and enhanced program delivery based on the data generated thus far.

FATHERS AND ADOLESCENT WELL-BEING

As noted throughout this book, the role of the father in the family increasingly has been the focal point of studies conducted by family researchers in the latter part of the twentieth century, particularly due to several social changes that have occurred over the past two decades, such as the increased (a) number of women employed outside of the home, (b) number of father-absent families, and (c) awareness of new types of fathers, extending beyond traditional, biological fathers, to include stepfathers, cohabitating fathers, gay fathers, young fathers, and low-income fathers (Tamis-LeMonda & Cabrera, 1999). In addition, significant legislative initiatives (e.g., paternity establishment, custody laws, parental leave) and national research initiatives (e.g., Early Head Start Evaluation, Fragile Families and Child Well-Being) have been launched to purposefully include fathers and their contributions to the family as a primary focus (Tamis-LeMonda & Cabrera, 1999).

However, one area of research that has been neglected is the father's contribution to his adolescent's problematic functioning and our understanding of the characteristics of the father–adolescent dyad in the context of adolescent dysfunction (Dadds, 1995; Phares, 1999; Phares & Compas, 1992). Specifically, Phares (1997) notes that research on maternal contributions (primarily *negative* contributions) far outweighs the study of paternal contributions and that "mother blaming reflects the tendency to consider and investigate maternal contributions to the development of psychopathology in children while not considering or investigating paternal contributions to the same phenomena" (p. 262). In addition, Phares and Compas (1992) identified several possible explanations for the limited focus on fathers, including the notions that children have less frequent contact with their fathers and that fathers are less willing or able to participate in therapy and research studies.

Recently, though, studies have emerged that concentrate on the fathers' influence on those adolescents who exhibit various forms of dysfunction that reflect internalizing behaviors such as depression (Cole & McPherson, 1993; Sheeber, Hops, Andrews, Alpert, & Davis, 1998; Weller et al., 1994), as well as externalizing behaviors such as delinquency and conduct disorder (Conger and Conger, 1994; Frick et al., 1992; Henggeler, Edwards, & Bourdin, 1987). Hence, these studies have begun to examine salient paternal mental health factors and characteristics of the father–adolescent dyad that impact the development and continuance of adolescent dysfunction of both internalizing and externalizing phenomena. Further research in this area undoubtedly will assist theorists, clinicians, and researchers interested in reformulating the erroneous notion that fathers do not play a significant role in their adolescent's mental health.

FATHERS AND FAMILY PROGRAMMING

At the same time, family scholars and practitioners have noticed the particular promise of family-based prevention and intervention programs to ameliorate adolescent problematic behaviors including depression (Asarnow, Jaycox, & Tompson, 2001; Burns, Hoagwood, & Mrazek, 1999; Fristad, Gavazzi, & Soldano, 1998), disruptive behaviors (Burns, Hoagwood, & Mrazek, 1999; Molgaard, Spoth, & Redmond, 2000), and substance use (Kumpfer & Tait, 2000). Unfortunately, maternal involvement in family-based programs has been discussed in the literature to a much greater extent than fathers' participation, largely because of men's lower rates of participation in programming (Klitzner, Bamberger, & Gruenewald, 1990; Lengua et al., 1992).

Initial work on paternal participation in programming primarily consisted of theoretical arguments and personal commentaries on how to increase paternal involvement in various forms of family-based programs (Carr, 1998; Hecker, 1991). Often based on clinical anecdote alone, family therapists have suggested numerous ways that fathers can be drawn into therapeutic endeavors, such as consulting with fathers on what changes they want for the family, as well as considering the unique ways in which many men communicate and cope with family problems (Carr, 1998; Hecker, 1991).

Although this information is useful, the systematic empirical study of how to maximize recruitment and retention that incorporates the fathers' and other family members' views of the father's role in treatment is warranted. In fact, research in this area must continue to evolve toward a greater understanding of such critical matters as (a) important pragmatic concerns that serve as barriers to paternal involvement, (b) which types of fathers are more likely to participate in programming, and (c) how fathers' perceptions of their role in their adolescent's condition influence their decisions to participate in family programs. Findings revealed through this type of focused research can enhance our knowledge of why some fathers do, in fact, participate in family programming while others do not and will correct the erroneous view that fathers are essentially uninvolved in programs for problematic adolescents and their families. In addition, empirical studies that incorporate quantitative measures serve as tools for obtaining valuable data directly from large samples of diverse father figures.

Pragmatic Issues

Having studied the literature on fathers and child development, Meyers (1993) proposed several changes that must occur to increase male participation in family programs. One area of change encompasses structural or pragmatic issues related to programming. For example, the strategic distribution of recruitment materials and program information directly to the father, the offering of programs at convenient times and locations for the father, and the enlistment of male group discussants and

8. FAMILY-BASED PROGRAMMING

members all should be incorporated into the structure of the program to enhance paternal participation.

Additional research on various types and formats of resource/service needs of fathers has expanded on Meyers' contentions. For example, in a study of fathers of developmentally disabled children, Hadadian and Merbler (1995) gathered data from 189 urban and rural fathers pertaining to needs/information that would assist them in improving their role as caregiver for their child. Responses showed that fathers preferred specific formats and types of services that included receiving specific information about the child's condition in the forms of films, tapes, and parent newsletters. Another study of barriers to participation in an intervention aiming to prevent mental health problems and substance use among youth gathered focus-group data from difficult-to-reach families, of which one group was specifically convened to include only fathers (Lengua et al., 1992). Group responses cited the provision of childcare and refreshments as ways in which the program would be viewed as more attractive by fathers, who by and large had reported very low levels of interest in their participation in a parent-training program.

Spoth and colleagues (Spoth & Redmond, 1992; Spoth, Redmond, Hockaday, & Shin, 1996) also conducted research focusing on pragmatic barriers to participation in family-based preventions and interventions targeting adolescents at-risk for engaging in substance abuse. Brief telephone interviews and mail questionnaires were completed by families who did not choose to participate in the project. These nonparticipants were asked a series of questions related to reasons for participation refusal. Although the majority of the data consisted of maternal reports, analyses of the reasons for nonparticipation revealed that scheduling conflicts/lack of time, length of project commitment, and general privacy issues all contributed to their decision of participation refusal. Notably, fathers were significantly more likely than mothers to report concerns with privacy issues as a reason for refusal (Spoth et al., 1996).

To expand our understanding of the pragmatic issues related to paternal participation rates in family-based programs, we should obtain detailed questionnaire data directly from the fathers. Also, this area of research could be strengthened by incorporating a qualitative methodology in order to capture any and all issues that fathers may raise and discuss as barriers to their participation and that may not have been included on a brief questionnaire with a limited number of items.

Predictors of Father Participation

In addition to pragmatic issues regarding program delivery that have been cited in the literature, variables related to family demographics, father characteristics, and fathers' perceptions (of their offspring, the program's applicability, and their parenting competence) also have been identified as factors likely to predict paternal participation in family programs.

154   GAVAZZI AND SCHOCK

Family Demographics. Several family demographic variables have been investigated in relation to fathers and their participation in programming. For example, Gavidia-Payne and Stoneman (1997) examined the predictive ability of family income on fathers' involvement in an intervention program for their severely developmentally disabled children, finding that financially secure fathers were most likely to participate in such a program. Spoth and colleagues found that fathers in families with lower socioeconomic status (SES) were more likely to cite privacy and research-related concerns (i.e., discussing family issues with others and completing interviews/questionnaires) as reasons for participation refusal. These findings suggest that fathers in low SES families may be much more wary of family program initiatives and may require different strategies for recruitment than do more economically advantaged fathers (Spoth et al., 1996).

In addition, Lengua and colleagues (1992) found that parents from middle-class, two-parent families were more willing to participate in their focus groups on barriers to program participation of high-risk families than were lower income, single-headed families. (It should be noted, though, that this finding was presented for overall *family* income levels in the study, and that the mean income level of the father-only focus group was average in relation to the other focus-group partici-pant's family incomes.) The authors offer several explanations for this disparity, such as lower income families were less knowledgeable regarding their child's needs, less aware of the important influence of parenting on their child's devel-opment, more likely to cite location/transportation problems, and more likely to have an unfounded suspicion that law enforcement agencies may be involved.

Clearly, family demographic data can help identify which fathers from unique family situations will choose to participate in certain types of family programs. However, it will be important to supplement these findings with additional research strategies that permit the formulation of explanations based on these findings, such as qualitative research methodologies that can elicit more detailed, in-depth information from fathers.

Father Characteristics. Certain characteristics of the father have been re-ported to be related to paternal participation in family programs, especially the father's level of education and his prior use of parenting resources. For instance, Spoth and colleagues reported that the father's educational level was a predictor of his agreement to be videotaped as a requirement of his involvement in a family skills intervention program (Spoth & Redmond, 1992; Spoth et al., 1996); that is, less educated fathers were more likely to refuse participation because of privacy issues related to the videotaping of interactions with their adolescents. In a related study, Spoth and colleagues examined a model of predictor variables influencing parents' inclination to participate in (a) the initial project assessment and then (b) the subsequent intervention in the same family-based program mentioned pre-viously. Again, findings showed that higher levels of educational attainment and higher levels of family income were related to increased assessment participation;

8. FAMILY-BASED PROGRAMMING

but only a higher level of education was related to actual increased participation in the intervention. Although nearly 70 percent (68.9%) of the 1,192 parents surveyed were mothers and no comparative analyses were conducted between mothers and fathers, it appears that educational attainment is a parental characteristic that is consistently predictive of program participation, both at the initial assessment and subsequent intervention stages.

Additionally, in another study involving the same sample, Spoth and Redmond (1995) tested a model of family context factors and health beliefs in predicting inclination to enroll in parenting skills programs. Findings showed that a positive effect of past parenting resource use, such as reading newspaper/magazine articles about parenting and participating in parenting skills programs, was related to perceived program benefits and inclination to enroll in a future intervention program if one were offered. Although this study failed to provide information regarding father-specific findings, it seems reasonable to infer that mothers and fathers who typically partake in activities to improve their parenting skills are more likely to consider involvement in a proposed parenting program as well as to cite the program as a useful source of information and worthy of their time commitment.

The study of father characteristics and program participation helps to reformulate the notion that fathers are largely uninvolved in interventions targeting their adolescents. However, as researchers continue to gather information on fathers who are likely to participate in family programs, it will also be important to study the characteristics of those fathers who refused participation and to examine the relationship between paternal variables and fathers' differential levels of involvement throughout the duration of the program offering (e.g., total number of sessions attended).

Fathers' Perceptions. Fathers' attitudes toward the condition of their adolescent, program characteristics, and their own parenting competence also have been examined in relation to how these perceptions are linked to program participation. For example, the father's perception of the existence and severity of the adolescent's problem behavior has been identified as a predictor of his program participation. Specifically, fathers who report that their adolescent is not at risk for the negative behaviors that the intervention is focusing on or that the intervention would not be useful to their family are not as likely to participate in the program (Lengua et al., 1992; Spoth & Redmond, 1992; Spoth, Redmond, Kahn, & Shin, 1997). Lengua and colleagues (1992) emphasize that the parent's view of his or her teen's susceptibility for developing a drug/alcohol problem was the most salient attitudinal difference found between mothers and fathers in the focus groups. Specifically, fathers, more often than mothers, expressed the belief that teen drug and alcohol abuse was a problem for society (e.g., within the political and legal systems), whereas mothers recognized substance abuse to be an immediate problem for their communities and families. Consequently, these fathers showed little interest in a parenting skills program curriculum involving this topic.

Extending these findings, paternal reports of perceived intervention benefits and perceived barriers to participation were found to be associated with the actual completion of an initial assessment phase of a family-focused prevention/intervention project (Spoth et al., 1997). In particular, fathers who believed that (a) eight parenting-skills-building topics in the program would not be useful to them and (b) certain barriers (e.g., needing child care, lengthy traveling distance to the meetings, having to pay 20 dollars for the program manual) existed for them were less likely to participate in the project assessment. However, it is noteworthy that these two paternal perceptions did not significantly predict actual participation in the intervention. Thus, the authors contend that these variables should be assessed in greater depth (beyond a limited number of 3-point likert type items) along with other factors that may be related to complete program involvement in all stages of the intervention.

One study to date has examined the potential link between the father's view of his own parenting competency and program participation (Spoth, Redmon, Haggerty, & Ward, 1995). To assess parental self-competence, the authors used an eight-item measure of parents' beliefs regarding their ability to perform certain types of parenting behaviors being targeted in a parenting-skills intervention to prevent adolescent conduct problems and substance abuse. Results revealed that the parental competence score was positively related to intervention attendance, yet this association was stronger for mothers than for fathers. Thus, findings that highlight the significant association between fathers' individual views and their participation rates especially emphasize the need to employ qualitative methodologies that can aid in uncovering fathers' personal beliefs through in-depth conversations, in conjunction with detailed quantitative measures inclusive of items that address fathers' perspectives on various topics (e.g., fathering skills/competency, program characteristics).

Summary

Although there is very little research on paternal involvement in family interventions, the literature suggests several variables that may be related to fathers' participation. These issues include the following:

- *Pragmatic/Structural Program Issues*: Scheduling matters, the provision of practical materials and services, and privacy-related concerns have all been related to paternal participation.
- *Family Demographics*: Married parents (versus nonmarried, coresidential couples) and higher levels of household income have been associated with higher participation rates.
- *Father Characteristics*: Higher educational levels and past experiences with any family-based interventions/services have been associated with higher participation rates.

8. FAMILY-BASED PROGRAMMING

- *Father's Perceptions*: The father's perception of greater severity problem behaviors of his offspring; the father's positive expectations for the program and the belief in the program's applicability to the family's situation; and the father's positive view of his parenting competency have been associated with higher participation rates.

Limitations

As the literature on factors related to father participation in family-based programming is emerging, current studies suffer from several limitations. These shortcomings can be classified into two areas: limits regarding the samples of families included in the studies, and limits regarding the research methodology that has been used in extant research.

Sample Limits. Families that have been included in the study of fathers' participation in programming have been restricted to a narrow group of fathers. First, paternal involvement in family programming has largely focused on fathers of preschool and elementary-school-age children, yielding much less information on fathers of *adolescents*. Second, there is very little knowledge about the father's role in *interventions* for youth who are exhibiting problematic and/or unhealthy behavior, as most of the literature has focused on the father's participation in prevention programming. Third, as teen problem severity has been "measured" only by the father's perception of the problem behaviors, it would be valuable to obtain the *adolescent's own report* of his or her symptomology in addition to the father's perspective. Fourth, as paternal participation has simply been classified as those fathers who did participate versus those fathers who did not, fathers' *differential levels of participation* (e.g., number of program sessions attended) should be assessed. Fifth, samples have been limited to two-parent, married, Caucasian families; there has been no study of *nonresidential and/or nontraditional fathers* from different ethnic backgrounds. This fifth limitation is especially problematic to the study of families with at-risk adolescents, as many of these youth do not reside in intact households. Therefore, there is a need to focus on fathers' involvement in the treatment of adolescent problem behaviors that includes ethnically diverse fathers from various family structures.

Methodological Limits. Within the limited number of studies that have investigated fathers and family programming, the common methodology has been the collection of brief, questionnaire data. Furthermore, information on factors related to fathers' participation has consisted mainly of mother's reports of simple demographic data on the family and/or limited-item self-report instruments assessing barriers. For example, Spoth and colleagues (1996) obtained a limited amount of sociodemographic measurements from white, rural families and also asked

parents (usually mothers) to rate how important potential participation barriers were on a three-point scale. Fathers were largely underrepresented, and neither mothers nor fathers were permitted to generate their own responses to the question of which barriers were specifically related to their participation. Thus, existing studies failed to incorporate the father's perspective of his role, including his view of individual barriers related to his level of participation, in family programming. In addition, research has only begun to identify correlates to fathers' participation, with no clear understanding of the detailed decision-making process and the factors that influence the father's decision to participate in programming. Specifically, there is a need to expand existing research by utilizing methods beyond single-item surveys to identify *why fathers of certain demographic groups choose to participate or fail to participate in family-based programming*.

EMPIRICAL WORK

We now present findings from two studies intended to expand our understanding of factors related to father involvement in a diversion program for the families of juvenile offenders who have been seen by the juvenile courts for delinquent acts, truancy, or incorrigible/unruly behaviors. Specifically, the first study examines the relationship between several family demographic variables, father characteristics, father's perceptions, and adolescent-reported variables and levels of paternal participation in the family diversion program. The second study uses a qualitative methodology to further investigate (a) specific factors contributing to the father's decision to be involved in the diversion program and (b) reasons why fathers, in general, may be less likely than mothers to participate in family-based programming.

The Family-Based Program

Both of the studies utilize data gathered from families who were referred to the Growing Up FAST: Families and Adolescents Surviving and Thriving Program (Gavazzi, 1995; Gavazzi, Wasserman, Partridge, & Sheridan, 2000), a diversion program that targets families of adolescents engaged in delinquent acts, truancy, or incorrigible/unruly behaviors (Gavazzi, Yarcheck, Wasserman, & Partridge, 2000). The main purpose of this family-based program is to strengthen the family's ability to recognize and support the adolescent's developmental needs in negotiating his or her way through the transition to a healthy, successful adult (Gavazzi & Law, 1997; Law & Gavazzi, 1999; Wasserman et al., 1999). Adolescents referred to the Growing Up FAST Program by court officials typically are first- and second-time misdemeanant or status offenders, although versions of this program exist that target more serious juvenile offenders and their families (Gavazzi, Rhine, & Partridge, in press; Partridge, Gavazzi, & Rhine, 2001).

8. FAMILY-BASED PROGRAMMING

159

Within 1 week of the time of referral, the family receives a phone call from the program's intake interviewer, and after an initial screening, the program facilitator schedules an initial assessment appointment with the family. Families who neglect to return more than two phone messages or who neglect to attend more than one scheduled appointment receive letters of inquiry regarding their continued interest. If there is no response to the letter, the family is terminated from the program and the court is informed. During the initial assessment appointment, family members complete an assessment battery that includes demographic information and measurements of family functioning, social supports/community resources, parental mental health symptoms, and the adolescent's risk behaviors. In addition, the family agrees to participate in two follow-up phone interviews: The first interview is conducted 2 weeks after the last in-person contact with the family; the second interview is conducted 6 months following the first interview. Further, a subsample of fathers are contacted during and following their participation (or decision to not participate) and invited to be involved in the postparticipation interviews, which were conducted in the second study discussed in this chapter.

STUDY #1

The goal of the first study was to examine salient variables expected to be related to father involvement in a family-based diversion program for at-risk adolescents and to further the current literature by focusing on fathers' *differential levels of participation* in an *intervention* program for at-risk *adolescents*. Analysis of the quantitative data gathered from families who were referred to the Growing Up FAST Program was conducted on questionnaire data that was classified into four categories: family demographic variables, father characteristics, father's perceptions, and adolescent-reported variables. *Family demographic variables* included family structure, household income, and the family's past use of community services/resources. *Father characteristics* included age, ethnicity, average amount of time per week spent at his place of employment. *Father's perceptions* included the father's report on the problem-solving subscale of the Family Assessment Device (FAD; Epstein, Baldwin, & Bishop, 1983). *Adolescent-reported variables* included the adolescent's age, gender, and the severity and nature of his or her problem behaviors.

Sample

Data were collected from 78 fathers of adolescents (45 males, 33 females; mean age, 14.7 years) who had been referred to the Growing Up FAST Program. The mean age of the sample of fathers was 42.8 years, and the sample was predominantly Caucasian: White, 84.6%; Black, 10.3%; Hispanic, 2.6%; Asian, 1.3%;

other, 1.3%. The percentages of fathers' reports on their present family structure were as follows: Married, biological parents, 42.3%; single-mother headed, 5.1%; single-father headed, 17.9%; stepfamily, 25.6%; other, 9.0%. The fathers' residential status (as indicated by the family members in attendance at the time of the initial assessment appointment) was reported to be 68 residential fathers and 10 nonresidential fathers. Annual household incomes ranged from $15,000 to $100,000 or more, with over half (53.9%) of the total household incomes falling in the $45,000 to $99,000 range.

All fathers in this sample attended the initial assessment appointment and completed a series of questionnaires prior to their participation (or nonparticipation) in the first session of the GFAST Program. The fathers completed the Brief Symptom Inventory (BSI) and the FAD; the adolescents completed the BSI; and the family (father, adolescent, and mother, when present) collaboratively answered the Child and Adolescent Services Assessment (CASA) questionnaire and responded to a demographic questionnaire.

Instruments

BSI. The Brief Symptom Inventory is a brief self-report form of the Psychiatric Symptoms Checklist-90 that assesses symptomology and current mental health functioning (Derogatis & Melisaratos, 1983). Respondents rate the degree to which they have felt distressed, bothered, or worried about a list of problems during the past few months on a likert-type scale (1 = not at all to 5 = extremely). The BSI includes 53 items that are scored on nine symptomology dimensions: somatization, obsessive compulsive, interpersonal sensitivity, paranoid ideation, depression, anxiety, hostility, phobia, and psychotocism.

CASA. The Child and Adolescent Services Assessment (Ascher, Farmer, Burns, & Angold, 1996) is a questionnaire completed by the entire family that asks members to report on their previous utilization of services that provide help to families. The CASA includes 12 categories of services: psychiatric, juvenile justice system, out-of-home placements, day treatments, home-based services, private practice, school-based services, social/children's services, religious services, volunteer services, family help, and other services.

FAD. Fathers also completed the problem-solving subscale of the Family Assessment Device (Epstein et al., 1983). Fathers identified how well they agreed with five questions that described the family's problem-solving strategies.

Demographic Questionnaire. A questionnaire was constructed to assess fathers' reports of demographic information pertaining to the family (family structure, household income, and number of household arrests), the father (age,

8. FAMILY-BASED PROGRAMMING 161

ethnicity, occupation/hours spent at work per week, residential status, relationship to adolescent, and his own relationship status), and the adolescent (age, ethnicity, last grade completed, and prior offense data).

Program Participation. Paternal program participation was operationalized by the number of sessions that the father attended in the GFAST program beyond the initial assessment appointment. Fathers' level of involvement was classified into three groups: low involvement = 0–1 sessions ($n = 24$); medium involvement = 2 sessions ($n = 30$); and higher involvement = 3 sessions ($n = 24$).

Data Analyses

Each analysis that was conducted tested for a significant relationship between the independent variable (level of paternal program participation) and the targeted dependent variable. A one-way analysis of variances (ANOVA) was performed for each of the dependent variables classified as continuous variables (BSI, CASA, and FAD scores); the categorical variables (father's age, ethnicity, residential status, relationship to the adolescent, current relationship status, and average amount of time per week spent at his place of employment; the adolescent's age, gender, and ethnicity; the family structure; and household income) were analyzed using a chi-square test for independence.

Results

One significant relationship was found between the family demographic variables and fathers' participation. Total scores on the CASA were associated with program participation, such that fathers who reported using a greater number of past services for their adolescent were more likely to complete a greater number of GFAST sessions, $F(2, 63) = 3.223$, $p < .05$.

Although none of the father characteristics proved to be significantly related to participation, the father's perception of the family's problem-solving skills was found to be significantly related to program participation. Total scores on the FAD problem-solving subscale were associated with program participation, such that fathers who reported poorer family problem-solving abilities were more likely to complete a greater number of GFAST sessions, $F(2, 77) = 5.484$, $p < .01$.

Of the adolescent-reported variables, one variable was found to be related to program participation. The severity of the adolescent's psychological symptoms, as assessed by the adolescent's report on the BSI, was related to fathers' participation. Specifically, adolescents' higher scores on 5 of the 9 BSI subscales (indicating higher symptomology levels) were significantly related to greater levels of fathers' program participation: somatization, $F(2, 58) = 5.070$, $p < .01$; paranoid

ideation, $F(2, 58) = 4.580$, $p < .05$; anxiety, $F(2, 58) = 3.959$, $p < .05$; hostility, $F(2, 58) = 8.843$, $p < .001$, and phobia, $F(2, 58) = 3.356$, $p < .05$.

Summary

Consistent with previous research, a higher level of paternal participation in the family-based program was significantly related to the fathers' reports of greater use of past family services, the father's perception of poorer family problem-solving skills, and more severe problem behaviors reported by the adolescent. In addition, fathers who completed a greater number of sessions were likely to be residential, married, biological fathers. These findings lend support to past studies and extend the research by operationalizing paternal participation in the program by including the high-medium-and low-level classifications of involvement. As other researchers have noted (e.g., McCurdy & Daro, 2001; Spoth, Redmond, Kahn & Shin, 1997), it is important to investigate predictors of father involvement at the initial assessment and throughout the levels/sessions of the program to better understand factors contributing to fathers' attrition rates. However, it would also be useful to obtain information on the father's view of the severity of his adolescent's problem behaviors and the father's individual past use of family resources/programs. Hence, the present study is limited in that it fails to obtain a comprehensive analysis of the reasons/factors that influence the father's decision to participate or not participate in programming. Specifically, there is a need to expand existing research by utilizing methods beyond limited-item surveys to identify *why* fathers of certain demographic groups choose to participate or fail to participate in family-based programming.

STUDY #2

Rationale for a Qualitative Study

To date, there is no in-depth research that examines fathers' subjective decision-making processes regarding their involvement in family programming. Therefore, a qualitative methodology, using a grounded-theory approach (i.e., theory that emerges from the data and is analyzed throughout the research process; Strauss & Corbin, 1994), was conducted in the second study to inductively identify important concepts and develop theory from interview data to yield a more profound understanding of factors that influence paternal participation. A central characteristic of grounded theory, similar to other qualitative approaches, is the assertion that the participants in the study identify salient issues by prescribing meaning to certain experiences in their lives. It is the researcher's main task, then, to interpret and build theory based on, or grounded in, these meaningful experiences. Stated another way, Strauss and Corbin (1994) contend that, "Interpretations must

8. FAMILY-BASED PROGRAMMING

include the perspectives and voices of the people whom we study... Interpretations are sought for understanding the actions of individual or collective actors being studied" (p. 274).

Grounded theory also differs from other qualitative methods in several ways, but most notably by the concept that theory is developed throughout the research process and is directly drawn from the data. In other words, unlike other qualitative analytic techniques that impose a certain perspective on the data during analysis (e.g., feminist theory), grounded theorists have no a priori assumptions and let theory emerge from the data. A grounded-theory methodology is appropriately used in the second study because (a) the study is exploratory and represents a new area of inquiry, (b) the study's objective focuses on discovering the details of fathers' decision-making processes and thus denotes a research area that is difficult to assess with quantitative methods, and (c) no preconceived theory will be forced upon the data, but rather the data will inform and guide theory development (Stern, 1980; Strauss & Corbin, 1994).

Sample

The sample consisted of fathers of adolescents who were invited to participate in the GFAST family-based diversion program described earlier. Consistent with recent research that acknowledges numerous types of father figures, such as stepfathers, cohabiting fathers, adopted fathers, and other surrogate fathers (e.g., uncles, grandfathers) (Tamis-LeMonda & Cabrera, 1999), the second study utilized a very broadly defined classification of "father" within the sample. Specifically, all men who considered themselves to be significant parental figures in the adolescent's life were permitted to participate in the study.

A total of 20 fathers from families who were referred to the family-based diversion program were included in this study. The 20 fathers were selected by using a purposeful sampling procedure (Strauss & Corbin, 1998). Purposeful sampling, or theoretical sampling, refers to the intentional selection of participants to maximize the variety of experiences shared regarding the research topic under investigation (Bogdan & Biklen, 1998; Strauss & Corbin, 1998). This method was used (a) to ensure representation of descriptive, multiple perspectives from a diverse sample of fathers, (b) to allow for cross-case analyses of the data based on certain descriptive variables, and (c) with consideration of the availability/limited contact with ethnically diverse families referred to the GFAST program. Thus, the sample of fathers was strategically selected to represent a diverse group of men, so that fathers of male and female adolescents displaying a range of behavioral problems and fathers from different ethnicities, family structures, and educational levels would be recruited to participate in the study.

Participating Fathers. Data were collected from 10 fathers of adolescents (5 males, 5 females; mean age, 15.2 years; age ranges: 2 adolescents aged

164   GAVAZZI AND SCHOCK

11–13 years, 3 adolescents aged 14–15 years, 5 adolescents aged 16–18 years)
who *had participated* in at least one program session. The mean age of the fathers was 43.3 years (ages ranged from 32 to 56), and the fathers' ethnic backgrounds were as follows: Caucasian, 6; African-American, 3; Native-American,
1. The fathers' reports on their family structure at the time of the adolescent's
referral were as follows: single-father headed, 3; married, biological parents, 3;
stepfamily, residential father, 2; stepfamily, nonresidential father, 1; single-mother
headed, 1. Annual household incomes ranged from $15,000 to $100,000 or more:
$15–$25,000, 2; $25–$35,000, 1; $45–$55,000, 1; $55–$100,000, 4; $100,000 or
more, 2.

Nonparticipating Fathers.   Data were also collected from 10 fathers of adolescents (1 male, 9 females; mean age, 15.2 years; age ranges: 1 adolescent aged
11–13 years, 5 adolescents aged 14–15 years, 4 adolescents aged 16–18 years)
who *had not participated* in any program sessions. The mean age of the fathers
was 46.4 years (ages ranged from 37 to 72), and the fathers' ethnicity backgrounds
were as follows: Caucasian, 8; African-American, 2. The fathers' reports on their
family structure at the time of the adolescent's referral were as follows: single-
father headed, 2; married, biological parents, 2; stepfamily, residential father, 1;
stepfamily, nonresidential father, 1; single-mother headed, 2; other, 2. Annual
household incomes ranged from $15,000 to $100,000 or more: $15–$25,000, 1;
$25–$35,000, 1; $35–$45,000, 4; $45–$55,000, 1; $55–$100,000, 3.

All 20 fathers in this sample attended the initial assessment appointment and
completed a series of questionnaires prior to their participation (or nonparticipation) in the first session of the GFAST Program.

Procedure

After determination of the father's participation group status, initial contact was
made with the fathers by telephone calls to describe the study and answer any
immediate questions. Also during the telephone contacts, the primary investigator
scheduled a time for the interview with those fathers who expressed a willingness to
participate. Follow-up phone calls were made, when necessary, with those fathers
who wished to think about their decision or needed to verify scheduling availability.

Semi-Structured Interviews.   The face-to-face interviews, which were conducted by the primary investigator in a university conference room, lasted 60–75
minutes. The questions focused on influential factors associated with the fathers'
decisions to participate in the family-based program. It was anticipated that the
interview protocols (one for participating fathers; one for nonparticipants) would
be loosely followed across interviews in order to allow for fathers' responses to
transpire and guide the dialogue during the interview process. Accordingly, the

8. FAMILY-BASED PROGRAMMING 165

primary investigator would choose to revise or expand the interview protocols with the identification of new areas of inquiry that emerged during ongoing analysis of the collected data (Strauss & Corbin, 1998).

For the initial interviews, a set of research questions and probes were reserved by the interviewer to guide the dialogue if necessary. However, as expected, fathers' experiences transpired during the interview and salient factors/issues related to participation were further explored in subsequent data collection efforts. Consistent with qualitative interviewing strategies, Strauss and Corbin (1998) offer the following suggestion:

> Initial interview questions or areas of observation might be based on concepts derived from literature or experience, or better still, from preliminary fieldwork. Because these early concepts have not evolved from 'real' data, if the researcher carries them with him or her into the field, then they must be considered provisional and discarded as data begin to come in. Nevertheless, early concepts often provide a departure point from which to begin data collection ... (p. 205).

The semi-structured interview protocols addressed the following research topics or themes:

1. How have previous experiences with prior family-based programming/ services influenced the father's perception of his present role in the adolescent's treatment?
2. How might the father's perception of the program's value and/or applicability to his adolescent's condition be related to his decision to participate?
3. What potential barriers/facilitators to participation, within and outside of the family, exist for the father?
4. What unique skills or characteristics does the father feel that he possesses *as a father* that can help the family cope with the adolescent's problematic behavior? Also, in what ways could the father improve his relationship with his adolescent?
5. How could a family intervention that target's their family's special needs be further developed/modified to maximize fathers' participation? What would this program look like?

Demographic Questionnaire. Demographic data from all fathers who are referred to the Growing Up FAST Program are collected at the initial assessment appointment. Thus, when this information was available, reports of demographic information pertaining to the family, the father, and the adolescent were obtained for this study. However, to ensure current and correct demographic information from the fathers in this second study, a brief questionnaire was verbally administered to the fathers immediately following the face-to-face interviews.

Data Analysis

All interviews were audiotaped and fully transcribed at a later time, post-interview. The verbatim transcripts were entered into a word processing program and served as the major source of data to be analyzed. Initially, the primary investigator handcoded the transcripts using paper and pencil methods, and a codebook was constructed, revised, and used throughout the data analysis to record emerging concepts and subcategories. In addition, the use of the computer program NVivo (NUDIST Version 5) assisted in data management and subsequent analyses of the interview text.

Procedures for investigating the data consisted of ongoing content analyses used to identify and organize themes within the interview text (Glesne & Peshkin, 1999). Specifically, first the transcripts were read thoroughly several (2–3) times, with the initial reading conducted in tandem with close review of the audiotaped interview. After several reviews of the interviews were completed, preliminary or open coding occurred. Open coding is "the analytic process through which concepts are identified and their properties and dimensions are discovered in the data" (Strauss & Corbin, 1998, p.101). Following the open coding, axial coding took place. In axial coding, "categories are systematically developed and linked with subcategories" (Strauss & Corbin, 1998, p. 142). Next, selective coding, or the integration of categories to formulate theories, was used. In short, the analysis evolved from labeling concepts, to grouping concepts into categories and subcategories, and then to integrating categories into theories throughout the research process. These steps occurred in a circular manner, each informing the other, throughout data collection and analyses of all of the transcribed interviews (Glesne & Peshkin, 1999). This constant comparative method (i.e., the ongoing exchange between research and theory development) is an important feature of the grounded-theory methodology and was used to guide data analysis in the present study (Glaser, 1978; Glaser & Strauss, 1967). Data collection continued to inform the further development of categories and theories until the point of theoretical saturation occurred—until the incorporation of additional data was unlikely to contribute to new properties, dimensions, or relationships during the analysis (Strauss & Corbin, 1998). Also, data displays, such as tables, graphs, and matrices were used, when appropriate, to visually organize the data (Glesne & Peshkin, 1999).

Analyses were separately conducted by the study's two authors and subsequently discussed at periodic meetings in order to continually revise existing coding schemes and to enhance theory development. Because the study's focus was on the subjective experience of the father's decision to participate, analysis was first conducted on an individual case level: each of the 20 fathers' interviews was analyzed for categories and themes. Following this process, patterns across groups of fathers were explored. Hence, the demographic data were used to organize subsamples of fathers to allow for cross-case analyses of the interview data, such that relationships between the sociodemographic variables and emerging themes could be examined.

RESULTS

Specific Factors Influencing Fathers' Participation

The primary intent of the interviews was to identify specific factors that contributed to the father's decision to participate in family-based programming. Hence, among the descriptive accounts that the fathers shared during the interviews involving various topics related to fathering a problematic adolescent, all fathers responded to the following question: "What specific factors influenced your decision to participate in the Growing Up FAST Program?" Fathers' responses to this question—both at the time the question was initially posed in the interview, and also if further factors were discussed at a subsequent time in the interview—were coded and grouped together for later analysis.

Participating Versus Non-Participating Fathers. Responses to the question regarding their decision to participate were analyzed separately between two groups of fathers: Participating Fathers (i.e., fathers who had participated in at least one program session) and Non-Participating Fathers (i.e., fathers who had not participated in any program sessions). Total responses given by the two groups of fathers will be presented separately in order to distinguish between the experiences of articipating and non-participating fathers.

Family Structure. In addition to the creation of two groups of fathers based on participation status, within group analyses of the participating and non-participating fathers showed that themes emerged among the participants based on the father's family structure. In other words, fathers who belonged to a particular family structure (i.e., single residential fathers; two-parent married fathers–biological fathers or stepfathers; and non-residential fathers) seemed to share and voice similar factors that influenced their decisions to participate in the program. Family structure was identified at the time of the interview during the father's completion of the demographic questionnaire, and all fathers were asked to identify their family structure status as it was at the *time of their referral to the diversion program*, as many of the living situations had changed between the time of their initial contact with the program and the time of the fathers' interviews.

Before discussing the themes, I will provide a brief description of each of the individual fathers that will include demographic data and relevant background information. Then, as the themes are presented, fathers' verbatim quotes will be lifted from the interview text to be used as examples to substantiate the respective themes. Finally, any exceptions (i.e., any fathers who did not correspond with the respective categories or any fathers who voiced multiple influencing factors, some of which were not within the categories that have been constructed) will be discussed as disconfirming evidence.

PARTICIPATING FATHERS

Single, Residential Fathers ($n = 3$)

Chip. Chip was a 41–year-old, Caucasian single father of an 18-year-old daughter who, to Chip's surprise, was caught shoplifting (her first and only offense). Chip was divorced from the biological mother who lived in another city in the same state and saw her daughter 4 to 5 times per year.

Sam. Sam was a 53-year-old, Caucasian single father of a 16-year-old daughter. He was a widow and was raising his daughter and her twin brother on his own. His daughter was caught shoplifting, but she had also experienced some mental health issues (depression) in the past and Sam's contact with the diversion program represented just one of his numerous attempts to obtain assistance with his daughter.

Ned. Ned was a 32-year-old, Caucasian single father of a 12-year-old son. At the time of his son's referral to the diversion program (for assaulting his teacher at school), Ned had been cohabitating with his girlfriend. However, at the time of the interview, Ned was in the process of moving to a new residence with only his two sons. The biological mother lives in another city in the same state but is typically uninvolved due to a fairly severe physically and verbally abusive relationship that she has with her son.

It was court ordered ... I didn't have a choice.

- "The fact that he has to be there."
- "I really felt like it was something that had to be done, and like I said, I mean, it was a more or less court ordered kind of thing so, and, I was the only parent around, so I didn't really know."
- "I'm here because I went to court people and they sent her here."

These three single fathers all expressed a feeling of being obligated to participate because they were the only residential parent. Also, because all three adolescents were given the option to participate in the program as an alternative to being seen by the juvenile courts, these fathers chose to participate in order for their adolescent to avoid any involvement with the juvenile justice system. Thus, the fathers felt that it was their obligation as the sole residential parent to ensure their family's attendance and circumvent contact with the juvenile courts.

Two-Parent, Residential Fathers ($n = 5$)

Andrew. Andrew was a 45-year-old, Native-American biological father of a 15-year-old daughter, and he was still married to the biological mother. During the interview, Andrew expressed obvious dislike for his daughter's older boyfriend

8. FAMILY-BASED PROGRAMMING

and after several incidences of her skipping school with the boyfriend, Andrew and his wife had contacted the diversion program. Andrew was also experiencing a particularly frustrating situation with his family due to the increasing conflict between his wife and his two daughters. He shared how he had been, and continued to be, unsuccessful in finding a "neutral" position at home among his wife and daughter.

Tim. Tim was a 44-year-old, Caucasian biological father of a 16-year-old son, and he was still married to the biological mother. Tim's son had been the victim of sexual abuse several years earlier, and Tim believed that his son had recently begun to express problematic behaviors as a result of the abuse. The adolescent and his family were referred to the diversion program by the juvenile courts as a result of a shoplifting incident.

Scott. Scott was a 47-year-old, Caucasian biological father of a 17-year-old son, and he was still married to the biological mother. Scott's son was caught by the local police with a small amount of marijuana and came into contact with the program as a result of this drug possession. Scott had only been able to attend one session of the program due to his very busy work schedule (more than 60 hours/week).

Hal. Hal was a 34-year-old, African-American biological father of a 12-year-old son. Hal's son had always lived with him and the son rarely saw his biological mother. Hal had been remarried for five years. After an incident in which the adolescent had been caught shoplifting on a school fieldtrip, Hal and his wife contacted the diversion program to prevent further problem behaviors.

Lee. Lee was a 43-year-old, African-American biological father of a 15-year-old son. Lee's son had resided with him since birth and the son seldom had contact with his biological mother. Lee had been remarried for 11 years. Lee and his wife had contacted the diversion program to obtain assistance regarding their son's persistent lying and theft in the home.

It is my responsibility to do something to fix the problem.

- "I knew something had to be done."
- "Whatever it takes."
- "Well, I feel I've got a responsibility to raise my kids . . . If there's a problem and I can't fix it, I will have to ask for help."
- "And I felt all of us should be in the program . . . If there's somebody out there that can help me help them or help them with me, or help them by themselves without me."
- "It was a given."
- "Usually, we're always there for him. Both of us together."

Although these fathers were all involved in a committed relationship with the biological mother or stepmother at the time of the program referral, these men also described an obligation or inherent responsibility as the father to participate in the diversion program. They matter-of-factly stated that as one of the two residential parents, it was a part of their role as the father to take appropriate action in attempt to "fix the problem." For these fathers, little thought was given to whether or nor to be involved, as they believed that their participation in the family-based program was simply an unspoken duty.

Nonresidential Fathers ($n = 2$)

Dan. Dan was a 38-year-old, Caucasian biological father of a 15-year-old daughter. Immediately prior to her referral, the daughter had been living with Dan and his new wife. However, at the time of the program referral and the interview, Dan's daughter was residing with her biological mother and stepfather. After a recent evening when the adolescent snuck out and stayed overnight with a new boyfriend, Dan and the biological mother contacted the program to prevent further problematic behaviors. According to Dan, although he was concerned about his daughter, he did not feel that her behaviors were too severe.

Matt. Matt was a 56-year-old, African-American biological father of a 16-year-old daughter who had been referred to the program as a result of multiple school suspensions due to fighting and incorrigibility at school. At the time of the program referral and during the family's participation in the program, the daughter was living with her biological mother. However, at the time of the interview, the daughter had just recently moved from her mother's home and was now living with Matt and his girlfriend. Matt had fathered several other children who were now much older, and he was very outspoken during the interview when describing his firm and punitive parenting style.

I wanted to be there for my child to show that I care.

- "We care about you and this is why we're going."
- "When it was mentioned, going to the meeting, if the father wanted to go, he could go. And I wanted to go."

These two non-residential fathers clearly stated that they had definitely planned to participate in the program and really had given little thought to their decision. In addition, it seemed to be important for these two fathers to show that they cared for their adolescents and they wanted to demonstrate their support for their daughters by being present at the program. Both of the fathers also reported having relatively amicable relationships with their daughters' biological mothers and they were able to easily communicate with their ex-wives regarding their adolescent's well-being.

8. FAMILY-BASED PROGRAMMING 171

NONPARTICIPATING FATHERS

The numerous responses voiced by the nonparticipating fathers showed similarities that suggested a further classification into 1 of 4 groups. Specifically, when discussing their main reasons for not being involved in the program, the nonparticipating fathers made reference to the:

- *Adolescent* (e.g., I didn't go because she ran away)
- *Father's personal concerns* (e.g., It wasn't necessary for me to be there)
- *Program* (e.g., I lacked confidence in what the program could do for me and my family)
- *Biological mother* (e.g., The child's mother never notified me about the program)

Interestingly, the fathers' family structure classification was related to these response categories, such that (a) single, residential fathers mentioned adolescent-related factors, (b) two-parent residential fathers cited father-related and program-related factors, and (c) nonresidential fathers communicated mother-related factors as the primary factors contributing to their lack of participation in the program.

Single, Residential Fathers ($n = 2$)

Mike.   Mike was a 52-year-old, Caucasian biological father of a 17-year-old daughter. He was divorced from the biological mother and had been raising his daughter on his own since his divorce for nearly 2 years. Because his daughter had frequently been skipping school and traveling out of state with friends, Mike decided to file a missing persons report. The adolescent was found and detained by police in another state, yet after Mike retrieved her and she returned home, her incorrigible behaviors continued and she ran away soon after referral to the program. Thus, although his daughter was residing with Mike at the time of the program referral, at the time of the interview, his daughter had run away and Mike thought that she was currently living with her mother in Jamaica.

Bart.   Bart was a 41-year-old, Caucasian biological father of a 17-year-old daughter who was also "sneaking out" and running away from home. Bart suspected that she was being sexually active with an older boyfriend and he eventually filed an unruly police report, which led to his contact with the program. Bart had been divorced from the biological mother for 15 years, but had just recently received custody of his daughter and her sister 3 years prior to the referral due to their mother's substance abuse problem. Although his daughter was residing with Bart at the time of the program referral, at the time of the interview, his daughter had run away and Bart was currently unaware of her whereabouts.

Adolescent-Related Factors

She ran away / Moved in with her mother.

- "She never shows up ... I can't find her and that was the same way with all the programs."
- "They set up somebody to talk to me. I think it was about two weeks later they called me, well within the very next week, my daughter ran away again. So I couldn't very well get her into any of the meetings."

When asked about the factors that influenced their decision to not participate in the program, these single, residential fathers responded that they would have been involved, but because their daughter had run away or returned to live with their biological mother immediately after referral to the diversion program, they were unable to participate with their adolescent. These fathers also described numerous previous efforts to receive help for their adolescent (i.e., Children's Services, community mentorship programs), but these attempts had been unsuccessful because of their daughters' repeated refusal to stay committed to the services. It was clear that these fathers were frustrated with the current situation involving their adolescent.

Two-Parent, Residential Fathers ($n = 4$)

Samuel. Samuel was a 49-year-old, African-American stepfather of a 15-year-old daughter. Samuel had been cohabitating with the daughter's biological mother for the past 7 years, and they had been married for 1 year. During the interview, it was clear that the adolescent's biological mother was the primary disciplinarian in the household, and that Samuel's role was to enforce his wife's rules when she was unable to be present. According to Samuel, his stepdaughter's school had notified Children's Services about visible bruises that she had, and Children's Services suggested that the family attend the diversion program.

Randy. Randy was a 45-year-old, Caucasian biological father of a 15-year-old daughter, and he was still married to the biological mother. The adolescent was referred to the program because she had stolen another student's purse at school. Although Randy, a law enforcement officer, initially appeared suspicious about the interview, he gradually opened up and later described how his recent anger and disappointment with his daughter made it difficult for him to want to participate in the program and to have the close relationship that he had shared with his daughter in the past.

Tom. Tom was a 41-year-old, Caucasian biological father of a 15-year-old daughter, and he was still married to the biological mother. Tom and his wife

8. FAMILY-BASED PROGRAMMING

had discovered that their daughter had begun drinking alcohol, and to prevent further problem behaviors from developing, Tom's wife had contacted the diversion program.

Monty. Monty was a 37-year-old, African-American uncle of a 16-year-old daughter. Monty and his wife had been raising their niece for 2 years and had decided to contact the diversion program in order to "scare" their niece and discourage further unruly behaviors that she had recently been exhibiting. The adolescent's father (Monty's brother) had passed away when she was 5 years old, and since then, the girl had been living with her mother. However, the biological mother had become chemically dependent and was currently unable to provide a home for her daughter. Monty was extremely verbose and eager to share his frustrating experiences involving his niece during the interview.

Father-Related Factors

I am not a part of this problem ... Why should I be involved?

- "I myself, personally, I felt like, hey, I didn't do any of this, so why should I get involved in it?"

She will open up more without me there.

- "I think part of me felt it might be better for her, because I'm so hard and opinionated, that it was better for her and her mother to be in the sessions and not me there with them."

I need to feel in control of my own life.

- "My biggest thing with all of it is that I want to feel in control of my world and I know I'm not. Even though I feel I'm at that point where I know I'm not, I'm still not as likely to share that with somebody else."

Program-Related Factors

I have a lack of confidence in therapy.

- "The lack of confidence that it was going to result in any changes in her."

It is difficult for me to seek help outside of the family.

- "My thing would be is that I don't know if they would consider it a sign of weakness or what if you have to go to someone else for help ... I know I'm reluctant to talk with someone else."
- "I'm the type of person, if I have to look outside the family for help within the family, then that would be hard for me to do."

Privacy ... I wanted to keep the problem within the family.

- "It's a family problem, we're going to keep it within the family. Why am I going to go talk to somebody that don't know me? Or don't know her or don't know the situation? "
- "We didn't do because we were trying to keep the privacy within her because the gossip is so rampant in our community because of her prior issues."

These fathers were still married to the adolescent's biological mother or had been involved with same woman (stepmother or step aunt) for several years, and therefore, were currently residing in a fairly stable two-parent household. However, unlike the participating fathers in two-parent homes, these fathers chose to not participate due to either father-related or program-related factors.

The father-related factors that were voiced, clearly indicate that these fathers did not characterize their role as the father as one in which their participation in the program was necessary or beneficial to the family's problematic situation. In other words, these fathers believed that if they did not personally have the behavioral problem, or if they would not be able to positively influence their adolescent's situation, why was it imperative that they attend the diversion program? One father also expressed his personal concern with needing to have a sense of command over his life, and that his involvement with this family-based service might weaken that feeling of control.

These fathers also voiced several program-related factors that influenced their decision to not participate, such as a lack of confidence in the effectiveness of the program and therapy in general, and a reluctance to seek assistance from nonfamily members who would not be familiar with the family's situation and who may compromise their rights of privacy. Interestingly, most of these fathers did not strongly object to the mother's and the adolescent's participation in the program, but they did not believe that their attendance was an obligatory part of their role as the father.

Non-Residential Fathers ($n = 3$)

Bud. Bud was a 43-year-old, Caucasian biological father of a 14-year-old daughter. Bud had been separated from the biological mother for 8 years and the daughter was, and had been, living with her biological mother since their separation. Due to a legal matter, Bud had been without a driver's license for several years and he stated that because of this obstacle, his communication with his daughter was limited to occasional telephone conversations. Bud suspected that the mother and daughter were asked to attend the diversion program as a result of police involvement in a physical fight that had occurred between the adolescent and her mother.

Rett. Rett was a 40-year-old, Caucasian biological father of a 16-year-old daughter. According to Rett, his daughter was referred to the program after her school had received an anonymous phone call notifying the school about incidents of physical abuse between the biological mother and Rett's daughter. At the time

8. FAMILY-BASED PROGRAMMING 175

of the program referral, the daughter was living with her biological mother and stepfather. However, shortly thereafter and at the time of the interview, the daughter had moved in with Rett and was currently residing with him.

Kent. Kent was a 44-year-old, Caucasian biological father of a 14-year-old son. Kent was divorced from the biological mother and the son was living with his biological mother and stepfather. Kent knew very little about his son's initial involvement with the diversion program, but he thought that it may have been related to an incident in which his son had been caught by the local police for trespassing on school grounds late one night. Kent was initially wary of the interview and he remained extremely guarded and hesitant throughout the conversation—especially regarding any discussion of his ex-wife and their ongoing conflict about parenting their son.

Mother-Related Factors

I didn't know about it.

- "No, I didn't know that he was involved in the program."
- "I didn't know about this growing up fast and I never heard of it before."
- "I've never had contact with it. When you called me, it was a complete shock."

I was ever asked to go.

- "I wasn't never asked."

Conflict with ex-wife would have been a problem.

- "No, I did not ask because we're at the stage and time in life where if we don't have to be around each other, we're better off and so is the kids. We do not see eye to eye on a lot of things."

In their responses to why they did not participate in the diversion program, these fathers all made references to the biological mother of the adolescent and her neglect to notify them about the program. In fact, two of the three fathers stated that they had been completely unaware of their adolescent's involvement in the program until they were contacted and invited to take part in the present study's interviews. It was clear that these fathers had limited contact with the biological mother, and often times, interactions with their ex-wives were characterized by conflict and disagreement.

EXCEPTIONS

Flint. Flint was a 72-year-old, Caucasian step grandfather of a 13-year-old adolescent who had been unruly in school and was continually running away from their home. Flint was married to the adolescent's grandmother and, at the time of

the referral, they had been raising the girl. The adolescent had lived with Flint, his wife, and his wife's son (the biological father) since the girl was 1 year old. However, the biological father had moved out of the home 2 years prior, and Flint and his wife had gained custody. At the time of the interview, though, the adolescent had moved and was currently living with her biological mother and her mother's boyfriend. Flint cited the adolescent's recent move as the reason for which they did not participate in the diversion program:

- "We would have went into that program, we would have tried anything actually, but, of course, we just dropped everything because when her mom tried to take her."

Thus, although Flint stated that he would have wanted to try the diversion program, their family did not participate because the adolescent had moved out of their residence to live with her biological mother. Because of his relation to the adolescent, and due to the family's constantly fluctuating living arrangements, Flint's experience does not exactly correspond with the other fathers' situations and with the classifications that have been presented.

Bud. In addition to the mother-related factors (not being "asked" to participate in the program and acknowledgment of a discordant relationship with the biological mother), Bud, one of the nonresidential fathers, also gave a third reason for why he did not participate in the program toward the end of his interview:

- "Not for me because I don't even think I'm the problem in this anyhow, any shape. Because I do anything and everything to the best of my ability that I can do. What I basically want to do is see if this program is working for them or not. The way I see it, they're the one's who've got the problem."

According to Bud, he did not have a significant role in any aspect of his adolescent's current situation, as he assumed no part in contributing to the existence of the problematic behaviors, or in the treatment of his daughter's problematic behaviors. It is likely that because Bud was a nonresidential father who had limited contact with his daughter and the biological mother, he did not feel that it was his responsibility to make an effort to attend the program. In any event, Bud talked about multiple reasons for why he did not participate in the program throughout the duration of the interview.

FACTORS INFLUENCING FATHERS' PARTICIPATION—IN GENERAL

A second related goal of the study was to better understand why fathers, in general, are less likely than mothers to participate in family-based programs. Thus all of the fathers were asked the following question: "Why do you think that fathers, in

8. FAMILY-BASED PROGRAMMING

general, do not participate as often as mothers do in our—or most—family-based programs?" Conversation regarding this topic typically followed the previously discussed question concerning specific factors that influenced the father's decision to participate, unless it was appropriate to inquire about this issue at another time in the interview. All fathers' responses to this question—at the time the question was initially posed in the interview and if further thoughts were raised at a subsequent time in the interview—were coded and grouped together for later analysis.

Interestingly, despite the fathers' participation status and despite the fathers' family structure, the responses were very similar among all 20 fathers. In particular, fathers' responses to this question could be classified into 1 of 2 thematic groups, and fathers often voiced multiple examples supporting one or both of the themes: (1) traditional mother/father roles in the family and (2) feelings of inadequacy.

In their responses, many fathers clearly identified and described the existence of traditional male and female roles within the household as a main reason for why fathers participate in family programming less often than mothers. Specifically, these fathers described the man's role in the family as primarily one of breadwinner and provider. In addition, they expressed the opinion that most men are mere onlookers to family life, and that fathers rarely discipline or communicate with their adolescents. Hence, according to these fathers, they believed that most men believe that it is the mother's job to raise their offspring and manage any issues related to the family. These 20 fathers also talked about feelings of inadequacy as a reason for why fathers are not as likely as mothers to be involved in family-based programming. For example, many of the fathers described specific feelings of being a failure, being weak, being uncomfortable, and being embarrassed as barriers to their involvement in family-based programs and services. In the following presentation of these two themes, fathers' verbatim quotes from the interviews are used to illustrate the thematic groups.

Traditional Father/Mother Roles in the Family

Fathers as providers:

- "The one males, there's a few of them I know wouldn't go 'cause they just live in the old world where the woman of the house does this. The man of the house does this. I take care of work and bringing home the money, doing whatever I want to do. You take care of the home and the family."
- "I'm sure there are cases where the father is saying it's the wife's job to raise the kids. I provide the money, the wife takes care of the family."
- "In general, I think they feel probably that they are busy, that their primary obligation of their family is monetary, money, providing."
- "Um, they're busy. They're busting their butt to work, they think they must. I gotta work. It's the societal pressure that says the man must be the provider."

Fathers are outsiders to home/family life:

- "Usually the father is basically the outsider to the house. He is just basically on the outside looking in. Watching his kids grow up but not making them grow up."
- "Fathers in general, I don't think participate in the family all that much. I mean, regardless of the work roles, mom still deals with the family issues and that sort of thing. I don't think fathers get down to the nitty gritty family level as much as moms do."

Mothers have the job to raise and discipline the children:

- "It's just like I said before, they leave all the disciplinary stuff to the mother."
- "They just handle it better because they tend to be more focused on taking care of the child. Fathers don't get to take care of children very much."
- "Bringing up the kids, that's mom's job."

Mothers are closer to and more emotionally involved with their children:

- "You know, moms seem to be more involved in the emotional well-being of their kids. I think moms care more maybe or they just seem to get more involved. They are more hands-on emotionally with kids than dads are. At least that's the way it was when I was growing up."
- "I don't think fathers know how to communicate as well with their children as well as what a mother might. I'm sure that goes for each individual is different. I'm not saying that's always the rule, but I would say 8 out of 10 times or 9 out of 10 times, a mother is going to have a better or closer relationship with their child, whether it be a male or a female."
- "I think moms are always there for their kids. I think all kids are just closer to their moms than they would be their fathers. Not that they don't love them any less, but it's their mother. I think that's why moms 'cause they're just closer to their children than the father would be."

Feelings of Inadequacy

Failure:

- "I guess just from, I'd use the word fear. Being afraid to face other people who may seem to be questioning your parenting skills."
- "They don't want to go in and be a failure—a father that failed because their child is not performing up to their standards."

8. FAMILY-BASED PROGRAMMING 179

- "Could be a father who is thinking he may be considered a failure . . . a failure as a father."

Embarrassment/pride:

- "Um, pride and embarrassment."
- "Maybe for a male, it's an embarrassment type thing or ego type thing that someone in their family may have a problem."
- "Could be a father who is thinking he may be considered a failure, could be embarrassed."
- "One, they're embarrassed."
- "Some are probably ashamed, I'm sure."
- "I think it's a sense of embarrassment."

Sign of weakness:

- "My thing would be is that I don't know if they would consider it a sign of weakness or what if you have to go to someone else for help."
- "They don't want to admit that they have a problem that they can't handle with their own kids.
- That's tough for a man to do, to say. . . Hey, I need help."

General discomfort:

- "Maybe because they think it's going to be that kind of a thing where they're going to get put on the spot."
- "I would say maybe they would just feel uncomfortable. They just wouldn't be, some people out of their elements aren't very comfortable."

In conclusion, when asked why paternal participation rates in family programs are generally lower than mothers' rates of participation, all 20 fathers voiced detailed and strikingly similar responses that evidenced one of two themes: traditional mother/father roles in the family and feelings of inadequacy. In addition, their replies were independent of the father's participation status in the diversion program and their family structure status at the time of referral to the program.

DISCUSSION

This chapter sought to accomplish two major goals: the further reconceptualization of father involvement to include the topic of paternal participation in family-based programming, and the advancement of multimethod efforts to generate empirical

information on fathers and families. A review of existing literature on father participation in programming efforts provided a framework for the gathering and analysis of both quantitative and qualitative data from fathers regarding their participation in a family-based diversion program. The focus of this chapter now turns to a discussion of how our findings may provide direction to future research efforts and contribute to more effective delivery of programs to fathers and families.

Analysis of the quantitative data included the finding that fathers who had used services in the past were more likely to get further in the diversion program offering. It may be that fathers are in fact willing and able participants once they gain some initial exposure to programming. Thus, it is important to make initial contact directly with the father, and it may be helpful to "advertise" the program in a manner that emphasizes the father's attendance as an essential contribution to the family's improvement. For instance, it may be useful to highlight the fact that other fathers have consistently attended program sessions, to present fathers with data that show improvements made by other fathers and their families as a result of their program involvement, or to recruit past participating fathers who would be willing to talk about their positive experiences with interested fathers during initial telephone contacts. Future research efforts, in the meantime, could bolster these findings with additional attention paid to more specific factors related to service utilization, including questions regarding fathers' satisfaction with past services, the ease of availability of those services, and modifications that could be made to improve existing programs.

The second finding from the quantitative data analysis is the significant negative relationship between fathers' perceptions of family problem-solving skills and the length of their program participation. Here, fathers reporting less family problem-solving skills were more likely to participate in greater numbers of sessions. The third and final quantitative finding to be noted here is the significant positive relationship between adolescents' reports of psychological symptoms and fathers' program participation. Fathers of adolescents reporting more somatization, paranoid ideation, anxiety, hostility, and phobia symptoms were more likely to participate in family programming for longer periods of time.

Because fathers who are experiencing their family members as less effective problem-solvers are more likely to remain in a family-based program for a longer amount of time, it may be the case that participating fathers are displaying a rather keen understanding of their family's needs (i.e. "If I think that we really need help as a family, I'm going to participate for as long as it takes") while nonparticipating fathers are simply being pragmatic ("If I don't think that we need the help, I'm not going to get involved at all"). Possible questions about the accuracy of fathers' assessments of their family members' needs are attenuated by the findings regarding adolescent psychological symptoms. However, future research efforts could be directed toward a better understanding of the consistency or discrepancy between fathers' and other family members' perceptions of the workings of their family, and the way that the convergence or divergence of viewpoints contributes

8. FAMILY-BASED PROGRAMMING

to overall participation rates. In turn, program developers might be able to increase the participation rates of fathers who might not see their families as being in need of a great deal of help through an emphasis on the adage that "an ounce of prevention is worth a pound of cure."

Analysis of the qualitative data from participating and nonparticipating fathers has shed further light on these quantitative findings. Residential fathers who participated in the family-based program reported doing so either because they felt that they were mandated to by an outside authority (i.e. the court) or by a sense of obligation to take care of matters inside the family. Embedded in this finding is the notion that residential fathers experience a sense of accountability—either to an external or an internal source—when making the choice to participate. Nonresidential fathers who chose to participate, on the other hand, reported being concerned about displaying their ability to be present for their adolescent in a time of need. This decision to participate may be an important way for non-residential fathers to meet the challenge of being a significant presence in their adolescent's life, even when they are not physically located in the same household.

Of the nonparticipating fathers, married residential fathers more often mentioned factors related to themselves or the program as the determining factor in their decision to not participate. However, even those fathers who talked about the perceived limits of the program seemed to be indicating that they lacked confidence in their own personal ability to get something out of the participation process itself. Hence, the married residential fathers most often mentioned factors that were under their control. In contrast, single residential fathers more often mentioned adolescent-related factors as the reason behind their lack of participation in the family-based program. These fathers seemed to be reporting that control of their participation in the program was "out of their hands" and instead was determined by their adolescent's problem behavior, and more specifically, by the adolescent's refusal to attend the program. Finally, the nonresidential fathers indicated that mother-related factors were the primary reasons behind their lack of participation in the program. While similar to the single residential fathers in that there was more often a reference to forces outside of themselves as shaping their choice to not participate, these nonresidential fathers generally reported more passive difficulties related to a total lack of communication with the biological mother and/or unresolved conflict from the past that served as a mental barrier to consideration of their participation.

Future research necessarily might include instruments that measure locus of control issues in the lives of fathers in order to explore the potential impact of such perceptions on their program participation. In turn, program developers might be able to increase program participation through efforts to help fathers gain enough of a sense of empowerment so as to feel confident that their participation is an important part of the family-based work that is being implemented. These last ideas about future empirical and intervention efforts offer a logical segue to the results of the second part of the qualitative study. Here, fathers were asked to

report their thoughts about why fathers in general seem to participate less often than mothers. The two themes that emerged from their responses centered on beliefs related to fathers not having a traditional role in these types of activities and, in related fashion, the feelings of inadequacy that fathers would experience in attempting to become engaged in such family matters.

While all of these findings have been discussed in terms of their impact on how fathers make decisions to participate in family-based programming, there are more widespread implications regarding the literature on father involvement. Fathers may need encouragement and assistance in trying out lots of activities that traditionally have been the purview of mothers, not just participation in a family-based program. The relationship between locus of control issues and father involvement might be examined in a variety of empirical ways as well. Finally, researchers and program developers alike might do well to address the combination of topics related to the father's personal authority and the obligations he carries for his offspring. The resulting synthesis of issues related to self-empowerment and just caring for others might advance the application of such empirical work and intervention efforts beyond the parochial interests of the fathers and families literature and into the consciousness of more mainstream society.

REFERENCES

Asarnow, J. R., Jaycox, L. H., & Tompson, M. C. (2001). Depression in youth: Psychosocial interventions. *Journal of Community Psychology, 30*, 33–47.

Ascher, B. H., Farmer, E. M., Burns, B. J., & Angold, A. (1996). The Child and Adolescent Services Assessment (CASA): Description and psychometrics. *Journal of Emotional & Behavioral Disorders, 4*, 12–20.

Bogdan, R. C., & Biklen, S. K. (1998). *Qualitative research in education: An introduction to theory and methods* (3rd ed.). Boston: Allyn & Bacon.

Burns, B. J., Hoagwood, K., & Mrazek, P. J. (1999). Effective treatment for mental disorders in children and adolescents. *Clinical Child and Family Psychology Review, 2*, 199–254.

Carr, A. (1998). The inclusion of fathers in family therapy: A research based perspective. *Contemporary Family Therapy, 20*, 371–383.

Cole, D. A., & McPherson, A. E. (1993). Relation of family subsystems to adolescent depression: Implementing a new family assessment strategy. *Journal of Family Psychology, 7*, 119–133.

Conger, K. J., & Conger, R. D. (1994). Differential parenting and change in sibling differences in delinquency. *Journal of Family Psychology, 8*, 287–302.

Dadds, M. R. (1995). *Families, children, and the development of dysfunction.* Thousand Oaks, CA.: Sage.

Derogatis, L. R., & Melisaratos, N. (1983). The Brief Symptom Inventory: An introductory report. *Psychological Medicine, 13*, 595–605.

Epstein, N. B., Baldwin, L. M., & Bishop, D. S. (1983). The McMaster Family Assessment Device. *Journal of Marital and Family Therapy, 9*, 171–180.

Frick, P. J., Lahey, B. B., Loeber, R., Stouthamer-Loeber, M., Christ, M. A., & Hanson, K. (1992). Familial risk factors to oppositional defiant disorder and conduct disorder: Parental psychopathology and maternal parenting. *Journal of Consulting and Clinical Psychology, 60*, 49–55.

8. FAMILY-BASED PROGRAMMING

Fristad, M. A., Gavazzi, S. M., & Soldano, K. W. (1998). Multi-family psychoeducation groups for childhood mood disorders: Program description & preliminary efficacy data. *Contemporary Family Therapy, 20(3)*, 385–402.

Gavazzi, S. M. (1995). The Growing Up FAST: Families and adolescents surviving and thriving program. *Journal of Adolescence, 18*, 31–47.

Gavazzi, S. M., & Law, J. C. (1997). Therapeutic utility of the Growing Up FAST program. Journal of Family Psychotherapy, 8, 21–39.

Gavazzi, S. M., Yarcheck, C. M., Rhine, E. E., & Partridge, C. P. (in press). Building bridges between parole officers and the families of serious juvenile offenders. *International journal of offender Therapy and Comparative Criminology.*

Gavazzi, S. M., Wasserman, D., Partridge, C. R., & Sheridan, S. (2000). The Growing Up FAST Diversion Program: An example of juvenile justice program development for outcome evaluation. *Aggression and Violent Behavior, 5*, 159–175.

Gavazzi, S. M., Yarcheck, C., Wasserman, D., & Partridge, C. (2000). A balanced and restorative approach to juvenile crime: Programming for families of adolescent offenders. In G. L. Fox & M. L. Benson (Eds.), *Contemporary issues in family research series, Families and crime millennium volume* (pp. 381–405). Stamford, CT: JAI Press.

Gavidia-Payne, S., & Stoneman, Z. (1997). Family predictors of maternal and paternal involvement in programs for young children with disabilities. *Child Development, 68*, 701–717.

Glaser, B. (1978). *Theoretical sensitivity*. Mill Valley, CA: Sociology Press.

Glaser, B., & Strauss, A. (1967). *The discovery of grounded theory: Strategies for qualitative research.* Chicago: Aldine.

Glesne, C., & Peshkin, A. (1999). Finding your story: Data analysis. In C. Glesne (Ed.), *Becoming qualitative researchers* (2nd ed., pp. 127–149). New York: Longman.

Hadadian, A., & Merbler, J. (1995). Fathers of young children with disabilities: How do they want to be involved? *Child & Youth Care Forum, 24*, 327–338.

Hecker, L. L. (1991). Where is dad? Twenty-one ways to involve fathers in family therapy. *Journal of Family Psychotherapy, 2*, 31–45.

Henggeler, S. W., Edwards, J., & Bourdin, C. M. (1987). The family relations of female juvenile delinquents. *Journal of Abnormal Child Psychology, 15*, 199–209.

Klitzner, M., Bamberger, E., & Gruenewald, P. J. (1990). The assessment of parent-led prevention programs: A national descriptive study. *Journal of Drug Education, 20*, 111–125.

Kumpfer, K. L., & Tait, C. M. (2000). F*amily skills training for parents and children*. Washington, DC: U.S. Department of Justice, Office of Justice Programs, Office of Juvenile Justice and Delinquency Prevention.

Law, J. C., & Gavazzi, S. M. (1999). Definitions of adulthood: From the voices of parents and adolescents. *Family Science Review, 11*, 318–335.

Lengua, L. J., Roosa, M. W., Schupak-Neuberg, E., Michael, M. L., Berg, C. N., & Weschler, L. F. (1992). Using focus groups to guide the development of a parenting program for difficult-to-reach, high-risk families. *Family Relations, 41*, 163–168.

McCurdy, K., & Daro, D. (2001). Parent involvement in family support programs: An integrated theory. *Family Relations, 50*, 113–121.

Meyers, S. A. (1993). Adapting parent education programs to meet the needs of fathers: An ecological perspective. *Family Relations, 42*, 447–452.

Molgaard, V., Spoth, R. L., & Redmond, C. (2000). *Competency training: The Strengthening Families Program for parents and youth 10–14*. Washington, DC: U.S. Department of Justice, Office of Justice Programs, Office of Juvenile Justice and Delinquency Prevention.

Partridge, C., Gavazzi, S. M., & Rhine, E. E. (2001). Working with the families of serious juvenile offenders: The Growing Up FAST parole program. *Contemporary Family Therapy, 23*, 403–417.

Phares, V. (1997). Psychological adjustment, maladjustment, and father–child relationships. In M. E. Lamb (Ed.), *The role of the father in child development* (3rd ed., pp. 261–283). New York: Wiley.

Phares, V. (1999). *"Poppa" psychology: The role of fathers in children's mental well-being*. Westport, CT: Praeger.

Phares, V., & Compas, B. E. (1992). The role of fathers in child and adolescent psychopathology: Make room for Daddy. *Psychological Bulletin, 111*, 387–412.

Sheeber, L., Hops, H., Andrews, J., Alpert, A., Davis, B. (1998). Interactional processes in families with depressed and non-depressed adolescents: Reinforcement of depressive behavior. *Behavior Research & Therapy, 36*, 417–427.

Spoth, R. L., & Redmond, C. (1992). Study of participation barriers in family-focused prevention: Research issues and preliminary results. *International Quarterly of Community Health Education, 13*, 365–388.

Spoth, R. L., & Redmond, C. (1995). Parent motivation to enroll in parenting skills programs: A model of family context and health belief predictors. *Journal of Family Psychology, 9*, 294–310.

Spoth, R. L., Redmond, C., Haggerty, K., & Ward, T. (1995). A controlled parenting skills outcome study examining individual difference and attendance effects. *Journal of Marriage and the Family, 57*, 449–464.

Spoth, R. L., Redmond, C., Hockaday, C., & Shin, C. (1996). Barriers to participation in family skills preventive interventions and their evaluations: A replication and extension. *Family Relations, 45*, 247–254.

Spoth, R. L., Redmond, C., Kahn, J. H., & Shin, C. (1997). A prospective validation study of inclination, belief, and context predictors of family-focused prevention involvement. *Family Process, 36*, 403–429.

Stern, P. N. (1980). Grounded theory methodology: Its uses and processes. *Image, 12*, 20–23.

Strauss, A., & Corbin, J. (1994). Grounded theory methodology: An overview. In N. K. Denzin & Y. S. Lincoln (Eds.), *Handbook of qualitative research* (2nd ed., pp. 273–285). Thousand Oaks, CA: Sage.

Strauss, A., & Corbin, J. (1998). *Basics of qualitative research: Techniques and procedures for developing grounded theory* (2nd ed.). Thousand Oaks, CA: Sage.

Tamis-LeMonda, C. S., & Cabrera, N. (1999). Perspectives on father involvement: Research and policy. *Social Policy Report, 2*, 1–26.

Wasserman, D. L., Gavazzi, S. M., & Randall, A. P. (1999). Furthering prevention-intervention linkages in family strengthering. Programs: The creation of a follow-up phase for the Growing Up FAST Program. Family Science Review, 11, 300–317.

Weller, R. A., Kapadia, P., Weller, E. B., Fristad, M. A., Lazaroff, E., & Preskorn, S. H. (1994). Psychopathology in families of children with major depressive disorders. *Journal of Affective Disorders, 31*, 247–252.

9

Fathering in a Beijing, Chinese Sample: Associations with Boys' and Girls' Negative Emotionality and Aggression

Chongming Yang, Craig H. Hart,
David A. Nelson, Christin L. Porter,
Susanne F. Olsen, Clyde C. Robinson
Brigham Young University

Shenghua Jin
Beijing Normal University

Whether specific patterns of parenting are similarly associated with child outcomes in diverse cultural contexts has been a topic of inquiry for the past several decades. Most recently, attention has focused on Asian parenting and the indigenous meanings of parental control among specific Asian groups as contrasted with Western cultures (Chao & Tseng, 2002). Recent debates in this literature center on whether coercive parenting has similar meanings for mainland Chinese and North American children and their parents (e.g., Grusec, 2002; Lau & Yeung, 1996). To further address the question of whether there is a universal nature to parenting and its linkages to child behavioral outcomes, we designed this chapter to consider whether coercive fathering in mainland China is related to childhood aggression in a manner similar to that which has been discovered in other cultural contexts (e.g., Hart, Nelson, Robinson, Olsen, & McNeilly-Choque, 1998). When referring to mainland China, we recognize that it is a vast country comprised of many

ethnic and minority groups. The available research synthesized in this chapter and explored in our Beijing sample captures only a small fraction of that population. Although a somewhat coherent picture is beginning to emerge, one should not assume that the findings discussed here are representative of what might be occurring with fathers and their children in the Chinese culture at large. Nevertheless, this and recent studies conducted in various parts of China provide a beginning point for understanding ways that Chinese fathering might be linked to child behavioral outcomes.

Most of past research on parenting styles has focused on maternal effects. In this review, we identify what is known about linkages between maternal coercion and childhood aggression in an effort to understand how paternal coercion might also be associated with negative child outcomes. In so doing, Chinese cultural context takes center stage. Whether relations between parenting and childhood aggression vary for boys and girls, depending on the sex of the parent and child temperament, is also considered. An important part of this chapter also involves measurement issues. We discuss methodological (e.g., self-report, spouse-report) and data analytic strategies (categorical versus continuous approaches) that have implications for studying how father behavior may be tied to child behavioral outcomes. These different approaches are then applied in a structural equation modeling analysis that explores linkages among difficult child temperament, maternal and paternal coercive parenting, and child peer group aggression in a Beijing sample.

COERCIVE PARENTING CONSTRUCTS

Recent research has empirically identified both positive (e.g., responsive/ authoritative) and negative (e.g., coercive and psychological control) forms of parenting in certain mainland Chinese cultures (e.g., Chen, Dong & Zhou, 1997; Chen, Liu, & Li, 2000; Olsen et al., 2002; Wu et al., 2002). The thrust of these studies is consistent with many North American findings suggesting that punitive, power-assertive discipline is associated with childhood physical aggression and other disruptive peer-group behavior (e.g., Gershoff, 2002; Hart, DeWolf, & Burts, 1992a,b; Hart, Nelson et al., 1998; McFadyen-Ketchum, Bates, Dodge, & Pettit, 1996). Although some research has called into question the universal nature of this relation (Baumrind, 1996; Coie & Dodge, 1998; Deater-Deckard & Dodge, 1997), it has long been assumed that parental physical and verbal coercion elicits resistance and animosity toward parents, which in turn hinders children's internalization of control (e.g., Hoffman, 1960). Such coercive parenting methods also imply that physical force is an acceptable form of social interaction and may help to satisfy children's instrumental needs (e.g., Hart et al., 1992a; Hart, Ladd, & Burleson, 1990). In the Chinese culture, few studies have examined the correlates or consequences of coercive parenting upon children's behaviors. Exceptions include the work of Chen et al. (1997, 2001, 2002) and Chang, Schwartz, Dodge,

and McBride-Chang (2002), who have shown that coercive parenting, on the part of mothers and fathers, is predictive of older and younger children's externalizing (aggressive/disruptive) behaviors. This chapter expands upon these contributions by examining relations between different types of parental coercion (with specific emphasis on fathering) and different forms of childhood aggression in same- and cross-sex parent–child interaction dyads.

Another form of hostile parenting includes the use of psychological control, in which parents seek conformance by manipulating and exploiting the parent–child bond. For example, love withdrawal, guilt induction, and value-laden expressions of disappointment and shame are all relevant strategies for this style of parenting (Barber, 1996). In our previous cross-cultural work, we identified the psychological control construct in Russian, Chinese, and U.S. parenting styles (Hart, Nelson et al., 1998, 2000; Olsen et al., 2002; Wu et al., 2002). Furthermore, the extant literature on Chinese parenting also supports the idea that Chinese parents may employ psychological control strategies. In particular, Ho (1986) summarizes literature in which Chinese mothers, as compared to their American counterparts, reported using more "love-oriented" methods of discipline, such as threatening to withdraw their love and attention when a child misbehaves. As noted earlier, love withdrawal is an important component in the practice of psychological control. Fung (1999) also identified shaming as a tool that many Chinese parents may employ in the socialization of their children. Some of the more extreme shaming behaviors utilized by Chinese parents, such as derogatory remarks and threats of abandonment, are consistent with the psychological control construct. In regard to child outcomes, our research has demonstrated that psychological control on the part of Chinese mothers is associated with preschool boys' externalizing behavior with peers (Olsen et al., 2002). This finding parallels those obtained in numerous studies that explore the negative effects of parental psychological control on children's social competence in a variety of cultural contexts (see Barber & Harmon, 2002). Because most of the research in China has focused on maternal psychological control, our data addresses the role that psychological control strategies may play in fathering as well. In particular, we seek to identify linkages between both paternal and maternal psychological control and subtypes of childhood aggressive behavior.

FATHERING INFLUENCES
AND CULTURAL CONTEXT

The study of how fathers' use of coercion and psychological control is related to different forms of childhood aggressive behavior is a relatively new area of inquiry. In the past, fathering scholars have focused attention on the narrow issue of fathers' absence or presence in the family or household. More recently, researchers have seen the need to study fathers' connections with households and families, focusing on cultural variations as well as the complexity and fluidity of those connections

with family members (Marsiglio, Amato, Day, & Lamb, 2001). Accordingly, a plethora of refined conceptualizations of paternal involvement have emerged to more fully characterize the diverse ways in which fathers are involved in their families and influence their children's lives (e.g., Hawkins & Dollahite, 1997). For example, Palkovitz (1997) expanded notions of father involvement by identifying 15 different categories of involvement, including such activities as monitoring, teaching, and planning. The overarching rubric for many dimensions of paternal involvement is the father–child relationship (i.e., whether fathers interact with their children in coercive or emotionally supportive ways). In that vein, this chapter focuses on the nature of parent–child interaction styles with special emphasis on father–child relationships in a Chinese cultural context.

Research over the past decade has illuminated many ways that fathers' and mothers' interaction styles make important contributions to children's competence in the peer group and to other aspects of their development in a variety of cultural contexts (see Hart, Newell, & Olsen, 2003; Marsiglio et al., 2001; Parke et al., 2002; Russell, Hart, Robinson, & Olsen, 2003, for recent reviews). For example, Russian family process research suggests that when mother and father influences are entered together in the same statistical models, differential linkages to child behavioral outcomes are observed. In line with recent work by Ross Parke and his colleagues with North American samples, playful and responsive fathering appears to carry the weight of influence with regard to reducing aggressive behavior with peers (Hart, Nelson et al., 1998). Mothers, however, seem to matter more in facilitating sociable peer group behavior when it comes to reasoning with children about the consequences of their actions (Hart, DeWolf, Wozniak, & Burts, 1992b).

Despite recent advances in our understanding of paternal influences, many questions remain. In particular, negative father–child interaction styles, as associated with childhood aggressive outcomes, have been relatively unexplored in Asian and other cultural contexts. Accordingly, this chapter focuses on examining how parental coercion and psychological control is associated with child behavioral outcomes in a sample from Beijing, China, with particular emphasis on fathering. As we consider the role of Chinese fathers, it is important to connect with current conceptualizations of Chinese fatherhood, as well as bridge this literature to the current knowledge of fathering in North American contexts. In so doing, we examine linkages between child temperament, paternal/maternal parenting, and childhood aggression. We also investigate specific parent–child linkages on the basis of the sex of the parent and child (i.e., father–daughter compared to mother–daughter linkages, etc.). Finally, we intend to demonstrate how certain methodological and data-analytic approaches may enhance or diminish the ability of researchers to assess these parent–child relationships.

Examining fathering in the Chinese culture presents a seldom-explored opportunity to make connections between specific dimensions of parenting and child outcomes in non-Western settings. For instance, studies have shown that relative to their Western counterparts, Chinese fathers engage in fewer play activities with

9. FATHERING IN A BEIJING CHINESE SAMPLE 189

their children (e.g., Ho, 1987; Roopnarine, Lu, & Ahmedezzaman, 1989). Rather than serving as a playmate, they apparently are more heavily involved in their children's training and education and are considered largely responsible for their children's social and academic progress (Chen et al., 2000; Ho, 1987; Stevenson, Chen, & Lee, 1992). Chinese fathers are, therefore, viewed as the predominant authority figure and are expected, more so than mothers, to help children achieve greater social and academic competence (Chao & Tseng, 2002; Chen et al., 2000). Thus, Chinese fathers are conceptualized as being more critical in their children's development (e.g., social and academic outcomes) than fathers in many Western cultural settings. Accordingly, research examining Chinese fathering, in relationship to Chinese mothering, may prove illuminating.

To help their children achieve social and academic competence, Chinese parents employ practices that are typically more restrictive and controlling than American socialization practices (Chiu, 1987; Wu et al., 2002). For example, Chinese mothers and fathers are rated by their spouses as more verbally and physically coercive in their parenting styles than U.S. parents (Porter et al., 2002). Chinese fathers are also viewed as being more coercive than Chinese mothers (Berndt, Cheung, Lau, Hau, & Lew, 1993; Ho, 1986, 1989; Lau & Cheung, 1987; Porter et al., 2002). The cultural meaning of this type of control has been the subject of significant debate over the past decade (Chao, 2001; Chen et al, 2000; Wu et al., 2002). One perspective forwarded by some scholars is that the coercive control exhibited by traditional Chinese parents is qualitatively different from control strategies found in many Western cultures (Chao & Tseng, 2002). This type of control, called *Guan Jiao* in Mandarin Chinese, is hypothesized to be reflective of parental involvement and concern, and thus considered to be positive and beneficial rather than destructive (Chao, 1994; Wu, 1981). Accordingly, Chinese children may perceive parental control positively, in alignment with high parental expectations (Chao & Sue, 1996). Others dispute this claim, however, based on evidence indicating that Chinese, like Western children, similarly view more controlling parental behavior (authoritarian/restrictive) as adverse (Lau & Yeung, 1996). If this latter perspective is true, we would expect to see more negative child outcomes occurring in the face of coercive parental control.

This issue regarding the meaning of more coercive control in Chinese parenting is especially relevant for studying fathering. Since fathers are typically viewed as prominent authority figures in Chinese homes, it may well be that efforts to help children develop appropriate behaviors, using more coercive means, in some cases may result in the opposite effect. In particular, children with difficult temperaments (e.g., negative emotionality) may elicit greater coercive discipline and control by their parents, thus exacerbating the child's difficult tendencies, which may be manifest in more frequent peer-group altercations (Hart et al., 2003). In this chapter, we hope to provide more information about ways that childhood temperament and fathers' and mothers' childrearing styles are associated with different types of childhood aggression using data from a mainland Chinese sample.

SUBTYPES OF CHILDHOOD AGGRESSION

Historically, research in childhood aggression has predominantly focused on physical forms of aggression (e.g., pushing, hitting, kicking, and threats of physical harm). Recent work (e.g., Crick & Grotpeter, 1995) has expanded our conceptualization of aggression to include relational aggression, which is defined as harming others through manipulation of or damage to social relationships (e.g., using social exclusion or spreading malicious rumors). Several researchers have found that girls tend to rely on more indirect, relational forms of aggression rather than on the physical forms of aggression that are more commonly found in boys (Crick, Casas, & Mosher, 1997; McNeilly-Choque, Hart, Robinson, Nelson, & Olsen, 1996). Accordingly, studies of relational aggression are particularly promising for increasing our understanding of the development of girls. Furthermore, our previous research has shown that these subtypes of aggression can be differentiated among young children in many cultural settings, including China (Hart, Nelson et al., 1998; Hart, Yang et al., 2001; Russell et al., 2003). Given that aggression of either type is generally associated with concurrent and long-term negative effects for the aggressors and victims (see Coie & Dodge, 1998, and Crick et al., 1999, for relevant reviews), it is important for researchers to identify antecedents that may form the basis of prevention and intervention work.

SOCIAL LEARNING AND CHILDHOOD AGGRESSION

One logical framework for investigating the possibility of unique developmental trajectories of relational and physical aggression is social learning theory. Within the context of this theory, it is presumed that children learn and adopt aggressive strategies by observing and/or interacting with aggressive models, such as their parents (Bandura, 1973, 1977). Certain forms of coercive or controlling parenting, for example, may contribute to a child's aggressive tendencies and carry over into peer relationships. As noted earlier, in this study we decided to focus upon physically and verbally coercive parenting as well as parenting that includes psychological control strategies.

The social learning model suggests that parental physical and verbal coercion are likely to be related to children's use of physical aggression, whereas parenting tactics that focus on psychological and relationship manipulation (psychological control) are more likely to be associated with children's use of relational aggression. Previous studies that addressed this question, however, did not demonstrate this level of specificity, with coercive parenting and psychological control each being associated with both forms of aggression in early- and middle-childhood samples (e.g., Hart, Nelson et al., 1998; Nelson & Crick, 2002). This may not be surprising, given that physical and relational forms of aggression tend to be highly

correlated and therefore are thought to occur simultaneously in the behavioral repertoires of many children (Crick et al., 1999).

Because the amount of research in this area is quite limited, further study of the relationships between parental psychological control strategies in the development of aggression, is warranted especially in young children from various cultural contexts. Given the conceptual similarity that exists between the constructs of psychological control and relational aggression, it is not unreasonable to assume that parental psychological control might be translated by children into relationally aggressive altercations in peer-group settings (Nelson & Crick, 2002). Some support has been offered for this hypothesis. For example, Nelson and Crick (2002) found that fathers' psychological control was significantly associated with their third-grade daughters' reputation for relational aggression in the peer group. A similar relationship was found for Russian mothers and their preschool-age children (Hart, Nelson et al., 1998). However, it should be noted that parental psychological control and coercion have not always been examined in tandem when predicting child outcomes. Thus, one aim of this study was to conduct further tests of these relationships in the Chinese culture, using both parental coercion and psychological control as predictors of childhood aggression. Although maternal psychological control has been found to predict externalizing behaviors in Chinese preschoolers (Olsen et al., 2002), it is unknown whether this relationship is maintained when controlling for parental coercion effects. Furthermore, the association between psychological control and negative child outcomes has not been explored with Chinese fathers. Thus, using the Chinese data reported in this chapter, we get psychological control to compete statistically with coercion in predicting the subtypes of aggression.

ISSUES REGARDING CHILD TEMPERAMENT

Several researchers have theorized that difficult temperament and peer aggression are linked in direct or indirect ways (Chen et al., 2002; Rothbart & Bates, 1998; Sanson, Hemphill, & Smart, 2002). A direct effects model links children's difficult temperament to their externalizing behaviors, even after controlling for parenting (Maziade, Cote, Bernier, Boutin, & Thivierge, 1989; Prior, Smart, Sanson, & Oberklaid, 1993; also see Rothbart & Bates, 1998). In contrast, an indirect model implies that the child's adverse temperament may evoke coercive parenting, which escalates over time in parent–child exchanges and subsequently promotes aggressive episodes in the child's peer group (Patterson, 1986; Reid & Patterson, 1989). However, this latter position has not been well supported by empirical findings (Rothbart & Bates, 1998). Another position is that the link of temperament to childhood aggression, either directly or indirectly (such as through parenting styles), may be moderated by the sex of the child (Russell et al., 2003). However, available

192   YANG ET AL.

evidence in support of this position is often in conflict and, therefore, inconclusive (Rothbart & Bates, 1998).

Even though mainly studied in Western cultures, subdimensions of temperament have also been identified in Chinese samples (e.g., Ahadi, Rothbart, & Ye, 1993; Hsu, 1985; Zhou & Yao, 1992), using various conceptualizations of temperament. For example, some Chinese cultural studies have focused on Thomas and Chess's (1977) nine dimensions, whereas others have used the three dimensions represented by Buss and Plomin's (1984) emotionality, activity, and sociability/shyness (EAS) model of temperament. Zhang's (1997) culturally derived conceptualizations of temperament suggest a fair degree of conceptual overlap between typical Chinese views of child temperament and Buss and Plomin's (1984) EAS. One of the prominent features of Chinese parental perceptions of child temperament is centered on negative features of children's emotionality (Porter et al., 2002; Zhang, 1997). Similar to research in Western cultures (e.g., Bates, 1980, 1989; Mebert, 1991), Chinese parents tend to associate negative features of children's emotionality with more difficult temperament (Porter et al., 2002). For this reason, the emotionality component of the EAS was selected in this study as a proxy for difficult temperament. In line with results of research on parenting and temperament conducted in Western and mainland Chinese settings, we anticipated that negative emotionality would be related to more hostile/adverse parenting (e.g., Crockenbert & Acredolo, 1983; Porter et al., 2002; Sanson & Rothbart, 1995). The current research effort is significant in that few studies have looked at associations between difficult temperament and psychological control (Morris et al., 2002). We also sought to examine whether hostile parenting (fathering and mothering) mediated the relation between children's negative emotionality and aggression (Baron & Kenny, 1986; Mize, Pettit, & Meece, 2000).

DIFFERENCES IN PARENT–CHILD INTERACTIONS BY PARENT–CHILD DYAD

The relation between several adverse parenting styles and childhood aggression is evident for both boys and girls. However, as implied above, specific relations between parenting and child outcomes may vary for boys or girls, depending on child temperament and the sex of the parent (Fagot, 1995; Jacklin, 1989; Russell & Saebel, 1997; Snyder, 1998). Accordingly, father–son, father–daughter, mother–son, and mother–daughter relationships should not be viewed as equivalent (Russell et al., 1998; Snyder, 1998). Previous research suggests that mother–daughter and father–son relationships are stronger than mother–son or father–daughter relationships (e.g., Chen, Wang, Chen, & Li, 2002; Isley, O'Neil, Clatfelter, & Parke, 1999; Lytton & Romney, 1991); thus, same-sex versus cross-sex relationships may yield differential patterns of child outcomes. Similarly, findings from the Chinese culture suggest that fathers, as compared to mothers, are more coercive toward sons

9. FATHERING IN A BEIJING CHINESE SAMPLE 193

than toward daughters (Ho, 1986, 1989). Although not always found to be the case (Chen, Wu, Chen, Wang, & Cen, 2001), paternal coercion in Chinese samples appears more likely to be associated with sons' than with daughters' aggressive behavior (Chen et al., 2002; Chang et al., 2002). However, when child temperament is taken into account, a somewhat different picture may emerge (Rothbart & Bates, 1998). For example, Sanson and Rothbart (1995) concluded from a number of studies that fathers, more so than mothers, are less accepting of difficultness in girls than in boys. If so, this may result in more paternal coercive and/or psychologically controlling behaviors directed toward daughters. This may play out in ways that cause girls to interact aggressively with peers. Partial support for this pattern arises from findings noted earlier (Nelson & Crick, 2002), where it appears that in middle childhood, parental psychological control is related to childhood relational aggression in father–daughter dyads but not in mother–daughter dyads. Alternatively, other recent findings indicate that there is no cross-sex differentiation. In mainland Chinese and North American samples, for example, negative child emotionality was found to be associated with more coercive parenting from both mothers and fathers, regardless of the sex of the child (Porter et al., 2002). Yet to be investigated in this line of work are Chinese parenting linkages to childhood relational and physical aggression. Our data set provides a unique opportunity to further explore parent–child interactions associated with childhood aggression and whether they vary depending on the sex of parent or sex of the child while taking difficult child temperamental characteristics into account.

MEASUREMENT ISSUES

Based on the literature reviewed thus far, we sought to investigate specific linkages involving negative emotionality, two parenting constructs, and two subtypes of aggression (see Fig. 9.1 in a later section). The model used to guide our analyses was partially derived from Hart, Olsen, Robinson, and Mandleco (1997). In general, we anticipated that negative emotionality would be associated with more hostile parenting (i.e., more coercive and psychologically controlling), and that hostile parenting, in turn, would be associated with more aggressive child outcomes. Furthermore, because Chinese fathers are highly involved in child rearing and are typically more coercive than Chinese mothers, we anticipated relationships between parenting and child aggression to be more pronounced among father–son and father–daughter dyads than among mother–son and mother–daughter dyads. In exploring the associations in this model, we relied on innovative ideas about measurement to better illuminate possible connections between the variables in the model. Indeed, despite progress in understanding ways that parents are important for children's development, how we gather and analyze data to understand these processes can enhance or diminish our ability to reach meaningful conclusions. In the following sections, we briefly discuss methodological (e.g., self-report,

spouse-report) and data-analytic issues that are relevant to the study of parenting and how different conclusions can be reached when using different methods of data gathering and analysis.

Self-Report vs. Proxy-Subjects Approaches to Parenting Measurement

Different ways that parent–child interactions are measured can influence how knowledge is created concerning linkages between fathering and child peer-group outcomes. Two decades ago, Brody and Endsley (1981) described a continuum of research approaches to the study of parent–child interaction, ranging from self-reports on one end to naturalistic observations on the other, with lab-based analogs in the middle. It was generally concluded that naturalistic observations provide the most trustworthy sources of data, with self-reports being the least acceptable (cf. Chamberlain & Patterson, 1995). Notwithstanding this conclusion, self-report (e.g., Hart, Nelson et al., 1998), simulation (e.g., Hart et al., 1992a,b), and observational techniques (e.g., Dishion, 1990; Isley et al., 1999), or combinations of all three approaches (e.g., Pettit, Bates, & Dodge, 1997) have often yielded similar findings (see Hart, Newell, & Olsen, 2003).

Although some studies indicate a modest correspondence between observed and self-reported parenting (e.g., Kochanska, Kuczynski, & Radke-Yarrow, 1989; Pettit, Clawson, Dodge, & Bates, 1996; Pettit et al., 1997), most research indicates weak evidence for these associations (Holden, Ritchie, & Coleman, 1992). This may be due, in part, to a reliance on global self-reported parenting patterns being correlated with distant behavioral acts in limited samples of parent observational data (Holden & Edwards, 1989). Similarly, many behaviors accessed by self-report parenting questionnaires may happen infrequently and therefore, are less likely to be observed (Deater-Deckard, 2000).

More recently, in an effort to minimize concerns about the use of self-report measures, some researchers have started using spouse-report measures (Nix et al., 1999; Russell et al., 2003). Because couples living together can observe each other's behavior over a sustained period of time and because spouses report on the behavior of another, rather than their own behavior, spouse reports may be less prone to social desirability and thereby may provide a more objective assessment. Using spouse reports of parenting in place of self-reports can be referred to as a proxy-subjects approach, where someone who knows the target person well is questioned (Nederhof, 1983).

To most effectively compare findings gained from parental self-reports or spouse reports, this study employed a structural equation modeling (SEM) approach. One advantage of SEM over traditional statistical analysis is that it accounts for random measurement error. Therefore, one important aim of this chapter is to explore whether the measurement of negative parenting styles might differ between

9. FATHERING IN A BEIJING CHINESE SAMPLE 195

parental self-reports and spouse reports in SEM. Furthermore, linkages between aspects of negative parenting (self and spouse reports) and peer perceptions of childhood aggression will also be assessed in our model. These associations have typically been small (e.g., Maccoby & Martin, 1983; Rothbaum & Weisz, 1994). The complications associated with a self-report approach, instead of a proxy-subjects approach, may partially explain the generally weak findings regarding the effects of parenting.

Continuous vs. Categorical Data

Another factor that is likely to cause confusion in findings about parenting and fatherhood in general is the persistent use of Likert-type scales as true interval measures in linear statistical analyses. Ever since Stevens' (1946) classification of the four psychological scales (nominal, ordinal, interval, and ratio) and the advocacy of corresponding nonparametric and parametric statistical treatments, there has been controversy over whether ordinal scales should be treated as interval variables for linear statistical analyses (e.g., Merbitz, Morris, & Grip, 1989). On one side of the debate, it is argued that ordinal scales should not be treated as interval data in parametric analyses because transformations cannot preserve a sense of ranking. In addition, it is proposed that means and standard deviations of data based on ordinal scales should be avoided because their meanings are interpreted in ways that go beyond rankings. In contrast, others have argued that measurement assumptions should not be mixed with statistical criteria and that any numbers meeting certain statistical assumptions can be used in corresponding parametric statistical analyses (see Gaito,1980, and Gardner, 1975, for details).

Many psychological constructs are assumed to have continuous interval-level distributions (O'Brien, 1985). When measured with ordinal scales or categorical responses, the underlying interval dimensions are categorized, and two types of errors may occur. Grouping errors occur when several values of the latent scale are collapsed into the same categories, leaving some values of the latent variable either overestimated or underestimated. Transformation errors may result if the arbitrary values of the ordinal scale do not correspond linearly with the latent variable (Coenders & Saris, 1995; Johnson & Creech, 1983). When the underlying construct is assumed to be normally or symmetrically distributed, as is often the case with social and psychological constructs (Borgata & Bohrnstedt, 1972), skewed ordinal scales would imply the existence of transformation errors (Coenders & Saris, 1995). In addition, ordinal scales may have limited ranges that fail to match the theoretical assumption of the latent construct (Snijders & Bosker, 1999). Accordingly, using raw ordinal or categorical scores as true measures for linear statistical analyses has been criticized as this procedure may produce distorted findings (Muthén, 1983; Merbitz et al., 1989; Wilson, 1971; Wright, 1999).

For testing full models that simultaneously incorporate factor analytic, path analysis, and regression components, it has been argued that a more appropriate approach to analyzing ordinal data is structural equation modeling that uses tetrachoric or the polychoric correlations as data input (Muthén, 1984; Muthén & Muthén, 1999; Muthén & Satorra, 1995). Using this approach, we can assume that two observed dichotomous variables x and y reflect two latent variables x' and y', which have a bivariate normal distribution. The tetrachoric correlation refers to the correlation of x' and y' that is estimated from the probability of x and y as summarized in a 2×2 contingency table (De Leeuw, 1983). The same notion can be applied to situations where the observed ordinal scales are supposed to be reflections of two polychotomized latent variables that are bivariate normally distributed. The polychoric correlation is the estimated correlation of the latent variables. Due to the presumed bivariate normal distribution in the estimation process, tetrachoric and polychoric correlations have, therefore, theoretically corrected the categorization errors (Coenders & Saris, 1995). Random errors are also taken into account in SEM when constructs are measured by several ordinal indicators.

The consequences of ignoring the noninterval and nonlinear nature of ordinal scales or categorization errors are reflected in various comparative studies. Compared with polychoric correlations, several studies have shown that the product-moment correlation of two categorical variables can seriously attenuate the correlation of latent continuous variables. This is more serious when either of the two variables has fewer categories (e.g., less than 5) in addition to being skewed in opposite directions (Bollen & Barb, 1981; Olsson, 1979a; Martin, 1978). In confirmatory factor analysis, factor loadings are underestimated with the magnitude negatively related to number of categories and degree of the skewness and kurtosis (Babakus, Ferguson, & Jöreskog, 1987; Bollen, 1989; Muthén & Kaplan, 1992; Olsson, 1979b; Rigdon & Ferguson, Jr., 1991). In addition, categorization errors appear as large random and correlated errors or as misspecifications of a model (Coenders & Saris, 1995), which could reduce the goodness of fit.

Many empirical researchers either are not aware of the problems posed by categorical data or do not consider them to be serious (Bernstein & Teng, 1989). Because our Chinese parenting and child temperament data consisted of ordered categorical data derived from Likert-type scales, a preliminary exploration of the data was conducted and, as anticipated, it indicated skewed distributions. Therefore, another important aim of the current chapter is to compare and contrast categorical and continuous approaches in our data analysis. Based on our reading of the literature, categorical approaches may be a more appropriate treatment of this type of data. Accordingly, our analyses were designed to contrast the linkages of two parenting constructs with two child aggression outcomes in our Chinese sample. We anticipated differences in the respective models, given that the path coefficients may be attenuated when the structural equation model is based on traditional product moment correlations rather than polychoric correlations of the ordinal variables.

METHOD

Subjects

Participants in this study included 216 children (100 boys, 116 girls) from nine classes in two Beijing preschools. Ages ranged from 46 to 76 months, with an average age of 61 months. Class sizes ranged from 15 to 39 children. In addition, 162 fathers and 177 mothers participated in this study. Families in which both parents participated (162 total) were included in subsequent analyses. Furthermore, as outlined earlier, the analyses were conducted separately by parent–child dyad. Accordingly, there were 76 mother–son dyads, 86 mother–daughter dyads, 76 father–son dyads, and 86 father–daughter dyads. The average age of parents was 34.1 years, with a range from 26 to 52 years. The average years of formal education for parents was 13.9 years, with a range from 5 to 22 years. Parents with a bachelor's or more advanced degree made up 32.8% of the sample, making it a highly educated sample.

Measurements and Procedure

Assessment of Child Aggression Subtypes. Children's relational and physical aggression scores were obtained via a peer behavior nomination procedure. For each behavior nomination item, children could nominate up to six classmates whom they perceived to engage in physical and relational aggression. The full list of behavioral nomination items are listed in Table 9.1. The number of behavioral nominations that children received for each of the items was standardized within each classroom. Further analyses were based on these standardized scores. All classrooms had a minimum of 75% participation in the peer behavioral nomination procedures (see McNeilly-Choque et al., 1996, for more detail).

TABLE 9.1
Standardized Factor Loadings of the Aggression Constructs

Constructs & Content	Loadings
Physical aggression:	
Who likes to mess up or knock down other children's things?	.83
Who grabs toys or things from other children?	.87
Who pushes other kids out of the way to get something they want?	.76
Who starts fights (physical) with other children?	.82
Relational aggression:	
Who won't let some of the other kids play with them, and they even might tell other kids to go away?	.73
Who tells other kids they cannot play unless they do what everyone wants them to do?	.68
Who won't let some kids sit beside them because they don't like them?	.69
Who tells some other kids not to be friends with someone?	.64

198   YANG ET AL.

Assessment of Parenting Styles. Parents were asked to independently rate themselves and their spouses' parenting styles on five-point scale items adapted from a measure developed to assess Baumrind's authoritarian, authoritative, and permissive typologies (Hart, Nelson et al., 2000; Robinson, Mandleco, Olsen, & Hart, 2001). Physical and verbal coercion items from this measure, shown in Table 9.2, have been used in prior research with mothers and fathers and were the parental coercion scale used in this study (see Hart, Nelson et al., 1998). Psychological control items shown in Table 9.2 were derived from measures developed in earlier research conducted in the Chinese, U.S., and Russian cultures that assessed this construct (see Barber, 1996; Olsen et al., 2002). In comparing self- and spouse reports in the analyses outlined below, self-reports were paired with spouse reports (i.e., for maternal comparisons, mothers' self-reports and fathers' reports of the mothers' behavior were contrasted).

Assessment of Child Temperament/Emotionality. The negative emotionality construct was adopted from the EAS (Buss & Plomin, 1984), a scale that includes three subscales: emotionality, activity, and sociability. For this study, both parents rated their child's temperament. The EAS constructs have been shown in past research to be appropriate for use with Chinese children (Zeng, 1998) and to be invariant across Chinese mother and father ratings of child temperament (Porter et al., 2002). The emotionality construct of temperament used in this study was defined by three EAS items: (a) child cries easily; (b) child often fusses and cries; and (c) child gets upset easily. Porter et al.'s previous study on temperament showed that these three items were the best indicators of the construct in a Chinese sample. Mother reports of child emotionality were used in subsequent analyses involving mother–child dyads and father reports were used in father–child dyads.

RESULTS

Analyses were conducted using Mplus, a program that allows for continuous and categorical variables at both the observed and latent levels (Muthén & Muthén, 1999). In structural equation modeling, Mplus uses Pearson product–moment correlation matrices of the observed variables when data are treated as continuous. Alternatively, it can use polychoric correlation matrices of the Likert-type scales/variables when data are treated as ordered categorical. We first delineated subtypes of children's aggression in our measurement model, followed by analyses of the parental coercion and psychological control constructs (self- and spouse reports). The second set of analyses explored whether father/mother parenting styles differed for sons versus daughters. The final model focused on linkages among the constructs in the different parent–child dyad groups, testing whether parenting mediated the relationship between child emotionality and child aggression.

9. FATHERING IN A BEIJING CHINESE SAMPLE

TABLE 9.2

Standardized Factor Loadings of Items Based on Different Informants and Data Treatment

Constructs & Contents	Mothers		Fathers	
	Self	Spouse	Self	Spouse
Physical & verbal coercion:				
Spanks when our child is disobedient	.80 (.77)	.64 (.63)	.63 (.63)	.95 (.84)
Yells or shouts when our child misbehaves	.59* (.55)	.59 (.56)	.73* (.71)	.79 (.72*)
Grabs our child when child is disobedient	.67* (.63)	.71 (.70)	.68* (.63)	.43 (.41*)
Explodes in anger toward child	.62 (.58)	.76 (.73)	.77 (.74)	.73 (.70*)
Uses physical punishment as a way of discipline	.67 (.59)	.62 (.46)	.56 (.53)	.74 (.63)
	$\phi = .62(.55)$	$\phi = .59(.57)$	$\phi = .68(.68)$	$\phi = .43(.34)$
Psychological control:				
Brings up child's past mistakes when criticizing our child	.57 (.53)	.45 (.35)	.38 (.32)	.56 (.48)
Becomes less friendly with our child if our child does not see things his/my way	.65* (.54)	.54 (.46)	.69* (.63)	.63 (.51*)
Goes back and forth between being warm and critical towards our child	.56* (.48)	.66 (.59)	.68* (.57)	.53 (.43*)
Tells our child that we get embarrassed when she/he does not meet our expectations	.37 (.38)	.49 (.47)	.52* (.51)	.33 (.36)
Tells our child he/she is not as good as other children	.63 (.59)	.64 (.58)	.48* (.45)	.60 (.61)
Goodness of fit	$\chi^2 = 30.60$	$\chi^2 = 29.26$	$\chi^2 = 26.00$	$\chi^2 = 28.73$
	$df = 21$	$df = 21$	$df = 21$	$df = 19$
	$p = .08$	$p = .11$	$p = .21$	$p = .07$
	$\chi^2_{diff} = 55.21$	$(\chi^2_{diff} = 15.60)$	$\chi^2_{diff} = 54.30$	$(\chi^2_{diff} = 37.45)$
	$df = 4$	$(df = 8)$	$df = 6$	$(df = 3)$
	$p < .01$	$(p < .05)$	$p < .01$	$(p < .01)$

Note.

a. Numbers in the parentheses are based on treatment of data as continuous.

b. An asterisk indicates that the maximum likelihood estimate of factor loading significantly differs between self- and spouse reports.

c. χ^2_{diff} indicates the chi-square difference between the two models, a model with all the factor loadings constrained to be equal and a model with the asterisked items unconstrained to be equal.

d. ϕ indicates the correlations between the two constructs, psychological control and physical/verbal coercion.

Measurement of Subtypes of Childhood Aggression

The standardized scores of peer behavioral nominations of aggression were normally distributed and continuous. Thus, the measurement model of physical and relational aggression was estimated with a multigroup (for boys and girls) confirmatory factor analysis. A baseline model was first estimated with all the factor loadings freely estimated across the two groups, which yielded a marginally acceptable goodness of fit index ($\chi^2 = 58.41$, df $= 36$, $p = .01$). The second model had all factor loadings constrained to be invariant across the two groups of children. The goodness of fit index (chi-square) increased nonsignificantly ($\chi^2_{dif} = 11.97$, $df_{dif} = 6$, $p > .05$). This finding indicated that the factor loadings are statistically equivalent for boys and girls; therefore, only one set of factor loadings are shown in Table 9.1. Further analysis showed that the two aggression constructs were moderately to highly intercorrelated ($\phi \approx .90$; Pearson $r = .80$ boys and .60 girls; .75 total). To test whether the physical and relational aggression constructs were well distinguished, a one-factor model combining items from both of these dimensions was compared to a two-factor baseline model. The change in the goodness of fit index ($\chi^2_{dif} = 7.05$, $df_{dif} = 2$, $p < .05$) indicated that the two-factor model (physical and relational aggression) fit the data better than the one-factor model.

Measurement of Parental Physical/Verbal Coercion and Psychological Control

To assess the viability of measuring the contribution of fathering constructs in relation to mothers, two sets of analyses were conducted using both continuous and categorical data estimations employing confirmatory factor analytic techniques. The first set compared factor loadings between self- and spouse reports for fathers and mothers, while the second set involved an examination of latent mean differences between fathering and mothering constructs for sons and daughters. Results in Table 9.2 show that for both fathers and mothers, factor loadings derived from data when treated as continuous were attenuated when compared to results of categorical data analyses. Both the continuous and categorical approaches yielded goodness of fit indices that were nonsignificant, indicating that the variables satisfactorily reflected the constructs. As noted earlier, prior research suggests that underestimation problems may arise when treating ordinal data as continuous (e.g., Babakus et al., 1987). These findings reinforce the need for fathering researchers to address these concerns.

Having established the factor structure of our parenting constructs, we next tested for invariance of factor loadings across self- and spouse reports for both fathers and mothers. Items in Table 9.2 that did not have equivalent factor loadings across the reports for either categorical or continuous data estimation strategies are

9. FATHERING IN A BEIJING CHINESE SAMPLE 201

asterisked. Though the standardized factor loadings may be similar or close across informants, the weighted least-square estimates suggested that the factor loadings for these items differed between the informants in measuring the constructs. This was shown by the significant chi-square difference (χ^2_{dif}) between a model with and a model without constraints of factor loading equality, and the corresponding change in degrees of freedom. The differences in factor loadings suggest that self-reports and spouse reports do not measure these parenting constructs similarly. Of the 15 items that differed between informants, 11 were attributable to the fathering measures from both self- and spouse reports. Whether using self- or spouse reports, these findings suggest that mothers' perceptions of fathering and fathers' perceptions of mothering relative to their own self-perceptions are different.

The second set of analyses explored whether father/mother-parenting styles differed for sons versus daughters. Given that our prior analyses showed that the continuous estimation approach underestimated the factor loadings for the parenting constructs, we decided to use the categorical approach for analysis comparing latent mean differences. Additionally, because variance in the factor loadings existed between fathers' and mothers' parenting constructs, we tested for parental differences in the constructs by using a regression approach with dummy-coded variables, as recommended by Muthén (1989). More specifically, father/mother differences in the two parenting constructs were estimated using a series of structural equation models with sex of parent and sex of child as dummy-coded exogenous variables (males $= 0$ and females $= 1$). This model was estimated for each child or parent group in order to adhere to the requirements of Mplus for categorical data (due to all categories in the Likert-type scale not being used for each group). Positive betas reflected higher parenting scores for fathers; negative betas reflected lower parenting scores for fathers relative to mothers.

Based on the self-reports, fathers were more coercive and psychologically controlling with daughters than were mothers ($\beta = .23$, $z = 2.57$, $p < .05$; $\beta = .29$, $z = 2.87$, $p < .05$, respectively). However, fathers were less psychologically controlling with sons than with daughters ($\beta = -.24$, $z = 2.20$, $p < .05$) but were more physically and verbally coercive with sons than with daughters ($\beta = .33$, $z = 3.78$, $p < .05$). Comparisons based upon spouse reports demonstrated that fathers were also more coercive with daughters than were mothers ($\beta = .19$, $z = 2.17$, $p < .05$) but did not differ with respect to sons. However, unlike the self-reports, spouse reports revealed that fathers were more psychologically controlling with sons than with daughters ($\beta = .25$, $z = 2.40$, $p < .05$).

Collapsing across sex of child, findings suggested that when using self-reports, fathers viewed themselves as being more psychologically controlling than mothers ($\beta = .15$, $z = 2.13$, $p < .05$); however, fathers and mothers did not view themselves differently on coercion. Alternatively, when looking at spouse reports, fathers were rated as being more coercive than mothers ($\beta = .13$, $z = 2.02$, $p < .05$), whereas spouses did not view each other differently on the use of psychological control.

Linkages of the Constructs

As anticipated from our literature review, categorical approaches to data analysis yielded a greater number of significant findings than when data were treated as continuous, and when spouse reports, rather than self-reports, were used (see Table 9.3). Because prior research indicates that Chinese fathers use higher levels of coercion than mothers, we anticipated relationships between parenting and child aggression to be more pronounced among father–son and father–daughter dyads than among mother–son and mother–daughter dyads. These linkages were estimated for each parent–child dyad group. To assess the specific contributions of the parenting variables, psychological control was set to statistically compete with coercion in predicting child physical and relational aggression. The structural coefficients and goodness of fit indices are listed in Table 9.3. For brevity, only the results of the spouse-report, categorical data analyses are discussed here. Mediational paths were not examined due to the lack of relationship between negative child emotionality and aggression in any of the models tested (Mize et al., 2000; Tabachnick & Fidell, 1996).

In the father–son dyad group (see Figure 9.1), boys' negative emotionality was significantly associated with paternal coercion, and paternal coercion was significantly related to children's sons' physical and relational aggression. No findings were obtained for psychological control in father–son dyads. In the father–daughter dyads (see Figure 9.2), girls' emotionality was significantly linked with paternal coercion, which in turn was significantly related to physical and relational aggression. Furthermore, paternal psychological control, though unrelated to negative emotionality, was significantly associated with both types of aggression in daughters. In contrast, for the mother–son dyad group, only maternal psychological control was significantly related to boys' physical aggression. Because there was only one significant path estimate, a figure representing the mother–son dyad model is not provided. Finally, in the mother–daughter dyads (see Figure 9.3), girls' negative emotionality was significantly associated with both maternal coercion and psychological control. Maternal psychological control also significantly predicted both physical and relational aggression in daughters, but maternal coercion was not directly related to any of the girls' aggressive behaviors.

Note: The mother–son dyad model is not included because it has only one significant path estimate.

IMPLICATIONS

The aims of this study were to further examine linkages between Chinese fathering and children's outcomes. Similar to findings in other cultural settings, results from this well-educated Beijing sample generally supported the notion that coercive parenting, particularly on the part of fathers, has negative consequences for children.

TABLE 9.3
Structural Parameters and Model Fit Indices

Parent–child Dyad & Paths	Self Reports		Spouse Reports	
	Categorical	Continuous	Categorical	Continuous
Father–son:				
Emotionality→Coercion	.37*	.38*	.30*	.18
Emotionality→Psychological control	−.07	−.16	−.01	−.23
Coercion→Physical aggression	.08	.11	.25*	.22
Psychological control→ Physical aggression	.12	.11	−.03	−.14
Coercion→Relational aggression	.09	.12	.28*	.23
Psychological control→Relational aggression	.33*	.23	−.07	−.15
Goodness of fit	$\chi^2 = 59.23$	$\chi^2 = 215.53$	$\chi^2 = 35.39$	$\chi^2 = 215.25$
	$df = 36$	$df = 182$	$df = 28$	$df = 180$
	$p = .01$	$p = .05$	$p = .16$	$p = .04$
Father–daughter:				
Emotionality→Coercion	.42*	.22	.38*	.17
Emotionality→Psychological control	.40*	.07	.25	.09
Coercion→Physical aggression	.10	.08	.36*	.39*
Psychological control→Physical aggression	.01	−.05	.36*	.27
Coercion→Relational aggression	.08	.11	.48*	.38*
Psychological Control→Relational aggression	.01	−.18	.50*	.38
Goodness of fit	$\chi^2 = 41.29$	$\chi^2 = 219.81$	$\chi^2 = 50.87$	$\chi^2 = 205.12$
	$df = 26$	$df = 182$	$df = 37$	$df = 169$
	$p = .03$	$p = .03$	$p = .06$	$p = .03$
Mother–son:				
Emotionality→Coercion	.12	.08	.05	.05
Emotionality→Psychological control	.40	.54	.01	.09
Coercion→Physical aggression	.13	.16	.13	.11
Psychological control→Physical aggression	.37	.31	.32*	.31
Coercion→Relational aggression	.20	.18	.08	.10
Psychological control→Relational aggression	.42	.41	.25	.21
Goodness of fit	$\chi^2 = 59.63$	$\chi^2 = 236.88$	$\chi^2 = 25.79$	$\chi^2 = 208.86$
	$df = 34$	$df = 182$	$df = 29$	$df = 182$
	$p = .00$	$p = .00$	$p = .36$	$p = .08$
Mother–daughter:				
Emotionality→Coercion	.22	.16	.25*	.10
Emotionality→Psychological control	−.15	−.12	.51*	.59*
Coercion→Physical aggression	.01	−.05	.14	−.25
Psychological control→Physical aggression	.26	.18	.37*	.30
Coercion→Relational aggression	−.09	−.13	−.01	−.19
Psychological control→Relational aggression	.16	.07	.47*	.51*
Goodness of fit	$\chi^2 = 30.45$	$\chi^2 = 227.03$	$\chi^2 = 49.66$	$\chi^2 = 219.55$
	$df = 31$	$df = 182$	$df = 35$	$df = 173$
	$p = .49$	$p = .01$	$p = .05$	$p = .01$

*The maximum likelihood indicate of factor loading significantly differs between self- and spouse reports.

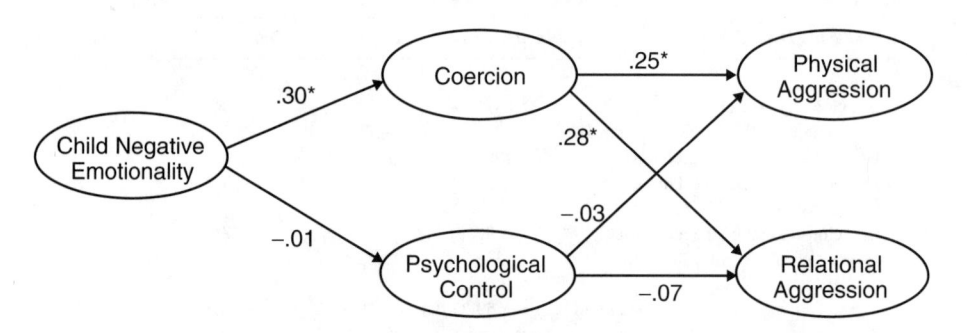

FIG. 9.1. Model linkages for the father–son dyads.

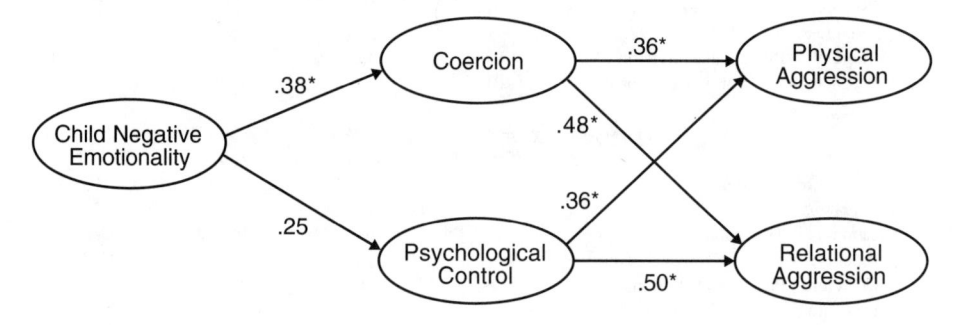

FIG. 9.2. Model linkages for the father–daughter dyads.

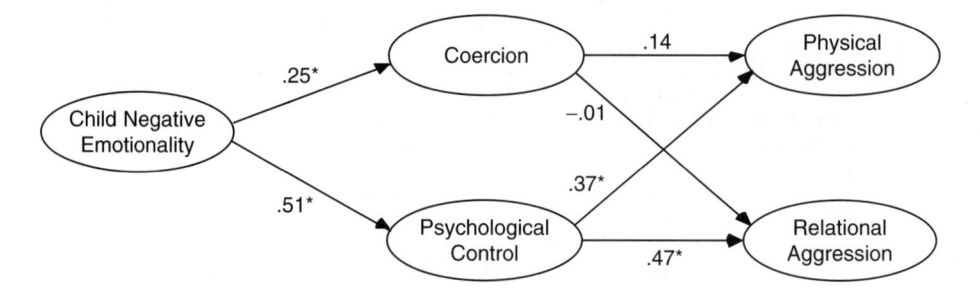

FIG. 9.3. Model linkages for the mother–daughter dyads.

9. FATHERING IN A BEIJING CHINESE SAMPLE

Contrary to views that Chinese children may view and respond to coercive parental control in positive ways, our findings are more in line with other recent data from limited samples suggesting that Chinese children's peer-group behavior is more aggressive in the face of coercive parenting styles (Chen et al., 1997; 2002). More large-scale studies are needed to affirm these findings with more representative Chinese samples as current results may not generalize to the entire mainland Chinese population and all of its socioeconomic and ethnic groups. We also sought to better understand how different methodological and statistical issues pertain to the measurement of fathering. As anticipated, spousal reports and categorical treatment of the data yielded findings that were consistent with our conceptualizations outlined in the beginning.

More specifically, the goals of our study were accomplished by examining stylistic dimensions of hostile parenting as associated with child temperament and child aggression. This effort was unique in several ways. First, we were able to successfully measure the constructs of interest in the mainland Chinese cultural context, using parent reports and child behavior nominations. This suggests that these constructs, derived primarily from Western conceptualizations, may be similarly perceived across cultures and thus represent more universal constructs (e.g., Hart, Nelson et al., 2000; Wu et al., 2002). Second, we focused on parent–child associations that are relatively unexplored in past research. For example, previous work on temperament has consistently noted a relation between difficult child temperament, coercive parenting, and negative child outcomes. Few studies, however, have specifically considered how parental psychological control may be associated with child temperament and negative child outcomes (c.f., Morris et al., 2002). Furthermore, relative to past research, analyses were further refined to pit psychological control against coercion when examining their associations with different types of childhood aggression. All of these associations were explored within various parent–child dyads (e.g., father–son, father–daughter).

Chinese fathers are viewed as the predominant authority figure in Chinese families and have been found in past research to be more coercive in their parenting styles than mothers; therefore, we anticipated more significant linkages between fathering and child temperament and child behavior. Our findings supported prior research showing that higher levels of negative emotionality in children are associated with more coercive parenting styles and more negative parenting perceptions (Porter et al., 2002). Furthermore, evidence for this association was seen in model linkages for Chinese fathers, wherein associations were obtained for both girls and boys. These findings imply that young children who tend to be more easily upset or fussy may make more taxing demands on fathers in this particular Chinese sample. Such behaviors often require immediate attention to alleviate the accompanying stress on parents (Bates, 1980). Fathers who apply more coercive parenting may do so in an attempt to bring about immediate, albeit short-term changes in their children's behavior (Grusec & Goodnow, 1994; Maccoby, 1998). In this vein, it is notable that children's negative emotionality (for both boys and girls) was

associated with more coercive control rather than psychological control by Chinese fathers. These findings imply that, in response to difficult child behaviors, psychological control strategies may be less favored by Chinese fathers. Past research in Western cultures does indicate that fathers tend to use less love-oriented methods of discipline in favor of more verbal and physical coercion in disciplinary contexts (Maccoby, 1998). This may also apply to Chinese fathering.

These findings contrast with those of Chinese mothers, where psychological control and coercion were both associated with negative child emotionality in daughters. Chinese mothers may endorse multiple forms of control in their parenting efforts, at least with girls. This notion is indirectly supported by research showing that Chinese mothers tend to report more love-oriented control strategies than their American counterparts (Ho, 1986). The evidence that there were no relationships between hostile parenting and negative emotionality in mother–son dyads suggests that mothers may be particularly sensitive or overreactive when daughters are more easily upset or fussy. A possible explanation may be that in the Chinese culture, where drawing attention to self is discouraged, negative emotionality may be considered antithetical to cultural norms. This may be particularly true for daughters who are expected to be more reserved, relative to boys (cf., Cheung, 1996). Additional research is needed to further delineate the nature of these relationships.

The evidence that Chinese fathers are more coercive toward sons and daughters who exhibit high levels of negative emotionality actually contradicts earlier findings in Western cultures, which indicate that fathers, relative to mothers, typically tolerate difficult temperament in boys but not in girls (Sanson & Rothbart, 1995). Negative features of child temperament may evoke more coercive fathering in China, which is directed toward both boys and girls. This in turn appears to be associated with physical and relational aggression in daughters and sons. As noted earlier, Chen et al. (1997) established a connection between coercive parenting and children's aggressive/disruptive behavior in a Chinese school-age sample. Our study also finds this connection in an early childhood sample, and extends this body of literature by considering parenting style associations with negative temperament. However, since parenting was not found to statistically mediate the relationship between children's negative emotionality and aggression, future studies should focus more on examining potential mediating and moderating effects (Baron & Kenny, 1986). Recent research is starting to move more in this direction (e.g., Chen et al., 2001; Paterson & Sanson, 1999; Russell et al., 2002).

Interestingly, coercive mothering was not associated with boys' or girls' aggression. Alternatively, coercive fathering was associated with both forms of childhood aggression in father–son and in father–daughter dyads. Past research indicates that mothers' coercion may carry the weight of influence regarding childhood aggressive behaviors relative to that of fathers (Hart, Nelson et al., 1998; Rothbaum & Weisz, 1994), and that Chinese mothers' coercion is associated with both boys' and

9. FATHERING IN A BEIJING CHINESE SAMPLE 207

girls' emotional regulation, which is associated, in turn, with childhood aggression (Chang et al., 2002). In contrast, the current data suggest that Chinese fathers may be relatively more important in this regard for both girls' and boys' aggression, perhaps because they might play a more dominant disciplinary role (Chen et al., 2000). These findings partially support and contradict those of prior research that indicate that Chinese fathers' (but not mothers') coercion is directly associated with boys' but not girls' aggression in some studies (Chen et al., 2002; Chang et al., 2002) but is related to girls' but not boys' aggression in others (Chen et al., 2001). Such discrepant findings across studies are not that unusual. As noted in a recent meta-analysis (Gershoff, 2002), there appear to be no consistent patterns of linkages between coercive parenting (i.e., corporal punishment) and children's behavior problems for any combination of parent and child gender. To sort out these contradictions, more formal statistical tests using dominance analysis techniques for assessing the *relative importance* of Chinese mothers and fathers in facilitating boys' and girls' aggression would be an important next step in future research (cf. Hart, Nelson et al., 1998; Stolz, 2002).

This is the first study to examine the relation between psychological control strategies and different forms of aggression in a mainland Chinese sample. Results showed that fathers' use of psychological control strategies was associated with both physical and relational forms of aggression in daughters but not in sons. This suggests that, in the father–son dyad, psychological control does not have the same effects in evoking aggression that it does for daughters. Although this finding might initially imply that girls are somehow learning aggressive behavior by interacting with their fathers as suggested by reciprocal role theory (Johnson, 1963; 1975), it should be recalled that psychological control on the part of mothers is also associated with both forms of aggression in daughters (but not in sons). It may well be that love-oriented methods of discipline elicit more resistance and animosity in girls than in boys, regardless of which parent administers it, primarily due to the greater sensitivity of girls to relational slights (e.g., Cross & Madsen, 1997; Leadbetter, Blatt, & Quinlan, 1995; Maccoby, 1998).

In addition, analysis of mean differences based on the self-reports revealed that Chinese fathers reported using more psychological control with daughters than with sons. Spouse reports, however, demonstrated the converse relationship, with fathers characterized as using more psychological control with sons than with daughters. It is interesting to note that the meaningful linkages between fathers' psychological control and daughters' aggression emerged from the spouse reports rather than from fathers' self-reports. Even though the majority of our meaningful findings were found when using spouse reports, this caveat well illustrates how mothers' and fathers' perceptions of their own and each other's parenting differ. Presently our data do not address whether these discrepancies in perceptions between fathers and mothers are due to possible social desirability biases, access to information, different meanings for similar phenomena, or differential reference

points or response sets reflecting levels of awareness/sensitivities (Triandis, 1994). Future fathering research needs to address these perceptual/methodological issues.

Measurement and analysis issues also proved to be an important aim of this chapter. In line with our expectations, spouse reports rather than self-reports, as well as categorical rather than continuous approaches to data analysis, yielded findings most consistent with trends and hypotheses in the research literature. Attention to these methodological and analytical issues should further enhance the study of fatherhood. Meaningful connections were further illuminated by comparing and contrasting findings for various parent–child dyads (e.g, father–son, father–daughter; cf. Isley et al., 1999).

In summary, the findings presented in this chapter contribute to the literature regarding associations among negative child temperament, aggression, and negative parenting. Examination of these linkages was particularly illuminating for father–child relationships. For example, consistent with prior research (e.g., Nelson & Crick, 2002), fathers apparently play an important role in the development of children's aggression. This is especially important in the consideration of relational aggression, an area of research that holds promise for understanding the unique developmental trajectories of girls. Taken together with research conducted in the Chinese cultural context that illustrates more positive influences of fathers on children's development (e.g., Chen et al., 2000), these findings emphasize the collective importance of father influence in the mainland Chinese cultural context. It is our hope that the issues raised in this chapter may bring greater focus to the study of father–child relationships in diverse cultural contexts.

ACKNOWLEDGMENTS

The authors express gratitude to the College of Family, Home, and Social Sciences, the Camilla Eyring Kimball Endowment, the David M. Kennedy Center for International Studies, the Zina Young Card Williams Professorship (awarded to Craig H. Hart), and the Family Studies Center at Brigham Young University for providing funding for this work.

REFERENCES

Ahadi, S. A., Rothbart, M. K., & Ye, R. (1993). Children's temperament in the US and China: Similarities and difference. *European Journal of Personality, 7*, 359–377.

Babakus, E., Ferguson, Jr., C. E., & Jöreskog, K. (1987). The sensitivity of confirmatory maximum likelihood factor analysis to violations of measurement scale and distributional assumptions. *Journal of Marketing Research, 24*, 222–228.

Bandura, A. (1973). *Aggression: A social learning approach*. Englewood Cliffs, NJ: Prentice-Hall.

Bandura, A. (1977). *Social learning theory*. Englewood Cliffs, NJ: Prentice-Hall.

9. FATHERING IN A BEIJING CHINESE SAMPLE 209

Barber, B. K. (1996). Parental psychological control: Revisiting a neglected construct. *Child Development, 67*, 3296–3319.

Barber, B. K., & Harmon, E. L. (2002). Violating the self: Parental psychological control of children and adolescents. In B. K. Barber (Ed.), *Intrusive parenting: How psychological control affects children and adolescents* (pp. 15–52). Washington, DC: American Psychological Association.

Baron, R. M., & Kenny, D. A. (1986). The moderator–mediator variable distinction in social psychological research: Conceptual, strategic, and statistical considerations. *Journal of Personality and Social Psychology, 51*, 1173–1182.

Bates J. E. (1980). The concept of difficult temperament. *Merrill–Palmer Quarterly, 26*, 299–319.

Bates, J. E. (1989). Concepts and measures of temperament. In G. A. Kohnstamm, J. E. Bates, & M. K. Rothbart (Eds.), *Temperament in childhood* (pp. 483–508). New York: Wiley.

Baumrind, D. (1996). The discipline controversy revisited. *Family Relations, 45*, 405–414.

Baumrind, D., & Black, A. E. (1967). Socialization practices associated with dimensions of competence in preschool boys and girls. *Child Development, 38*, 291–327.

Berndt, T. J., Cheung, P. C., Lau, S., Hau, K. T., & Lew, W. J. F. (1993). Perceptions of parenting in Mainland China, Taiwan, and Hong Kong: Sex differences and societal differences. *Developmental Psychology, 29*, 156–164.

Bernstein, R. H., & Teng, G. (1989). Factoring items and factoring scales are different: Spurious evidence for multidimensionality due to item categorization. *Psychological Bulletin, 105*, 467–477.

Bollen, K. A. (1989). *Structural equations with latent variables*. New York: Wiley.

Bollen, K. A., & Barb, K. H. (1981). Pearson's R and coarsely categorized measures. *American Sociological Review, 46*, 232–239.

Borgata, E. F., & Bohrnstedt, G. W. (1972). How one normally constructs good measures. *Sociological Methods & Research, 1*, 3–12.

Brody, G. H., & Endsley, R. C. (1981). Researching children and families: Differences in approaches of child and family specialists. *Family Relations, 30*, 275–280.

Buss, H. A., & Plomin, R. (1984). Theory and measurement of EAS. In A. H. Buss & R. Plomin (Eds.), *Temperament: Early developing personality trait* (pp. 84–104). New Jersey: Lawrance Erlbaum Associates.

Chamberlain, P., & Patterson, G. R. (1995). Discipline and child compliance in parenting. In M.H. Bornstein (Ed.), *Handbook of parenting: Applied and practical parenting, Vol. 4*, (pp. 205–226). Hillsdale, NJ: Lawrence Erlbaum Associates.

Chang, L., Schwartz, D., Dodge, K., & McBride-Chang, C. (2002, August). *Harsh parenting in relation to child emotion regulation and aggression: Evidence from mothers and fathers and sons and daughters*. Paper presented at the International Society for the Study of Behavioral Development Meetings, Ottawa, Canada.

Chao, R. K. (1994). Beyond parental control and authoritarian parenting style: Understanding Chinese parenting through the cultural notion of training. *Child Development, 65*, 1111–1119.

Chao, R. K. (2001). Extending research on the consequences of parenting style for Chinese Americans and European Americans. *Child Development, 72*, 1832–1843.

Chao, R. K., & Sue, S. (1996). Chinese parental influence and their children's school success: A paradox in the literature on parenting styles. In S. Lau (Ed.), *Growing up the Chinese way* (pp. 93–120). Hong Kong: The Chinese University Press.

Chao, R. K., & Tseng, V. (2002). Parenting of Asians. In M. H. Bornstein (Ed.), *Handbook of parenting: Volume 4: Social conditions and applied parenting* (pp. 59–93). Mahwah, NJ: Lawrence Erlbaum Associates.

Chen, X., Dong, Q., & Zhou, H. (1997). Authoritarian and authoritative parenting practices and social and school performance in Chinese children. *International Journal of Behavioral Development, 21*, 855–873.

Chen, X., Liu, M, & Li, D. (2000). Parental warmth, control, and indulgence and their relations to adjustment in Chinese children: A longitudinal study. *Journal of Family Psychology, 14*, 401–419.

Chen, X., Wang, L., Chen, H., & Liu, M. (2002). Noncompliance and child-rearing attitudes as predictors of aggressive behaviour: A longitudinal study of Chinese children. *International Journal of Behavioral Development, 26*, 225–233.

Chen, X., Wu, H., Chen, H., Wang, L., Cen, G. (2001). Parental affect, guidance, and power assertion and aggressive behavior in Chinese children. *Parenting: Science and Practice, 1*, 159–183.

Cheung, F. (1996). Gender role development. In S. Lau (Ed.), *Growing up the Chinese way* (pp. 45–67). Hong Kong: The Chinese University Press.

Chiu, L. H. (1987). Child-rearing attitudes of Chinese, Chinese-American, and Anglo-American mothers. *International Journal of Psychology, 22*, 409–419.

Coenders, G., & Saris, W. E. (1995). Categorization and measurement quality: The choice between person and polychoric correlations. In W. E. Saris & Á. Münich (Eds.), *The multitrait-multimethod approach to evaluate measurement instruments* (pp. 125–144). Budapest: Evõtvõs University Press.

Coie, J. D. & Dodge, K. A. (1998). Aggression and antisocial behavior. In W. Damon (Series Ed.) & N. Eisenberg (Vol. Ed.), *Handbook of child psychology: Vol. 3, Social, emotional and personality development* (pp. 779–862). New York: Wiley.

Crick, N., Casas, J. J., & Mosher, M. (1997). Relational and overt aggression in preschool. *Developmental Psychology, 33*, 579–588.

Crick, N., & Grotpeter, J. K. (1995). Relational aggression, gender, and social-psychological adjustment. *Child Development, 66*, 710–722.

Crick, N. R., Werner, N. E., Casas, J. F., O'Brien, K. M., Nelson, D.A., Grotpeter, J. K., & Markon, K. (1999). Childhood aggression and gender: A new look at an old problem. In D. Bernstein (Ed.), *Nebraska symposium on motivation: Gender and motivation* (Vol. 45, pp. 75–141). Lincoln, NE: University of Nebraska Press.

Crockenberg, S. B., & Acredolo, C. (1983). Infant temperament ratings: A function of infants, of mothers, or both? *Infant Behavior and Development, 6*, 61–72.

Cross, S. E., & Madsen, L. (1997). Models of the self: Self-construals and gender. *Psychological Bulletin, 122*, 5–37.

Deater-Deckard, K. (2000). Parenting and child behavioral adjustment in early childhood: A quantitative genetic approach to studying family processes. *Child Development, 71*, 468–484.

Deater-Deckard, K., & Dodge, K. A. (1997). Externalizing behaviors problems and discipline revisited: Nonlinear effects and variation by culture, context, and gender. *Psychological Inquiry, 8*, 161–175.

Deater-Deckard, K., Dodge, K. A., Bates, J. E., & Pettit, G. S. (1996). Physical discipline among African American and European American mothers: Links to children's externalizing behaviors. *Developmental Psychology, 32*, 1065–1072.

De Leeuw, J. (1983). Models and methods for the analysis of correlation coefficients. *Journal of Econometrics, 22*, 113–137.

Dishion, T. J. (1990). The family ecology of boys' peer relations in middle childhood. *Child Development, 61*, 874–892.

Embreston, S. E. (1996). The new rules of measurement. *Psychological Assessment, 8*, 341–349.

Fagot, B. I. (1995). Parenting boys and girls. In M. H. Bornstein (Ed.), *Handbook of parenting. Vol. 1: Children and parenting* (pp. 163–183). Hillsdale, NJ: Lawrence Erlbaum Associates.

Fung, H. (1999). Becoming a moral child: The socialization of shame among young Chinese children. *Ethos, 27*, 180–209.

Gaito, J. (1980). Measurement scales and statistics: Resurgence of an old misconception. *Psychological Bulletin, 87*, 564–567.

Gardner, P. L. (1975). Scales and statistics. *Review of Educational Research, 45*, 43–57.

Gershoff, E. T. (2002). Corporal punishment by parents and associated child behaviors and experiences: A meta-analytic and theoretical review. *Psychological Bulletin, 128*, 539–579.

9. FATHERING IN A BEIJING CHINESE SAMPLE 211

Grusec, J. E. (2002). Parental socialization and the acquisition of values. In M. H. Bornstein (Ed.), *Handbook of parenting. Volume 5: Practical issues in parenting* (pp. 143–167). Mahwah, NJ: Lawrence Erlbaum Associates.

Grusec, J. E., & Goodnow, J. J. (1994). Impact of parental discipline methods on the child's internalization of values: A reconceptualization of current points of view. *Developmental Psychology, 30*, 505–529.

Hart, C. H., DeWolf, M. D., & Burts, D. C. (1992a). Linkages among preschoolers' playground behavior, outcome expectations, and parental disciplinary strategies. *Early Education and Development, 3*, 265–283.

Hart, C. H., DeWolf, M. D., Wozniak, P., & Burts, D. C. (1992b). Maternal and paternal disciplinary styles: Relations with preschoolers' playground behavioral orientations and peer status. *Child Development, 63*, 879–892.

Hart, C. H., Ladd, G. W., & Burleson, B. R. (1990). Children's expectations of the outcomes of social strategies: Relations with sociometric status and maternal disciplinary styles. *Child Development, 61*, 127–137.

Hart, C. H., Nelson, D. A., Robinson, C. C., Olsen, S. F., & McNeilly-Choque, M. K. (1998). Overt and relational aggression in Russian nursery-school-age children: Parenting style and marital linkages. *Developmental Psychology, 34*, 687–697.

Hart, C. H., Nelson, D. A., Robinson, C. C., Olsen, S. F., McNeilly-Choque, M. K., & McKee, T. R. (2000). Russian parenting styles and family processes: Linkages with subtypes of victimization and aggression. In K. A. Kerns, J. M. Contreras, & A. M. Neal-Barnett (Eds.), *Family and peers: Linking two social worlds* (pp. 47–84). Westport: Praeger.

Hart, C. H., Newell, L. D., & Olsen, S. F. (2003). Parenting skills and social/communicative competence in childhood. In J. O. Greene & B. R. Burleson (Eds.), *Handbook of communication and social interaction skill* (pp. 752–797). Mahwah, NJ: Lawrence Erlbaum Associates.

Hart, C. H., Olsen, S. F., Robinson, C. C., & Mandleco, B. L. (1997). The development of communicative competence in childhood: Review and a model of personal, familial, and extrafamilial processes. *Communication Yearbook, 20*, 305–373.

Hart, C. H., Yang, C., Nelson, D., Jin, S., & Nelson, L. (1998). Peer contact patterns, parenting practices, and preschoolers' social competence in China, Russia, and the United States. In P. Slee & K. Rigby (Eds.), *Peer relations amongst children: Current issues and future directions* (pp. 1–30). London: Routledge & Kegan Paul.

Hart, C. H., Yang, C., Nelson, L. J., Robinson, C. C., Olsen, J. A., Nelson, D. A., Porter, C. L., Jin, S., Olsen, S. F., & Wu, P. (2000). Peer acceptance in early childhood and subtypes of socially withdrawn behaviour in China, Russia, and the United States. *International Journal of Behavioral Development, 24*, 73–81.

Hart, C. H., Yang, C., Robinson, C. C., Wu, P., & Olsen, S. F. (2001, April). *Physical and relational aggression: Gender and coercive parenting linkages in China and the United States*. Paper presented at the *Understanding Parenting and Its Associations From a Cross-Cultural Perspective*. Symposium conducted at the Biennial Meeting of the Society for Research in Child Development, Minneapolis, MN.

Hawkins, A. J., & Dollahite, D. C. (Eds.). (1997). *Generative fathering: Beyond deficit perspectives*. Thousand Oaks, CA: Sage.

Ho, D, Y. F. (1986). Chinese patterns of socialization: A critical review. In M. H. Bond (Ed.), *The psychology of the Chinese people* (pp. 1–37). New York: Oxford University Press.

Ho., D. Y. F. (1987). Fatherhood in Chinese culture. In M. E. Lamb (Ed.), *The father's role: Cross-cultural perspectives* (pp. 227–245). Hillsdale, NJ: Lawrence Erlbaum Associates.

Ho, D, Y. F. (1989). Continuity and variation of Chinese patterns of socialization. *Journal of Marriage and the Family, 51*, 149–163.

Hoffman, M. L. (1960). Power assertion by the parent and its impact on the child. *Child Development, 31*, 129–143.

Holden, G. W., & Edwards, L.A. (1989). Parental attitudes towards child rearing: Instruments, issues, and implications. *Psychological Bulletin, 106*, 29–58.

Holden, G. W., Ritchie, K. L., & Coleman, S. D. (1992). The accuracy of maternal self-reports: Agreement between reports on a computer simulation compared with observed behavior in the supermarket. *Early Development and Parenting, 1*, 109–119.

Hsu, C. (1985). Characteristics of temperament in Chinese infants and young children. In W. S. Tseng & D. Y. H. Wu (Eds.), *Chinese culture and mental health*. Orlando, FL: Academic Press.

Isley, S. L., O'Neil, R., Clatfelter, D., & Parke, R. D. (1999). Parent and child expressed affect and children's social competence: Modeling direct and indirect pathways. *Developmental Psychology, 35*, 547–560.

Jacklin, C. N. (1989). Female and male: Issues of gender. Special issue: Children and their development: Knowledge base, research agenda, and social policy application. *American Psychologist, 44*, 127–133.

Johnson, D. R., & Creech, J. C. (1983). Ordinal measures in multiple indicator models: A simulation study of categorization error. *American Sociological Review, 48*, 398–407.

Johnson, M. M. (1963). Sex role learning in the nuclear family. *Child Development, 34*, 319–333.

Johnson, M. M. (1975). Fathers, mothers, and sex typing. *Sociological Enquiry, 45*, 15–26.

Kochanska, G., Kuczynski, L., & Radke-Yarrow, M. (1989). Correspondence between mother's self-reported and observed child-rearing practices. *Child Development, 60*, 56–63.

Lau, S., & Cheung, P. C. (1987). Relations between Chinese adolescents' perception of parental control and organization and their perception of parental warmth. *Developmental Psychology, 23*, 726–729.

Lau, S., & Yeung, P. P. W. (1996). Understanding Chinese child development: The role of culture in socialization. In S. Lau (Ed.), *Growing up the Chinese way* (pp. 29–44). Hong Kong: The Chinese University Press.

Leadbetter, B. J., Blatt, S. J., & Quinlan, D. M. (1995). Gender-linked vulnerabilities to depressive symptoms, stress, and problem behaviors in adolescents. *Journal of Research in Adolescence, 5*, 1–29.

Lytton, H., & Romney, D. M. (1991). Parents' differential socialization of boys and girls: A meta-analysis. *Psychological Bulletin, 109*, 267–296.

Maccoby, E. E. (1998). *The two sexes: Growing up apart, coming together*. Cambridge, MA: Harvard University Press.

Maccoby, E. E., & Martin, M. (1983). Socialization in the context of the family: Parent–child interaction. In P. Mussen (Ed.), *Handbook of child psychology, Vol. 4. Socialization, personality, and social development* (4th ed., pp. 1–101). New York: Wiley.

Marsiglio, W., Amato, P., Day, R. D., & Lamb, M. E. (2001). Scholarship on fatherhood in the 1990s and beyond. *Journal of Marriage and the Family, 62*, 1173–1191.

Martin, W. S. (1978). Effects of scaling on the correlation coefficient: Additional considerations. *Journal of Marketing Research, 15*, 304–308.

Maziade, M., Cote, R., Bernier, H., Boutin, P., & Thivierge, J. (1989). Significance of extreme temperament in infancy for clinical status in pre-school years: II. Patterns of temperament change and implications for the appearance of disorders. *British Journal of Psychiatry, 154*, 544–551.

McFadyen-Ketchum, S. A., Bates, J. E., Dodge, K. A., & Pettit, G. S. (1996). Patterns of change in early childhood aggressive-disruptive behavior: Gender differences in predictions from early coercive and affectionate mother–child interactions. *Child Development, 67*, 2417–2433.

McNeilly-Choque, M. K., Hart, C. H., Robinson, C. C., Nelson, L. J., & Olsen, S. F. (1996). Overt and relational aggression on the playground: Correspondence among different informants. *Journal of Research in Childhood Education, 11*, 47–67.

Mebert, C. J. (1991). Dimensions of subjectivity in parents' rating of infant temperament. *Child Development, 62*, 353–361.

Merbitz, C., Morris, J., & Grip, J. C. (1989). Ordinal scales and foundations of misinference. *Archives of Physical and Medical Rehabilitation, 70*, 308–312.

9. FATHERING IN A BEIJING CHINESE SAMPLE 213

Mize, J., Pettit, G. S., & Meece, D. (2000). Explaining the link between parenting behavior and children's peer competence: A critical examination of the "mediating-process" hypothesis. In K. A. Kerns, J. M. Contreras, & A. M. Neal-Barnett (Eds.), *Family and peers* (pp. 137–168). London: Praeger.

Morris, A. S., Steinberg, L., Sessa, F. M., Avenevoli, S., Silk, J. S., & Essex, M. J. (2002). Measuring children's perceptions of psychological control: Developmental and conceptual considerations. In B. K. Barber (Ed.), *Intrusive parenting: How psychological control affects children and adolescents* (pp. 235–262). Washington, DC: American Psychological Association.

Muthén, B. O. (1983). Latent variable structural equation modeling with categorical data. *Journal of Econometrics, 22*, 43–65.

Muthén, B. O. (1984). A general structural equation model with dichotomous, ordered categorical, and continuous latent variable indicators. *Psychometrika, 49*, 115–132.

Muthén, B. O. (1989). Latent variable modeling in heterogeneous population. *Psychometrika, 54*, 557–585.

Muthén, B., & Kaplan, D. (1992). A comparison of some methodologies for the factor analysis of non-normal Likert variables: A note on the size of the model. *British Journal of Mathematical and Statistical Psychology, 45*, 19–30.

Muthén, L. K., & Muthén, B. O. (1999). *Mplus user's guide*. Los Angeles, CA: Muthén & Muthén.

Muthén, B. O., & Satorra, A. (1995). Technical aspects of Muthén's LISCOMP approach to estimation of latent variable relations with a comprehensive measurement model. *Psychometrika, 60*, 489–503.

Nederhof, A. J. (1983). Methods of coping with social desirability bias: A review. *European Journal of Social Psychology, 15*, 263–280.

Nelson, D. A., & Crick, N. R. (2002). Parental psychological control: Implications for childhood physical and relational aggression. In B. K. Barber (Ed.), *Intrusive parenting: How psychological control affects children and adolescents* (pp. 161–189). Washington, DC: American Psychological Association.

Nix, R. L., Ellen, E. P., Dodge, K. A., Bates, J. E., Pettit, G. S., & McFadyen-Ketchum, S. A. (1999). The relation between mothers' hostile attribution tendencies and children's externalizing behavior problems: The mediating role of mothers' harsh discipline practices. *Child Development, 70*, 896–909.

O'Brien, R. M. (1985). The relationship between ordinal measures and their underlying values: Why all the disagreement? *Quality and Quantity, 19*, 265–277.

Olsen, S. F., Yang, C., Hart, C. H., Robinson, C. C., Wu, P., Nelson, D. A., Nelson, L. J., Jin, S., & Wo, J. (2002). Maternal psychological control and preschool children's behavioral outcomes in China, Russia, and the United States. In B. K. Barber (Ed.), *Intrusive parenting: How psychological control affects children and adolescents* (pp. 235–262). Washington, DC: American Psychological Association.

Olsson, U. (1979a). On the robustness of factor analysis against crude classification of observations. *Multivariate Behavioral Research, 14*, 485–500.

Olsson, U. (1979b). Maximum likelihood estimation of the polychoric correlation coefficient. *Psychometrika, 44*, 443–460.

Palkovitz, R. (1997). Reconstructing "involvement": Expanding conceptualizations of men's caring in contemporary families. In A. J. Hawkins & D. C. Dollahite (Eds.), *Generative fathering: Beyond deficit perspectives* (pp. 200–216). Thousand Oaks, CA: Sage.

Parke, R. D., Simpkins, S. D., McDowell, D. J., Kim, M., Killian, C., Dennis, J., Flyr, M. L., Wild, M., & Rah, Y. (2002). Relative contributions of families and peers to children's social development. In P. K. Smith & C. H. Hart (Eds.), *Handbook of childhood social development* (pp. 156–177). Oxford, UK: Blackwell.

Paterson, G., & Sanson, A. (1999). The association of behavioural adjustment to temperament, parenting and family characteristics among 5 year-old children. *Social Development, 8*, 293–309.

Patterson, G. R. (1986). The contribution of siblings to training for fighting: A microsocial analysis. In D. Olweus, J. Block, & M. Radke-Yarrow (Eds.), *Development of antisocial and prosocial behavior: Research, theories, and issues*. New York: Academic Press.

Pettit, G. S., Bates, J. E., & Dodge, K. A. (1997). Supportive parenting, ecological context, and children's adjustment: A seven-year longitudinal study. *Child Development, 68*, 908–923.

Pettit, G. S., Clawson, M. A., Dodge, K. A., & Bates, J. E. (1996). Stability and change in peer-rejected status: The role of child behavior, parenting, and family ecology. *Merrill–Palmer Quarterly, 42*, 267–294.

Porter, C. L., Hart, C. H., Yang, C., Zeng, Q., Robinson, C. C., & Jin, S. (2002). An exploratory study of child temperament and parenting: Chinese and U.S. comparisons. Unpublished manuscript, Brigham Young University.

Prior, M, Smart, D., Sanson, A., & Oberklaid, F. (1993). Sex differences in psychological adjustment from infancy to 8 years. *Journal of the American Academy of Child and Adolescent Psychiatry, 32*, 291–305.

Reid, J. B., & Patterson, G. R. (1989). The development of antisocial behavior patterns in childhood and adolescence. *European Journal of Personality, 3*, 107–119.

Rigdon, E. E., & Ferguson, Jr., C. E. (1991). The performance of the polychoric correlation coefficient and selected fitting functions in confirmatory factor analysis with ordinal data. *Journal of Marketing Research, 28*, 491–497.

Robinson, C. C., Mandleco, B., Olsen, S. F., & Hart, C. H. (2001). The parenting styles and dimensions questionnaire (PSDQ). In B. F. Perlmutter, J. Touliatos, & G. W. Holden (Eds.). *Handbook of Family Measurement Techniques. Vol. 2*. Instruments and Index (p. 190). Thousand Oaks, Sage.

Roopnarine, J. L., Lu, M., & Ahmedezzaman, M. (1989). Parental reports of early patterns of caregiving play and discipline in India and Malaysia. *Early Child Development and Care, 50*, 109–120.

Rothbart, M., & Bates, J. (1998). Temperament. In N. Eisenberg (Ed.), *Handbook of child psychology*, (Vol. 3, pp. 105–176). New York: Wiley.

Rothbaum, F., & Weisz, J. R. (1994). Parental caring and child externalizing behaviors in nonclinical samples: A meta-analysis. *Psychological Bulletin, 116*, 55–74.

Russell, A., Aloa, V., Feder, T., Glover, A., Miller, H., & Palmer, G. (1998). Sex-based differences in parenting styles in a sample with preschool children. *Australian Journal of Psychology, 50*, 89–99.

Russell, A., Hart, C. H., Robinson, C. C., & Olsen, S. F. (2003). Children's sociable and aggressive behavior with peers: A comparison of the U.S. and Australia and contributions of temperament and parenting styles. *International Journal of Behavioural Development, 23*, 74–86.

Russell, A., Russell, G., & Midwinter, D. (1992). Observer influences on mothers and fathers: Self-reported influences during a home observation. *Merrill–Palmer Quarterly, 38*, 263–283.

Russell A., & Saebel, J. (1997). Mother–son, mother–daughter, father–son, father–daughter: Are they distinct relationships? *Developmental Review, 17*, 111–147.

Sanson, A., Hemphill, S. A., & Smart, D. (2002). Temperament and social development. In P. K. Smith & C. H. Hart, (Eds.), *Handbook of childhood social development* (pp. 97–116). Oxford, UK: Blackwell.

Sanson, A., & Rothbart, M. K. (1995). Child temperament and parenting. In M. H. Bornstein (Ed.), *Handbook of parenting: Vol. 4. Applied and practical parenting* (pp. 299–321). Hillsdale, NJ: Lawrence Erlbaum Associates.

Shield, A., & Cicchett, D. (1998). Reactive aggression among maltreated children: The contributions of attention and emotion dysregulation. *Journal of Clinical Child Psychology*, 381–395.

Snijders, T. A. B., & Bosker, R. J. (1999). *Multilevel analysis: An introduction to basic and advanced multilevel modeling*. Thousand Oaks, CA: Sage.

Snyder, J. R. (1998). Marital conflict and child adjustment: What about gender? *Developmental Review, 18*, 390–420.

Stevens, S. S. (1946). On the theory of scales of measurement. *Science, 103*, 677–680.

9. FATHERING IN A BEIJING CHINESE SAMPLE 215

Stevenson, H. W., Chen, C., & Lee, S. (1992). Chinese families. In J. L. Roopnarine & D. B. Carter (Eds.), *Parent–child socialization in diverse cultures: Advances in applied developmental psychology* (pp. 17–33). Norwood, NJ: Ablex.

Stolz, H. (2002). *Disentangling maternal and paternal effects: Conceptual and methodological issues.* Unpublished doctoral dissertation, Brigham Young University.

Tabachnick, B. G., & Fidell, L. S. (1996). *Using multivariate statistics.* New York: HarperCollins.

Takane, Y., & De Leeuw, J. (1987). On the relationship between item response theory and factor analysis of discretized variables. *Psychometrika, 52,* 393–408.

Thomas, A., & Chess, S. (1977). *Temperament and development.* New York: Brunner/Mazel.

Triandis, H. C. (1994). *Culture and social behavior.* New York: McGraw-Hill Inc.

Wilson, T. P. (1971). Critique of ordinal variables. *Social Forces, 49,* 432–444.

Wright, B. D. (1999). Fundamental measurement for psychology. In S. E. Embretson and S. L. Hershberger (Eds.), *The new rules of measurement: What every psychologist and educator should know* (pp. 65–104). Mahwah, NJ: Lawrence Erlbaum Associates.

Wu, D. H. (1981). Child abuse in Taiwan. In J. E. Korbin (Ed.), *Child abuse and neglect: Cross-cultural perspectives* (pp. 139–165). Los Angeles: University of California Press.

Wu, P., Robinson, C. C., Yang, C., Hart, C. H., Olsen, S. F., Porter, C. L., Jin, S., Wo, J., & Wu, X. (2002). Similarities and differences in mothers' parenting of preschoolers in China and the United States. *International Journal of Behavioural Development, 26,* 481–491.

Zeng, Q. (1998). An exploratory study of child temperament and parenting: A Chinese perspective. Unpublished dissertation, Brigham Young University.

Zhang, Y. (1997). *Chinese children's personality and its development: Based on parents' perceptions.* Unpublished dissertation, Beijing University.

Zhou, S., & Yao, K. (1992). The relationship of temperament, environment, and behavioral problems in children age 2–3 years. *Chinese Mental Health Journal, 6,* 160–163.

10

Measuring Father Involvement in Divorced, Nonresident Fathers

Kay Pasley
University of North Carolina at Greensboro

Sanford L. Braver
Arizona State University

Data from the U.S. Census Bureau (Fields & Casper, 2001) show that many children do not reside in two-parent families nor are all such families biological. In fact in 2000, 30.7% of children aged 17 years and younger were residing with one parent, usually a single mother (80%). Other estimates (U.S. Census Bureau, 1998) show that about 11% of children have a nonresident, divorced or separated father. These figures have remained about the same since 1992. Given that there is no expectation of a dramatic decline in the number of children affected by divorce, continued focus on the experiences of these fathers is warranted.

In this chapter we examine the ways father involvement has been conceptualized and measured in studies of divorced, nonresident fathers. We discuss how those studies fall short by failing to adequately recognize and address (a) the consequences of the structural changes caused by divorce that affect fathers involvement, (b) the gendered context that promotes a deficit perspective by invalidating men's voices and experiences, (c) the breadth of ways fathers are involved after divorce, and (d) the developmental appropriateness of decreased involvement over time. Also, concern over the accuracy of reporting and inherent reporter biases in our measures of involvement are discussed, and we present a promising method

of triangulating biases. We end the chapter by offering recommendations for addressing some of these limitations.

MEASURES OF FATHER INVOLVEMENT

Early conceptualizations of father involvement for divorced fathers assumed that fathers were either present or absent based on their marital status. Thus, married fathers were automatically considered to be present, and divorced fathers were considered to be absent. (We see this in the early work on boundary ambiguity in families by Boss in 1977.) Ahrons' (1981) study of coparenting in families of divorce was one of the first to assess parental involvement by questioning both fathers and mothers; she assumed that many divorced fathers, in fact, were involved and the important question was how frequently they were involved. More recently, the construct of father involvement in studies of nondivorced and divorced fathers typically has been conceptualized as economic provision and other forms of behavioral involvements (Marsiglio, Amato, Day, & Lamb, 2000; Marsiglio, Day, & Lamb, 2000) with some recent scholarship on fathering also examining the motivations for involvement. We briefly describe some of the measures used to assess these constructs. Studies are cited as examples only and are not meant to be inclusive.

Using economic provision as a measure of father involvement, scholars commonly ask divorced fathers and/or their former spouses about his payment or her receipt of child support and the amount of such payments "in the past year" (Berkman, 1986; Braver, Fitzpatrick, & Bay, 1991; King, 1994). Other studies query respondents about the amount and regularity (on-timeness) of child support payments (Berkman, 1986), as well as contributions that do not include the exchange of money, such as the purchase of clothes, presents, dental care, and medical insurance (Teachman, 1991).

Measures that assess other forms of behavioral involvement in studies of divorced fathers often use the same measures applied to studies of intact, two-parent families with a few exceptions. Typical indicators of father involvement include the frequency of participation in a series of activities (Ahrons, 1983; Aldous, Mulligan, & Bjarnason, 1998; Amato & Rivera, 1999; Bruce & Fox, 1999; Clarke-Stewart & Hayward, 1996; Guidubaldi, Duckworth, Perry, & Redmond, 1999). Many of these activities reflect the constructs of engagement, accessibility, and social/emotional support, such as preparing meals, teaching a skill, attending events, doing household chores together, transporting to dental/medical appointments, discussing problems, being available for problems, providing emotional support. Fewer studies include indicators of the cognitive domain of behavioral involvement, such as reasoning, planning, evaluating, and monitoring (Palkovitz, 1997). Of these studies that have assessed the cognitive domain, the effects of monitoring on child outcomes is the typical focus. No study was found that addressed

10. DIVORCED, NONRESIDENT FATHERS   219

other aspects of cognitive involvement, although there are data available to assess planning (see report of the Federal Interagency Forum on Child and Family Statistics, 1998). Even fewer studies include measures of the affective domain of behavioral involvement (e.g., emotions, feelings, affection; Amato & Rivera, 1999), although Palkovitz (1997) offered a strong rationale for its inclusion and other scholars agree (Marsiglio, Amato, et al., 2000). In fact, when affective involvement is measured, respondents are asked to report the quality of the father–child relationship often in terms of closeness/connection and perceived supportiveness (Amato & Rivera, 1999; Arditti & Keith, 1993; Barber, 1994; Buchanan, Maccoby, & Dornbusch, 1996; Emery, 1999).

Measures of behavioral involvement unique to studies of divorced fathers included general assessments of the frequency, regularity, and duration of visits (face-to-face contact) and the frequency of phone calls, letters, and e-mail, usually referencing behaviors within the past year or the past month (see as examples, Argys, Peters, Brooks-Gunn, & Smith, 1998; Beller & Graham, 1986; Buchanan et al., 1996). Other measures include estimates of time, such as the number of weeks the child visited or lived with the nonresident father (see studies using data from the National Survey of Families and Households, NSFH, 1998) or the percentage of time the child spent in the care of the father (Braver, Wolchik, Sandler, Fogas, Zvetina, 1991; Maccoby & Mnookin, 1992). Still other measures attempted to assess the subjective nature of contact by asking about visitation quality (Arditti & Keith, 1993).

Marsiglio, Day, and Lamb (2000) suggest that the motives or perceptions associated with fathering are important to our understanding of men's behavior. To this end, scholars have examined some of the motivations of divorced fathers. Studies have assessed the effects of perceived competence, role salience, satisfaction, investment, employment status, and conditions of employment on involvement (Arendell, 1995; Fox & Bruce, 1999; Minton & Pasley, 1996a; Futris & Pasley, 1997). Other research has addressed the influence of the coparental relationship on father involvement after divorce, particularly the ways in which mothers may restrict involvement (Arendell, 1995; Braver, Wolchik, et al., 1991; Maccoby, 1995; Minton & Pasley, 1996b). However, most studies of coparenting focus on the influence of the coparental relationship on child outcomes rather than on father involvement (Lamb, 1997; Hetherington & Stanley-Hagan, 1997).

HOW MEASURES OF INVOLVEMENT IN DIVORCED FATHERS FALL SHORT

We argue that the measures just described above and many of the measurement strategies themselves are problematic for scholars seeking to understand father involvement in divorced, nonresident fathers. Next we outline these problems and

offer some recommendations for reconceptualizing and measuring father involvement following parental divorce.

Structural Changes Affecting Involvement

When divorce occurs, the pattern of family life is disrupted and new patterns must be negotiated and developed. Several issues relevant to the study of father involvement following divorce stem from these changes. For example, divorce means that decisions must be made regarding the care of dependent children, and such decisions translate into formal legal arrangements regarding the access parents have to children (e.g., legal and physical custody, visitation schedules). Legal custody connotes which parent assumes the rights and responsibilities for making decisions affecting the health, education, and welfare of the child (Emery, 1994). Thus, joint legal custody arrangements continue the predivorce circumstance in which decisions affecting the child are shared by the parents. In contrast, sole legal custody means that only one parent is recognized legally to have this decision-making right and responsibility. Physical custody is distinct from legal custody, as it indicates who is going to provide care for the child on a daily basis. As such, great variation can and does occurs in divorced families regarding the arrangement of physical custody. A common custody arrangement is the awarding of joint legal custody in combination with primary physical custody to the mother, although the definition of primary physical custody can vary (Gunnoe & Braver, 2001; Maccoby & Mnookin, 1992).

The distinction between legal and physical custody is more complicated than would appear from our earlier comments, because evidence suggests that informal changes in both types of custody can and do occur, so the formal (*de jure*) award of custody does not necessarily reflect what happens in daily (*de facto*) life (Maccoby & Mnookin, 1992). Consider a couple that is awarded joint legal custody with primary physical custody to the mother. In one such couple, the father may abdicate his decision-making responsibilities to his former wife, but they equally divide the child's time so each parent provides half of the child's care. Another couple with this same custody arrangement finds the father highly involved in decisions, whereas the mother has most of the daily care of the child except during visitation with the father every other weekend.

Two points are germane to our argument about the consequences of the structural changes imposed legally or informally on families after divorce. First, as a result of divorce, most fathers simply do not have "at-will" access to their children, as they did prior to divorce. Although some custody arrangements are such that fathers have more access and contact than others, in nearly all cases it is impossible to duplicate the earlier pattern of resident fathering, no matter how much they might desire to do so. In reality, many fathers are relegated to a restricted visitation/access schedule, designated as every other weekend. Thus, when compared with nondivorced fathers, the structural barrier of the limited custody arrangement means that divorced fathers will appear less involved on most behavioral measures.

10. DIVORCED, NONRESIDENT FATHERS

In addition, family life on the weekends, when divorced fathers are most likely to engage in face-to-face contact with children, is different than that during the week. Weekends typically have less routinized patterns and activities, and there is greater involvement in leisure pursuits. In contrast, behaviors such as planning (e.g., making dental/medical appointments) occur during the week, when the mother generally has responsibility for primary care. Applied to studies of father involvement, the nature and dynamics of the interaction during weekends would be expected to be different from that of weekly daily involvement. Yet, we could find no study that examined involvement within this structural reality.

Clarity of Referent. Many measures of involvement ask about the frequency of participation in an activity from a series. Such measures often lack a specific anchoring to time, and other measures require respondents to report a specific time frame (e.g., within the past month, within the past year). In either case, divorced fathers, their former spouses, and, in some cases, their children may answer such queries using different referents. Some may refer to the frequency of what occurs during weekend visits; others may consider frequency by comparing weekends with fathers to weekends without fathers as the referent; still others may refer to the combination of weekdays and weekends regardless of where the child resides at either time. Clear references to time allow us to make comparisons across groups and provide greater assurance that the response of one participant is similar to that of another. We could find no study that did this explicitly beyond the typical reference to "in the past month" or "in the past year."

Boundary Issues. We argue that behavioral involvement is influenced by the overt boundaries established between parental households following divorce and the accompanying behaviors of the parents and children. For example, the divorce decree ordinarily spells out the "visitation privileges." Whereas these privileges vary considerably from family to family, the most common provision is one that limits contact to every other weekend. Thus, to visit more frequently could actually be a violation of the law. We could find no research that took this structural limitation into account, although one way to do so is calculating "percentage compliance" for visitation (the amount of visits taking place divided by the amount of contact allowed, by the decree, or otherwise).

Regardless of what the decree says, a father's contact with his child could be virtually limitless, if the custodial mother permitted it to be so. She could easily—and with no outside interference—permit him to visit more than their decree stipulated. This fact puts a focus on the behavior of the former spouse and the nature of the coparental relationship in limiting father involvement. Both quantitative (Braver & O'Connell, 1998; Rettig, Leichtentritt, & Stanton, 1999) and qualitative data (Arendell, 1995; Pasley & Minton, 1997) reveal the negative side of "gatekeeping" and continued coparental conflict. In fact, some evidence shows that when fathers and their young adult children are asked, both wanted more contact than either the mothers or the decree allowed (Fabricius & Hall, 2000). Other evidence (Rettig

et al., 1999) indicates the negative influence of continued conflict between former spouses on father involvement. That is, many former wives encourage more contact between the father and his children than is outlined in any formal order, only to be disappointed when the father does not respond, although this pattern seems less common than the reverse (Braver, Wolchik et al., 1991.) We would be remiss if we failed to recognize that many fathers and mothers work hard to promote and maintain a cooperative coparenting relationship and that the gate swings both ways (Walker & McGraw, 2000). Important to our argument is that the potential variation in boundary maintenance means that measures of involvement should include indicators of court-ordered access, as well as desired and allowed access. In this way additional insight into the complexity of involvement by divorced fathers would result.

Mobility, Relocation, and Proximity. Another commonly occurring structural change after divorce involves mobility and relocation, which dramatically alter the pattern of family life. Researchers recognize geographic proximity as an important variable affecting fathers' behaviors, and greater distance from a child is associated with less contact (Braver & O'Connell, 1998; Stewart, 1999). For example, Braver and O'Connell showed that 34% of mothers moved "more than an hour's drive away from what used to be the family home," and in another 28% of families, the fathers moved (when both moved, these figures describe the parent who moved first). Thus, such relocations are normative and make face-to-face daily involvement impossible, such that special handling of the resulting measurement issues is required.

We note that proximity (distance) is used as a control variable in many studies of divorced, nonresident fathers; however, few attempts are made to tease out any differential effects of distance on various aspects of involvement (c.f., Braver & O'Connell, 1998.) All else being equal, fathers who have adequate resources can continue to have access to and involvement with children who live at a distance via phone, e-mail, and letter writing, when distance and expenses prohibit face-to-face contact. However, we could find no study that recognized the greater effort and expense required to maintain contact at a distance. This greater effort and expense may undermine involvement, and inclusion of changes in location, distance, effort, and the associated expenses might better inform our understanding of father involvement. Because most nondivorced, resident fathers have ready access daily, less effort and expense is needed to maintain the father–child relationship. Divorced fathers who maintain contact in the face of relocation may represent a select group—one that is both more responsible and resourceful and that possesses the necessary economic resources. To date, scholars have done little to explore the nature and frequency of father involvement "from a distance."

Economic Provision. Divorce also results in heightened awareness of how the provider aspects of father involvement influence the patterns of family life. Although nondivorced fathers have this responsibility also, their involvement in

10. DIVORCED, NONRESIDENT FATHERS

economic provisioning is taken for granted and commonly measured by their employment status and income. The legal context of divorce makes this responsibility explicit. Some variation across states regarding court orders for child support exists, and these differences result in higher or lower percentages of fathers being ordered to pay. For example, 83% of those in California were ordered to pay child support (Maccoby & Mnookin, 1992); 75% were ordered to do so in Wyoming (personal communication, Office of Family Services, December 2000). Not only are there variations in whether fathers are ordered to pay, but there also are variations in how much they are ordered to pay (Emery, 1999; Pirog, Klotz & Byers, 1998). Morgan and Lino (1999) analyzed child support guidelines in every state and found enormous variability. For an identical family size and parental income scenario, a presumptive order varied from a low of $550 per month in Mississippi to a high of $1,054 in Nebraska. According to Venohr and Williams (1999), about half the states provide significant reductions based upon the percentage of time fathers spend with children in determining the award, but, with two or three exceptions, only if that percentage is substantial (the "shared parenting adjustment").

For measurement purposes and in light of such variation, we believe that it is reasonable to divide the amount of child support paid by the amount of child support ordered to establish a "compliance ratio" instead of, or in addition to, simply asking about the amount paid. Whereas some data sets ask about court orders/awards (see the NSFH, 1998) and enable calculation of this ratio, other data sets do not include this query (e.g., ADD-Health, Udry, 1997). Also, researchers who worked with a data set that had the information available failed to make these calculations (e.g., King & Heard, 1999).

Additional complications arise because some fathers who are not ordered to pay do so anyway, informally and voluntarily (Argys, et al., 1996; Greene & Moore, 1999). Fabricius, Braver, and Mack (2003) studied the financial support divorced fathers provided for their young adult children's college expenses. Because the children were no longer minors, they were under no legal obligation to pay anything; however, substantial support was provided, especially among fathers with joint legal custody, who, after adjusting for differential income, provided proportionately more than did custodial mothers.

Failure to differentiate the economic contributions made voluntarily from those made under court order erroneously treats all divorced fathers as a homogeneous group. How would our reporting change if the research questions were about economic responsibility or compliance? If we included additional indicators of economic involvement by measuring responsibility (court-ordered), amount, and regularity of child support payments, designating involvement would be even more complicated. Typical measures do not account for these complex variations among divorced, nonresident fathers and their experiences, although we believe these measurement issues should be addressed.

A related problem in asking about financial provision has to do with the interpretation respondents make of a query. Consider an item that asks about the timeliness of payments. A father who directly mails his payment to his former spouse by the

due date or has the payment automatically withdrawn from his paycheck and for-warded to a collection agency typically will report making his payment "on time." Because it takes time for the payment to arrive (e.g., the agency has to process the payment or the mail system to deliver it), the former spouse may report the payment as "late" because it is not received on the designated date. Other questions may ask about the regularity of payments (whether they are made "regularly"), and these also can be more or less problematic depending on the specificity of the query. When questions allow respondents to define "regularity" for themselves, we cannot be confident that the query is interpreted in a similar fashion. Greater care must be exercised in selecting terminology and clearly articulating questions so more accurate reporting is possible.

Gendered Context and the Deficit Perspective of Divorced Fathers

Some scholars acknowledge that divorce occurs in a context in which gender bias is enacted (e.g., Arendell, 1995; Buehler, 1995; Braver & O'Connell, 1998; Maccoby & Mnookin, 1992; Pasley & Minton, 1997). Fineman (1991) suggested that the presumption of gender neutrality and gender equality served as a guid-ing principle in many of the statutory reforms related to property division and spousal support, stemming from the view of marriage as a economic partnership. Buehler (1995) argued that contributions by husbands to family life occur pri-marily through employment and secondarily through household/family work, and the reverse pattern is true for women. These primary and secondary role-related responsibilities connote gender bias that influences the ways in which we concep-tualize and measure father involvement. For example, early studies focused on the financial contributions fathers made in terms of child support, so interest was on amount, frequency, and regularity of such payments (Cassetty, 1978; Chambers, 1979). Often compliance was viewed as a reflection of father involvement, and men have been disparaged for noncompliance as "deadbeat dads," although such beliefs have been effectively challenged (Braver & O'Connell, 1998).

The gendered presumption that men are economically responsible for families is apparent in research comparing the payment of child support by nonresident mothers and nonresident fathers. Findings shows that nonresident mothers are less likely to pay (Brown, 2000; Stewart, 1999), the amount is frequently less than that ordered of fathers with equivalent standards of living, and mothers pay less regularly (e.g., Meyer & Garasky, 1993). However, we do not see the same negative labels (e.g., "deadbeat moms") applied to women who are noncompliant.

Another area in which gender bias is evident is in custody decisions. Many scholars (Buehler, 1995; Mason, 1994; Maccoby & Mnookin, 1992) note that, despite laws to the contrary, custody decisions are hardly gender neutral, and figures indicate that about 85% of divorced nonresident parents are fathers (U.S. Census Bureau, 1998). In this culture, parenting is conducted primarily by mothers,

10. DIVORCED, NONRESIDENT FATHERS 225

and most parents prefer and adopt this pattern of role responsibilities. Although only one state (Minnesota) has a primary caretaker criterion as a formal part of its custody statute (meaning custody should be awarded to the parent who served as primary caretaker during the marriage; Crippen, 1990), judges in most states frequently apply a primary caretaker preference anyway (Buehler, 1995; Emery, 1994; Kelly & Lamb, 2000). The result is gender biased, because men rarely fit these criteria.

Further, the gender bias is apparent in many of the commonly used measures of father involvement because most are derived from measures developed and used primarily with mothers as respondents, implicitly suggesting that fathers should do what mothers do. As a result, most measures assess engagement activities; this kind of face-to-face contact, especially that which is instrumental in nature, is more characteristic of the types of behaviors mothers engage in than that of fathers, who are more likely to be accessible and engage in recreational activities (Lamb, 1997). Often there is little if any recognition of father's involvement in play activities with children, even though research shows this is a prominent way for fathers to spend time with young children. Given the structural barriers to engagement for divorced, nonresident fathers, we believe that measures of accessibility must be further explored, as accessibility is less affected by the structural changes that come with divorce. For example, whereas physical accessibility is common in nondivorced families, accessibility by phone might be expected when fathers are not in close proximity to the child as is the case in many divorced families. Also, because many fathers are restricted to having face-to-face contact with their children on weekends, we would do well to acknowledge that leisure activities commonly occur on weekends in most families, not just divorced families.

Breadth of Father Involvement After Divorce

Much of the empirical work has not addressed the structural constraints of the divorced family context. Therefore, we have been unsuccessful in understanding the full breadth of father involvement among divorced fathers, and more work is needed on measures that assess accessibility, responsibility, and the emotional and cognitive domains of father involvement. We noted earlier that accessibility (and engagement) can and is restricted by the legal context, geographic proximity, and the nature and quality of the continuing coparenting relationship. Further, the child's response to the structural changes resulting from parental divorce can and does affect his or her willingness to connect with the father (Maccoby & Mnookin, 1992; Emery, 1999), and both mothers and fathers are known to limit access because of what they believe is best for the child (e.g., Arendell, 1995; Wolchik, Fenaughty & Braver, 1996; Pasley & Minton, 1997). Yet measures typically do not account for children's responses or parental responses in light of children's responses.

Moreover, we believe that the typical measures of responsibility (e.g., payment of child support, monitoring) inadequately address other dimensions of responsibility, such as protecting the child, meeting commitments (e.g., picking the child up on time, attending school-related activities), or teaching the child certain skills (e.g., appropriate social behavior). In fact, we know of no study of divorced, nonresident fathers that asked about their level of responsibility in a variety of parenting activities typically asked of fathers and mothers in nondivorced families (see Pleck, 1997). Thus, we do not know the answer to questions concerning who and at what level a parent is responsible for certain aspects of parenting, under what conditions (such as divorce) this responsibility changes, and how it changes.

We also believe an important aspect of father involvement remains virtually unexplored: the cognitive domain (Palkovitz, 1997). Research shows that divorced fathers and mothers are highly concerned/worried about the possible effects that their decision to divorce can have on their children (Hetherington & Stanley-Hagan, 1997; Kitson, 1992). Findings suggest that they are cognizant of their children's responses to the divorce, and fathers comment that these concerns prompt them to disengage from their children (Braver & O'Connell, 1998; Futris & Pasley, 1997). Buehler and Pasley (1993) argued that the cognitive or psychological presence of the child to the father is likely heightened after divorced. Although this construct (psychological presence) may provide a unique understanding of some cognitions associated with fathering after divorce from both the father's and the child's perspectives, it has yet to be studied adequately. Because psychological presence reflects concern and worry about one's child, fathers may choose to limit their involvement in the hope that this reduces the children's stress (Arendell, 1995; Braver & Griffin, 2000; Futris & Pasley, 1997). Interestingly, using data from the Minton and Pasley (1996a) study, we found that the level of psychological presence of the child did not differ significantly between nondivorced, resident fathers and divorced, nonresident fathers, (Minton & Pasley, 1996b). Thus, if psychological presence had been used as one indication of father involvement, these data would have shown that their level of this type of involvement is equivalent; however, the measure of engagement with this sample showed divorced, nonresident fathers as less involved.

Developmental Appropriateness of Involvement

Another limitation is that most studies of fathering after divorce fail to consider the developmental appropriateness of different kinds of involvement as the child matures. For example, the often cited study by Furstenberg, Peterson, Nord, and Zill (1983) shows a dramatic decline in fathers' contact in the first 2 years after divorce. Less often noted is that these target children were 11–16 years of age, an age when children's focus turns to peers and when visitation interferes with

10. DIVORCED, NONRESIDENT FATHERS

children's social agendas. Maccoby and Mnookin (1992) reported that for the youngest group of children (those under 6 at the beginning of their 3-year study), visiting with their fathers remained a positive experience. It was only among those children 12 and older that increasing resistance to visitation occurred over time; in part, this resistance may be expected during this stage of children's development. Not only does the involvement of fathers change over time, it may be differentially important at varying points in the child's maturation. Coatsworth (2000) found that divorced father's were, on average, less supportive of their college-age children than were divorced mothers. However, support from fathers accounted better than did support from mothers for the children's college adjustment. Clearly, more exploration of changes in father involvement over time in the context of the child's developmental needs is warranted.

Measures of behavioral involvement often do not address the developmental changes. Use of a scale such as Ahron's (1983) means that fathers of infants typically would answer *never* to "discussing problems with children," "religious and moral training," and "attending school or church related functions." If composite scores are used (a common practice), these fathers would appear less involved than fathers of school-age children where these items are developmentally appropriate. "Dressing and grooming" would be less appropriate behavioral involvement for fathers of school-age children or adolescents, and we would see the same problem surfacing.

Accuracy of Respondents' Reports

At the foundation of the four limitations mentioned thus far lie concerns regarding the accuracy of the reports and information derived from various informants. In the recent decade review of research on fathering, Marsiglio, Amato, and associates (2000) summarized the findings regarding "shared-method variance, discrepancies among respondents' reports and the reliability of observational data" (p. 1179). They described some of the issues and ways in which the extant literature has or is addressing these issues. We will not summarize their comments here but will limit our discussion to several key points for studying divorced, nonresident fathers.

Biased Reporting. Generally, the biases of informants appear to be of two sorts: a "self-serving" bias when the informant describes him/herself in terms of more socially desirable behavior and less undesirable behavior than is warranted (Braver & Rohrer, 1978; Cialdini, Braver, & Lewis, 1974; Miller & Ross, 1975; Sicoly & Ross, 1977); and an "ex-spouse-bashing" bias (Braver, Fitzpatrick, & Bay, 1991) characterized by exactly the opposite tendencies when the informant describes the former spouse. For example, scholars (Ahrons,1983; Braver, Wolchik, et al., 1991; Braver et al., 1993) found that a father's reports of his contact and emotional involvement with the child were significantly greater than were reports by his former spouse (the child's mother) on his behavior. Interestingly, other

research shows that nonresident mothers also have a tendency to report higher levels of contact with nonresident children than others report (Greif & Kristall, 1993; Warshak, 1992). Braver, Fitzpatrick, and Bay (1991) and Sonenstein and Calhoun (1990) found similar results for child support payment and compliance. One clear methodological implication of these biases for descriptive work on father involvement arises when only one former spouse, most commonly the mother, provides data. Generally, the researcher accepts the mother's report as a proxy for the father's, a practice that should be recognized as virtually guaranteed to produce misleading results. This practice is less problematic in hypothesis or model testing research than in purely descriptive studies because the former commonly relies on correlations between the matched reports, which are typically quite substantial and positive (e.g., Braver, Fitzpatrick, & Bay, 1991), despite the significant mean differences found in the absolute amount of involvement reported.

Obtaining Objective (or Less-Biased) Data. Because of these two well-documented biases in measuring father involvement after divorce, it is desirable to attempt to "triangulate" reports to get at the truth by obtaining both mother's and father's responses whenever feasible. Obtain some more objective data in the form of archival or administrative data when possible, in addition to the parent's reports. The child support aspect of father involvement appears most amenable to this desideratum; however, this goal has proven elusive because trustworthy administrative databases do not appear to exist (Braver & O'Connell, 1998; Garfinkel, 1985; Schaeffer, Seltzer, & Klawitter, 1991). Further, for most other father involvement indicators, administrative or official records simply do not exit.

Another alternative for a less-biased data source that often is overlooked is the child's report of father involvement which should contain neither self-serving nor other-bashing biases. Although children may respond with biases of their own, they are less likely to be systematic than those previously mentioned. For many studies, however, such as the Panel Study of Income Dynamics and the National Survey of Families and Households, querying the child may be difficult but not impossible. Even when it is practical, questions arise about the trustworthiness of the data when the child is too young to be a credible informant.

These latter problems are alleviated if we recruit older children as informants, such as late adolescents or young adults. Not only is this child old enough to be credible, but also she or he should not be as biased as the parents are to either overreport or underreport involvement. Because young adults often have achieved some independence, distance, and perspective on family dynamics and may no longer reside in either parent's house, the biases of young adult children of divorce are less obvious and more complex, and these children might conceivably be entirely unbiased. Thus, we believe using young adult samples can provide valuable insights into father involvement. One way such a sample can be obtained is to screen the potential primary respondent in nationally representative data sets for age (e.g., selecting those ages 18–22) and parental divorce status. An easier method, albeit

10. DIVORCED, NONRESIDENT FATHERS

not nationally representative, is to obtain responses about father involvement from college students.

A chief advantage of using college student samples is that their reports are among the easiest data to obtain. The numbers are adequate, they congregate in the exact domain of researchers (college campuses), and little or no financial resources are required to obtain responses. Of course, reports of college students about father involvement may contain a different bias: sample representativeness. College students are plausibly disproportionally from better adapted and more functional families because, after all, somehow the young adult had the "capital" (social, human) to attend college. Thus, young adult children of divorce who go to college, may be a select sample with biased levels of father involvement. Diminishing that argument, however, findings from several recent surveys at a large state university (Fabricius & Hall, 2000; Fabricius, Braver & Mack, 2003) indicate that the proportion of college students who describe their parents as divorced was consistent at about 30%, corresponding well with national figures. For example, Bumpass and Sweet (1989) found that 31% of children whose parents are married are expected to experience parental divorce (see also National Center for Health Statistics, 1990, Table 1-31.)

We believe that using college student samples may be an important first step in identifying the areas in which multiple informants are needed. In the following section, as an illustration of the utility of this readily available sample, we describe the sample acquisition method and response rate results of a study recently undertaken as an honors thesis by Diana Coatsworth (2000) under the supervision of the second author. Then we report some intriguing results with this sample.

COLLEGE STUDENTS AS RESPONDENTS: AN EXAMPLE

After receiving approval from the University Institutional Review Board, we recruited college students for the study in the following way. During one class session before a scheduled exam, six introductory psychology classes received an announcement that students had an opportunity to receive extra course credit toward their final grade by participating in our survey. Our interest in surveying them and their parents was explained, and the students were instructed to bring their parents' addresses to the next exam in order to address a questionnaire packet to each parent. Parents were recruited by telling them in a letter that their child would be given additional points toward their final grade if they returned the survey but that no penalty would befall their student if they decided not to participate. The survey was one of several extra credit options. Students had the opportunity to earn 1 or 2 extra credit points per survey (depending on the instructor), allowing them 3 to 6 extra credit points maximum per student, a total of about 1.5% of their final semester grade.

On the scheduled exam day, students had the opportunity to indicate their desire to participate in the study as they left the classroom following the exam. The incentive was described again. Each student signed a prepared letter to each parent, explaining the study and our request of them. If the student knew each parent's address, they provided it at that time. If the child did not have the addresses with them, their e-mail address was requested as a way of communicating to obtain the parents' addresses later. Students had the option of completing their survey at that time or submitting the completed survey later to a designated place. The parent packets included a prepaid return envelope. After all surveys were returned, the student received the promised extra credit points.

Approximately 725 students (about 120 students in each section) were enrolled in the six sections of the course, Fall 2000. From responses on a previous survey ($n = 644$), 189 (29.3%) indicated that their parents were divorced. (Of these 189 students presuming this number was correct as of the day of the exam), 166 (88%) chose to participate in the study by taking the materials for themselves and their parents. Of the students who took the materials, 34 (20.5%) of the students did not return their questionnaire by the deadline (2.5 to 3.5 weeks after the surveys were distributed), leaving 132 students whose data were analyzed. Of the 332 potential parents of the potentially participating 166 students, 31 father questionnaires and 5 mother questionnaires were not mailed because of address problems; 9 father questionnaires and 2 mother questionnaires were not mailed because they were either deceased or unable to complete a questionnaire for medical reasons; 15 father questionnaires were not mailed because the student indicated they had absolutely no contact with the father and no way of obtaining an address. This resulted in 111 father questionnaires and 159 mother questionnaires being mailed. Of the 270 questionnaires mailed, 243 were completed and returned (for mothers $N = 141$, for a response rate of 88.7%; for fathers $N = 102$, for a response rate of 91.9%), an extremely high rate for a mailed questionnaire. Restricting attention to the 132 students who returned their questionnaire, 128 mother questionnaires were mailed (97% of the actually participating students), and 109 were returned (83% of the eligible mothers; an 85% response rate of those mailed). Again for the 132 responding students, 42 father questionnaires were unable to be mailed for reasons listed above, leaving 90 father questionnaires that were mailed (68% of the actually participating students), and 81 were returned (61.4% of the eligible fathers; a 90% response rate of those mailed).

Sample Findings About Father Involvement

Clearly, using this method a variety of aspects of father involvement questions can be asked in parallel of the divorced mother, divorced father, and child. Questions can be asked retrospectively about involvement at earlier stages of the divorce or about indices of current involvement. As an illustration of the retrospective

10. DIVORCED, NONRESIDENT FATHERS

TABLE 10.1

Retrospective Reports of Father Involvement by Divorced Mothers, Divorced
Fathers, and Their College-Age Children in Percent

Informant	Lived 20% Time or More With Dad	Had Own Bedroom at Dad's House	Had Own or Shared With Sibling a Bedroom at Dad's House
Father's report	51%	35%	68%
Mother's report	40%	28%	54%
Child's report	56%	30%	59%

questions students and parents were asked: "Considering the entire time since the divorce, when [you were/the child was] either with [your mother or your father/you or your ex-spouse], what was the approximate breakdown of that time with each?" An example of possible answers was "about 10% of the time with [dad/me], 90% of the time with [mom/my ex-spouse]." Percentages of each of the matched responses reporting 20% or more time with the father appear in Table 10.1.

Another retrospective item construed as an indicator of father involvement asked of the child: "During the first 2 years after the divorce, when you stayed in the home of the parent you did not primarily live with, which of the following best describes where you stayed? I had a bedroom of my own; I had a bedroom I shared with one or more siblings; or I didn't have a bedroom I stayed in." (For parents, the question was phrased "During the first 2 years after the divorce, which of the following best describes the bedroom situation in the home of the parent the child did NOT primarily live with?"). Results also are shown in Table 10.1. Together, these results show fathers reporting substantially more involvement than mothers, with college-age children most often being intermediate. However, on one variable the young adults reported more involvement than did either parent.

As one example of current involvement in the area of the financial support, we asked, "How much money is [your/your father's/your mother's] household (including [your/her/his] [new husband/new wife] or live-in partner or [boy/girl]friend, if any) contributing to [your/your child's] total college expenses per year (tuition, books, room and board, fees, etc)?" We also asked each parent to make their "best guess about how much money your ex-spouse's household was contributing." The results are displayed in Figure 10.1. Fathers reported that they provide significantly more college expense support than mothers reported fathers providing. Mothers reported that they provide significantly more college expense support than fathers reported mothers providing. The children's report was intermediate but substantially more similar to the fathers' than to the mothers' profile.

A second example of current involvement concerned the degree of "small extras" the parents provided the college-age child (small extras was defined as small presents, treats, additional clothing, spending money, free meals, etc.). This item

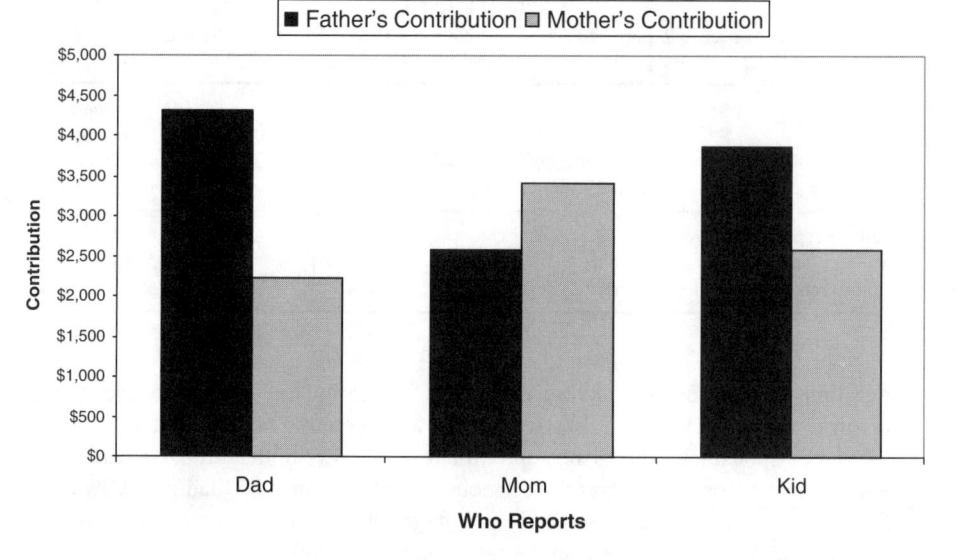

FIG. 10.1. Divorced parents' contributions to college expenses.

was answered on a 0 to 5 scale, with 0 representing none, and 5 representing a lot. Again, each respondent answered about the small extras given both by the father and by the mother. The interaction was highly significant, $F(2, 61) = 13.23$, $p < .001$, and the means are displayed in Figure 10.2. Fathers reported that they provided more extras than mothers provided, whereas mothers reported that they provided many more extras than did fathers. Again children's reports were intermediate but this time bore substantially more similarity to the mothers' than to the fathers' profile.

A third pattern was found for the next example of current involvement: the answer to the question "To what extent is [the parent] really there for [the student] when [the student] needs [the parent] to be?" As before, matched questions were asked of all three informants about both the father's and the mother's "really there"-ness. The answers were on a 0 to 8 scale with 0 representing *not at all*, and 8 labeled as *extremely*. Results are displayed in Figure 10.3. The fathers reported that they were slightly (and nonsignificantly) more "really there" than the mothers were, the mothers reversal of that pattern was highly significant, $F(1, 61) = 93.4$, $p < .001$. Again, the child was intermediate, but in this instance, the child's report about the father was closer to the father's report than to the mother's, whereas the child's report about the mother was closer to the mother's report than to the father's.

This technique also can be used about other important family issues in addition to father involvement, such as the extent of family violence. Research on this issue has frequently obtained findings rife with reporter biases (Archer, 2000; Sternberg, Lamb, & Dawud-Noursi, 1998; Szinovacz, 1983). For example, with a

10. DIVORCED, NONRESIDENT FATHERS 233

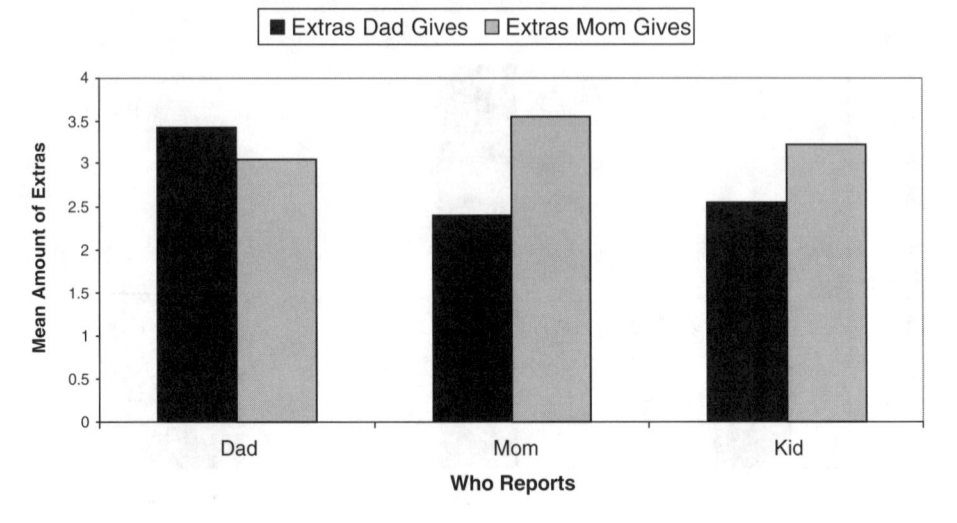

FIG. 10.2. Amount of small extras given to the child.

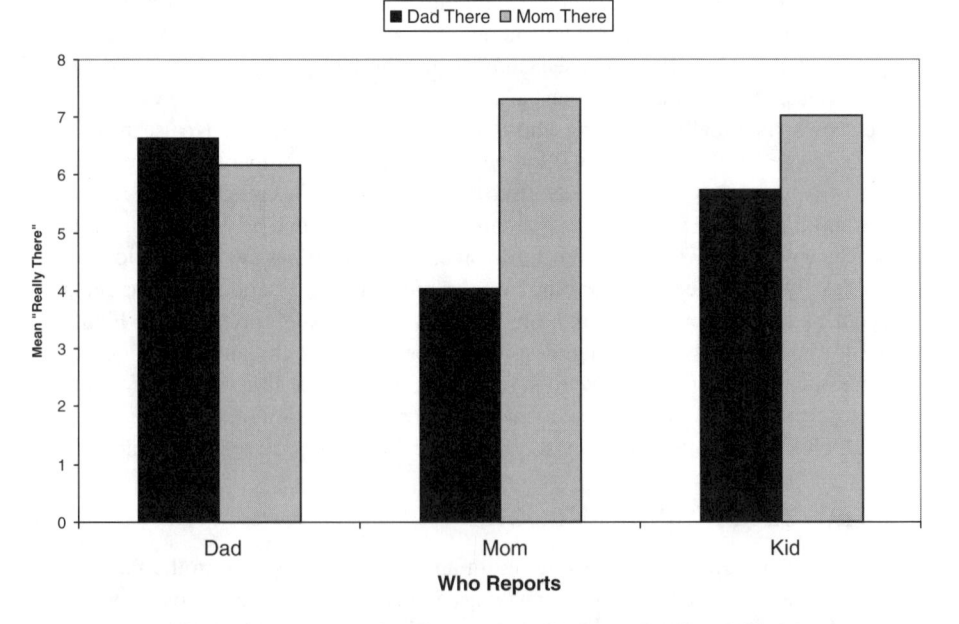

FIG. 10.3. Extent the parent is "really there" for the child.

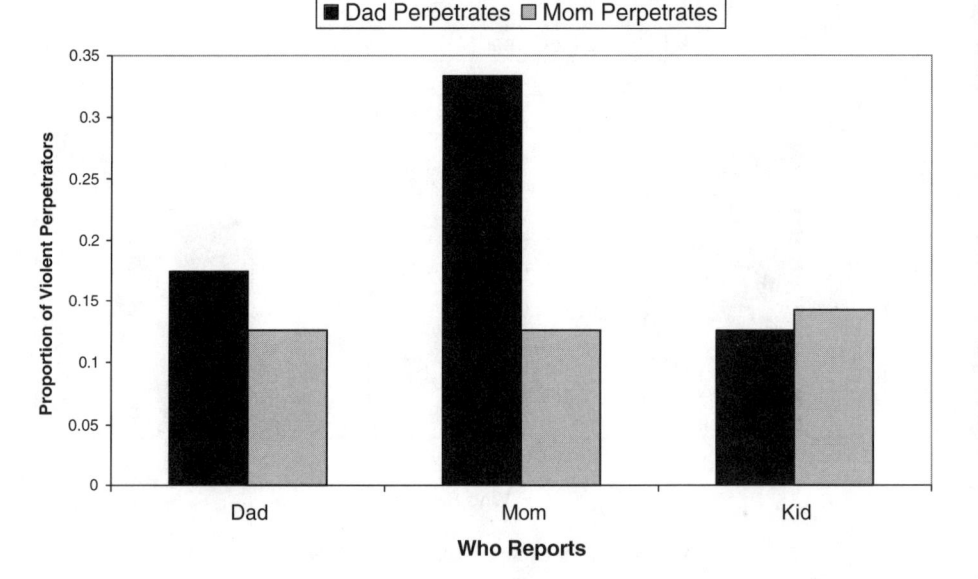

FIG. 10.4. Child-witnessed domestic violence before divorce.

sample of recently divorced couples, Williams, Schnidt, Braver, and Griffin (2000) reported that both mothers and fathers reported roughly three times more violence perpetrated by the former spouse against them than they perpetrated upon the former spouse. Most authors bemoan the lack of any external or validating evidence to detect who is actually assaulting whom. The current study attempted to use the now college-age child as this external source and, to maintain comparability, we asked all respondents to confine their reports to only before-divorce violence witnessed by the child. The exact wording was [parents' first/child's second]: "While [your child was/you were] growing up before the divorce, how many times did [your child/you] witness [you/your ex-spouse/your dad/your mom] hitting, slapping, or punching [your ex-spouse/you/your mom/your dad]?" The results are presented in Figure 10.4. The findings suggest that, despite mothers reporting that they were victims three times as often as they were perpetrators, and despite fathers admitting that they perpetrated slightly more violence than they were victim of, the now-young-adult children reported that their mothers were the slightly more violent parent.

Analyzing Multiple Reports

A number of strategies might be used in analyzing responses from the family's multiple informants (father, mother, young adult child). When the purpose is purely descriptive, we recommend individually reporting each respondent's answer, with a commentary on discrepancies and likely biases. Recall that we have found consistent and predictable differences between mothers' and fathers' reports, but no

10. DIVORCED, NONRESIDENT FATHERS

consistent or predictable pattern of where children's reports fall. For model or hypothesis testing research, combining responses into a composite might be more appropriate, depending upon whether the intercorrelations between the informant's responses is high enough. For example, in the violence data reported earlier, informants correlated between .39 and .48 about fathers' violence, which would probably permit aggregation, but only from .12 to .30 about mothers' violent acts, for which forming a composite might be questionable. Composites might be formed by simple summing or averaging or by forming latent constructs. An interesting strategy is to determine whether adding various respondents' responses to such a composite strengthens the relationships found (comparable to adding additional items on a scale to increase reliability and validity). Another appealing strategy is to model the error term and determine whether the direction and degree to which certain informants' answers (e.g., the mothers') diverge from the composite of the remaining informants to predict anything interesting.

RECOMMENDATIONS AND CONCLUSIONS

From our discussion, we offer several recommendations that may enhance future assessment of father involvement in divorced, nonresident fathers. We believe that both the gendered nature of the context in which fathering after divorce occurs and the structural changes resulting from divorce places divorced fathers at a disadvantage, especially when studies of father involvement compare divorced and nondivorced fathers. Although such comparisons may be warranted, greater care must be exercised in making these comparisons. Specifically, we suggest that any assessment of involvement should factor in the percent of time divorced fathers are allowed to spend with their children. For example, if divorced fathers spend only weekends with their children, then the most realistic comparison would result from examining the weekend behavior of nondivorced fathers with that of divorced fathers. However, in the case where a divorced father is supposed to see his children every other weekend, but his former wife does not allow him to do so, then using a measure that fails to recognize this reality will result in his appearing less involved.

We advocate for research on father involvement that assumes heterogeneity among divorced fathers and uses within-group comparisons rather than between-group comparisons. In doing so, it is imperative that behavioral indicators go beyond allowed involvement to distinguish among father involvement behaviors that are ordered, desired, performed, and allowed. This will provide greater clarity of the complex nature of fathering after divorce. One way to do this is through examining gatekeeping as part of the coparental relationship with measures that assess how the gate swings in both ways. Needless to say, careful development and pretesting of items is imperative, if the measures are to resonate with the experiences of the range of divorced fathers and if the queries and referents used are to reflect a common understanding/meaning across informants. For example,

we can envision that a measure of performed behavior in terms of accessibility and responsibility might vary depending on the father's proximity to the child, the age of the target child, and the nature of any formal or informal coparental agreements, including the payment of child support.

Further, measures must reflect what men do with children, so new measures must do more to tap the recreational dimension of divorced fathers who see their children on weekends and assess the emotional and cognitive aspects of involvement. (Only 3 of the 10 items on the Ahron's measure, 1983, reflect recreational activities; 4 of the 16 items used by Pasley in a 1998 study of divorcing parents were recreational, and this measure was adapted from the 10-item Ahron's scale.) Marsiglio, Amato, et al. (2000) called for studies of the motivations for father involvement, and we concur that studying the emotional and cognitive aspects of fathering is an important step in furthering our understanding of fathering after divorce. Using measures such as those that assess psychological presence may be one way of doing so.

Given our discussion of accuracy of reporting issues and resulting biases, we advocate for greater use of young adult samples like the convenience sample described here with college-age students and their parents. We believe the advantages associated with this alternative are considerable, particularly in the initial testing of important research questions where multiple informants can provide greater insight into family life following divorce. However, we agree with Marsiglio, Amato, and associates (2000) that certain questions may not require multiple informants. Using the method we outline here may allow us to determine when multiple respondents are needed. Some recent work by Pasley, Futris, and Skinner (2002) on reflected appraisals (a father's perception/belief about his spouse's perceptions/beliefs about him as a father) with a sample of nondivorced, resident fathers showed that reflected appraisals were a strong statistical predictor of father involvement. Although not reported in that article, additional analysis showed a similarly strong link between reflected appraisals in divorced fathers. Our point is that his perceptions of her perceptions of him as a father may offer more explanatory power than either his perceptions of his own behavior or her self-reported perceptions of him. Had Pasley and Futris collected data using the method we outline here, they would have been able to test the value of using multiple informants.

Lastly, we believe that several areas warrant further attention. Little is known about father involvement in terms of responsibility for decision-making, whether it is legally warranted or not. Future conceptualizations of involvement should include this cognitive dimension. Also, we could find little that taps the accessibility of divorced fathers except for the few studies that comment on gatekeeping as an inhibitor to involvement. We see both assessing responsibility and accessibility with students as multiple informants to be especially useful in exploring the range of behaviors that reflect these constructs. Also, students make good testing ground for understanding the structural and motivational barriers to involvement. For example, some evidence indicates that divorced fathers see themselves as accessible to their children (e.g., "my child knows they can call me if they need to," Futris & Pasley,

1997); however, limited information has been derived from either the child or the former spouse, who may attach a different meaning to accessibility. Only through carefully constructed measures with carefully constructed prompts can we better tap the complexity of father involvement across the diversity inherent in any population of divorced, nonresident fathers.

REFERENCES

Ahrons, C. R. (1981). The continuing coparental relationship between divorced spouses. *American Journal of Orthopsychiatry, 51*, 415–428.

Ahrons, C. R. (1983). Predictors of paternal involvement postdivorce: Mothers' and fathers' perceptions. *Journal of Divorce, 6*(3), 55–69.

Aldous, J., Mulligan, G. M., & Bjarnason, T. (1998). Fathering over time: What makes a difference? *Journal of Marriage and the Family, 60*, 809–820.

Amato, P. R., & Rivera, F. (1999). Paternal involvement and children's behavior problems. *Journal of Marriage and the Family, 61*, 375–384.

Archer, J. (2000). Sex differences in aggression between heterosexual partners: A meta-analytic review. *Psychological Bulletin, 126*, 651–689.

Arditti, J. A., & Keith, T. Z. (1993). Visitation frequency, child support payments, and the father–child relationship postdivorce. *Journal of Marriage and the Family, 55*, 699–712.

Arendell, T. (1995). *Fathers and divorce.* Thousand Oaks, CA: Sage.

Argys, L. M., Peters, H. E., Brooks-Gunn, J., & Smith, J. R. (1998). The impact of child support dollars on cognitive outcomes. *Demography, 35*(2), 159–173.

Barber, B. L. (1994). Support and advice from married and divorced fathers: Linkages to adolescent adjustment. *Family Relations, 43*, 433–438.

Beller, A. H., & Graham, J. W. (1986). The determinants of child support income. *Social Science Quarterly, 67*, 353–364.

Berkman, B. G. (1986). Father involvement and regularity of child support in post-divorce families. *Journal of Divorce, 9*, 67–84.

Boss, P. (1977). A clarification of the concept of psychological father presence in family experiencing ambiguity of boundary. *Journal of Marriage and the Family, 39*, 141–151.

Braver, S. L., Fitzpatrick, P., & Bay, C. (1991). Noncustodial parent's reports of child support payments. *Family Relations, 40*, 180–185.

Braver, S. L., & Griffin, W. A. (2000). Engaging fathers in the post-divorce family. *Marriage and Family Review, 29*, 247–267.

Braver, S. L., & O'Connell, E. (1998). *Divorced dads: Shattering the myths.* New York: Puttman.

Braver, S. L., & Rohrer, V. (1978). Superiority of vicarious over direct experience in interpersonal conflict resolution. *Journal of Conflict Resolution, 22*, 143–155.

Braver, S. L., Wolchik, S. A., Sandler, I. N., Fogas, B. S., & Zvetina, D. (1991). Frequency of visitation or divorced fathers: Differences in reports by fathers and mothers. *American Journal of Orthopsychiatry, 61*, 448–454.

Braver, S. L., Wolchik, S. A., Sandler, I. N., Sheets, V. L., Fogas, B. S., & Bay, R. C. (1993). A longitudinal study of noncustodial parents: Parents without children. *Journal of Family Psychology, 7*, 9–23.

Brown, B. V. (2000). The single-father family: Demographic, economics, and public transfer use characteristics. *Marriage and Family Review, 29*(2/3), 203–200.

Bruce, C., & Fox, G. L. (1999). Accounting for patterns of father involvement: Age of child, father–child coresidence, and father role salience. *Sociological Inquiry, 69*, 458–470.

Buchanan, C. M., Maccoby, E. E., & Dornbusch, S. M. (1996). *Adolescents after divorce*. Cambridge, MA: Harvard University Press.

Buehler, C. (1995). Divorce law in the United States. *Marriage and Family Review, 21*(3/4), 99–120.

Buehler, C., & Pasley, K. (1993, November). *Child's views of parents and stepparents: A construct validity study of three measures*. Paper presented at the Annual Meeting of the National Council on Family Relations, Baltimore, MD.

Bumpass, L. L., & Sweet, J. A. (1989). Children's experience in single parent families: Implications of cohabitation and marital transitions. *Family Planning Perspectives, 21*, 256–260.

Cassetty, J. (1978). *Child support and public policy*. Lexington, MA: Lexington Books.

Chambers, D. L. (1979). *Making fathers pay: The enforcement of child support*. Chicago: University of Chicago Press.

Cialdini, R. B., Braver, S. L., & Lewis, S. K. (1974). Attributional bias and the easily persuaded other. *Journal of Personality and Social Psychology, 30*, 631–637.

Clarke-Stewart, K. A., & Hayward, C. (1996). Advantages of father custody and contact for the psychological well-being of school-age children. *Journal of Applied Developmental Psychology, 17*, 239–270.

Coatsworth, D. (2000). Emotional, instrumental and financial support by divorced parents of their college aged children. Unpublished honors thesis, Arizona State University.

Crippen, G. (1990). Stumbling beyond best interests of the child: Reexamining custody standard setting in the wake of Minnesota's four year experiment with the primary caretaker preference. *Minnesota Law Review, 75*, 427–503.

Emery, R. E. (1994). *Renegotiating family relatonships: Divorce, child custody, and mediation*. New York: Guilford.

Emery, R. E. (1999). *Marriage, divorce, and children's adjustment (2nd ed.)*. Thousand Oaks, CA: Sage.

Fabricius, W. V., Braver, S. L., & Mack, K. (xxx). Divorced parents' financial support of their children's college expenses. *Family Courts Review, 41*, 224–241.

Fabricius, W. V., & Hall, J. A. (2000). Young adults' perspective on divorce: Living arrangements. *Family and Conciliation Courts Review, 38*, 446–441.

Federal Interagency Forum on Child and Family Statistics (1998). *Nurturing fatherhood: Improving data and research on male fertility, family formation, and fatherhood*. Washington, DC: U.S. Government Printing Office.

Fields, J., & Casper, L. M. (2001). American's families and living arrangements: March 2000. *Current Population Reports*, P29–537. US Census Bureau, Washington DC.

Fineman, M. A. (1991). *The illusion of equality: The rhetoric and reality of divorce reform*. Chicago: University of Chicago Press.

Fox, G. L., & Bruce, C. (1999). The anticipation of single parenthood: A profile of men's concerns. *Journal of Family Issues, 20*, 485–506.

Furstenberg, F. F., Jr., Peterson, J. L., Nord, C. W., & Zill, N. (1983). The life course of children of divorce: Marital disruption and parental contact. *American Sociological Review, 48*, 656–668.

Futris, T. G., & Pasley, K. (1997, November). *The father role identity: Conceptualizing and assessing within-role variability*. Paper presented at the Theory Construction and Research Methodology Workshop, National Council on Family Relations, Washington, DC.

Garfinkel, I. (1985). *Preliminary report on the effects of the Wisconsin child support reform demonstration*. Madison, WI: University of Wisconsin, Institute for Research on Poverty.

Greene, A. D., & Moore, K. A. (1999). Nonresident father involvement and child well-being among young children in families on welfare. *Marriage and Family Review, 29*, 2–3.

Greif, G. L., & Kristall, J. (1993). Common themes in a group for noncustodial parents. *Families and Society, 74*, 240–245.

Guidubaldi, J., Duckworth, J., Perry, J., & Redmond, C. (1999, September). *Reviving fatherhood: Empirical foundations from three independent samples*. Paper presented at the Children's Right Council 12th National Conference, Alexandria, VA.

10. DIVORCED, NONRESIDENT FATHERS 239

Gunnoe, M. L., & Braver, S. L. (2001). The effects of joint legal custody on mothers, fathers, and children, controlling for factors that predispose a sole maternal vs. joint legal award. *Law and Human Behavior, 25*, 24–43.

Hetherington, E. M., & Stanley-Hagan, M. (1997). The effects of divorce on fathers and their children. In M. E. Lamb (Ed.), *The father's role in child development* (pp. 191–211). New York: Wiley.

Kelly, J. B., & Lamb, M. E. (2000). Using child development research to make appropriate custody and access decisions for young children. *Family and Conciliation Courts Review, 38*, 297–311.

King, V. (1994). Nonresident father involvement and child well-being. *Journal of Family Issues, 15*, 78–96.

King, V., & Heard, H. E. (1999). Nonresident father visitation, parental conflict, and mothers' satisfaction: What's best for child well-being? *Journal of Marriage and the Family, 61*, 385–396.

Kitson, G. C. (1992). *Portrait of divorce: Adjustment to marital breakdown.* New York: Guilford.

Lamb, M. E. (1997). Noncustodial fathers and their impact on the children of divorce. In R. A. Thompson & P. R. Amato (Eds.), *The postdivorce family: Children, parenting, and society* (pp.105–126). Thousand Oaks, CA: Sage.

Lamb, M. E., Pleck, J. H., Charnow, E. L., & Levine, J. A. (1987). A biosocial perspective on parental behavior and involvement. In J. B. Lancaster, J. Altmann, A. S. Rossi, & L. R. Sherrod (Eds.), *Parenting across the lifespan: Biosocial dimensions* (pp. 11–142). New York: Aldine de Gruyter.

Maccoby, E. E. (1995). Divorce and custody: The rights, needs, and obligations of mothers, fathers, and children. In G. B. Melton (Ed.), *The individual, the family, and social good: Personal fulfillment in times of change* (pp. 135–172). Lincoln, NE: University of Nebraska Press.

Maccoby, E. E., & Mnookin, R. H. (1992). *Dividing the child: Social and legal dilemmas of custody.* Cambridge, MA: Harvard University Press.

Marsiglio, W., Amato, P. R., Day, R. D., & Lamb, M. E. (2000). Scholarship on fatherhood in the 1990s and beyond. *Journal of Marriage and the Family, 62*, 1173–1191.

Marsiglio, W., Day, R. D., & Lamb, M. E. (2000). Exploring fatherhood diversity: Implications for conceptualizing father involvement. In H. E. Peters, G. W. Peterson, S. K. Steinmetz, & R. D. Day (Eds.), *Fatherhood: Research, interventions, and policies* (pp. 269–294). Binghamton, NY: Haworth.

Mason, M. A. (1994). *From father's property to children's rights: The history of child custody in the United States.* New York: Columbia University Press.

Meyers, D. R., & Garasky, S. (1993). Custodial fathers, mothers' realities, and child support policy. *Journal of Marriage and the Family, 55*, 73–90.

Miller, D. T., & Ross, M. (1975). Self-serving biases in the attribution of causality: Fact or fiction? *Psychological Bulletin, 82*, 213– 225.

Minton, C., & Pasley, K. (1996a). Father's parenting role identity and father involvement: A comparison on nondivorced and divorced, nonresident fathers. *Journal of Family Issues, 17*, 26–45.

Minton, C., & Pasley, K. (1996b, November). *The effect of the coparental relationship on fathers' parenting role identity and father involvement: A comparison of nondivorced and divorced, nonresident fathers.* Paper presented at the symposium "Interpersonal Relationships and Identity Development: Theoretical and Methodological Issues," Annual Meeting of the National Council on Family Relations, Kansas City, MO.

Morgan, L. W., & Lino, M. C. (1999). A comparison of child support awards calculated under states' child support guidelines with expenditures on children calculated by the U.S. Department of Agriculture. *Family Law Quarterly, 33*, 191–218.

National Center for Health Statistics (1990). *Vital statistics of the United States. 1988, Vol, 1: Natality.* (DHHS Publication No. PHS-90-1100), Public Health Service. Washington, DC: U.S. Government Printing Office.

National Survey of Families and Households. (1998). http://www.ssc.wisc.edu/nsfh/home.htm.

Palkovitz, R. (1997). Reconstructing "involvement": Expanding conceptualizations of men's caring in contemporary families. In A. J. Hawkins & D. C. Dollahite (Eds.), *Generative fathering: Beyond deficit perspectives* (pp. 200–216). Thousand Oaks, CA: Sage.

Pasley, K. (1998). *Evaluating the Effectiveness of the Seminar for Successful Coparenting and the SUCCEED Program: Final Report.* Fort Collins, CO: Center for Divorce and Remarriage.

Pasley, K., Futris, T. G., & Skinner, M. L. (2002). The effects of commitment and psychological centrality on the fathering. *Journal of Marriage and Family, 64,* 130–138.

Pasley, K., & Minton, C. (1997). Generative fathering after divorce and remarriage: Beyond the "disappearing dad." In A. J. Hawkins & D. C. Dollahite (Eds.), *Generative fathers: Beyond deficit comparisons* (pp.118–133). Thousand Oaks, CA: Sage.

Pirog, M. A., Klotz, M. E., & Byers, K. V. (1998). Interstate comparisons of child support orders using state guidelines. *Family Relations, 47,* 289–296.

Pleck, J. H. (1997). Parental involvement: Levels sources, and consequences. In M. E. Lamb (Ed.), *The role of the father in child development* (3rd ed., pp. 66–103). New York: Wiley.

Rettig, K. D., Leichtentritt, R. D., & Stanton, L. M. (1999). Understanding noncustodial fathers' family and life satisfaction from resource theory perspective. *Journal of Family Issues, 20,* 507–538.

Schaeffer, N. C., Seltzer, J. A., & Klawitter, M. (1991). Estimating nonresponse and response bias: Resident and nonresident parents' reports about child support. *Sociological Methods Research, 20,* 30–59.

Sicoly, F., & Ross, M. (1977). Facilitation of ego-biased attributions by means of self-serving observer feedback. *Journal of Personality and Social Psychology, 35,* 734–744.

Sonenstein, F. L., & Calhoun, C. A. (1990). Determinants of child support: A pilot survey of absent parents. *Contemporary Policy Issues, 8,* 75–94.

Sternberg, K. J., Lamb, M. E., & Dawud-Noursi, S. (1998). Using multiple informants to understand domestic violence and its effects. In G. W. Holden, R. Geffner, & E. N. Jouriles (Eds.), *Children exposed to marital violence* (pp. 121–156). Washington, DC: American Psychological Association.

Stewart, S. D. (1999). Disneyland dads, Disneyland moms? How nonresident parents spent time with absent children. *Journal of Family Issues, 20,* 539–556.

Szinovacz, M. E. (1983). Using complete data as a methodological tool: The case of marital violence. *Journal of Marriage and the Family, 45,* 633–644.

Teachman, J. D. (1991). Who pays? Receipt of child support in the United States. *Journal of Marriage and the Family, 53,* 759–772.

Udry, J. R. (1997). *The National Longitudinal Study of Adolescent Health (ADD HEALTH), Wave I, 1994–1996.* Los Altos, CA: Sociometrics.

U.S. Census Bureau. (1998). Marital status and living arrangements: March 1998 (update). *Current Population Reports* (PS20–514). Washington, DC: U.S. Government Printing Office.

Venohr, J. C., & Williams, R. G. (1999). The implementation and periodic review of child support guidelines. *Family Law Quarterly, 33,* 7–38.

Walker, A. J., & McGraw, L. A. (2000). Who is responsible for responsible fathering? *Journal of Marriage and the Family, 62,* 563–569.

Warshak, R. A. (1992). *The custody revolution.* New York: Simon & Schuster.

Williams, J., Schmidt, J., Braver, S. L., & Griffin, W. A. (2000). *Matched reports of domestic violence among the recently divorced.* Paper presented at the Fifth International Conference on Family Violence, San Diego, CA.

Wolchik, S. A., Fenaughty, A. M., & Braver, S. L. (1996). Residential and nonresidential parents' perspectives on visitation problems. *Family Relations, 45,* 230–237.

11

Early Father Involvement
in Fragile Families

Marcia J. Carlson
Columbia University

Sara S. McLanahan
Princeton University

INTRODUCTION

The proportion of children born to unmarried parents has risen dramatically in the past 40 years, with fully one-third of births now occurring outside of marriage; the proportions are even higher among minority populations—42% among Hispanics and 69% among African Americans (Ventura & Bachrach, 2000). The rise in the fraction of nonmarital births, along with demographic changes in marriage and divorce, has yielded a growing group of "fragile families"—unmarried parents who are raising their children together. Such families are deemed fragile because of the multiple risks associated with nonmarital childbearing (including poverty) and the vulnerability of the parents' relationship. New research shows that more than four-fifths of unmarried couples are in a romantic relationship—and just under half are living together—at the time of their child's birth, indicating that they may be more "family like" than typically perceived (McLanahan, Garfinkel, Reichman, & Teitler, 2001). To understand how unmarried-parent families may differ from more traditional families and the consequences for children, it is important to examine the nature of fathering across various types of fragile families.

A growing number of studies have explored the consequences of father involvement for children, with an emerging consensus that (positive) involvement by fathers is generally beneficial to child wellbeing (Lamb, 1997; Marsiglio, Amato, Day, & Lamb, 2000). Yet, most of the extant research has focused on married or previously married fathers, or is limited to special samples of unwed fathers such as teen fathers. Therefore, understanding the factors associated with involvement by unmarried fathers—and the consequences for children—is an important new area for research. The Fragile Families and Child Wellbeing Study provides a unique opportunity to examine this understudied group of fathers using a large nationally representative sample of nonmarital births.

In this paper, we use data from the Fragile Families Study to examine five measures of involvement by unmarried fathers around the time of a child's birth. After briefly reviewing the relevant literature, we present descriptive information about fathers' characteristics and their involvement. Then, we present our multivariate analyses and note specific characteristics that appear to be strongly linked to greater father involvement. Finally, we discuss particular methodological issues related to father involvement using the Fragile Families data.

CONCEPTUAL FRAMEWORK AND PREVIOUS RESEARCH

Various researchers have explored the individual attributes and contextual factors that are most conducive to greater paternal participation. Belsky's model of the determinants of parenting points to three broad categories of factors that are likely to affect fathers' involvement with their children: (1) fathers' personal characteristics, (2) characteristics of the child, and (3) social-contextual influences (Belsky, 1984, 1990; Woodworth, Belsky, & Crnic, 1996).[1] We discuss each category of determinants in turn, noting possible theoretical mechanisms that may account for the influence of particular characteristics on fathers' involvement.

Fathers' Characteristics

While cultural understandings of fathering have broadened beyond the provider role in recent decades, breadwinning remains a central element of the father role in most segments of society (Lamb, 1997). Thus, all else being equal, we would expect fathers' socioeconomic status or earnings capacity—measured as education, employment experience, and health—to affect their involvement with children

---

[1] A number of useful typologies for factors influencing father involvement have been developed (see for example, Lamb et al., 1987; Pleck, 1997). We utilize Belsky's model here because it is parsimonious yet broadly considers how individuals and processes within the family influence fathering.

11. FRAGILE FAMILIES
243

(Marsiglio & Cohan, 2000). Earnings capacity should affect fathers' financial support because fathers with more income can afford to give more to their children. Also, earnings capacity should affect nonfinancial contributions because fathers who cannot meet the expectations of the breadwinner role may disengage from their families out of a sense of shame or inadequacy (Lamb, 1997; Liebow, 1967). Alternatively, fathers who are unemployed or otherwise unable to provide resources to the child may be "pushed out" of the family—or not be given access to the child—by mothers (Edin & Lein, 1997; Marsiglio & Cohan, 2000).

Socialization theory tells us that past and present experiences are also important in shaping fathers' attitudes and behaviors toward their children. Men's experiences in their families of origin inevitably shape their understanding of what it means to be a father. Thus, we would expect men who were exposed to "good" fathering to mirror this behavior with their own children. Of course, the mechanism could work in the opposite direction as men who were exposed to "poor" fathering try to compensate for their own fathers' lack of involvement by demonstrating high levels of involvement (Pleck, 1997). Because religious institutions typically promote familial investments (Wilcox, 2002), we would also expect fathers who actively participate in a religious community to be more involved with their children than fathers who are not religious. Finally, identity theory suggests that men who identify strongly with being a father and the associated roles (provider, nurturer, etc.) are more likely to invest in their children than men who view fatherhood as less salient (Ihinger-Tallman, Pasley, & Buehler, 1993; Rane & McBride, 2000).

The empirical literature provides some support for the earnings capacity, role modeling (socialization), and identity hypotheses. With respect to earnings capacity, studies show that fathers of higher socioeconomic status (particularly as reflected by education and employment status) are more likely to live with their children or to exhibit positive parenting behaviors (or both) than fathers of lower status (Coley & Chase-Lansdale, 1999; Cooksey & Craig, 1998; Landale & Oropesa, 2001; Woodworth et al., 1996), although the evidence is not entirely consistent (see Pleck, 1997 for a review). Some research shows that earnings capacity is strongly related to the amount of child support paid by nonresident fathers but is less important to how often fathers see their children (Garfinkel, McLanahan, & Hanson, 1998). Also, fathers who suffer from depression (Blair & Hardesty, 1994, cited in Pleck, 1997) or have a problem with drugs (Waller & Bailey, 2002) are less likely to demonstrate positive paternal engagement.

With respect to socialization theory, some evidence suggests that men who grow up apart from their fathers are less likely to form successful relationships in adulthood and thus are less likely to live with their children than men who live with their fathers during childhood (McLanahan & Sandefur, 1994). Moreover, men who identify strongly with the father role are likely to exhibit greater involvement with their children than men for whom the father role is less salient

(Ihinger-Tallman et al., 1993). Whether fathers primarily identify as parent or worker does not appear to affect their interaction which children (underscoring that breadwinning remains a key element of fathering); however, identifying more strongly with a nurturing role in particular is linked to more frequent father–child interaction (Rane & McBride, 2000).

Fathers' socio-demographic characteristics would also be expected to influence their involvement with children. Strong kinship ties among African-Americans may promote father-child interaction by black fathers relative to other race/ethnic groups (Hofferth, 1984), although the lower socioeconomic status of minority groups relative to whites may operate in the opposite direction (Seltzer & Bianchi, 1988). Some studies do find that black (or non-white) fathers are more involved with children (Danziger & Radin, 1990; King, 1994; Lerman & Sorenson, 2000; Marsiglio, 1991; Seltzer, 1991), but others find no relationship between race/ethnicity and paternal involvement (Cooksey & Craig, 1998; Selzter & Bianchi, 1988). Evidence on the effect of fathers' age on involvement is also not consistent; this may be because older fathers have greater maturity and resources (which promote involvement), while father involvement may be increasing—at least among some groups or with respect to certain types of involvement—among more recent (younger) cohorts of men (Cooksey & Craig, 1998).

Child Characteristics

Several characteristics of children are likely to affect fathers' involvement, including sex, age, and temperament. We might expect fathers to be more involved with boys than with girls for two reasons. First, fathers may feel they can identify more with a same-sex child and may have greater incentive toward—and perceived rewards from—active involvement with boys. Second, there may be greater external pressure and expectations that fathers spend more time with boys and serve as role models for them. While other child characteristics such as age and temperament may be important for father involvement later on, such attributes are not relevant for newborn children. Finally, an additional factor that may affect father involvement is whether the father wanted the pregnancy in the first place. We would expect a father's interest in and involvement with his child to be lower if he did not intend to have a child.

Some empirical evidence suggests that fathers are more involved with boys than with girls (Harris & Morgan, 1991; Marsiglio, 1991; Pleck, 1997) and that this greater involvement reduces the risk of divorce among couples with sons (Lundberg & Rose, 1999; Morgan, Lye, & Condran, 1988). However, the difference in involvement by child gender is not always consistant and may vary by child age or type of involvement (Cooksey, & Craig, 1998; Pleck, 1997). Evidence also indicates that unintended pregnancies are associated with a higher risk of divorce and lower father involvement among unmarried Puerto Rican fathers (Landale & Oropesa, 2001).

Social-Contextual Characteristics

Finally, the social-contextual environment is expected to shape the nature of fathers' involvement. The key factor in this domain is the father's relationship with the child's mother. Two aspects of the parents' relationship are expected to affect father involvement—whether the parents live in the same household and whether they have a high-quality relationship. There are at least three reasons why coresidence should increase father involvement. First, when fathers live with their children, they automatically spend time and money on the child. Second, living with the child increases a father's information and empathy, which in turn should increase involvement. Finally, when fathers live apart from their child they cannot be sure that the money they contribute is actually going to the child, and thus they may be reluctant to pay child support (Weiss & Willis, 1985).

The quality of the mother–father relationship could also affect father involvement. First, for fathers (who are typically less emotionally expressive than mothers), the relationship with the mother may provide an important source of information about the child. Heimer and Staffen (1998) note that men's ties to their children are often mediated by their connection to the child's mother, with the sexual union (and the accompanying "pillow talk" by which mothers convey information to fathers about the child) playing an important role in fostering the father–child bond. Following this logic, we would expect that fathers who are closely involved with the child's mother would exhibit the highest levels of involvement with children because they would have the greatest access to information and, ultimately, the greatest understanding of the child. Second, for men who live apart from their child, the problem of monitoring how their resources are allocated is related to the quality of the parents' relationship. If the father trusts the mother and believes that she has the interest of the child at heart, he is likely to contribute more to the child. Similarly, if the mother trusts the father, she is likely to encourage his involvement and facilitate his access to the child. Finally, if the mother–father relationship is negative or hostile, interacting with the mother may be painful for the father, and he may withdraw from the child in order to avoid interacting with the mother.

Previous research corroborates the hypothesis that fathers are more likely to be involved with their children if the relationship with the child's mother, particularly within marriage, is positive (Belsky, Youngblade, & Rovine, 1991; Gottman, 1998). For unmarried parents, a conflicted mother–father relationship discourages positive father involvement, while an amicable relationship supports healthy father–child interaction (Coley & Chase-Lansdale, 1999; Danziger & Radin, 1990; Seltzer, 1991).

The diagram in Fig. 11.1. depicts the conceptual model used in our analyses. We expect that characteristics in each of the three domains are linked to fathers' involvement but that the father's and child's characteristics may operate in part through the status and quality of the mother–father relationship.

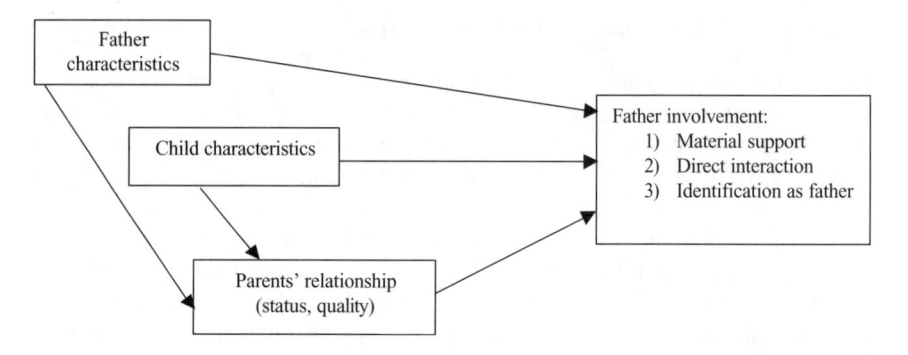

FIG. 11.1. Conceptual model of factors affecting father involvement.

DATA, VARIABLES, AND METHODS

Data

We use data from the Fragile Families and Child Wellbeing Study, a new national survey designed to track the conditions and capabilities of unmarried parents and their children over time subsequent to a nonmarital birth (Garfinkel, McLanahan, Tienda, & Brooks-Gunn, 2001). The survey provides detailed information about the characteristics of fathers, the nature of parents' relationships, and the extent to which fathers are involved with their children. The study follows a birth cohort of about 3,700 children born to unmarried parents in 20 U.S. cities; the sample is representative of all nonmarital births to parents residing in cities with populations over 200,000. Also, a comparison group of married parents is included for each of the 20 cities; the sample of married births is approximately 1,200. New mothers are interviewed in person at the hospital within 48 hours of having given birth, and fathers are interviewed in person either in the hospital or are located as soon as possible thereafter. Follow-up interviews are/will be conducted when the child is about 1, 3, and 5 years old.

In this paper, we use data from the baseline survey in all 20 cities in the Fragile Families Study.[2] Our sample includes 2,776 unmarried fathers who completed the baseline interview, which is 75% of the fathers of children born outside of marriage in the Study. Response rates varied greatly according to fathers' relationship status with the mothers at the time of birth: 90% for cohabiting fathers, 73% for fathers who were romantically involved with the mother but not cohabiting, 53% for fathers who were "just friends" with the mother, and 26% for fathers who had

---

[2]The twenty cities are Oakland, CA; San Jose, CA; Jacksonville, FL; Chicago, IL; Indianapolis, IN; Boston, MA; Baltimore, MD; Detroit, MI; Newark, NJ; New York, NY; Toledo, OH; Philadelphia, PA; Pittsburgh, PA; Nashville, TN; Austin, TX ; Corpus Christi, TX; San Antonio, TX; Norfolk, VA; Richmond, VA; and Milwaukee, WI.

11. FRAGILE FAMILIES   247

little or no contact with the mothers. Thus, the Fragile Families Study is much more representative of fathers who are more closely connected to the mothers of their children than those who are no longer romantically involved.[3]

Variables

We examine five indicators of father involvement, as reported by mothers.[4] Conceptually, we divide the father involvement items into three categories. The first includes two indicators of the father's material contributions during the pregnancy—whether he gave money or provided another kind of (tangible) help to the mother.[5] The second category includes only one item of fathers' direct participation around the time of the birth—whether he visited the mother in the hospital. The third category includes two items that reflect the extent to which the father is willing to be identified as the father—whether his name is on the child's birth certificate and whether the child will take his last name.[6]

We include variables in each of the three categories of independent variables deemed to be important in previous research—fathers' characteristics, child characteristics, and characteristics of the mother–father relationship.[7]

Fathers' Characteristics. We include a variety of self-reported information about fathers. Demographic characteristics include categorical variables for fathers' age (younger than 20, 20 to 24, 25 to 29, and 30 and older), race (White, non-Hispanic; Black, non-Hispanic; Hispanic; and other/don't know), and educational attainment (less than high school, high school degree, and some college or higher). We also include a variable indicating whether the father is an immigrant (i.e., not born in the United States), a dummy variable for whether the father was working in the week prior to the survey,[8] and a continuous variable for fathers'

---

[3]This has implications for the generalizability of our findings. Our estimates of involvement by fathers are likely upper bound estimates, because fathers who participated in the survey are probably more engaged in their child's life than their counterparts who did not participate. This is particularly the case for fathers not romantically involved with the baby's mother.

[4]We use mothers' reports to avoid shared-method variance (Marsiglio et al., 2000) as most of our independent variables are based on fathers' reports. See the section on methodological issues for additional discussion about using mothers' versus fathers' reports.

[5]The question asked of mothers about other kinds of help is: "Did [baby's father] help you in other ways, such as providing transportation to the pre-natal clinic or helping with chores?"

[6]We recognize that the father's name being on the birth certificate and the child taking his surname are also influenced by mothers' wishes and intentions, particularly for couples who are not romantically involved. Yet, most (94%) mothers report that they want the father to be involved with the child.

[7]We did not include mothers' demographic characteristics as they are significantly correlated with those of the fathers.

[8]More detailed information is not available about the father's employment history. Thus, we use whether the father worked in the previous week as a proxy for his overall labor force attachment.

hourly wage rate (in dollars).[9] In addition, we include a variable indicating that the father has other biological children, as fathers with other children may have less time to spend with a new child.

Beyond the basic demographic and socioeconomic characteristics, fathers' physical and mental health are also indicators of fathers' earnings capacity. We include an indicator that the father reports his health to be "poor" or "fair"; self-reported health status has been shown to be strongly linked to actual health problems (Farmer & Ferraro, 1997). Also, we include a variable that indicates whether the father reported that his drinking or drug use interfered with his work or personal relationships in the past year. Finally, we measure depression using an abbreviated version of the Center for Epidemiologic Studies Depression (CES-D) scale. The CES-D was designed to measure the frequency of depressive symptoms that have been identified in the clinical literature on depression as well as in other existing depression inventories (Radloff, 1977). The shortened version contains 12 items that correspond to two emotional components—depressed mood and psychomotor retardation. Respondents indicate the frequency that each symptom occurred in the previous week, from 0 to 7 days, and responses are summed across items.

We include variables for how involved was the father's own father—very involved (omitted category), somewhat involved, not very involved, and never knew own father. Also, we include a measure that reflects father's interest in and commitment to fathering. We combine scores from three indicators of fathers' attitudes toward fathering, each of which has four response choices ranging from 1 (strongly disagree) to 4 (strongly agree); the three items are "Being a father and raising children is one of the most fulfilling experiences a man can have," "I want people to know that I have a new child," and "Not being a part of my child's life would be one of the worst things that could happen to me." Factor analysis indicated that these three items were similar and could be represented by a single factor (alpha =.728). We include a measure of the frequency that the father attends religious services (ranging from 1 "not at all" to 5 "once a week or more").

Child Characteristics. We include a dummy variable indicating the sex of the baby (girl is omitted). Also, we represent whether the father wanted the pregnancy by the mother's report about whether he suggested that she have an abortion.

Social-Contextual Characteristics. We examine two related dimensions of the mother–father relationship. First, we assess the particular status of the couple's relationship around the time of the child's birth based on the mother's report; relationship status includes four possible categories—cohabiting (omitted), visiting

---

[9]For the 14% of fathers for whom the wage information is missing, we impute their hourly wage rate based on fathers' age, education, race/ethnicity, immigrant status, has condition that limits work, substance problem, and city of residence at the time of the baby's birth.

11. FRAGILE FAMILIES 249

(romantically involved but living separately), just friends, and not in any relationship (determined by the mother's report that she and the father "never" or "hardly ever" talk).

Second, we examine the quality of the parents' relationship (across all relationship types) in two areas based on mothers' reports—frequency of conflict and level of supportiveness. For the conflict items, mothers indicate whether they have (1) never, (2) sometimes, or (3) often had conflict over the following in the last month: money, spending time together, sex, the pregnancy, drinking or drug use, and being faithful. We created an index of the overall frequency of conflict ranging from 1 to 3 by averaging scores from each of these six items (alpha = .657). It is important to note that the timing of the inquiry vis-à-vis the frequency of conflict between parents may affect the nature of the reports. For mothers who are romantically involved with the father at the time of interview, their reports refer to the month prior to the survey (and thus, the month prior to the birth); for mothers who are not romantically involved at the time of the survey, their reports refer to "when [they] were last together." For couples that are romantically involved at the time of the birth, we might expect that the month prior to the birth was a particularly positive time given the anticipation of the baby. Yet, for couples no longer together, the month before the birth may have been a particularly contentious time. Thus, differences in levels of conflict between couples that are and are not romantically involved may be somewhat exaggerated.

Supportiveness in the relationship is measured by mothers' reports about how often the father does the following: (1) is fair and willing to compromise when they have a disagreement, (2) expresses affection or love, (3) insults or criticizes her or her ideas (coding is reversed), and (4) encourages or helps her to do things that are important to her. Again, response options are (1) never, (2) sometimes, and (3) often; for the item reflecting negative behaviors (insults or criticizes), "never" is coded as high. No specific timeframe for the assessment of frequency is given.[10] The items are averaged to obtain an overall supportiveness score (range = 1 to 3), with higher scores indicating a greater level of supportiveness reported by the mother about the father (alpha = .620).[11]

Methods

After presenting some descriptive statistics about fathers, we estimate logistic regression models for each of our five measures of father involvement. For each outcome, we estimate two models. The first model includes fathers' characteristics, and the two characteristics about the baby—sex and whether the pregnancy was wanted. In the second model, we add the three variables that reflect the nature of

---

[10]The question reads: "Thinking about your relationship with [baby's father], how often would you say that . . ."

[11]Table 6 provides information comparing the effects of mothers' versus father's reports about supportiveness on father involvement.

relationship between the father and the mother—status at the time of interview, frequency of conflict, and level of supportiveness. We expect that some of the father and child characteristics may operate through the parents' relationship, so we are interested in examining the father and child characteristics first separately and then simultaneously with the mother–father relationship characteristics.

DESCRIPTIVE RESULTS

Table 11.1 presents frequencies on the indicators of father involvement for all fathers interviewed, overall and by relationship status. We show mothers' reports of fathers' behavior as well as fathers' own reports as a point of comparison. Overall, the vast majority of unmarried fathers are involved in one or more ways during the pregnancy and around the time of their child's birth. Fathers report slightly higher levels of involvement on each of the indicators than do mothers. According to the mothers, 90% of fathers gave money or bought things for the baby, 88% helped in another way (such as providing transportation or helping with chores), and 88% came to visit in the hospital; 91% of mothers indicate that the father's name is on the baby's birth certificate, and 87% of mothers report that the child will take the father's surname.

Despite the high overall levels of father involvement, dramatic differences in involvement are noted by the nature of relationship between the mother and father shortly after the child's birth. Across all items, cohabiting fathers demonstrate the highest level of involvement, with more than 90% of fathers involved in each of the five ways. Fully 96% of cohabiting fathers have their name on the birth certificate, indicating their intention to self-identify as the baby's father. Involvement among visiting fathers (those romantically involved with the mother but living separately from her) is somewhat lower than among cohabitors. Still, 88% of visiting fathers contributed materially during the pregnancy, 81% visited in the hospital; 87% of mothers in visiting relationships say that the father's name is on the birth certificate, and 80% of visiting mothers report that the child will take the father's surname. Thus, being in a romantic relationship with the mother appears to provide a context that facilitates a high level of involvement by unmarried fathers, at least around the time of a new baby's birth.

Levels of involvement are notably lower for fathers who are not romantically involved with the mother, although fathers who are "just friends" with the mother are much more involved than those no longer in any kind of relationship with her. Fifty-five percent of fathers who are friends with the child's mother contributed financially, 46% helped in another way, and more than two-thirds visited the mother in the hospital. Even though not romantically attached to the mother, most fathers who are friends are willing to be identified as the father of the baby—86% of mothers report that the father's name is on the child's birth certificate, and 76% of mothers report that the baby will have his surname.

TABLE 11.1
Indicators of Father Involvement

	Fathers' Report	Mothers' Report About Fathers				
		All Interviewed Fathers	Cohabiting	Visiting	Friends	Not in Relationship
Material support during pregnancy:						
Gave money or bought things for baby	91.2	89.8	97.2	88.0	54.6	30.1
Helped in another way	90.4	88.0	97.8	83.9	45.6	16.5
Direct involvement:						
Visited baby's mother in hospital	NA	88.3	97.2	80.8	69.4	23.1
Identification as father:						
Father's name is on birth certificate	93.4	91.3	96.0	86.7	86.3	55.4
Child will take father's surname	89.5	86.5	93.5	80.2	76.1	31.6
Unweighted number of cases (n)	2,776	2,776	1,601	926	156	93

Note. All figures are weighted by national sampling weights; NA = not available.

Fathers who are no longer in any kind of relationship with the baby's mother (based on her report that they "hardly ever talk" or "never talk") are least likely to be involved with the child along all the measures examined here. Only 30% of the fathers provided some sort of financial assistance during the pregnancy, 17% provided another kind of help to the mother, and 23% visited the mother in the hospital. Not surprisingly, only 32% of mothers not in any relationship with the father report that the child will have the father's last name; just over half of these mothers report that the father's name is on the birth certificate. It is important to note that the fathers who had minimal contact with the mother but agreed to participate in the survey are likely to be a very select group of men; namely, they are likely to place a high value on fatherhood.

Table 11.2 provides information on the characteristics of the father, the child, and the quality of parents' relationship for all fathers interviewed overall and by relationship status. Of all fathers interviewed, three-fifths are in their twenties, 27% are age 30 and older, and 13% are in their teens (less than age 20). Fifty-four percent of the sample is non-Hispanic Black, 32% is Hispanic, 20% is non-Hispanic White, and 4% is of another race. Sixteen percent of fathers are immigrants. With respect to educational attainment, 38% of fathers have less than a high school degree, 35% have a high school degree, and 26% have some college or higher. These figures are notably lower than national averages—of all persons ages 15 and older in the United States, only 22% have less than a high school degree (U.S. Census Bureau, 2000). Most fathers—more than three-fourths—reported having worked the week prior to the survey, and mean hourly wages were $10.80. Half of fathers in the sample have other biological children.

With respect to their own father's involvement in their lives, most fathers interviewed report that their father was very involved (38%) or somewhat involved (27%) in their lives, while 27% report that their father was not very involved in their lives, and 8% say they never knew their father. Asked the extent to which they agree with three statements about the importance to them of being a father, the mean score for the average of all three statements was close to "strongly agree" (3.71 out of 4), indicating that this group of fathers highly esteems the father role. Again, it is important to note that fathers who were interviewed in the Fragile Families Study are likely more attached to their children than the fathers who were not interviewed, so we would expect noninterviewed fathers to hold somewhat less positive attitudes toward fathering than those included in the sample. Most fathers we interviewed do not participate frequently in organized religion—only one-quarter of fathers attend religious services at least several times a month. The typical father reports attending religious services between "hardly ever" and "several times a year."

Most fathers appear to be in good health, with only 9% reporting that their health is "poor" or "fair." Also, only 7% report that substance use interfered with their work or relationships in the past year; however, it is important to note that fathers may underreport their use of harmful or illegal substances. With respect to depression, the typical father scores quite low on the abbreviated CES-D measure;

TABLE 11.2
Descriptive Characteristics by Relationship Status

	All Fathers Interviewed	Cohabiting	Visiting	Friends	Not in Relationship
Father Characteristics:					
Demographics					
Age					
Less than 20	12.9	9.8	17.0	24.9	12.7
Ages 20–24	37.7	35.5	40.9	39.2	46.3
Ages 25–29	22.1	24.5	18.3	20.1	15.1
30 and older	27.4	30.3	23.8	15.8	26.0
Race					
White, non-Hispanic	19.7	25.9	8.2	13.2	19.6
Black, non-Hispanic	43.7	33.5	63.9	46.9	45.3
Hispanic	32.4	37.6	21.8	30.5	34.1
Other	4.2	3.1	6.0	9.5	1.4
Immigrant	16.0	17.9	13.1	11.6	14.3
Education					
Less than high school	38.3	37.7	39.3	34.2	46.2
High school degree	35.4	35.1	36.2	34.0	36.3
Some college or higher	26.3	27.2	24.5	31.9	17.5
Worked last week	78.9	84.4	69.8	75.8	63.6
Mean hourly wage rate (SD)	$10.80 (7.46)	$10.83 (6.69)	$10.48 (6.79)	$12.39 (15.33)	$10.58 (7.30)
Has other biological children	51.0	53.4	48.2	44.75	43.03
Fathering background and religiosity					
Own father's level of involvement					
Never knew father	8.1	9.0	7.4	5.1	3.4
Not very involved	27.0	24.5	29.7	38.7	30.2
Somewhat involved	26.9	27.9	25.8	21.8	27.1
Very involved	38.0	38.6	37.1	34.5	39.3

(Continued)

TABLE 11.2
(Continued)

	All Fathers Interviewed	Cohabiting	Visiting	Friends	Not in Relationship
Attitudes toward fathering (range = 1–4)[1]					
Being a father is one of most fulfilling experiences	3.71	3.75	3.67	3.61	3.53
Father wants people to know has new child	3.71	3.79	3.65	3.52	3.24
Not being in child's life would be one of worst things	3.72	3.78	3.68	3.57	3.42
Overall mean (SD)	3.71 (.45)	3.77 (.38)	3.66 (.46)	3.56 (.70)	3.37 (.66)
Frequency of religious attendance					
Not at all	23.1	23.4	21.0	25.5	31.5
Hardly ever	30.6	32.2	27.4	37.9	18.7
Several times a year	21.1	21.0	24.0	10.9	12.1
Several times a month	11.8	11.6	12.1	11.4	13.3
Once a week or more	13.5	11.8	15.5	14.3	14.3
Mean score, range = 1–5 (SD)	2.62 (1.32)	2.56 (1.29)	2.73 (1.34)	2.51 (1.36)	2.80 (1.60)
Health and wellbeing					
Health is poor or fair	8.9	7.6	11.1	7.8	13.8
Substance use interfered with work/relationships	6.8	6.0	7.5	6.7	15.9
Mean CES-D depression score, range = 1–7 (SD)	1.14 (1.23)	1.06 (1.14)	1.15 (1.28)	1.65 (1.45)	1.75 (1.56)
Child characteristics:					
Child is boy	52.3	50.4	56.7	54.4	43.0
Pregnancy not wanted[2]	10.0	5.5	13.2	27.2	35.5
Parents' relationship quality[3]:					
Supportiveness, range = 1–3 (SD)	2.65 (.36)	2.72 (.31)	2.63 (.34)	2.35 (.49)	2.10 (.49)
Frequency of conflict, range = 1–3 (SD)	1.44 (.38)	1.40 (.35)	1.49 (.43)	1.55 (.45)	1.55 (.40)
Unweighted number of cases (n)	2,776	1,601	926	156	93

Note. All figures weighted by national sampling weights; SD = standard deviation.
[1] Range is from 1 "strongly disagree" to 4 "strongly agree."
[2] Mother reports that father suggested that she have an abortion.
[3] Mothers' reports: Supportiveness is her assessment of the father's behavior in four areas. Frequency of conflict is her assessment of how often they have conflict in six areas.

when asked the number of days they have experienced 12 symptoms, ranging from 0 days to 7 days—the mean score for the 12 items was 1.14. Consistant with other research using the Fragile Families data (Wilson & Brooks-Gunn, 2001), we find that the association between the health indicators and parents' relationship status is not entirely linear: the healthiest fathers are those who are cohabiting or who are friends with the mother, whereas fathers not in any relationship with the mothers have the highest frequencies of poor health and substance problems.[12]

Also shown on Table 11.2 are two characteristics related to the child: sex and pregnancy intentions. For about half the fathers, their new baby was a boy. Ten percent of fathers did not necessarily want the pregnancy, based on mothers' reports that the father suggested that she have an abortion. Not surprisingly, the proportion of fathers who suggested the mother get an abortion varies notably by parents' relationship status, ranging from 6% of cohabiting fathers to 36% of fathers not in a relationship with the mother.

With respect to the quality of relationships between mothers and fathers, there is a rather linear pattern of quality decline along the spectrum of relationship types, from most to least attached. The level of supportiveness (as evidenced by mothers' reports about fathers) is highest in cohabiting relationships (mean score of 2.72 out of 3), followed by visiting (2.63), friends (2.35), and those not in a relationship (2.10). The pattern of conflict scores is similar (in the opposite direction), with the lowest mean conflict score noted among those in cohabiting relationships (1.40 out of 3), followed by visiting (1.49), friends (1.55), and those not in a relationship (1.55).

REGRESSION RESULTS

We present log odds ratios from logistic regression equations for our five dependent variables in Tables 11.3 through 11.5. Table 11.3 presents results for the two indicators of whether the father provided some sort of material support to the mother during the pregnancy. Model 1 includes characteristics of the father and the child; Model 2 adds characteristics of the mother–father relationship. With respect to giving money, father's employment status is strongly linked to his giving money or buying things for the baby during the pregnancy—employed fathers are one and a half times as likely to give money as those fathers not working at the time of the survey, even when characteristics of the parents' relationship are controlled. This finding is consistent with the breadwinner hypothesis. Otherwise, none of the other indicators of earnings capacity appear to affect fathers' monetary contributions— neither education, physical health, nor mental health.[13] Fathers' wage rates are

---

[12]Since the men who participated in the survey are a select group and may be better off than all fathers in this category overall, these figures may actually understate the health problems of this group.

[13]Fathers with substance problems are less likely to give money, but this association is no longer significant once we control for parents' relationship characteristics.

TABLE 11.3

Estimated Log Odds Ratios From Logistic Regression Models: Father's Provision
of Material Support During the Pregnancy

	Gave Money		Helped in Other Ways[1]	
	Model 1	Model 2	Model 1	Model 2
Father characteristics:				
Age (omitted = 30 and older)				
Less than 20	.724	.789	.594*	.663
Ages 20–24	.890	.903	.670*	.669*
Ages 25–29	.781	.803	.752	.836
Race (omitted = Black, non-Hispanic)				
White, non-Hispanic	.956	.714	1.566[+]	1.107
Hispanic	1.162	.878	1.554*	1.116
Other	.964	.973	.866	.735
Father is immigrant	1.063	.837	1.054	.750
Education (omitted = some college or more)				
Less than HS degree	.821	.801	1.085	1.098
High school degree/GED	1.034	.987	1.385[+]	1.481*
Father worked last week	1.565**	1.555**	1.420*	1.398*
Father's hourly wage rate (in dollars)	1.004	1.013	.991	.997
Father has other biological children	.700*	.634**	1.079	1.025
Fair or poor health	.819	.926	.897	1.069
Substance use interfered with work/relationships	.617*	.725	.771	.886
Depression score (range = 1–7)	.930	.977	.926	.980
Involvement of own father (omitted = very involved)				
Never knew father	1.038	.997	1.160	1.125
Not very involved	.989	.945	1.097	1.122
Somewhat involved	1.261	1.347	1.133	1.154
Positive attitudes toward fathering	1.414**	.953	1.717**	1.156
Frequency of religious attendance	.896*	.913	.896*	.920
Child characteristics:				
Child is boy	.981	.937	.815	.763[+]
Pregnancy not wanted	.296**	.551**	.364**	.757
Parents' relationship:				
Status (omitted=cohabiting)				
Visiting (romantic but living separately)		.362**		.172**
Friends		.125**		.042**
Not in relationship (hardly/never talk)		.041**		.029**
Quality				
Supportiveness		3.679**		4.937**
Frequency of conflict		.983		1.493*
Log likelihood	−824.246	−680.927	−889.249	−678.298
Chi-square	110.48**	397.11**	117.54**	539.44**
Pseudo R-squared	.063	.226	.062	.285
Number of cases (*n*)	2,616	2,616	2,616	2,616

[+] $p < .10$; *$p < .05$; **$p < .01$.

[1] Such as providing transportation to the prenatal clinic or helping with chores.

11. FRAGILE FAMILIES 257

not related to whether fathers contributed. Thus, it appears that having any employment increases the likelihood of fathers' contributing at all, while it could be that the level of earnings increases the amount or frequency that the father contributes (not reflected in our dichotomous measure). Fathers who have other biological children are significantly less likely to make financial contributions than fathers without other children.

We also find some support for the argument that fathers who identify more strongly with being a father will be more involved; those fathers who express positive attitudes about the importance of the father status are more likely to have given money. Yet, this association diminishes once we control for parents' relationship status and quality; this is because fathers who hold positive attitudes about being a father are also likely to be closely connected to the mother. Surprisingly, however, fathers who attend religious services frequently are about 10% *less* likely to have given money to the mother. This puzzling finding runs counter to expectations of religiosity leading to greater father involvement, but this result has been corroborated in other analyses using the Fragile Families data (Johnson, 2001). Finally, the kind of fathering a man received growing up does not affect his financial contribution.

At least one characteristic related to the child appears to affect father involvement. Not having wanted the pregnancy (determined by the mother's report that he suggested she have an abortion) is strongly associated with a lower likelihood that the father gives money to the mother. This effect persists even when we control for the variables describing parents' relationship. The sex of the child is not related to whether the father contributes financially.

Model 2 shows that the status and quality of the parents' relationship are strongly linked to whether the father contributed money during the pregnancy. Compared to fathers in a cohabiting relationship with the baby's mother, fathers in all other relationship types are much less likely to have contributed; visiting fathers are 44% less likely, friends are 77% less likely, and those not in relationships are 96% less likely to have given money than cohabiting fathers. Holding relationship status constant, the quality of the relationship is also strongly linked to the likelihood that the father gave money. However, only the positive dimension of relationship quality appears to matter—level of supportiveness is strongly linked to whether the father gave money, while frequency of conflict shows no association. This implies that even for parents who are not romantically involved, the ability to relate to one another in a positive, supportive manner facilitates the father's involvement.

Similar results are noted for the second indicator of fathers' provision of material support during the pregnancy—whether the father helped the mother in some other way, such as providing transportation or helping with chores. Employed fathers are significantly more likely to have helped. Also, fathers with a high school degree are more likely to have provided such help than those with some college or higher. It may be that fathers with higher education have jobs that require greater work hours, so they are less available to provide instrumental support. Positive fathering

attitudes are linked to the provision of nonmonetary assistance, although this effect is not significant when relationship status and quality are controlled. As with giving money, religiosity is negatively related to the provision of help when only father and child characteristics are included; however, this effect is no longer significant in Model 2. Also, if the child is a boy, the father is less likely to have helped than if the child is a girl (marginal significance); it is unclear why the sex of the baby might be significantly related to fathers' help in this way, particularly prior to the child's birth.

Again, aspects of the parents' relationship are strongly associated with helping in another way (Model 2). Visiting fathers are 83% less likely to have helped in some other way than cohabiting fathers, and those who are friends or not in a relationship with the mother are about 96% less likely to have provided such help. Similar to the results for giving money, level of supportiveness in the relationship is strongly associated with the father's helping in a nonmonetary way. For this outcome, the frequency of conflict is also associated with a *greater* likelihood of providing such help. It could be that providing help is the result of conflict between the parents (about his lack of involvement), while on the other hand, being together while the father is providing help may create a context in which more conflict will occur. Given the cross-sectional nature of the data, it is impossible to determine the direction of the effect.

Estimates for logistic regression models predicting the likelihood that the father visited the mother in the hospital are shown in Table 11.4. While fathers' race is not significant for whether the father provided material support to the mother (Table 11.3), non-Hispanic White fathers are significantly more likely to have visited the mother in the hospital. Hispanic fathers also are more likely to have visited the mother in the hospital, but this characteristic is no longer statistically significant when relationship characteristics are controlled in Model 2 (Hispanic fathers are disproportionately cohabiting). Less educated fathers are much less likely to have visited the mother than their more educated counterparts with some college or higher. Employment status is a strong predictor of whether the father visited the mother in the hospital; employed fathers are more than twice as likely to have visited as fathers who are not employed around the time of the child's birth, even after controlling for relationship status and quality. Having other biological children is associated with a lower likelihood of visiting the mother in the hospital, and depressed fathers and those with substance problems are also less likely to have visited.

Fathers who never knew their own father are more likely to have visited the mother in the hospital than those whose own father was highly involved; this result provides support for the notion that some fathers compensate for the lack of involvement by their own father. Positive fathering attitudes are strongly related to whether the father visited. Again, frequent religious attendance is significantly linked to a *lower* likelihood that the father visited the mother in the hospital, a rather unexpected finding; it could be that highly religious fathers are reticent to publicly acknowledge a nonmarital birth.

TABLE 11.4

Estimated Log Odds Ratios from Logistic Regression Models: Father's Direct
Interaction with Mother and Child

	Visited Mother in Hospital	
	Model 1	Model 2
Father characteristics:		
Age (omitted = 30 and older)		
Less than 20	1.266	1.570[+]
Ages 20–24	1.023	1.148
Ages 25–29	1.023	1.207
Race (omitted = Black, non-Hispanic)		
White, non-Hispanic	2.476**	2.515**
Hispanic	1.544*	1.217
Other	.875	.800
Father is immigrant	1.446	1.291
Education (omitted = some college or more)		
Less than HS degree	.559**	.501**
High school degree/GED	.662*	.609*
Father worked last week	2.562**	2.615**
Father's hourly wage rate (in dollars)	.998	1.002
Father has other biological children	.802	.709*
Fair or poor health	1.259	1.359
Substance use interfered with work/relationships	.573**	.579*
Depression score (range = 1–7)	.853**	.869**
Involvement of own father (omitted = very involved)		
Never knew father	1.932*	1.664[+]
Not very involved	1.081	1.024
Somewhat involved	1.325[+]	1.360[+]
Positive attitudes toward fathering	1.765**	1.290**
Frequency of religious attendance	.787**	.803**
Child characteristics:		
Child is boy	.986	.960
Pregnancy not wanted	.616**	.973
Parents' relationship:		
Status (omitted = cohabiting)		
Visiting (romantic but living separately)		.234**
Friends		.111**
Not in relationship (hardly/never talk)		.024**
Quality		
Supportiveness		1.340
Frequency of conflict		1.948**
Log likelihood	−851.920	−733.211
Chi-square	208.76**	446.17**
Pseudo R-squared	.109	.233
Number of cases (*n*)	2,618	2,618

[+]*p* < .10; *p* < .05; **p* < .01.

As with the previous two outcomes, attributes of the parents' relationship are strongly associated with whether the father visited the mother in the hospital. Compared to cohabiting fathers, those in visiting relationships are 77% less likely, those who are friends with the mother are 89% less likely, and those not in any relationship are 98% less likely to have visited the mother in the hospital. However, contrary to our findings for both measures of fathers' material contributions, level of supportiveness is not significantly linked to whether the father visited the mother in the hospital. By contrast, when the mother reports more frequent conflict, the father is more likely to have visited; again, this could simply indicate that having more contact provides greater opportunities for conflict.

Table 11.5 presents results for the two indicators of the extent to which the father is willing to identify himself legally as the father. While the father's name being on the birth certificate is not synonymous with a declaration of paternity, it is an important precursor to paternity establishment. Also, whether the child takes the father's surname has potentially long-term implications for his being publicly identified as the child's father.

With respect to the father's name being on the birth certificate, few characteristics of fathers are significantly associated, once parents' relationship characteristics are controlled. Unlike for any other outcome, fathers' wages have a significant positive relationship with his name being on the birth certificate; each additional dollar of hourly wages is associated with a 5% greater likelihood that his name is on the birth certificate. Since paternity establishment is necessary for establishing a child support order, fathers with higher earnings may be more able/willing to take financial responsibility for their child and/or mothers may make greater efforts to establish paternity if the father has higher earnings potential. Fathers whose own fathers were not very involved are much less likely to be identified as the father on the baby's birth certificate.

Not wanting the pregnancy is highly associated with a lower likelihood that the father's name is on the birth certificate in Model 1, but this association dissipates when parents' relationship characteristics are controlled. As to parents' relationship, cohabitation is again a strong predictor of the father's name being on the birth certificate. Supportiveness is a strong predictor, while there is no effect of the frequency of conflict.

Turning to the outcome for whether the child will have the father's last name, children of teenage fathers are significantly more likely to have their father's last name, once parents' relationship characteristics are controlled. Children of Hispanic fathers are much more likely to take his surname. Education is positively related to the baby having the father's surname as is fathers' being employed.

As with the previous indicators, parents' relationship status is an important factor for this outcome as well. Compared to cohabiting fathers, for fathers in all three other relationship types the child is significantly less likely to take his last name. Also, holding constant the relationship status, the level of supportiveness in

TABLE 11.5

Estimated Log Odds Ratios From Logistic Regression Models: Father's Identification as the Baby's Father

	Father's Name Is on Birth Certificate		Child Will Have Father's Last Name	
	Model 1	Model 2	Model 1	Model 2
Father characteristics:				
Age (omitted = 30 and older)				
Less than 20	1.080	1.251	1.392	1.653*
Ages 20–24	1.108	1.192	1.207	1.316
Ages 25–29	.814	.874	1.079	1.205
Race (omitted = Black, non-Hispanic)				
White, non-Hispanic	.541**	.419**	1.158	.954
Hispanic	1.394	1.117	2.981**	2.654**
Other	.966	.955	1.326	1.363
Father is immigrant	1.151	.999	1.505	1.380
Education (omitted = some college or more)				
Less than HS degree	.817	.820	.577**	.566**
High school degree/GED	.810	.797	.677*	.646*
Father worked last week	1.165	1.061	1.349*	1.288+
Father's hourly wage rate (in dollars)	1.044*	1.051*	1.005	1.009
Father has other biological children	.840	.787	1.135	1.130
Fair or poor health	.907	.987	.776	.812
Substance use interfered with work/relationships	.792	.955	.710+	.854
Depression score (range = 1–7)	.946	.976	.961	.991
Involvement of own father (omitted = very involved)				
Never knew father	.858	.773	1.326	1.287
Not very involved	.660*	.615*	.999	.954
Somewhat involved	.889	.888	1.027	1.020
Positive attitudes toward fathering	1.699**	1.281	1.627**	1.289*
Frequency of religious attendance	.885*	.919	.950	.980
Child characteristics:				
Child is boy	1.175	1.177	1.197	1.206
Pregnancy not wanted	.442**	.747	.529**	.876
Parents' relationship:				
Status (omitted = cohabiting)				
Visiting (romantic but living separately)		.393**		.481**
Friends		.226**		.220**
Not in relationship (hardly/never talk)		.065**		.057**
Quality				
Supportiveness		1.682*		1.603**
Frequency of conflict		1.055		.845
Log likelihood	−637.183	−579.240	−967.774	−877.936
Chi-square	69.68**	185.56**	139.83**	319.51**
Pseudo R-squared	.052	.138	.067	.154
Number of cases (*n*)	2,596	2,596	2,596	2,596

+ *p* < .10; *p* < .05; **p* < .01.

the relationship is positively associated with the child taking the father's surname, while the frequency of conflict shows no relationship to this outcome.

DISCUSSION

This research adds to the literature about fathers' involvement with their children by focusing on unmarried fathers and examining the characteristics of the father, the child, and the parents' relationship that are associated with paternal involvement at the very beginning of a child's life. We assess three types of fathers' involvement—material contributions during the pregnancy, direct interaction around the time of the child's birth, and legal identification as the father. Because our data are cross-sectional, we provide a descriptive portrait of the characteristics associated with father involvement around the time of a child's birth, but we cannot infer causal relationships between any of the individual predictors and the involvement outcomes.

Overall, we observe that several attributes of the father are important across multiple domains of involvement. We find the father's ability to fulfill the provider role—demonstrated by his higher education, being employed, or higher wages—is linked to each of the outcomes. Fathers who are employed are more likely to provide material support during the pregnancy and to visit the mother in the hospital, a relatively public acknowledgment of paternity. Having a job may both increase the resources a father has available to contribute financially and cause him or the mother (or both) to feel that he can "legitimately" participate in the nonmonetary aspects of fathering. The fact that employment status is also linked with whether the child has the father's surname indicates that breadwinning capabilities are a factor in parents' long-term thinking as well, since taking his name implies that he will be identified as the child's father indefinitely.

By contrast, employment status is not an important factor for whether the father's name is on the birth certificate. Instead, the father's hourly wage rate is the only significant economic characteristic. Because the proportion of fathers named on the birth certificate is much lower for men who are not in a relationship with the mother (as compared to fathers in all other relationship types), this group may be largely driving the effect of the wage rate. It may be that earnings potential is a key factor that distinguishes involved from uninvolved fathers among those who have no relationship with the mother; that is, men with a better financial status may anticipate that they can "afford" to be involved in the future and thus be more willing to become the legal father. Likewise, mothers may perceive greater benefits to having higher-earning fathers involved over time (even without having any other relationship with him), so they may make greater efforts to ensure that the father is legally connected to the child at the time of birth. Further research would be instructive to determine which characteristics are most salient for the father being seen as an adequate provider and whether this effect on father involvement operates through fathers' self-perceptions, mothers' perceptions of fathers, or both.

11. FRAGILE FAMILIES 263

Other demographic characteristics of the father—his age, race, immigrant status, education, and having other children—are not consistent predictors of his involvement. Fathers' personal health and wellbeing are also not strongly linked to involvement. Only the outcome of visiting the mother in the hospital is affected by fathers' mental health: depressed fathers and those with substance problems are less likely to have visited. Subsequent follow-up interviews in the Fragile Families Study will provide greater information that will allow a more in-depth investigation of how fathers' mental health affects their involvement with children.

With respect to fathering background and religiosity, fathers' positive attitudes about fathering are significantly linked to greater involvement when only father and child characteristics are included; however, once characteristics of the parents' relationship are controlled, fathers' attitudes no longer matter for three of the outcomes (but persist for hospital visiting and the child taking his surname). That this association diminishes in several cases is because fathers who are more committed to and invested in the father role are also more likely to be closely attached to the mother. This confirms our expectation that some of the fathers' characteristics are mediated by the mother–father relationship. Fathers' experiences with their own fathers while growing up does not appear to be consistently related to the fathering they demonstrate around the time of a child's birth. Surprisingly, frequency of fathers' religious attendance is *negatively* associated with visiting the mother in the hospital, even after characteristics of the parents' relationship are controlled; this finding merits further investigation.

Also, characteristics related to the child are not strong predictors of fathers' involvement. The child's gender is only linked (marginally) to whether the father provided nonmonetary help; if the child was a boy, it is less likely that the father provided such help. It is unclear why this might be true, particularly since the help is during pregnancy before the gender of the child is known with certainty. Whether the father wanted the pregnancy is initially significant for all five outcomes when only father and child characteristics are included, but after accounting for parents' relationship, whether the pregnancy was wanted is no longer significant; this is because wantedness is closely associated with the parents' relationship status at the time of birth.

The nature of the parents' relationship with one another is the most consistent predictor of whether the father will be involved during the pregnancy and around the time of the child's birth. Two aspects of parents' relationship are key—the status of their relationship around the time of birth, and the level of supportiveness between them. Compared to fathers in cohabiting relationships with the child's mother, fathers in all other types of relationships are significantly less likely to be involved in each of the ways examined here. This implies that the decision to cohabit by the time a nonmarital birth occurs is an important indicator of the parents' intentions to raise their child together. For each of the five measures of father involvement, being romantically involved but not living together is not equivalent to cohabitation in terms of the likelihood that the father will be involved. Thus, coresidence provides

an important initial context for highly involved fathering, and future research with these data will demonstrate whether cohabiting unions remain stable and whether fathers who start out in such unions at the time of their child's birth continue to demonstrate positive involvement over time.

For four of the five outcomes, we find that beyond the particular relationship status itself, having a high-quality relationship (evidenced by mothers' reports of fathers' supportiveness) is also associated with a greater likelihood that the father will be involved.[14] Also, more frequent conflict is linked with the father's providing (nonmonetary) support and his visiting the mother in the hospital. We expect that this association is more driven by the fact that for couples with contentious relationships, greater interaction provides additional occasions where conflict can occur—not that conflict directly promotes father involvement. While relationship status is linked to relationship quality (i.e., cohabitors generally have higher-quality relationships than, say, parents who are just friends with one another), the association is not perfect, and variation in quality is noted within (as well as across) relationship types. Therefore, regardless of the parents' determination about whether to pursue a romantic relationship, their ability to relate in a positive manner with one another appears to have benefits for whether the father is involved with the child.

As a point of comparison, we also estimated models using the fathers' reports about his involvement for each of the five outcomes (except that fathers were asked whether they were present at the baby's birth instead of whether they visited the mother in the hospital). Our basic findings about the fundamental importance of fathers' economic capabilities and of the mother–father relationship are unchanged. The one exception is that fathers' employment is not significant for whether the child will have the father's surname when the father's report for this measure is used. Also, fathers' positive attitudes about fathering are more strongly linked to the father involvement outcomes when his report of the latter is used. This is not surprising given the shared variance from having the same reporter provide information about both the independent and dependent variables.

METHODOLOGICAL ISSUES

As highlighted throughout this volume, methodological and conceptual issues have significant bearing on our understanding of the determinants, nature, and consequences of father involvement. These issues clearly merit further theoretical

---

[14]Our results that both cohabitation and relationship quality matter for involvement are contrary to those of Coley and Chase-Lansdale (1999), who find that the effect of paternal coresidence is entirely mediated by parents' emotional closeness. This could be because they are evaluating involvement (and coresidence) when the child is 3 years old, as relationship status and quality may become more highly correlated over time. Also, their sample of cohabiting fathers is small ($n = 16$).

11. FRAGILE FAMILIES 265

consideration and empirical investigation in future research. We discuss here several key methodological issues (particularly related to data and measurement) that arise from the present investigation.

The Fragile Families and Child Wellbeing Study has a unique design that presents both opportunities and challenges for studying father involvement (see Reichman, Teitler, Garfinkel, & McLanahan, 2001, for information about the research design of the study). First, because it follows a birth cohort, the study allows investigators to control for the conditions that exist at the time of the child's birth. This paper explores father involvement at the very beginning of a child's life. As additional data become available, we will be able to describe both change and continuity in fathers' involvement with children over time and to analyze how such involvement affects children's wellbeing, controlling for the initial social and economic context into which the child is born.

Second, the study has an innovative data collection strategy, with parents being interviewed in the hospital shortly after their child's birth. While this might seem an unlikely venue and time to successfully conduct survey interviews, early pretests for the Fragile Families Study showed that hospitals were a better location for reaching fathers than prenatal clinics, which had been originally intended as the interview site. Collecting data on fathers has been a notable challenge in family research generally, and fathers (particularly nonresident fathers) have historically been underrepresented in national surveys (Garfinkel et al., 1998). By interviewing three-quarters of all eligible fathers, the Fragile Families Study provides data that are significantly more representative of fathers than most previous studies. Still, one-quarter of all fathers are missing, so we do not have direct information from this group of men. Anticipating this problem, the Fragile Families baseline survey asked mothers a number of questions about fathers so that some information is available about all fathers. Because the results presented in this paper are based on the more detailed information provided by fathers themselves, we cannot infer information about involvement of the "missing" fathers. The Fragile Families data (from the father interviews) are most representative of cohabiting fathers (90% response rate) and least representative of fathers who are no longer in any kind of relationship with the child's mother at the time of birth (26% response rate). Moreover, among the latter group, the men who participated in the study are likely to be a highly select group of men; namely men who are unusually committed to the child and/or the mother. Thus, our estimates of father involvement represent an "upper bound" estimate of the involvement among unmarried fathers, particularly with respect to this latter group.

Finally, both mothers and fathers are interviewed at each survey wave, which allows us to compare each parent's report about fathers' involvement, relationship quality, and other variables. While having two reports on the same topic offers additional information, it also represents a challenge. In cases where the reports differ, we must wonder whether one parent's report is more "correct" than the other's report, or whether the differences simply reflect the fact that perceptions of

266   CARLSON AND McLANAHAN

social experiences are intrinsically subjective. With respect to fathers' involvement with their children, parents' reports may differ for at least two reasons. First, fathers may be more likely to overreport their involvement because they view it as socially desirable. Second, parents may have different assessments about whether a particular type of involvement actually occurred. We would expect less ambiguity about outcomes that are more concrete (e.g., father's name being on the birth certificate); but for some items, the definition of involvement may be more ambiguous (e.g., "helping in another way" could include a broader or more narrow set of helping tasks depending on one's perspective).

Comparing the four father involvement indicators used in this paper for which we have identical reports from mothers and fathers, we find quite a high degree of corroboration overall. Agreement is highest about whether the father's name is on the birth certificate (88.5%), followed by whether the father gave money or bought things for the baby (84.6%), whether the baby will have the father's last name (83.3%), and whether the father helped in another way during the pregnancy (83.3%).

We also explored differences in parents' reports about the quality of their relationship with each other, and here we find much less consensus. For the frequency-of-conflict measure, parents' reports are correlated at $r = .302$ ($p < .001$). Thus, while the correlation is statistically significant, parents have notably different perceptions about the level of conflict in their relationship. For the measure of supportiveness, the decision about whose report to use is even more consequential because the items refer to the behavior of the other parent, as opposed to the relationship per se. In other words, mothers report on the fathers' behavior and fathers report on the mothers' behavior. These are fundamentally different constructs that have different theoretical implications. Mothers' and fathers' reports about the other parent are correlated at $r = .264$ ($p < .001$).

To further investigate how the source of the report affects estimates of parents' relationship and father involvement, we estimated a series of regression models with various possible combinations. Table 11.6 shows the log odds ratios from models predicting whether the father gave money or bought things for the baby and whether his name is on the child's birth certificate, using mothers' versus fathers' reports of involvement and relationship quality. (These models include all the covariates in Model 2 in the main analyses). We examine three measures of each of the two dependent variables in columns across the top—mothers' reports of fathers' involvement, fathers' reports of fathers' involvement, and both parents' reports of involvement. Then, in rows on the side we show three measures of the supportiveness in the parents' relationship—mothers' reports about fathers, fathers' reports about mothers, and both parents' reports about each other.

Based on these two outcomes, it is difficult to discern a consistent pattern. We find that the mother's assessment of the father's supportive behavior is linked to fathers' financial contributions, regardless of who is reporting about the latter. Fathers' assessment of how the mother behaves in the relationship appears to

TABLE 11.6
Estimated Log Odds Ratios From Logistic Regression Models: Comparing Mother and Father Reports of Father Involvement and of Other Parent's Supportiveness

	Father Gave Money or Bought Things for the Baby			Father's Name is on the Child's Birth Certificate		
Supportiveness in the Parents' Relationship	Mother Report (yes = 89.8%)	Father Report (yes = 91.2%)	Both Parents (yes = 84.6%)	Mother Report (yes = 91.3%)	Father Report (yes = 93.4%)	Both Parents (yes = 88.5%)
Mother's assessment of father's behavior	3.679**	1.790**	2.904**	1.682**	1.341	1.609*
Father's assessment of mother's behavior	.997	1.953**	1.277	1.237	2.155**	1.813**
Both parents' assessments of each other's behavior						
Mother about father	3.940**	1.694*	2.949**	1.789**	1.231	1.537*
Father about mother	0.828	1.929**	1.096	1.166	2.196**	1.738**

+ $p < .10$; * $p < .05$; ** $p < .01$.

have less bearing on his contributions; only when the father is reporting about his financial contributions does mothers' supportiveness matter, indicating some shared assessment on his part. The pattern is slightly different for the outcome of whether the father's name will be on the birth certificate. Each parent's report of the other's supportiveness is linked to their own report of whether the father's name is on the birth certificate and to both parents' consensus report. This pattern is replicated when both parents' reports about whether his name will be on the birth certificate are included in the same model.

Beyond the data and measurement issues related to father involvement and parents' relationship, there are important questions about the causal order of variables that the present research cannot answer. In addition to positive mother–father relationships promoting father involvement (the direction of effects posited in this paper), we also would expect active participation in childrearing to enhance parents' relationship quality (or lack of involvement to foster greater conflict). Alternatively, unmeasured attributes of fathers may positively affect both fathers' involvement with their children and their ability to be supportive and maintain a high-quality relationship with the mothers. Although we include variables for fathers' attitudes toward fathering and fathers' experiences growing up (potential "third" variables), other personal characteristics of the father—such as a general commitment to and investment in family roles or his self-efficacy—have not been taken into account. Although family relationships and dynamics are inherently interconnected, future research using longitudinal data and more sophisticated analytic techniques may yield important new information about the direction of these causal relationships. More generally, it is important to consider father involvement at any particular time and circumstance in the context of a father's overall fertility and family history. Applying a life course perspective with attention to a father's current and past commitments to children and partners would enrich our understanding of whether, when, and how fathers are involved and what are the implications of such involvement for children, families, and the fathers themselves.

CONCLUSION

This paper provides new information about factors associated with greater involvement by unmarried fathers around the time of a child's birth. We find support for the importance of the provider role in facilitating fathers' overall involvement, and our results confirm the centrality of the mother–father relationship for understanding fathers' contributions to their children. Further research is requisite to examine change and continuity in fathers' involvement with their children over time and the extent to which the personal and contextual characteristics shown to be important in this paper continue to shape the nature of fathers' interactions with their children.

ACKNOWLEDGMENTS

We thank Kristin Moore and the Editors of this volume for useful comments. We appreciate the generous financial support of the Fragile Families and Child Wellbeing Study provided by a consortium of government agencies and private foundations. The Fragile Families and Child Wellbeing Study is funded by the National Institute of Child Health and Human Development (NICHD), the California Healthcare Foundation the Center for Research on Religion and Urban Civil Society at the University of Pennsylvania, the Commonwealth Fund, the Ford Foundation, the Foundation for Child Development, the Fund for New Jersey, the William T. Grant Foundation, the Healthcare Foundation of New Jersey, the William and Flora Hewlett Foundation, the Hogg Foundation, the Christina A. Johnson Endeavor Foundation, the Kronkosky Charitable Foundation, the Leon Lowenstein Foundation, the John D. and Catherine T. MacArthur Foundation, the A. L. Mailman Family Foundation, the Charles S. Mott Foundation, the National Science Foundation, the David and Lucille Packard Foundation, the Public Policy Institute of California, the Robert Wood Johnson Foundation, the St. David's Hospital Foundation, the St. Vincent Hospital and Health Services, and the U.S. Department of Health and Human Services (ASPE and ACF).

REFERENCES

Belsky, J. (1984). The determinants of parenting: A process model. *Child Development, 55*, 83–96.

Belsky, J. (1990). Parental and nonparental child care and children's socioemotional development: A decade in review. *Journal of Marriage and the Family, 52*, 885–903.

Belsky, J., Youngblade, L., & Rovine, M. (1991). Patterns of marital change and parent–child interaction. *Journal of Marriage and the Family, 53*, 487–498.

Blair, S. L., & Hardesty, C. (1994). Parental involvement and the wellbeing of fathers and mothers of young children. *Journal of Men's Studies, 3*, 49–68.

Coley, R. L., & Chase-Lansdale, P. L. (1999). Stability and change in paternal involvement among urban African American fathers. *Journal of Family Psychology, 13*(3), 1–20.

Cooksey, E. C., & Craig, P. H. (1998). Parenting from a distance: The effects of paternal characteristics on contact between nonresidential fathers and their children. *Demography, 35*(2), 187–200.

Danziger, S., & Radin, N. (1990). Absent does not equal uninvolved: Predictors of fathering in teen mother families. *Journal of Marriage and the Family, 52*(3), 636–642.

Edin, K., & Lein, L. (1997). *Making ends meet: How single mothers survive welfare and low-wage work.* New York: Russell Sage Foundation.

Farmer, M. M., & Ferraro, K. F. (1997). Distress and perceived health: Mechanisms of health decline. *Journal of Health and Social Behavior, 39*, 298–311.

Garfinkel, I., McLanahan, S., & Hanson, T. (1998). A patchwork portrait of nonresident fathers. In I., Garfinkel, S. McLanahan, D. Meyer, & J. Seltzer (Eds.). *Fathers under fire: The revolution in child support enforcement* (pp. 31–60). New York: Russell Sage Foundation.

Garfinkel, I., McLanahan, S. S., Tienda, M., & Brooks-Gunn, J. (2001). Fragile families and welfare reform: An introduction. *Children and Youth Services Review, 23*(4/5), 277–301.

Gottman, J. M. (1998). Toward a process model of men in marriages and families. In A. Booth & A. C. Crouter (Eds.), *Men in families: When do they get involved? What difference does it make?* (pp.149–192). Mahwah, NJ: Lawrence Erlbaum Associates.

Harris, K. H., & Morgan, S. P. (1991). Fathers, sons and daughters: Differential paternal involvement in parenting. *Journal of Marriage and the Family, 53,* 531–544.

Heimer, C. A., & Staffen, L. R. (1998). *For the sake of the children: The social organization of responsibility in the hospital and the home.* Chicago: The University of Chicago Press.

Hofferth, S. L. (1984). Kin networks, race, and family structure. *Journal of Marriage and the Family, 47,* 93–115.

Ihinger-Tallman, M., Pasley, K., & Buehler, C. (1993). Developing a middle-range theory of father involvement postdivorce. *Journal of Family Issues, 14,* 550–571.

Johnson, W. E., Jr. (2001). Parental involvement among unwed fathers. *Children and Youth Services Review, 23*(6/7), 513–536.

King, V. (1994). Variation in the consequences of nonresident father involvement for children's well-being. *Journal of Marriage and the Family, 56,* 963–972.

Lamb, M. (Ed.). (1997). *The role of the father in child development.* New York: Wiley.

Lamb, M. E., Pleck, J. H., Charnov, E. L., & Levine, J. A. (1987). A biosocial perspective on paternal behavior and involvement. In J. B. Lancaster, J. Altman, A. Rossi, & L. R. Sherrod (Eds.), Parenting across the lifespan: Biosocial perspectives (pp. 11–42). New York: Academic.

Landale, N. S., & Oropesa, R. S. (2001). Father involvement in the lives of mainland Puerto Rican children: Contributions of nonresident, cohabiting and married fathers. *Social Forces, 79,* 945–968.

Lerman, R. & Sorenson, E. (2000). Father involvement with their nonmarital children: Patterns, determinants, and effects on their earnings. *Marriage & Family Review, 29*(2/3), 137–158.

Liebow, E. (1967). *Tally's corner: A study of negro streetcorner men.* Boston: Little, Brown.

Lundberg, S. & Rose, E. (1999). The determinants of specialization within marriage. Working paper, University of Washington, Department of Economics.

Marsiglio, W., (1991). Paternal engagement activities with minor children. *Journal of Marriage and the Family, 53,* 973–986.

Marsiglio, W., Amato, P., Day, R. D., & Lamb, M. E. (2000). Scholarship on fatherhood in the 1990s and beyond. *Journal of Marriage and Family, 62*(4), 1173–1191.

Marsiglio, W., & Cohan, M. (2000). Contextualizing father involvement and paternal influence: sociological and qualitative themes. *Marriage & Family Review, 29*(2/3), 75–95.

McLanahan, S., & Sandefur, G. (1994). *Growing up with a single parent: What hurts, what helps.* Cambridge, MA: Harvard University Press.

McLanahan, S., Garfinkel, I., Reichman, N., & Teitler, J. (2001). Unwed parents or fragile families?: Implications for welfare and child support policy. In L. L. Wu, & B. Wolfe (Eds.), *Out of Wedlock: Trends, Causes, and Consequences of Nonmarital Fertility* (pp. 202–228). New York: Russell Sage Foundation.

Morgan, S. P., Lye, D. N., & Condran, G. A. (1988). Sons, daughters, and the risk of marital disruption. *American Journal of Sociology, 94*(1), 110–129.

Pleck, J. H. (1997). Paternal involvement: Levels, sources, and consequences. In M. E. Lamb (Ed.), *The Role of the Father in Child Development.* New York: Wiley.

Radloff, L. S. (1977). The CES-D scale: A self report depression scale for research in the general population. *Applied Psychological Measurement, 1,* 385–401.

Rane, T. R. & McBride, B. A. (2000). Identity theory as a guide to understanding fathers' involvement with their children. *Journal of Family Issues, 21*(3), 347–366.

Reichman, N., Teitler, J., Garfinkel, I., & McLanahan, S. (2001). Fragile Families: Sample and design. *Children and Youth Services Review, 23*(4/5), 303–326.

Seltzer, J. A., & Bianchi, S. M. (1988). Children's contact with absent parents. *Journal of Marriage and the Family, 50,* 663–677.

11. FRAGILE FAMILIES

Seltzer, J. (1991). Relationships between fathers and children who live apart: The father's role after separation. *Journal of Marriage and the Family, 53*, 79–101.

U.S. Census Bureau (2000). *Educational Attainment in the U.S.: March 2000* (P20–536). http://www. census.gov/population/www/socdemo/education/p20–536.html.

Ventura, S. J. & Bachrach, C. A. (2000). Nonmarital childbearing in the United States, 1940–99. *National Vital Statistics Reports, 48*(16). Hyattsville, MD: National Center for Health Statistics.

Waller, M., & Bailey, A. (2002). How do fathers' negative behaviors shape relationships with their children. Center for Research on Child Wellbeing, Princeton University, Working Paper 02-18-FF.

Weiss, Y., & Willis, R. J. (1985). Children as collective goods and divorce settlements. *Journal of Labor Economics, 3,3*, 268–292.

Wilcox, W. B. (2002). Religion, convention, and paternal involvement. *Journal of Marriage and Family, 64*(3), 780–792.

Wilson M., & Brooks-Gunn, J. (2001). Health status and behaviors of unwed fathers. *Children and Youth Services Review, 23*(4/5), 377–401.

Woodworth, S., Belsky, J., & Crnic, K. (1996). The determinants of father involvement during the child's second and third years of life: A developmental analysis. *Journal of Marriage and the Family, 58*, 679–692.

12

Youth Ratings of Family Processes and Father Role Performance of Resident and Nonresident Fathers

Randal D. Day
Brigham Young University

Alan Acock
Oregon State University

Researchers interested in father involvement have focused on the relationships between parents and their younger children (Hosley & Montemayor, 1997; Lamb, 1997; Marsiglio, Day, Amato, & Lamb, 2000). Whereas the research on father involvement has blossomed in recent years, the focus on father involvement with regard to adolescent children is still in its infancy (Hosley & Montemayor, 1997). The purpose of this chapter is to explore an important measurement issue that is relatively underresearched. How can we assess teen's perceptions of family processes (social capital) and role performance of fathers compared to mothers? We show that researchers can use existing large national data sets to assess this important construct and specifically explain how to use data from the National Longitudinal Survey of Youth-97 to gather important information about teen–father relationships.

In particular, we compare how fathers are viewed differently by their children as a function of family status, focusing on biological and nonbiological fathers and whether they resident in the same home as the reporting child. We also examine differences in the perceptions across racial/ethnic groups and by the gender of the youth.

273

We suggest that a greater understanding of youth perceptions of father involvement may lead to better intervention strategies designed to increase effective father involvement in children's lives. Fathers in different cultural and/or family structural conditions may have particular challenges to face as they try to discover better strategies to connect to, mentor, and affect the lives of the teens in their homes.

Father Involvement

The research community has endorsed the notion that father involvement in children's lives is a significant social issue (Marsiglio et al., 2000; Lamb, 1997). Additionally, researchers, theorists, and practitioners have embraced the idea that the father's role in the lives of children in multifaceted. When physically and/or emotionally present in the lives of their children, men often do more than simply provide financial stability (Palkowitz, 1997; Lamb, 1997).

A standard view of the father's role is that he has several strategic functions within family life and he influences the well-being of his children. He is typically viewed as a moral guide, protector, model, and primary supporter of his spouse/partner (Marsiglio et. al., 2000). In an important conceptual advancement about the role(s) that men play in families, Palkowitz (1997) suggested that researchers move from a deficit model of father involvement (i.e., what happens when fathers are absent) to a proactive model suggesting that fathers do many activities resulting in positive father involvement (Pleck, 1997). In fact, this shift in thinking reflects a move toward the degendering of the father role, and in work of Palkovitz and many others the shift has been toward an examination of "parent involvement." The implication, of course, is that gender is less important than the quality of the activities performed. Palkovitz's categories cover a wide array of activities and include caring for and thinking about the children, doing errands, planning events, teaching the child, and providing for physical maintenance, in addition to the typical breadwinning and mentoring. One could extrapolate that what a teenager perceives his or her parents as doing with regard to these activities shapes the teen's connection and interaction with and trust of the parents.

Again, we care about each of these kinds of activities and children's perception of them because the research suggests (cf. Marsiglio et. al., 2000) that increases in these kinds of activities by parents enhance the child's well-being. For the most part, however, we know very little about how children and teenagers in particular scrutinize and value these activities. Also, we know very little about how an adolescent's view of a parent varies by gender, ethnic, and family structural differences. We assume that to some degree, perception is reality and, although we have no objective measures of performance by parents, we assume that when teens view their parents' parenting activities in a relatively positive light that the transfer of social and financial capital will be facilitated. When respect, trust, valuation, and connection are low in families, we propose that social capital will be difficult to be transferred from parent to succeeding generations of children and grandchildren.

We do not assess this theoretical notion in this chapter; instead we are proposing it as a solid rationale for studying and assessing this aspect of family processes.

FAMILY PROCESSES AND
SOCIAL CAPITAL

The National Institute of Child Health and Development's (NICHD) Child and Family Well-Being Network has suggested several important topics that social scientists should pay attention to in coming years (Thornton, 2001); two are featured in this chapter. First, the Network echoed the voice of many contemporary researchers in suggesting that increased attention needs to be given to "the study of fathers and their family relationships across all types of family situations, including both residential and non-residential fathers" (Thornton, 2001, p. 439).

Second, the Network suggested that researchers pay more attention to the importance of family processes. The Network called for

> additional research concerning family processes. Here the emphasis is upon relationships and interactions among family members. Examples of important family processes . . . (are) the amount of individuality and belonging, conflict and violence, and caring, kindness, and love. Understanding of such central family processes is important both because they are central dimensions of well-being and because they can have important influences on other aspects of family and child well-being (Thornton, 2001, p. 439).

The purpose of this chapter is to bring those two research areas into closer proximity by suggesting that the research about fatherhood can be expanded within a family process/social capital perspective. We suggest that a strong conceptual link exists between family processes (as identified by family scientists and clinicians) and social capital (as the term is commonly used by sociologists and economists).

Another important aspect of this research is to explore what adolescents generally think of their parents' performance; specifically we examine how they view key aspects of family functioning. Knowing what they think about family functioning is key to understanding how resources are created in families that result from interaction (Coleman, 1990). Coleman's argument is that social capital is created when "the relations among persons change in ways that facilitate action" (p. 304).

By definition, family processes are the strategies used by families to attain goals, sustain ideological beliefs, and respond to disruption created by expected and unexpected crises (Day, Gavazzi, and Acock, 2001). Examples of family processes are degree and style of parental monitoring (Hetherington, Cox, & Cox, 1982); use of effective family routines (O'Connor, Hetherington, & Clingempeel, 1997); and parenting style (Baumrind, 1991). Sampson and Laub (1993) showed that

such family processes have significant and long-term influences on the criminal behavior of teens and their continued arrest and conviction records into adulthood. For example, the monitoring used by parents was especially valuable in predicting whether a teen had ever been arrested. It is important that this conceptual framework be expanded to include the idea of social capital (Coleman, 1990).

Family Process and Social Capital

We suggest that an important family process that needs more exploration relative to men in families is the mechanism by which social capital is created and transferred within families. Family scientists and sociologists have, in recent years, found utility in describing a key family process in terms of human and/or social capital (Coleman, 1988; 1990; Furstenberg, 1998; Furstenberg & Hughes, 1995; Hagan, MacMillian, & Wheaton, 1996; Seltzer, 1998). In particular, Coleman (1990) expanded upon the work of Loury (1977; 1987) and refined the term social capital to describe the resources "that inhere in family relations and in community social organization and that are useful for the cognitive or social development of the child" (p. 300). He goes on to explain that there is a fiction in Western culture that society consists of sets of "independent individuals" who are tangible and observable as they make decisions and solve problems. Instead he asserts that social capital is not lodged in the individual but is a property of social connection and "it is embodied in the *relations* among persons" (p. 304). Social capital is not the private property of one individual; instead it is the essence of relationships. It is also important to note that social capital is not tangible. It cannot be taken to the bank as can financial capital. Social capital, according to Coleman, is created when "the relations among persons change in ways that facilitate action" (p. 304).

An example of how social capital is formed in family life can be found in the literature on distance regulation (Gavazzi, 1994). In this complicated family process, trust, contracts, and negotiations occur in families to control the distance between and among individuals in the system. According to this line of research, families spend large amounts of emotional and physical energy controlling or regulating intimacy and individuality (Gavazzi, 1994). Coleman would add that such control, when appropriately applied, is productive, enabling, family members to make better decisions, use resources better, and accomplish more tasks that are representative of deeply held goals when distance regulation is optimal.

Research about Teen Perception of Parents

Our focus here narrows. We suggest that one way to begin to understand the linkages among family processes, social capital, and teen outcomes is to better understand how teenagers view their parents. Again, we suggest that when their view of a parent is positive (i.e., full of respect, trust, deference, care, and love)

the social capital within the parent–child dyad will increase as will the ability to transfer the social capital of that parent to connections that are extrafamilial. In like manner, when teens have trust, respect, care, and high positive regard for the routines and structure of their family life, we expect their well-being to flourish and the creation and transference of social capital to increase.

So, we begin our search for this conceptual linkage with the assessment that teens make about their parents. Most research about children's perceptions of their parents focuses on older adolescents, usually college-age students in convenience samples. (For a review of this research see Burbach & Borduin, 1986.) Additionally, most of these studies use measures of parental behavior (a notable exception is Phares & Renk, 1998). Of course, behavioral assessments limit what a child can report on a nonresident parent.

There is a glaring absence of literature about teen–father relationships. One of the few examples of research about teens' evaluation of their fathers is a study done by Miller and Lane (1991). They found that college students are more likely to call and talk with their mothers than their fathers (again a behavior measure). According to Hauser, et al., (1987), both boy and girl teens are more likely to talk with their dads about problems, and they perceive these fathers as less restrictive, more engaging, and more open to their needs than their mothers are.

A few other researchers reported that a teen's perception of his or her father's involvement is more selective and more likely to be aimed at the instrumental features of the parent–child interaction (Noller & Bagi, 1985; Youniss & Smollar, 1985). Other studies suggest that the teen's evaluation of father interaction often lacks emotional content or discussion of personal problems (Larson & Richards, 1994) but instead centers on school performance and the problems of managing life.

Most teens report feeling closer to their mothers than to their fathers (Barnes & Olson, 1985; Kenny, 1987; Miller & Lane, 1991). The research further indicates that sons' perceive their relationships with their fathers as having fewer expressions of affection and disclosure than with their mothers (Ebery, Montemayor, & Flannery, 1993).

Many of these studies used limited, self-selected samples of teens and parents, and, until recently, large national data sets have not included information on how teens view their parents, particularly their fathers. While perceptions of parental performance is quite a different question than more objectively observed measures of performance, we assert that an important starting point for understanding human behavior is in understanding the meaning and definition the actor places upon relationships.

Note that we are proceeding without specific hypotheses. There is no extant literature to guide us in this regard. Instead we begin with general research questions: With increasing trends toward alternative family arrangements, we specifically want to know how a teen's perception of his parents may be different from (or possibly similar to) those of teens who live with their biological parents. Additionally,

278   DAY AND ACOCK

if a father is not present in the home, what does he give up or lose in terms of the
perception his child(ren) have about his performance as a father? Does it matter
whether the mother lives alone with the children or has a new father or father
figure in the home? Does the race/ethnicity or gender of the youth influence perceptions of parental role performance? To answer these basic research questions,
we analyzed the NLSY-97 data set with its extensive cross-national sample.

METHODOLOGY

This study uses the National Longitudinal Survey of Youth 1997 (NLSY-97). This
is the newest panel of the National Longitudinal Surveys (NLS) program (Center
for Human Resource Research, 2000). NLSY-97 is a nationally representative
survey of 8,984 adolescents age 12 to 16 as of 12/31/96. Our analysis is limited
to youth who were 12–14 as of 12/31/96 because these where the only youth who
were asked the appropriate questions.

Outcome Variables

The first wave of this panel included a series of items measuring selected family
process variables. We focus on a subset of these measures that broadly represent
a youth's perception of how his or her father performs his role. To provide a
comparison, we include measures of how the youth rates his or her resident mother,
resident father or father figure (if there is one), and nonresident father. Our measures
include the youth's report of (a) parental monitoring, (b) the parent doing a good
job, (c) the parent doing a bad job, and (d) family routines.

Youth Report of Parental Monitoring

The youth's report on parental monitoring was measured using a four-item scale
asking how much the parents know about (1) your close friends, (2) your close
friend's parents, (3) who you are with when you are not at home, and (4) who
your teachers are and what you are doing in school. The response options ranged
from 0 for "knows nothing" to 4 for "knows everything." The mean was computed
resulting in a range of 0 to 4. The means and standard deviations for cases included
in our analysis appear in Table 12.1. Only youth age 12–14 were asked these
questions in 1997. The monitoring scale was developed by Child Trends (1999)
and has been used by Hetherington et al., (1982), Maccoby & Mnookin (1992), and
Otto and Atkinson (1997). The reported reliabilities are alpha = .71 for mothers,
alpha = .81 for residential fathers, and alpha = .85 for nonresident fathers. For the
actual subsample utilized in our analysis, the corresponding alphas are .71, .81,
and .89.

12. YOUTH RATINGS OF FAMILY AND FATHERS

TABLE 12.1

Means, Standard Deviations, and Sample Sizes for Outcome Variables Used
in the Analyzes

Outcome Variable Based on Youth Report	Parent	Mean	Standard Deviation	Alpha	Sample Size
	Resident mother	2.62	.79	.71	4098
Monitoring of parent,	Resident father/father figure	2.07	.99	.81	3008
range is 0–16	Nonresident biological father	.93	.93	.89	532
	Resident mother	3.09	.71	.75	4096
Positive view of parent,	Resident fathers/father figure	2.94	.86	.85	3005
range is 0–4	Nonresident biological father	2.24	1.08	.89	664
	Resident mother	.72	.67	.53	4095
Negative view of parent,	Resident fathers/father figure	.68	.69	.59	3006
range is 0–4	Nonresident biological father	.75	.70	.56	528
Index of family routines,	Family level variable				
range is 0–28		15.06	5.41	NA	4096

Youth Report of Positive View of Parent

Child Trends (1999) also developed a scale measuring the youth's relationship with each of his or her parents. After doing a factor analysis of this scale, we found two clear factors: a positive view of parent and a negative view of parent. We treat the items loading on the two factors as separate scales. Youths aged 12–14 were asked to rate their resident mother, resident father or father figure (if present), and nonresident biological father on four positive items. These included (1) wants to be like the parent, (2) enjoys time with the parent, (3) is praised by the parent, and (4) the parent helps the youth on things that are important to the youth. The first two items were rated on a 0–4 scale with 0 being "strongly disagree" and 4 "strongly agree." The last two items were rated on a 0–4 scale with 0 representing never and 4 representing always. Positive view of parent is the mean of these four items (see Table 12.1) and has a possible range of 0–4. Alpha = .75 for view of mothers, .85 for fathers or father figures, and .89 for nonresident fathers.

Youth Report of Negative View of Parent

Youths aged 12–14 were asked to rate each of their parents on three negative items. These included how often the parent (1) criticizes the youth, (2) blames the youth for his or her own problems, and (3) makes plans only to cancel them. The three items were rated on a 0–4 scale with 0 for "never" and 4 "always." Negative view of parent is the average of these three items (see Table 12.1) and has marginal reliability with alpha = .53 for negative view of mothers, .59 for fathers or father figures, and .56 for nonresident fathers.

Youth's Perception of Family Routines

Child Trends (1999) developed an Index of family routines that was designed to tap the youth's sense of belonging to a family (Henry & Lovelace, 1995; Jenson, James, Bryce, & Hartnett, 1983; O'Connor et al., (1997). The index was administered to youths aged 12–14. It asked about four activities: (1) days per week youth eats dinner with family, (2) days per week housework gets done, (3) days per week the family has fun together, and (4) days per week the family does something religious together. Response categories ranged from 0 to 7 days per week. The items were summed to form the index (means and standard deviations appear in Table 12.1. This is an index rather than a scale, hence alpha has not been computed. Family routine is a family-level variable applied to the family in which the child resides at the time of the interview. The index has a possible range of 0–28.

Predictors

We have three predictors: (1) family type, (2) race/ethnicity, and (3) gender. We restricted our analysis to four types of families including families with (1) both biological parents present, (2) a biological mother but no father or father figure in the household, (3) a biological mother with a stepfather, and (4) a biological mother with a father figure who is not a stepfather. A stepfather may be adoptive or not. A father figure who is not a stepfather is typically a male cohabiting partner, but may be a male relative. A father figure is defined from the point of view of the youth. A cohabiting partner from the point of view of the mother is not a father figure unless the youth says he is. Similarly, a male relative who lives in the home may be a father figure from the youth's perspective.

We include three race/ethnicity groups in our analysis: (1) non-Hispanic African Americans, (2) non-Hispanic Whites, and (3) Hispanic. The race is the self-report of the youth.

Control Variables

We controlled for three variables: (1) the youth's age at the date of the interview, (2) the mother's age, and (3) the poverty ratio for the household. It was important to control for the youth's age at 12/31/96 because of the age range. By the time the interviews were completed, the ages varied from 12 to 15 with a handful who were 16. There was a great deal of missing data on all of the family income variables. Using the poverty ratio, we first used an expectation maximization imputation of members of our subsample who had missing values on family poverty ratio. We did not do this with any of the other variables because there were relatively few missing values.

We restricted the sample in the following ways: (a) youth was 12–14 on 12/31/96, (b) youth was Hispanic, non-Hispanic African-American, or

12. YOUTH RATINGS OF FAMILY AND FATHERS 281

non-Hispanic White, (c) youth had contact with the nonresident father, (d) youth lived in one of the four family types we analyzed, and (e) youth had no missing values for any of the variables (except for poverty ratio). These restrictions reduced our sample size but provided greater clarity to our analysis. The actual sample sizes appear in all tables.

Estimation of Effects

The general linear model was used to estimate the effects of family type, race, and gender on each outcome variable, while treating youths' age, mothers' age, and the household poverty ratio as covariates. Our analysis focused on adjusted means for each outcome. All possible interactions were tested.

RESULTS

Although our primary interest is on the perception youth have of resident and nonresident fathers, we include their perceptions of mothers as a shared reference. Table 12.1 shows that mothers have the highest rating on monitoring and being viewed positively by their teenagers. The mean for the mother on monitoring corresponds to knowing between "some things" and knowing "most things." By contrast, the mean on monitoring for resident fathers corresponds to knowing "some things" and the mean for nonresident fathers corresponds to knowing between "nothing" and knowing "just a little." However, mothers have no advantage when it comes to rating parents for negative behavior. The means on negative view of parents are consistently low (i.e., not negative) regardless of whether the referent is the mother, resident father, or nonresident biological father.

Table 12.2 shows these patterns are true across the four family types. Table 12.3 shows this is true for all race/ethnicity groups, and Table 12.4 shows this is true for both male and female children.

The Importance of Family Type

This section relies on Table 12.2. The four family types appear as columns and are labeled A through D. In addition to the overall probability, statistically significant contrasts are shown as paired letters. For example, A-D signifies that the mean in Column A (biological mother with no father figure) is significantly different from the mean in Column D (biological mother with biological father). The sample size on which each mean is based appears in parentheses below the mean. Although our primary interest is on the perception youth have of resident and nonresident fathers, we include their perceptions of mothers as a shared reference point.

TABLE 12.2
Youth's Perceptions of Parental Characteristics by Family Type: Estimated Means With Controls[1]

Outcome Variable Based on Youth Report	Type of Household (all contain the biological mother)				Overall Probability	Significant Contrasts[2]
	No Father Figure in Household A	Stepfather in Household B	Father Figure Not Stepfather in Household C	Biological Father in Household D		
Monitoring by resident mother	2.50 (1989)	2.50 (407)	2.64 (132)	2.65 (2469)	.001 (4098)	A-D, B-D
Monitoring by resident father/father figure	NA	1.62 (407)	1.64 (132)	2.11 (2469)	.001 (3008)	B-D, C-D
Monitoring by nonresident father	.95 (362)	.71 (125)	.87 (45)	NA	NS (532)	A-B
Resident mother does a good job	3.01 (1090)	3.14 (407)	3.15 (132)	3.14 (2467)	.001 (4096)	A-B, A-C, A-D
Resident father/father figure does a good job	NA	2.50 (407)	2.62 (132)	3.00 (2466)	.001 (3005)	B-D, C-D
Nonresident father does a good job	2.27 (471)	2.19 (144)	2.36 (49)	NA	NS (664)	NS
Resident mother does a bad job	.84 (1090)	.77 (407)	.78 (131)	.70 (2467)	.001 (4095)	A-D
Resident father/father figure does a bad job	NA	.77 (407)	.73 (132)	.68 (2467)	NS (3006)	B-D
Nonresident father does a bad job	.76 (360)	.72 (124)	.87 (44)	NA	NS (528)	NS
Family routines[3]	14.09 (1090)	15.34 (407)	15.12 (132)	15.42 (2467)	.001 (4096)	A-B, A-C, A-D

[1] Control variables include the youth's age at the date of the interview, the mother's age, and the poverty ratio for the household; sample sizes N are in parentheses.
[2] Contrasts refer to significant differences between means in the columns indicated. A-D, for example, shows that the mean for the youth report in households consisting of a biological mother and biological father is significantly different from the youth report in the households consisting of a biological mother and no father figure living in the household.
[3] Rescaled by dividing score by 100.

12. YOUTH RATINGS OF FAMILY AND FATHERS   283

TABLE 12.3

Youth's Perceptions of Parental Characteristics by Race/Ethnicity of the Youth:
Estimated Means With Controls[1]

Outcome Variable Based on Youth Report	Race/Ethnicity of Youth			Overall Probability	Significant Contrasts[2]
	African-American A	Hispanic B	White C		
Monitoring by resident mother	2.54	2.53	2.64	NS	A-C, B-C
	(944)	(932)	(2222)	(4098)	
Monitoring by resident father/father figure	1.63	1.81	1.93	.027	A-B, A-C
	(494)	(680)	(1834)	(3008)	
Monitoring by nonresident biological father	.70	.72	1.11	.001	A-C, B-C
	(183)	(95)	(255)	(532)	
Resident mother does a good job	3.14	3.11	3.10	NS	NS
	(944)	(932)	(220)	(4096)	
Resident father/father figure does a good job	2.66	2.70	2.76	NS	NS
	(494)	(679)	(1832)	(3005)	
Nonresident father does a good job	2.18	2.24	2.41	NS	NS
	(247)	(125)	(292)	(664)	
Resident mother does a bad job	.80	.82	.69	.007	A-C, B-C
	(944)	(931)	(2220)	(4095)	
Resident father/father figure does a bad job	.72	.72	.74	NS	NS
	(494)	(680)	(1832)	(3006)	
Nonresident father does a bad job	.85	.74	.75	NS	NS
	(181)	(94)	(253)	(535)	
Family routines[3]	15.17	15.02	14.80	NS	NS
	(944)	(932)	(2220)	(4096)	

[1]Control variables include the youth's age at the date of the interview, the mother's age, and the poverty ratio for the household; sample sizes N are in parentheses.

[2]Contrasts refer to significant differences between means in the columns indicated. A-C, for example, shows that the mean for the White-non-Hispanic youth report is significantly different from the African-American, non-Hispanic youth report.

[3]Score divided by 100.

Monitoring

Table 2 shows that mothers receive their highest rating on monitoring in families with a biological father or a father figure who is not a stepfather. They receive their lowest rating in families where there is no father figure ($M = 2.50$) present, or there is a stepfather ($M = 2.50$). They receive their highest ratings when a biological father is present ($M = 2.65$) or a father figure who is not a stepfather ($M = 2.64$). Families with no father figure or a stepfather are statistically significantly lower in their rating on monitoring than families in which there is a biological father. The differences, however, are small with an effect size of about .11. For mothers, the means are all between the mother knowing "some things" and knowing "most things."

TABLE 12.4

Youth's Perception of Parental Characteristics by Gender of Youth: Estimated
Means with Controls*

Outcome Variable Based on Youth Report	Gender of the Youth		Probability
	Male	Female	
Monitoring by resident mother	2.50	2.64	.002
	(2084)	(2014)	(4098)
Monitoring by resident father/father figure	1.78	1.80	NS
	(1580)	(1428)	(3008)
Monitoring by nonresident biological father	.84	.84	NS
	(251)	(281)	(532)
Resident mother does a good job	3.13	3.11	NS
	(2083)	(2013)	(4096)
Resident father does a good job	2.82	2.60	.001
	(1578)	(1427)	(3005)
Nonresident father does a good job	2.48	2.07	.003
	(307)	(357)	(664)
Resident mother does a bad job	.82	.72	.013
	(2082)	(2013)	(4095)
Resident father/father figure does a bad job	.78	.67	.034
	(1578)	(1428)	(3006)
Nonresident father does a bad job	.80	.76	NS
	(249)	(281)	(528)
Family routines	15.03	14.96	NS
	(2084)	(2012)	(4096)

*Control variables include the youth's age at the date of the interview, the mother's age, and the poverty ratio for the household; sample sizes N are in parentheses.

Resident biological fathers have much higher ratings on monitoring ($M = 2.11$) than either stepfathers ($M = 1.62$) or father figures ($M = 1.64$). Both differences have substantial effect sizes of .5. Thus, teens do not perceive either stepfathers or father figures as substitutes for a biological father when it comes to monitoring.

As might be expected because they are not living in the household, nonresident fathers have the lowest ratings on monitoring (means are .71 to .95). The nonresident fathers have their highest rating ($M = .95$) when there is no father figure in the household, an intermediate rating when there is a father figure who is not a stepfather in the household ($M = .87$), and the lowest rating when there is a stepfather in the household ($M = .71$). These results suggest that the presence of stepfathers creates monitoring limitations for every parent—mother, biological father, and even themselves. Although the overall differences are not statistically significant, the difference between having no father figure in the household and having a stepfather is significant. This is a moderate effect size of about .25. An important qualification on any differences is the fact that the mean scores of nonresident fathers fall between knows "nothing" and knows "very little" across all types of families.

12. YOUTH RATINGS OF FAMILY AND FATHERS

Positive View of Parent

Teenagers express some concern about how well their mothers do when there is no father or father figure in the household ($M = 3.01$). Any resident father including a biological father, stepfather, and father figure has a positive effect on how teens rate their mothers.

How good is the relationship between fathers and their children? Table 12.2 shows that biological fathers in the household have the highest mean ($M = 3.00$), resident father figures are intermediate ($M = 2.62$), and resident stepfathers have the lowest mean ($M = 2.50$). Both the resident stepfathers and the resident father figures have significantly lower ratings on a good relationship than does the resident biological father. Both of these differences are strong effect sizes. Interestingly, the mother has a better rating than the father in all types of two-parent families. However, a biological father in a two-parent household has virtually the same rating as a single-parent mother.

Nonresident fathers have comparable ratings on a good relationship, regardless of whether there is a stepfather or father figure in the household and even if there is no father figure in the household. The means range from 2.19 to 2.36 and none of the differences approach statistical significance. The results are inconsistent with the popular press assertions that youth's view of a nonresident father is threatened when there is a father figure in the household. All the means for nonresident fathers reflect a fairly neutral rating on a scale that ranges from 0 to 4. By contrast, the teens rated their mothers as going a good job (3 or more on a 0–4 scale), regardless of family type.

Negative View of Parent

In rating their relationships to their fathers on negative criteria, the teenagers rate the biological resident fathers as less negative ($M = .68$) than the resident father figures ($M = .73$) or stepfathers ($M = .77$), but only the difference between stepfathers and resident biological fathers is statistically significant. The effect sizes for these differences are quite small and all the means are low considering the scale ranged from 0 (never negative) to 4 (always negative). Also, neither resident nor nonresident fathers are viewed as substantially more negative than the mother. The low negative ratings of nonresident fathers needs to be balanced by the fact that we excluded youths who had no contact with their biological father. Still, there is no evidence that teens who are in contact with their biological father have a negative view of him.

Family Routines

Family routines are remarkably similar (means are between 15.12 and 15.42) across family types, except for single-parent, mother-headed families ($M = 14.09$). The effect sizes show that families with no father figure in the household are between

a fifth and a fourth of a standard deviation lower on family routines. Thus, the presence of a father or father figure contributes to the ability of the family to maintain family routines regardless of whether the father is the biological father, stepfather, or father figure.

The Importance of Race/Ethnicity

Table 12.3 shows the differences in the outcome variables between African-American non-Hispanic, Hispanic, and White non-Hispanic teenagers. Fully 6 of the 10 comparisons show no significant differences by race/ethnicity. Youth from all three of these race/ethnicity backgrounds do not differ significantly on family routines or whether the resident or nonresident father does either a good or bad job. They are also similar in the rating of how good a job the mother does.

A key difference for race/ethnicity is on the monitoring variable for rating their resident father. White youth ($M = 1.93$) and Hispanic youth ($M = 1.81$) give their resident fathers higher monitoring rates than African-American youth ($M = 1.63$) give their resident fathers. These differences represent moderate effect sizes.

For nonresident fathers, the effect of race/ethnicity on monitoring is even greater. White non-Hispanic youth report significantly and substantially greater monitoring ($M = 1.11$) than either African-American ($M = .70$) or Hispanic ($M = .72$) youth. These results represent perceived disengagement of nonresident Hispanic and African-American fathers from their children's lives.

Gender Differences

Half the tests in Table 12.4 are not statistically significant. The monitoring level of fathers is virtually the same, whether the youth is male or female and whether the father is resident are not. However, mothers have higher reported monitoring of daughters ($M = 2.64$) than of sons ($M = 2.50$).

Daughters are more critical than sons. Daughters rate resident and nonresident fathers lower on doing a good job than do sons. This difference is weak for resident fathers but moderate in the case of the nonresident father with daughters giving them a mean rating of 2.07 compared to sons' mean rating of 2.48. This is a moderate effect size. Sons rate their mothers and resident fathers/father figures as doing a worse job ($M = .82$ and $M = .78$, respectively) than daughters ($M = .72$ and $M = .67$, respectively). These are small effect sizes. Overall, sons are more likely to rate parents better on doing a good job and worse on doing a bad job than daughters.

Interaction Effects

The previous discussion has been limited to main effects, which can be misleading when there is an interaction effect. The general linear model procedures allowed us to test for interaction. Significant interaction was found for just two

12. YOUTH RATINGS OF FAMILY AND FATHERS 287

TABLE 12.5

Youth's Perception of Parental Characteristics by Family Type and Race/Ethnicity
of Youth: Estimated Means with Controls[1]

Type of Household	Youth's Race/Ethnicity	Youth Report: Monitoring by Mother[2]
Biological mother with no father figure	African-American	2.54 (450)
	Hispanic	2.45 (252)
	White	2.53 (388)
Biological mother with stepfather	African-American	2.30 (88)
	Hispanic	2.66 (72)
	White	2.53 (247)
Biological mother with father figure, not stepfather	African-American	2.71 (61)
	Hispanic	2.43 (28)
	White	2.78 (43)
Biological mother and biological father	African-American	2.61 (345)
	Hispanic	2.58 (580)
	White	2.73 (1544)

[1]Control variables include the youth's age at the date of the interview, the mother's age, and the poverty ratio for the household; sample sizes N in parentheses.

[2]$p = .011$.

variables, both involving monitoring. The first interaction is between family type and race/ethnicity when predicting monitoring by the resident mother. The second interaction is between race/ethnicity and gender when predicting monitoring by the resident father.

The interaction between family type and race/ethnicity requires us to qualify our findings from Tables 12.2 and 12.3. Table 12.2 reports that having a father figure other than a stepfather has a positive effect on the rating of the mothers' monitoring. Table 12.5 shows that this is especially true for African-American and White youth, but not for Hispanic youth. Moreover, African-American youth are especially harsh on mothers when a stepfather is present, but Hispanic youth give mothers a good rating on monitoring when a stepfather is present. Finally, the data show that Hispanic youth with no father figure in the household rate the mothers low on monitoring. These results suggest that Hispanic youth are harsh on their mothers when there is no legally sanctioned father (biological or stepfather) in the household and African-American youth are harsh on their mothers when there is a stepfather in the household.

Table 12.6 shows the interaction effects between race/ethnicity and gender when predicting the monitoring by the resident father. The most notable interaction effect in this table is that White females rate their resident father and father figure much higher on monitoring than do African-American or Hispanic females; they also rate them higher than males of any race/ethnicity.

TABLE 12.6
Youth's Perception of Parental Characteristics by Race/Ethnicity and Gender of
Youth: Estimated Means With Controls[1]

Race/Ethnicity of Youth	Gender of Youth	Youth Report: Monitoring by Resident Father/Figure[2]
African-American, non-Hispanic	Male	1.62 (253)
	Female	1.60 (250)
Hispanic	Male	1.81 (354)
	Female	1.75 (336)
White, non-Hispanic	Male	1.83 (994)
	Female	2.07 (859)

[1]Control variables include the youth's age at the date of the interview, the mother's age, and the poverty ratio for the household; sample sizes N in parentheses.

[2]$p = .024$.

DISCUSSION

What does the nonresident father give up or lose? Does it matter whether the mother lives alone with the children or has a new father or father figure in the home? Does the race/ethnicity or gender of the youth influence perceptions of parental role performance? The results of our analysis allow us to provide initial answers to these and related questions.

Not surprisingly, nonresident fathers have very low levels of monitoring their child. Figure 12.1 illustrates this finding for African-American youth. The light gray bars show that nonresident fathers are much lower than resident fathers and especially resident mothers on monitoring. Nonresident fathers, regardless of race, youth's gender, or family type are seen as knowing "nothing" or just "a little" about what their youth are doing.

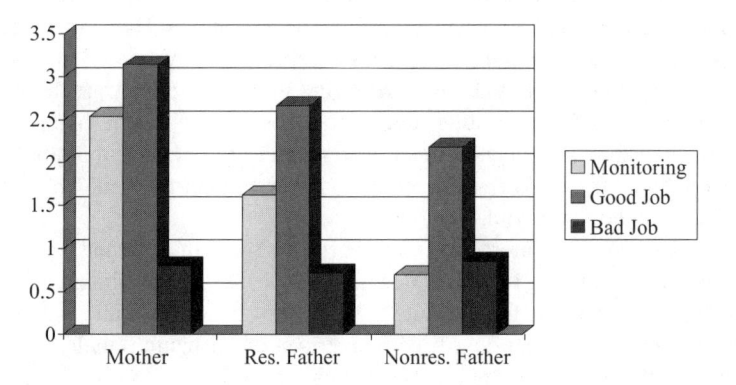

FIG. 12.1. Perceived role performance of parents of African-American youth.

The medium gray bars show that there is a less dramatic drop off on how favorably youth rate nonresident fathers on positive aspects of their role performance. Importantly, Figure 12.1 highlights that there is no significant drop off in how youth rate nonresident fathers on negative actions. Nonresident fathers are not rated as substantially more negative than resident fathers or resident mothers. A similar pattern can be shown for Hispanic and White youth.

The absence of a father or father figure in the household has important implications for how youth rate their mothers. In general, single-parent mothers have lower ratings than mothers who have a father or father figure in this home. When mothers have no father or father figure in the household they have the lowest rating on monitoring, the lowest rating on doing a good job, the highest rating on doing a bad job, and the lowest level of family routines. It is important to emphasize that these ratings are the perception of their child rather than an objective measure of the mothers' role performance. Still, an important consequence of having a father or father figure in the home is the validation of the role performance of the mother.

Nonresident biological fathers may believe their role is threatened by a new father figure or a stepfather. The new father in the household may replace the nonresident father's importance to his child. We see inconsistent evidence for this concern. Figure 12.2 shows that nonresident fathers are neither more positive nor less negative when the mother lives with a new father or father figure. Hence, nonresident fathers do not need to fear that their role will be devalued by their youth if a new father enters the child's home.

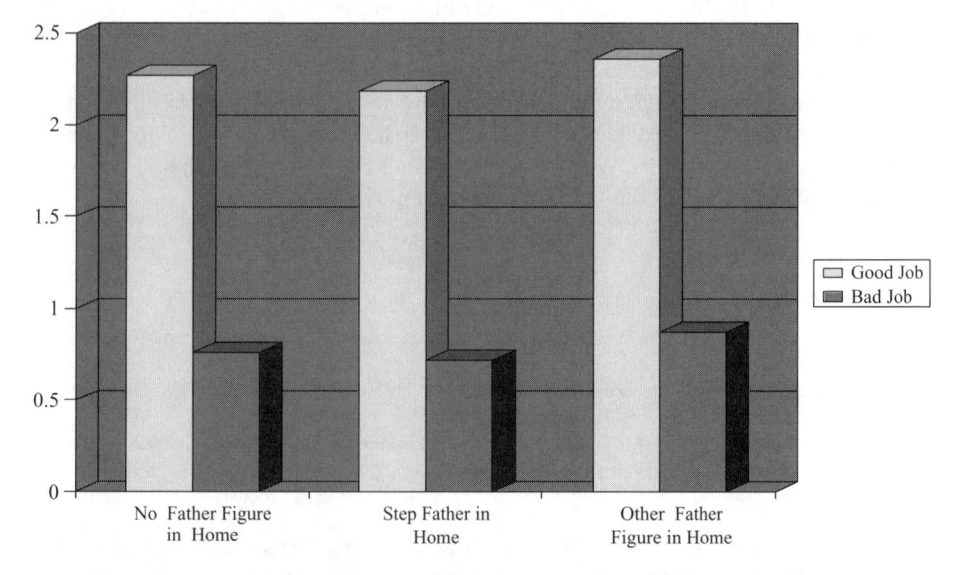

FIG. 12.2. Nonresident fathers do not lose respect when mothers remarry or have new father figures in their homes.

However, the nonresident biological father may do less monitoring and be less involved when there is a new father in the home. It is useful to compare monitoring by nonresident fathers when the mothers' marital status changes. Although this is cross-sectional data we note that when there is no father figure present in the household the nonresident father has a significantly higher score on monitoring than when there is a stepfather. This suggests that the presence of a stepfather may diminish the monitoring role and hence involvement of the biological father.

There is an important qualification on these findings. First, there is significant interaction between race/ethnicity and family type. The interaction effect shows that Hispanic youth are especially harsh on mothers when there is no legally sanctioned father (biological or stepfather) in the household and African-American youth are harsh on mothers when there is a stepfather in the household.

Race/ethnicity makes little difference outside of monitoring. African-American youth report the least monitoring by their mother, resident father, and nonresident father. Among nonresident fathers, both African-American and Hispanic youth report very low levels of monitoring. African-American youth report that their mothers are much more involved than White youth. Both African-American and Hispanic youth report that their mothers are less likely to be permissive.

Another important gender difference is that sons give more polar responses than daughters. Sons are more likely to rate their parents as more likely to be doing a good job and worse on doing a bad job than daughters. Daughters see mothers as providing more monitoring than do sons.

An important limitation of this analysis is that it does not use parental ratings of self or partner. Parents may have different ratings and the actual role performance of parents may be different again.

It is important that we do not blame parents for the ratings of their children. For example, single-parents mothers often have lower ratings by their children but may be working very hard supporting their families and have limited time for monitoring and routines. An impoverished single-parent mother should not be blamed because she lacks time for routines and monitoring.

REFERENCES

Barnes, H., & Olson, D. (1985). Parent–adolescent communication and the circumplex model. *Child Development, 56*, 438–447.

Baumrind, D. (1991). The influence of parenting style on adolescent competence and substance use. *Journal of Early Adolescence., 11*, 256–272.

Burbach, D. J. & Borduin, C. M. (1986). Parent–child relations and the etiology of depression: A review of methods and findings. *Clinical Psychology Review, 6*, 133–153.

Center for Human Resource Research. 2000. *NLSY97 user's guide.* Columbus OH: Ohio State University.

Child Trends. (1999). *NLSY97 codebook supplement main file round I: Appendix 9: Family process and adolescent outcome measures.* Columbus OH: Center for Human Resource Research, Ohio State University.

12. YOUTH RATINGS OF FAMILY AND FATHERS

Coleman, J. S. (1988). Social capital in the creation of human capital. *American Journal of Sociology, 94*(Supplement), S95–S120.

Coleman, J. S. (1990). *Foundations of social theory.* Cambridge, MA: Harvard University Press.

Ebery, M. B., Montemayor, R., & Flannery, D. J. (1993). Variation in adolescent helpfulness toward parents in a family context. *Journal of Early Adolescence, 13,* 228–244.

Gavazzi, S. M. (1994). Advances in assessing the relationship between family differentiation and problematic functioning in adolescents. *Family Therapy, 21,* 249–259.

Furstenberg, F. F., Jr, & Hughes, M. (1995). Social capital and successful development among at-risk youth. *Journal of Marriage and the Family, 57*(3), 580–592.

Furstenberg, F. F., Jr. (1998). Social capital and the role of fathers in the family. In Booth, A., & Crouter, A. C. (Ed.), *Men in families: When do they get involved? What difference does it make?* (pp. 295–301). Mahwah, NJ: Lawrence Erlbaum Associates.

Hagan, J., MacMillan, R., & Wheaton, B. (1996). New kid in town: Social capital and the life course effects of family migration on children. *American Sociological Review, 61*(3), 368–385.

Hauser, S. T., Book, B. K., Houlihan, J., Powers, S., Weiss-Perry, B., Follansbee, D., Jacobson, A. M., & Noam, G. G. (1987). Sex differences within the family: Studies of adolescent and parent family interactions. *Journal of Youth and Adolescence, 16,* 199–220.

Henry, C. S., & Lovelace, S. G. (1995). Family resources and adolescent family life satisfaction in remarried family households. *Journal of Family Issues, 16,* 765–786.

Hetherington, E. M., Cox, M., & Cox, R. (1982). Effects of divorce on parents and children. In M. E. Lamb (Ed.), *Nontraditional families* (pp. 233–288). Hillsdale, NJ: Lawrence Erlbaum Associates.

Hosley, C. A. & Montemayor, R. (1997). Fathers and adolescents. In M. E. Lamb (Eds.), *The role of father in child development* (3rd ed., pp. 162–178). New York: Wiley.

Jensen, E. W., James, S. A., Bryce, W. T., & Hartnett, S. A. (1983). The family routines inventory: Development and validation. *Social Sciences Medicine, 17,* 201–211.

Kenny, M. E. (1987). The extent and function of parental attachment among first year college students. *Journal of Youth and Adolescence, 16,* 17–29.

Lamb, M. (1997). *The role of father in child development* (2nd ed.). New York: Wiley.

Larson, R., & Richards, M. (1994). *Divergent lives: The emotional lives of mothers, fathers, and adolescents.* New York: Basic Books.

Loury, G. C. (1977). A dynamic theory of racial income differences. In Wallace, P., & La Mond, A. M. (Ed.), *Women, minorities, and employment discrimination* (pp. 153–186). Lexington, MA: Heath.

Loury, G. C. (1987). Why should we care about group inequality? *Social Philosophy and Policy, 5*(1), 249–271.

Maccoby, E. E., & Mnookin, R. H. (1992). *Dividing the child: Social and legal dilemmas of custody.* Cambridge, MA: Harvard University Press.

Marsiglio, W., Day, R. D., Amato, P., & Lamb, M. (2000). Fatherhood in a social context. *Journal of Marriage and the Family, 62,* 439–460.

Miller, J. B., & Lane, M. (1991). Relations between young adults and their parents. *Journal of Adolescence, 14,* 179–194.

Noller, P., & Bagi, S. (1985). Parent–adolescent communication. *Journal of Adolescence, 8,* 125–144.

O'Connor, T. G., Hetherington, E. M., & Clingempeel, W. G. (1997). Systems and bi-directional influence in families. *Journal of Social and Personal Relations, 14,* 491–504.

Otto, L. B., & Atkinson, M. P. (1997). Parental involvement and adolescent involvement. *Journal of Adolescent Research, 12,* 68–89.

Palkovitz, R. (1997). Reconstruction "involvement": Expanding conceptualizations of men's caring in contemporary families. In A. J. Hawkins & D. C. Dollahite (Eds.), *Generative fathering: Beyond the deficit perspective* (pp. 200–216). Thousand Oaks, CA: Sage.

Phares, V., & Renk, K. (1998). Perceptions of parents: A measure of adolescents' feelings about their parents. *Journal of Marriage and the Family, 60,* 646–659.

Pleck, J. H. (1997). Paternal involvement: Levels, sources, and consequences. In M. E. Lamb (Eds.), *The role of father in child development* (3rd ed., pp. 66–103). New York: Wiley.

Sampson, R. J., & Laub. J. H. (1993). *Crime in the making*. Cambridge, MA: Harvard University Press.

Seltzer, J. A. (1998). Men's contributions to children and social policy. In Booth, A., & Crouter, A. C. (Ed.), *Men in families: When do they get involved? What difference does it make?* (pp. 303–314). Mahwah, NJ: Lawrence Erlbaum Associates.

Thornton. (2001). Compelling family processes. In (Eds.), *The well-being of children and families* (pp. 438–440). City: Publisher.

Youniss, J. & Smollar, J.(1985). *Adolescent relations with mothers, fathers, and friends*. Chicago: University of Chicago Press.

13

Father Involvement and the Diversity of Family Context

Kathleen Mullan Harris
Suzanne Ryan
University of North Carolina at Chapel Hill

This research examines variations in father involvement according to the family context of parental figures inside and outside children's homes. Using data from the National Longitudinal Study of Adolescent Health (Add Health), we measure both the quantity and quality of paternal involvement and we document differences in levels of father involvement for resident biological fathers, resident nonbiological fathers, and nonresident biological fathers, according to the family structure of children defined by the constellation of parental figures available to the child. We then develop a simple theoretical model of parenting strategies among two resident parents and among resident parents and nonresident biological fathers that elaborates how parents coordinate and negotiate their involvement with children. Family contexts that matter most for the involvement of fathers are those linked to the process of becoming a parent (i.e., biology, adoption) or marked by a chaotic or traumatic family history (children living with no biological parents). Collective parenting strategies are more evident when resident parents are of the same type (two adoptive or two biological parents) and less evident in stepfamilies or when biological parents live apart.

Rising public interest in the roles and responsibilities of fathers over the last few decades has produced a substantial body of research on father involvement (reviews in Cabrera, Tamis-LeMonda, Bradley, Hofferth, & Lamb, 2000; Furstenberg, 1988; Lamb, 1997, 1999; Pleck, 1997; Seltzer, 1994a). Theoretical and conceptual work on the ways in which fathers participate in the lives of children and how such participation fosters their healthy development has provided a solid framework for measuring the key components of father involvement (Amato, 1987; Lamb, Pleck, Charnov, & Levine, 1987; Radin, 1994; Parke, 1996). Some standard measures of father involvement have worked their way into most of the leading national studies on children and youth, while in-depth, qualitative studies continue to elucidate the ways in which fathers interact with and influence their children.[1] Although the academic community has made considerable progress in thinking about how fathers can make a difference in children's lives, we are only beginning to understand how father involvement varies according to the diversity of family contexts in America today, and whether our concepts and measures of father involvement are appropriate for fathers in different contexts.

Fathers' behaviors and participation in the family are affected by many factors including their immediate social surroundings, especially those defined by family structure and residential arrangement. The growing diversity of life course and residency patterns for men and children has fostered new perceptions about fathers' roles (Gerson, 1993; Griswold, 1993; Marsiglio, 1995). One consequence of these patterns is that, compared to a few decades ago, a decreasing proportion of all children today live in households with their biological fathers, and at no time in U.S. history have so many children had biological fathers living elsewhere (Bianchi, 1995; Mintz, 1998). Moreover, many children have stepfather figures living with them on a regular or irregular basis, and growing numbers of men are assuming the role of custodial single father (Eggebeen, Snyder, & Manning, 1996; Garasky & Meyer, 1996; Seltzer, 1994b). These remarkable social and family changes have expanded the images of who fathers are and what they do.

This chapter examines variations in father involvement according to the family context of parental figures inside and outside children's homes. The few studies that have analyzed levels of father involvement by family structure provide hints of how family context conditions the roles and involvement of fathers in the family (Blair, Wenk, & Hardesty, 1994; Cooksey & Fondell, 1996; Harris, Heard, & King,

---

[1]For example, questions about how close children feel to their resident fathers and how frequently they do things together are available in the National Survey of Children, the Child Supplement of the Panel Study of Income Dynamics, the National Longitudinal Survey of Youth, the National Longitudinal Study of Adolescent Health (Add Health), and the National Survey of Families and Households. Questions tapping the components of paternal engagement, availability, and responsibility are included in the Early Childhood Longitudinal Study, Early Head Start, Birth Cohort 2001 and the Early Childhood Longitudinal Study, Kindergarten Class of 1998–99. The National Institute of Health and Human Development Early Child Care Study conducted in-depth interviews with fathers and extensive videotaping of father–child interactions.

13. DIVERSITY OF FAMILY CONTEXT

2000). The general finding is that stepfathers are much less involved in children's lives than biological fathers in two-parent families (Blair et al., 1994; Cooksey & Fondell, 1996; Marsiglio, 1991), with the implication that fathers invest less in children with whom they have no biological link (Harris et al., 2000). We take the biological relationship between the father and the child as a point of departure in this research and conduct an in-depth analysis of variations in father involvement by family structure for biological fathers separately from nonbiological fathers and from nonresident biological fathers. Most analyses of family structure differences confound biology with structure with regard to the parent–child relationship. We argue that to understand how family structure conditions levels of father involvement, one must hold constant the biological relationship that exists between the father and the child.

A second layer of context for the father–child relationship is the residence status of the biological father. It is becoming as common for biological fathers to live apart from children as it is for them to coreside, representing meaningful differences in the ways in which biological fathers can participate in their children's lives. Children living apart from biological fathers can live in various nonintact family forms, some that include nonbiological resident fathers, which may further condition the involvement of the nonresident biological father. Our research delves into these complexities in family context for the father–child relationship by examining how resident biological fathers differ in their involvement with children across various family structures, how resident nonbiological fathers differ in their involvement with children across various family structures, and how nonresident biological fathers differ in their involvement with children living in various nonintact family structures.

At the heart of our understanding of potential differences in father involvement by family context is the constellation and involvement of various mother figures inside the home and the presence and involvement of resident nonbiological and nonresident biological fathers for children living in nonintact families. For example, biological fathers can live with children's biological mother, stepmother, or alone (no mother figure). Nonbiological fathers, however, can have different relationships with children, as well as live with varying mother figures. Nonbiological father figures can be step, adoptive, or foster or other surrogate fathers and live with children's biological mother, adoptive mother, or foster or other surrogate mother. We argue that father involvement is dependent upon the type of mother figure in the home and her involvement with the children. Further, the involvement of nonresident biological fathers is likely conditioned by the presence and involvement of resident nonbiological fathers.

Using data from the National Longitudinal Study of Adolescent Health (Add Health), we first document differences in levels of father involvement by family structure for resident biological fathers, resident nonbiological fathers, and nonresident biological fathers, attributing differences that we find to the family context of parental figures available to children inside and outside the home. We then develop

a simple theoretical model of parenting strategies between two resident parents and among nonresident biological fathers and resident parents that elaborates how parents coordinate and negotiate their involvement with children. We investigate the presence of such strategies by exploring how levels of father involvement vary by levels of mother involvement and by levels of resident mother and father involvement for children who live with a nonbiological father and have contact with their nonresident biological father.

Although our analysis is largely descriptive, it contributes new data to the literature on father involvement in several ways. We know of no other research that examines father involvement by the detailed constellation of biological and nonbiological parental figures inside and outside the home. Prior research has mainly contrasted father involvement of stepfathers with that of biological fathers, neglecting the diversity of family forms in the United States, where children increasingly live apart from their biological fathers and often have multiple father figures with whom they have a relationship (Bianchi & Casper, 2000). The cooperation and negotiation among such parental figures with respect to time with and responsibilities for children is becoming a common facet of family life in America. Most data sets do not provide sufficient numbers of cases for such an in-depth analysis of this growing family diversity. Because Add Health has a unique sample design that oversampled youth living in rare family settings and contains a fairly large sample size (over 20,000 youth), we are able to conduct such a detailed analysis. Most studies of father involvement focus only on biological or resident fathers (Amato, 1994). Our study incorporates mothers, nonresident fathers, and other surrogate fathers, expanding our knowledge of how men's involvement with children is influenced by and is dependent on other parental figures. Finally, we measure both the quantity and the quality of paternal involvement using nationally representative data on school-age adolescents. The large majority of studies on father involvement focuses on young children. Our study examines the father–child relationship during the formative years of adolescence, a socially and emotionally dynamic period for children and families.

THE DIVERSITY OF FAMILY CONTEXT

To illustrate the current diversity of family forms in America and to present the analytic framework for our study, we show in Table 13.1 the national distribution of adolescents living with biological and nonbiological father figures by family structure with the data we use from Add Health (described subsequently). We analyze separately three sets of father–child relationships: teens who live with their biological fathers shown in panel A; teens living with nonbiological fathers in panel B; and teens who live in nonintact families where the biological father is nonresident in panel C. Among all adolescents in the United States in 1995, more than half, or 59.0%, lived with their biological fathers. The distribution

13. DIVERSITY OF FAMILY CONTEXT

TABLE 13.1

Distribution of Adolescents Living With Biological and
Nonbiological Father Figures, by Family Structure
(weighted percentages, raw *n*s)

A. Teens With Resident Biological Fathers

Child Lives With:	%	N
2 Biological parents	90.4	9,686
Bio dad/stepmom	4.4	506
Single father	5.2	583
Total	100.0	10,775

B. Teens With Resident Nonbiological Fathers

Child Lives With:	%	N
Stepdad/bio mom	80.6	2,490
Adaptive father	4.2	369
Surrogate father	15.2	535
Total	100.0	3,394

C. Teens With Nonresident Biological Fathers

Child Lives With:	%	N
Stepdad/bio mom	35.8	2,305
Single mother	52.2	3,646
Nonparent	12.1	844
Total	100.0[a]	6,795

[a]Totals may not sum to 100 because of rounding.

of family forms for youth living with biological fathers is shown in panel A. The majority (90.4%) live with both their biological mother and father, but a substantial minority live in other family forms–4.4% with their biological father and stepmother and 5.2% with their single biological father (no mother figure). We show the unweighted *N*s from Add Health for each of these family forms on which subsequent analyses are based.

Panel B represents the increasing number of youth who lived with a nonbiological father, amounting to 16.9% of all school-age adolescents in 1995. The first family structure involving resident nonbiological fathers is the more common stepfamily composed of the biological mother and stepfather. In our data a stepfather is any nonbiological father who lives with or is married to the youth's biological mother.[2] Among all youth living with nonbiological fathers, 80.6% live with a stepfather. Adoptive fathers make up the second category of nonbiological

---

[2]A stepfather can be the youth's step, foster, adoptive, or some other surrogate father, or the youth's mother's partner.

fathers. Adoptive fathers live with the child's adoptive mother or, in a few cases, with some other nonbiological mother figure. Only 4.2% of youth live with adoptive fathers. A sizable percentage of youth (15.2%) live with surrogate fathers, or male adults who act like father figures according to youth. Surrogate fathers can be foster fathers, relatives, or nonrelatives, and may live with surrogate mothers or no mother figure.

Panel C shows the 35.3% of all U.S. adolescents who live in nonintact families where the biological father is nonresident.[3] Here variation in family structure is represented by the family structure in which the child lives. Among all youth who live apart from their biological father, 35.8% live in a stepfamily with their biological mother and stepfather, 52.2% live with a single mother, and 12.1% live with surrogate parents or no parent (e.g., group home or alone).

Note that the groups of youth in panels B and C are not mutually exclusive. Youth who live with a nonbiological father in panel B are also represented in panel C if they know who their biological father is and he is still alive. Relationships with multiple parental figures are not uncommon any more. Over 14% of school-age adolescents have both resident nonbiological fathers and nonresident biological fathers. The increasing complexity of family relations is creating new contexts for mother and father roles in the lives of children, and the relationships forged by fathers and children are surely a function of these changing contexts.

WHY CONTEXT MATTERS

Fathers' behaviors and interactions with children cannot be understood without considering the role of the resident mother. Although individual factors may influence father involvement, fathers' behaviors and emotional investment in children are inextricably linked to mothers' behaviors and expectations for such investment within a family context. Fathers may take their cues from mothers in how and when to participate in children's lives whether they live with or apart from children. Moreover, father involvement may hold different meanings for youth according to the father's relationship to the child and the mother's relationship to the child (or, by extension, the father's relationship to the mother). Expectations for father involvement are normally greater for biological fathers than for surrogate fathers and may vary according to the type of mother figure in the home. Variations in the configuration of parental figures in the home therefore have implications for the ways in which we measure father involvement and for the salience of the relationships fathers forge with children.

We therefore examine variations in father involvement by family context where family context is defined by the configuration of mother and father figures in the

---

[3]The remaining 6% of youth who do not live with their biological father either know nothing about their biological father (e.g., adopted youth) or their biological father died.

13. DIVERSITY OF FAMILY CONTEXT

home, controlling for the biological relationship and residence of the father and child. For children who live with biological fathers, family context is defined by the type of mother figure in the home. If we believe that the father's relationship with his resident biological children is influenced by mother type, then we expect to see differences in levels of father involvement by family structure. For example, a biological father who is married to the biological mother of his children may feel less motivated to participate in children's lives than a biological father who has remarried and lives with his children, knowing that his wife, as a stepmother, is less invested in the care and well-being of his children. In addition, single biological fathers may display greater levels of involvement to make up for the lack of another resident parent.

Family contexts for resident nonbiological fathers are subject to more sources of variation in parental figures including the father type, defined by the relationship of the father to the child, and the mother type. For example, resident nonbiological fathers can be stepfathers (married or living with the child's biological mother), adoptive fathers, or surrogate fathers. A stepfather becomes a parent through his relationship to the child's mother. Thus, stepfathers may not necessarily choose to become fathers, but assume that role secondarily to their role as the mother's partner. This notion of "choice" may underlie the lower levels of investment by stepfathers in the lives of their stepchildren that research has consistently documented (Blair et al., 1994; Cooksey & Fondell, 1996; Harris et al., 2000; Marsiglio, 1991). On the other hand, adoptive fathers assume the parental role by choice as adoption requires purposeful and legal action on the part of the father in assuming financial and social responsibility for the child. Nearly all mother types living with adoptive fathers are adoptive mothers, further reflecting a desire and motivation to become parents at the couple level. We therefore expect greater involvement by adoptive fathers than stepfathers.

Finally, surrogate fathers are men who act like father figures to youth and therefore represent a select group of fathers as well. Although a surrogate father may not have chosen to be a social father, his parental behavior and involvement is demonstrated by the fact that youth identify him as a father figure in a home in which no biological parent lives. On the other hand, a surrogate father may find himself the social parent to a child in much the same way a stepfather does. Children who do not live with either biological parent are likely to have experienced significant family upheaval or trauma (e.g., parents' death, institutionalization, or illness) and may be sent to live with relatives or other adults who must assume the role of surrogate parents. While surrogate fathers accept this role by the fact that they live with the child and act as their parent, their lack of choice may diminish their active involvement. There may be a surrogate mother figure in the home who, if present, may also be a parent figure out of family obligation or as person of last resort. Thus, we expect that surrogate fathers will be similar to or perhaps more involved with youth than stepfathers but less involved than adoptive fathers.

Children who live in nonintact families but have contact with their nonresident biological fathers experience varying contexts according to the presence and type of parental figures in the home. Children who have a relationship with their nonresident biological fathers can either live with a stepfather and biological mother or a single mother, or in a nonparental home (with surrogate parents or no parents). We suspect that nonresident biological fathers' involvement with children may be a function of these contexts. For example, nonresident biological fathers may be less apt to frequently see and do things with their children if they live with a stepfather, either because of competition or jealousy or because they feel that children are sufficiently attended to by the stepfather. Conversely, the nonresident biological father may be especially involved for the same reasons or because he wishes to influence and socialize his children according to his own values. On balance, the presence of a resident stepfather in the lives of children is likely to reduce involvement by nonresident biological fathers, especially compared to children living with a single mother, because of less encouragement or perceived need for such involvement.

Children living with single mothers and in nonparental homes do not have a self-identified father figure in the home, making the involvement of nonresident biological fathers especially important for these youth. We might therefore expect greater involvement by nonresident fathers when there is no self-selected father figure in the home compared to children living with stepfathers. There is considerable research examining the constraints nonresident fathers face in remaining in contact and being involved in their children's lives (Furstenberg & Harris, 1992; King, 1994; Marsiglio, 1993; Seltzer, 1994a), including such structural factors as propinquity, work schedules, and the relationship between former spouses or partners. Note that we are not considering these constraints in our analysis (nor do our data have this information).

PARENTING STRATEGIES OF INVOLVEMENT

We argue that family context matters because the family system, and parenting in particular, is a collective enterprise. Coresident mothers and fathers coordinate their parenting responsibilities and activities. In the previous section we argued that the presence of different mother figures in the home would influence levels of father involvement, and here we extend this argument to propose that what mothers do matters as well. Research shows that mothers are much more involved in children's lives than fathers are, reflecting normative role prescriptions and different time constraints (Harris & Morgan, 1991; Nock & Kingston, 1988; LaRossa, 1988). Because mothers are still the primary figures in children's lives—managing and supervising their daily care and organizing childrearing activities—it is likely that fathers' involvement is highly dependent on mothers' involvement. This codependency is expressed through the development of various parenting strategies

13. DIVERSITY OF FAMILY CONTEXT 301

that reveal how parents coordinate their responsibility and involvement with children as a collective enterprise.

We consider a simple theoretical model depicting two kinds of parenting strategies. One strategy is cooperative parenting, which involves collaborative efforts in which parents relate to and interact with children in similar ways, reinforcing each other's parenting styles at the same level of involvement. A second joint-parenting strategy reflects compensating efforts in which one parent is highly involved and the other parent is less involved with their children. Parents decide who is better able (according to their personalities, time constraints, and interests) to provide the emotional support and developmental guidance of children and then that parent specializes in those aspects of raising children.

We expect that cooperative parenting strategies are more common in family structures in which the parents are of a similar type—two biological parents, two adoptive parents, or two surrogate parents. Because there is similar selection into parenthood and more equal investment in the child by parent figures of a similar type, we assume that parents will adopt and reinforce similar levels of involvement with children. In two-parent families where there is a biological parent and a nonbiological parent, we expect more compensatory strategies, simply because nonbiological parents tend to be less involved, leaving the biological parent to make up for this lack of investment with greater involvement.

Similar parenting strategies may develop between resident and nonresident parents in the coordination and negotiation of time and activities with children. Again, relationships between nonresident fathers and children cannot be understood without considering the role of the resident mother. Although the resident mother is typically less willing to support and sustain the identity and role status of the biological father when he lives outside the children's home, she continues to orchestrate and control the father's relationship with his children (Seltzer, 1994a). Highly involved mothers may demand that nonresident fathers be as involved as possible, representing a cooperative strategy. Without such encouragement, nonresident fathers can also "cooperate" with relatively uninvolved mothers by being uninvolved themselves. On the other hand, nonresident fathers may feel less need to participate in children's lives if mothers are highly involved, engaging in a compensatory strategy. And of course, highly involved mothers may sabotage nonresident fathers' efforts to be involved, feeling they can compensate for, as well as prefer, the lack of father involvement. The ways in which nonresident father involvement varies by levels of resident mother involvement may reveal how former spouses or partners negotiate parenting strategies once parents live apart.

Although there is less theoretical support for the notion of joint parenting strategies by multiple father figures, the involvement of nonresident biological fathers may also be a function of the level of involvement by resident nonbiological fathers. If the resident nonbiological father is relatively uninvolved with the youth, the nonresident father may compensate by increasing his involvement. On the other hand, if the resident nonbiological father is highly involved, nonresident fathers

may disengage further from their children. Similarly, resident nonbiological fathers may develop strategies of involvement with children that are dependent on the level of involvement by nonresident biological fathers. When the nonresident biological father is not in contact or relatively uninvolved with his children, resident nonbiological fathers may compensate with greater involvement than when nonresident biological fathers are highly involved. Compensatory strategies seem more likely between multiple father figures because mother figures may encourage involvement by at least one father and fathers may compete for the father role and place constraints on the other's involvement. Arguments for a cooperative strategy are weaker, as there is no normative expectation for multiple father figures to collaborate in their involvement with children.

MEASUREMENT OF FATHER INVOLVEMENT

Lamb et al., (1987) developed the concept of paternal involvement as including three components: (1) paternal engagement (direct interaction with the child in the form of caretaking, or play or leisure), (2) accessibility or availability to the child, and (3) responsibility for the care of the child, as distinct from the performance of care. They argued that this construct should be content-free and concerned with only the quantity of fathers' behavior, time, or responsibility with their children. Other measures were soon developed, however, to assess paternal involvement in certain activities with children that are not just indicators of overall time spent with the child but are specific activities likely to promote development. For example, the 1987—1988 National Survey of Families and Households (NSFH) asked men with school-age (5–18) children to report on their frequency of leisure activities, working on projects or play at home, having private talks, and helping with reading and doing homework (Marsiglio, 1991). Amato's (1987) summary variable of "paternal support" incorporates positive paternal activities along with reports about whether the father is a favorite person to have talks with and the person in the family the child tells if he or she is really worried.

Thus, the concept and measurement of father involvement has evolved from a quantitative measure that was content-free to one that, in addition to the quantitative level of involvement, also assesses the content or quality of paternal involvement. Our research follows in this tradition by measuring two distinct dimensions of paternal involvement representing both the quantity and the quality of involvement (Parke, 1996). We measure the quantity of involvement by assessing the number of different shared activities in which fathers and youth engage. The activities cover a wide range and are intended to capture some indication of the time fathers and children spend together. The quality of father involvement is measured by an index of the degree of closeness, warmth, communication, and satisfaction in the father–child relationship. This measure represents the strength of the emotional

13. DIVERSITY OF FAMILY CONTEXT 303

bond between fathers and children by focusing on feelings adolescents express for their fathers.

Both our quantity and quality measures tap the three theoretical components of father involvement that Lamb and his colleagues (1987) proposed. Paternal engagement occurs when fathers and children spend time together in shared activities and when they engage in communication with each other. Fathers who do things with their children are assuming responsibility for their care (especially when activities involve school work). Children have an essential need to be loved and cared for, and this is expressed in our quality measure. Finally, the accessibility of fathers is implicit in our measures by the quantitative levels of both shared activities and communication and closeness between fathers and children. Thus, fathers who are highly involved according to our measures are demonstrating paternal behavior that is high in engagement, accessibility, and responsibility with children.

We are interested in both the separate quantity and quality dimensions of father involvement, and in the complete package of involvement that is represented by the father's physical availability, emotional investment, and behavioral interaction. We argue that fathers who spend a lot of time with children in shared activities are most likely to foster a close bond with children, but it is possible that there is little communication and much conflict during the shared activities that detract from the quality of the relationship. The packaging of the quantity and quality dimension of involvement may represent the essence of how and why fathers matter to children. We therefore combine the two measures and create an overall involvement index that captures the bundle of activities, interactions, and emotions that fathers and adolescents share.

DATA AND MEASURES

Data come from the National Longitudinal Study of Adolescent Health (Add Health), a nationally representative study of more than 20,000 adolescents in grades 7 through 12 in the United States in 1995. Add Health was designed to help explain the causes of adolescent health and health behavior with special emphasis on the effects of multiple contexts of adolescent life. The study used a multistage, stratified, school-based, cluster sampling design. A stratified sample of 80 high schools was selected with probability proportional to size.[4] For each high school, a feeder school was also selected with probability proportional to its student contribution to the high school. The school-based sample therefore has a pair of schools in each of 80 communities.[5]

---

[4] Schools were stratified by region, urban/rural status, school sector type (public/private/parochial), ethnic mix, and size. School dropouts were not included in the sample.

[5] Some high schools spanned grades 7 through 12 and therefore served as their own feeder school, so the pair was in fact a single school. There are 132 schools in the study.

An in-school questionnaire was administered to every student who attended each selected school on a particular day during the period of September 1994 to April 1995. In a second level of sampling, adolescents and parents were selected for in-home interviews. From the school rosters, a random sample of some 200 students from each school pair was selected to produce the core in-home sample of about 12,000 adolescents. A number of special over-samples were also selected for in-home interviews using screeners from the in-school questionnaires, including physically disabled adolescents, Black adolescents from highly educated families, several ethnic samples (Cuban, Puerto Rican, and Chinese adolescents), a genetic sample (identical and fraternal twins, full siblings, half siblings, and unrelated adolescents in the same household), and saturated samples in 14 schools.

The in-home interviews were conducted between April and December 1995, yielding the Wave I data. The core sample plus the special samples produced a sample size of 20,745 adolescents in Wave I. A parent, generally the mother, was also interviewed in Wave I. All adolescents in grades 7 through 11 in Wave I were followed up 1 year later for the Wave II in-home interview in 1996. Bearman, Jones, and Udry (1997) provide a more detailed description of the Add Health study.

Our analysis uses data from Wave I and includes all adolescents who live with a resident father or have contact with their nonresident biological father and who have valid sampling weights. All analyses use the sampling weights to adjust for the complex sampling design.

Family Structure

Family structure (and the type of father and mother figure in the home) is defined according to a household roster in which the adolescent respondent lists all household members and his or her relationship to each member. Questions about father involvement and father–child relations are only asked of adolescents who identify a father figure living in the household. Thus, a cohabiting partner of the adolescent's mother who is listed as "mother's boyfriend" will have no data on father involvement, but a cohabiting partner who is identified by the youth as a "step" father will. In addition, youth who do not list any household member as a father are asked if there is anyone in their household who is like a "father figure" to them.[6] Youth who respond in the affirmative are then asked to identify the household member who acts as a father figure. Among youth who live in a nonparental family (no biological, step, foster, or adoptive parent), about one-third identify a father figure, usually a grandfather, older brother, uncle, other relative, or nonrelative adult male. We refer to these father figures as "surrogate fathers."

Because of the special genetic sample that over-sampled half siblings, step siblings, and unrelated adolescents living in the same household, Add Health data

---

[6]The same procedure is followed for mother figures.

13. DIVERSITY OF FAMILY CONTEXT

provide exceptional richness in the variety of family forms in which adolescents have a relationship with a father figure. We examine differentials in involvement by *resident biological fathers* with adolescents who live in three different family structures as shown in Table 13.1: two biological parents ($N = 9,686$), biological father and stepmother ($N = 506$), and single father ($N = 583$). We examine variations in father involvement by *resident nonbiological fathers* with adolescents who live in three different family structures: stepfather and biological mother ($N = 2,490$), adoptive father and adoptive mother ($N = 369$), and surrogate father and surrogate or no mother (including foster fathers and relative and nonrelative surrogate fathers; $N = 535$). Finally, we examine differentials in involvement by *nonresident biological fathers* with adolescents who live in three different family structures: stepfather and biological mother ($N = 2,305$); single mother ($N = 3,646$); and nonparent(s) (either surrogate parent(s) or no parent figures, $N = 844$).[7] Such refinement of the family context in which the paternal involvement of biological and nonbiological fathers is measured represents an important contribution of this research.

Father Involvement

Measures of father involvement are based on adolescent reports from the Wave I interview. The quantity of paternal involvement is measured by a count of the number of activities in which the father and adolescent engaged in the last 4 weeks among the following five activities: attending religious services or church-related events; shopping; playing a sport; going to a movie, play, museum, concert, or sports event; and working on a school project. This question is asked about resident fathers and mothers and nonresident biological parents. Weighted sample means for the three groups of fathers are 1.31 activities with resident biological fathers, 0.99 activities with resident nonbiological fathers; and 0.80 activities with nonresident biological fathers.

The quality of the resident parent–adolescent relationship is measured by an index of four items relating to affective relations. Father–child closeness is constructed as the mean response (ranging from $1 =$ low to $5 =$ high) of adolescent reports on the level of closeness, satisfaction, warmth, and satisfaction with communication in the father–child relationship. The internal reliability of this index as measured by Cronbach's alpha is .89. Consistent with most of the research on resident fathers (Harris, Furstenberg, & Marmer, 1998), adolescents report relatively high levels of closeness with biological fathers, averaging 4.18 in our sample, and somewhat lower levels of closeness with resident nonbiological fathers, averaging 3.85.

---

[7]Too few adolescents who live with adoptive parents know anything about or have any contact with their nonresident biological fathers to be included as a separate category in the analysis of involvement by nonresident biological fathers.

Only the closeness item was asked about nonresident biological fathers. Adolescents were asked, "How close do you feel to your [nonresident] biological father?" Responses range from 1 (not close at all) to 5 (extremely close). We use the response to this single item for our measure of the quality of the father–child relationship with nonresident biological fathers. Mean closeness with nonresident biological fathers is 3.07, considerably lower than with resident fathers.

We construct our overall index of father involvement for resident and nonresident fathers by summing the quantity and quality measures, resulting in a scale ranging from 1 to 10. For descriptive purposes we then transform this scale into a three-category involvement measure where involvement scores of 1 to 3 are classified as "low involvement," scores of 4 to 6 as "medium involvement," and scores over a threshold of 6 as "high involvement." Sample averages indicate that 31.8% of resident biological fathers fall into the high involvement category, whereas 19.5% of resident nonbiological fathers and 15.5% of nonresident biological fathers are classified as highly involved.

We note that our measures of father involvement are somewhat limited. Although there are other indicators of parental behavior in Add Health, they do not refer specifically to the father or the mother, but rather to "parents," which would not suit our purposes here. The measures must also be available for all resident father and mother figures and for nonresident biological fathers and mothers, placing high demands on the data. While we gain a unique perspective on father involvement according to the diversity of family forms in America, we lose some richness in measuring the variety of ways in which fathers are involved in children's lives.

Control Variables

The focus of our analysis is on variations in father involvement by family context defined by the constellation of parental figures inside and outside the home. Our goal is not to model levels of father involvement but simply to understand how family context conditions father involvement with adolescent children. Our analysis is a straightforward comparison of means by family structure for each of the three sets of fathers. Because previous research has consistently shown that levels of father involvement vary by demographic characteristics of children, we adjust our means for age, gender, race, ethnicity, and family socioeconomic status (SES) (Blair et al., 1994; Cooksey & Fondell, 1996; Harris & Marmer, 1996; Harris & Morgan, 1991; Hofferth, 1999; Marsiglio, 1991; Mosley & Thomson, 1995; Nord, Brimhall, & West, 1997; Pleck, 1997).

Age is measured in years. Race and ethnicity is measured as a five-category variable including non-Hispanic White, non-Hispanic Black, Asian, Native American or "other" race, and Hispanic. Family socioeconomic status is based on the sum of an occupation scale and education scale for resident parents. The occupation scale ranges from 0 to 5 with the categories, not in the labor market (0), unskilled,

13. DIVERSITY OF FAMILY CONTEXT   307

skilled, blue collar, white collar, and professional (5). The education scale ranges from 1 (less than high school grad) to 5 (more than college degree). Socioeconomic status is calculated for both mothers and fathers and ranges from 1 to 10. When there are two resident parents, we use the higher value to represent family socioeconomic status.

FATHER INVOLVEMENT
BY FAMILY CONTEXT

Differentials in father involvement by family structure according to the three types of father–child relationships are shown in Table 13.2.[8] Panel A shows levels of father involvement by *resident biological fathers* for children who live with two biological parents, a biological father and stepmother, and a single father. In general, there is little variation in our measures of father involvement by family structure. Adolescents report a weaker affective bond with single fathers (these differences are statistically significant) and engage in fewer shared activities with biological fathers who have remarried (i.e., stepmother present), but overall indicators of high involvement vary little by family structure. Closeness is highest in the biological father–child relationship in stepfamilies, but fathers in two-biological-parent families are nearly as high and they most frequently engage in shared activities with youth. Single fathers are also actively involved in shared activities with youth, perhaps making up for the lack of a mother figure in the home. Almost a third of all resident biological fathers are highly involved according to our measure of overall involvement, with biological fathers living with nonbiological mothers the least highly involved at 27.3% (these differences are not significant).

More variation in father involvement is found among *resident nonbiological fathers* in panel B of Table 13.2. Adoptive fathers enjoy the closest bonds with adolescents, followed by surrogate fathers. Stepfathers have the weakest bonds with youth (all differences are statistically significant). The same pattern of involvement is shown in the shared activities measure, although the difference between surrogate fathers and stepfathers is less (but still significant). The overall measure of involvement reveals that adoptive fathers are quite involved in their adoptive children's lives, as 42% are highly involved, greater than the percentage among biological fathers in two-biological-parent families. In contrast, only 14.7%

---

[8]Sample sizes reduce somewhat from Table 13.1 to Table 13.2 because of missing values on the control variables and father involvement. The numbers change dramatically for certain groups because of missing values on father involvement. For example, children living with stepfathers, and to lesser extent with surrogate fathers, were more likely to not respond to questions about the father–child relationship than children living with biological or adoptive fathers. In addition, there is considerable missing data on father–child relationships with nonresident biological fathers because children may know of their biological father but have little or no contact with him.

TABLE 13.2

Father Involvement by Family Structure (weighted means, adjusted for gender, age, race/ethnicity, and SES)

A. Resident Biological Fathers

Child Lives With:	2 Biological Parents	Bio Dad/ Stepmom	Single Father
Closeness index (1–5)	4.15	4.18	4.01[a]
Shared activities (0–5)	1.28	1.17	1.26
% Highly involved	30.7	27.3	29.1
Number of respondents	9,284	477	518

B. Resident Nonbiological Fathers

Child Lives With:	Stepdad/ Bio Mom	Adaptive Father	Surrogate Father
Closeness index (1–5)	3.72	4.27	4.00[b]
Shared activities (0–5)	0.91	1.62	0.97[b]
% Highly involved	16.9	42.0	14.7[c]
Number of respondents	1,532	346	441

C. Nonresident Biological Fathers

Child Lives With:	Stepdad/ Bio Mom	Single Mother	Nonparent
Closeness index (1–5)	3.06	3.06	2.93
Shared activities (0–5)	0.79	0.85	0.58
% Highly involved	16.0	15.3	9.2
Number of respondents	1,700	2,690	538

[a] Differences in levels of closeness with single fathers are statistically significant from levels of closeness with fathers in two biological parent and bio dad, stepmom families.

[b] Differences across all groups are statistically significant.

[c] Differences between adoptive fathers and stepfathers/surrogate fathers are significant.

of surrogate fathers and 16.9% of stepfathers are highly involved with youth in the emotional and interactive dimensions of fathering. Despite the higher levels of closeness and shared activities surrogate fathers display compared to stepfathers, evidently the surrogate fathers who forge close relations with youth are a different group than those who frequently engage in shared activities with youth. Therefore, the overall package of emotional support and active participation is less among surrogate fathers than stepfathers. Although stepfathers are less involved in the separate dimensions of involvement, those who are involved are likely to participate in adolescents' lives along the multiple dimensions of time together, communication, and emotional support.

13. DIVERSITY OF FAMILY CONTEXT

These different patterns of involvement may be related to the mother figure in the home.[9] Clearly, the motivation to be a parent is displayed by the high levels of involvement by adoptive fathers living with adoptive mothers. Mothers surely reinforce this commitment and self-selection into parenthood. Surrogate fathers may or may not live with a surrogate mother, and this could explain why different sets of surrogate fathers participate in adolescents' lives along different dimensions. Nevertheless, the relatively high levels of closeness in the surrogate father–child relationship probably reflect the special bond youth feel for an adult man who acts like a father figure in the absence of traditional parental figures. Finally, although stepfathers display less investment in stepchildren consistent with previous research, the fact that their involvement is a more complete package of both emotional and behavioral involvement may be a reflection of the biological mother encouraging or orchestrating such involvement.

Turning to panel C in Table 13.2, we observe differences in levels of father involvement by *nonresident biological fathers* according to the family structure in which children live. Nonresident biological fathers are least involved with children who live in nonparental homes (with surrogate parents or no parents). Low involvement may reflect a family history of crises and upheaval because these children do not live with either of their biological parents or with any traditional parent figure. These adolescents live with foster parents, grandparents, aunts, uncles, siblings, nonrelative adults, or in a group home situation. They are unique in that they even have a relationship with their nonresident biological father, but this relationship is tenuous, with little time shared together and less than 10% with a highly involved father.

Father involvement by nonresident biological fathers differs little for children living in stepfamilies compared to children living with single mothers. Contrary to our expectations, nonresident fathers may engage in slightly more activities with youth living with single mothers than those living in stepfamilies, but overall levels of involvement are nearly identical at 16% for youth in stepfamilies and 15.3% for youth in single-mother families with a highly involved nonresident biological father.

Overall, family context exerts less influence on levels of father involvement than we anticipated. Although certain contexts seem to foster greater involvement by the father, such as two adoptive parents, the main distinctions in levels of father involvement lie in the father–child relationship and in his residence status. In particular, resident biological fathers are much more involved with youth than nonbiological fathers (with the exception of adoptive fathers), who are more involved with youth than nonresident biological fathers. As a result, the family contexts that matter most for the involvement of fathers are those linked to the process of

---

[9]We also investigated whether levels of stepfather and surrogate father involvement varied by whether the adolescent had contact with his or her nonresident biological father, but differences were substantively minor and statistically insignificant.

becoming a parent (i.e., biology, adoption) or marked by a chaotic or traumatic family history (children living with no biological parents).

UNCOVERING PARENTING STRATEGIES

We now investigate patterns of involvement by resident and nonresident fathers according to levels of resident mother involvement to uncover possible parenting strategies of cooperation or compensation. We use the three-category measure of overall involvement (low, medium, and high) for mothers and fathers. Table 13.3 shows levels of father involvement (row variable) by levels of mother involvement (column variable) by the family structure of resident parents (panels A through E). These data address two questions about patterns of joint parenting. First, do levels of father involvement vary by levels of mother involvement? Second, are there distinct patterns in the combinations of parental involvement, suggesting the adoption of particular parenting strategies? We present Pearson's correlation (ρ) and the significance level of the chi-square test statistic for independence between levels of mother and father involvement to more formally address the first question.

Panel A of Table 13.3 shows how father involvement is related to mother involvement in two-biological-parent families. Scanning across the rows of the table, we see that father involvement indeed varies by levels of mother involvement. As mother involvement increases from low levels to high levels, high levels of father involvement increase and low levels of father involvement decrease. This interdependence is furthermore reflected in the high correlation of .47 and a highly significant chi-square statistic. The pattern of joint involvement reveals a strong relationship along the diagonal of the table, indicating that biological mothers and fathers tend to engage in similar levels of involvement with children, suggesting a cooperative parenting strategy. When mothers have low involvement with children, 61% of fathers are similarly uninvolved; and when mothers are highly involved with youth, 54% of fathers are also highly involved. Given that mothers remain the primary parent who organizes and supervises adolescents' time and activities, it seems likely that mothers set the context for parental involvement in families, either encouraging fathers to be highly involved with children or organizing activities that involve the entire family, or discouraging fathers from involvement by not taking the lead themselves.

In panel B we observe the relationship between levels of mother and father involvement in biological father, stepmother families. Again, father involvement varies by level of mother involvement ($\rho = .35$; p of $X = .000$), but here we see some different patterns of joint parenting. When mothers are highly involved, fathers cooperate by displaying high involvement as well. But when mothers are less than highly involved, which is more often the pattern for stepmothers, fathers seem to compensate somewhat by displaying medium to high levels of involvement. Here we see more movement off the diagonal in the direction of greater

TABLE 13.3

Degree of Resident Father Involvement by Resident Mother Involvement
and Family Structure (weighted means)

A. Teen Lives With 2 Bio Parents ($\rho = .47$; prob of X $= .000$)

Degree of resident Father Involvement	Degree of Resident Mother Involvement		
	Low	Medium	High
Low	61.3	24.3	8.3
Medium	33.6	60.1	37.9
High	5.0	15.7	53.9
Total	100.0[a]	100.0[a]	100.0[a]
n	898	4,559	4,202

B. Teen Lives With Bio Dad/Stepmom ($\rho = .35$; prob of X $= .000$)

Degree of resident Father Involvement	Degree of Resident Mother Involvement		
	Low	Medium	High
Low	30.0	16.8	7.4
Medium	51.9	63.0	30.5
High	18.0	20.2	62.1
Total	100.0[a]	100.0	100.0
n	131	167	75

C. Teen Lives With Stepdad/Bio Mom ($\rho = .43$; prob of X $= .000$)

Degree of resident Father Involvement	Degree of Resident Mother Involvement		
	Low	Medium	High
Low	75.9	43.3	21.6
Medium	22.9	49.9	39.5
High	1.2	6.9	39.0
Total	100.0	100.0[a]	100.0[a]
n	199	823	619

D. Teen Lives With Adoptive Parents ($\rho = .50$; prob of X $= .000$)

Degree of resident Father Involvement	Degree of Resident Mother Involvement		
	Low	Medium	High
Low	66.1	22.1	6.2
Medium	30.7	53.9	35.1
High	3.2	23.9	58.7
Total	100.0	100.0[a]	100.0
n	50	153	166

E. Teen Lives With Surrogate Parents ($\rho = .47$; prob of X $= .000$)

Degree of resident Father Involvement	Degree of Resident Mother Involvement		
	Low	Medium	High
Low	72.6	25.1	14.4
Medium	27.4	67.2	46.9
High	0.0	7.7	38.7
Total	100.0	100.0	100.0
n	68	249	156

[a]Totals may not sum to 100 because of rounding.

involvement by fathers, especially when mothers have low levels of involvement. Thus, there appears to be some compensation on the part of biological fathers for the lower levels of involvement by stepmothers.

When the biological parent is the mother in a stepfamily, a different pattern emerges in panel C. We see little cooperation among stepfathers and biological mothers, except for the clustering on the diagonal at the low end of involvement. This might be considered a cooperative strategy by default—when the mother is uninvolved with biological children, so is the stepfather. Among biological mothers with low levels of involvement, 76% of stepfathers also display low levels of involvement with children. Stepfathers are less likely to compensate for the low involvement of the biological mother than are biological fathers for the low involvement of the stepmother (panel B). In addition, medium and highly involved biological mothers are less able to pull the father into a cooperative strategy whereby he is just as involved. Here we see movement off the diagonal in the direction of less involvement by stepfathers relative to the levels of involvement by mothers, representing compensation in a downward direction.

Patterns of joint parenting among adoptive parents in panel D resemble those of two biological parents with high levels of interdependence ($\rho = .50$; p of $X = .000$). Clustering along the diagonal represents cooperative parenting styles. When adoptive mothers are highly involved with youth, 59% of adoptive fathers are also highly involved, more than the percentage among biological fathers in two-biological-parent families (54%).

In panel E, we observe patterns of parental involvement among surrogate parents. At the medium and low ends of surrogate mother involvement, we do not observe a compensatory parenting strategy on the part of surrogate fathers in which they might increase their involvement relative to the mother's involvement to make up for her lower levels. Rather we again see "cooperation by default" in that fathers are as engaged or disengaged as mothers are with children. However, when surrogate mothers are highly involved, we see movement off the diagonal toward less involvement by surrogate fathers in a downward compensatory fashion.

In summary, we find cooperative parenting strategies among two resident biological parents and adoptive parents. There is a strong relationship between levels of mother involvement and levels of father involvement, with the implication that when mothers are highly involved, so are fathers. Compensatory strategies in parental involvement are mainly adopted by remarried biological fathers living with their children. Biological fathers tend to have higher involvement with children when stepmothers have low involvement. For all other types of fathers, we do not see any upward compensation in involvement when mothers are uninvolved. We do see downward compensation, however, among stepfathers and surrogate fathers when mothers are highly involved. Nonbiological fathers may see the high involvement of the mother as leeway to disengage. Finally, in all family structures except biological father/stepmother, when mothers are uninvolved with children, so are fathers, a rather sobering finding.

13. DIVERSITY OF FAMILY CONTEXT

STRATEGIES WHEN PARENTS LIVE APART

Because nonresident biological fathers must negotiate and coordinate their time and activities with their children with the children's resident parents, mainly the mother, we now explore patterns of parenting among nonresident biological fathers and resident mothers and fathers in Table 13.4. Panel A shows how levels

TABLE 13.4

Degree of Nonresident Father Involvement by Resident Mother and Father Involvement (weighted means)

A. Teen Lives With Step Dad/Bio Mom or With Single Mother
($\rho = .12$; *prob of X* = .000)

Degree of nonresident Father Involvement	Degree of Resident Mother Involvement		
	Low	Medium	High
Low	73.3	64.3	57.4
Medium	16.2	21.8	21.5
High	10.5	14.0	21.1
Total	100.0	100.0[a]	100.0
n	577	2,316	1,868

B. Teen Lives With Step Dad/Bio Mom ($\rho = .13$; *prob of X* = .000)

Degree of nonresident Father Involvement	Degree of Resident Father Involvement		
	Low	Medium	High
Low	71.1	62.9	56.2
Medium	16.8	18.6	18.2
High	12.1	18.5	25.6
Total	100.0	100.0	100.0
n	468	512	196

C. Teen Lives With Surrogate Father in Nonparental Home
($\rho = .19$; *prob of X* = .000)

Degree of nonresident Father Involvement	Degree of Resident Father Involvement		
	Low	Medium	High
Low	72.7	69.1	49.1
Medium	24.9	25.8	33.8
High	2.4	5.2	17.1
Total	100.0	100.0[a]	100.0
n	86	175	66

[a]Totals may not sum to 100 because of rounding.

of nonresident biological father involvement varies by levels of biological mother involvement for youth living in stepfamilies and single-mother families. A dramatic pattern emerges. First, there is very little variation in father involvement by level of mother involvement, reflected in the low correlation of .12 (although the interdependence is still significant with X significant at the .000 level). We do see a similar pattern of low levels of father involvement decreasing and high levels of father involvement increasing when levels of mother involvement increase from low to high, but the increase in involvement is much less than it was among resident parents in Table 13.3. Rather, the general finding from panel A is that levels of nonresident father involvement are much more likely to be low, regardless of the level of mother involvement. Second, we do not observe cooperative or compensating parenting strategies among parents who live apart, but rather we see a pattern of parallel parenting in which mothers and fathers maintain separate and segregated relations with their children and have a tacit agreement not to interfere in each other's lives (Furstenberg & Cherlin, 1991).

Next we examine joint patterns of father involvement among nonresident and resident fathers. We are curious as to whether nonresident biological father involvement varies by level of resident father involvement. If a nonresident father sees that a stepfather, who has supplanted him as the father figure in the home, is actively involved with his children, does he further disengage from his children? Panel B addresses this question by showing the joint patterns of involvement for resident stepfathers and nonresident biological fathers. Consistent with the previous panel, levels of nonresident father involvement are relatively independent of the degree of stepfather involvement ($\rho = .13$). There is a sense that when stepfather involvement increases, so does nonresident father involvement, but again, the general pattern is one of low involvement by nonresident fathers, regardless of the level of stepfather involvement.

Panel C addresses this same relationship for resident surrogate fathers. Similar patterns emerge, except that high involvement by nonresident fathers is even less likely when children live with surrogate fathers, regardless of the surrogate father's level of involvement. In sum, there does not seem to be much coordination of parenting styles between nonresident biological fathers and resident parents with the overall pattern one of low involvement by nonresident fathers.

Although involvement by nonresident biological fathers seems to be unrelated to resident father involvement, step and surrogate father involvement may be a function of levels of nonresident father involvement. If the resident father sees that the biological father is highly, involved, he may back off in his engagement with children. That does not seem to happen (results not shown), but we do see more compensation by resident fathers when nonresident fathers are uninvolved such that 55% display medium to high involvement when the nonresident father has low involvement.

CONCLUSION

This research examined how levels of father involvement varied according to family context defined by the configuration of parent types inside and outside the home and by the involvement of parent figures with children. To sort out the family context influences of biology, residency, and family structure, we contrasted measures of father involvement for children who have the same biological link to their fathers and who coreside or live apart from fathers. Variations in family structure, then, are not due to the biological relationship between fathers and children but to the presence of different mother and father figures in the home.

This close attention to family context has produced additional insights into parenting processes in diverse family settings. For example, levels of father involvement by resident biological fathers are relatively unaffected by the context of mother figures in the home. Among resident nonbiological fathers, adoptive fathers are by far the most involved parents of all father types. Nonresident fathers are unaffected by the presence of other father figures living with their children, displaying rather low levels of involvement with children, especially children living in nonparental homes.

These results, however, lead to the conclusion that the structure of our analysis is our strongest finding: biology and father residence are the most important contextual factors for father involvement. Resident biological fathers display higher levels of emotional and behavioral involvement with children than resident nonbiological fathers and than nonresident biological fathers. Moreover, biology and residence are the most important factors in the development of successful parenting strategies. Cooperative parenting strategies, in which both mothers and fathers coordinate their involvement such that highly involved mothers draw fathers into high involvement as well, are found only in two-biological-parent families and adoptive parent families.

When resident parents are nonbiological, their levels of involvement are lower and they tend to disengage further if the resident biological parent is highly involved. Evidence of a compensatory parenting strategy in which one parent is highly involved and the other less involved is mainly found in stepfamilies, with the biological parent always the more highly involved. Compensation does not operate in the other direction such that when biological parents are relatively uninvolved, stepparents increase their involvement. In summary, collective parenting in which parents coordinate their responsibilities and activities with children is probably not operating in families with nonbiological parents.

The ways in which family context matters for the involvement of fathers conform with notions of selection into parenting. Biological and adoptive parents choose to become parents. Given the many circumstances involving biological parenthood, the choice to become a parent is probably stronger and purer among

adoptive parents, and this is reflected in the findings. Adoptive fathers are the most highly involved fathers according to our measures, followed by biological fathers regardless of family structure. When biological and adoptive fathers live with the same mother types, most children benefit by their parents' cooperative strategies. Because biological and adoptive fathers display the highest levels of involvement, and mothers are typically more involved with children than fathers, most children living in two-adoptive- or biological-parent families enjoy high levels of involvement from parents who support, engage, and interact with them at similar levels. Stepfathers, and to a lesser extent surrogate fathers, do not choose to become parents, but end up assuming the parental role through other family relationships—the stepfather through marriage or partnering with children's biological mother, and the surrogate father through a family or friendship obligation. This type of selection into parenthood results in lower levels of father involvement and less engagement in collective parenting strategies with resident biological or other surrogate parents. Differences in how the selection process of becoming a parent influences parental involvement is best illustrated by the family context of stepmother and biological father. When biological fathers remarry, they increase their involvement with their resident children to make up for lower levels of involvement among step-mothers.

Last, once biological fathers no longer live with their children, participation in their lives is stifled and collective parenting strategies for parental involvement are precluded. The family context of children who live apart from biological fathers makes little difference for the consistently low levels of involvement by nonresident fathers. Rather, the context defined by nonresidence seems to overpower any small influence that other parental figures may have. This suggests that structural constraints such as distance, work schedules, and relationships between former spouses or partners may pose the same barriers to father involvement across all family contexts. Our analysis of the interdependency of father and mother involvement suggests that men may relate to their children in large part through their wives or partners. Resident mothers are less willing to identify and support the role status of the father when he lives outside the children's home. This loss of role validation marginalizes the father from the collective family system and likely contributes to his disengagement from children's lives.

Perhaps our most important finding is that one cannot understand father involvement without taking into consideration the presence and involvement of mothers in children's lives. One cannot study father involvement in isolation from family context. Levels of resident father involvement are highly related to levels of resident mother involvement, reinforcing the notion that mothers organize, structure, and coordinate children's activities and family engagement, and are likely to provide the stimulus or the constraint for fathers' involvement and participation with children. Further advances in our knowledge about paternal engagement, accessibility, and responsibility for children can only be made by paying close attention to the context and involvement of all parental figures in the home.

13. DIVERSITY OF FAMILY CONTEXT   317

Taking this perspective one step farther, future directions for fatherhood research should involve the collection and analysis of data on couples, in which mothers and fathers in the same family report on their involvement with children. Most research to date examines variations in parental involvement across families, making inferences about what is happening within families, as we do here. Insights into how fathers and mothers coordinate their parenting strategies and how involvement by mothers and fathers matter to children's development can better be gained with couple data that permit analysis of within-family differences in parental involvement.

To further explore father involvement across the diversity of family forms in America, national studies need to incorporate the rich, detailed indicators of parental investment and involvement often found in small local studies of families. National samples give us the sample size to study family diversity, but they often must prudently limit the number of measures of parental involvement and behavior in order to provide a range of topics for interdisciplinary research. Future studies of father involvement must take this increasing diversity of family life into consideration by combining national sampling with detailed family process indicators to improve our measurement of father involvement and understand the salience of father involvement for children, mothers, and fathers in different family contexts.

ACKNOWLEDGMENTS

This chapter is based on data from the Add Health project, a program project designed by J. Richard Udry (PI) and Peter Bearman, and funded by grant P01-HD31921 from the National Institute of Child Health and Human Development to the Carolina Population Center, University of North Carolina at Chapel Hill, with cooperative funding participation from 17 other federal agencies. We gratefully acknowledge research support to Harris from the National Institute of Child Health and Human Development through grant 1 P01 HD31921–01 as part of the Add Health program project and grant 1 U01 HD37558-01 as part of the NICHD Family and Child Well-Being Research Network.

REFERENCES

Amato, P. R. (1987). *Children in Australian families: The growth of competence.* New York: Prentice-Hall.
Amato, P. R. (1994). Father–child relations, mother–child relations, and offspring psychological well-being in early adulthood. *Journal of Marriage and the Family, 56,* 1031–1042.
Bearman, P. S., Jones, J., & Udry, J. R. (1997). *The National Longitudinal Study of Adolescent Health: Research design.* www.cpc.unc.edu/projects/addhealth/design.html.
Bianchi, S. M. (1995). The Changing Demographic and Socioeconomic Characteristics of Single Parent Families. In S. M. H. Hanson, M. L. Heims, D. J. Julian, and M. B. Sussman (Eds.), *Single parent families: Diversity, myths, and realities* (pp. 71–97). Binghamton, NY: Haworth.

Bianchi, S. M., & Casper, L. M. (2000). American families. *Population Bulletin, 55*(4), 1–42.

Blair, S. L., Wenk, D., & Hardesty, C. (1994). Marital quality and paternal involvement: Interconnections of men's spousal and parental roles. *Journal of Men's Studies, 2*, 221–237.

Cabrera, N. J., Tamis-LeMonda, C. S., Bradley, R. H., Hofferth, S., & Lamb, M. E. (2000). Fatherhood in the twenty-first century. *Child Development, 71*, 127–136.

Cooksey, E. C., & Fondell, M. (1996). Spending time with his kids: Effects of family structure on fathers' and children's lives. *Journal of Marriage and the Family, 58*, 693–707.

Eggebeen, D. J., Snyder, A. R., & Manning, W. D. (1996). Children in single-father families in demographic perspective. *Journal of Family Issues, 17*, 441–465.

Furstenberg, F. F., Jr. (1988). Good dads–bad dads: The two faces of fatherhood. In A. J. Cherlin (Ed.), *The changing American family and public policy* (pp. 193–218). Washington, DC: Urban Institute Press.

Furstenberg, F. F., Jr., & Cherlin, A. J. (1991). *Divided families*. Cambridge, MA: Harvard University Press.

Furstenberg, F. F., Jr., & Harris, K. M. (1992). The disappearing American father? Divorce and the waning significance of biological parenthood. In S. J. South & S. E. Tolnay (Eds.), *The changing American family: Sociological and demographic perspectives* (pp. 197–223). Boulder, CO: Westview.

Garasky, S., & Meyer, D. R. (1996). Reconsidering the increase in father-only families. *Demography, 33*, 385–393.

Gerson, K. (1993). *No man's land: Men's changing commitments to family and work*. New York: Basic Books.

Griswold, R. L. (1993). *Fatherhood in America: A history*. New York: Basic Books.

Harris, K. M., & Marmer, J. K. (1996). Poverty, paternal involvement, and adolescent well-being. *Journal of Family Issues, 17*, 614–640.

Harris, K. M., & Morgan, S. P. (1991). Fathers, sons, and daughters: Differential paternal involvement in parenting. *Journal of Marriage and the Family, 53*, 531–544.

Harris, K. M., Furstenberg, F. F., Jr., & Marmer, J. K. (1998). Paternal involvement with adolescents in intact families: The influence of fathers over the life course. *Demography, 35*, 201–216.

Harris, K. M., Heard, H., & King, V. (2000, March). *Resident father involvement: Differences by family structure, race and ethnicity, and social class*. Paper presented at the Annual Meeting of the Population Association of America, Los Angeles, CA.

Hofferth, S. L. (1999). *Race/ethnic differences in father involvement* (working paper 004-99). Ann Arbor: University of Michigan, Center for the Ethnography of Everyday Life.

King, V. (1994). Nonresident father involvement and child well-being: Can dads make a difference? *Journal of Family Issues, 15*, 78–96.

Lamb, M. E. (Ed.). (1997). *The role of the father in child development*. New York: Wiley.

Lamb, M. E. (Ed.). (1999). *Parenting and child development in nontraditional families*. Mahwah, NJ: Lawrence Erlbaum Associates.

Lamb, M. E., Pleck, J. H., Charnov, E. L., & Levine, J. A. (1987). A biosocial perspective on paternal behavior and involvement. In J. B. Lancaster, J. Altman, A. Rossi, & L. R. Sherrod (Eds.), *Parenting across the lifespan: Biosocial perspectives* (pp. 11–42). New York: Academic Press.

LaRossa, R. (1998). Fatherhood and social change. *Family Relations, 37*, 451–457.

Marsiglio, W. (1991). Paternal engagement activities with minor children. *Journal of Marriage and the Family, 53*, 973–986.

Marsiglio, W. (1993). Contemporary scholarship on fatherhood: Culture, identity, and conduct. *Journal of Family Issues, 14*, 484–509.

Marsiglio, W. (1995). Fathers' diverse life course patterns and roles: Theory and social interventions. In W. Marsiglio (Ed.), *Fatherhood: Contemporary theory, research, and social policy* (pp. 1–20). Thousand Oaks, CA: Sage.

13. DIVERSITY OF FAMILY CONTEXT   319

Mintz, S. (1998). From patriarchy to androgyny and other myths: Placing men's family roles in historical perspective. In A. Booth and N. Crouter (Eds.), *Men in families: When do they get involved? What difference does it make?* (pp. 3–30). Mahwah, NJ: Lawrence Erlbaum Associates.

Mosley, J., & Thomson, E. (1995). Fathering behavior and child outcomes: The role of race and poverty. In W. Marsiglio (Ed.), *Fatherhood* (pp. 148–165). Newbury Park, CA: Sage.

Nock, S., & Kingston, P. (1988). Time with children: The impact of couples' work-time commitments. *Social Forces, 67,* 59–85.

Nord, C., Brimhall, D. A., & West, J. (1997). *Fathers' involvement in their children's schools.* Washington, DC: Office of Educational Research and Improvement, U.S. Department of Education.

Parke, R. (1996). *Fatherhood.* Cambridge, MA: Harvard University Press.

Pleck, J. H. (1997). Paternal involvement: Levels, sources, and consequences. In M. E. Lamb (Ed.), *The role of the father in child development* (pp. 66–103). New York: Wiley.

Radin, N. (1994). Primary-caregiving fathers in intact families. In A. E. Gottfried and A. W. Gottfried (Eds.), *Redefining families: Implications for children's development* (pp. 55–97). New York: Plenum.

Seltzer, J. A. (1994a). Consequences of marital dissolution for children. *Annual Review of Sociology, 20,* 235–266.

Seltzer, J. A. (1994b). Intergenerational ties in adulthood and childhood experience. In A. Booth & J. Dunn (Eds.), *Stepfamilies: Who benefits? Who does not?* (pp. 89–96). Hillsdale, NJ: Lawrence Erlbaum Associates.

14

Multiple Determinants of Father Involvement: An Exploratory Analysis Using the PSID–CDS Data Set

Brent A. McBride, Sarah J. Schoppe,
Moon-Ho Ho
University of Illinois at Urbana-Champaign

Thomas R. Rane
Washington State University

Fathers as active, involved parents began to attract the attention of social scientists in the 1970s (Greenberg & Morris, 1974; Lamb, 1975; Parke, 1981; Parke & Sawin, 1976). This interest was in contrast to research on fathers conducted in the prior few decades: which primarily focused on consequences for children of father absence (Biller, 1971). The refocused interest on fathers as active parents increased dramatically in the ensuing years with considerable attention given to father involvement in direct child-rearing activities (Barnett & Baruch, 1987; Cowan & Cowan, 1987; Crouter, Perry-Jenkins, Huston, & McHale, 1987; Darling-Fisher & Tiedje, 1990; Deutsch, Lussier, & Servis, 1993; Grossman, Pollack, & Golding, 1988; Larson, 1993; Levy-Shiff & Israelashvili, 1988; Marsiglio, 1991; McBride & Rane, 1997). In the past decade researchers were joined by policymakers and the popular media in a continued and explicit focus on fathers and fathering (Coltrane & Allen, 1994; Furstenburg, 1995; Griswold, 1993; Lamb, 1997; LaRossa, 1997; LaRossa, Gordon, Wilson, Bairan, & Jaret, 1991; Marsiglio, 1995; Meyer, 1992; Snarey, 1993; Tamis-LeMonda & Cabrera, 1999; Thomas, 1998).

As outlined in the introduction to this volume and articulated in many of the chapters, several factors have contributed to this increased interest in fathers and

fatherhood (e.g., the changing societal conceptions of parental roles, increases in maternal employment, a growing body of literature outlining the impact of father involvement on child development, shifts in the demographic profile of modern families, and increased policy debates over the well-being of children). This increased interest has resulted in a rapidly expanding body of research literature on fathers and fatherhood, especially during the past decade (Cabrera, Tamis-LeMonda, Bradley, Hofferth, & Lamb, 2000; Marsiglio, Amato, Day, & Lamb, 2000). Given the interrelatedness of many of the factors that have influenced this research agenda and the ongoing debates and concerns over various issues, it seems certain that the focus on fathers and fathering in both the research and policy arenas will not abate any time soon.

Two fundamental contributions have been made by researchers studying fathers and fathering during the past three decades: (1) the explicit effort to clarify and broaden conceptualizations of fathering (Doherty, Kouneski, & Erickson, 1998; Hawkins & Dollahite, 1997; Lamb, Pleck, Charnov, & Levine, 1985, 1987; Palkovitz, 1997; Pleck, 1997) and (2) concerted attempts to articulate and model critical antecedents of fathers' involvement with their children (Lamb et al., 1987; Levine & Pitt, 1995; Pleck, Lamb, & Levine, 1986; Pleck, 1997; Volling & Belsky, 1991; Woodworth, Belsky, & Crnic, 1996).

This paper is primarily concerned with the second of these major contributions of fathering researchers. Specifically, our aim is to provide a brief description of the Lamb, Pleck et al. (Lamb et al., 1987; Pleck, 1997; Pleck et al., 1986) model of influences on father involvement (see Fig. 14.1), and then to draw upon data from an existing data set to conduct a full assessment of the model.

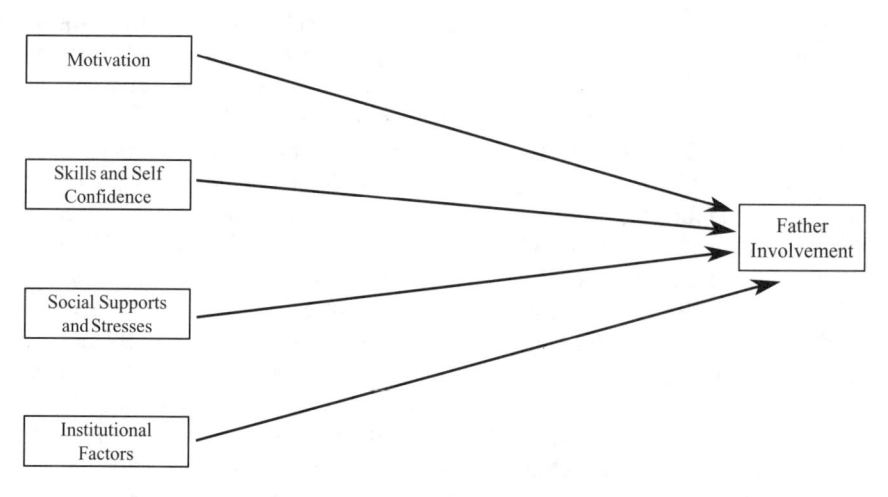

FIG. 14.1. Lamb, Pleck et al. (1987). Model of the Determinants of Father Involvement.

Lamb, Pleck, and colleagues presented a four-factor model of influences on father involvement. The four factors in the Lamb–Pleck model are (1) Motivation, or the extent to which fathers want to be involved with their children, (2) Skills and Self-Confidence, or the actual physical skills and techniques needed to be successful and effective in providing care for children, and perhaps more important, fathers' perceived competence and confidence in being able to develop and employ such skills, (3) Social Supports and Stresses, or the extent to which others in the social network, primarily mothers, are supportive of or resistant to increased involvement by fathers, and (4) Institutional factors and practices, or the degree to which workplace practices and policies (which often are a reflection of broader societal expectations) serve to inhibit or facilitate increased involvement by fathers. Lamb, Pleck, and colleagues (Lamb, 1987; Pleck, 1997; Pleck et al., 1986) suggested that these factors operate in sequence; for example, in the absence of motivation on the part of a father to be involved with his child(ren), lack of skills or support or presence of workplace barriers to the father's involvement or both will not be an issue.

This model has served implicitly to shape much recent research on father involvement (Doherty, Kouneski, & Erickson, 1998). This influence is clearly reflected in Pleck's (1997) comprehensive review of the research on paternal involvement. Pleck used the model as a framework for the review and provided extensive discussion of research that could be categorized according to each of the four factors. For example, under the category of motivation, Pleck summarized research on fathers' developmental history and socialization experiences, fathers' personality characteristics and gender-role orientation, and fathers' "paternal identity." Under the category of skills and self-confidence, Pleck focused on studies of the effect of fathers' perceived competence in interacting with children, along with the impact of various skills-based interventions on fathers' involvement. With regard to social supports and stresses, Pleck focused on maternal employment characteristics and marital dynamics. Finally, in considering institutional factors and practices as influences on father involvement, Pleck reviewed the research on fathers' employment characteristics and work–family conflicts, as well as the direct effects of such workplace policies as flextime and paternal leave. However, notwithstanding the careful articulation of the Lamb–Pleck model and its implicit influence on recent fathering research, no one to date has explicitly set out to simultaneously assess the relationships between the four factors in the model and various aspects of father involvement within a single study. Furthermore, with the exception of one conference paper drawing on data from a subsample of 309 males in the National Survey of Adolescent Males (Stueve & Pleck, 1997), no studies have investigated the interrelationships between the factors in the model and their potential cumulative influence on father involvement (Pleck, 1997). In addition, Pleck and Stueve (2001) argued that the model could be more useful if expanded to specify in more detail how particular aspects of each of the four predisposing factors are associated with different kinds of involvement activities. These are the specific goals that guided the research reported here.

METHOD

Background

Data for this investigation were obtained from the 1997 Child Development Supplement (CDS) of the Panel Study of Income Dynamics (PSID) (Hofferth, 1998). Begun in 1968, the PSID is a 30-year longitudinal survey of a representative sample of U.S. families (Hofferth & Anderson, this volume; Hofferth, Yeung, & Stafford, 1997). The CDS is a supplement to the core PSID data that was begun in 1997 with funding from the National Institute of Child Health and Human Development (NICHD) to provide researchers with a nationally representative database of children and their families. For the CDS, data from approximately 2,500 families (a subset of the larger PSID sample) were collected regarding 3,563 children aged 0–12 years (including one or two randomly selected children per family). The CDS survey was conducted from March 1997 to December 1997 (Hofferth & Anderson, this volume). Data were collected from the children themselves and from both the children's primary caregiver and a secondary caregiver where applicable (Hofferth, Davis-Kean, Davis, & Finkelstein, 1998). Ninety percent of the families in the core PSID sample contacted about the CDS agreed to participate. Eighty-four percent of families who were contacted for the first time in 1997 as part of an immigrant "refresher" sample of families who emigrated to the United States after 1968 agreed to participate (Hofferth & Anderson, this volume). The combined response rate for the CDS sample was 88% and the combined sample was made nationally representative by using weights based on the 1997 Current Population Survey (Hofferth & Anderson, in press).

The Present Study

For the purposes of this study, we are focusing on a PSID–CDS subsample of 2,215 children (51% boys, 49% girls; average age = 6 years) who have been identified as living with a mother and a secondary caregiver who is the child's biological father, stepfather, or father figure. In addition, our sample contains only children from the two largest demographic groups represented in the CDS data (Caucasian, 66% of respondents; and African-American, 34% of respondents). For the questionnaires we used in this investigation, the response rates for the primary caregiver household booklet and the other caregiver instruments are approximately 65% and 50%, respectively (Hofferth et al., 1998). Weights are also employed to adjust for the lower response rate by "other caregivers" to the survey instruments (Hofferth & Anderson, this volume).

Variables

We were interested specifically in information that mapped onto the Lamb–Pleck model of the determinants of father involvement. First, we examined the CDS database and selected items theorized to represent the different factors of the

14. MULTIPLE DETERMINANTS   325

Lamb–Pleck model. Second, we employed data reduction and factor analysis procedures to select the best representative items for each factor. Third, we formed composite variables representing different dimensions of the factors and checked them using confirmatory factor analysis techniques to ensure the unidimensionality of the constructs. Finally, we used these composites in the path analyses. The composite variables included under each conceptual factor are detailed next, including the number of items in each composite and item examples.

Motivation. The variables included under this conceptual factor of the model are fathers' reports of parenting socialization (e.g., "Did you take parenting classes?"), desire for a better life for their kids (e.g., "Have you ever moved to a different neighborhood, reduced/increased work hours to make a better life for your child(ren)?"), information about their own fathers' involvement (e.g., "How involved was your father figure in raising you?"), and beliefs regarding the role of the father in the family (e.g., degree of endorsement of the statement: "A father should be as heavily involved in the care of his child as the mother").

Skills and Self-Confidence. One variable is included as a measure of fathers' perceptions of their parenting skills and self-confidence. This variable consists of four items assessing parenting stress (e.g., degree of endorsement of the statement: "I feel trapped by my responsibilities as a parent").

Social Supports and Stresses. Six variables are included to assess social supports and stresses. The first represents the primary caregiver's (i.e., mother's) perceptions of economic stress (e.g., "In the last month have you postponed medical care, fallen behind in paying bills, etc., due to economic problems?") and is composed of 16 items. The second variable consisted of a combination of mothers' reports of self and spouse neighborhood involvement using 18 (9 for self, 9 for spouse) items (e.g., "Have you and/or your spouse participated in neighborhood watch, church, etc. in the past month?"). The third and fourth variables consist of items regarding fathers' perceptions of interparental conflict regarding specific activities (nine items) and more general life goals (six items). Examples of items in these two variables include: "How often do you and the child(ren)'s mother disagree about disciplining children or your job/career plans?" (respectively). The fifth variable consists of mothers' reported social support, using four items. An example item in the fifth variable is the following question: "In the past month, have you given/received help with things like child care, transportation, repairs, etc.?" The sixth variable was made up of three items assessing the mother's attitudes about the role of the father in the family, and consisted of the same items described earlier for fathers' beliefs regarding the paternal role.

Institutional Factors. One variable was chosen to represent the institutional factors component of the Lamb–Pleck model. This variable consists of fathers' reports of total time spent working, compiled from the total minutes fathers reported

working as an "activity," using a time-use report table contained in the "other caregiver" household questionnaire.

Father Involvement. The construct of father involvement was operationalized using five variables. The first represents responsibility and consists of six items assessing both mothers' and fathers' reports (three items each) of which partner had responsibility (self vs. other vs. shared) for child-related management tasks (e.g., pediatrician, child care). A second variable assesses fathers' reports of their own displays of warmth and affection toward their children, using six items (e.g., "How often in the past month have you told the child that you love him/her?"). The third and fourth variables assess fathers' reports of participation with their children within the last month in two categories of specific activities: household-centered (six items) and child-centered (seven items). An example of a household-centered item is doing the dishes together. An example of a child-centered item is "working on homework together." The fifth variable consists of eight items representing an aspect of father involvement known as paternal monitoring, or the extent to which fathers are involved in setting limits and guidelines for their children's activities. Example items included in this variable are setting limits on how late children can stay up at night and controlling who the children spend time with.

Time diary information (a record of time spent in various activities and with whom, and who was present during activities) for 1 weekday and 1 weekend day was available for a subset of children in the sample. The information was provided by the child's primary caregiver (with the child's collaboration if the child was 3 years of age or older). Although time diary information is one of the best ways to accurately examine temporally focused aspects of paternal involvement, unfortunately a large amount of data was missing for the time diary records. Initial inclusion of the time diary information reduced our sample size from approximately 2,200 to 700–800 children. Thus, although time diary information can be valuable, the reduced sample size would have precluded examination of our full model, so we did not include it in further analyses.

Demographic Factors. Several demographic variables were also included as controls in the initial conceptualization of the model. These variables included: child gender, race, and age, the child's relationship to his or her residential father or father figure (i.e., biological father vs. stepfather or other father-figure), family size, and father/mother age, education, and hours spent in paid employment (per week).

RESULTS

Prior to fitting the full combined model to the data, we tested the composite variables in each of the factors in the Lamb–Pleck model for the significance of their individual direct paths using the structural equation modeling (SEM) program Mplus

14. MULTIPLE DETERMINANTS   327

(Muthen & Muthen, 2000).[1] The five composites representing father involvement were treated as response variables in this round of analyses. We regressed these five composites on the composite variables comprising the five predictors: Motivation, Skills and Self-Confidence, Social Supports and Stresses, Institutional factors, and Demographic factors. Variables with paths significant at the $p < .05$ level were maintained for inclusion in the testing of the full model. Nonsignificant variables were dropped from further analyses. Table 14.1 details all the variables considered in the initial rounds of testing and indicates which variables were maintained or dropped.

Preliminary Analyses

For the variables comprising the Motivation factor, fathers' reports of parenting socialization were positively associated with fathers' reports of displays of warmth/affection toward their children ($\beta = .07$, $p < .05$) and participation in both household-centered ($\beta = .08$, $p < .05$) and child-centered ($\beta = .16$, $p < .05$) activities. Fathers' reported desires for a better life for their children were positively associated with combined maternal and paternal reports of responsibility ($\beta = .08$, $p < .05$), and negatively associated with fathers' reports of paternal monitoring ($\beta = -.09$, $p < .05$). Fathers' reports of their own fathers' involvement were positively associated with their self-reported affection toward their children ($\beta = .08$, $p < .05$) and their reports of paternal monitoring ($\beta = .27$, $p < .05$). In turn, fathers' attitudes regarding the role of the father in the family were negatively associated with combined maternal and paternal reports of responsibility ($\beta = -.07$, $p < .05$), fathers' self-reports of affection toward their children ($\beta = -.31$, $p < .05$) and participation in child-centered ($\beta = -.14$, $p < .05$) activities, but positively associated with fathers' reports of paternal monitoring ($\beta = .17$, $p < .05$). Thus, all variables included in the Motivation factor were maintained for inclusion in the full model.

The one variable in the Skills and Self-Confidence factor (fathers' perceptions of parenting stress) was found to be negatively associated with fathers' reports of affection toward their children ($\beta = -.10$, $p < .05$) and positively associated with fathers' reports of paternal monitoring ($\beta = .20$, $p < .05$). This variable was maintained for inclusion in the full model.

For the Social Supports and Stresses Factor, four of the six original variables were maintained for inclusion in the full model. The combined self-and-spouse score for neighborhood involvement was positively associated with fathers' participation in child-centered activities ($\beta = .11$, $p < .05$), but negatively associated with fathers' reports of paternal monitoring ($\beta = -.18$, $p < .05$). Fathers' reports of interparental conflict regarding specific activities were positively associated

---

[1]Missing data were handled using procedures outlined by the Mplus (Muthen & Muthen, 2000) path analysis program.

TABLE 14.1
Operationalization of the Determinants of Father Involvement, and Variables Maintained in Full Model

Construct/Factor	Responsibility	Showing Warmth/Affection	Father/Child Household-Centered Activities	Father/Child Child-Centered Activities	Paternal Monitoring	Maintained in Full Model
Motivation:						
Parenting socialization		+.07*	+.08*	+.16*	-.09*	Y
Better life for kids	+.08*	+.08*			+.27*	Y
Own father's involvement		-.31*			+.17*	Y
Skills & Self-Confidence:						
Paternal perceptions of role of father	-.07*			-.14*		Y
Parenting stress		-.10*			+.20*	Y
Social Supports & Stress:						
Economic stress						N
Neighborhood involvement				+.11*	-.18*	Y
Interparental disagreements (activities)	+.08*	+.15*	+.07*	+.08*	+.22*	Y
Interparental disagreements (life goals)		-.07*	+.11*	+.09*	+.19*	Y
Social support						N
Institutional Factors:						
Maternal perceptions of role of fathers	-.11*	-.13*		-.08*	-.07*	Y
Time spent working						Y
Basic Demographics:						
Child gender		-.08*	+.16*	+.13*		N
Race		-.42*	+.11*	-.28	-.14*	Y
Child age		-.07*				Y
Family size	-.17*					Y
Father's age					+.17*	Y
Mother's age	.09*	.14*				Y
Father's education	-.10*				-.12*	Y
Mother's education	-.11*		-.07*			N
Father's total employment						Y
Mother's total employment		-.06*		-.12*		Y
Father's biological status						Y

* $p < .05$.

14. MULTIPLE DETERMINANTS   329

with combined maternal and paternal reports of responsibility ($\beta = .08$, $p < .05$), fathers' reports of affection toward their children ($\beta = .15$, $p < .05$), fathers' participation in household- ($\beta = .07$, $p < .05$) and child-centered activities ($\beta = .08$, $p < .05$), and fathers' reports of paternal monitoring ($\beta = .22$, $p < .05$). In turn, fathers' reports of interparental conflict involving larger life goals were negatively associated with fathers' reports of affection expressed toward their children ($\beta = -.07$, $p < .05$), but positively associated with fathers' reports of participation in household-($\beta = .11$, $p < .05$) and child-centered ($\beta = .09$, $p < .05$) activities, and fathers' reports of paternal monitoring ($\beta = .19$, $p < .05$). Maternal attitudes regarding the role of the father in the family were negatively associated with combined maternal and paternal reports of responsibility ($\beta = -.11$, $p < .05$), paternal reports of affection toward their children ($\beta = -.13$, $p < .05$) and participation in child-centered ($\beta = -.08$, $p < .05$) activities. Maternal reports of economic stress and social support were not associated with any of the measures of father involvement and thus were dropped from further analyses.

The one variable representing Institutional factors (fathers' reports of total time spent working) was negatively associated with fathers' reports of paternal monitoring ($\beta = -.07$, $p < .05$), and thus was maintained for the full model testing.

Of all the Demographic factors considered, most were found to be associated with the measures of father involvement and included in the full model. Race was negatively associated with fathers' reports of affection toward their children ($\beta = -.08$, $p < .05$) and positively associated with fathers' reports of participation in both household- ($\beta = .16$, $p < .05$) and child-centered ($\beta = .13$, $p < .05$) activities. Child age was positively associated with fathers' participation in household-centered activities ($\beta = .11$, $p < .05$). Family size was negatively associated with fathers' reports of affection toward their children ($\beta = -.07$, $p < .05$) and fathers' reports of paternal monitoring ($\beta = -.14$, $p < .05$). Father's age was negatively associated with paternal responsibility ($\beta = -.17$, $p < .05$). Mother's age was positively associated with fathers' reports of affection toward their children ($\beta = .14$, $p < .05$) and paternal monitoring ($\beta = .17$, $p < .05$). Father's education was positively associated with paternal responsibility ($\beta = .09$, $p < .05$), while mother's education was negatively associated with paternal responsibility ($\beta = -.10$, $p < .05$) and monitoring ($\beta = -.12$, $p < .05$). Father's total hours spent in paid employment (per week) was negatively associated with combined maternal and paternal responsibility scores ($\beta = -.10$, $p < .05$) and fathers' participation in household-centered activities ($\beta = -.07$, $p < .05$). The biological status of the child's father was negatively associated with fathers' reports of affection towards their children ($\beta = -.06$, $p < .05$) and fathers' participation in child-centered activities ($\beta = -.12$, $p < .05$). Child gender and mother's total hours in paid employment (per week) were not associated with any of the measures of father involvement, and thus were dropped from further analyses.

Full-Model Testing

Next, all of the variables retained from the first round of testing were entered into a full model, testing all direct paths simultaneously. The overall model, using only variables with significant paths in the first round of analyses, fit the data well ($\chi^2(49) = 86.85$, $p = .0007$). A good fit was also indicated by the model's root mean square approximation (RMSEA = .019). Table 14.2 presents the significant

TABLE 14.2

Results From the Path Analysis of the Full Model of the Multiple Determinants of Father Involvement

Construct/ Factors	Responsibility	Showing Warmth/ Affection	Father/Child Household- Centered Activities	Father/Child Child-Centered Activities	Paternal Monitoring
Motivation:					
Parenting socialization		+	+	+	
Better life for kids	+				−
Own father's involvement					+
Paternal perceptions of role of father		−			+
Skills & Self-Confidence:					
Parenting stress					+
Social Supports & Stresses:					
Neighborhood involvement				+	−
Interparental disagreements (activities)	+	+	+		+
Interparental disagreements (life goals)			+	+	+
Maternal perceptions of role of father	−				
Institutional Factors:					
Time spent working					
Basic Demographics:					
Race		−	+	+	
Child age		−	−	−	
Family size		−			−
Father's age					
Mother's age					
Father's education					
Mother's education					
Father's total employment					
Father's biological status				−	

Note. Significant predictors are denoted by + (positive prediction) or − (negative prediction). See Fig. 14.2 for standardized parameter estimates for the path coefficients.

Model summary. $\chi^2 = 86.85$, $df = 49$, $p = .0007$, $n = 2215$, RMSEA = .019.

14. MULTIPLE DETERMINANTS   331

paths (and the direction of effects) from the testing of the full model. Figure 14.2 presents a diagram of the significant paths in the full model and the standardized parameter estimates for the path coefficients.

For the Motivation factor, fathers' reports of parenting socialization were positively associated with fathers' reports of affection toward their children ($\beta = .06$, $p < .05$), and participation in both household- ($\beta = .08$, $p < .05$) and child-centered ($\beta = .14$, $p < .05$) activities. In addition, fathers' desire for a better life for their children was positively associated with combined maternal and paternal reports of responsibility ($\beta = .08$, $p < .05$), but negatively associated with fathers' reports of paternal monitoring ($\beta = -.06$, $p < .05$). Fathers' reports of their own fathers' involvement were positively associated with their reports of paternal monitoring ($\beta = .18$, $p < .05$). In turn, fathers' attitudes regarding the role of the father in the family were negatively associated with fathers' reports of affection toward their children ($\beta = -.17$, $p < .05$), but positively associated with fathers' reports of paternal monitoring ($\beta = .14$, $p < .05$).

The one variable in the Skills and Self-Confidence factor, fathers' reports of parenting stress, was found to be positively associated only with fathers' reports of paternal monitoring ($\beta = .11$, $p < .05$).

For the Social Supports and Stresses factor, self-and-spouse combined neighborhood involvement was positively associated with fathers' reports of participation in child-centered activities ($\beta = .06$, $p < .05$), but negatively associated with fathers' reports of paternal monitoring ($\beta = -.13$, $p < .05$). Fathers' reports of interparental conflict regarding activities were positively associated with combined maternal and paternal reports of responsibility ($\beta = .07$, $p < .05$), fathers' reports of affection toward their children ($\beta = .08$, $p < .05$), fathers' reports of participation in household-centered ($\beta = .08$, $p < .05$) and child-centered ($\beta = .07$, $p < .05$) activities, and fathers' reports of paternal monitoring ($\beta = .17$, $p < .05$). Similarly, fathers' reports of conflict regarding life goals were positively associated with fathers' reports of participation in both household- ($\beta = .09$, $p < .05$) and child-centered ($\beta = .09$, $p < .05$) activities as well as fathers' reports of paternal monitoring ($\beta = .13$, $p < .05$). Alternatively, maternal attitudes regarding the role of the father in the family were negatively associated with combined maternal and paternal reports of responsibility ($\beta = -.10$, $p < .05$).

The one variable included in the full model representing Institutional factors (fathers' reports of total time spent working) was not found to be significantly associated with any of the measures of father involvement.

Of the demographic factors considered, many but not all remained significant in the full model. Race remained significantly associated with father involvement. Specifically, race was negatively associated with fathers' reports of affection toward their children ($\beta = -.07$, $p < .05$) but positively associated with fathers' reports of participation in both household- ($\beta = .15$, $p < .05$) and child-centered ($\beta = .13$, $p < .05$) activities. Child age also remained important for the full model in that this variable was found to be negatively associated with fathers' reports of

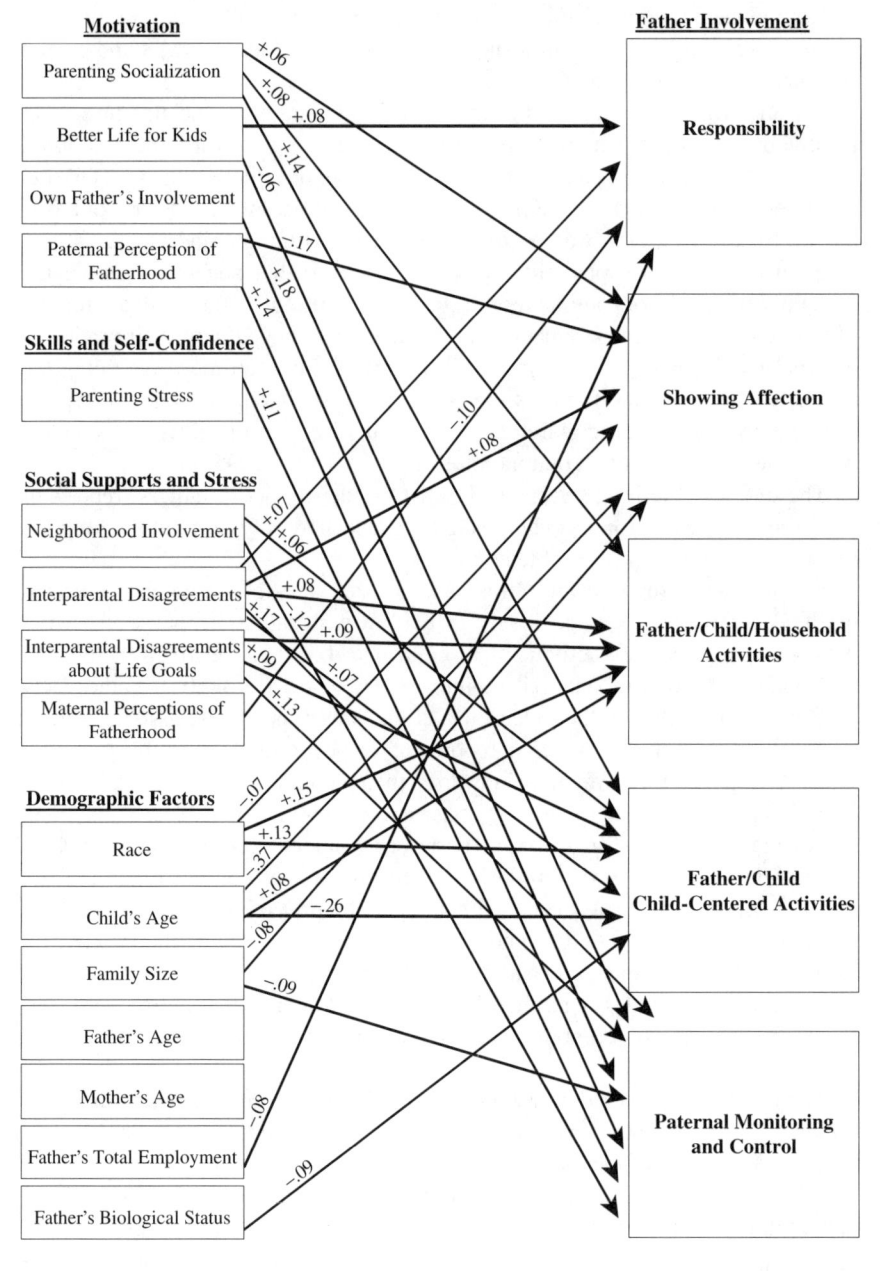

FIG. 14.2. Results from the path analysis of the multiple determinants of father involvement. Note: Only significant paths depicted. Values represent standardized parameter estimates for the path coefficients.

14. MULTIPLE DETERMINANTS

affection toward their children ($\beta = -.36, p < .05$) and participation in household-centered ($\beta = -.08, p < .05$) and child-centered ($\beta = -.26, p < .05$) activities. In addition, family size continued to be negatively associated with fathers' reports of affection toward their children ($\beta = -.08, p < .05$) and fathers' reports of paternal monitoring ($\beta = -.09, p < .05$). Maternal and paternal age and education levels were no longer significantly associated with any of the five measures of father involvement. Fathers' total hours spent in paid employment (per week) remained negatively associated with combined maternal and paternal responsibility scores ($\beta = -.08, p < .05$), and father's biological status remained negatively associated with fathers' participation in child-centered activities ($\beta = -.09, p < .05$).

DISCUSSION

Results from this exploratory study provide partial support for the Lamb–Pleck model of the determinants of father involvement. Furthermore, because they are based on a multidimensional view of father involvement, these findings underscore the value of simultaneously exploring how different aspects of each of the four factors outlined in the model are associated with different forms of paternal involvement, something that has been neglected in previous research. Results from this work hold implications for researchers, educators, practitioners, and policymakers as they explore the impact of changing societal expectations for parental roles. Given the nature and focus of this book, a majority of the discussion section of this chapter will be devoted to measurement issues related to father involvement as opposed to conceptual issues.

Consistent with previous research (see Pleck, 1997, for a comprehensive review), when we examined the relationships between individual variables represented in the factors outlined in the Lamb–Pleck model, all four factors included variables with significant direct paths to the various father involvement measures. The paternal monitoring dimension of father involvement emerged with the broadest relationships, with 8 of the possible 12 direct paths being significant. The most consistent and strongest individual predictor of all forms of father involvement was paternal perception of the role of fathers. Those fathers who held perceptions of the paternal role that went beyond that of financial provider reported greater participation in responsibility behaviors, showed more affection toward their children, participated more with their children in household tasks and child-centered activities, and engaged in higher levels of monitoring of their children. In contrast to previous research, the time spent working variable (Institutional factor in the model) was found to be significantly related only to paternal monitoring, with those fathers working longer hours reporting higher monitoring.

As expected, several significant patterns emerged when exploring the relationship of individual demographic variables and paternal involvement measures. Most

notable were race, family size, and fathers' biological status. Caucasian fathers reported more warmth and affection with their children, while African-American fathers were more involved in household tasks and child-centered activities with their children. Fathers with larger families and stepfathers/father figures reported showing less warmth and affection and participated in fewer child-centered activities with the target children. Surprisingly, child gender did not emerge as a significant individual predictor of any of the father involvement measures.

In testing simultaneously all direct paths of the predictor variables when examining the fit of the Lamb–Pleck model, we found that the Institutional factor was not significantly related to the paternal involvement measures. Paternal perceptions of the role of fathers (a Motivation variable) emerged as the strongest predictor during testing of the full model. Fathers who reported less traditional perceptions of fatherhood reported showing more affection with their children and more monitoring of their children. Fathers' reports of interparental conflicts about specific activities (Social Supports and Stresses) emerged as a significant predictor of all five father involvement variables in the full-model testing. Those fathers experiencing less disagreement reported greater responsibility behaviors, more affection toward their children, and greater participation in household-centered and child-centered activities with their children. These fathers also reported lower levels of paternal monitoring. The full-model testing also revealed the differential relationship between race and father involvement measures: Caucasian fathers reported showing more warmth and affection to their children, whereas African-American fathers reported spending more time in household tasks and child-centered activities with their children. As observed when testing the individual paths, child age again emerged as a significant predictor of three of the four measures of father involvement in the full-model testing. Several other significant paths emerged · from the Motivation and Social Supports and Stresses factors when we tested the full model (see Fig. 14.2). These findings lend partial support to the utility of the Lamb–Pleck four-factor model of the determinants of father involvement as a means of describing why some fathers may assume a more active role in raising their children.

Analyses from the current study underscore several conceptual and statistical issues related to the measurement of father involvement that can benefit researchers' discussions. Although the PSID–CDS is a comprehensive compilation of data outlining various aspects of parental functioning and child outcomes, it has limitations that must be acknowledged, especially for projects focusing on paternal roles. One major limitation is the small number of noncustodial, nonresident biological fathers (i.e., approximately 280) in the sample. This relatively low response rate for nonresident biological fathers precluded the use of this family type in the current analyses and will limit research, policy, and programmatic implications to be drawn from analyses focused on this important ecological context for fathering. A second major limitation of this data set involves the ethnicity of families represented. Forty-six percent of the respondents were Caucasian and 41% were African

American. The numbers of Hispanic (267), Asian (64), and Native-American (19) families clearly underrepresent these populations in the CDS data set and introduce potential bias in the data on paternal roles. Such bias will require special considerations in analyses focused on cultural variations in father involvement. A third limitation of the PSID–CDS relates to the relatively low response rate on some of the instruments used for data collection. The overall response rate of PSID families contacted for the Primary Caregiver and Other Caregiver questionnaires (major sources of data used in the analyses for the present study) was 65% and 50% respectively. Although not an unusually low response rate for such a data set, it still raises questions of potential bias in data from those families who did respond. Future research is needed to explore any potential differences between PSID families who did and those who did not choose to participate in the CDS.

A fourth limitation of the PSID–CDS relates to the format of the time diary data. Although these data include information about fathers' activities with their children, it is drawn from time diary interviews with mothers. The use of mother reports on paternal engagement activities raises questions regarding the reliability and validity of the data for assessing important temporally focused dimensions of father involvement. A related problem is the large amount of missing data for these time diary entries. Whether the problem stems from the lack of information recorded in the time diaries or from the way the data were encoded is unclear. Further exploration is needed on ways to use this important source of information on father involvement.

One final limitation of the PSID–CDS that needs to be acknowledged is the problem of how to handle missing data. In conducting analyses for the current study, we used the MAR (missing at random) function of the Mplus statistical software program to handle missing data. The MAR function allows the probabilities of missing values to be computed by predicting the values based on variables that are not missing. Without inputting the missing values, the sample size drops from 2,215 to 433 complete cases. There are no easy solutions to this problem. Simply dropping incomplete cases fails to capitalize on the richness of the data set and introduces potentially biased parameter estimates. The use of mean values for variables when data are missing from individual subjects, an alternative often used for missing data, also introduces biased parameter estimates. Although the use of the MAR function with the Mplus statistical software provides a compromise solution, the problems and limitations associated with missing data need to be acknowledged when dealing with and interpreting findings from the PSID–CDS data set.

In spite of these limitations, the richness of the PSID–CDS allowed the current study to overcome many of the shortcomings of previous research on paternal roles. A major strength of this data set is its inclusion of several dimensions of paternal behaviors (e.g., responsibility, showing warmth and affection, time engaged in child-centered activities). Much of the previous research on father involvement used simple time-use measures of paternal engagement or focused

on only one dimension of paternal behavior (Hawkins & Palkovitz, 1999). Data in the PSID–CDS allow for the use of multiple measures that simultaneously tap into several different dimensions of paternal roles. A second major strength of the PSID–CDS is its multiple sources of information on the contexts in which parenting behaviors occur (e.g., mother and father reports on father's responsibility behaviors) as well as information on a variety of potential influences on parenting (e.g., maternal and paternal perceptions of the role of fathers). Beitel and Parke (1998) suggested that father–child relationships must be viewed in the context of a network of mutually interdependent relationships within the family that are part of their shared ecologies. Data in the PSID–CDS allow for such relationships to be explored.

A third strength of the PSID–CDS is its focus on child-specific fathering behaviors as opposed to generic fathering within families. Many large-scale surveys fail to identify a target child when assessing father involvement and thus do not take into account potential variations in paternal behaviors based on family composition and functioning (Cabrera, Tamis-LeMonda, Lamb & Boller, 1999; Pleck, 1997). In linking information on father involvement to a specific child, the PSID–CDS data can overcome this problem. A related advantage of the PSID–CDS involves the age ranges of the target children used for data collection. Most studies of father involvement focus on one specific age range (e.g., preschool, school-age, or adolescence), yet findings from previous research suggest there may be differences in paternal involvement patterns based on the age of the child (Pleck, 1997). Findings from the current study underscore these differences in paternal behaviors based on the age of the child and highlight how the inclusion of a wide range of ages in the target children in participant families (i.e., 3 to 12 years of age) allows the PSID–CDS data set to overcome this limitation found in previous research.

FUTURE DIRECTIONS

In conclusion, the overall richness of the PSID–CDS with its large, nationally representative database of U.S. children and their families has allowed the current study to use a multidimensional, multiperspective view of paternal parenting behaviors to provide an overall test of the Lamb–Pleck four-factor model of the determinants of father involvement. Herein lies the greatest strength of the PSID–CDS (i.e., a large, comprehensive data set that allows for testing of theoretical perspectives on the antecedents of father involvement). A relatively small number of theoretical orientations have served as the framework for much of the research examining the determinants of father involvement (e.g., the Lamb–Pleck four-factor model, Belsky's process model of parenting, identity theory, etc.). Although these theoretical perspectives have been used widely by researchers and practitioners in implicitly influencing fathering research and program development, to date little work has been conducted which explicitly sets out to simultaneously assess the

14. MULTIPLE DETERMINANTS 337

relationships between factors outlined in the models with various aspects of father involvement within a single study. The PSID–CDS provides an excellent opportunity to begin exploring the appropriateness of using these theories as frameworks for researchers as they attempt to describe, explain, and predict fathering behaviors.

As researchers begin using the PSID–CDS to test the theories that have guided much of the work done in this area, they must be cognizant of the cross-sectional nature of the data set. Information on family functioning (e.g., characteristics of the father, contextual sources of stress), father involvement, and child outcomes within the PSID–CDS data set was collected at one point in time, thus limiting the ability to make definitive conclusions about the causal relationship between the factors being examined. Even with the use of sophisticated statistical procedures, definitive causal evidence can only be extrapolated from carefully designed experimental studies. SEM and similar statistical procedures are often mistakenly used by researchers to suggest the existence of a "cause and effect" relationship among variables of interest (Schumacker & Lomax, 1996; Thompson, 2000). This is not to suggest that analyses using the PSID–CDS data set to evaluate the utility of theoretical models will be without merit. As suggested by Licht (1995), one can gain a better understanding of the nature of a phenomenon by identifying those factors with which it co-occurs. Although not conclusive, it is likely that co-occurring factors either are causally related to one another or have other causative factors in common. At a minimum, information of co-occurrence helps define the theoretical constructs involved in the phenomenon under study. In addition, one's inferences of causation can be improved by ruling out plausible alternative causal explanations. Preferably, these alternative causal explanations would be excluded by means of experimental controls in the design of future studies. The comprehensive nature of the PSID–CDS data set will allow investigators to explore and control for specified alternative explanations of causation as they test the models commonly used to guide research on fatherhood. Because little work has been done that simultaneously explores the relationships among the factors outlined in these models, the PSID–CDS provides an excellent mechanism for researchers and practitioners to test why some men are more engaged in parenting tasks than others.

ACKNOWLEDGMENTS

This research was supported in part by a grant from the American Educational Research Association which recives funds for its "AERA Grants Program" from the National Science Foundation and the National Center for Educational Statistics and Office of Educational Research and Improvement (U.S. Depaartment of Education) under NSF Graant #RED-9980573. Opinions reflect those of the authors and do not necessarily reflect those of the granting agencies. The authors would like to acknowledge the helpful comments of Joe Pleck on an earlier version of the manuscript.

REFERENCES

Barnett, R. C. & Baruch, G. K. (1987). Determinants of fathers' participation in family work. *Journal of Marriage and the Family, 49*, 29–40.

Biller, H. B. (1971). *Father, child and sex role*. Lexington, MA: Heath.

Beitel, A. H., & Parke, R. D. (1998). Parental involvement in infancy: The role of maternal and paternal attitudes. *Journal of Family Psychology, 12*, 268–288.

Cabrera, N. J., Tamis-LeMonda, C. S., Lamb, M. E., & Boller, K. (1999). *Measuring father involvement in the Early Head Start evaluation: A multidimensional conceptualization*. Paper presented at the National Conference on Health Statistics, Washington, DC.

Cabrera, N. J., Tamis-LeMonda, C. S., Bradley, R. H., Hofferth, S., & Lamb, M.E. (2000). Fatherhood in the twenty-first century. *Child Development, 71*, 127–136.

Coltrane, S. & Allan, K. (1994). "New" fathers and old stereotypes: Representations of masculinity in 1980's television advertising. *Masculinities, 2*, 1–25.

Cowan, C. P. & Cowan, P. A. (1987). Men's involvement in parenthood: Identifying the antecedents and understanding the barriers. In P. W. Berman & F. A. Pedersen (Eds.), *Men's transitions to parenthood: Longitudinal studies of early family experience* (pp. 145–174). Hillsdale, NJ: Lawrence Erlbaum Associates.

Crouter, A. C., Perry-Jenkins, M., Huston, T. L., & McHale, S. M. (1987). Processes underlying father involvement in dual-earner and single-earner families. *Developmental Psychology, 23*, 431–440.

Darling-Fisher, C. S., & Tiedje, L. B. (1990). The impact of maternal employment characteristics on fathers' participation in child care. *Family Relations, 39*, 20–26.

Deutsch, F. M., Lussier, J. B., & Servis, L. J. (1993). Husbands at home: Predictors of paternal participation in childcare and housework. *Journal of Personality and Social Psychology, 65*, 1154–1166.

Doherty, W. J., Kouneski, E. F., & Erickson, M. F. (1998). Responsible fathering: An overview and conceptual framework. *Journal of Marriage and the Family, 60*, 277–292.

Furstenburg, F. F., Jr. (1995). Fathering in the inner city: Paternal participation and public policy. In W. Marsiglio (Ed.), *Fatherhood: Contemporary theory, research, and social policy* (pp. 41–56). Thousand Oaks, CA: Sage.

Greenberg, M. & Morris, N. (1974). Engrossment: The newborn's impact upon the father. *American Journal of Orthopsychiatry, 44*, 520–531.

Griswold, R. L. (1993). *Fatherhood in America*. New York: Basic Books.

Grossman, F. K., Pollack, W. S., & Golding, E. (1988). Fathers and children: Predicting the quality and quantity of fathering. *Developmental Psychology, 24*, 82–91.

Hawkins, A. J., & Dollahite, D. C. (1997). *Generative fathering: Beyond deficit perspectives*. Thousand Oaks, CA: Sage.

Hawkins, A. J., & Palkovitz, R. (1999). Beyond ticks and clicks: The need for more diverse and broader conceptulizations and measures of father involvement. *Journal of Men's Studies, 8*, 11–32.

Hofferth, S. L. (1998). *Report on 1997 data collection for the PSID Child Development Supplement*. PSID website, http://www.isr.umich.edu.src/child-development/home.html.

Hofferth, S. L., Davis-Kean, P. E., Davis, J., & Finkelstein, J. (1998). *User guide for the Child Development Supplement of the Panel Study of Income Dynamics*. PSID website, http://www.isr.umich.edu.src/child-development/home.html.

Hofferth, S. L., Yeung, W. J., & Stafford, F. (1997). *Panel Study of Income Dynamics*. PSID website, http://www.isr.umich.edu.src/child-development/index.html.

Lamb, M. E. (1975). Fathers: Forgotten contributors to child development. *Human Development, 18*, 254–266.

Lamb, M. E. (1987). Introduction: The emergent American father. In M.E. Lamb (Ed.), *The father's role: Cross-cultural perspectives* (pp. 3–25). Hillsdale, NJ: Lawrence Erlbaum Associates.

Lamb, M. E. (Ed.). (1997). *The role of the father in child development* (3rd ed.). New York: Wiley.

Lamb, M. E., Pleck, J. H., Charnov, E. L. & Levine, J. A. (1985). Paternal behavior in humans. *American Zoologist, 25,* 883–894.

Lamb, M. E., Pleck, J. H., Charnov, E. L. & Levine, J. A. (1987). A biosocial perspective on paternal behavior and involvement. In J. Lancaster, J. Altmann, A. Rossi & L. Sherrod (Eds.), *Parenting across the lifespan: Biosocial dimensions* (pp. 111–142). New York: Aldine de Gruyter.

LaRossa, R. (1997). *The modernization of fatherhood: A social and political history.* Chicago: University of Chicago Press.

LaRossa, R., Gordon, B. A., Wilson, R. J., Bairan, A., & Jaret, C. (1991). The fluctuating image of the 20th century American father. *Journal of Marriage and the Family, 53,* 987–997.

Larson, R. W. (1993). Finding time for fatherhood: The emotional ecology of adolescent–father interactions. *New Directions for Child Development, 62,* 7–25.

Levine, J. A. & Pitt, E. W. (1995). *New expectations: Community strategies for responsible fatherhood.* New York: Families and Work Institute.

Levy-Shiff, R. & Israelashvili, R. (1988). Antecedents of fathering: Some further exploration. *Developmental Psychology, 24,* 434–440.

Licht, M. H. (1995). Multiple regression and correlation. In L. Grimm & P. Yarnold (Eds.), *Reading and understanding multivariate statistics* (pp. 19–64). Washington, DC: American Psychological Association.

Marsiglio, W. (1991). Paternal engagement activities with minor children. *Journal of Marriage and the Family, 53,* 973–986.

Marsiglio, W. (Ed.). (1995). *Fatherhood: Contemporary theory, research, and social policy.* Thousand Oaks, CA: Sage.

Marsiglio, W., Amato, P., Day, R. D., & Lamb, M. E. (2000). Scholarship on fatherhood in the 1990s and beyond. *Journal of Marriage and the Family, 62,* 1173–1191.

Meyer, D. R. (1992). Paternity and public policy. *Focus, 14,* 1–10.

McBride, B. A., & Rane, T. R. (1997). Role identity, role investments, and paternal involvement: Implications for parenting programs for men. *Early Childhood Research Quarterly, 12,* 173–197.

Muthen, L., & Muthen, B. (2000). *Mplus: User's guide.* Los Angeles, CA: Authors.

Palkovitz, R. (1997). Reconstructing "involvement": Expanding conceptualizations of men's caring in contemporary families. In A. J Hawkins & D. C. Dollahite (Eds.), *Generative fathering: Beyond deficit perspectives* (pp. 200–216). Thousand Oaks, CA: Sage.

Parke, R. D. (1981). *Fathers.* Cambridge, MA: Harvard University Press.

Parke. R. D., & Sawin, D. B. (1976). The father's role in infancy: A reevaluation. *The Family Coordinator, 25,* 365–371.

Pleck, J. H. (1997). Paternal involvement: Levels, sources, and consequences. In M. E. Lamb (Ed.), *The role of the father in child development* (3rd ed., pp. 66–103). New York: Wiley.

Pleck, J. H., Lamb, M. E., & Levine, J. A. (1986). Epilog: Facilitating future change in men's family roles. In R. A. Lewis & M. Sussman (Eds.), *Men's changing roles in the family* (pp. 11–16). New York: Haworth.

Pleck, J. H., & Stueve, J. L. (2001). Time and paternal involvement. In K. Daly (Ed.), *Minding the time in family experience: Emerging perspectives and issues* (pp. 205–226). Oxford, UK: Elsevier Science.

Radin, N. (1994). Primary-caregiving fathers in intact families. In A. E. Gottfried & A. W. Gottfried (Eds.), *Redefining families: Implications for children's development* (pp. 11–54). New York: Plenum.

Schumacker, R. E., & Lomax, R. G. (1996). *A beginner's guide to structural equation modeling.* Mahwah, NJ: Lawrence Erlbaum Associates.

Snarey, J. (1993). *How fathers care for the next generation: A four decade study.* Cambridge: Harvard University Press.

Stueve, J., & Pleck, J. H. (1997, November). *Paternal engagement: Its caretaking and development-promoting components in a diverse national sample of young adult residential fathers.* Paper presented at the National Council on Family Relations Annual Conference, Crystal City, VA.

Tamis-LeMonda, C., & Cabrera, N. (1999). Perspectives on father involvement: Research and policy. *Social Policy Report: Society for Research in Child Development, 13*(2), 1–26.

Thomas, N. G. (Ed.). (1998). U.S. policy initiative on fathering. *Social Policy Report: Society for Research in Child Development, 12*(1), 22–23.

Thompson, B. (2000). Ten commandments of structural equation modeling. In L. Grimm & P. Yarnold (Eds.), *Reading and understanding multivariate statistics* (pp. 261–283). Washington, DC: American Psychological Association.

Volling, B.L., & Belsky, J. (1991). Multiple determinants of father involvement during infancy in dual-earner and single-earner families. *Journal of Marriage and the Family, 53,* 461– 474.

Woodworth, S. J., Belsky, J., & Crnic, K. (1996). The determinants of fathering during the child's second and third years of life: A developmental analysis. *Journal of Marriage and the Family, 58,* 679–692.

15

Measuring Mother and Father Shared Caregiving: An Analysis Using the Panel Study of Income Dynamics–Child Development Supplement

Allison Sidle Fuligni
University of California, Los Angeles

Jeanne Brooks-Gunn
Teachers College, Columbia University

The concept of the role of fathers in families has been evolving in recent years. Rather than being primarily responsible for the material support of the family as prescribed by the traditional American father role, fathers are now considered to have an important role to play in the daily lives of their children. Fathers are expected to directly interact with their children, be available to them, and be responsible for their care (Lamb, Pleck, Charnov, & Levine, 1987). Concurrently with the expansion of the father's expected role, rates of employment among married mothers of young children have been rising dramatically, making the two-working-parent family the predominant pattern in two-parent households with children under 5 years of age. The higher rates of employment of mothers with young children opens the possibility and opportunity (as well as potential necessity) for fathers in these families to contribute greater amounts of time and responsibility to the daily care of their children.

Data from a number of studies suggest that the amount of time fathers spend engaged with their children has been increasing since as early as 1924, and certainly

341

from the 1960s to the present (Pleck, 1997). Such findings provide evidence that the expanded expectation for fathers to interact with their children is accompanied by a true increase in the time fathers contribute to such interactions. However, although there is an ideal and an actual increase in the engagement of fathers in their children's lives, this involvement should be considered in the context of mothers' involvement with children. Mothers typically provide the majority of daily care for young children, even though contemporary fathers spend more time with their children than fathers of previous generations. In the 1970s and 1980s researchers reported that fathers' engagement with children was about a third that of mothers (Lamb, Pleck, & Levine, 1985; Goldberg, Michaels, & Lamb, 1985) and rose to about 43% of mothers' engagement in the 1990s (Pleck, 1997). Thus, the historical increase in the time fathers spend with children has not displaced mothers from the primary caregiving role, with respect to the amount of time each contributes to interacting with their children.

In this chapter, we explore patterns of father involvement in daily caregiving responsibilities with young children and consider these patterns relative to mother's involvement. By exploring father involvement within the context of its effects on mother involvement, we examine the notion of "shared caregiving." Using data from a nationally representative sample of American families, we present two approaches to measuring the extent to which caregiving is shared by mothers and fathers across multiple domains of caring for young children. The overall prevalence of shared caregiving is described, including consideration of the specific domains in which fathers show higher and lower rates of involvement and the effects of father involvement on patterns of maternal involvement across various domains of caregiving.

We begin with a brief theoretical overview. In this introduction, we (a) justify our focus on young children in two-parent families by framing it within the context of the transition to parenthood and the developmental significance of the first 3 years of life, (b) briefly review the literature on father involvement with young children, and (c) develop the concept of shared caregiving in two-parent families with young children.

THE TRANSITION TO PARENTHOOD

The arrival of a new baby in a family is a significant transition period for both first-time parents and those who already have children. New parents must adjust their roles within the family to accommodate the newcomer, who is virtually helpless and requires feeding, changing, and soothing 24 hours a day. The care that young children require is physically demanding, emotionally intense, and continuous; the transition to being a new parent is therefore both physically and emotionally challenging (Antonucci & Mikus, 1998). New parents must navigate the emotional challenges of redefining their roles as new parents or parents of a

15. MOTHER AND FATHER SHARED CAREGIVING   343

now-larger family while generally suffering from a sudden constant lack of sleep that typically characterizes this period.

We focus our analysis on two-parent families and their patterns of caring for children under 3 years of age. We have chosen this young age group for several reasons. First, the time period from birth to 3 years old has received much recent attention from developmentalists, policymakers, and the popular press as more information has emerged identifying the importance of infants' experiences on the brain development occurring during these years (Shonkoff & Phillips, 2000). Second, as we mentioned before, as we are interested in the patterns that couples arrange for themselves during their transition to parenthood. We believe early parenting patterns will set the stage for the division of parenting responsibilities later in the child's life. Third, the continuing growth in maternal employment rates for children under age 3 means that fewer mothers will be taking sole responsibility for caregiving in the early years, which could result in other patterns of family caregiving.

Father Involvement

Pleck's (1997) review of paternal involvement studies conducted in the 1980s and 1990s summarized child and father characteristics that are related to levels of paternal involvement. Generally, studies find that fathers spend more time with sons than with daughters, although this gender difference is not documented for very young children. Fathers' involvement declines as children get older, but their involvement with children relative to mothers' involvement with children increases over time. Some studies find that fathers' proportional share of interactions with children is higher in families with more children and that fathers tend to be more involved with their first-born children than their later-born children. There is not a straightforward relationship between father characteristics of race, education, occupation, or income and paternal involvement with young children. However, some characteristics of mothers are related to levels of father involvement. In particular, fathers take on larger proportions of involvement with their children when mothers are employed outside the home, but there has been no relationship found between mothers' educational attainment and fathers' involvement.

Father involvement in direct interaction with children can provide benefits to children. When fathers perform 40% or more of the total family child care, preschool children exhibit positive outcomes in cognitive and social–emotional domains (Radin, 1994). In addition, paternal involvement with a new baby can be beneficial for the father—it is associated with better adjustment to parenthood and more positive marital outcomes (Goldberg et al., 1985). Mothers who are responsible for the vast majority of the care of the new baby report more marital difficulties (Goldberg et al., 1985). When couples share equally in the care of their children, there are positive consequences for the family: more successful parent–child relationships and enhanced child development, which is supported by the stability of commitment from both parents (Biller, 1993).

Measuring Father Involvement

Traditional approaches to measuring father involvement have tended to focus on either the overall amount of time fathers spend with children or reports of which spouse tends to be responsible for which family or household duties. Some investigators have reported absolute amounts of time that fathers spend with their children, on a daily or weekly basis, and comment on historical patterns (Pleck, 1997; Yeung, Sandberg, Davis-Kean, & Hofferth, 2001). Others focus on fathers' time use relative to that of mothers, reporting variations in the proportional contribution of fathers (Almeida, Maggs, & Galambos, 1987). When looking at reports of household and childrearing responsibility, researchers typically rely on self- or spouse-reported answers to stylized questions, revealing perceptions about whether family members consider themselves to be primarily responsible for certain areas or whether responsibility is shared.

Both the proportional-time use and the shared-responsibility approaches encompass an underlying notion of measuring "shared caregiving." In this paper, we propose various ways of measuring shared caregiving. We consider this concept to encompass the extent to which two parents share responsibility for childrearing by (1) spending comparable amounts of time caring for the child, (2) spending time in childrearing together, and (3) reporting shared responsibility across a range of childrearing domains.

How can estimates of father involvement provide a picture of the involvement's effect on the functioning of the family? Can a measure of "shared caregiving" help to illustrate the caregiving provided by mothers and fathers, separately and together, across various domains of caregiving activities? In the analyses presented below, we attempt to address the following research questions:

1. How much time do fathers of young children spend in activities with them? Which types of activities do fathers engage in most?
2. How does the amount of time fathers spend with children relate to the time mothers spend in these activities with children alone (i.e., without the father)? Do relatively higher levels of time involvement by fathers result in more coparenting time, or do they reduce the amount of time that mothers devote to interacting with children?
3. How do spouse reports of responsibility for caregiving relate to the actual amount of time parents spend with their children in different caregiving activities?

Some of our previous research in the area of self-reports of child-caregiving responsibilities suggests that a fair number of fathers share this responsibility with their spouses (Fuligni & Brooks-Gunn, 2002). In a nationally representative sample of 1,549 two-parent families with children under 3 years, we found that 36% of the survey respondents (who were both mothers and fathers) felt that they

15. MOTHER AND FATHER SHARED CAREGIVING 345

shared responsibility for child caregiving equally with their spouse or partner. Furthermore, we found that mothers and fathers seem to be in agreement about who provides the majority of care. Thirty-seven percent of fathers and 36% of mothers said they shared the daily care of their child about equally with their spouse or partner. Of the mothers, 62% claimed they had primary responsibility and 2% said that their spouse did. Consistent with these figures, 3% of fathers reported providing the majority of care for their young child, and 60% said their spouse or partner provided more. These figures support the common belief that mothers are the primary caretakers of very young children, but a sizable proportion of families seem to be practicing some form of shared caregiving.

However, these data came from a single interview item and reflect a global perception of child-care responsibility. To address the complexities of caring for young children across many domains of caregiving (including bathing, feeding, dressing, playing, disciplining, and managing children's activities), we turned to the Panel Study of Income Dynamics–Child Development Supplement (PSID–CDS), which includes extensive details about patterns of caregiving in terms of perceptions of responsibility as well as time committed to caregiving.

METHODS

The Panel Study of Income Dynamics (PSID) is a longitudinal, nationally representative survey that has been collecting data annually since 1968 on the income, employment, composition, and demographic changes of U.S. families. In 1997, the PSID added a Child Development Supplement (CDS) to collect data from parents and their 0- to 12-year-old children on child development, parenting, and schooling ($N = 3,563$). To answer our questions about shared caregiving of young children, we extracted a subsample of 534 two-parent families with a child under age 3. After randomly selecting only one sibling per family in cases where 2 children under age 3 came from one family, the sample size was 493. This sample is 71% White, with 94% of fathers employed and 55% of mothers employed outside the home (see Table 15.1).

Measuring Shared Caregiving in the PSID–CDS

There are two main sources of information on childrearing patterns in the PSID–CDS: (1) a household questionnaire ($N = 332$), which is an interview with the child's primary caregiver (who in 99% of cases was the mother of the child); and (2) a time diary of children's activities during two 24-hour periods, including one weekday and one weekend day ($N = 476$).

To create a measure of *perceived shared caregiving*, we used responses to a set of items in the household questionnaire. A set of 16 questions asked the primary caregiver to indicate who generally does various household tasks, including

TABLE 15.1
PSID–CDS Two-Parent Families With Children
Under 3 Years

Characteristics	Percent of Sample
Mother's education:	
High school or less	46
Some college or more	54
Father's education:	
High school or less	46
Some college or more	54
Parent employment:	
Employed mothers	55
Employed fathers	94
Child race/ethnicity:	
White	70
Black	8
Hispanic	15
Asian and other	7
Child age:	
Under 12 months	25
12–23 months	35
24–35 months	40

child-related responsibilities. Respondents answered "self," "shared with someone in the household," or "someone else in the household." Although the "shared" answer choice does not explicitly specify that the other person in the household is the father, we feel that this answer choice represents a reasonable estimate of shared responsibility with fathers, given that all of these are two-parent households with fathers present. Nevertheless, it is important to remember when interpreting these results that some nonfather household residents may be included in the "shared" responses. These might be other relatives, including grandparents or older siblings. Although we loosely interpret this category to imply tasks that are shared with the father, it can certainly be considered to represent mothers' perceptions that she shares responsibility for these tasks with someone in the household.

When the 16 items in this questionnaire were entered into a factor analysis, seven of the child-related tasks loaded onto a single factor, whereas the item "buying children's clothes" loaded onto another factor with the rest of the daily household tasks. Based on this result, we created an overall score for *perceived shared caregiving* based on the first seven items listed in Table 15.2. These items were recoded as 1 = shared and 0 = not shared, and the seven items were averaged. Therefore, scores on this scale range from 0 to 1 and can be thought of as the proportion of childrearing tasks that are considered to be shared (i.e., 1 = all seven tasks are shared; 0 = all seven tasks are not shared). The scale had an acceptable reliability of Cronbach's alpha = .76. The overall mean was .60, indicating that primary caregivers perceive 60% of these childrearing tasks to be shared.

15. MOTHER AND FATHER SHARED CAREGIVING

TABLE 15.2
Caregiving and Household Responsibilities

Activity	Shared	Mother	Someone Else
Child-related tasks:			
Playing with children	89%	10%	1%
Bathing/changing diapers	56%	42%	2%
Disciplining children	85%	14%	1%
Driving children to activities	54%	40%	6%
Choosing children's activities	66%	32%	3%
Making pediatrician appts.	23%	75%	2%
Selecting child care	49%	49%	2%
Daily household tasks:			
Buying children's clothes	33%	65%	2%
Preparing meals	27%	68%	6%
Washing dishes	39%	54%	7%
Cleaning house	40%	54%	6%
Grocery shopping	37%	57%	6%
Washing, ironing, mending	24%	72%	4%
Paying bills	26%	50%	24%
Household maintenance	30%	9%	61%
Auto maintenance	16%	5%	79%

Note: Data from Household Questionnaire; *N*s are 317–332.

Other information about patterns of shared caregiving came from time diaries completed by parents describing all of the child's activities over two 24-hour periods (1 weekday and 1 weekend day). In our sample of two-parent families with young children, 476 completed a time diary. For these young children, a parent completed the time diaries, specifying for the 24-hour period each activity of the child, its duration, and the person or people who participated in each activity with the child. Based on this information, we were able to identify the total amount of time that the child spent with his or her mother, father, or both parents. We calculated these times for a variety of domains of activity. The main categories of activity that young children engaged in with their parents were *personal care activities* (including dressing, bathing, diaper changing, and being fed), *meals* (including joint eating activities—not passively being fed, but eating together), *active play* (outside play, rough-and-tumble play, motor activity), *quiet play* (indoor games, pretend play, coloring), *TV*, *reading* (including being read to), *shopping*, *social interaction* (conversation, visiting or receiving visitors, attending church and other social functions), and *travel to activities*.[1]

---

[1]Categories not included in this list because of extremely low daily participation rates with parents are school/child care, housework, other activities (such as musical activities, lessons, watching others do activities), and sleep. When children's total time in all of these categories are added together, including those described in the text above and the low-parent-involvement categories mentioned here, they account for most of a young child's day (an average of 23 hours, 37 minutes).

To explore the extent that fathers contribute to child caregiving, as well as the effect of fathers' interaction time on the amount of time that mothers interact with children, we calculated both absolute and proportional estimates of fathers' time in activities with children. For each activity category, we calculated the average number of minutes children spent in activities with their mother alone (father not involved), father alone (mother not involved), and with both parents together. Using these values, we calculated a *father time proportion* for weekdays and weekends. This proportion differs from the traditional approach of dividing father time by mother time. Instead, we constructed the father time proportion to represent the amount of time that a child spent with any parent in which the father was engaged. Using the traditional father/mother time ratio would result in a loss of any cases in which mothers' time was zero and father time was not zero. For example, on a given day a child may spend 60 minutes playing outside with her father, and no time in active play with her mother. These cases are of extreme importance in our estimates: We want to be certain to include those cases when the full amount of parenting time a child received was with the father. Therefore, we calculated the total parenting time in each activity (mother and father together + father alone time [without mother] + mother alone time [without father]). Next, we calculated the proportion of this total parenting time in which the father was engaged (all father time/total parenting time). Using this measure, a value of 1.00 indicates that 100% of time the child spent with a parent was spent with the father involved, and .5 means that the father was engaged during half of parenting time.

This approach to creating a proportional measure of father involvement is useful for several reasons. First, as already mentioned, it preserves important cases in the data set in which fathers were the only parent who spent time with the child in a particular activity. Preserving these cases is important when considering fathers' proportional time contribution because we are conducting analyses of specific activity categories rather than simply reporting total time across activities. There are some activities during any given day that a parent may not engage in with a child. For instance, in the case of quiet indoor play, there were 66 cases in which mothers did not spend any time with their child on a weekend day, but fathers did. Thus the sample of children with a valid father-time proportion for this category was 311 and included the 66 cases where fathers provided 100% of parental interaction in that activity on that day. Scores are only missing in this method of calculation if there was no time spent by either parent in each activity.

Another advantage to using total parenting time as the denominator when calculating fathers' proportional time contribution is that it sets the range of possible values at 1.0. Traditional father/mother time ratios have an essentially limitless range of possible values. A father may spend a full hour with a child and mother 1 minute, resulting in a score of 60 (60/1). If that mother spent 2 minutes with the child, the score would be cut in half to 30 (60/2). Using total parenting time as the denominator, the scores in these two scenarios would be 60/61 = 98% and

15. MOTHER AND FATHER SHARED CAREGIVING   349

$60/62 = 97\%$, respectively, more accurately portraying the proportion of the child's time in which the father was involved.

RESULTS AND DISCUSSION

In Table 15.2, we present the response paterns for the perceived shared caregiving questionnaire items. The pattern of responses reveals that the highest rates of perceived shared responsibility are in the areas of playing with and disciplining children. The more managerial tasks such as making pediatrician appointments tend to fall more heavily on the mother. Although one might conceive of an approach to "shared caregiving" in which parents divide up the tasks, with one parent taking primary responsibility for some and the other parent taking responsibility for the others, we did not find evidence of this type of sharing. According to these reports, all childrearing tasks are either shared or primarily the mother's responsibility.

Patterns of time use in activities with parents on weekdays and weekend days are presented in Table 15.3. For each day, the first two columns show the average amount of time that the mother or father was engaged in each activity with the child and without the other parent. The third column shows time that both parents interacted with the child together. The fourth column presents the father-time proportion as described earlier.

The data presented in Table 15.3 provide information on several types of variation in parent–child interaction time. First, the data illustrate the amount of time parents spend in different activities with children. We can see that for children under 3 years of age, a fair amount of time is spent with parents eating meals, playing indoors, and traveling (i.e., driving to activities). Another category that has a high total time with parents is personal care. As we might expect, children under 3 years require a fair amount of adult participation in daily dressing, feeding, and bathing activities. Surprisingly low, however, is the average number of minutes parents spend in reading activities with their young children. Although children spend 21 minutes with one or both parents watching television on weekdays, they spend only an average of 8 minutes together in reading activities. It is difficult to compare this finding with data from other studies because there is no comparable source of time-use data for this age group. However, other studies of early childhood have shown that parents report any daily reading to their children under age 3 at relatively low rates (e.g., Britto, Fuligni, & Brooks-Gunn 2002; Love et al., 2001).

Second, we can compare the amounts of time each parent spends with the child, both within and across activity categories. On weekdays, for instance, mothers spend substantially more time in each activity than fathers. The largest discrepancies appear in the categories that represent the most time overall: meals, playing, and personal care. Fathers contribute the most time in absolute terms to playing with children, and the most joint mother-and-father time is spent in mealtime engagement.

TABLE 15.3
Time in Activities With Parents

	Weekday (N = 439)				Weekend Day (N = 431)			
Activity	Mother-Only Time	Father-Only Time	Mother and Father Time	Father Proportion	Mother-Only Time	Father-Only Time	Mother and Father Time	Father Proportion
Personal care	0:36	0:06	0:01	.19	0:39	0:09	0:03	.23
Meals	0:45	0:07	0:18	.41	0:39	0:09	0:33	.54
Active play	0:13	0:06	0:03	.39	0:11	0:09	0:14	.63
Quiet play	0:49	0:19	0:09	.45	0:27	0:22	0:32	.66
TV	0:12	0:04	0:05	.46	0:11	0:07	0:13	.68
Reading	0:06	0:01	0:01	.30	0:03	0:02	0:02	.50
Shopping	0:11	0:01	0:03	.28	0:13	0:01	0:13	.56
Social interaction	0:08	0:02	0:02	.39	0:13	0:05	0:23	.57
Travel to activities	0:32	0:05	0:08	.30	0:19	0:05	0:32	.68
Total*	3:49	0:58	0:55	.42	3:10	1:19	2:59	.60

Note. The "Total" category includes time with parents in all of the above categories plus a small "other" category and does not necessarily add directly from the numbers in the column above because of slightly different sample sizes for each activity category.

15. MOTHER AND FATHER SHARED CAREGIVING   351

Third, we can determine how parenting time in each activity differs on weekends versus weekdays. It is noteworthy that the total amount of time each parent spends with children increases on weekends. (Father time increases by over 2 hours; from 2 hours 17 minutes to 4 hours, 37 minutes mother time by about 1.5 hours from 4 hours, 44 minutes to 6 hours 12 minutes.) A similar finding for the PSID–CDS sample as a whole has been reported elsewhere (Yeung et al., 2001).

Using the data in Table 15.3 to help conceptualize shared caregiving, we turn to the fourth column for each day: the father-time proportion. Note that on weekdays, this father-time proportion is less than 50% in every activity category, whereas on weekend days the proportion is over 50% in most categories. On weekdays, father-time proportions approach 50% for quiet play and watching TV. The category with the highest relative amount of father involvement is TV time on weekend days. Other activities with high proportions of father involvement on weekends are quiet play and traveling to activities. Based on these results, we might say that caregiving is truly shared on weekend days in almost every category except for personal care, which continues to be the mother's domain.

Another way to think of shared caregiving is to focus solely on the time that both parents actually spend together in caregiving activities. Higher values on this shared parenting time result in higher father-time proportions. When mothers spend more time without father participation in caregiving, the father-time proportion is lower. The columns from Table 15.3 representing the time mothers and fathers spend together in particular activities with their children reveal that on weekdays there is relatively little overlap between mothers' and fathers' time. Mothers are doing a lot of caregiving without fathers present on weekdays, which is not a surprising finding given the high rate of father employment in this sample. Presumably, these fathers do not have a lot of time to spend with their young children on weekdays, and the most efficient way to meet family needs may entail parents' engaging in childrearing activities in sequence rather than together. The values for the amount of time spent together in caregiving on weekend days give more of a sense of "shared caregiving," as there is much more time that mothers and fathers spend together with their young children. Again, however, much of this shared time is spent in play and watching TV.

The increased time investment by fathers on weekend days results in a reduction, not in the amount of time mothers are spending with their children, but the amount of time they are spending with their children without father involvement. In particular, mothers spend less time without fathers on weekend days in traveling to activities and having meals with children than they do on weekdays. On the other hand, there is virtually no change in the division of labor or shared caregiving in personal care on weekend days. Here, the father proportion time is lowest; even though fathers have increased their relative share of other activities on weekend days, mothers continue to be primarily responsible for personal care of young children.

Our two measures of shared caregiving, then, provide slightly different pictures. According to the measure of perceived sharing, 60% of child caregiving

responsibilities are shared. But fathers contribute half or more of parenting time in none of the child caregiving areas on weekdays and in eight of nine areas on weekend days. The father-time proportions across all activity categories are .42 on weekdays and .60 on weekends. So, how is perceived shared caregiving related to the time-use measures?

Bivariate correlations between these measures are significant but small: perceived sharing and weekday father-time proportion are correlated at .19 and perceived sharing and weekend time proportion are correlated at .17 ($p < .01$). (Bivariate correlations between the perceived shared caregiving measure and the amount of time parents spend together in caregiving were nonsignificant at .07 for mother and father time on weekdays and .08 for mother and father time on weekends.) To explore these associations further, we divided the questionnaire scale into those reporting that half or more of the caregiving tasks were shared (.50 or greater on the perceived shared caregiving scale) and those reporting that fewer than half of these tasks were shared (under .50). We found that when parents report higher rates of shared caregiving across the seven questionnaire items, fathers also exhibit higher proportions of parenting time, both on weekdays and weekends, but particularly on weekdays (see Fig. 15.1). Father time on weekdays is just under one-third of total parenting time in families who describe themselves as not sharing most childrearing duties. But in these self-reported low-sharing families, weekend father caregiving is still over 50% of the total time. On the other hand, in families where most caregiving is perceived to be shared, father's proportion

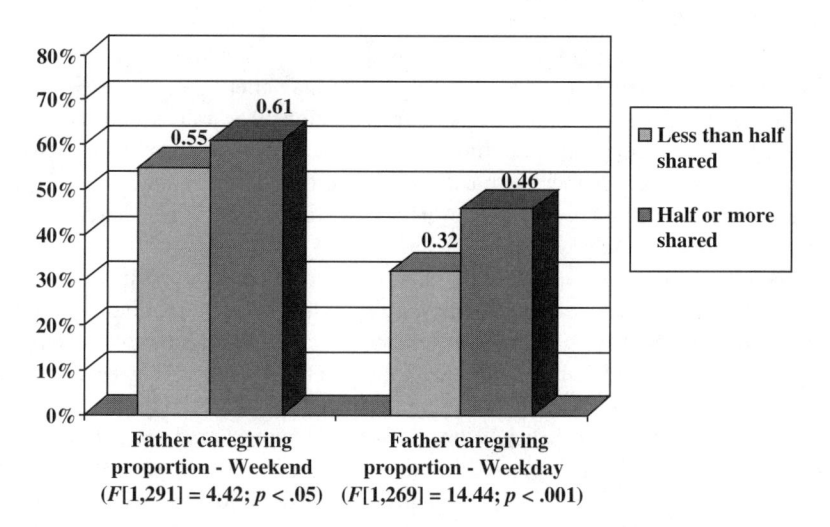

FIG. 15.1. Proportion of parenting time spent by father according to proportion of child caregiving activities that primary caregiver reports are shared.

15. MOTHER AND FATHER SHARED CAREGIVING   353

approaches half even on the weekdays. Thus we might conclude that perceived shared caregiving requires a substantial input during the week, and that mothers (the primary reporters on the perceived measure) do not consider higher levels of involvement on weekends only to constitute true sharing.

To explore the relationship between perceived shared caregiving and time use in more detail, we made similar comparisons for specific activity categories that seem analogous across the two measures. For instance, we compared patterns of parent time involvement in personal care activities for families who reported that responsibility for bathing and changing diapers" was shared versus those in which the mother claimed primary responsibility for these activities. Similarly, time use in the travel category was compared for families in which the mother said driving children to activities was shared and those in which the mother reported this to be her primary responsibility. Finally, both quiet play and active play time-use patterns were compared against mothers' reports of sharing responsibility for playing with children.

Results of these analyses are presented in Table 15.4. These numbers mimic to some extent the findings just presented regarding the more global measures of time use and perceived shared caregiving, but they illustrate some variation across activity categories. For the categories of personal care and travel (or driving children to activities), the perception that responsibility is shared is associated with higher father-time proportions on weekdays. In the case of personal care, perceived sharing of responsibility was also associated with a higher father-time proportion on weekends. Nevertheless, the father-time proportions for personal care remain well below 50% on both weekdays and weekends even in the families where such activities are perceived to be shared.

The item reflecting perceived shared responsibility for playing with children was less compelling in terms of its association with patterns of time use in parental playing with children. With respect to quiet indoor play, there was virtually no difference in father-time proportions when mothers reported shared responsibility or that they were primarily responsible for playing with children. In fact, when mothers reported sharing responsibility for playing with children, the father-time proportion on weekends was actually somewhat lower than in families whose mothers felt primarily responsible for playing. In the case of active play, perceived sharing followed the more general pattern in that it was associated with a higher father-time proportion on weekdays but not weekend days. Therefore, these findings generally support the notion that perceptions of shared caregiving are more strongly associated with patterns of fathers' time contributions on weekdays than on weekends. Also similar to the earlier findings, father-time proportions were under 50% on weekdays and well over 50% on weekends across all activities with a striking exception of personal care. Interestingly, when mothers perceived the responsibility for bathing and changing children to be shared, fathers' time contributions to personal care activities not only were higher but also varied little between weekends and weekdays.

TABLE 15.4
Time in Activities With Parents, According to Perceived Shared Responsibilities

Perceived Shared Caregiving Item/Activity	Weekday				Weekend Day			
	Mother-Only Time	Father-Only Time	Mother and Father Time	Father Proportion	Mother-Only Time	Father-Only Time	Mother and Father Time	Father Proportion
Bathing and changing/Personal care								
Mother	0:38	0:03	0:01	.11	0:42	0:07	0:01	.18
Shared	0:37	0:09	0:02	.23	0:39	0:11	0:04	.27
Driving children/Travel								
Mother	0:39	0:02	0:07	.18	0:24	0:02	0:27	.64
Shared	0:29	0:09	0:11	.40	0:15	0:06	0:33	.69
Playing with children/Quiet play								
Mother	0:58	0:11	0:11	.41	0:29	0:23	0:29	.72
Shared	0:44	0:20	0:10	.45	0:28	0:21	0:36	.67
Playing with children/Active play								
Mother	0:23	0:00	0:03	.12	0:13	0:02	0:41	.67
Shared	0:13	0:08	0:01	.38	0:12	0:09	0:12	.59

CONCLUSIONS AND IMPLICATIONS

In this paper we presented several ways of measuring and thinking about shared caregiving among two-parent families with children under 3 years of age. The findings show that variation exists in patterns of shared caregiving when specific domains of caregiving are measured and compared. For instance, in terms of absolute time, mothers and fathers spend more time eating meals together with children than in many other activities. Especially on weekdays, there are few other activities in which mothers and fathers engage for very many minutes on average together with their children. In terms of the proportion of parenting time that fathers contribute to caregiving, variation also exists according to activity category. Fathers are engaged for higher proportions of parenting time in activities like playing with children than in providing their personal care.

In addition, we argue that measurement of fathers' proportional contribution to parenting time should be conceived as a proportion of the total amount of time that the child engages with any parent, rather than as a straight ratio of fathers' time divided by mothers' time spent with children. Theoretically, this approach considers the experience of the child to be central and creates a range of possible values that is easier to interpret with respect to the child's experience of total time with parents. This approach also maximizes the number of valid cases, especially when analysis of categories with low participation rates makes this an important issue. We believe that both absolute parenting time and proportional time measures are necessary to illustrate the time contributions parents make to their children. For instance, in the case of reading, we found that father-time proportions were moderate (.30 on weekdays and .50 on weekends), however the actual absolute time spent by parents in this activity was low overall (average total parenting time was 8 minutes on both weekdays and weekend days). We presented absolute time measurements of the amount of time mothers and fathers spend together in caring for their children, allowing for comparison with the amount of time each parent spent in caregiving without the participation of the other parent. Each of these separate pieces of information (time parents spend together, time each spends alone, and the proportional father-time measure) allows for a more nuanced consideration of what may be considered to be shared caregiving.

The availability of separate time diary data for weekdays and weekend days also helped to illustrate variations in parenting. Consideration of the time parents spend together in caregiving as well as the father-time proportions revealed that fathers are able to contribute more time to caregiving on weekend days. Generally, fathers' increased time results in higher rates of caring for children together with mothers on weekend days, and reduces the burden on mothers who have higher rates of caring for children without fathers on weekdays.

In this paper we also found that patterns of shared caregiving vary by type of measure. We reported responses to survey items related to perceived shared caregiving, which appeared to reflect higher levels of shared caregiving than actual sharing in terms of time spent with children. We found that many fathers appear to be spending significant amounts of time on average with their young children, particularly on weekends, although this time is spent mostly in playing and leisure activities. Given these findings, and the higher rates of mother-and-father time and father-time proportions on weekends, we might conclude that these measures indicate more shared caregiving on weekend days than on weekdays. The inclusion of data on perceived shared caregiving adds another dimension to such a conclusion. For instance, fathers' time contribution to the personal care of their young children is low overall, even though mothers are likely to report that activities such as bathing and changing diapers are shared, suggesting that for this category even a low time contribution by fathers is perceived as sharing responsibility. Upon exploration of associations between perceived shared caregiving and parenting time use, we found that perceived shared caregiving in other activity domains was more strongly related to patterns of parental time contributions on weekdays than on weekends. In fact, patterns of fathers' time contribution on weekend days were relatively high regardless of whether the families reported high or low levels of perceived shared responsibility for caregiving.

In conclusion, these data argue for a more nuanced and expanded conceptualization of shared caregiving. Looking simply at overall levels of time that fathers spend with children overlooks the fact that much of this time is spent playing or engaging in meals. Measuring time use in specific activities reveals the very low levels of father involvement in providing direct physical care for their children during these early years. Furthermore, attention to variations across weekdays and weekend days and to the amount of time parents spend in caregiving activities together represents an important direction for research in this area. These data illustrate how increases in father engagement with children on weekends impact both the time use of the mother and the experience of the child, who receives more time with both parents together on weekends. Comparing the time data with the perceived sharing measure illustrates the limitations of drawing conclusions from only one of these types of data alone. Together, the data allow us to consider the value to mothers of fathers' increased engagement with children on weekdays.

We have not considered how these caregiving arrangements are negotiated or arrived at by families, nor how these variations affect the overall functioning and well-being of the family. Although the previous father involvement literature suggested that higher levels of father involvement, particularly in providing personal care for children, is beneficial to child development, we await the upcoming longitudinal follow-up of these families to assess the impact on children of shared caregiving in the various ways we defined it in this study.

ACKNOWLEDGMENTS

The authors are grateful for funding from the MacArthur Network on Family and the Economy and the National Institute of Child Health and Development's Child Well-Being Research Network.

REFERENCES

Almeida, D. M., Maggs, J. L., & Galambos, N. L. (1987). Wives' employment hours and spousal participation in family work. *Journal of Family Psychology, 7*(2), 233–244.

Antonucci, T. C., & Mikus, K. (1988). The power of parenthood: Personality and attitudinal changes during the transition to parenthood. In G. Y. Michaels & W. A. Goldberg (Eds.), *The transition to parenthood: Current theory and research* (pp. 62–84). Cambridge: Cambridge University Press.

Biller, H. B. (1993). *Fathers and families: Paternal factors in child development.* Westport, CT: Auburn House/Greenwood.

Britto, P. R., Fuligni, A. S., & Brooks-Gunn, J. (2002). Reading, rhymes, and routines: American parents and their young children. In N. Halfon, K. T. McLearn, & M. S. Schuster (Eds.). *Child rearing in America: Challenges facing parents with young children* (pp. 117–145). Cambridge: Cambridge University Press.

Deutsch, F. M. (2000). *Halving it all: How equally shared parenting works.* Cambridge, MA: Harvard University Press.

Fuligni, A. S., & Brooks-Gunn, J. (2002). Meeting the challenges of new parenthood: Responsibilities, Advice, and Perceptions. In N. Halfon, K. T. McLearn, & M. S. Schuster (Eds.), *Child rearing in America: Challenges facing parents with young children* (pp. 83–116). Cambridge: Cambridge University Press.

Goldberg, W. A., Michaels, G. Y., & Lamb, M. E. (1985). Husbands' and wives' adjustment to pregnancy and first parenthood. *Journal of Family Issues, 6,* 483–503.

Lamb, M. E., Pleck, J. H., Charnov, E. L., & Levine, J. A. (1987). A biosocial perspective on paternal behavior and involvement. In J. B. Lancaster, J. Altmann, A. S. Rossi, & R. R. Sherrod (Eds.), *Parenting across the lifespan: Biosocial perspectives* (pp. 111–142). Hawthorne, NY: Aldine.

Lamb, M. E., Pleck, J. H., & Levine, J. A. (1985). The role of the father in child development: The effects of increased paternal involvement. In B. Lahey & A. Kazdin (Eds.), *Advances in clinical child psychology* (Vol. 8, pp. 229–266). New York: Plenum.

Love, J. M., Kisker, E. E., Ross, C., M., Schochet, P. Z., Brooks-Gunn, J., Boller, K., Paulsell, D., Fuligni, A. S., & Berlin, L. J. (2001). *Building their futures: How Early Head Start programs are enhancing the lives of infants and toddlers in low-income families.* Washington, DC: U.S. Department of Health and Human Services.

Pleck, J. H. (1997). Paternal involvement: Levels, sources, and consequences. In M. E. Lamb (Ed.), *The role of the father in child development,* (3rd ed., pp. 66–103). New York: Wiley.

Radin, N. (1994). Primary-caregiving fathers in intact families. In A. E. Gottfried & A. W. Gottfried (Eds.), *Redefining families: Implications for children's development* (pp. 55–97). New York: Plenum.

Shonkoff, J., & Phillips, D. A. (Eds.). (2000). *From neurons to neighborhoods.* Washington, DC: National Academy Press.

Yeung, W. J., Sandberg, J. F., Davis-Kean, P. E., & Hofferth, S. L. (2001). Children's time with fathers in intact families. *Journal of Marriage and the Family, 63,* 136–154.

16

Violent Men, Bad Dads? Fathering Profiles of Men Involved in Intimate Partner Violence

Greer Litton Fox
University of Tennessee

Michael L. Benson
University of Cincinnati

The extensive research and clinical literature on family violence gives surprisingly little attention to the father roles of men who batter their female partners (Holden, Stein, Ritchie, Harris, & Jouriles, 1998; Sternberg, 1996). Likewise, the growing literature on fathering has largely ignored the subset of fathers who are physically violent toward the mothers of their children (Booth & Crouter, 1998; Phares, 1992; Silverstein & Phares, 1996). This paper helps to fill this gap in the literature by focusing on evidence of the involvement in fathering of men who have been identified as physically aggressive toward their wives or partners in intimate relationships and comparing violent men to their nonviolent counterparts.

National data on rates and types of intrafamilial assault indicate that at least some men who are assaultive in one role, such as husband/partner, are also assaultive in other familial and extrafamilial relationships (Saunders, 1993). Data from a subsample of two-parent families with at least one child from the 1985 National Family Violence Survey suggest that of 512 families with self-reported violent incidents involving an assaultive husband/father, 31% involved child abuse only, 23% involved both wife and child abuse, and 45% involved wife assault but not child abuse (Hotaling, Straus, & Lincoln, 1989; our recalculations of their Table 11,

359

pp. 360–361). Data from the Study of Marital Instability over the Life Course, a national panel survey of 2,034 married couples, indicated the co-occurrence of marital and child physical aggression in a substantial subset of ongoing marriages (McNeal & Amato, 1998). The occurrence of physical violence in relationships that subsequently dissolve is higher than that found in ongoing relationships (DeMaris, 2000), and in studies that include dissolving as well as ongoing relationships, cited rates of the co-occurrence of child abuse and wife assault range from 30 to 70% (Jaffe & Geffner, 1998).

Many have noted the difficulty in differentiating between men who batter and men in general in terms of sociodemographic or personality characteristics (Gondolf, 1993; Hotaling & Sugarman, 1986). Where social correlates with violence are found, typically in large sample surveys, younger age, Black racial identity, and lower socioeconomic status are often associated with battering (Greenfeld et al., 1998; Rennison & Welchans, 2000). Small clinical studies have attempted to identify predominant character traits of men who batter (Stuart & Holtzworth-Munroe, 1995). Batterers have been found to express shame, but they also lack empathy, show an inability to assess the impact their violent behavior has on others, minimize and discount its effects, and resist taking responsibility for their battering (Adams, 1988; Gondolf, 1993; Matthews, 1995). Observational research on maritally violent couples by Gottman and colleagues identified two types of batterers based on heart rate reactivity: one set of men, those for whom violent interactions had a calming influence, were more antisocial, sadistic and aggressive in relationships beyond their violent marriages (Gottman, Jacobson, Rushe, & Shortt, 1995; Jacobson & Gottman, 1998). The carryover to parenting relationships was not described in this research, but anecdotal evidence suggests that children were not uncommon targets of their father's brutalities (Jacobson & Gottman, 1995, p. 133).

The value of focusing on the fathering profiles of men who have been or who currently are violent in intimate partner relationships can be argued on several grounds. First, there is plentiful evidence of serious, harmful, and long-term outcomes for children who witness parental marital violence (Holden, 1998). The damaging impact of parental marital violence on children can be substantial, whether or not the marital relationship is severed (Cummings & Davies, 1993; Holden, 1998; McCloskey, Figueredo, & Koss, 1995; McNeal & Amato, 1998). It is not clear whether children who are exposed to but never actually see their parents' violent physical behaviors are subject to negative outcomes in the same degree as children who are physically present during violent episodes. However, even when children are not direct witnesses to their parents' physical violence, it is difficult to argue that they are unaware of and thus unaffected by the tensions and abusive verbal exchanges that typically precede or accompany physically violent interactions (Cummings, 1998). It is also not clear whether interparental violence itself has a direct effect on child outcomes, or whether it operates indirectly through effects on subsequent parenting behaviors of either or both partners, or whether there is

16. ARE VIOLENT MEN BAD DADS? 361

some other pathway altogether or some combination of all of these (Cummings, 1998; Graham-Bermann, 1998). Nonetheless, the potential for causing significant, long-term harm to their children merits close attention to maritally violent fathers.

Second, without a clear picture of the nature of parenting by men who have shown themselves capable of marital violence, contemporary social policy initiatives that encourage marital preservation rather than dissolution of conflict-filled marriages may be shortsighted. Such policies have received widespread support on the grounds that they serve the interests of children by shielding them from the economic consequences of divorce. Until it can be shown convincingly that maritally violent fathers pose no threat to their children's safety, however, the broader social costs of marital preservation policies may be far greater than currently reckoned. Moreover, policies that mandate joint custody and continued father involvement following divorce or partnership dissolution may be premature and arguably not in the best interests of those children whose fathers are known to have engaged in physical violence against the child's mother. Several have debated the merits of restrictions on batterers' visitation privileges or custody rights to children (Jaffe & Geffner, 1998; McMahon & Pence, 1995; Silverstein, 1993; Sternberg, 1996). The poor empathic abilities of men who batter have been cited as evidence that such men may be challenged by or incapable of establishing nurturant relationships with children (Forte, Franks, Forte, & Rigsby, 1996, pp. 68–69). Yet another debate concerns the ability of men to separate their partner/spouse role from their fathering behaviors. In describing batterers' motivations to maintain contact with their children, Silverstein (1993, p. 9) observed that some men who demand access to their children have instrumental motives of intimidation or domination of their wives/partners; but "others may be more capable of a connection with their children that is not embroiled in the dynamics of the marital relationship."

It is especially problematic that there is so little in the empirical or clinical literature that specifically addresses the nature of violent men's relationships with their children and the quality of the father–child relationship. The goal of this paper is to examine the parenting behaviors of fathers who have been identified as having engaged in physical violence toward their partners in ongoing adult intimate relationships. To do so, we rely upon the two waves of the National Survey of Families and Households, supplemented by census tract data from the 1990 U.S. Census. Two questions guide this analysis: first, are maritally violent men notably different from nonviolent men in their fathering attitudes, practices, and assessments of relationship quality with their children? Second, does knowing a man's history of marital violence add significantly to an explanation of his parenting behaviors, and does it do so even after taking into account several sociodemographic factors that are known precursors of intimate violence? These questions test the hypothesis (and its null) that batterers are substantively different (or not) from other men in their interpersonal relationships with their children, hypotheses that underlie the debates about the appropriate social policies governing the relationships of maritally violent men with their children.

METHODS

Data

Data are drawn from waves 1 and 2 of the National Survey of Families and Households (NSFH) and from the 1990 Census. Completed in 1988, the first wave of the NSFH included interviews with a probability sample of 13,007 respondents, representing 9,637 households, with oversamples of minority households and cohabiting couples. In wave 1, face-to-face interviews were conducted with a randomly selected primary respondent from each household. To facilitate the collection of sensitive information, portions of the interview with the primary respondent were self-administered. The primary respondent's spouse or cohabiting partner was given a shorter self-administered questionnaire (Sweet, Bumpass, & Call, 1988). In wave 2, completed in 1994, interviews were conducted with all surviving members of the original sample ($n = 10,007$) and with the current spouse or cohabiting partner of the primary respondent ($n = 5,624$) (Sweet & Bumpass, 1996).

Our use of national sample survey data rather than clinical samples is consequential for this analysis. The severity of incidents of physical violence can vary dramatically from a simple shove to homicide. It is important to note that the items used to assess marital violence in the data set we use most likely tap only what has been termed "common couple violence" and not "intimate terrorism" (Holtzworth-Munroe & Stuart, 1994; Johnson, 1995; Johnson & Ferraro, 2000). Intimate terrorism refers to repeated, long-term, extreme physical and psychological abuse. This extreme form of intimate violence is quite common in clinical or shelter-based samples of victims of batterers but is relatively rare in nationally representative samples (Johnson & Ferraro, 2000). Although women suffering from intimate terrorism may be present in the NSFH sample, the available measures of marital violence are not well suited to identifying them. A recent meta-analysis suggested that studies based on community surveys yield weaker effects of violence than do studies using clinic-based samples (Stith et al., 2000). This implies that the probability of Type II errors, that is, failing to identify significant relationships where in fact they exist, are increased and that our results are likely to be conservative and may underestimate rather than overstate underlying relationships. The NSFH, however, has a compensatory design strength that makes it especially useful for the analyses proposed: Both male and female respondents and their partners were interviewed, which is essential for establishing the credibility of self-report measures of violence (Szinovacz & Egley, 1995).

Our analyses are based on wave-specific subsamples of households in which respondents were married or cohabiting at the time of the interview and lived in a child-present household with the biological children aged 18 or younger of the primary respondent or his or her partner (wave 1 $n = 2,930$; wave 2 $n = 3,171$). We eliminated from the subsamples couples who reported that there were no biological children aged 18 or younger of one or both partners present in the household in

16. ARE VIOLENT MEN BAD DADS?

either wave 1 or wave 2 or both. In the interwave period, 564 new bio-child-present couples were formed, offsetting the 323 bio-child-present couples lost to followup. Because the data are longitudinal, we evaluated whether there was evidence of selective attrition as a function of intimate violence. Probit analysis of participation in wave 2 indicates that violence is not a predictor of exclusion from wave 2. However, there is some selectivity on violence. Couples experiencing violence in wave 1 were more likely to disrupt between waves of the NSFH (DeMaris, 2000). The wave 2 subsample used here likely has experienced some selectivity, which means that the use of this subsample makes for a conservative test of our hypotheses because males who engage in violence against their partners are the ones most likely to separate and thus not show up in the subsample of couples present in wave 2.

Measures

Intimate Violence.   NSFH respondents were asked how often during the past year arguments with their spouse or partner resulted in the respondent hitting, shoving, or throwing things at their spouse or partner. Respondents also were asked how often arguments resulted in the spouse or partner becoming similarly violent toward the respondent. The five-category response set ranged from "none" to "four or more" times. Because responses to the violence items were extremely skewed, we created a dichotomous variable in which 0 indicates that neither partner reported violence and 1 indicates that either the male reported becoming physically violent with the female, or the female reported that the male became physically violent with her, or both. In cases where the reports did not agree, we assigned a code of 1 (indicating wife assault) provided that at least one partner reported violence against the female partner. Identical measures were created for both wave 1 and wave 2. In the first wave, 264 (9.0%) of 2,930 fathers were violent; in the second wave, 251 (7.9%) of 3,171 fathers were violent. We also created a second violence variable applicable only to those respondents who were represented in both waves ($n = 2,607$). This variable distinguishes among male respondents based upon their violence trajectories across the two interview waves and includes fathers who were never violent (88.2%), fathers violent in wave 1 only (5.3%), fathers violent in wave 2 only (4.1%), and fathers who were violent in both waves (2.4%).

Measures of Fathering.   The NSFH contains a plethora of self-report questions about parenting activities, attitudes, and behaviors. We used only a few items from wave 1, which are presented seperately for male primary respondents and secondary respondents. We relied primarily on measures from wave 2 for two reasons: The wave 2 data are richer in content coverage and the exact replicates of questions and question sequences were used for both primary and secondary respondents, allowing the creation of measures for all male respondents in the

survey. In wave 2 many of the parenting questions have a focal child as their referent, and others pertain to children of the household in general. We included both kinds of questions from wave 2 and grouped them into the following four general categories: measures of activities fathers report participating in with their child; indicators of relationship quality; fathers' assessments, aspirations, and expectations for their children, and measures of parenting style including monitoring and discipline techniques. We constructed several summary measures from wave 2 items. These include a count of the problems fathers identify for all children in the household, including such behaviors as truancy, trouble with the police, and so forth; an index of 27 problematic characteristics fathers attribute to focal children aged 5–17 (Cronbach's alpha = .92); a similar index of 17 characteristics of focal children aged 3–4 (Cronbach's alpha = .82); a summary measure of the frequency of arguments about four specific issues (such as how late to stay out, the child's sexual behavior) with focal children aged 12–17 and arguments about six specific issues (such as how to dress, helping out at home) with focal children aged 17 and under. We also created a family assessment index, based upon the father's agreement with five items that describe positive and negative qualities of family life. For this measure, items were scored and averaged such that higher scores indicate a more negative assessment of the quality of family life. Finally, for both waves we constructed summary indexes of harsh parenting styles. The wave 2 measure is based upon five different items and assigns a score of zero to fathers who report never engaging in hitting, yelling, or threatening the withdrawal of privileges. Two points are assigned for each answer indicating use of hitting or slapping a child, and 1 point for each answer indicating frequent use of yelling or threats to take away privileges. Scores on the index range from 0 to 6, with a mean of 2.99 and standard deviation of 1.38 (Cronbach's alpha = .63). Two measures were constructed for wave 1 fathers, one for male primary respondents and one for men who were secondary respondents, that is, who were spouses or partners of the primary female respondent. Primary respondents answered the five items in terms of a focal child aged 5–17; secondary respondents answered in terms of children aged 3–18. Each measure is an average of men's responses to five questions about their frequency (on a 1- to 4-point response scale) of hugging, praising, involving the child in setting rules, yelling at, and spanking the focal child. Three of the items were reverse scored so that higher scores indicate a more coercive or harsh parenting style.

Control Variables. Although the primary focus of this study is on the parenting behaviors of men distinguished by their violence toward intimate partners, several other sociodemographic measures are included in our final models as controls because of their of their known correlations with domestic violence. Previous research consistently found that intimate violence is more common among Blacks than Whites or others and among couples of lower-class standing (Greenfield et al., 1998). Hence, our predictive model includes race (entered as two dummy variables: Black = 1, else = 0; and Hispanic = 1, else = 0), educational attainment,

16. ARE VIOLENT MEN BAD DADS? 365

employment status, household debt level, and an income-to-needs ratio, (a measure of income adequacy that takes into account household composition). Previous research also indicates that intimate violence is inversely related to age and the duration of a couple's union. Because age and duration of union are very highly correlated we include only the father's age in the model. As measures of family composition, we include the following four variables based upon the presence (wave 1) or number (wave 2) of children of different ages: his children aged 0–4 in the household, children aged 5–17 in the household, children aged 18–23 in the household (wave 2 only), and his children living elsewhere.

Finally, we include an index of neighborhood economic disadvantage, modeled on the work of Sampson and colleagues (Sampson, Morenoff, & Earls, 1999). We demonstrated in other work the significance of neighborhood economic disadvantage to intimate violence beyond the effects of race and social class measured at the individual level (Benson, Fox, DeMaris, & VanWyk, 2000). The index of neighborhood disadvantage is based on five census tract measures from the 1990 U.S. Census, including the percentage of single parents, percentage of non-White residents, percentage of unemployed, percentage of families on public assistance, and percentage below the poverty line. After transforming the items to z-scores, we summed them and divided by the number of indicators to form the index of concentrated disadvantage (Cronbach's alpha = .93 in wave 1; .92 in wave 2). Sampson and Wilson (1995) argued that the crime-related effects of community disadvantage are not linear across levels of disadvantage. Rather, they tend to appear only in the most distressed neighborhoods as "concentration effects" (Sampson & Wilson, 1995). Following this line of reasoning, we investigated and found that our index of neighborhood disadvantage has a nonlinear relationship with intimate violence. We grouped the respondents into deciles based on their score on the wave 2 disadvantage index and compared rates of intimate violence across deciles. Over the first seven deciles the rate of violence fluctuates randomly between 2.5 and 5.8%. In the eighth decile the rate rises to 9.8%, to 10.6% in the ninth decile, and then climbs to 10.8% in the last decile. Accordingly, we dichotomized our indexes of concentrated disadvantage at the 70th percentile. Census tracts that fall into the upper 30% are considered disadvantaged.

Analysis Plan

To assess whether men who have engaged in violence toward intimate partners differ from nonviolent men in their fathering profiles, we conducted independent sample t-tests for all outcome variables for fathers represented in wave 1 ($n = 2,930$) and wave 2 ($n = 3,171$) respectively. To assess for differences in fathering among men with distinct violence histories, one-way analyses of variance were conducted for the subsample of fathers represented in both waves ($n = 2,607$). As a final step, we conducted a series of regression analyses to examine the contribution of intimate violence to explanations of variance in fathering behaviors once the sociodemographic controls have been taken into account.

All tests of significance are two-tailed, which allows for the consideration of the competing hypotheses that, on the one hand, men who have been violent in their relationships with an adult intimate partner are no different from nonviolent men in their attitudes and behaviors toward children and, on the other, they are different (with no specification as to the direction of that difference). Although it is likely that maritally violent men are also aggressive or coercive in their parental disciplinary styles, for many other aspects of father involvement, it is more difficult to specify the directionality of a difference between maritally violent and nonviolent fathers. Is there reason to expect, for example, that violent men monitor their children's television viewing more or less carefully than nonviolent fathers? Is there reason to anticipate that nonviolent fathers rate their children's health more or less positively than violent fathers? While one-tailed tests are preferable because they specify directionality and have a larger critical region (thus making the detection of significant differences in the hypothesized direction more likely), the nature of most of the fathering measures used in the NSFH makes posing and testing directional hypotheses conceptually unsupportable, given the limitations of the existing literature on maritally violent fathers.

FINDINGS

Table 16.1 displays the distributions of the wave 1 and wave 2 samples of fathers by their violence status across the several sociodemographic descriptor variables used in this analysis. As can be seen, the familiar bivariate correlations of violence with lower socioeconomic status, short union duration, and large family size are evident. The next four tables present the individual fathering measures from wave 2 for violent and nonviolent fathers. Looking first at Table 16.2, which displays results for the behavioral engagement items from wave 2, we see little difference between fathers in terms of the amount of time they report that they spend with their children (assessed for a focal child aged 5–17), the type of child-focused activities in which they participate, or the time they spend with their children in family, extended family, and neighborhood contexts. Most fathers, regardless of their violence toward partners, report spending private time with the designated focal child, assisting the child with homework on a regular basis, and querying the child about school. Moreover, fathers report having talked seriously during the past month with the focal child about things worrying or simply of interest to the child. Fathers, regardless of their violence status, spend much more time with children's sports teams than with other youth-based activities, reporting at least some involvement with community groups on a weekly basis. Finally, if fathers' reports are to be believed, the dinner hour is family time on average at least half of the evenings each week. In short, these data suggest that intimate violence does not significantly diminish or increase the amount of time fathers report spending with their children or their families.

TABLE 16.1
Sociodemographic Indicators by Violence Status of Fathers, NFSH Wave 1 and Wave 2

Sociodemographic Indicators	Wave 1 Fathers								Wave 2 Fathers							
	Nonviolent			Maritally Violent					Nonviolent			Maritally Violent				
	N	X	SD	N	X	SD	p	N	X	SD	N	X	SD	p
Black (1 = yes; 0 = no)	2666	.11	.31	264	.16	.37	.031	2920	.12	.32	251	.18	.39	.008
Hispanic (1 = yes; 0 = no)	2406	.08	.27	201	.08	.28	.860	2920	.09	.28	250	.08	.27	.588
Neighborhood disadvantage index (1 = disadvantaged; 0 = not)	2666	.24	.60	264	.38	.78	.007	2907	.194	.39	250	.30	.46	.000
Educational attainment	2308	13.5	2.76	245	12.6	2.58	.000	2558	13.4	2.85	226	12.7	2.62	.000
Income/needs ratio	2291	4.12	4.62	233	3.67	5.63	.171	2888	4.00	3.56	248	3.29	2.53	.002
Number of debts	2666	1.35	1.12	264	1.59	1.26	.003	2920	1.40	1.20	251	1.68	1.27	.000
Employment status (1 = employed; 0 = not)	2298	.94	.23	244	.88	.33	.002	2388	.93	.25	189	.87	.33	.019
Marital/union duration (months)	2655	95.0	74.4	264	75.1	66.3	.000	2884	94.3	71.4	247	69.9	56.0	.000
Respondent's age	2313	33.5	7.17	246	31.0	6.49	.000	2571	38.7	7.23	226	35.3	6.74	.000
Children 0–4 in the home (Wave 1: 1 = yes; 0 = no) (Wave 2: number)	2270	.36	.48	208	.51	.50	.000	2572	.53	.740	226	.69	.83	.004
Children 5–17 in the home (Wave 1: 1 = yes; 0 = no) (Wave 2: number)	2270	.86	.35	208	.80	.40	.038	2572	1.48	1.06	226	1.46	1.12	.698
Children 18–23 in the home (Wave 1: not available) (Wave 2: number)	—	—	—	—	—	—	—	2572	.15	.43	226	.10	.39	.049
Children <18 living elsewhere (Wave 1: 1 = yes; 0 = no) (Wave 2: number)	2666	.10	.30	264	.18	.39	.001	2572	.32	.72	226	.36	.83	.464

Note. Tests of significance are two-tailed t-tests. Sample sizes vary due to missing data and to question content.

TABLE 16.2

Fathers' Reports of Time Spent in Activities With Children by Intimate Partner
Violence Involvement, NSFH wave 2

Activity	Nonviolent			Maritally Violent			
	N	X	SD	N	X	SD	p
Time with focal child (fc) aged 5–17:							
Spend any private time with fc in past week? (1 = yes, 2 = no)	1400	1.17	.37	115	1.18	.39	.655
Checks on fc homework (days/wk)	1393	3.53	2.39	114	3.79	2.35	.261
Helps fc with homework (days/wk)	1341	1.81	1.75	106	1.92	1.78	.560
Talks with fc about school (days/wk)	1382	3.52	1.89	112	3.44	1.77	.669
Talks about what fc learns in school (days/wk)	1377	3.41	1.85	112	3.28	1.79	.469
Talks about fc's worries (times in past month)	1707	4.21	1.35	147	4.24	1.41	.777
Talks w/fc about fc (times in past month)	1709	2.69	1.30	147	2.77	1.40	.466
Number of school meetings attended in past year	1685	1.79	2.47	143	1.57	3.03	.324
Number of fc's school performances attended in past year	1663	5.50	9.78	142	4.83	10.0	.783
Time spent in community activities (hours/week in past year):							
Community youth group	844	0.58	3.09	71	0.52	1.79	.883
PTO or school-based organization	841	0.69	2.83	71	0.63	1.69	.861
Faith-based youth group	842	0.54	1.68	71	0.69	2.43	.496
Sports or coaching	850	1.82	5.00	71	1.49	3.08	.591
Average hrs/week in community activities	842	0.88	2.16	71	0.83	170	.848
Time spent with family:							
# evenings Dad ate dinner with any child in past week	1004	5.29	1.93	88	5.06	2.09	.270
# evenings entire family had dinner together	1005	4.47	2.19	88	4.49	2.39	.922
Frequency over past year of get-togethers with fc and relatives	1005	3.85	1.38	88	4.05	1.30	.194
Frequency over past year of get-togethers with fc and neighbors	993	3.47	1.49	88	3.78	1.41	.057

Note. All significance tests are two-tailed. Sample sizes vary due to missing data and to question content.

16. ARE VIOLENT MEN BAD DADS? 369

Table 16.3 shows results of comparisons across wave 2 fathers' assessments of and aspirations for their children. As with the behavioral engagement measures, few differences are seen here. Fathers do not differ in their willingness to identify any of the children in the households as especially easy or difficult or as having limiting physical, mental, or emotional conditions. They do differ, however, in the problematic character assessments with which they rated the focal child, and in the total number of problems they suggested that children in the household displayed ($p = .045$, one-tailed test). In data not shown on the individual items comprising the problematic character assessments, violent fathers are significantly more likely to feel that their focal child aged 5–17 is accurately described as unhappy, disobedient at school, paranoid, feeling unloved, cheating and lying, arguing too much, having difficulty concentrating, easily confused, and tense and nervous. Violent fathers with a focal child aged 3–4 are significantly more likely to describe the child as disobedient at home, impulsive, stubborn, sullen, having a strong temper, one who cheats and lies, iimpulsive, and cruel to others.

No differences emerge when fathers with a focal child aged 5–17 rate their focal child's health, the child's music, art, sports, and mechanical skills, or the focal child's likely ultimate educational attainment. However, when rating in importance a series of achievements or accomplishments for the focal child as an adult, and violent fathers are more likely than nonviolent fathers to attach a high value to a child's achieving career and financial success and eventual parenthood.

Table 16.4 presents several items from wave 2 related to relationship quality, including fathers' estimates of the frequency of arguments with the focal child about a variety of issues over the 3 months preceding the survey. Fathers with a focal child aged 5–17 were asked about arguments over money, how to dress, the child's choice of friends, helping out at home, getting along with other family members, and school. Fathers with a focal child aged 12–17 were also asked about the frequency of arguments with the child about his or her friends, how late the child may stay out at night, sexual behavior, and the use of cigarettes, alcohol, or drugs. As can be seen in Table 16.4, maritally violent fathers differ significantly from nonviolent fathers in the frequency of arguments about the focal child's helping out at home, as well as on the overall index of argument frequency. There are no significant differences between violent and nonviolent fathers of teenage focal children in the frequency of arguments over adolescent issues. The next two measures are single-item indicators of the global quality of the father's relationship with the focal child aged 5–17 and 0–4, respectively; violent fathers differ from nonviolent fathers on neither of these measures. The next item asks fathers to assess how well children in his family get along with one another compared to other families, and again there is no difference between violent and nonviolent fathers. The final measure is the five-item assessment of the quality of family life. On this measure maritally violent fathers perceive their families as significantly more negative than do nonviolent fathers, although the average rating for both sets of fathers is toward the positive side of the scale.

TABLE 16.3

Fathers' Assessments, Aspirations, and Expectations for Children by Father's
Intimate Partner Violence Involvement, NSFH Wave 2

Assessments, Aspirations, Expectations	Nonviolent			Maritally Violent			
	N	X	SD	N	X	SD	p
Any children 5–17 especially easy? (1 = yes)	2033	.60	.49	174	.59	.49	.774
Any children 5–17 especially difficult? (1 = yes)	2154	.17	.38	189	.21	.41	.287
Number of problems any children 5–17 have	2920	.46	.97	251	.59	1.17	.090
Any children 5–17 with physical limitations? (1 = yes)	2155	.04	.19	189	.03	.18	.684
Any children 5–17 with emotional or mental problems? (1 = yes)	2149	.07	.25	187	.07	.26	.895
Any children 0–4 especially easy? (1 = yes)	934	.58	.49	101	.53	.50	.367
Any children 0–4 especially difficult? (1 = yes)	516	.11	.31	55	.16	.37	.278
Any children 0–4 with physical limitations? (1 = yes)	1005	.01	.12	109	.01	.10	.683
Any children 0–4 with emotional or mental problems? (1 = yes)	1003	.01	.11	109	.01	.10	.797
Problem rating index for focal child aged 5–17 (average for 27 items)	1650	1.41	.31	141	1.48	.29	.013
Problem rating index for focal child aged 3–4 (average for 17 items)	156	1.41	.20	14	1.53	.16	.014
Health rating of focal child aged 5–17 (1 = excellent, 5 = poor)	739	1.62	.85	56	1.61	0.80	.887
Dad's rating of sports skills of focal child aged 5–17 (1 = one of the best, 5 = one of the worst)	1704	2.50	1.00	145	2.43	1.05	.418
Art skills	1695	2.47	.91	146	2.49	.98	.771
Music skills	1681	2.73	1.03	141	2.80	.97	.453
Mechanical skills	724	2.94	1.05	56	2.89	1.14	.766
Educational expectations for focal child aged 5–17 (1 = not finish high school, 7 = graduate degree)	1691	5.25	1.62	144	5.03	1.66	.128
Importance to Dad that focal child (age 5–17) graduate from high school (7 = extremely important)	1664	6.86	.62	144	6.82	0.60	.398
Get a college degree	1661	6.05	1.34	144	6.05	1.20	.984
Have a steady job	1661	6.37	1.16	144	6.41	1.06	.680
Get to the top in a career	1662	5.29	1.56	144	5.67	1.42	.005
Have lots of money	1663	4.67	1.58	144	5.24	1.39	.000
Get married	1663	4.64	1.69	143	4.75	1.73	.456
Have children	1662	4.56	1.73	143	4.85	1.69	.049
Become a community leader	1662	4.22	1.77	143	4.51	1.87	.062
Live nearby	1663	4.56	1.73	144	4.76	1.80	.200

Note. All significance tests are two-tailed. Sample sizes vary due to missing data and to question content.

16. ARE VIOLENT MEN BAD DADS?

TABLE 16.4

Fathers' Reports of His Relationship Quality With Focal Child and Overall Family
Relations by Intimate Partner Violence Involvement, NSFH Wave 2

Relationship Quality Indicators	Nonviolent			Maritally Violent			
	N	X	SD	N	X	SD	p
Frequency of arguments in past 3 months with focal child aged 5–17 about money							
(1 = never or rarely; 6 = almost every day)	1710	1.49	1.04	145	1.60	1.15	.229
How to dress	1710	1.72	1.20	146	1.92	1.42	.104
Friends	1707	1.27	0.73	146	1.40	0.86	.086
Helping out at home	1710	2.69	1.51	146	2.97	1.51	.029
Getting along with other family members	1709	2.61	1.67	146	2.81	1.65	.167
School	1707	1.69	1.20	144	1.81	1.29	.248
Total argument frequency across 6 issues	1713	11.47	4.56	144	12.49	4.77	.011
Frequency of arguments with focal child aged							
12–17 about boy or girl friends	454	1.26	0.85	28	1.25	0.93	.974
How late focal child may stay out at night	673	1.30	0.72	40	1.50	0.88	.156
Sexual behavior	671	1.06	0.36	40	1.10	0.38	.507
Smoking, drinking, using drugs	673	1.07	0.39	40	1.18	0.64	.287
Total argument frequency across 4 issues	451	4.78	1.64	28	5.07	1.63	.349
Global relationship with focal child 5–17							
(1 = extremely poor; 10 = extremely good)	1712	8.50	1.44	146	8.30	1.65	.158
Global relationship with focal child 0 –							
(1 = extremely poor; 10 = extremely good)	226	1.98	2.48	21	2.24	2.76	.654
Assessment of how well children get along with one another at home (1 = much better than other families; 5 = much worse)	885	2.41	0.81	73	2.52	0.71	.205
Family relationship index (average of 5 items, higher scores = more negative rating)	994	1.93	0.61	88	2.07	0.65	.036

Note. Probability values are based upon regression analyses with violence at wave 2 as the predictor. All significance tests are two-tailed. Sample sizes vary due to missing data and to question content.

Table 16.5 displays findings that profile the use of various monitoring strategies by maritally violent and nonviolent fathers in wave 2. With one exception there are no significant differences between the groups of fathers in their reports of their monitoring standards and actions, including knowing the focal child's good friends, permitting the focal child to be home alone under various conditions, and monitoring the amount and type of television programs watched by the focal child. Violent fathers are slightly less likely to permit a child to be home alone overnight while the father is gone.

Tables 16.6 and 16.7 show fathers' reports of disciplinary strategies for wave 1 and wave 2, respectively. Among wave 1 fathers who were primary respondents, differences by violence status are found for self-reports of the frequency fathers praised, spanked, yelled at, and permitted their focal child aged 5–17 to participate

TABLE 16.5

Fathers' Parental Style by Intimate Partner Violence Involvement, NSFH Wave 2

Parental Style	Nonviolent			Maritally Violent			
	N	X	SD	N	X	SD	p
Monitoring of focal child aged 5–17:							
How many of focal child's good friends does he know? (1 = all of them; 5 = none of them)	1395	2.19	1.11	114	2.33	1.27	.253
OK for focal child to be home alone after school? (1 = yes or sometimes; 2 = no)	788	1.57	.50	71	1.66	.48	.129
OK for focal child to be home alone at night when dad is out late? (1 = yes or sometimes; 2 = no)	785	1.76	.43	71	1.83	.38	.114
OK for focal child to be home alone when dad is gone overnight? (1 = yes or sometimes; 2 = no)	786	1.92	.26	70	1.97	.17	.038
TV Restrictions:							
Dad attempts to restrict TV time for focal child (1 = yes; 2 = no)	1392	1.51	.50	115	1.50	0.50	.824
Dad attempts to restrict TV programs for focal child (1 = yes; 2 = no)	1392	1.20	.40	115	1.17	0.38	.576
Dad attempts to restrict TV time for focal child aged 0–4 (1 = yes; 2 = no)	201	1.49	.50	16	1.56	0.51	.566
Dad attempts to restrict TV programs for focal child aged 0–4 (1 = yes; 2 = no)	201	1.13	.34	16	1.25	0.45	.327

Note. All significance tests are two-tailed. Sample sizes vary due to missing data and to question content.

in setting rules. Violent men are less likely to praise their children or let them help set rules and more likely to spank and yell at their children. There are no significant differences in the self-reports of parenting among primary respondents with a very young focal child. Secondary respondents answered similar items but with a wider age range for the reference child, and there are no significant differences between violent and nonviolent secondary respondents. Finally, the harsh parenting indexes show significant differences between violent and nonviolent fathers for both the primary and secondary respondents, with the violent men reporting themselves as harsher fathers than the nonviolent men.

A different set of questions was used in wave 2 to assess disciplinary style. The first two items in Table 16.7 query fathers about a consultative decision-making style, that is, how frequently they consult with their children before making decisions that affect the children, and the frequency with which fathers take their children's views into account in setting rules for them. As can be seen in the table, violent fathers do not differ significantly from nonviolent fathers on these measures. The next two items measure the frequency of positive affective behaviors (hugging) and negative affective behaviors (spanking) of the father toward the focal

16. ARE VIOLENT MEN BAD DADS? 373

TABLE 16.6

Fathers' Reports of Discipline Style With Focal Child by Intimate Partner
Violence Involvement, NSFH Wave 1

Discipline Style	Nonviolent			Maritally Violent			
	N	X	SD	N	X	SD	p
Fathers who were primary respondents in wave 1:							
Praise child 5–17 (1 = never; 4 = very often)	574	3.54	.61	47	3.32	.69	.018
Allow child 5–17 to help set rules (1 = never;							
4 = very often)	558	2.66	.82	45	2.40	.69	.039
Spank child 5–17 (1 = never; 4 = very often)	573	2.02	.81	48	2.33	.72	.009
Hug child 5–17 (1 = never; 4 = very often)	575	3.71	.55	48	3.54	.77	.134
Yell or shout at child 5–17 (1 = never;							
4 = very often)	575	2.65	.74	48	2.94	.78	.010
Praise child 0–4 (1 = never; 4 = very often)	268	3.76	.52	29	3.83	.47	.490
Spank child 0–4 (1 = never; 4 = very often)	268	2.06	.86	29	2.21	.94	.373
Hug child 0–4 (1 = never; 4 = very often)	268	2.05	.86	29	2.21	.94	.373
Yell or shout at child 0–4 (1 = never;							
4 = very often)	268	2.32	.86	29	2.49	.66	.718
Fathers who were secondary respondents in wave 1:							
Praise child 3–18 (1 = never; 4 = very often)	809	3.49	.66	85	3.36	0.70	.105
Allow child 3–18 to help set rules (1 = never;							
4 = very often)	803	2.47	.86	85	2.38	.83	.333
Spank child 3–18 (1 = never; 4 = very often)	806	2.09	.78	86	2.15	.83	.471
Hug child 3–18 (1 = never; 4 = very often)	806	3.66	.61	86	3.56	.78	.291
Yell or shout at child 3–18 (1 = never;							
4 = very often)	806	2.71	0.81	85	2.82	.77	.200
Harsh parenting indexes:							
(range = 1–4; high scores = harsher parenting)							
Male primary respondents with focal child							
5–17	574	1.95	.40	48	2.20	.35	.000
Male secondary respondents with children							
3–18	806	2.13	.46	85	2.13	.46	.045

Note. All significance tests are two-tailed. Sample sizes vary due to missing data and to question content.

child aged 5–17. Again, there are no significant differences between violent and nonviolent fathers on these items. The next four items ask about different influence techniques fathers may use with the focal child, including reasoning, offering extra privileges, threatening to take privileges away, and yelling or shouting at he child. Violent fathers are significantly more likely to offer extra privileges and to yell in order to influence the focal child to do something. Four items ask fathers how they respond when the focal child is "especially bad." Under these conditions, maritally violent fathers are significantly more likely than are nonviolent fathers to report that they yell at the focal child; there are no significant differences on the

374   FOX AND BENSON

TABLE 16.7
Fathers' Reports of Discipline Style With Focal Child by Intimate Partner
Violence Involvement, NSFH Wave 2

	Nonviolent			Maritally Violent			
Discipline Style	N	X	SD	N	X	SD	p
Frequency he consults children about decisions (1 = all the time; 5 = never)	883	2.04	.99	73	2.24	1.13	.128
Frequency he takes children's views into account in rule-making (1 = all the time; 5 = never)	882	3.77	.69	73	3.62	.81	.123
Number of times he hugged focal child aged 5–17 in past week	1389	8.74	12.62	114	9.53	16.29	.533
Number of times he spanked or hit focal child aged 5–17 in past week	1399	.12	.47	114	.19	.62	.219
Frequency he explained his reasoning to influence focal child 5–17 in past week (1 = never; 5 = always)	1399	4.03	1.00	114	3.90	1.13	.259
Frequency he offered extra privileges to influence focal child 5–17 in past week (1 = never; 5 = always)	1398	2.31	1.12	114	2.58	1.24	.025
Frequency he threatened to take away privileges to influence focal child 5–17 in past week (1 = never; 5 = always)	1399	2.66	1.14	114	2.72	1.08	.565
Frequency he yelled or shouted to influence focal child 5–17 in past week (1 = never; 5 = always)	1399	2.36	1.04	114	2.68	1.00	.002
When focal child 5–17 is especially bad, frequency he talks with fc about what s/he did wrong (1 = never; 5 = always)	1401	4.44	1.01	114	4.38	1.04	.525
When focal child 5–17 is especially bad, frequency he yells at focal child (1 = never; 5 = always)	1366	2.79	1.27	112	3.21	1.19	.001
When focal child 5–17 is especially bad, frequency he takes away privileges (1 = never; 5 = always)	1359	2.64	1.24	112	2.66	1.13	.875
When focal child 5–17 is especially bad, frequency he spanks or slaps focal child (1 = never; 5 = always)	1343	1.46	0.77	111	1.58	0.73	.126
Harsh parenting index (range = 0–6; higher scores indicate harsher parenting)	1399	2.96	1.37	114	3.43	1.32	.000

Note. All significance tests are two-tailed. Sample sizes vary due to missing data and to question content.

other items. The final item is the constructed index of harsh parenting for wave 2.
On this measure the maritally violent fathers scored as significantly more harsh in
their parenting behaviors.

In analyses not shown, we also categorized the violent fathers who were in
intimate relationships that continued over the two waves of the survey into three
groups according to their violence trajectories (violent at both waves, violent at
wave 1 only, violent at wave 2 only) and examined how they compared with one

16. ARE VIOLENT MEN BAD DADS?

another and with the nonviolent fathers on all of the parenting measures. The most consistent finding was that the groups of fathers generally did not differ significantly from one another, when differences appeared, the primary distinction was between the nonviolent fathers and the three subsets of violent fathers. These results are adequately subsumed under the results presented in Tables 16.2 to 16.6, in which the three violence trajectories are undifferentiated and comparisons are made between all men who were violent versus those who were not.

The final set of analyses is shown in Tables 16.8 and 16.9, in which the harsh parenting indexes for wave 1 and wave 2 respectively are regressed onto different sets of control variables along with the measure of intimate partner violence. This set of analyses permits a determination of whether the relationships found between fathers' violence toward his intimate partner and harsh parenting styles are a function of the sociodemographic differences between violent and nonviolent fathers noted in Table 16.1. If the effect for violence, noted in the bivariate condition, fails to retain its significance in the presence of the sociodemographic controls, we will have evidence that the connection between intimate violence and parenting behaviors is spurious and could conclude that both intimate violence and harsh parenting are a function of social processes stemming from or shaped by a father's sociodemographic characteristics. On the other hand, if the effect of violence remains significant in the explanation of harsh parenting, then we can have more confidence in asserting that there are important connections among aggressive, abusive behaviors across a man's familial roles.

Table 16.8 shows regression results from wave 1 for the primary and secondary respondents in the first and second panels respectively. Model 1 in both panels shows that the effect of violence by itself on harsh parenting is significant. Model 2 introduces variables for race, ethnicity, and social contextual disadvantage. The effect for violence is only minimally reduced for primary respondents and enhanced among secondary respondents with the introduction of these controls. Model 3 introduces socioeconomic controls. Among primary respondent fathers, educational attainment significantly reduces the degree of harsh parenting, whereas being employed has a positive effect on harsh parenting. However, these two variables operate largely independently of violence, which retains its substantial effect on harsh parenting. Among secondary respondents, educational attainment and the availability of discretionary income beyond the family's needs deter harsh parenting but being employed significantly enhances fathers' reliance upon harsh parenting. As with the primary respondents, the effect of violence is not diminished by the introduction of these controls into the model, suggesting that intimate violence operates independently of these socioeconomic factors in influencing the nature of men's parenting. Model 4 introduces family composition variables into the model. As can be seen in the table, the effect of violence is not substantially affected by the entry of these family composition variables into the

TABLE 16.8
Regression Models for Harsh Parenting Index for Primary and Secondary Respondents, NSFH Wave 1

Violence Status and Control Variables	Primary Respondents					Secondary Respondents				
	Model 1	Model 2	Model 3	Model 4	Model 5	Model 1	Model 2	Model 3	Model 4	Model 5
Wave 1 violence	.166**	.152***	.151***	.137***	.110**	.067*	.077*	.081*	.081*	.093*
Black		.019			.009		.024			.007
Hispanic		−.068			−.125**		−.011			−.046
Neighborhood disadvantage		.057			.040		−.017			−.042
Educational attainment			−.176***		−.195***			−.087*		−.091*
Income/needs ratio			−.046		−.023			−.152***		−.146**
Number of debts			−.003		−.004			.036		−.018
Employment status			.086*		.091*			.112**		.071†
Father's age				−.194***	−.156***				−.126**	−.103*
Children 0–4 in the home				.115**	.116**				−.065	−.062
Children 5–17 in the home				.077†	.101*				−.003	.017
Children <18 living elsewhere				−.049	−.049				.039	−.020
Adjusted R^2	.026	.026	.059	.085	.117	.003	.002	.046	.017	.050

Note. † $p < .10$, * $p < .05$, ** $p < .01$, *** $p < .001$. Cell entries are standardized beta coefficients. All models for the primary respondents are significant at the $p < .001$ level. For the secondary respondents, Model 1 is significant at the $p < .05$ level, Model 2 is not significant; Model 4 is significant at the $p \leq .01$ level, and Models 3 and 5 are significant at the $p < .000$ level.

16. ARE VIOLENT MEN BAD DADS? 377

TABLE 16.9
Regression Models for Harsh Parenting Index, NSFH Wave 2

Violence Status and Control Variables	Wave 2 Fathers				
	Model 1	Model 2	Model 3	Model 4	Model 5
Wave 2 violence	.091***	.097***	.095***	.055*	.065**
Black		−.067*			−.042
Hispanic		−.048†			−.051†
Neighborhood disadvantage		−.018			−.001
Educational attainment			.034		.012
Income/needs ratio			−.056†		−.010
Number of debts			.078**		.060*
Employment status			.078**		.042
Father's age				−.178***	−.176***
Children 0–4 in the home				.113***	.125***
Children 5–17 in the home				.008	.006
Children 18–23 in the home				−.059*	−.045†
Children <18 living elsewhere				−.090***	−.061*
R^2	.008	.014	.021	.085	.095

Note. †$p < .10$, *$p < .05$, **$p < .01$, ***$p < .001$. Cell entries are standardized beta coefficients. All models are significant at the $p < .000$ level.

model. Father's age has a significant impact on harsh parenting, such that older fathers are significantly less likely than younger fathers to engage in harsh parenting; this is true both for primary and secondary respondents. The presence of young children significantly enhances the use of harsh parenting, and the presence of school-age children marginally, increases harsh parenting but only among the primary respondents. Among secondary respondents the age composition of children in the household does not add to the explanation of harsh parenting. Model 5 enters all the sociodemographic controls into the model. Among primary respondents, violence retains its significant impact on harsh parenting, although its effect is reduced to 34% when all the other predictor variables are taken into account. Among the secondary respondents, the effect of violence is actually enhanced by 39% when all 11 sociodemographic controls are in the model simultaneously. In sum, the results for wave 1 respondents suggest that a man's violence toward his intimate partner has a strong, positive effect on his reliance upon harsh parenting behaviors with his children, an effect that persists when sociodemographic correlates of violence are taken into account.

Table 16.9 presents similar models for the index of harsh parenting for wave 2 fathers. Although a slightly different configuration of sociodemographic variables is significant in each model for wave 2 as compared to wave 1, the overall results are quite consistent. The effect of violence on harsh parenting retains significance in each of the models when sociodemographic controls are introduced. The family composition variables in Model 4 have the largest impact on the effect

TABLE 16.10
Fathering Profiles of Men Who Batter:
Parenting Differences Between Maritally Violent
and Nonviolent Fathers

Parenting Differences

Maritally violent fathers:
  Argue with children more frequently
  Rate family more negatively
  Rate children more negatively
  Value career success more
  Value money more
  Are more restrictive in monitoring their focal child
  Praise less often
  Involve and consult children less often
  Spank more often
  Yell more often
  Offer extra privileges more often
  Engage in harsher parenting

of violence, reducing the effect size by 40%, but even in this model violence is a significant predictor of harsh parenting. Model 5 shows that violence retains just over 70% of its original impact once all 11 sociodemographic variables are in the model as simultaneous predictors.

Table 16.10 is a text table that summarizes the significant differences found across all of our comparisons of maritally violent and nonviolent fathers. As such, it yields a profile of violent fathers, showing these men as holding more negative assessments of their children and their families, engaging more often in punitive behaviors and less often in positive parenting behaviors, and relying more often on aggressive verbal techniques for persuasion and correction.

CONCLUDING DISCUSSION

The purpose of this paper was to examine fathering profiles of men who had been abusive toward their intimate partners and to compare their fathering attitudes and behaviors with men who had not been violent in their marriages or partnerships. In doing so, we tested the competing hypotheses that, on the one hand, maritally violent men are indistinguishable from nonviolent men in their fathering, and on the other, that maritally violent men are notably different from nonviolent men when it comes to fathering. In fact, we found evidence for both hypotheses. Tables 16.2 through 16.5 showed only a few differences between the groups of fathers, while Tables 16.6 through 16.9 showed evidence of consistent differences between

maritally violent and nonviolent fathers. How important are the similarities and differences?

When the mundane activities of parenting and family life are examined, fathers do not differ in the amounts of time they say they spend with the focal child or the family or engaged in youth-focused community activities. Taken at face value, these results suggest that perhaps in the day-in, day-out minutiae of family life, men's abusive behaviors toward their wives are not translated into abusive behaviors toward children. And yet, the items available in the NSFH assess only the amounts of time spent in different activities, not the quality of time. Fox, Sayers, and Bruce (2001), citing field notes from their observations of batterers' counseling groups, report, "[Asked] what they remembered most about being a child elicited episodes of commonplace paternal brutality, perhaps all the more striking because of the dispassionate way in which the men [recounted their memories] to the knowing nods of the others in the group . . . suppers thrown to the floor, broken furniture and dishes, cursing, yelling. Fishing trips, hunting trips, working on cars remembered not for the male camaraderie we associate with such father–son activities but rather for their coerced participation and menace." Unfortunately, the items in the NSFH do not allow us to push beyond the quantities of time men claim to devote to their children to explorations of how that time is spent or how fathers behave during the time they spend engaged with their children and their activities. Such information is crucial to understanding the nature of father involvement and the meaning of activity-based measures, such as those in the NSFH.

When men's feelings about their children and of their hopes and aspirations for them are examined, the differences are few but sobering. Maritally violent fathers are marginally more likely to report greater numbers of problems their children had experienced, problems ranging from school truancy to difficulties with police. The reporting of such problem behaviors is less a function of the father's perception than are some of the other measures in the analyses. The higher frequencies of these objectively verifiable, troubled behaviors may simply reflect the reality of life among children from distressed neighborhoods and lower socioeconomic standing, or they may reflect the negative behavioral outcomes commonly found among children exposed to marital violence, or both (Osofsky, 1998). Fathers' monitoring styles show very few differences based on men's violence status. Maritally violent fathers are marginally less likely to allow their children to be home alone under varying circumstances, but this may reflect the disadvantaged neighborhood contexts of violent fathers as much as the fathers' predilections or assessments of the child's maturity. This interpretation is supported by the fact that when we control for neighborhood concentrated disadvantage, the link between marital violence and monitoring is no longer significant.

Other differences in fathers' perceptions of their children are more troubling. Specifically, not only are violent fathers of older focal children more likely to assess their children in negative terms, but so too are the violent fathers of very

young focal children, although here the numbers are quite small. By the time children had reached age 3 or 4, their fathers already perceived them (and rated them to interviewers) negatively. With the NSFH data we cannot trace how negative perceptions are translated into behaviors toward the child, but other research has suggested how such perceptions on the part of parents are associated with less positive parenting (Cummings, 1998; Graham-Bermann, 1998). This implies that it is less important that the perceptions are accurate than that they are negative. That maritally violent fathers of very young and older focal children alike perceive their children in such negative terms, and significantly more so than nonviolent fathers, gives rise to concern. Corroborating these data are those on relationship quality. Here again, few differences emerge on single items. However, maritally violent fathers have significantly more arguments with their focal child than do nonviolent fathers, and they also perceive family life in more negative terms. The comparisons of fathers on their expressions of positive affect toward their children and their controlling and punitive behaviors show that maritally violent men are more likely to engage in harsh verbal and physical discipline of their children. These differences are confirmed in the regression models, in which the importance of a man's violence status in accounting for harsh parenting behaviors persists across four different predictive models. Despite the fact that the effects are small, the consistency of results across three different samples of fathers and two different measures of harsh parenting lends credence to these findings. It is these analyses that provide the most convincing evidence for the hypothesis that maritally violent men are different—harsher, meaner—from men who have never been violent in their intimate partnerships.

Adding to this picture are the results we did not present in detail from the comparisons across the three groups of violent men (those violent in both waves, wave 1 only, and wave 2 only). There were few statistically or substantively significant differences among the three groups of men, but substantial differences between the nonviolent men and the three groups of violent men. This suggests that neither the timing nor the persistence of violence in the adult intimate relationship affects parenting behaviors as much as the fact of being violent at all.

It was our intention to provide as thorough an inventory of fathering attitudes and behaviors as possible within the constraints of the NSFH, and our analyses have offered a good, but preliminary, overview of the contours of maritally violent men's fathering behaviors. The analytic template of independent group comparisons was appropriate for the largely descriptive purposes of this paper, but our multivariate analyses point to the fruitfulness of testing more sophisticated models of violence and parenting. Thus, we caution that these analyses need to be followed up and extended in several ways. Certainly, future analyses with the NSFH need to include data on parenting from the wives and partners and to extend these analyses to patterns of marital violence constructed from both partners' behavior, rather than solely the male partner. Further work should look more closely

16. ARE VIOLENT MEN BAD DADS? 381

at respondents whose marriages or partnerships dissolved between waves 1 and 2, and look carefully at the fathers who were lost to followup after wave 1. We also have not addressed the question of how the parenting behaviors of maritally violent fathers shape outcomes among the focal children, a question that can and should be addressed using the NSFH data. When Wave 3 of the NSFH becomes available, longer term effects of parental marital violence on adult children can be traced, perhaps using hierarchical linear modeling such as latent growth curve analysis.

We regard the NSFH as a valuable resource for examining the broad outlines of "common couple" marital violence as it affects family quality and stability and child outcomes. However, we reiterate that the effects of more severe forms of intimate violence on fathering are likely to be muted in these analyses because of our inability to distinguish among types of violent men with these data. Clearly, neither the NSFH nor other broad-scope, national sample surveys can be used alone to portray the fullness of the fathering role and maritally violent men's reactions to that role. There is great need for more research using a variety of methodological approaches on fathering among men whose family lives are lived, overtly or covertly, on the margins of acceptability.

We reiterate that our analyses have provided evidence for both of the competing hypotheses about violent fathers. The underlying extensions of these competing hypotheses have been left unstated to this point, and we close by making them explicit. The "no difference" hypothesis can be extended as follows: "Maritally violent fathers do not differ from nonviolent fathers, and therefore these men pose no realistic threat to their children, which means that restrictions on parental contact or custody are wholly unnecessary." The "vast difference" hypothesis likewise can be extended: "Maritally violent fathers differ significantly from nonviolent fathers, and because these men can pose a significant threat to their children, they should be monitored closely when they have contact with their children, if indeed they are allowed contact with their children at all." The stakes are high in making either a Type I error (that is, rejecting a true hypothesis) or Type II error (accepting a false hypothesis as true) in assessing these competing hypotheses. The frequent news accounts of the lethal outcomes of the propensity of violent husbands to carry their domestic wars to their children give potent evidence of the costliness of rejecting the "vast difference" hypothesis. At the same time, the legions of men who are denied access to their children while their violence against their wives or girlfriends is adjudicated by the courts—fathers who can tally great costs to the emotional bonds they have with their children—give evidence of the costs of misapplying the "vast difference" hypothesis. Nonetheless, this limited review of the evidence available in the National Survey of Families and Households convinces us that there is reason to be concerned about the parenting behaviors of men who have been violent toward their intimate partners, even those who have engaged in the relatively less severe "common couple" violence. And there is much reason for caution in

pushing forward with social policies of marital preservation and mandatory joint custody in child-present divorce proceedings without fully taking into account the potential presence and impact of abusive and violent marital behaviors.

REFERENCES

Adams, D. 1988. Treatment models for men who batter: A profeminist analysis. In K. Yllo & M. Bograd (Eds.), *Feminist perspectives on wife abuse* (pp. 176–199). Newbury Park, CA: Sage.

Benson, M. L., Fox, G. L., DeMaris, A., & VanWyk, J. (2000). Violence in families: The intersection of race, poverty, and community context. In G. L. Fox and M. L. Benson (Eds.), *Families, crime, and criminal justice* (pp. 91–109). Amsterdam: JAI/Elsevier Science.

Booth, A., & Crouter, A. C., (Eds.). (1998). *Men in families.* Mahwah, NJ: Lawrence Erlbaum Associates.

Cummings, E. M. (1998). Children exposed to marital conflict and violence: Conceptual and theoretical directions. In G. W. Holden, R. Geffner, & E. N. Jouriles (Eds.), *Children exposed to marital violence: Theory, research, and applied issues* (pp. 55–93). Washington, DC: American Psychological Association.

Cummings, E. M., & Davies, P. 1994. *Children and marital conflict: The impact of family dispute and resolution.* New York: Guilford.

DeMaris, A. (2000). "'Til discord do us part": The role of physical and verbal conflict in union disruption. *Journal of Marriage and the Family, 62,* 683–692.

Forte, J. A., Franks, D. D., Forte, J. A., & Rigsby, D. (1996). Asymmetrical role-taking: Comparing battered and nonbattered women. *Social Work, 41,* 59–73.

Fox, G. L., Sayers, J., & Bruce, C. (2001). Beyond bravado: Fatherhood as a resource for rehabilitation of men who batter. *Marriage and Family Review, 30,* 137–163.

Gondolf, E. W. (1993). Male batterers. In R. L. Hampton, T. P. Gullotta, G. R. Adams, E. H. Potter III, & R. P. Weissberg (Eds.), *Family violence: Prevention and treatment* (pp. 230–257). Newbury Park, CA: Sage.

Gottman, J. M., Jacobson, N. S., Rushe, R. H., Shortt, J. W. (1995). The relationship between heart rate reactivity, emotionally aggressive behavior, and general violence in batterers. *Journal of Family Psychology, 9,* 227–248.

Graham-Bermann, S. A. (1998). The impact of woman abuse on children's social development: Research and theoretical perspectives. In G. W. Holden, R. Geffner, & E. N. Jouriles, (Eds.) *Children exposed to marital violence: Theory, research, and applied issues* (pp. 21–54). Washington, DC: American Psychological Association.

Greenfeld, L. A., Rand, M. R., Craven, D., Klaus, P. A., Perkins, C., Warchol, G., Maston, C., & Fox, J. S. (1998). *Violence by intimates: Analysis of data on crimes by current or former spouses, boyfriends, and girlfriends.* Washington, DC: U.S. Department of Justice.

Holden, G. W. (1998). Introduction: The development of research into another consequence of family violence. In G. W. Holden, R. Geffner, & E. N. Jouriles (Eds.), *Children exposed to marital violence: Theory, research, and applied issues* (pp. 1–18). Washington, DC: American Psychological Association.

Holden, G. W., Stein, J. D., Ritchie, K. L., Harris, S. D., & Jouriles, E. N. (1998). Parenting behaviors and beliefs of battered women. In G. W. Holden, R. Geffner, & E. N. Jouriles (Eds.), *Children exposed to marital violence: Theory, research, and applied issues* (pp. 289–334). Washington, DC: American Psychological Association.

Holtzworth-Munroe, A., & Stuart, G. L. (1994). Typologies of male batterers: Three subtypes and the differences among them. *Psychological Bulletin, 116,* 476–497.

16. ARE VIOLENT MEN BAD DADS? 383

Hotaling, G. T., Straus, M., & Lincoln, A. J. (1989). Intrafamilial violence, and crime and violence outside the family. In L. Ohlin & M. Tonry (Eds.), *Family violence* (pp. 315–375). Chicago: University of Chicago Press.

Hotaling, G. T., & Sugarman, D. B. (1986). An analysis of risk markers in husband to wife violence: The current state of knowledge. *Violence and Victims, 1*, 101–124.

Jacobson, N. S., & Gottman, J. M. (1998). *When men batter women*. New York: Simon & Schuster.

Jaffe, P. G., & Geffner, R. (1998). Child custody disputes and domestic violence: Critical issues for mental health, social service, and legal professionals. In G. W. Holden, R. Geffner & E. N. Jouriles (Eds.), *Children exposed to marital violence: Theory, research, and applied issues* (pp. 371–408). Washington, DC: American Psychological Association.

Johnson, M. P. (1995). Patriarchal terrorism and common couple violence: Two forms of violence against women. *Journal of Marriage and the Family, 57*, 283–294.

Johnson, M. P., & Ferraro, K. J. (2000). Research on domestic violence in the 1990s: Making distinctions. *Journal of Marriage and the Family, 62*, 948–963.

Matthews, D. J. (1995). Parenting groups for men who batter. In E. Peled, P. G. Jaffe, & J. L. Edleson (Eds.), *Ending the cycle of violence* (pp.106–120). Thousand Oaks, CA: Sage.

McClosky, L. A., Figueredo, A. J., & Koss, M. P. (1995). The effects of systemic family violence on children's mental health. *Child Development, 66*, 1239–1261.

McMahon, M., & Pence, E. (1995). Doing more harm than good? Some cautions on visitation centers. In E. Peled, P. G. Jaffe, & J. L. Edleson (Eds.), *Ending the cycle of violence* (pp. 186–206). Thousand Oaks, CA: Sage.

McNeal, C., & Amato, P. R. (1998). Parents' marital violence: Long-term consequences for children. *Journal of Family Issues, 19*, 123–139.

Osofsky, J. D. (1998). Children as invisible victims of domestic and community violence. In G. W. Holden, R. Geffner, & E. N. Jouriles (Eds.), *Children exposed to marital violence: Theory, research, and applied issues* (pp. 95–117). Washington, DC: American Psychological Association.

Phares, V. (1992). Where's Poppa? The relative lack of attention to the role of fathers in child and adolescent psychopathology. *American Psychologist, 47*, 656–664.

Rennison, C. M, & Welchans, S. (2000). Intimate partner violence. *Special report*. Washington, DC: U.S. Department of Justice, Bureau of Justice Statistics NCJ178247.

Sampson, R. J., Morenoff, J. D., & Earls, F. (1999). Beyond social capital: Spatial dynamics of collective efficacy for children. *American Sociology Review, 64*, 633–660.

Sampson, R. J., & Wilson, W. J. (1995). Toward a theory of race, crime, and urban inequality. In J. Hagan & R. D. Peterson (Eds.), *Crime and inequality* (pp. 37–54). Stanford, CA: Stanford University Press.

Saunders, D. (1993). Husbands who assault: Multiple profiles. In Z. Edwards (Ed.), *Legal responses to wife assault* (pp. 9–36). Newbury Park, CA: Sage.

Silverstein, L. B. (1993). Primate research, family politics, and social policy: Transforming "cads" into "dads." *Journal of Family Psychology, 7*, 267–282.

Silverstein, L. B., & Phares, V. (1996). Expanding the mother–child paradigm: An examination of dissertation research 1986–1994. *Psychology of Women Quarterly, 20*, 39–53.

Sternberg, K. (1996). Fathers: The missing parent in research on family violence. In M. E. Lamb (Ed.), *The role of the father in child development* (pp. 284–308). New York: Wiley.

Stith, S. M., Rosen, K. H., Middleton, K. A., Busch, A. L., Lundeberg, K., & Carlton, R. P. (2000). The intergenerational transmission of spouse abuse: A meta-analysis. *Journal of Marriage and the Family, 62*, 640–654.

Stuart, G. L., & Holtzworth-Munroe, A. (1995). Identifying subtypes of maritally violent men: Descriptive dimensions, correlates and causes of violence, and treatment implications. In S. M. Stith and M. A. Straus (Eds.), *Understanding partner violence: Prevalence, causes, consequences, and solutions* (pp. 162–172). Minneapolis: National Council on Family Relations.

Sweet, J. A., & Bumpass, L. L. (1996). *The National Survey of Families and Households B Waves 1 and 2: Data description and documentation*. Center for Demography and Ecology, University of Wisconsin-Madison (http://ssc.wisc.edu/nsfh/home.htm).

Sweet, J. A., Bumpass, L. L., & Call, V. (1988). *The design and content of the National Survey of Families and Households*, NSFH Working Paper No. 1, Center for Demography and Ecology, University of Wisconsin, Madison, WI.

Szinovacz, M. E., & Egley, L. C. (1995). Comparing one-partner and couple data on sensitive marital behaviors: The case of marital violence. *Journal of Marriage and the Family, 57*, 995–1010.

17

Fathering Indicators for Practice and Evaluation: The Fathering Indicators Framework

Vivian L. Gadsden
*National Center on Fathers and Families (NCOFF),
University of Pennsylvania*

Jay Fagan
Temple University and NCOFF

Aisha Ray
The Erikson Institute and NCOFF

James E. Davis
Temple University and NCOFF

Efforts to increase the quality of fathers' engagement with their children have been at the center of discussions on fathers and families over the past decade. This emphasis is evident in both the numbers of basic and policy studies conducted and the emergence of preventive and intervention programs designed to (re)engage fathers with their children and families. Such programs are estimated to exceed more than 1,000 nationally and are located in a vast range of settings: from small local enclaves in rural and urban settings, to larger community-based organizations, to federal and state programs such as Head Start. They focus disproportionately on the needs of low-income, noncustodial, nonresidential fathers. Until recently, however, the availability of measures of father engagement and indicators of father involvement has been limited. The lack of rigorous research tools in this area is

particularly noteworthy given the growing number of programs that serve fathers and the expectation that these programs, along with increased public awareness of the importance of responsible fathering, will reduce father absence, increase father involvement, and improve the lives of children.

Despite heightened interest in providing services to fathers and new state and federal policy initiatives on welfare and families, there is relatively little knowledge about what occurs in programs that serve fathers, what the relative effects of men's participation are, or what the dimensions of positive behavioral change are. On the one hand, these matters clearly involve program content and participant engagement. On the other, they are singularly issues of assessment and the methodological considerations that must occur in order to determine and implement appropriate measures, designs, and approaches that assist in identifying indicators of change and uncovering the nature of change.

The National Center on Fathers and Families (NCOFF) has developed a framework of indicators for fathering behaviors that can help practitioners, policymakers, and researchers assess, measure, and evaluate behavioral change as occasioned by fatherhood programs, promoted through major policy initiatives, or examined through basic and applied research. This chapter focuses on a description of NCOFF's *Fathering Indicators Framework* (FIF), an evaluation tool that provides indicators of fathering behaviors—within and outside of programs—particularly as they reflect changes in the quality of life for children and families (Gadsden, Fagan, Ray, & Davis, 2001). In the pages that follow, we concentrate on issues relevant to research, practice, and evaluation that are contributing to the construction of a conceptual framework for developing and implementing such fathering indicators using the FIF.

The chapter is organized into four sections. The first section provides a context for the discussion on indicators and considerations for developing an indicators framework. The second section describes the approach, design, and development of the FIF. The third section draws upon data from a field study with fathering and family practitioners to highlight the complexities that may arise in implementing the framework in programs. The final section provides a concluding summary of our findings and closing considerations.

THE ISSUES AND INDICATORS
IN CONTEXT

Traditionally, academic research on families as well as program and policy efforts have focused on mothers or children largely because (1) mothers' have immediate access to children through childbirth, (2) there is a related social expectation that mothers assume the primary responsibility for childrearing, and (3) father absence from the homes of their children is on the rise. However, newly developed family assistance programs often embrace a variety of goals relating to the encouragement

of father involvement—from increasing paternity establishment at birth and the provision of child support, to teaching parenting skills to new fathers, to fostering positive contact between fathers and children (see Barnow & The Lewin Group, 1997; Gadsden, Rethemeyer, & Iannozzi, 2001).

One of the emerging challenges—perhaps the greatest challenge—for any developing field is to determine whether the new policies and concepts emanating from research are making a difference or have the potential to do so. In that sense, the field of responsible fathering is no different. As the field begins to mature, lingering questions remain concerning research and evaluation, as well as larger practice and policy considerations: What counts as positive change, and how do we measure and understand the effects of that change for children, families, and communities?

Beyond this basic assessment are similar questions that are drawn from and inform conceptual and methodological considerations: What specific changes should we strive to effect for children and families through the promotion of improved fathering? Other questions emerge from this line of inquiry: What indicators of positive father engagement, family efficacy, community involvement, and public policies and investments can serve as markers of change? How do we measure and describe accurately the impact of individual programs without setting overly optimistic expectations? The responses to these and related questions will have important implications for researchers who study these issues and conduct evaluations of programs; for practitioners in social service agencies, schools, and community-based organizations who wish to provide onsite, useful services to children, families, and their communities; for communities that want to support children and families and increase father involvement; for families who seek to eliminate social vulnerability and risk for their children; and for policymakers who must formulate effective initiatives that support children and families within the constraints of limited budgets. They contribute to a range of conceptual and methodological issues that serve as a backdrop to developing indicators and shaping an appropriate framework, as described next.

Conceptual Considerations in Developing an Indicators Framework

Although little has been written about fathering measurement and evaluation strategies, the data that are available suggest that when attempts are made to determine the scope of the problem, the focus tends to be on broad indicators of social problems (e.g., rates of unemployment, school dropout, teenage pregnancy, and child support payment) rather than on targeted indicators of fathering or father behavioral change in relation to identified child or family outcomes (Gadsden, Pitt, & Tift, 2001). In short, there is a dearth of sound measures of father involvement designed specifically to assess positive outcomes for fathers, families, and children and to reduce the constraints to developing the field. Thus, a more balanced and informed

model, both conceptually and theoretically, of fathering and its consequences for children is needed—one that focuses directly on fathers, fathering, and the positive contributions better fathering can make to child outcomes. To create such a model, a range of potentially problematic issues must be considered. Discussed next are five such issues: (1) definitions of "father", (2) naive dichotomies, (3) fathers' roles as caregivers, (4) cultural variations within and across fathers and families, and (5) quantity versus quality of paternal involvement.

Defining the Term Father. Family specialists often make assumptions about what is meant by the term father, typically assuming that it refers to a biological father. Few studies attempt to ascertain the family's definition of the figure who is doing the work of the father. In some cases, children relate to several individuals who function as father, including the biological father, stepfather, mother's partner, or a male relative who acts as a father to the child. Defining what father means also leads to a sampling consideration that relates to the shifting nature of households. As Cherlin and Griffith (1998) suggested, perhaps the most fundamental methodological problem we face is also a conceptual one. For example, in studying fathers, "the household survey, the basic data gathering tool for demographic and behavioral science research on the family, the labor force, and fertility, was based on assumptions that no longer hold" (Federal Interagency Forum, 1998, p. 179). Until recently, we assumed that complete and accurate information could be collected from a single household, typically in a single visit or phone call. The need to cross household boundaries to obtain accurate information from (and about) fathers— along with the need to focus on at-risk populations and the desire to examine the experiences of men as parents—has expanded the conceptual frameworks, which has encouraged methodological innovations in fatherhood research and promoted a more general review of federal data collection efforts in this area (Federal Interagency Forum, 1998). Thus, research on fathering measurement or indicators will need to find methods for assessing the involvement of multiple individuals in the life of a child in order to obtain a full picture of the involvement of men in families and to construct broader definitions of father.

Using Naive Dichotomies. Because fatherhood research is relatively new, it has not always been clear what hypotheses should be tested, especially in large-scale surveys (see Moore et al., this volume). By default, global rates of marriage, divorce, and nonmarital birth have been used as proxies for father presence, and coresidence has been assumed to signify father involvement. Although these institutional and residential arrangements tell us something about potential paternal availability, they do not inform us about actual father–child contact and interaction or fathers' assumption of responsibility for children. Furthermore, they tend to simplistically divide issues: For example, involved versus uninvolved father, intact versus father-absent homes, and financially contributing versus financially irresponsible fathers. An alternative to these dichotomous representations

17. THE FATHERING INDICATORS FRAMEWORK 389

of fatherhood is the use of a continuum of father involvement in which multiple points of entry and exit are considered, and the nature of change—namely when it occurs, how it occurs, and what the implications of change are for child and family well-being—is tracked.

Constructing Fathers' Roles as Caregivers. Fathers' roles in caregiving continue to both fascinate and frustrate researchers and practitioners. The dilemma of determining these roles is due in part to shifting societal expectations of fathers within the growing complexity of family lives. Indeed, researchers require more informed models of fathers' behaviors that will help uncover the particular features of caregiving—that is, to distinguish fathers' roles as caregivers from those provided by mothers—to understand the combined influences of fathers and mothers, to address economics as a factor in paternal caregiving, and to identify the unique character and contributions of familial caregiving. In addition, it is crucial that we examine the development and evolution of caregiving as part of the father's identity, beliefs, and behaviors over the father's and the family's life-course (Gadsden & Hall, 1996).

Capturing Cultural Variations. Fathering indicators must be defined and refined in light of different cultural and community values of appropriate paternal roles: e.g., how different cultural and ethnic groups construct notions of fatherhood and the significance that those notions have for father behavior and child development within different community and cultural contexts. This reconsideration suggests a need to develop two levels of indicators—broad categories that are general enough to apply to most communities and more specific variables that capture the concerns, values, and resources of particular communities or family structures within different cultural contexts.

Inherent in any construction of fathering indicators are the values and beliefs held by those who have formulated the indicators—values and beliefs that may be inconsistent with aspects of the father's role as constructed by particular cultures or communities. For example, developers of indicators may have a shared definition of "cooperative parenting" that is at odds with the definition held by members of a given community. Or program evaluators, researchers, and practitioners may not sufficiently comprehend definitions of father involvement that reflect contextual and cultural patterns. For example, cultures differ in their expectations regarding paternal involvement in child care. If fathers are not expected to care for infants and young children or are less involved in the care of girls than of boys, whose definition of their role should be used in the development of appropriate constructs of caregiving? These issues are complicated by the existence in many communities and neighborhoods of multiple ethnicities and cultures (and variations within those cultures) that sometimes make the development of "universal" fathering indicators for all groups difficult, if not problematic. Such differences should be acknowledged and incorporated into fathering indicators. To be useful, fathering indicators

must be easily modified, expanded, rejected, or reshaped to reflect particular cultural and community-level factors.

Measuring the Quantity Versus Quality of Paternal Involvement. A significant number of data collection strategies in father involvement studies rely on either large-scale surveys with representative samples or small-scale studies that often involve interviews with the mother (Marsiglio, Amato, Day, & Lamb, 2000). Because these data collection strategies primarily require quantitative analyses, they are expected to provide an accurate measure. Typically, they do. However, they often fail to identify equally important measures of the quality of father–child interaction or the underlying processes that may be related to father–child interaction, making it essential that data on the nature and quality of father involvement be collected along with the quantity of time spent in various activities and contexts. The conceptual question involves determining the parameters of the behaviors that the researcher, practitioner, or evaluator seek to measure. Assessment of quality can be captured in surveys by adding qualitative questions asking fathers, mothers, and children to assess the affective dimension of fathers' participation in various domains (Lewin Group, 1997). For example, recording the number of minutes per day that the father spends in direct interaction with the child is an important indicator of father presence, but the potential impact of that interaction will be tempered by the qualitative nature of the interaction. Marsiglio et al. (2000) also suggest that national surveys could develop more effective ways to collect information about the intimate aspects of father involvement such as emotional displays. Furthermore, researchers are discovering that how a father, mother, and child feel about an interaction is more consequential than simply the amount of time spent together.

METHODOLOGICAL CONSIDERATIONS

Indicators, such as those in the FIF, must adhere to practical needs as well as scientific principles. They should be amenable to data collection using phone, mail, or in-person interviews as normally done for sample surveys and federally assisted program evaluations (see Child Trends, 1998; DHHS Fathers' Work Group, 1997; Doolittle and Lynn, 1998; Federal Interagency Forum, 1998; Lewin Group, 1997; National Center for Children in Poverty, 1997, 1999). In addition, they should respond to a variety of data collection issues, as described in the following paragraphs.

Use of Multiple Methods. Each proposed indicator can and should be measured using multiple methods and raters. Social scientists, program evaluators, and policymakers agree that multiple methods and data sources are necessary for assessing, understanding, and evaluating father involvement. Identifying different

17. THE FATHERING INDICATORS FRAMEWORK

methods is insufficient, however. It is essential to determine which method is most effective for which purpose and to think carefully about how each method and the data obtained inform the collection of subsequent information. To understand the social and behavioral processes involved in various fathering practices, to assess fathers' influence on their children, to evaluate service programs for fathers, and to monitor the social impacts of government support for fathers, the field requires a multidimensional approach to research methods and data collection. Considerable attention and planning should be given to decisions about the kinds of information that are needed and their application for program development, intervention, policy considerations, or basic research. It leads to a simple but crucial question: To what end will the results of a study or evaluation be used?

To supplement the types of information that can be collected in sample surveys, we believe that intensive observational studies of the interaction patterns of fathers, father figures, mothers, and children must be conducted. Such research allows for the discovery and description of the nature of affective, cognitive, and social processes that characterize father involvement (Lamb, 1997; Parke, 1996). It is also important to include qualitative methodologies—focus groups, in-depth interviews, participant observation, case studies, and ethnographic approaches—in the study of fathers (Coltrane, 1996). Such approaches are especially appropriate to consider at the beginning of the process of selecting relevant variables and refining study questions, but they are also helpful in answering questions about the cultural relevance of various instruments and interpreting data.

Data Sources. Collecting data about fathers from mothers alone introduces substantial bias into survey results. Similarly, collecting information from fathers only creates a biased and partial picture (Coltrane, 1996). Indicators of paternal care must include the perspectives of children who receive care in multiple households and from different kinds of paternal figures. In such cases, absolute and relative measures of time and frequency should be collected and reported. Only by collecting data from mothers, fathers, children, and, as necessary, other family members and observers can both types of father involvement measures be constructed. Such measures are essential in any research or evaluation effort to assess the potential impact of father–child involvement on child development.

Joint Use of Alternative Data Collection Strategies. There is increasing recognition that various research approaches can be compatible and that joint use of alternative data collection strategies can yield a more complete picture of the father's role. For example, multistage sampling procedures are becoming more common because they combine the benefits of generalizability from a representative survey sample and deeper understanding from more intensive observational strategies. Recent examples include studies of the effects of unshared environments on children in stepfamilies (Reiss, Plomin, & Hetherington, 1994). After employing a representative national sampling strategy, these investigators subsequently

videotaped the interaction of family members. Although expensive and time-consuming, this staged-sampling, multimethod strategy advanced an understanding of complex issues. Beitel and Parke (1998) utilized a more modest example of this approach in their study of maternal "gatekeeping." A large sample of mothers was surveyed concerning their attitudes toward, and perceived levels of, paternal involvement, and a subsample of this larger group was chosen for observational analysis.

Reliance on traditional strategies may be insufficient for addressing such enduring issues as the direction of effects measured by quantitative research, the specific impacts of fathers on children and families, and how programs can enhance those impacts. Although the general goal is to increase the level of father involvement in the hope of improving a child's life chances, experimental interventions to test theoretical propositions are also needed. This recommendation serves as a reminder that intervention (often viewed as an applied concern) and theory testing (often viewed as a basic research theme) are quite compatible. Experimental designs have been underutilized in studies of fathers and fathering support programs. By experimentally modifying either the type of paternal behavior or the level of father involvement studied, firmer conclusions concerning the direct causative role that fathers play in modifying their children's and partner's development can be made. Often the use of control groups in experimental studies highlights ethical issues concerning the withholding of needed programs and services for fathers and families. However, the use of waiting lists for control groups in program evaluations is a responsible way to use experimental designs in the assessment of father involvement (Barnow & The Lewin Group, 1997).

Limitations. One limitation of using the indicators with existing data sets is the lack of information regarding how to obtain more in-depth data from various sources. In other words, these indicators only tell us very generally what the potential sources might offer. For example, the number of divorces/separations, the time spent in direct caregiving, or the proportion of fathers employed provide a minimal understanding of the nature and quality of the father's relationship with the child and the family.

Constructing the Indicators Framework

The FIF emerged out of a collaborative process involving researchers, practitioners, and policymakers convened by the National Center on Fathers and Families (NCOFF) and the Annie E. Casey Foundation. The group, which came to be called the NCOFF Working Group on Fathering Indicators, set out to develop a set of themes and indicators as well as to create a framework for measurement—a method of inquiry and understanding—that would have credibility and utility to evaluate father-focused programs, efforts, and activities. The FIF was also intended

17. THE FATHERING INDICATORS FRAMEWORK

to guide research on fathering behaviors and practices. Further, it was meant to be applicable to different populations of fathers (i.e., married fathers present in the home; never-married fathers; noncustodial, nonresidential fathers involved with their children; and noncustodial, nonresidential fathers making the transition to responsible fatherhood).

The Working Group initially identified five indicator categories. A larger group of fathering and family researchers and practitioners from around the country were then commissioned by NCOFF to further develop the indicators. At least one researcher was assigned as the lead contributor and was asked to do the following: review the potential indicators listed in the assigned category; add to, delete from, or refine the list, as necessary; and write a short background and application summary for the category. Practitioners collaborated with researchers on the development of both the category items and the resulting matrix.

A draft report of the FIF was subsequently reviewed by the Working Group and other father and family-focused specialists. Comments from the reviews were compiled and analyzed along with comments from other specialists who were interviewed either face-to-face or by telephone, and suggestions were integrated to create the six categories that currently constitute the FIF: (1) father presence, (2) caregiving, (3) child social competence and academic achievement, (4) cooperative parenting, (5) healthy living, and (6) material and financial contribution. A matrix was developed for each category, listing: (a) potential indicators, (b) existing or potential sources of information, and (c) methodological approaches (see Table 17.1). The next section provides a brief background of each category.

TABLE 17.1
Fathering Indicators Framework Categories

Fathering Indicator Category	Operational Definitions
Father presence	A three-part process involving father engagement, availability, and responsibility in relation to the child
Caregiving	Providing nurturance and performing routine tasks necessary to maintain the child's emotional well-being, physical health, and appearance
Children's social competence and academic achievement	Actively engaging with children and others in developing and enhancing their social competence and academic achievement
Cooperative parenting	Father, mother, and other caregivers establishing a supportive, cooperative interdependent relationship aimed at optimal child development
Fathers' healthy living	Providing a role model through healthy lifestyle and appropriate social behaviors that teach work and personal ethics, as well as social norms to help the child grow and become a productive member of society
Material and financial contribution	Engaging in consistent activities that provide material and financial support to children

The Father Presence Indicator Category. Father presence involves the capacity of fathers to form and maintain significant supportive attachments to a child and his or her caregivers over the life-course. It includes the ability to adapt to maturational changes in the child, in other caregivers, and in the father himself so that optimal child development is achieved (Hawkins, Dollahite, & Brotherson, 1997; NCOFF, 1998). As our principal concern is optimal child development, our indicators highlight those aspects of father presence that are most influential in promoting social, emotional, and intellectual competence in children. To that end, research (Pleck, 1977) suggests that indicators of father–child presence should include the quality and quantity of father–child interactions; fathers' accessibility to children; their assuming responsibility for helping their children develop; their ability to work constructively with other caregivers (see also the section on cooperative parenting indicators); and related aspects of father involvement (Table 17.2).

The Caregiving Indicator Category. Caregiving is a critical and universal aspect of childrearing, encompassing all of those nurturing and life-sustaining acts that help to ensure optimal child outcomes, especially physical, emotional, and psychological development. It requires that the caregiver have an understanding of

TABLE 17.2
Sample Father Presence Indicators

Indicators	Current or Potential Sources of Information
Frequency and quality of play, games, and recreation Frequency of meals eaten with children Frequency of shared housework activities with children present	Father, mother, child reports, service programs Time diaries, surveys, observations, interviews, administrative records (courts, schools, employment) Ethnographies, in-depth interviews, focus groups
Number of fathers coresiding in two-parent households* Number of fathers living in father-only households*	Demographic indicators from national surveys (CPS, NLSY, NSFH, PSID, etc.) (See Federal Interagency Forum on Child and Family Statistics, 1998; Lewin Group, 1997; National Center for Children in Poverty, 1997) Other potential sources for demographic information include parent reports, school records, program case files, CSE, etc.
Number of unmarried fathers coresiding with their children and their children's mother*	Survey and agency estimates
Number of father contacts with children*	Parents, programs, court records Surveys, time diaries, interviews, and observations

*Demographic indicators should be transformed into regional and group-specific rates for comparison and longitudinal analysis.

17. THE FATHERING INDICATORS FRAMEWORK

TABLE 17.3
Sample Caregiving Indicators

Indicators	Current or Potential Sources of Information
Father presence at birth	Father, mother, child, and other caregivers' reports
Time spent in direct caregiving	
Provides physical care to the children (i.e., changing diapers, grooming, bathing, dressing)	
Nature and quality of father–child interaction during solo care	
Frequency and quality of father providing solo care of children	
Nature and quality of father–child interaction during solo care	

children's developmental needs, a capacity to respond effectively to those needs, and an ability to work with other caregivers to enhance the child's development (Hans, Ray, Bernstein, & Halpern, 1995). The search for appropriate indicators of responsible fathering by family advocates, practitioners, researchers, and policy-makers has expanded beyond traditional descriptors of breadwinning to include an array of tasks and behaviors such as nurturing and caregiving formerly associated with the maternal role. See Table 17.3 for sample indicators.

The Children's Social Competence and Academic Achievement Indicator Category. Fathers, mothers, and other significant caregivers of children play an important role in the social competence and academic achievement of their children. Although the degree of parental involvement is highly important in all areas of children's development, the quality of that involvement is also critical to positive child outcomes (Amato, 1998). For this category, we focus on fathers' behaviors that influence various social competence and academic achievement outcomes of children within home, school, and other settings (see Table 17.4). We draw heavily on two frameworks from the developmental literature: Darling and Steinberg's (1993) definitions of parenting styles and behaviors and Baumrind's (1991) typology of parenting styles.

The Cooperative Parenting Indicator Category. Unlike other categories in this framework, cooperative parenting indicators do not focus primarily on changes in the one-on-one relationships between fathers and their children. Instead, this category charts changes in the ability of fathers to work along with mothers (in terms of both cooperative and uncooperative behaviors) to enhance children's well-being. Parents' ability to work with each other depends on a process of establishing cooperation, collaboration, and shared expectations of the responsibilities caregivers have. Despite the practical advantages of creating and sustaining positive, cooperative parenting relationships and the increasing potential of cooperative

TABLE 17.4

Sample Children's Social Competence and Academic Achievement Indicators

Indicators	Current or Potential Sources of Information
Is responsive to children	Father, mother, child reports
Is accepting of children	
Demands mature behavior, but is not overly demanding	
Encourages children to be assertive, responsible, cooperative, and self-regulating	
Makes time for children to do homework	
Expresses interest in children's schoolwork	
Listens attentively to children when they talk	
Communicates with children's teachers	Father, mother, child, teacher reports
Shares with the mother, and where necessary, assumes full responsibility to meet children's health, educational, social, physical, and psychological needs	Father, mother, pediatrician or family physician, teacher reports

TABLE 17.5

Sample Cooperative Parenting Indicators

Indicators	Current or Potential Sources of Information
Maintains mature and respectful relationships with others in the childrearing network	Father, mother, child reports
Resolves differences with others in the childrearing network through effective problem-solving measures	Surveys
Models appropriate ways to deal with feelings and differences in relating to others in the childrearing network	In-depth interviews
Values the importance of the other parent in fostering children's growth and development	
Respects and values the judgments of the other parent	

parenting for responsible fatherhood, there is currently no systematic body of work in research, programs, or policy that addresses issues of cooperative parenting as it relates to father involvement and its implications for child well-being. Sample indicators are given in Table 17.5.

The Fathers' Healthy Living Indicator Category. This category focuses on fathers' healthy living variables (see Table 17.6) that contribute to their ability to care for, be committed to, and foster the well-being and positive development of children. The emphasis is specifically on adolescent fathering, substance abuse, family violence, emotional and physical health, and antisocial behavior.

17. THE FATHERING INDICATORS FRAMEWORK 397

TABLE 17.6

Sample Fathers' Healthy Living Indicators

Indicators	Current or Potential Sources of Information
Makes periodic and regular visits to a family physician	Father, mother, child reports Surveys
Attends to one's physical health needs and illnesses	In-depth interviews
Increased recognition that personal use of substances (alcohol, illegal drugs, nicotine) interferes with paternal responsibilities	
Decrease in child abuse and neglect perpetrated by fathers and other men	
Number and severity of incidents of domestic violence witnessed by child (spouse, sibling)	
Number of fathers who avoid use and possession of substances that could lead to legal interventions	Surveys
Decrease in severity of fathers' criminal activities	
Number of fathers in prison or on parole or probation	Child Welfare League
Decrease in first births to adolescent females and males	U.S. Census Bureau
Decrease in second births to adolescent females and males	

Adolescent and young adult fathering is included as a healthy living variable because of the multiple risks associated with early childbearing.

Each healthy living variable draws on literature showing how such variables become barriers to parenting and their consequences for children and studies demonstrating how a father's disconnection from his children adversely affects his own well-being. Practitioners are keenly aware of the strong connection between fathers' well-being and the capacity of fathers to be active participants in their children's lives. However, practitioners seldom have a positive impact on fathers' abilities to care for their children when the father's own health and well-being are not being considered (Johnson, Levine, & Doolittle, 1999).

The Material and Financial Contribution Indicator Category. Until recently, fathers were seen as the primary economic providers for both children and their mothers. As women increasingly move into the workforce, fathers no longer necessarily have the primary or only role as breadwinner (Cohen, 1993; Perry-Jenkins, Repetti, & Crouter, 2000). Despite these changes, societal expectations are that men will be wage earners and will contribute to their children's financial welfare. As a result, the key indicators used to represent fathers' contributions typically refer to earnings and income for fathers who reside with their children and child support or informal support for those who do not. However, fathers contribute in a number of financial and other material ways to support their children (Sorenson & Turner, 1996). Table 17.7 lists sample indicators.

TABLE 17.7
Sample Material and Financial Contribution Indicators

Indicators	Current or Potential Sources of Information
Proportion of fathers employed	(CPS)
Proportion of fathers who pay any child support	(SIPP)
Number/proportion of fathers with earnings	(SPD)
at least 100%, 150%, and 200% of poverty level	(CSE)
Number and change in the number of households	
with children living at 100%, 150%, and 200%	
of poverty level	
Amount and regularity of formal child support paid	CPS, SIPP, SPD, CSE, special surveys, ethnography
Degree to which fathers' increased financial	Father, mother, grandparent or other family
contributions result in improved resources	member reports
and opportunities for children	Surveys and ethnography

THE FIF AND FATHERING PRACTITIONERS: POTENTIAL APPLICATION WITHIN PROGRAMS

An embedded question in creating fathering indicators concerns how practitioners—for whose programs the indicators have been designed—will interpret, understand, and potentially apply them. To gain some insights into practitioners' responses to this question, NCOFF conducted a small field study during Fall 2000, collecting data from five focus groups of practitioners in child-, father-, and family-focused programs. The total number of participants in the five focus groups was 36: 7 women and 29 men, comprising practitioners from a large Southeastern city, a rural/small-town Northeastern city, a large Northeastern city, a large Western city, and a large Midwestern city. As practitioners, the participants provided an array of services (e.g., early-unwanted fatherhood prevention, employment and job training, and domestic violence reduction) to various populations (e.g., adolescent fathers, incarcerated fathers, and unemployed fathers). See Tables 17.8 and 17.9 for a description of the programs and the fathers participating in them.

Upon arrival at the focus group session, practitioners completed a questionnaire, which asked them to read a scenario and then rate the fathering indicators in the pages that followed. The scenario read as follows:

Your program/organization has received almost 90% of its support from two funders during the past three years. Both funding agencies recently informed you that they will make decisions about whether to increase, continue, or discontinue funding programs such as yours, stating that they are not sure whether such programs are making a difference. They want to know whether your program has made a difference

17. THE FATHERING INDICATORS FRAMEWORK

TABLE 17.8

Practitioners' Programmatic Backgrounds

Program Type	Number
Responsible fathering	27
Early/teen fatherhood support	20
Parenting	20
Incarcerated fathers	19
Workplace and work-related support	10
Divorce support	7
Early/unwanted fatherhood prevention	5
Abusive household support	5

Note. Number does not total 36 because of multiple program offerings in many organizations. On average, each practitioner works in an organization that offers three types of programs.

TABLE 17.9

Descriptive Analyses of the Program Participants

Fathers' Characteristics	Mean Percent for All Programs
Race/ethnicity of participants:	
Asian American	1.25
African American	50.65
Hispanic	20.21
Native American	.18
European American	26.05
Number of fathers served per year (median)	101–150
Household income of fathers:	
50–100% of poverty line	40.00
100–150% of poverty line	36.00
150–200% of poverty line	7.72
200–250% of poverty line	4.86
More than 250% of poverty line	10.79

in helping fathers and their children and families. They indicate that in order for your program to be considered for continued funding, you will need to demonstrate how the program has affected its participants. You contact a local evaluator who suggests that you use the FIF. You then select from the FIF indicators that you think would be most appropriate to represent your program's participants.

Practitioners were then asked to consider the indicators in relationship to changes that are desirable in fathers, children, and families based upon their experiences in the field and their work in programs. They were also informed that their ratings should reflect the level of importance assigned to each indicator. A three-point response format was used, with 1 being "not very important," 2 being "somewhat

important," and 3 being "very important." Practitioners were instructed further to rate indicators as being "very important" if they truly felt that the indicator was a critical area of change or progress that most fathers should make as a result of participating in a program. Following completion of the questionnaire, the focus group moderator initiated a group discussion about the indicators, specifically focusing on why practitioners assigned the different ratings to indicators and how they might use them in their agencies or programs.

Findings From the Survey

The descriptive analysis of survey results was designed to respond to two questions: (1) What is the relative importance of the six indicator categories to the ongoing work of fathering practitioners? and (2) What is the differential value assigned to items within each category? To determine the relative importance of the six categories, we calculated the mode as the measure of central tendency for each of the categories (e.g., father presence). After calculating the mode for each individual indicator item, the percentage of items within each indicator category with a mode of 3 ("very important") was then determined. As Table 17.10 reveals, the healthy living category contained the largest percentage (59%) of items rated as being very important. The financial contribution indicator category contained the lowest percentage (39%) of items with a mode of 3. For the other indicator categories (e.g., presence, caregiving, social competence, and cooperative parenting), the percentage of items with a mode of 3 was fairly similar, with proportions ranging from 46% for the father presence category to 54% for the social competence category.

Tables 17.11 to 17.16 list the items within each category that received the highest and lowest practitioner ratings. The highest rated items in the father presence category (Table 17.11) were those pertaining to the quality of the father–child relationship (e.g., frequency and quality of communication and quality of father's emotional attachment). Practitioners also gave high ratings to items such as increased number of father contacts with children and increased number of visitations with children. The lowest rate items in the presence category were those that assessed family structure variables (e.g., number of divorces, number of marriages,

TABLE 17.10

Percentage of Indicators Within Each Indicator
Category With a Mode of 3

Indicator Category	Percentage
Father presence	46
Caregiving	49
Social competence	54
Cooperative parenting	49
Healthy living	59
Financial contributions	39

TABLE 17.11

Practitioners' Ratings of the Importance of Fathering Indicators: Father Presence

| | Number of Respondents (N = 36) | | |
| | Very | Somewhat | Not |
Indicator	Important	Important	Important
Highest rated items:			
Quality of father's emotional attachment	32	2	2
Frequency of communication	31	4	1
Quality of communication	31	4	1
Frequency of emotional interchanges	30	4	2
Quality of emotional interchanges	30	4	2
Quality of children's emotional attachment	30	3	3
Number of father contacts with children	29	5	2
Number of fathers who initiated contact with children for the first time	26	6	4
Number of father visitations with children	25	9	2
Frequency of play, games, and recreation	22	10	4
Number of legal paternity establishments	16	8	12
Lowest rated items:			
Number of divorces	4	11	21
Number of marriages	5	10	21
Responsibility for vacations, outings, travel	6	15	15
Frequency of meals eaten with children	8	19	9
Number of fathers residing in two-parent households	8	14	14

and number of fathers coresiding in two-parent households) or those that require a father's presence at a routine family event (e.g., eating meals with children).

The items rated the highest in the caregiving category (Table 17.12) were "awareness of children's social-emotional development" and "responsiveness to children's emotions." Practitioners rated "interest in children's health" and "children feeling safe in the presence of the father" as being very important. Most practitioners also indicated that "the nature and quality of fathers' solo child care" and "the provision of physical care to children" (e.g., changing diapers) are very important. Consistent with the findings from the father presence category, the results suggest that practitioners are most concerned about caregiving activities that lead to fathers' emotional attachments to their children. The items that were rated the lowest tended to be those pertaining to fathers assuming responsibility for planning and organizing caregiving (e.g., maintenance tasks related to children or willingness to drop off and pick up child from child care and after-school programs). The ability of fathers to achieve these goals may be constrained because many of the fathers receiving services from father practitioners do not reside with their children.

With respect to fathers' involvement in fostering children's social competence and academic achievement (Table 17.13), practitioners rated "being accepting and supportive of children" the highest, followed by "listening attentively to children

TABLE 17.12

Practitioners' Ratings of the Importance of Fathering Indicators: Caregiving

	Number of Respondents ($N = 36$)		
Indicator	Very Important	Somewhat Important	Not Important
Highest rated items:			
Awareness of children's social-emotional dev.	30	4	1
Responsive to children's emotions	26	7	2
Interest in children's health	25	9	1
Children feel safe in presence of father	25	9	2
Nature and quality of father–child interaction during solo care	24	6	6
Provides physical care to the children (i.e., changes diapers)	22	9	5
Consistently arranges safe environment and monitors children's safety	22	11	3
Improvement in children's mental health	22	10	3
Time spent in direct caregiving	21	11	4
Father presence at birth	18	8	10
Frequency of providing solo care to children	18	13	5
Lowest rated items:			
Maintenance tasks related to children	8	15	12
Drops off and picks up from child care and after-school program	9	18	9
Arranges child care	9	20	7
Responsibility for arranging child's health care	9	20	7
Responsibility for child maintenance	10	14	11

when they talk" and "being responsive to children." Practitioners also appeared to support fathers making at least a minimal effort to learn about child development and parenting. Most practitioners indicated that it is very important for fathering programs to encourage fathers to teach their children about the dangers of substance abuse. They also assigned high ratings to items such as expressing interest in children's schoolwork and praising children for their achievements. These results suggest that practitioners place the greatest emphasis on fathering behaviors that lead to children's sense of security and overall well-being. The lowest ratings were given to items related to teaching specific skills, such as how to use public transportation or how to use the telephone. Low ratings were also given to items pertaining to the provision of opportunities for children to develop their social competence (e.g., visiting peers or relatives).

The highest rated items in the cooperative parenting category (Table 17.14) were those that pertained to maintaining open and respectful communication between adults relative to meeting the needs of children. Practitioners also placed considerable emphasis on fathers' abilities to resolve differences with others in the childrearing network through effective problem-solving. Most practitioners

17. THE FATHERING INDICATORS FRAMEWORK

TABLE 17.13
Practitioners' Ratings of the Importance of Fathering Indicators: Social
Competence

	Number of Respondents (N = 36)		
Indicator	Very Important	Somewhat Important	Not Important
Highest rated items:			
Is accepting of children	29	4	3
Is supportive of children	29	5	2
Listens attentively to children when they talk			
Is responsive to children	27	7	2
Makes at least a minimal effort to learn about child development			
Teaches children about the dangers of substance abuse	25	8	3
Expresses interest in children's schoolwork	25	8	3
Shares with the mother, and where necessary, assumes full responsibility to meet the children's health, educational, social, physical, and psychological needs	25	6	5
Praises children for their achievements	25	8	3
Reads to young children	24	6	6
Teaches children to use nonviolent means to resolve conflicts	23	9	4
Is aware of individual children's needs at each stage of development	24	9	2
Lowest rated items:			
Takes children to visit peers	5	15	16
Teaches children how to use public transportation when it is available	8	14	14
Takes children to visit relatives	9	13	14
Teaches children how to speak on the telephone	9	12	15

also indicated that it is very important for fathers to discuss and negotiate childrearing goals with others in the childrearing network. Considering that many practitioners work with fathers who have strained relationships or minimal contact with the mothers of their children, it is not surprising that the emphasis would be placed on fostering open and mature communication between fathers and mothers. The item rated lowest, although still perceived to be important by practitioners, was the father's flexibility in maintaining a schedule that meets the other parent's and child's expectations. Because of the economic constraints, however, many low-income fathers, who appear to constitute the majority of clients of fathering practitioners, may have few choices about altering their schedules.

Within the healthy living category (Table 17.15), the highest rated indicators were related to decreased incidents of child abuse, child neglect, and other forms of domestic violence. "Improved communication of needs and wants" and "decreased

TABLE 17.14

Practitioners' Ratings of the Importance of Fathering Indicators: Cooperative
Parenting

	Number of Respondents (N = 36)		
Indicator	*Very Important*	*Somewhat Important*	*Not Important*
Highest rated items:			
Maintains mature and respectful relationships with others in the childrearing network	20	9	7
Resolves differences with others in the childrearing network through effective problem-solving	19	11	6
Discusses and negotiates childrearing goals with others in the childrearing network	19	10	7
Models appropriate ways to deal with feelings and differences in relating to others in the childrearing network	15	15	6
Stated or contracted plan for cooperative parenting in relation to different areas of child development (noncustodial parents)	15	13	8
Lowest rated item:			
Flexibility of schedule to meet other parent's and child's expectations	12	14	10

personal use of substances" were also rated as being a high priority. Practitioners placed considerable emphasis on fathers' improved emotional and psychological well-being. According to these findings, it appears that practitioners are concerned about the behaviors and emotional issues that are obstacles to fathers' positive involvement with their children.

The healthy living items that received the lowest ratings by practitioners were those that reflected population trends (e.g., number of fathers in prison, on parole, or on probation and decrease in first births to adolescent females). Somewhat surprising was the relatively low emphasis by practitioners on fathers' physical and mental health or on periodic and regular visits to a family physician. A growing body of evidence indicates that low-income fathers, particularly African-American and Latino fathers, do not pay sufficient attention to their physical and mental health, reflected, in part, by their infrequent visits to the family physician for preventive care.

The financial contributions category (Table 17.16) was rated the lowest of all the indicator categories, although many of the items were still regarded as being very important for fathers. The items rated the highest in this category relate to paying child support (e.g., proportion of fathers who pay any child support and increase in the number/proportion of fathers who pay child support). Most practitioners also indicated that a measure of success in their efforts to work with fathers

17. THE FATHERING INDICATORS FRAMEWORK 405

TABLE 17.15

Practitioners' Ratings of the Importance of Fathering Indicators: Healthy living

| | Number of Respondents (N = 36) | | |
| | Very | Somewhat | Not |
Indicator	Important	Important	Important
Highest rated items:			
Decrease in child abuse and neglect perpetrated			
by fathers and other men	28	4	4
Number of incidents of domestic violence	27	7	2
witnessed by the child			
Improvement in fathers' effective communication			
of needs and wants	26	8	2
Improvement in coping with stressors without			
relying on substances	25	8	4
Improvement in resolving conflicts with related			
adults without violence	24	8	4
Increasing recognition that personal use of			
substances interferes with paternal			
responsibilities	24	10	2
Improvement in resolving conflicts with unrelated			
adults without violence	23	6	7
Decrease in sexual abuse perpetrated by fathers			
and other men	23	4	9
Attends to one's emotional and psychological			
challenges by seeking out resources	23	10	3
Number of fathers who avoid use and possession			
of substances that could lead to legal			
interventions	23	9	4
Maintains mature and respectful relationships			
with others	22	10	4
Resolves differences with others through effective			
problem-solving	22	11	3
Decrease in severity of fathers' criminal activity	22	7	7
Lowest rated items:			
Makes periodic and regular visits to the family			
physician	12	13	11
Number of fathers in prison, parole, or probation	13	10	13
Decrease in first births to adolescent females and			
males	15	5	16
Decrease in second births to adolescent females			
and males	15	7	14

is the proportion of fathers who are employed. Interestingly, practitioners were also concerned about the extent to which fathers' increased financial contributions result in improved opportunities for children. Practitioners placed less emphasis on the indicators pertaining to fathers' education beyond high school and fathers' increased earnings and ability to move out of poverty. Although regarded as being

TABLE 17.16

Practitioners' Ratings of the Importance of Fathering Indicators: Financial Contributions

	Number of Respondents ($N = 36$)		
Variable	Very Important	Somewhat Important	Not Important
Highest rated items:			
Proportion of fathers who pay any child support	21	9	6
Increase in the number/proportion of fathers who pay child support	18	11	7
Proportion of fathers employed	17	13	6
Degree to which fathers' increased financial contributions result in improved opportunities for children	17	12	7
Number of fathers entering, re-entering the labor force	16	14	6
Proportion of fathers who pay all child support	15	13	8
Amount/regularity of formal child support paid	15	13	8
Number of fathers who complete job training and GED programs	14	13	9
Lowest rated items:			
Number of fathers who complete degree programs beyond high school	10	14	12
Number/proportion of fathers who have children covered on their medical insurance	11	13	12
Number/proportion of fathers with earnings at least 100%, 150%, and 200% of poverty level	11	10	15
Change in number/proportion of fathers with earnings at least 100%, 150%, and 200% of poverty level	11	11	14
Number of households with children living at 100%, 150%, and 200% of poverty level	11	11	14
Amount and regularity of informal material and financial contributions made to the child	13	15	8

important, fathers' completion of job training and GED programs received somewhat less emphasis. The high ratings given to paying child support may result from the fathering field's emphasis on child support enforcement. It is worth noting that practitioners did not rate movement out of poverty and educational achievement as high priorities for fathers. This finding is particularly compelling considering the increased focus on workforce investment and the intergenerational poverty experienced by many fathers and families in urban and rural settings.

Findings From Focus Group Interviews

Focus groups conducted with practitioners who completed the survey were designed to elicit information from practitioners about their rationale for rating the indicators and to seek out the nuanced issues that informed their choices. All of the practitioners stated that the father presence category was important in their work with fathers. Many of the practitioners work with noncustodial fathers and

17. THE FATHERING INDICATORS FRAMEWORK

place considerable emphasis on fathers' contacts and visits with their children. However, some types of contact were regarded as more important than others. For example, quality and frequency of communication were important, but frequency of meals and frequency of shared housework were not considered to be of equal value. The practitioners argued that improved communication helps fathers, many of whom have minimal contact with their children, to become emotionally available and supportive of their children. They suggested that increased number of meals eaten with children and shared housework are more relevant to the lifestyles of middle-income, two-parent families than they are to low-income, single-parent families being served by the fathering programs, mainly because of the increased likelihood that middle-income fathers have more flexible work schedules.

While many practitioners commented on the significance of indicators that reflected the quality of the father–child relationship, there was some disagreement about the relative importance of the "quality" versus "quantity" indicators, particularly within the father presence and caregiving categories. One practitioner commented, "The quantity of time is not nearly as important as the quality of time spent with children. That is very important in what I hope to accomplish with fathers." Another practitioner emphasized the quality of fathers' emotions. "The emotions of a family help to keep families from splitting apart."

However, a number of practitioners argued that in their work with fathers, quantity is oftentimes more important than quality, at least in the initial phases of reconnecting fathers with their children. One practitioner noted, "We deal with a lot of men who haven't seen their children in a long time. We want to see these fathers have increased contact with their children." This practitioner seemed to suggest that quality issues could not be addressed until fathers first have some regular contact with their children. Another practitioner commented that the quantity and quality of fathers' presence are important for both residential and nonresidential fathers. He noted that while he works with many nonresidential fathers who are estranged from their children, he also works with many residential fathers "who do not have any emotional or significant contact with [their children], or don't spend much time with them. They come home after the children are asleep or they're watching television and not interacting."

Several practitioners suggested that the presence category was more important than the caregiving category of indicators. As one practitioner shared, "I expect more presence because presence leads to caregiving." Another practitioner placed more emphasis on presence than caregiving because many of the fathers with whom she works "have not visited their children in a long time—are out-of-touch fathers." This practitioner also indicated that the major objective of her work is to increase the number and frequency of contacts (presence); caregiving, she stated, follows if the father increases his presence with his children.

Practitioners reached no uniform agreement that presence is more important than caregiving. One practitioner suggested that the presence and caregiving categories are equally important: "You can't have one without the other. A father sitting on the couch not caring for his children is not worth much." Many focus group

members agreed that the caregiving indicators are important, but they may not be addressed; they noted that programs may not have the capacity to respond to these issues and the fathers who participate may not be prepared to assume the full scope of responsibilities associated with caregiving. As one practitioner stated, "Some of the [caregiving] items were related more so to the tasks of the custodial parent, such as knowledge of the children's daily routine, so I rated them as less important."

There was considerable agreement among the practitioners that fathers play an important role in fostering the social competence and academic achievement of their children. Many of the practitioners stated that they place greater emphasis on the social competence indicators that reflected fathers' emotional support and acceptance of children than on indicators that reflected parental involvement in teaching specific developmental tasks (e.g., enhancing children's communication skills, teaching children to ride a bicycle, or encouraging children to be assertive). Several practitioners also stated that they chose indicators that appeared to focus on enhancing children's self-esteem.

Quite a few of the practitioners in one focus group expressed concerns about the degree to which they could be held accountable for promoting children's social competence and academic achievement through their work with fathers. Several practitioners indicated that the children whose fathers they typically serve are preschool-age or toddlers. As one practitioner stated, "With most of the fathers that we have, the children are preschool-age and toddlers. Looking at it in that context, yeah it is important, but it doesn't apply." Hence, they suggest, early intervention with the father would not have an impact on social competence or academic achievement—developmental areas that they perceived to be more relevant to older children.

Similarly, several practitioners remarked that they would not expect to see children make short-term gains in the areas of social competence and academic achievement as a result of their work with fathers for a year: "You would really have to evaluate on a long-term scale in order to [expect change]. Academically, you don't see it in the generation that you have here, but you see it in the following generation." Another practitioner was concerned about the many factors that can influence children's outcomes, in addition to fathers' involvement, commenting: "It is hard to tease it out and say that a program is not successful when there are so many other influences on children." Although the practitioners in this group were skeptical about being able to measure change in children's social competence as a result of their work with fathers, they did not disagree that the ultimate goal of their work is to enhance the outcomes for children.

Many practitioners commented that the cooperative parenting indicators are extremely important to their work with fathers, noting that nonresidential fathers in particular often have longstanding conflict with the mothers of their children. The practitioners see their role as assisting fathers in having a respectful relationship with the mothers of their children in order to increase father–child involvement. They also see themselves as providing an important source of support to fathers

17. THE FATHERING INDICATORS FRAMEWORK

who often find it difficult to refrain from reacting to differences with their children's mother. As one practitioner stated, "We get a lot of anger toward wives. For a lot of [the fathers], it is educating them to be a parent first. We emphasize, still love your kids."

There was general agreement among the practitioners that the healthy living indicators are extremely important to the fathers in their programs. Nearly all the practitioners indicated that they promote healthy living among their fathers. Many practitioners are concerned about substance abuse and violent behavior. One practitioner stated, "We place a lot of emphasis on nonviolent means of solving problems." Several other practitioners suggested that raising fathers' self-esteem is a priority. Another practitioner commented, "A lot of men are so wounded they just don't feel like they're worthy of taking care of [the child]. It's very hard to turn that around until they feel nurtured and supported." While there was little disagreement about the importance of fathers' health for involved parenting, practitioners also stated that community services are not always responsive to the needs of fathers. Few practitioners addressed issues of domestic violence within the healthy living category. In only one focus group site did practitioners discuss domestic violence issues in detail, indicating that these concerns are poorly addressed in programs for fathers.

The financial contributions indicator category sparked controversy among the focus group participants. A number of practitioners took the position that fathers do not need to be good providers in order to be good parents. One practitioner, who shared that he gave a low rating to the financial contributions indicators, stated, "There are fathers who stay at home and are still good fathers. Being there is more important than what you earn. Child support is overrated." Another practitioner stated that he emphasizes the notion of "working with what you have." He stated further, "You can still do a lot of things for free with your children. Your children will remember that you spent time with them, not how much money you spent." Other practitioners took the position that child support is important. As one participant stated, "After being a single father [myself] for ten years, I haven't found a father who has paid enough." Although there was considerable disagreement about the extent to which financial contributions should be emphasized, practitioners concurred that the child support enforcement system often does not treat fathers well, and there is nearly always the assumption that fathers are trying to avoid payment of child support.

SUMMARY AND CLOSING CONSIDERATIONS

The FIF is an evaluation tool for assisting practitioners, researchers, and policymakers in determining changes that can be expected of fathers within responsible fathering initiatives and programs. As a framework, the FIF also has the potential to assist programs and research in developing a broader view of the range

of behaviors that can be addressed in daily practice with fathers and similarly to facilitate the enhancement of both research and practice.

This chapter addressed the conceptual and methodological considerations in developing an indicators framework, focusing on the specific needs of diverse audiences. Because practitioners and other program specialists are fundamental to the effort—although they sometimes are minimally involved as an audience for measurement and evaluation issues—and because they constitute a major potential audience for the framework, we presented practitioners' responses and assessments of the relevance of the FIF to fathers receiving their services. Their commentaries reinforce the notion that a conceptual understanding of the issues is inextricable from the methodological considerations in developing indicators. Consider, for example, that practitioners reported in the survey that they perceived all the major indicator categories (e.g., presence, caregiving, and children's academic and social competence) to be relevant to their work with fathers. The relatively similar weight given to the six indicator categories suggests that practitioners are thinking holistically about the needs of the fathers with whom they work. Practitioners in the fathering field work primarily with men who have a multitude of needs. Although some are out of touch with their children, those who are involved may be inexperienced as parents, struggling with personal development issues, and burdened by the lack of financial resources to improve their own lives and that of their children. Practitioners' commentaries suggest that the field will need to design programs that are comprehensive in their approach to addressing fathers' needs and that change will have to be measured in multiple areas of child, father, and family development in order to assess adequately the larger influence of the fathering field.

Practitioners also demonstrated consistency in their denotations of important subareas for each indicator and the limitations of collecting data on specific indicators, noting in several instances that a specific fathering behavior or family activity/need is not addressed by the program or, based on practitioners' experience, the issue is not considered to be conceptually or temporally relevant to the programs' missions. Where there were differences in the degree of importance given to some categories over others, the extent of the difference in each instance was relatively small. In particular, practitioners' responses indicated a need for the detailed type of information that quantitative analyses yield, as well as the descriptive and in-depth data that qualitative analyses provide, for seeking information from multiple sources in the family and for considering contextual, temporal, and transitional issues in interpreting results. The sensitivity of issues around context, temporality, and transition is most obvious in practitioners' discussion of the appropriateness to their work of indicators for children's social and academic competence. They emphasized, for example, the importance of transitions—that is, recognizing, as in the case of children's social and academic competence, that fathers' behaviors at the outset of the program differs from their behaviors after participating and that assessing the effects of fathers' engagement over the course of a program without

17. THE FATHERING INDICATORS FRAMEWORK 411

focusing on the effects after fathers' participation is unrealistic and not especially useful in determining the long-term impact.

Indicators are a specific subset of measurement tools. They assist the researcher/evaluator in assessing whether change occurred as well as the parameters of such change. Depending upon how the indicators are used and the approaches implemented to ensure sound data collection and analysis, indicators have the potential to yield important information about how change is occurring— in what ways, for whom, with what barriers and incentives, and within what time-frame(s). As such, indicators are likely to be compared to bean counting and may be utilized within small, focused program evaluations as well as larger, in-depth studies.

The challenge in developing appropriate indicators to inform the work of practitioners, researchers, and policymakers lies in the construction of more balanced and informed models of fathering and its effects on children. An expansive vision of what fathering is, what it does, and what its consequences are for the lives of children and families is at the heart of considerations for applying the FIF. In our conceptualization of the indicators, we have focused on several questions raised during our review of the literature and interviews with practitioners. Many of these issues have the potential to inform, direct, guide, and facilitate better research on parenting.

First, the data and review of programmatic and research reports raise a fundamental question about whether some indicators are inappropriate because of the unavailability of data or inaccessibility of data sources. Our findings suggest that, from practitioners' points of view, some indicators are not applicable, in part, because the activities fall outside the missions and the duration of the programs or are considered unessential to the core work of the programs. The practitioners' candid discussion of the FIF category on children's academic and social competence is one example, which points to larger conceptual and methodological concerns that are useful for researchers, practitioners, and policymakers to consider: that is, providing the latitude to examine fathers and their children and families over time. Few research studies have actually followed families long enough to determine if the effects of fatherhood interventions occur long after the termination of the service, and there is little information on longitudinal or intergenerational effects that can be gleaned from current fathering studies. However, despite the relevance of the issues that the practitioners noted, they also may be missing an important point—that there are likely to be a number of immediate effects on children when fathers become more involved in positive ways with them. These more immediate effects may not be manifested in large-scale improvements in children's social competence or academic achievement but may be reflected in increased sense of well-being, more cooperative behavior, and higher motivation to succeed in tasks. On the other hand, the practitioners' concerns resonate with arguments for better longitudinal studies and support the possibility of indicators being a tracking mechanism that allows us to examine change over the long term: as a programmatic

evaluation device to inform practitioners of the status of their work and as a research tool that allows us to determine the intergenerational effects of fathering efforts on the individual father and his children, family, and community.

Secondly, specific indicators may need to be reconfigured to reflect the realities of programs and the lifestyles of the fathers themselves. This is particularly important for the cooperative parenting and material and financial contributions categories, for example. The indicators in the cooperative parenting category are among those with the greatest potential to be discordant with the cultural values and expectations of program participants, who represent a wide cultural spectrum. A similar mismatch may exist for some of the indicators in the material and financial contributions category, where the value assigned to financial contributions conflicts with the cultural value assigned to material contributions versus physical or caregiving support. In this second instance, however, the mismatch may not simply be between the expectations of the instrument designers and those of the fathers but also between the expectations of the instrument designers and the practitioners within programs who, as in the case of the practitioners in our field study, count financial contributions as an important but not a high priority. If such a mismatch exists, then the specific indicators should be examined and revised as necessary.

More generally, the FIF suggests a way to translate prescriptions into measurable quantities not only that practitioners, researchers, and policymakers can interpret but also that any parent may be able to understand. FIF is helpful to programs, but with some modification it may be useful in considering how it can assist in the creation of self-assessments for parents—an area of work that our findings suggest would be of value and which we are initiating. For example, parents can choose from a menu of outcomes they might want to explore for their children and family. An expanded framework that takes different constituent audiences into consideration would enable parents to measure their own behaviors—to see if they meet their own criteria of success using research-informed assessment tools.

The issue of mismatch in values and focus described earlier raises a related question about what the FIF tells us about the mismatch (if any exists) between the normative vision of good parenting that comes from research and the normative vision of good parenting that is evident in practice. What are the sources of that mismatch? If we accept that the academic normative view of parenting is correct, what do we know about helping parents reconfigure their values? Are these imposed reconfigurations appropriate? If yes, under what circumstances?

A third consideration relates to the specific issues of responsible fathering and responsible mothering and the fit between researchers' or programs' assumptions about and definitions of responsible fathering and mothering and those of the parents participating in research projects. The FIF creates an inventory that could be converted into an assessment tool housing the stated priorities of parents as well as scientific requirements of researchers. This functionality would provide a good check on researchers' biases and a road map for researchers to self-assess critically their own work throughout the research process.

17. THE FATHERING INDICATORS FRAMEWORK

Fourth, another general issue emerged during the process of constructing and revising the FIF and the interviews with practitioners: Can the FIF or any similar indicator tool be successfully translated into user-friendly instruments that still retain their scientific validity and integrity? Even if the instruments are user-friendly, there is a question of whether they are employed in the proper manner—to avoid measurement error. Thus, any work on fathering indicators should ask: Are these tools robust enough to avoid programs' error in their use?

Fifth, there is considerable consensus among practitioners and researchers that both quality and quantity of father involvement needs to be assessed. They highlight issues that practitioners identify as crucial in providing support to fathers and may have implications for determining the degree to which the work and expectations of practice cohere with policy mandates and research agendas and findings. To this end, the indicators must use quantitative studies and data sources. They must also attend more directly to quantitative issues. For example, one question in this line of inquiry is, Could the inventories presented here be used to create local, state, regional, or national profiles of fathering/mothering priorities/values, looking for differences across gender, race, ethnicity, class, and location? Another would be, How diverse is the perception of "responsible" fathering?

Researchers must also employ both qualitative and action research methodologies that permit the voices of community, family members, fathers, and children to be heard and the contexts of childrearing to be more fully understood and described. In particular, the definitions of fathers' roles and unique contribution within particular childrearing contexts, in relation to other caregiving roles, need to be examined systematically. This step is particularly important to promoting an understanding of cultural variations and their implications for practice, research, and advocacy.

The FIF is intended to provide a useful schematic summary of data sources, methods, and variables that can aid in the field's efforts. It identifies specific structural, interactional, and contextual indicators of father involvement. At the same time, many national, regional, and administrative data sources are beginning to include information on fathers. To understand better the behavioral processes and outcomes of fathering practices and to evaluate and monitor the effectiveness of fathering programs, the field needs authentic and reliable indicators. Equally necessary is the ongoing indictor measurement and development that reflects changes in the practice of fathers and families, research efforts that have developed, and knowledge that is most often ignored. The purpose of the FIF is to create a practical, flexible framework. However, when transitioning the FIF or any instrument from a research tool to a practical protocol (i.e., one that is time effective and cost effective, yet rich in the data it can yield), the field will need to develop practical approaches that practitioners and participants on the ground can use to conceptualize their work and assess their progress. In this way, researchers contribute to the building of broader notions of inquiry in which practice both is informed by and uses research—and in which research knowledge, in turn, draws effectively from practice.

ACKNOWLEDGMENTS

Parts of this paper were adapted from a larger report, *The Fathering Indicators Framework* (Gadsden et al., 2001). Earlier versions of this paper received textual contributions and review from our colleagues: Burt Barnow, Eric Brenner, Ruth Chao, Scott Coltrane, David McDowell, Ross Parke, and R. Karl Rethemeyer.

REFERENCES

Amato, P. R. (1998). More than money? Men's contributions to their children's lives. In A. Booth & A. C. Crouter (Eds.), *Men in families: When do they get involved? What difference does it make?* (pp. 241–278). Mahwah, NJ: Lawrence Erlbaum Associates.

Baumrind, D. (1991). Effective parenting during the early adolescent transition. In P. Cowan & E. M. Hetherington (Eds.), *Advances in family research: Vol. 2 Family transition* (111–163). Hillsdale, NJ: Lawrence Erlbaum Associates.

Beitel, A. H., & Parke, R. D. (1998). Paternal involvement in infancy: The role of maternal and paternal attitudes. *Journal of Family Psychology, 12*(2), 268–288.

Barnow, B. S., & The Lewin Group. (1997). *An evaluability assessment of responsible fatherhood programs: Final report.* Washington, DC: U.S. Department of Health and Human Services, Office of the Assistant Secretary for Planning and Evaluation.

Chao, R. K. (1994). Beyond parental control and authoritarian parenting style: Understanding Chinese parenting through the cultural notion of training. *Child Development, 65*, 1111–1119.

Chao, R. K. (1995). Chinese and European American cultural models of the self reflected in mothers' childrearing beliefs. *Ethos, 23*, 328–354.

Cherlin, A., & Griffith, J. (1998). Methodological issues in improving data on fathers. In *Nurturing fatherhood: Improving data on research on male fertility, family formation, and fatherhood.* (pp. ?). Washington, DC: Federal Interagency Forum on Child and Family Statistics.

Child Trends (1998). *Trends in the well-being of America's children and youth.* Washington, DC: U.S. Department of Health and Human Services, Office of the Assistant Secretary for Planning and Evaluation.

Coltrane, S. (1996). Why do couples share? In *Family man: Fatherhood, housework, and gender equity* (pp. 116–150). New York: Oxford University Press.

Cohen, T. F. (1993). What do fathers provide? Reconsidering the economic and nurturant dimensions of men as parents. In J. C. Hood (Ed.), *Men, work and family* (pp. 1–22). Newbury Park, CA: Sage.

Darling, N., & Steinberg, L. (1993). Parenting style as context: An integrative model. *Psychological Bulletin, 113*(3), 487–496.

Department of Health and Human Services. (1997). *Implementation strategy for President Clinton's initiative to strengthen the role of fathers in families. The first year implementation report.* Washington, DC: Author.

Doolittle, F., & Lynn, S. (1998). *Working with low-income cases: Lessons for the child support enforcement system from Parents' Fair Share.* New York: Manpower Demonstration Research Corp.

Federal Interagency Forum on Child and Family Statistics. (1998). *Nurturing fatherhood: Improving data and research on male fertility, family formation, and fatherhood.* Washington, DC: Author.

Gadsden, V. L. & Hall, M. (1996). Intergenerational learning: A review of the literature. National Center on Fathers and Families.

Gadsden, V., Fagan, J., Ray, A., & Davis, J. E. (Eds.). (2001). *The Fathering Indicators Framework: A Tool for Quantitative and Qualitative Analysis.* Philadelphia: National Center on Fathers and Families.

17. THE FATHERING INDICATORS FRAMEWORK 415

Gadsden, V. L., Pitt, E., and Tift, N. (2001). Fathers and families research and practice: Exploring potential areas for inquiry. In J. Fagan & A. Hawkins (Eds.), *Clinical and education interventions with fathers*. Binghamton, NY: Haworth.

Gadsden, V. L., Rethemeyer, R. K., & Iannozzi, F. (2001). Bay area fatherhood initiatives: Portraits and possibilities. Philadelphia: National Center on Fathers and Families.

Hans, S., Ray, A., Berstein, V., & Halpern, R. (1995). *Caregiving in the inner-city*. Final report to the Carnegie Corporation of New York and the Charles Stewart Mott Foundation. Chicago: University of Chicago, Department of Psychiatry, Unit for Research in Child Psychiatry and Development.

Hawkins, A. J., Dollahite, D. C., & Brotherson, S. E. (1997). Fatherwork: A conceptual ethic of fathering as generative work. In A. J. Hawkins & E. C. Dollahite (Eds.), *Generative fathering: Beyond deficit perspectives. Current issues in the family series, Vol. 3*. (pp. 17–35). Thousand Oaks, CA: Sage.

Johnson, E. S., Levine, A., & Doolittle, F. C. (1999). *Fathers' fair share: Helping poor men manage child support and fatherhood*. New York: Russell Sage Foundation.

Lamb, M. E. (Ed.). (1997). *The role of the father in child development* (3rd ed.). New York: Wiley.

Lewin Group, Inc. (1997, August). *An evaluability assessment of responsible fatherhood programs* (Final report). Washington, DC: Department of Health and Human Services and the Ford Foundation.

Marsiglio, W., Amato, P., Day, R. D., & Lamb, M. E. (2000). Scholarship on fatherhood in the 1990s and beyond. *Journal of Marriage and the Family, 62*, 1173–1191.

National Center for Children in Poverty & Harvard Family Research Project. (1997). *Starting points: Challenging the "Quiet Crisis". A description of the starting points sites*. New York: National Center for Children in Poverty.

National Center on Fathers and Families. (1998). *The fathers and families core learnings: An update from the field*. Philadelphia: Author.

Parke, R. D. (1996). Fatherhood: Myths and realities. In *Fatherhood* (pp. 1–16). Cambridge, MA: Harvard University Press.

Perry-Jenkins, M., Repetti, R. L., & Crouter, A. C. (2000). Work and family in the 1990s. *Journal of Marriage and the Family, 62*(4), 981–988.

Pleck, J. H. (1997). Paternal involvement: Levels, sources, and consequences. In M. E. Lamb (Ed.), *The role of the father in child development*(3rd ed., pp. 66–104). New York: Wiley.

Reiss D., Plomin R., Hetherington, E. M. (1994). Genetics and psychiatry: An unheralded window on the environment. *American Journal of Psychiatry, 48*, 283–291.

Sorenson, E., & Turner, M. (1996). *Barriers in child support policy: A literature review*. Philadelphia: National Center on Fathers and Families.

18

The DADS Initiative: Measuring Father Involvement in Large-Scale Surveys

Natasha Cabrera
University of Maryland

Kristin Moore,
Jacinta Bronte-Tinkew, Tamara Halle
Child Trends, Inc.

Jerry West
National Center for Educational Statistics

Jean Brooks-Gunn
Columbia University

Nancy Reichman,
Julien Teitler
Princeton University

Kirsten Ellingsen,
Christine W. Nord
Westat

Kimberly Boller
Mathematical Policy Research, Inc.

Although conceptualizations of what "good" fathers do or ought to do have proliferated in the last 10 years or so, methodological and measurement issues concerning how to recruit, interview, and retain fathers in research studies have progressed at a slower pace. Past approaches to the measurement of father involvement have been characterized by at least five limitations: (1) Mothers are often used as proxy for fathers, (2) the often interchangeable use of generic fathering versus child-specific fathering, (3) the limited generalization of findings from middle-class, European-American groups to other cultural groups, (4) the validity of fathers' self-report

data, and (5) the narrow or dichotomous (present/absent) definition of father involvement. However, in the last few years there have been serious and concerted efforts to improve on past methodologies.

In this chapter we discuss methodological, design, and measurement issues related to studying father involvement and its impact on child development in three large national studies: the Early Head Start National Research and Evaluation Project Father Studies (EHS), the Fragile Families and Child-Well Being Study (FF), and the Early Childhood Longitudinal Study Birth–Cohort (ECLS–B). These studies are part of a coordinating effort titled Developing a Daddy Survey (DADS). The general mission of DADS is to increase comparability across surveys, and provide an integrated view of father involvement that can inform the field and serve as a guide for future projects that measure father involvement. This effort has resulted in substantial comparability in using similar constructs and survey questions as well as the opportunity to share each other's experiences and challenges. Given this level of coordination, the DADS project has provided a unique opportunity to share strategies for engaging fathers in these studies and a forum for discussing the methodological challenges and opportunities for studying fatherhood in this population.

The specific goals of this paper are to (1) briefly present the historical context for this project, (2) describe the projects that are part of DADS, (3) provide an overview of the methodological challenges faced in collecting data on father involvement in the DADS studies that focus on "being a dad", and (4) briefly present the way these studies have overcome challenges and the lessons learned.

HISTORICAL BACKGROUND

The DADS project responds to an emerging need for better information about fatherhood. It builds on the expertise and work of researchers involved in measuring father involvement in several large-scale national surveys. It provides a forum for researchers to share knowledge and experience about how to design and implement studies of fathers. In this context, it seeks to increase comparability across surveys by providing an integrated view of how to measure father involvement.

The DADS project arose out of the fatherhood research initiative of the mid-1990s. In 1995, the Clinton Administration asked federal agencies to assume greater leadership in promoting father involvement by reviewing programs and policies to strengthen and highlight the importance of fathers in the lives of children, as well as improve data collection on fathers (Federal Interagency Forum on Child and Family Statistics, 1998). President Clinton asked for a review of agency activities in four areas:

- Ensure, where appropriate and consistent with program objectives, that programs seek to engage and meaningfully include fathers.

18. LARGE-SCALE SURVEYS 419

- Proactively modify programs designed to serve primarily mothers and children, where appropriate and consistent with program objectives, to explicitly include fathers and strengthen their involvement with their children.
- Include evidence of father involvement and participation, where appropriate, in measuring the success of programs.
- Incorporate fathers, where appropriate, in government-initiated research regarding children and their families. This area was taken as a further impetus to collaborate broadly to examine data, theory, measures, analyses, and data collection strategies regarding fathers, as well as what is known on the basis of research.

Under the leadership of the Federal Interagency Forum on Child and Family Statistics (the Forum), a number of groups including federal statistical agencies, federal and state policymakers, practitioners, and the broader family and child research community gathered to take stock of the research base on fertility, family formation, and fatherhood (Tamis-LeMonda & Cabrera, 1999). The result was a series of conferences held in 1996 and 1997 that came to be known as the "Fatherhood Initiative." While confirming the importance of fathers to children (and of children to fathers), these meetings highlighted major limitations of current research on fatherhood. These meetings were summarized in a report entitled *Nurturing Fatherhood: Improving Data and Research on Male Fertility, Family Formation, and Fatherhood* (Federal Interagency Forum on Child and Family Statistics, 1998), which presented a detailed analysis of the state of data collection and research on male fertility, family formation, and fathering and provided a foundation for additional data collection and research within the public and private sectors. The *Nurturing Fatherhood* report also recommended 10 targets of opportunity to improve data and research on fatherhood:

1. Publish a report on the state of data collection and research on male fertility, family formation, and fathering.
2. Publish a report on fatherhood indicators, including indicators of male fertility, family formation, and fathering.
3. Use the National Survey of Family Growth to increase our understanding of fertility and family formation by interviewing men directly.
4. Include measures of whether fathers live with and have contact with their children in surveys and routine administrative data collection. Additional measures of father–child interaction should be developed and incorporated as feasible.
5. Use the ECLS–B to expand our understanding of fathers' relationship to child development and school readiness by including a module on the involvement of both resident and nonresident fathers.
6. Use the NSLY-97 to increase our understanding of how sexual activity, fertility, marriage, and parenthood affect educational attainment and labor force participation for men.

7. Use the EHS Research and Evaluation project as a laboratory for conducting basic theoretical research on the meaning and nature of fathering for low-income men and their children.
8. Test, as part of a national survey, the experimental method for identifying individuals who are tenuously attached to households as developed by the U.S. Census Bureau and piloted in the Living Situation Survey.
9. Explore, with the Departments of Justice and Defense, the possibility of including military and prison populations in some surveys.
10. Explore the possibility of using state administrative data to augment national survey data about fathers.

These targets represent an agenda for specific opportunities and suggests a timeline for meeting these goals. The DADS project fulfills several of these targets.

The DADS project is one of a number of exciting pathbreaking activities in research and policy on child and family well-being that have been initiated in the past several years. Several innovative, large national studies of young children and their families are now in the field (as profiled in the Synthesis and Profile of Early Education and Development, SPEED, Brooks-Gunn et al., 2000; Fuligni & Brooks-Gunn, 2003). These studies pay particular attention to the varied contexts in which young children develop—families, child-care settings, schools, early childhood intervention programs, community programs, and neighborhoods.

The DADS project, which began in 1997 and builds on several of the new initiatives profiled in SPEED, would not have happened had it not been for the intellectual vision, generous input, and collaborative spirit of the people involved in this project. On a shoestring budget and determined to take advantage of the opportunity presented, several researchers and representatives of federal agencies met regularly to share measures and refine them with the goal of improving the design and development of father involvement measures. Principal investigators from studies that were further along also shared psychometric data, as they became available, with the group. This information was used to shape the questions being used, delete questions that were not reliable, and modify others (Bronte-Tinkew, Moore, & Cabrera, 2000).

The DADS project coordinates measurement across six surveys that are categorized into two sets—those that look at *becoming a dad* and those that focus on *being a dad*. The *becoming a dad* surveys include the National Longitudinal Survey of Youth 1997 (NLSY-97), the National Survey of Family Growth (NSFG), and National Longitudinal Study of Adolescent Health (Add Health). Those that focus on *being a dad* include the Early Head Start National Research and Evaluation Project Father Studies (EHS), the Fragile Families and Child Well-Being Study (FF), and the Early Childhood Longitudinal Study–Birth Cohort (ECLS–B). One caveat is important: Although the overall mission of DADS is to coordinate measures across the six aforementioned studies, in this paper we focus on the work that has been done to date to coordinate the studies that focus on *being a dad*

18. LARGE-SCALE SURVEYS   421

(i.e., EHS, FF, and ECLS–B). Efforts to ensure construct comparability across studies that focus on *becoming a dad* have followed a different trajectory and are not reported here.

The DADS project regarding the being a dad surveys has three immediate goals: (1) to make constructs scientifically, methodologically, and theoretically as uniform as possible across father studies that examine the process of being a father, (2) to assemble the survey items measuring father involvement into one document to provide state-of-the-art measures that can be used in other surveys, and (3) to establish validity and reliability for these measures.

The process of meeting these goals unfolded as the studies themselves were taking shape in the field. One result is two binders compiling measures of father involvement that are child-age-specific. The measures are catalogued by construct and sociodemographic variables and organized according to Lamb, Pleck, Charnov, and Levine's (1985, 1987) theoretical framework of father involvement and Palkovitz's (1997) extended definition of involvement (Table 18.1). The binders of measures are striking for two reasons: (1) They represent state-of-the art summaries of how cutting-edge conceptualizations of father involvement have been translated into survey instruments and (2) they show that there is considerable overlap among constructs and measures across the three DADS studies. This level of coordination is unprecedented and will facilitate analytic work across these studies using a similar conceptualization of father involvement. While the binders represent an important advance in the field, the validity and reliability of the measures have yet to be established. The next step for the *DADS* group is to establish their psychometric characteristics so that future researchers can use these measures with confidence.

The DADS Studies

To reiterate, the *being a dad* studies include the Fragile Families and Child Well-Being Study, the Early Head Start National Evaluation Father Studies, and the Early Childhood Longitudinal Study–Birth Cohort. The FF targets a representative sample of new, mostly unwed couples[1] in cities with populations of 200,000 or more. The ECLS–B is a nationally representative study of 15,000 children from birth to the time they enter school. The EHS evaluation sample is drawn from 17 EHS programs; within programs, families are randomly assigned either to the program group or the control group. Collectively these studies will provide rich and previously unavailable information on the type, nature, and frequency of father involvement in the United States. These studies were funded partly in response to some of the recommendations of the *Nurturing Fatherhood* report.

---

[1]These new parents and their children are called fragile families because of the multiple risk factors associated with nonmarital childbearing and to signify the vulnerability of the relationships within these families.

TABLE 18.1
Matrix of Measures/Constructs used in the EHS, ECLS–B and FF Studies

Father Involvement Constructs/ Items	Early Head Start (Father Interviews)						ECLS-B Father Interviews
	1mth	3mth (NI)	6mth	14mth	24mth	36th	9mth
Sociodemographics:							
Bio or Social Father	X		X	X	X	X	
Residence (e.g., type of home, number of moves)	X		X	X	X		X
Household composition/ Living situation	X		X	X	X		X
Marital/Partner Status	X	X	X	X	X		X
Number of biological children	X	X		X	X		X
Hispanic origin	X				X		
Race/ethnicity	X				X		
Age mth/yr born	X		X	X	X	X	X
Country of origin, citizenship/immigration*	X				X		X
Language (including literacy)	X		X	X	X		X
Employment status* (including off-the-books activities FF)	X		X	X	X		X
Occupation	X		X	X	X		X
Work schedule	X		X	X	X	X	X
Satisfaction w/ income/job	X		X	X	X	X	
Income (including monthly expenses FF)/Earnings	X		X	X	X	X	X
Education	X		X	X	X	X	X
Religion							X
Enrollment and training (including military service -FF)			X	X	X		X
Employment benefits							X
Income & ownership							
Family background:							
Family composition while growing up			X	X		X	X
Receipt of public assistance during childhood			X	X		X	X
Educational attainment of father's parents			X	X		X	X
Whether father's parents are still living							
Parents' country of origin			X	X		X	

(Continued)

TABLE 18.1
(Continued)

Father Involvement Constructs/ Items	Early Head Start (Father Interviews)						ECLS-B Father Interviews
	1mth	3mth (NI)	6mth	14mth	24mth	36th	9mth
Accessibility							
Lived with child since birth/last interview	X		X	X	X	X	X
How long father lived in HH or child lived with father	X		X		X	X	X
Since child born ever lived in same household	X		X	X	X	X	X
How old child when first met/when did you start living w/child	X		X	X	X	X	
How many miles/minutes away does dad live	X		X	X	X		X
How do you get to child	X			X			
How often spent 1 or more hrs a day w/child since birth/or past month	X	X	X	X	X		X
How many months able to see child on regular basis				X	X	X	
Separations from child and duration			X	X	X	X	X
How long since last contact with child							X
In past 12 month/since birth/past 30 days how often seen child							X
How often child's mother able to contact father when he's not at home							
Live in same household with (child)				X			
Reasons for low/no contact		X	X	X		X	
How often seen child since stopped living together							X
How often talk w/mother about child							X
How much of time is (child) living w/you							
Engagement:							
Number of hours with child and whether primary caretaker	X	X	X	X	X		
Prenatal support	X						X
Present at birth, visits soon after	X						X

(Continued)

TABLE 18.1
(Continued)

Father Involvement Constructs/ Items	Early Head Start (Father Interviews)						ECLS-B Father Interviews
	1mth	3mth (NI)	6mth	14mth	24mth	36th	9mth
Held newborn	X						X
Warmth/affection	X	X	X	X	X	X	X
Shared activities (e.g., sing songs, take to visit friends, meals together). Includes cog. stimulation items	X	X	X	X	X	X	X
Discipline/parenting style				X	X	X	
Volunteers at child care program					X		
Violence, abuse, neglect							
Limited setting/monitoring							
School Involvement							
Responsibility:							
Child-related maintenance (child care tasks including babysitting)	X	X	X	X	X	X	X
Purchase items for child (including pay for child care)	X	X		X	X		X
Role in deciding about child care	X		X	X	X		X
Input into child-related decisions	X	X	X	X	X		X
Provide health insurance coverage, paid for medical insurance, doctor bills, medicine		X	X	X	X		X
Given extra money to help out		X		X	X	–	X
Take child to sitter or child care			X	X	X	–	
How much child support due/how often paid			X	X	X	X	X
Type of child support arrangements (also informal)			X	X	X	X	X
Whether baby will have father's last name/Whether father's name will be on the birth certificate			X		X	X	X
Legal paternity established			X	X	X	X	X

(Continued)

426 CABRERA ET AL.

TABLE 18.1
(Continued)

Father Involvement Constructs/ Items	Early Head Start (Father Interviews)						ECLS-B Father Interviews
	1mth	3mth (NI)	6mth	14mth	24mth	36th	9mth
Professional treatment for emotional or mental problems							X
Father–mother relationships:							
Time w/mom before pregnancy	X	X					
Disagreements concerning child	X		X	X	X		X
General disagreements	X		X	X	X		X
Rating of relationship w/child's mother	X	X		X	X		X
Status of relationship (e.g., romantic/friendship)			X				
Past relationship w/child's mother/why relationship ended							
Plans for relationship in the future (e.g., marriage, cohabitation)							
Mother's view of father's involvement w/child							
Quality of current relationship							X
Feelings about interactions (w/spouse) (may not be bio-mom)			X	X			
Relationships w/ family members:							
Dad's relationship with other relatives	X	X	X	X	X	X	
Experiences w/ own father/father figure		X	X	X	X		
Present relationship w/own father/father figure		X	X	X	X		
Experiences w/ own mother/mother figure		X	X	X	X		
Present relationship w/own mother/mother figure		X	X	X	X		X
How problems w/family members are resolved				X		X	
Knowledge and attitudes about fatherhood:							
Feelings about pregnancy	X						X

(Continued)

TABLE 18.1
(Continued)

Father Involvement Constructs/Items	Early Head Start (Father Interviews)						ECLS-B Father Interviews
	1mth	3mth (NI)	6mth	14mth	24mth	36th	9mth
Share common household and child related expenses			X	X	X	X	
Plans for involvement in the future			X	X	X	X	X
Discuss child w/doctor, sitter etc.							
How many children live elsewhere							X
Provide support for children living elsewhere							X
Efforts to improve life of child							
Fertility, marital, partner history:							
Number of children ever sired	X	X		X	X	X	X
Age at child's birth (can be calculated)							X
Age when first became father						X	X
Marital status at birth of child							
Ever married/live with child's mother							
Complete Fertility History							
Marital/Cohabiting History							X
Number of biological children w/child's mother							
Health, mental health, stressful life events:							
Stressful life events	X			X	X	X	
Health status	X		X	X	X	X	X
Depression			X	X	X	X	X
Cigarette smoking, drug and alcohol use							X
Family history of: Cigarette smoking, drug & alcohol use, depression, mental disorders, asthma, learning disability							X
Self esteem							
Locus of control							
Limiting conditions							X

(Continued)

18. LARGE-SCALE SURVEYS

TABLE 18.1
(Continued)

Father Involvement Constructs/Items	Early Head Start (Father Interviews)						ECLS-B Father Interviews
	1mth	*3mth (NI)*	*6mth*	*14mth*	*24mth*	*36th*	*9mth*
Perceptions of fatherhood	X		X	X	X		X
Feelings about child	X		X	X	X		X
Rating of self as father	X	X	X	X	X		X
Plans for involvement w/ child	X	X					
Knowledge about raising a child	X		X	X	X	X	X
Stress related to fatherhood			X	X	X		
Importance of things dads do	X		X	X	X		X
Perceived rights and obligations of dads							
Marriage and gender role perceptions:							
Social support network	X	X	X	X		X	
Support of parenting role							
Guidance/parenting advice	X	X	X				
Material support from relatives and friends							
Emotional support							
Social involvement (excluding church attendance)							X
Neighborhood & environment:							
Public housing							
Neighborhood problems (e.g., litter, crime, traffic)							
Safe play areas							
Housing and/or financial problems							
Child-related services & government programs:							
Attends/invited to parenting training	X		X	X	X		
Attends/invited to programs for fathers/men				X	X		
Attends program's board meeting			X	X	X		
Where receive information about caring for child	X						
Program affiliated child care			X				
Program/agency visits home	X		X	X	X		

(Continued)

TABLE 18.1
(Continued)

Father Involvement Constructs/ Items	Early Head Start (Father Interviews)						ECLS-B Father Interviews
	1mth	3mth (NI)	6mth	14mth	24mth	36th	9mth
Welfare and child support policy in father's state							
Received help from agency or program							
Received income from program (e.g., welfare, food stamps, unemployment)							
Criminal justice system experience:							
Criminal charges							
Criminal convictions							
Incarceration/Probation							
Custodial fatherhood:							
Mother/child contact							
Child support from mother							
Child Behavior:						X	

Note. The X indicates that the item is measured in the study.

The Fragile Families and Child Well-Being Study. The FF addresses the following questions: (1) What are the conditions and capabilities of new unwed parents? (2) What is the nature of the relationship between unwed parents? (3) What factors push new unwed parents together? What factors pull them apart? In particular, how do public policies affect parents' behaviors and living arrangements? (4) What are the long-term consequences for parents, children, and society of new welfare regulations, stronger paternity establishment, and stricter child support enforcement? See Table 18.2 for program details.

The study follows a birth cohort of new, mostly unwed parents and their children and provides previously unavailable information about the conditions and capabilities of new parents and the well-being of their children. In addition to the core survey, FF includes several "add-on" studies, including an intensive substudy of 75 couples that entails ethnographic interviews with mothers and fathers separately and together, repeated over the first 3 years of the child's life. This substudy examines the type of relationships unwed couples have, with a special focus on conflict, cohesion, and bargaining.[2]

---

[2]This substudy is funded by the MacArthur Network on Work and the Family. Kathy Edin is the principal investigator.

18. LARGE-SCALE SURVEYS   429

TABLE 18.2
The Fragile Families and Child Well-Being Study—Main Study/Context

Purpose	To learn about the conditions and capabilities of new unwed parents.
Design	Longitudinal design following a representative panel of mostly unmarried parents (includes both mothers and fathers). Families drawn from 20 cities selected based on welfare and child support policies and labor market strength.
Sample	A hospital-based sampling procedure was used to enroll 4,700 families including 3,600 unmarried couples and 1,100 married couples.
Periodicity	In several waves of data collection from 1998 to 2000, parents were interviewed after the birth of their child. Follow-up interviews with both parents are scheduled for when the child is 12, 30, and 48 months old.
Topics covered/content	Family characteristics, child well-being and fathering, parent–parent and parent–child relationships, fathers, demographics, family support, environment and programs, health and health behavior, education and employment, income, incarceration, child care, and child abuse.
Data collection	See periodicity.
Principal investigators	Sara McLanahan & Irwin Garfinkel; Jeanne Brooks-Gunn, Marta Tienda, Nancy Reichman, and Julien Teitler are co-investigators.
Funders	NICHD, Ford Foundation, Robert Wood Johnson Foundation, William T. Grant Foundation, Public Policy Institute of California, California HealthCare Foundation, Hogg Foundation, St. David's Hospital Foundation, Commonwealth Fund, Fund for New Jersey, Healthcare Foundation of New Jersey, Foundation for Child Development, David and Lucile Packard Foundation, Kronkosky Charitable Foundation, A.L. Mailman Family Foundation, St. Vincent Hospital and Health Services, William and Flora Hewlett Foundation, Leon Lowenstein Foundation, Johan D. and Catherine T. MacArthur Foundation, and Charles Stewart Mott Foundation.
Limitations	Only large cities; only English and Spanish speaking parents.
Internet site and contact information	http://opr.princeton.edu/crcw/ff

Note. The fatherhood component has all the same program element descriptions.

The FF study addresses three areas of great interest to policymakers and community leaders—nonmarital childbearing, welfare reform, and the role of fathers—and brings these three areas together in an innovative, integrated framework. The study has collected data on approximately 900 births (700 nonmarital, 200 marital) in 75 hospitals in 20 cities across the United States.[3] In nearly all of the cities, at least 75% of the unwed fathers have been interviewed. The response rate is lowest for

---

[3] At the time of this writing, the baseline data from the last 13 cities have been collected but not yet fully processed. The data were collected by Mathematica Policy Research, Inc.

those fathers with whom the mothers reported they had no relationship at the birth of the child. Not only are the data on unwed fathers more complete than those from previous surveys (i.e., many fewer missing fathers), they allow for a comparison of fathers who were not interviewed with fathers who were interviewed based on information provided by the mothers.

The Early Head Start National Research and Evaluation Project. The EHS project began in 1995 and includes a study of the Early Head Start program and a longitudinal study of infants and toddlers in low-income families. EHS is a comprehensive, two-generation program that includes intensive services before the child is born. The EHS evaluation includes approximately 3,000 families living in 17 communities across the country who met the EHS income eligibility criteria and had a child younger than 12 months of age (Table 18.3).

As part of the experimental research design, families who applied were randomly assigned either to the EHS group and received program services or to the control group and received the services available in their communities. The evaluation includes measures of a broad range of child and family outcomes and extensive information about the programs and the individual families' experiences with them. Data on family demographics and service needs were collected prior to random assignment; families were interviewed at 6, 15, and 26 months after random assignment and at program exit. Child assessments, parent interviews, and parent–child interaction assessments were conducted when the children were 14, 24, and 36 months old. Preliminary findings reported by the Administration on Children, Youth, and Families (Love et al., 2002) indicate that there are modest program impacts on key child outcomes, the parent–child relationship, parenting, and quality of the home environment provided by parents when the children are about 2 years old. The 36-month child assessment and interviews were completed in July 2001 and a final report to Congress on program impacts when the children were 3 years old was released in 2002.

Unlike FF, the EHS families (usually mothers and their children) were enrolled first and fathers were recruited after mothers identified them. Questions for the mother about father and father figure involvement with the children were included in the first parent interviews (the primary caregiver in 95% of the cases was the child's mother) and in child assessments, conducted when the children were 14 months old. In 1997, data collection was expanded in 12 of the 17 research sites to include interviews with fathers and, in nine sites, father–child videotaped interactions. The result of these efforts is four strands of father research: (1) Father Involvement with Toddlers Study (FITS), (2) Father and Child Interaction during Toddlerhood Study (FACITS), (3) Father and Newborn Study (FANS), and (4) Participation in Fatherhood Programs and Services Use Study (PASS). Table 18.4 describes the EHS fatherhood component.

FITS is being conducted in 12 of the 17 EHS research sites when the children are 24 and 36 months of age. In all of the EHS sites, mothers are asked during

18. LARGE-SCALE SURVEYS

TABLE 18.3
EHS Research & Evaluation Project—Main Study

Purpose	Conduct an evaluation of Early Head Start, a two-generation program serving low-income families with infants and toddlers, from pregnancy until children are 36 months old. Also conduct local research and special policy studies on such topics as child-care, health and disabilities, welfare reform, and fatherhood.
Design	Seven-year, national study employing a randomized design with two conditions: EHS program group and a control group including eligible families who applied to EHS at one of the 17 research sites. EHS services began between the third trimester of pregnancy and the child's 12th month; services continue through age three. The control group does not receive an offer of EHS services but can receive any other community services. Design includes (1) an implementation study, (2) an impact evaluation, (3) local research studies, (4) policy studies, (5) father studies, and (6) continuous improvement activities.
Sample	Approximately 3,000 low-income families from 17 local EHS sites with children born between September 1995 and July 1998. Father sample of approximately 1,000 drawn from 12 local sites. The programs participating in the national evaluation are located in Russellville, AR; Venice, CA; Denver, CO; Marshalltown, IA; Kansas City, KS; Jackson, MI; New York City; Kansas City, MO; Pittsburgh, PA; Sumter, SC; McKenzie, TN; Logan, UT; Alexandria, VA; Kent, WA; Sunnyside, WA; and Brattleboro, VA
Periodicity	From 1996 to 2001, children were assessed and parents interviewed when children were 14, 24, and 36 months old; parents were also interviewed at 6, 15, and 26 months after enrollment, and when they exit the program. A follow-up study of the children and families is being planned. Public use files will be available after the final project impact report has been submitted to Congress.
Principal investigators	John Love, Ellen Kisker, and Jeanne Brooks-Gunn are co-PIs; Helen Raikes and Rachel Chazan Cohen are the project monitors for the national research; Esther Kresh is the project monitor for the local research studies. Kimberly Boller is PI for the father studies. The EHS Father Studies Workgroup includes representatives from the EHS Research Consortium (including Mathematica, Columbia University, program staff members, and their university-based research partners), and ACYF. In addition, Natasha Cabrera and Michael Lamb of NICHD, Linda Mellgren of ASPE, Frankie Gibson of the HS Bureau, and Virginia Davies Floyd from the Ford Foundation.
Funders	Administration on Children, Youth, and Families (ACYF). ACYF, NICHD, ASPE, and the Ford Foundation for the father studies.

(Continued)

TABLE 18.3
(Continued)

Topics covered/content	*IMPACT EVALUATION* : *Child*: Health, motor, cognitive, language, social, and emotional development, includes standardized assessments (e.g., Bayley Scales, PPVT-3, CDI, CBCL) and videotaped child–parent interactions (e.g., Nursing Child Assessment Teaching Scales) *Mother*: Household demographic information, education, employment, work and family issues, mental and physical health, the home environment, family routines and conflict, stress, social support, parenting attitudes and knowledge about child development, discipline, child care, parent-child activities, the parent-child relationship, and verbal ability. *Parenting behavior*: (via videotaped child–parent interactions): Ratings of sensitivity, intrusiveness, detachment, mutuality. *Neighborhood:* Program coordination with other community service providers, parental perception of community services, qualitative descriptions of the community, and assessments of community child-care quality. *Child-care*: Observations and provider interview in formal and informal settings. *IMPLEMENTATION STUDY*: *Parent services interview*: Perceived needs and resources, employment, educati on, child-care and home visits, health status/services, family support services. *Exit interview:* Early Head Start Program experiences and other services. *EHS ratings of program quality:* Quality of center-based care, aspects of home visits. *EHS ratings of program implementation:* Consensus-based ratings of early child development and health services, family partnerships, community partnerships, staff development and management systems and procedures along key dimensions tied to the Revised HS Program Performance Standards.
Limitations	Sample is not nationally representative programs selected to represent diversity of geographic, demographic, and program approach characteristics.
Internet site and contact information	Http://www.mathematica-mpr.com. Contact Judith Jerald for information on the Early Head Start program (jjerald@acf.dhhs.gov). Contact Helen Raikes (helen_raikes@gallup.com), Rachel Chazan Cohen (rcohen@acf.dhhs.gov), or John Love (jlove@mathematica-mpr.com) for information on the National Research and Evaluation Project.

their interviews about the child's biological father and his involvement with the child. If the biological father does not live with the mother and child, mothers are asked about any men in the child's life who might be "like a father" to the child. In the 12 FITS sites, at the end of the interview with the mother, the interviewer describes the father study, reviews the father interview section, and identifies the man who is most involved with the child. Approximately 76% of the completed

18. LARGE-SCALE SURVEYS

TABLE 18.4
EHS Research and Evaluation Project—Fatherhood Component

Purpose	Fathers added to the study to broaden understanding of the family context, learn about the role of fathers in the lives of low-income families, explore how fathers become involved in Early Head Start, and examine how EHS programs work to involve fathers in the program and in the lives of infants and toddlers.
Design	For the Father Study, the man who is most involved with the child at the time of the mother interviews was recruited. Fathers may be biological fathers or father figures who live with the child or not. The study includes quantitative and qualitative components and videotaping of father–child interactions in seven sites.
	For the Father of Newborns Study, the biological father was recruited around the time of the child's birth and followed longitudinally. The study includes quantitative and qualitative components, videotaping of father–child interactions, mother interviews, and child assessments.
	For the Practitioners Study, program staff members from the 17 research sites participated in the qualitative study components, including individual interviews, group interviews, and a single site case study. All EHS programs were recruited to participate in the survey of father involvement, which included a web-based survey followed by mail.
Sample	For the Father Study, approximately 1,000 fathers/father figures drawn from 12 of the 17 local sites.
	For the Father and Newborn Study, about 200 fathers, children, and mothers. For the Practitioners Study, staff members from the 17 research sites for the qualitative work and about 270 Early Head Start programs for the 1999 survey of father involvement.
Periodicity	For the Father Study, fathers are interviewed when the children are 24 and 36 months old.
	For the Father and Newborn Study, fathers are interviewed when the children are 1, 6, 14, 24, and 36 months old.
	For the Practitioners Study, qualitative work was conducted from 1997 to 2000, and the survey of father involvement was conducted in 1999.
	A follow-up study of the fathers and programs is being planned. Public use files will be available after the final project impact report has been submitted to Congress.
Topics covered/content	*FATHER STUDY*
	Father: Education, employment, work and family issues, mental and physical health, family conflict, stress, social support, parenting attitudes and knowledge about child development, discipline, father–child activities, the father–child relationship, attitudes toward fathering, and his experience with his father and mother.
	Father parenting behavior (via videotaped child–father interactions): Ratings of sensitivity, intrusiveness, detachment, mutuality.

(Continued)

TABLE 18.4
(Continued)

	Father beliefs about fathering (via audiotaped qualitative questions): Fathers responses to questions about what being a good father means to them, expectations of fatherhood, relationship with their own father, perceived support needed to be a father, and what makes them proud of their child.
	FATHER AND NEWBORN STUDY
	Unique contribution is early timing of interviews and videotaping of father–child interaction and ability to understand how father involvement changes over time. Includes all of the topics covered in the Father Study.
	PRACTITIONERS STUDY
	Qualitative study: How programs develop and implement father involvement activities.
	Survey of father involvement: Program descriptive information, families with fathers/father figures, extent of father/father figure involvement in the program, successes and barriers to father involvement, ways program has worked to become "father friendly," and overall rating of stage in father involvement.
Limitations	*FATHER STUDY*
	Sample is not nationally representative, nor is it representative of all EHS families in the study. Mother survey responses provide basis for drawing the father sample.
	FATHER AND NEWBORN STUDY
	Small sample but provides in-depth view of father participation from child's birth.
	PRACTITIONERS STUDY
	Possible lack of generalizability of the qualitative work to the other 600 EHS programs based on anecdotal evidence that the research interest in father activities may drive some of the program activities.
Internet site and contact information	Http://www.mathematica-mpr.com/EHSTOC.HTM Contact Kimberly Boller (kboller@mathematica-mpr.com) for information about the father studies.

mother interviews when the children were 24 months of age at the FITS sites yielded a viable father interview identification. Of the approximately 1,350 fathers identified, 800 participated in 24-month interviews. Approximately half of the father interviews completed were conducted with fathers of children in the EHS group and half were conducted with fathers of children in the control group. At 36 months, 745 father interviews were completed.

FACITS involves 9 of the 12 FITS sites. Father–child interaction assessments were conducted when the children were 24 and 36 months of age. Approximately 300 father–child interaction assessments for the 24-month study were completed. Of the 800 father interviews completed in the nine FITS sites, 76% included a father–child interaction assessment. The FACITS assessment activities comprised

18.   LARGE-SCALE SURVEYS   435

(1) a Nursing Child Assessment Satellite Training Programs teaching task, (2) a task where fathers chose what they wanted to do, (3) a structured play task with toys brought by the interviewer, and (4) a clean-up task. The teaching and structured play activities were identical to the mother–child interaction assessments, except that the actual materials used were changed so that children would not be bored. To help identify unique dimensions of father interaction with toddlers, the father studies workgroup developed the "Your Choice" task that included asking the fathers to do something for 5 minutes with their child that they would normally do. At 36 months, a problem-solving task with puzzles replaced the teaching task and the clean-up task was dropped.

FANS project is an EHS study of about 200 fathers, their infants, and partners. It addresses the following questions: (1) How do different degrees, timing, and intensity of father involvement influence infant/toddler development? (2) How do fathers interact and become involved with their newborns? (3) How do fathers' relationships with their children's mothers relate to their children's development? and (4) How does early father involvement predict later parental involvement? Interviews are conducted when the children are 1, 3, 6, 14, and 24 months old. Father–child interaction assessments are conducted when the children are 6, 14, and 24 months of age.

The PASS study describes how EHS program sites involve fathers, how fathers view their roles (and the support they would like to enhance their parenting), and how they feel supported by the EHS programs. During visits to all 17 of the EHS program, sites researchers collected data about program activities to engage fathers in the program and how successful programs were in involving fathers. Implementation of father program activities was rated based on the number of father-specific program activities sites made available as well as the number of fathers who participated. At one site, researchers conducted an in-depth study over 2 years of the father involvement activities (McCallister et al., 2000). The PASS study also includes a qualitative investigation of the evolution of program approaches to father involvement across all 17 EHS research sites (Raikes et al., 2000). This study entails group and individual interviews with program directors, fathers, and father involvement staff members.

The Early Childhood Longitudinal Study–Birth Cohort.   The ECLS–B is the first study in the United States to track a nationally representative sample of children from infancy to the time they enter school (Tables 18.5 and 18.6). The goal of the ECLS–B is to provide a comprehensive and reliable data set for studying the physical, cognitive, social, and emotional growth of children from birth through first grade. The ECLS–B is part of a longitudinal studies program comprising two cohorts, a birth cohort and a kindergarten cohort. The kindergarten cohort (ECLS–K) follows a group of children from the start of kindergarten through fifth grade, measuring aspects of children's development and their home and school environments. Similarly, the ECLS–B uses multiple modes of data collection and

TABLE 18.5
The Early Childhood Longitudinal Study–Birth Cohort—Main Study

Purpose	The study is being designed to provide detailed information on children's development, health, early care, and education. Three key areas are of particular interest: children's growth and development in critical cognitive and noncognitive domains; children's transitions to child care and early education programs and to school; and children's school readiness.
Design	A parent interview and direct child assessment will be conducted at each wave. The direct child assessment includes measures of the children's height and weight, and their motor and cognitive development. Videotaping is used to capture critical elements of mother–child interactions at 9 and 18 months. Children's child-care providers are interviewed at 18 and 48 months, and some of these providers are observed by trained field staff.
Sample	Approximately 15,000 children will be sampled from birth certificates. The sample will be nationally representative of all births occurring in the United States in 2001. The sample will include children from diverse socioeconomic and racial/ethnic backgrounds. Asian and Pacific Islander, Chinese, American Indian, twins, and low birth weight children will be oversampled.
Periodicity	Data are collected when children are 9, 24, and 48 months old and when they enter kindergarten and first grade.
Principal Investigators	Jerry West, NCES Christine W. Nord, Westat
Funders	National Center for Education Statistics, National Center for Health Statistics, National Institutes of Health, Administration for Children, Youth and Families, U.S. Department of Agriculture
Topics covered/content	Children's cognitive, social, emotional, and physical development; mother–child interactions; pregnancy and maternal care and health; adverse birth outcomes; child health and health care access; family health; children's family and living situation; marriage and partner relationships; home educational activities and environment; parental attitudes and childrearing practices; child-care arrangements and their characteristics; neighborhood quality and safety; social and community support; family routines; mothers' and fathers' education and employment; welfare and other public transfers; household income and assets.
Limitations	The study is national in scope and this serves to limit the types of data that can be captured. The requirement for a national field staff imposes some limits on the measures and methods that can be used. With some notable exceptions, the study relies on traditional survey methodology.
Internet site and contact information	Jerry West, NCES, http://nces.ed.gov.

18.   LARGE-SCALE SURVEYS   437

TABLE 18.6

The Early Childhood Longitudinal Study–Birth Cohort–Fatherhood Component

Purpose	The father component of the ECLS–B provides information for policymakers and researchers to better understand the role of men as fathers and the unique contributions that fathers make to the development of young children. Fathers themselves are asked about their attitudes and behaviors, and the quality and quantity of involvement with their children.
Design	For the 9-month field test, two different father instruments are used: a resident father and a nonresident father self-administered questionnaire. The nonresident father questionnaire is given to biological fathers who live apart from their children and have maintained at least some level of contact. *Resident father*: The resident father interview is estimated to take 20 minutes to complete. *Nonresident father*: The nonresident father questionnaire is estimated to take 10 minutes to complete.
Sample	*Resident father*: A nationally representative sample of approximately 13,500 children will be used in the main study. The preferred respondent for the main parent interview is the mother. The mothers identify a spouse or partner residing in the household who is given the resident father questionnaire. This person is usually the biological father, but may also be an adoptive, step, or foster father or other partner. *Nonresident father*: After receiving permission from the mother, the study child's biological father is contacted to complete a nonresident father questionnaire. Only biological fathers who have had contact with the study child or mother within 3 months of the parent interview are included in the nonresident father sample.
Periodicity	*Resident fathers*: Self-administered questionnaires are collected from resident fathers when the study child is 9, 24, and 48 months of age, and at the beginning of kindergarten and first grade. *Nonresident father*: A 9-month nonresident self-administered questionnaire is included in the field test.
Topics Covered/Content	The ECLS–B father questionnaires cover a range of topics including items that are compatible with Lamb's definitions of father involvement, which include engagement, responsibility, and availability. Also, some of the specific items selected to measure involvement, behaviors, health status, and experience parallel those from the ECLS–B parent interview. *Resident fathers*: The major constructs represented in the questionnaires are the following: father activities with his child, prenatal/neonatal experiences, knowledge about child development, discipline and parental control, attitudes about being a father, separations from child, influence in child-care decision making, current marital/partner relationship, father's childbearing & marital and partner history, background information, education, cognitive ability & employment, health, family background, social and support network.

(Continued)

TABLE 18.6

(Continued)

	Nonresident fathers: Similar to many of the major constructs in the resident father questionnaire, the 9-month field test nonresident questionnaire includes items concerning child support and time spent with child, relationship with child's mother, feelings about self as father, how he helps family and child, education and employment, depression, and income.
Limitations	*Resident father*: The need to keep the questionnaire short to increase response rate and reduce respondent burden limits the items and constructs that can be collected.
	Nonresident father: The following procedures may limit the generalizability of the father data:
	• The need to obtain permission from mothers to contact nonresident fathers.
	• Only biological and not social fathers are given the questionnaire.
	• Nonresident fathers must have had at least some contact with child or mother in the last 3 months.
Internet site and contact information	http://nces.ed.gov

seeks to identify factors at various ecological levels that influence children's development in multiple domains that are important to later school readiness and academic achievement. The ECLS–B will yield both descriptive and analytical information to more fully describe children's health, early experiences, and learning, and the multiple factors that influence their development and well-being (such as home environment, family, child-care settings, and neighborhood). Of particular interest are how transitions (e.g., from parental to nonparental care or from preschool to kindergarten) affect children's development and how their background and characteristics influence their transition to kindergarten and first grade.

The national sample consists of infants randomly selected from birth certificates and over-samples of important populations such as Asian- and Native-American infants, low-birth-weight infants, and twins. Families of approximately 13,500 infants born in 2001 have been asked to participate. Births that occurred in 100 primary sampling units throughout the United States were sampled using a two-stage, stratified design. Home visits occur when the study children are 9, 24, and 48 months of age and at kindergarten and first grade. During the home visit, the field staff conducts direct child assessments, takes physical measures, and conducts a computer-assisted interview with the child's mother. A self-administered questionnaire (SAQ) is completed by the resident fathers. At 24 and 48 months, children's child-care providers will be identified and telephone interviews conducted. A sample of these providers will be observed in order to collect data on the quality of the care settings.

At each data collection point resident fathers are given a 20-minute SAQ and asked to fill it out while the mother is being interviewed. The resident father

18. LARGE-SCALE SURVEYS

questionnaire covers a range of constructs such as father activities with his child, prenatal/neonatal experiences, knowledge about child development, discipline and parental control, attitudes about being a father, separations from child, influence in child-care decision-making, current marital/partner relationship, father's child-bearing and marital and partner history, background information, education, cognitive ability, employment, health, family background, and social support network. If the father is not at home during the visit, it is left with the mother to give to her spouse/partner and mail back in a self-addressed stamped envelope.

Nonresident fathers are identified from information provided by the children's mothers, located, contacted, and asked to complete a 10-minute nonresident father interview. These fathers are asked about child support, time spent with their children, their relationship with the children's mother, feelings about themselves as fathers, how they help the family and child, and their education, employment, and income as well as their mental health status (i.e., depression).

The father component of the ECLS–B provides an opportunity to examine the unique contributions fathers make to children's well-being and developmental outcomes over time. The ECLS–B is one of the few national U.S. studies to involve fathers through self–report, thus enabling fathers to describe their attitudes, experiences, and activities related to caregiving during the early years of their children's lives.

In combination with the main ECLS–B components, the father questionnaire will enable researchers to address the following type of questions: (1) What are fathers' perceptions of themselves as fathers and how do their perceptions change as their children grow older? (2) What factors influence the type and amount of activities that fathers do with their children? (3) What role do fathers play in early child-care and childrearing and how does their involvement with their children and families relate to school readiness and child well-being?

METHODOLOGICAL CHALLENGES

Multiple studies indicate that the fathers most likely to be missed in national surveys are never-married fathers, divorced fathers, and minority fathers (Cherlin & Griffith, 1998; Garfinkel, McLanahan, & Hanson, 1998; Rendall, Clarke, Peters, Ranged, & Verropolou, 1997). In addition, men in the military, prisons, jails, or other institutions are also typically excluded from household surveys. Underreporting is also a common problem, because absent male parents are included in survey interviews without any information or with inadequate information about their parental status. Issues regarding response burden, the length of questionnaires, and, for some, the difficulty of questions also plague data collection on father involvement. Another type of response burden is related to sensitive items (e.g., income, drug use, and sexual practices), which in most cases affect the respondent's feelings of privacy and confidentiality. Changing family structures also represent

a challenge for data collection. Many previous surveys did not measure the varied family forms that now exist, such as cohabiting unions, unmarried couples, single-parent families with nonresident fathers, never-married fathers, families with other relatives playing important parenting roles in children's lives, and families with extended networks beyond the household. Methods for addressing these challenges are inadequate (Cherlin & Griffith, 1998; Greene, Halle, Menestrel, & Moore, 1998). These scenarios make it difficult for researchers to collect reliable information that would help to understand the evolving role of the father and his level of involvement.

Biological fathers are better able to provide detailed, accurate information about themselves than mothers can on most topics, making them the best respondent for information about themselves. In particular, information on what the father feels and thinks is more reliably reported by the father than the mother (Marsiglio et al., 1998). Bates and Gerber (1994) claimed that complicated living situations and transient and tenuous attachments to households make it difficult to determine and count men as household members. Some mothers are not in regular contact with the child's father but will report the identity of the father. If identified, institutionalized fathers—in the military or in prison—can be reached by phone interview.

In some cases, women do not know who fathered their children or knew him so briefly that they lack basic information on social and demographic characteristics. In other cases, women cannot or will not reveal the identity of the father because they were raped or are the victims of domestic abuse. Mothers who have had children through unwanted sex may not want the father to know about the child or to know they know he is the father. These mothers may be willing to provide some social and demographic information about these men (Greene et al., 1998). Other mothers who fear that legal authorities will pursue the father for child support will refuse to share the identity of the father. Locating fathers under these circumstances may antagonize the mother. Therefore, information probably cannot be obtained from these fathers (Greene et al., 1998).

Depending on the purpose of the study, it might be important to collect information from stepfathers who live with children over a substantial portion of the childhood years or from men who are living with infants and toddlers who are not the child's biological fathers, or both. "Social fathers" such as grandfathers, boyfriends, and others may play an important role in the lives of young children. Collecting information from these men will give researchers a complete picture of extended-kin networks and social support to the mother (Greene et al., 1998). Although the father might be the best respondent, the mother is the one who decides who is a father and whether to identify him. In the case of unmarried mothers, the name of the father is often recorded on the birth certificate; if not, the name of the father can only be obtained from the mother.

Once fathers have been identified, the next hurdle becomes locating them. If the father's name is known, other sources of information can be used to locate him, but there is some risk of offending or alienating mothers if they disapprove

of fathers being contacted. In cases where the mother is likely to be the primary respondent, her cooperation is crucial because the mother is most likely to know of the father's whereabouts and contact information. Locating fathers becomes more challenging when mothers are not cooperating.

Trying to locate men who became fathers under extremely harmful conditions, or who refuse to acknowledge their children or do not know they fathered a child, may be futile or possibly even dangerous. Because these fathers are not in contact, they are not included in the universe of fathers with whom interviews are sought in most fatherhood studies and are not included in response rates (Greene et al., 1998). In FF, these types of fathers constitute less than 10% of all new fathers. In EHS, mothers only identify a father for the father interview study for about 60% of the children, even though close to 90% of the mothers report that there is some contact between the child and the father or father figure. The EHS Father Studies Workgroup is analyzing father identification and father contact reports by the mothers to help understand the gap between those two key components of the father-interview study response rates.

In sum, there are many reasons why men are missing from most national surveys and other research on fatherhood. Although a percentage of fathers will never be involved fathers, the majority of the "missing" men have been excluded from major data collection efforts for reasons other than their unwillingness to be an active part of their children's development. Following the work of the Fatherhood Initiative, there has been a surge of research on fatherhood that has tried to overcome many of the institutional and methodological reasons that have kept men out of surveys. These studies recognize that fathers are important components of families and of child well-being and have made great efforts to improve on past methodologies. The DADS studies are a case in point. These studies collect data from men across several socioeconomic groups, ask the fathers themselves about their involvement with their children, use a multidimensional definition of father involvement, and are longitudinal. As this discussion suggests, there are challenges associated with defining, identifying, locating, and keeping men in research studies. These challenges are discussed next from the perspective of the DADS studies.

Defining and Identifying Who is a Father

The issue of who is a father is not as simple as that of deciding who is a mother. Fathers can be biological, both residential and nonresidential, and social, both biologically related or romantically linked to the mother (Tamis-LeMonda & Cabrera, 1999). These categories of fathers are important considerations in designing and implementing father studies. If the study focuses on the child, then researchers want to collect data on all adults, parents and others, who come into contact with the child. If the study is about fathers themselves, then data collection efforts focus on locating the men and reducing attrition. The DADS studies fall under the latter category. The only studies that will collect information on a national sample of

men, thus bypassing the mothers' gatekeeping role, are the *becoming a dad* studies, that is, the NSFG, NLSY-97, and Add Health.

In the *being a dad* DADS studies, the mothers are the "gatekeepers" of the fathers. Mothers identify which fathers will be part of the study. These studies focus primarily on biological fathers. However, the EHS collects data on social fathers and the resident father SAQ for ECLS–B is given to the person that the mother (or parent interview respondent) indicates is the spouse or partner who currently resides in the household. That person may be the biological father or a social father. This is true for each round of data collection. At 9 months, the nonresident father is always the study child's biological father, but this may change over the life of the study. In all these studies the focus is the child; that is, data are collected from mothers and fathers with the goal of linking this information to child outcomes. If the family structure changes during data collection and the father is absent from the household at Time 1 but returns at Time 2, we will have missing data for that man at Time 1. If the biological father does not return during the study, the data will be collected from whomever the mother identifies as the father. This is true for EHS and ECLS–B. In ECLS–B, the child's resident father will be identified at each data collection. The same person could be the resident father at 9 months and 30 months but not at 18 months. In this case, there would be two father figures if the mother has a new partner at 18 months and this person is living in the child's home. The Fragile Families study is a study of children and their biological fathers, so at this time it does not collect data from any social father.[4] On the other hand, in the EHS newborn study, efforts will be made to locate the biological father who was identified at Time 1 but was not located at Time 2. The goal is to have information from the men themselves about why they left. All three studies will have some information collected from the mothers about the absent fathers. These data will improve our information base on the "missing men."

Each of the *DADS* studies employed a different method for enrolling fathers. During the initial phase of the Fragile Families project, a series of small-scale pilot studies was conducted in selected cities: Detroit, Chicago, Washington, DC, and Richmond. These early pretests revealed that researchers could gain permission to interview new parents in hospitals, that unwed mothers would provide contact information on fathers, and that many unwed fathers go to the hospital and would agree to be interviewed. The results of a pilot study conducted in Philadelphia showed that the response rate was somewhat higher for the mothers in prenatal clinics than for mothers in the hospital (90% versus 80%), yet the proportion of mothers who identified the fathers was about the same. However, the proportion of identified fathers who were located and interviewed was much higher in the hospital sample (70% versus 53%) because most of the fathers visited the mothers in the hospital, and it was therefore relatively easy to locate and interview them there.

---

[4]The FF team is seeking funds to add a social father component to the study.

18. LARGE-SCALE SURVEYS

In the EHS, fathers were enrolled as part of the National Research and Evaluation Project. This study follows the child and identifies the primary caregiver (usually the mother) as the respondent. The mother identifies the father. The father is defined from the perspective of the child to include the biological father as well as father figures (sometimes referred to as social fathers). Developing procedures for identifying the social father proved challenging. In the mothers interviews at 24 and 36 months, they are asked to name someone who is "like a father" to the child. Preliminary data showed that the identified men were not only romantic partners (some of whom were involved with the mother for only a short period of time), but also maternal and paternal relatives. Thus the investment of these social dads in the children depends on the relationship with the mother. While the presence of many father figures in the home is an index of turbulence, it is difficult to determine how invested these men are in their children and the resources that should be allocated to their participation in the study. Although these men were not asked whether they felt like a father to the child, they were asked about many dimensions of their relationship with the child and how involved they plan to be in the child's life in the future.

The ECLS–B sample of fathers is determined by the responses to the questions in the parent interview. The preferred respondent for the main parent interview is the infant's mother; the resident father is identified as the spouse or partner who is currently residing in the household. Information on any biological fathers who do not live in the same household as the child is obtained from the parent interview. Consistent with the EHS study, the adults included in the ECLS–B sample are selected according to their connection to the identified infant, although the ECLS–B adult sample originates from a nationally representative sample of infants.

Defining Father Involvement

Researchers on father involvement have struggled with defining an "involved father." Father involvement is a multidimensional concept that continually changes both at the level of scholarship and with levels of cultural awareness (Cabrera, Tamis-LeMonda, Lamb, Boller, & EHS workgroup, 1999). Current research has moved beyond early methodologies that relied on time-use data to assess the quantity of father involvement to research using more complex methodologies that try to measure not only the quantity but also the quality of father–child interactions (Cabrera et al., 1999).

A number of conceptual models of father involvement have been used to design questionnaires of father involvement (for a description of these models see Cabrera et al., 1999). However, few empirical data exist to test these models and it is unclear whether any single model is adequate. For example, the Lamb et al. (1985, 1987) model proposes three dimensions of father involvement: engagement, availability and responsibility. This model provides a framework for comparison across studies but does not assess how children and fathers in the context of families develop a

positive and nurturant relationship (Cabrera et al., 1999). Additionally, it is unclear whether this model captures variations in father involvement across socioeconomic and ethnic groups. What is clear is that we need instruments that can capture the quantitative and qualitative aspects of paternal involvement. This is a demanding, laborious, and complicated task. The DADS studies will provide data that either challenge or support the Lamb et al. model of father involvement.

In the DADS studies, father involvement is organized around Lamb's model of involvement because it provides a flexible and common understanding of what types of behaviors influence father involvement. The DADS studies also rely on a number of items that come from Palkovitz's (1997) conceptualization of involvement as well as an array of sociodemographic variables. These items include questions about paternity establishment, paternal leave, and child support.

Although there are similarities across the three studies, there are also differences. The Fragile Families study is unique in that it follows mostly unwed parents from the time their child is born. FF is a nationally representative sample of unwed parents in U.S. cities of 200,000 or more people. The clustered design also makes the data representative of each of the 20 cities and allows investigators to analyze effects of state and local policies and labor markets. The ECLS–B is a nationally representative study of 13,500 infants that will collect information on mothers, fathers, child-care providers, and children. In the EHS father studies, the father involvement questionnaire taps key dimensions of parenting and parent-child relationships using the same data collection procedures and measures used with mothers. This instrument goes beyond the "mother template" by assessing areas seen as unique to fathering. The quality of father–child interactions is examined during videotaped, semistructured play activities. In addition, there is an embedded qualitative study of fathers' responses to open-ended questions about how they see the father role, their experiences with their own fathers, and the support they need to be a father.

Despite our methodological advances, there are still barriers to overcome. Cabrera et al. (1999) pointed out that these include (1) the validity of fathers' self-reports, because they rely on respondents' estimates as opposed to full-scale time diaries, (2) the reporting of generic fathering versus specific fathering, because large-scale surveys do not always identify a target child, so fathers evaluate generic fathering rather than child-specific fathering, and (3) the generalization of findings from middle-class European-American groups to other cultural groups. The design of measures that capture what fathers do and are sensitive to variations across families, cultures, and ethnicities remains a challenge in father involvement research (Cabrera et al., 1999).

Locating Fathers

Whereas the task of locating resident fathers is uncomplicated because they live in the household, the task of locating nonresident fathers is a major challenge (Greene et al., 1998; Martin & Siegel, 1998; Sorenson, 1998). In either case,

18. LARGE-SCALE SURVEYS   445

mothers represent the best avenue for learning the identity of the father; they are likely to know the whereabouts of the father and the best way to reach him. Mothers often provide basic demographic and social information about fathers. Because mothers play an important gatekeeping role, under circumstances of conflict or misunderstanding they may prevent interviews with some fathers. In any case, the support of the mother is likely to increase the participation of the father and her lack of cooperation is likely to minimize the opportunity to locate fathers and obtain information from them (Greene et al., 1998; Marsiglio et al., 1998).

In the EHS father interview study, locating fathers has been a challenge, especially fathers who do not live with the mother and child. Locating resident fathers and father figures also has provided some challenges. For example, some of these men may have moved out between the time the mother identified them during her interview and the time attempts to locate the father for his interview were made. To reduce location problems, researchers have reduced the delay between father identification and attempts to locate and schedule the father interview. Depending on site staffing, the interviewer who conducts the mother interview may be able to schedule the father interview during the next visit to the home to complete the mother interview and child assessment. Locating nonresident fathers is challenging, but because the mother has identified the man as "involved" with the child, she is usually able to supply good contact information for him. The study team was surprised to find that it is more difficult to locate and schedule interviews with nonresident father figures than with biological fathers who do not live with the child. This difference in the success of locating and interviewing these two types of men may reflect the differences in commitment between these two groups of men or perhaps the quality of the contact information the mothers provide.

In Fragile Families, researchers interviewed the majority of fathers in the hospital when they were visiting the mother and new baby. Substantial efforts are required to locate these fathers in subsequent waves. However, mothers have often been willing to provide up-to-date information about the fathers.

In ECLS-B, resident fathers who are present during the home visit are handed a self-administered questionnaire to complete while the interviewer is conducting the mother interview. If the resident father is not home, the interviewer gives the mother a packet containing the resident father SAQ and a self-addressed stamped envelope to give her spouse or partner. As previously mentioned, locating resident fathers is not anticipated to be a challenge once the home visit has been arranged. However, interviewers face common problems associated with locating nonresident fathers, such as mothers who do not have the biological father's current address and phone number or who provide inaccurate contact information, as well as cases of disconnected phone numbers. After obtaining permission from the mother to contact the nonresident father, the interviewer asks the mother to provide an address and phone number of the child's biological nonresident father. For cases where the mother says she has frequent contact with the nonresident father, the

interviewer asks the mother if she is willing to hand him a packet containing the SAQ, a self-addressed stamped envelope, and a check. When the mother and the child's biological father are not in frequent contact, the interviewer attempts to contact the nonresident father by phone using the information that the mother provides during the parent interview. Field staff from the 1999 ECLS–B field test reported that some mothers who had no specific address for the father were still willing to give him the SAQ.

Retention and Response Rates

In general, men are more difficult to interview and to keep engaged in studies. There are a number of documented strategies to increase men's participation in surveys. These strategies include offering financial incentives for in-person interviews, explaining the purpose of the study in a way that motivates them to participate, matching the demographic characteristics (gender and race) of the interviewer to the respondent, being flexible in arranging interviews, and dissociating the study from government child support efforts. In addition, in-person interviews are more effective than telephone surveys because they allow interviewers to build rapport and trust with the respondent. Paper and pencil questionnaires afford privacy and are preferred by respondents to verbal questioning. Computer-assisted personal interviews when used in addition to financial incentives, have also been found to increase the response rates for sensitive topics (Turner, Forsyth, Reilly, & Miller, 1996).

In the EHS father interview study, we use a variety of strategies to get fathers to agree to the interview and continue with the study at the second data collection point. The interviewers attempt to be as flexible as possible about when and where to schedule the father interviews. Fathers with busy schedules appreciate this flexibility, and interviews have been conducted as early as 6 a.m., before the workday begins, and at a variety of locations in the community, including at the father's worksite. Researchers who conduct the father–child videotaped assessment offer to decouple the interview from the videotaping session if the father has enough time to complete only the videotaping in the home and prefers to do the interview by phone. This flexibility in scheduling has been important. To establish rapport with the men, interviewers use different rapport-building techniques with the fathers than they do with the mothers (more conversation about father-specific activities, sports, and work activities). The interviewers report that once they are able to get the interview started, most fathers spontaneously express how much they enjoy talking about their child and the videotaped interaction assessment. Fathers also report that they rarely have the opportunity to reflect on their role as fathers and that they appreciate having that experience. Modest financial incentives are used to reimburse fathers for their time and effort.

Fathers are given a monetary incentive for participating in the ECLS–B to help secure their cooperation, to convey a sense of the importance of the study, and to

18. LARGE-SCALE SURVEYS   447

recognize the importance of the respondent's contribution. Interviewers are also trained to identify and address hesitations or concerns that fathers express about participating in the study. Mothers who encourage the fathers to participate and discuss the study may contribute to the likelihood of a completed father questionnaire. In addition, both resident and nonresident fathers are given attractive study materials that explain the study and reasons for questioning fathers.

In Fragile Families, financial incentives are used to compensate respondents for their time and effort. A parent newsletter informing participants of general findings and policy relevance of the study is sent 1 month prior to each wave of interviews.

LESSONS LEARNED

Because of their varied purposes, designs, and populations, each of the DADS studies has important methodological, measurement, and design lessons to share with other researchers who are studying fathers. An important lesson from Fragile Families is that sampling from hospitals is much more efficient and desirable than sampling from prenatal clinics. The latter strategy leads to fewer completed father interviews and is less representative of all nonmarital births. This strategy revealed that unwed fathers do indeed go to the hospitals and will agree to be interviewed. Fragile Families data also revealed that hospital sampling is better than trying to find the father after the birth. Sampling was done from hospitals rather than from birth records because the former would result in higher response rates. Kalsbeek, Botman, Massey, and Liu (1994) noted that the 1988 National and Maternal Infant Health Survey, which sampled from birth records, was able to locate and complete interviews with only 80% of the mothers. Presumably, the response rate was even lower for unmarried mothers. Clustering of mothers along with intensive interviewer coverage and availability in the hospitals allows researchers to attain even higher response rates among mothers. One could also expect high response rates for fathers because so many come to visit the baby at the hospital. Additionally, interviewing in the hospital costs one-third less than conducting in-home interviews.[5]

Usually, because both mothers and fathers are to be interviewed and because there is generally more than one birth per hospital per day, multiple interviews can be conducted during each field worker hospital visit. In-home interviews, on the other hand, require a substantial amount of time for locating, scheduling, and traveling. Finally, researchers learned something substantive about the nature of the relationships between unwed mothers and fathers. According to mothers' reports in the early pretests, 54% of couples were still in romantic relationships when their babies were born and 25% had lived together at some point. More than

---

[5]This estimate does not consider the costs of obtaining access to the hospitals, which are substantial and amounted to approximately $300,000 over 2 years.

half the mothers believed that their chances of marrying the father were 50% or greater. Two-thirds of the fathers provided some type of financial support during the pregnancy. All told, 75% of unwed fathers either had a continuing romantic relationship or they (or their kin) provided support to the mother during pregnancy. Interestingly, these numbers were even higher later in actual data collection.

In the ECLS–B, two 9-month field tests (fall 1999 and fall 2000) were conducted to evaluate the reliability and manageability of the various instruments including a resident and non-resident father questionnaire. The experience of the first field test helped guide the structure and operation of the second. Although there are several components to the ECLS–B, the process of securing father participation and increasing the response rates for both resident and nonresident fathers benefited from the modifications to the fall 1999 field test approach. During the 1999 field test home visit, the interviewer gave either a $10 or $15 dollar incentive. In addition, some fathers received a check before completing a questionnaire and some afterward. The amount and timing of the incentive were randomly selected by case. The amount of money did not seem to affect response rates and no consistent pattern in response rate was discerned by whether fathers received their check prior to or after completing the SAQ.

In the 1999 field test, two versions of the nonresident father questionnaire were used. The response rate was generally higher when the shorter (10 minutes versus 20 minutes) questionnaire was administered. Also, hard-copy instruments tended to be better received by respondents than a computer-assisted interview, and some follow-up telephone calls evoked strong negative reactions from resident fathers. Not surprisingly, the frequency of the sampled child's mother's contact with the nonresident father was positively correlated with the likelihood of nonresident father participation. About 70% of the nonresident father respondents were in touch with the children's mothers every day or almost every day.

In the 2000 field test, the staff was instructed to give the resident father the SAQ at the beginning of the home visit. This minor change in field procedures increased the number of completed questionnaires interviewers had at the end of the home visit, thus reducing the time and cost of follow-up efforts.

CONCLUSION

Research on fatherhood has proliferated in the last 10 years. Given the recent policy impetus to include fathers in programs and policies, researchers have begun to address difficult questions, such as, Who are fathers? How are they involved in their children's lives? What impact does this involvement have on children's development? How does this happen? And how can public policies maximize father's involvement? The result is an emerging body of research on fathers that will advance our understanding of how mothers and fathers influence their children's well-being.

18. LARGE-SCALE SURVEYS 449

Although this new work is guided by conceptualizations of fatherhood that are more sophisticated and complex than they were 20 years ago, it has had to proceed in spite of the fact that theory and measurement are moving from infancy into the early childhood phase. The DADS project (here we focused on the *being a dad* studies more than on the *becoming a dad* studies) is an effort that has the potential to advance our understanding of how to measure what fathers do with their children, how they are involved, and the aspects of father involvement that are linked to child outcomes. These rich data will come from three large-scale surveys that collectively will be able to provide a complete picture of the type, nature, and frequency of father involvement in the United States. Each DADS study addresses a different set of research and policy questions. Collectively, the studies will provide data that will allow us to link father involvement, across socioeconomic and cultural backgrounds, to child outcomes. More important, the DADS project will give researchers the opportunity to analyze data across several studies using a similar model of father involvement. Making the binders of measures available to the research community will provide a public forum within which to continue to refine our measures. The DADS project has the potential to change the course of research on fatherhood by increasing comparability across studies and hence increasing their analytical power while also contributing to our methodological knowledge base.

REFERENCES

Amato, P. (1996, October). *More than money? Men's contributions to their children's lives.* Paper presented at the Men in Families Symposium, Pennsylvania State University.

Barclay-McLaughlin, G., & The EHS Research Consortium Father Studies Workgroup. (2000, April). *Father involvement in early head start: Listening to the voices of fathers, mothers, and program staff.* Paper presented at the National Family Resource Coalition Meetings, Chicago, IL.

Bates, N. A., & Gerber, E. (1994). A typology of temporary mobility patterns and reporting of usual residence. Unpublished, In *Proceedings of the Survey Research Methods Section of the American Statistics Association,* Bounpane, PA, 1991.

Boller, K., Barclay-McLaughlin, G., Cabrera, N., Shears, J., Summers, J., & The EHS Research Consortium Father Studies Workgroup. (1999, June). *The role of fathers and father figures in low-income families.* Paper presented at the American Psychological Society Meetings, Denver, CO.

Boller, K., Barclay-McLaughlin, G., Summers, J., & The EHS Research Consortium Father Studies Workgroup. (1999, January). *Research on fathers and father figures in EHS programs.* Paper presented at the Head Start Institute for Programs Serving Pregnant Women, Infants, Toddlers and Their Families, Washington, DC.

Boller, K., Summers, J., Barclay-McLaughlin, G., & The EHS Research Consortium Father Studies Workgroup. (2000, January). *The voices of fathers, mothers, and EHS staff members.* Invited symposium at the Head Start Institute for Programs Serving Pregnant Women, Infants, Toddlers and Their Families, Washington, DC.

Bronte-Tinkew, J., Moore, K. A., & Cabrera, N. (2000). *The Developing a Daddy Survey: Framework Paper.* Paper prepared for the National Institute for Child Health and Human Development, by Child Trends, Washington, DC.

Brooks-Gunn, J., Fuligni, A., & Berlin, L. (2003). *Early child development in the 21st century: Profiles of current research initiatives.* New York, NY: Teachers College, Columbia University.

Brophy-Herb, H. E., Gibbons, C., Omar, M.A., & Schiffman, R. (1999). Low-income fathers and their infants: Interactions during teaching episodes. *Infant Mental Health Journal, 20*, 305–321.

Burton, L. (1996). *Undercover parenting: Reframing paradigms for studying African American fathers.* Paper presented at the Conference on Developmental, Ethnographic, and Demographic Perspectives on Fatherhood, sponsored by the Demographic and Behavioral Sciences Branch and the Mental Retardation and Developmental Disabilities Branch of the National Institute of Child Health and Human Development, the Federal Interagency Forum on Child and Family Statistics, and the NICHD Family and Child Well-Being Research Network, Bethesda, MD.

Cabrera, N. J., Roggman, L., Bradley, R., & The EHS Research Consortium Father Studies Workgroup. (2000, July). *The Early Head Start father studies: How low-income men are involved in their children's lives.* Paper presented at the Seminar on Involving Low Income Fathers in the Lives of their Young Children: USA and UK Policy, Research & Practice, London.

Cabrera, N. J., Tamis-LeMonda, C.S., Bradley, R.H, Hofferth, S., & Lamb, M.E. (2000). "Fatherhood in the Twenty-First Century." *Child Development, 71*, 127–136.

Cabrera, N. J., Tamis-LeMonda, C., Lamb, M., Boller, K., & The EHS Research Consortium Father Studies Workgroup. (1999, July). *Measuring father involvement in Early Head Start: A multidimensional conceptualization.* Paper presented at the National Center for Health Statistics Meetings, Washington, DC.

Cherlin, A. J. (1992). *Marriage, divorce, and remarriage.* Cambridge, MA: Cambridge University Press.

Cherlin, A. J., & Griffith, J. (1998). Report of the working group on the methodology of studying fathers. In *Nurturing fatherhood: Improving data and research on male fertility, family formation and fatherhood.* Washington, DC: Federal Interagency Forum on Child and Family Statistics.

Early Head Start Research Consortium Father Studies Workgroup. (2000, June). *Fathers and early child development: Lessons learned from fathers' stories.* Symposium at Head Start's Fifth National Research Conference, Washington, DC.

Early Head Start Research Consortium Father Studies Workgroup. (2000, July). *24 months of fatherhood:Low- income men and their toddlers.* Symposium at the International Conference on Infant Studies, Brighton, England.

Federal Interagency Forum on Child and Family Statistics (1998). *Nurturing Fatherhood: Improving Data and Research on Male Fertility, Family Formation and Fatherhood.* Washington DC.

Garfinkel, I., McLanahan, S., & Hanson, T. (1998). A patchwork of nonresidential fathers. In I. Garfinkel, S. McLanahan, D. R. Meyer, & J. A. Seltzer (Eds.), *Fathers under fire*, 31–60. New York: Russell Sage Foundation.

Greene, A., Halle T., Menestrel S., & Moore, K. (1998). *Father involvement in young children's lives: Recommendations for a fatherhood module for the ECLS–B.* Paper prepared for the National Center for Education Statistics, by Child Trends, Washington, DC.

Greene, A., & Moore, K. A. (1996, October). *Nonresident father involvement and child outcomes among young children in families on welfare.* Paper presented at the Conference on Father Involvement, Bethesda, MD.

Greenstein, B., McBride, S., Raikes, H. H., Love, J. M., & The EHS Research Consortium Father Studies Workgroup. *Father involvement in the Early Head Start.* Presentation at the 12th National Training Institute of Zero to Three National Center for Infants, Toddlers and Families, Nashville, TN.

Hofferth S. (1999). *Race/ethnic differences in father involvement with young children.* Paper presented at the Urban Seminar on Fatherhood, Harvard University, Cambridge, MA.

Kalsbeek W. D., Botman S. L., Massey J. T., & Liu P. W. (1994). Cost-efficiency and the number of allowable call attempts in the National Health Interview Survey. *J Off Stat 10(2)*, 133–52.

Lamb, M. E. (1997). The development of father–infant relationships. In M. E. Lamb (Ed.), *The role of the father in child development.* (pp.104–120). New York: Wiley.

18. LARGE-SCALE SURVEYS

Lamb, M. E. (2000). The history of research on father involvement: An overview. *Marriage and Family Review, 29*, 23–42.

Lamb, M. E., (2000). Fatherhood in the twenty-first century. *Child Development 71*, 127–136.

Lamb, M. E., Pleck, J. H., Charnov, E. L., & Levine, J. A. (1985). The role of the father in child development: The effects of increased paternal involvement. In B. B. Lahey & A. E.Kazdin (Eds.) *Advances in clinical child psychology, 8*, 229–266. New York: Plenum.

Lamb, M. E., Pleck, J. H., Charnov, E. L., & Levine, J. A. (1987). A biosocial perspective on paternal behavior and involvement. In J. B. Lancaster, J. Altmann, A. S. Rossi, & L. R. Sherrod (Eds.), *Parenting across the lifespan: Biosocial dimensions* (pp. 111–142). New York: Aldine de Gruyter.

Laumann, E. O., Michael, R. T., & Browning, C. R. (1998). *Response and measurement error in studies of male sexual and fertility related behavior: An analysis of the national health and social life survey data*. Unpublished paper prepared for the NSFG Branch, National Center for Education Statistics.

Love, J. M., Boller, K., Raikes, H., McAllister, C., & The EHS Research Consortium Father Studies Workgroup. (1999, April). *Dads in Context: Early Experiences of Fatherhood, Parenting, and Program Involvement in Early Head Start*. Invited presentation at the Harvard University Urban Seminar on Fatherhood, Cambridge, MA.

Love, J. M., Kisker, E., Ross, C. M., Schochet, P., Brooks-Gunn, J., Paulsell, D., Boller, K., Constantine, J., Vogel, C., Fuligni, A., & Brady-Smith. (2002). *Making a difference in the lives of infants and toddlers and their families. The impacts of Hearly Head Start*. Mathematic Policy Research, Inc. Report.

Martin, E., & Siegel, P. (1998). New directions for exploring fathers' attachment to households. In *Nurturing Fatherhood: Improving data and research on male fertility, family formation and fatherhood*, 445–451 Washington DC: Federal Interagency Forum on Child and Family Statistics.

Marsiglio, W., Day, R., Braver, S., Evans, J., Lamb, M., & Peters, E. (1998). Report of the working group on conceptualizing male parenting. In *Nurturing Fatherhood: Improving data and research on male fertility, family formation and fatherhood*. Washington DC: Federal Interagency Forum on Child and Family Statistics.

McAllister, C.L. Mulvey, L, & Butler, J. (2000). *From sports fans to nurturers: A program's evolution toward involving fathers*. Paper presented at the Fifth National Head Start Research Conference, Washington, DC.

Morgan, P. S., Lye, N., Condran, G. A. (1988). Sons, daughters and the risk of marital disruption. *American Journal of Sociology, 94*, 110–129.

National Center for Education Statistics. (1999). *Early Childhood Longitudinal Study: Birth Cohort 2000*. ECLS-B website, http://nces.ed.gov/ecls/.

Nord, C.W. & Brimhall, D., & West, J. (1997). *Father's involvement in schools*. Washington, DC: U.S. Department of Education.

Palkovitz, R. (1997). Reconstructing involvement: Expanding conceptualizations of men's caring in contemporary families. In A. J. Hawkins & D. C. Dollahite (Eds.), *Generative fathering: Beyond deficit perspectives*, 200–216. Thousand Oaks, CA: Sage.

Parke, R. D. (1995). Fathers and families. In M. H. Bornstein (Ed.), *Handbook of parenting, 3*, 27–63. Hillsdale, NJ: Lawrence Erlbaum Associates.

Poister, T. H. (1978). *Public programs analysis*. Baltimore, MD: University Park Press.

Radin, N. (1986). The influence of fathers upon sons and daughters and implications for school social work. *Social Work in Education, 8*, 77 – 91.

Raikes, H., Boller, K., van Kammen, W., Love, J. M., Summers, J., Laible, D., Wilcox, B., Barclay-McLaughlin, G., McAllister, C., & the EHS Research Consortium Father Studies Workgroup. (2000, July). *Father involvement in Early Head Start: Promising practices, challenges, and stages of program activities*. Seminar on Involving Low Income Fathers in the Lives of their Young Children: USA and UK Policy, Research & Practice, London.

Raikes, H. H., Love, J. M., Mellgren, L., McAllister, C., Pan, B., Summers, J., & The EHS Research Consortium Father Studies Workgroup. (1999, April). *Research findings related to intervention*

programs and social policy. Paper presented at the biennial meeting of the Society for Research in Child Development, Albuquerque, NM.

Raikes, H., & The EHS Research Consortium Father Studies Workgroup. (2000, April). *Father involvement in Early Head Start: Listening to the voices of fathers, mothers, and program staff.* Invited presentation at the annual meeting of the National Head Start Association, Washington, DC.

Rendall, M. S., Clarke, L. Peters, H., Ranged, N., & Verropolou, G. (1997). *Incomplete reporting of male fertility in the United States and Britain: A research note.* Unpublished manuscript, Cornell University.

Roggman, L. A., Benson, B., & Boyce, L. (2000). Fathers with infants: Knowledge and involvement in relation to psychosocial functioning and religion. *Infant Mental Health Journal, 3,* 257–277.

Roggman, L. A., Boyce, L. K., & Benson, B. (1998, April). *What dads know about babies: Relations with attitudes, well-being, and social support.* Paper presented at the International Conference on Infant Studies, Atlanta, GA.

Sorensen, E. (1998). *Nonresident fathers: What we know and what's left to learn?* Paper presented at the NICHD Conference on Fathering and Male Fertility: Improving Data and Research, Bethesda, MD.

Summers, J., Raikes, H., Butler, J., Spicer, P., Pan, B., Shaw, S., Langager, M., McAllister, C., & Johnson, M. K. (2000). Low-income fathers' and mothers' perceptions of the father Role: A qualitative study in four Early Head Start communities. *Infant Mental Health Journal, 20,* 291–304.

Tamis-LeMonda, C. S., & Cabrera, N. (1999). Perspectives on father involvement: Research and policy, Social Policy Report, Vol. XIII, No. 2, Ann Arbor, MI: Society for Research in Child Development.

Tamis-LeMonda, C., Shannon, J., Bradley, R., Roggman, L., Boyce, L., Summers, J., & EHS Research Consortium Father Studies Workgroup. (1999, April). *Definitions of father involvement: A multidimensional conceptualization.* Paper presented at the biennial meeting of the Society for Research in Child Development, Albuquerque, NM.

Tanfer, K., Billy, J. O. G., & Grady, W. R. (1998). *Application of experience from the National Survey of Men to including males in the National Survey of Family Growth.* Seattle, WA: Battelle, Centers for Public Health Research and Evaluation.

Turner, C., Forsyth, B., Reilly, J., & Miller, H. (1996). *Automated self interviewing in surveys.* Paper presented at the International Conference on Computer Assisted Survey Information Collection, San Antonio, TX.

Working Group on Conceptualizing Male Parenting. (1997). *Social fatherhood and paternal involvement: Conceptual, data, and policymaking issues.* Paper presented at the NICHD Conference on Fathering and Male Fertility: Improving Data and Research, Bethesda, MD.

Author Index

A

Abidin, R. R., *92*
Acock, A., *2, 11, 275*
Acredolo, C., *192*
Adams, D., *360*
Adams, M., *23*
Ahadi, S. A., *192*
Ahmeduzzaman, M. E., *143, 189*
Ahrons, C. R., *218, 227, 234*
Aldous, J., *218*
Allan, K., *321*
Allen, S. H., *22, 28, 68, 92*
Allred, K. W., *109*
Aloa, V., *192*
Alpert, A., *151*
Amato, P., *45, 64, 129, 143, 188, 218, 219, 227, 234, 273, 274, 322, 390*
Amato, P. R., *294, 296, 302, 360, 395*
Anderson, E. A., *143*
Andrews, J., *151*
Angold, A., *160*
Anthony, E. J., *85*
Archer, J., *232*
Arditti, J. A., *219*
Arendell, T., *62, 77, 219, 221, 224, 225, 226*
Argys, L. M., *219, 223*
Asarnow, J. R., *152*
Ascher, B. H., *160*
Atkinson, M. P., *278*
Auerbach, C. F., *2*
Avenevoli, S., *192, 205*
Averett, S. L., *7*

B

Babakus, E., *196*
Backett, K. C., *47*
Bagi, S., *277*
Bailey, D. B., *119*
Bairan, A., *321*
Bakan, D., *75*
Baldwin, L. M., *159*
Bamberg, M., *86*
Bamberger, E., *152*
Bandura, A., *190*
Barb, K. H., *196*
Barber, B. K., *6, 187, 198, 219*
Barclay, L., *61, 62*
Barclay-McLaughlin, G., *435*
Barker, R. W., *51*
Barnes, H., *277*
Barnett, R. C., *131, 142, 145, 321*
Barnow, B. S., *387, 392*
Baron, R. M. *101, 192, 206*
Baruch, G. K., *131, 142, 145, 321*
Bates, J. E., *186, 191, 192, 193, 194, 205*
Bates, N. A., *440*
Baumrind, D., *186, 275, 395*
Bay, C., *218, 227, 228*
Beail, N., *42*
Bearman, P. S., *304*
Beck, M., *51*
Beckman, P. J., *119*
Beishon, S., *53*
Beitel, A., *22, 28, 92*
Beitel, A. H., *336, 392*
Beller, A. H., *219*
Belsky, J., *322*
Benedek, T., *85*

453

Bennett, T., *120*
Benson, M. L., *12, 365*
Berg, C. N., *150, 154, 155*
Berkman, B. G., *218*
Berndt, T. J., *189*
Bernier, H., *191*
Bernstein, R. H., *196*
Bernstein, V., *395*
Berthoud, R., *53*
Beuhler, C., *85*
Bhavnagri, N. P., *143*
Bianchi, S. M., *294, 296*
Biklen, S. K., *163*
Biller, H., *5, 6, 321*
Bishop, D. S., *159*
Bishop, L. C., *120*
Bjarnson, T., *218*
Bjornberg, U., *40*
Blair, S. L., *294, 295, 299, 306*
Blasco, P. M., *119*
Blatt, S. J., *207*
Blumer, H., *62, 69*
Bogdan, R. C., *163*
Bohrnstedt, G. W., *195*
Bollen, K. A., *196*
Boller, K., *336, 430, 435, 443, 444*
Book, B. K., *277*
Bookstein, F. L., *130*
Booth, A., *359*
Borduin, C. M., *277*
Borgata, G. H., *195*
Bosker, R. J., *195*
Boss, P., *218*
Botman, S. L., *447*
Bourdin, C. M., *151*
Boutin, P., *191*
Bowlby, J., *33*
Bradley, R. H., *294, 322*
Bradshaw, J., *40*
Brady-Smith, *430*
Brannen, J., *43, 45*
Branson, M. P., *143*
Braver, S. B., *11, 24, 217, 218, 219, 220, 221, 222, 223, 224, 225, 226, 227, 228, 229, 234, 440, 445*
Brimhall, D. A., *306*
Bristol, M. M., *111*
Broberg, A., *130*
Broderick, C., *103*
Brody, G. H., *194*
Bronte-Tinkew, J., *420*

Brooks-Gunn, J., *12, 219, 420, 430*
Brotherson, S. E., *109, 112, 118, 394*
Brown, B. V., *224*
Bruce, C., *63, 64, 67, 89, 218, 219, 379*
Bruner, J., *86*
Brunner, J. F., *92*
Bryce, W. T., *280*
Buchanan, A., *51*
Buchanan, C. M., *219*
Buehler, C., *6, 224, 225, 226*
Bumpass, L. L., *229, 362*
Burbach, D. J., *277*
Burgess, A., *41, 51*
Burghes, L., *44*
Buriel, R., *19, 24*
Burke, P. J., *85*
Burleson, B. R., *186*
Burns, B. J., *152, 160*
Burts, D. C., *186, 188, 194*
Busch, A. L., *362*
Buss, H. A., *192, 198*
Butler, J., *435*
Byers, K. V., *223*

C

Cabrera, N. J., *42, 151, 163, 294, 321, 322, 336, 419, 420, 441, 443, 444*
Calhoun, C. A., *228*
Call, V., *362*
Callender, C., *42*
Cameron, S., *41*
Carlson, M. J., *11*
Carlton, R. P., *362*
Carr, A., *152*
Casas, J. J., *190, 191*
Casper, L. M., *217, 295*
Cassetty, J., *224*
Cast, A. D., *85*
Cath, S. H., *85*
Cauce, A. M., *19, 21*
Cen, G., *193, 206*
Center for Human Resource Research, *278*
Chamberlain, P., *194*
Chang, L., *186, 193, 207*
Chao, R. K., *185, 189*
Chapa, J., *20*
Charnov, E. L., *12, 49, 64, 84, 130, 294, 303, 322, 421, 443*
Chen, C., *189*

AUTHOR INDEX

Chen, H., *186, 191, 193, 205, 206, 207*
Chen, X., *186, 189, 191, 192, 193, 205, 206, 207, 208*
Cherlin, A., *67, 314, 388, 439, 440*
Chess, S., *192*
Cheung, P. C., *189, 206*
Child Trends, *278, 279, 280, 390*
Chiu, L. H., *189*
Christ, M. A., *151*
Christiansen, S. L., *64*
Chuang, S. S., *10, 129*
Cialdini, R. B., *227*
Clarke, L., *8, 9, 39, 40, 42, 44, 439*
Clarke-Stewart, K. A., *218*
Clatfelter, D., *192, 194, 208*
Clawson, M. A., *194*
Clingempeel, W. G., *280*
Coatsworth, D., *227, 229*
Coenders, G., *195, 196*
Cohan, M., *42, 52, 61, 63*
Cohen, T. F., *62, 92, 397*
Coi, J. D., *186*
Coie, J. D., *190*
Cole, D. A., *151*
Coleman, J. S., *275, 276*
Coleman, S. D., *194*
Collett, P., *52*
Collier, R., *51*
Coltrane, S., *20, 23, 24, 143, 321, 391*
Combs, G., *86*
Combs-Orme, T., *63*
Compas, B. E., *150, 151*
Conger, K. J., *151*
Conger, R. D., *151*
Conners, L. J., *34*
Connolly, J., *51*
Constantine, J., *430*
Cooksey, E., *44, 294, 295, 299, 306*
Cooley, C. H., *74*
Corbin, J., *125, 162, 163, 165, 166*
COSSMHO, *21*
Cote, R., *191*
Cowan, C. P., *63, 321*
Cowan, P. A., *63, 321*
Cox, M., *275, 278*
Cox, R., *275, 278*
Craven, D., *360, 364*
Creech, J. C., *195*
Creswell, J. W., *62*
Crick, N., *190, 191, 193, 208*
Crippen, G., *225*

Crnic, K., *322*
Crockenberg, S. B., *192*
Cronin, N., *44*
Cross, S. E., *207*
Crouter, A. C., *321, 359, 397*
Cummings, E. M., *360, 361, 380*

D

Dadds, M. R., *151*
Daly, K. J., *62, 74*
Darling, N., *395*
Darling-Fisher, C. S., *321*
Daro, D., *162*
Davies, L., *49*
Davies, P., *360*
Davis, B., *151*
Davis, J., *323*
Davis, J. E., *25, 386*
Davis-Kean, P. E., *324*
Davis-Kean, P. M., *23*
Dawud-Noursi, S., *232*
Day, R. D., *2, 11, 24, 45, 64, 69, 72, 143, 188, 218, 219, 227, 234, 273, 274, 275, 322, 390, 440, 445*
De Leeuw, J., *196*
de St. Aubin, E., *86*
Deater-Deckard, *186, 194*
Del Campo, M., *24*
Delgado-Gaitan, C., *19, 20*
Deluca, D. A., *120*
DeMaris, A., *360, 363, 365*
DeMent, T., *19*
Dennis, N., *41, 48, 188*
Department for Education and Employment, *42*
Department of Trade and Industry, *42*
Derogatis, L. R., *160*
Deutsch, F. M., *321*
DeWolf, M. D., *186, 188, 194*
Dex, S., *41*
DHHS Fathers' Work Group, *390*
Diamond, A., *86*
Dishion, T. J., *194*
Dodge, K. A., *186, 190, 194, 207*
Doherty, W. J., *2, 64, 111, 322, 323*
Dollahite, D. C., *2, 6, 8, 10, 65, 109, 110, 111, 113, 114, 118, 120, 122, 124, 125, 188, 322, 394*
Dong, Q., *186, 205, 206*
Doolittle, F., *390, 397*

Dornbusch, S. M., *219*
Duckworth, J., *218*
Dunn, J., *49, 51*
Dunne, G., *51*
Dyches, T. T., *109*

E

Eadley, N., *51*
Earls, F., *365*
Easterbrooks, M.A., *142*
Eastman, G., *91*
Ebery, M. B., *277*
Edwards, J., *151*
Edwards, L. A., *194*
Eggebeen, D. J., *294*
Egley, L. C., *362*
EHS Research Consortium Father Studies
    Workgroup, *435, 443, 444*
Ellen, E. P., *194*
Emery, R. E., *219, 220, 223, 225*
Endsley, R. C., *193*
Epstein, J. L., *35*
Epstein, N. B., *159*
Erdos, G., *41*
Erikson, M. F., *64, 322, 323*
Essex, M. J., *192, 205*
European Commission Network on Childcare,
    40
Evans, J., *440, 445*
Evans, V. J., *24*

F

Fabricius, W. V., *221, 223, 229*
Fagan, J. A., *23, 386*
Fagot, B. I., *192*
Farmer, E. M., *160*
Farrell, M. P., *87*
Featherstone, B., *41, 52*
Feder, T., *192*
Federal Interagency Forum on Child and Family
    Statistics, *52, 54, 219, 388, 390, 418, 419*
Fenaughty, A. M., *225*
Ferguson, C. E., Jr., *196*
Ferraro, K. J., *362*
Ferri, E., *45*
Fewell, R. R., *119, 122*
Field, T., *22*

Fields, J., *217*
Figueredo, A. J., *360*
Fineman, M. A., *224*
Finkelstein, J., *323*
Fitzpatrick, P., *218, 22, 228*
Flannery, D. J., *277*
Flannery, W. P., *29*
Flouri, E., *51*
Flyr, M. L., *188*
Fogas, B. S., *219*
Follansbee, D., *277*
Fonagy, P., *49*
Fondell, M., *294, 295, 299, 306*
Forsyth, B., *446*
Forte, J. A., *361*
Forte, J. A., *361*
Forth, J., *42*
Fox, G. L., *12, 63, 64, 67, 89, 218, 219, 365,*
    379
Fox, J. S., *360, 364*
Franks, D. D., *361*
Freedman, J. M., *86*
Freeman, H., *33*
Frey, K. S., *119*
Frick, P. J., *151*
Fristad, M. A., *72, 152*
Frodi, A., *131, 145*
Frodi, M., *130, 131, 145*
Fthenakis, W., *40*
Fuligni, A. S., *12, 420, 430*
Fung, H., *187*
Furstenberg, F. F., Jr., *4, 62, 67, 92, 226, 276,*
    294, 300, 305, 314, 321
Futris, T. G., *219, 226, 234*

G

Gadsden, V., *13, 386, 387, 389, 414*
Gaito, J., *195*
Gallagher, J. J., *111*
Garasky, S., *224, 294*
Gardner, P. L., *195*
Garfinkel, I., *228, 439, 450*
Gavazzi, S. M., *2, 10, 72, 149, 152, 158, 275,*
    276
Gavidia-Payne, S., *153*
Geffner, R., *360, 361*
Gennetian, L. A., *7*
Gerber, E., *440*
Gergen, K. J., *62, 76, 86, 87*

AUTHOR INDEX

Gergen, M. M., *62, 76, 86, 87*
Gershoff, E. T., *186, 207*
Gershuny, J., *47*
Gerson, K., *6, 143, 294*
Ghate, D., *52*
Gilbreth, .G., *129*
Gilroy, R., *41*
Giovannini, D., *40*
Glaser, B., *62, 65, 166*
Glesne, C., *166*
Glover, A., *192*
Goldberg, S., *67, 119, 142*
Golding, E., *321*
Golding, J. M., *24*
Goldscheider, F. K., *131*
Goldsmith, R., *130*
Gondolf, E. W., *360*
Gonzales, N.A., *19, 21*
Goodman, M., *110*
Goodnow, J. J., *205*
Gordon, B. A., *321*
Gottman, J. M., *2, 360,*
Graham, J. W., *219*
Graham-Bermann, S. A., *361, 380*
Greenberg, M., *321*
Greene, A., *223, 440, 441, 444, 445*
Greenfeld, L. A., *360, 364*
Greif, G. L., *287*
Greunewald, P. J., *152*
Greven, P. J., *4*
Griffin, W. A., *226, 234*
Griffith, J., *388, 439, 440*
Grip, J. C., *195*
Griswold, R. L., *294, 321*
Grossman, F. K., *321*
Grotpeter, J. K., *190, 191*
Grusec, J. E., *10, 185, 205*
Guidubaldi, J., *218*
Gunnoe, M. L., *220*
Gurwitt, A., *85*

H

Hadadian, A., *153*
Hagan, J., *276*
Haggerty, K., *156*
Hall, J.A., *221, 229*
Hall, M., *389*
Halle, T., *440, 441, 444, 445*
Halpern, R., *395*

Halsey, A. J., *53*
Hans, S., *395*
Hanson, K., *151*
Hanson, T., *439*
Hantrais, L., *42*
Hardesty, C., *294, 295, 299, 306*
Harmon, E. L., *187*
Harris, K. M., *11, 294, 295, 299, 300, 305, 306*
Harris, S. D., *359*
Hart, C. H., *185, 186, 187, 188, 189, 190, 191, 192, 193, 194, 197, 198, 205, 206, 207*
Hartnett, S. A., *280*
Hau, K. T., *189*
Hauser, S. T., *277*
Hawkins, A. J., *6, 21, 22, 28, 65, 68, 72, 92, 109, 111, 114, 188, 322, 336, 394*
Hayward, C., *218*
Hazel, N., *52*
Heard, H. E., *223, 294, 295, 299*
Hearn, J., *51*
Hecker, L. L., *152*
Hemphill, S. A., *191*
Henggeler, S. W., *151*
Henriques, F., *48*
Henry, C. S., *280*
Henwood, K., *51*
Hermans, H. J. M., *86*
Herrera, R. S., *24*
Hetherington, E. M., *34, 219, 226, 275, 278, 280, 391*
Ho, D. Y. F., *187, 189, 193, 205*
Hoagwood, K., *152*
Hockaday, C., *153, 154, 157*
Hofferth, S. L., *23, 294, 306, 322*
Holden, G. W., *194, 359, 360*
Hollingshead, A. B., *131*
Holtzworth-Munroe, A., *360, 362*
Hood, J. C., *98, 101, 103*
Hopes, H., *151*
Hornby, G., *111*
Hosley, C. A., *273*
Hossain, Z., *22*
Hotaling, G. T., *359, 360*
Houlihan, J., *277*
Hsu, C., *192*
Hughes, M., *4, 276*
Hult, G., *130*
Hunter, A. G., *25*
Huston, T. L., *321*
Hutchinson, S., *51, 62, 63, 65, 70, 75, 78*

Hwang, C. P., *10, 129, 130, 131, 133, 143, 145*
Hymel, S., *34*

I

Iannozzi, F., *387*
Ihinger,-Tallman, M., *85, 86*
Ishii-Kuntz, M., *143*
Isley, S. L., *192, 194, 208*
Israelashvili, R., *321*

J

Jacklin, C. N., *192*
Jacobson, A. M., *277*
Jacobson, N. S., *360*
Jaffe, P. G., *360, 361*
James, A., *42*
James, S. A., *280*
Jaret, C., *321*
Jaycox, L. H., *152*
Jenks, C., *42*
Jenni, C., *67*
Jensen, E. W., *280*
Jin, S., *186, 187, 189, 191, 192, 193, 198, 205*
John, D., *23*
Johnson, D. R., *195, 207*
Johnson, E. S., *397*
Johnson, M. P., *362*
Jones, D., *48, 49, 143*
Jones, J., *304*
Jöreskog, K., *196*
Josselson, R. J., *109, 124*
Jouriles, E. N., *359*

K

Kagan, S., *19*
Kahn, J. H., *155, 156, 162*
Kalicki, B., *40*
Kalsbeek, W. D., *447*
Kaplan, D., *196*
Keating, N. C., *3*
Keefe, S. E., *19, 20, 27*
Keith, T. Z., *219*
Kelly, J. B., *6, 225*
Kenny, D. A., 10, *192, 206*

Kenny, M. E., *277*
Killian, C., *188*
Kim, M., *188*
King, V., *218, 223, 294, 295, 299, 300*
Kingston, P. W., *145, 300*
Kisker, E., *430*
Kitson, G. C., *226*
Klaus, P. A., *360, 364*
Klawitter, M., *228*
Klitzner, M., *152*
Klotz, M. E., *223*
Knight, G. P., *19, 21, 29*
Kochanska, G., *194*
Koss, M. P., *360*
Kouneski, E. F., *64, 322, 323*
Kraemer, S., *49*
Kristall, J., *287*
Kuczynski, L., *194*
Kumpfer, K. L., *152*

L

Ladd, G. W., *186*
Lahey, B. B., *151*
Laible, D., *435*
Lamb, M. E., *4, 5, 6, 10, 12, 18, 19, 24, 34, 45, 49, 64, 72, 84, 91, 98, 111, 129, 130, 131, 132, 133, 142, 143, 144, 145, 188 , 218, 219, 225, 227, 232, 234, 273, 274, 294, 303, 321, 322, 323, 336, 390, 391, 421, 440, 443, 444, 445*
Lane, M., *277*
Langford, W., *48*
LaRossa, M. M., *63*
LaRossa, R., *63, 85, 92, 300, 321*
Larson, R. W., *277, 321*
Latshaw, J. S., *109*
Lau, S., *10, 185, 189*
Laub, J. H., *275*
Laumann-Billings, E. O., *10, 111*
Law, J. C., *158*
Leach, P., *51*
Leadbetter, B. J., *207*
Lee, S., *189*
Leiblich, A., *109, 124*
Leichtentritt, R. D., R. D., *221*
Lengua, L. J., *150, 152, 153, 154, 155*
Leslie, L. A., *143*
Letablier, M. T., *42*
Levant, R. F., *143*

AUTHOR INDEX

Levenson, R., *2*
Levine, A., *397*
Levine, J. A., *12, 34, 49, 63, 64, 84, 130, 145,*
294, 303, 322, 323, 421, 443
Levy-Shiff, R., *321*
Lew, W. J. F., *189*
Lewin Group, The, *387, 390, 392*
Lewis, C., *40, 42, 46, 47, 48, 51, 52, 55, 130*
Lewis, S. K., *227*
Leyendecker, B., 18, *19*
Li, D., *186, 189, 207, 208*
Licht, M. H., *337*
Lincoln, A. J., *359*
Lino, M. C., *223*
Lissenburgh, S., *42*
Liu, M., *186, 189, 191, 192, 193, 205, 207, 208*
Liu, P. W., *447*
Lloyd, *52*
Loeber, R., *151*
Loiselle, J. E., *143*
Lomax, R. G., *337*
Longmore, M. A., *62*
Loury, G. C., *276*
Love, J. M., *430, 435*
Lovelace, S. G., *280*
Lu, M., *189*
Lundeberg, K., *362*
Lupton, D., *61, 62*
Lussier, J. B., *321*
Lynn, S., *390*
Lytton, H., *192*

M

Maccoby, E. E., *195, 205, 206, 207, 219, 220,*
223, 224, 225, 227, 278
Mack, K., *223, 229*
MacMillian, R., *276*
Madsen, L., *207*
Madsen, W., *19*
Malphus, J., *22*
Mandleco, B. L., *109, 193, 198*
Mandler, J. M., *86*
Manning, W. D., *294*
Mansfield, E., *86*
Markon, K., *190, 191*
Marks, L. D., *109, 114*
Marks, S. R., *92, 110, 113, 120*
Markus, H., *67*
Marmer, J. K., *305, 306*

Marshall, E. S., *109, 120*
Marsiglio, W., *8, 9, 24, 42, 45, 52, 61, 62, 63,*
64, 65, 68, 69, 70, 72, 75, 78, 84, 142, 188,
218, 219, 227, 234, 273, 274, 294, 295,
299, 300, 302, 306, 321, 322, 390, 440, 445
Martin, M., *195, 196*
Martin, P., *444*
Mason, M. A., *224*
Massey, D. S., *18*
Massey, J. T., *447*
Maston, C., *360, 364*
Matheson, J., *55*
Maton, K. I., *120*
Matthews, D. J., *360*
Maurer, T. W., *85*
Mauthner, N., *48*
May, J., *123*
Maziade, M., *191*
McAdams, D., *65, 74, 75, 86, 87, 88, 109, 124*
McAllister, C. L., *435*
McBride, B. A., *12, 34, 85, 142, 143, 321*
McBride-Chang, C., *187, 193, 207*
McCarthy, P., *51*
McCloskey, L. A., *360*
McCurdy, K., *162*
McDowell, D. J., *188*
McFayden-Ketchum, S. A., *186, 194*
McGraw, L. A., *222*
McHale, S. M., *321*
McKee, L., *40, 42, 48*
McKee, T. R., *198, 205*
McLanahan, S., *11, 439*
McLoyd, V. C., *19*
McMahon, M., *72, 87, 361*
McNeal, C., *360*
McNeilly-Choque, M. K., *185, 186, 187, 188,*
190, 191, 194, 197, 198, 205, 206, 207
McPherson, A. E., *151*
McQuire. J., *42*
Mebert, C. J., *192*
Meece, D., *192*
Melisaratos, N., *160*
Menestrel, S., *440, 441, 444, 445*
Merbitz, C., *195*
Merbler, J., *153*
Meyer, D. R., *294, 321*
Meyers, D. R., *224*
Meyers, S. A., *150, 152*
Michael, M. L., *150, 154, 155*
Middleton, K. A., *362*
Miller, D. T., *227*

Miller, H., *192, 446*
Miller, J. B., *277*
Mills, G., *142, 143*
Millward, N., *42*
Ministry of Social Affairs, *40*
Minton, C., *219, 221, 224, 225, 226*
Mintz, S., *4, 294*
Mirandé, A., *20, 23, 24*
Mize, J., *192*
Mnookin, R. H., *219, 220, 223, 224, 225, 227, 278*
Modood, T., *53*
Molgaard, V., *152*
Montemayor, R., *273, 277*
Moore, K., *223, 420, 440, 441, 444, 445*
Morales, R., *20*
Morenoff, J. D., *365*
Morgan, D., *51*
Morgan, D. H., *25*
Morgan, L. W., *223*
Morgan, S. P., *143, 300, 306*
Morgan-Lopez, A., *19, 21*
Morris, A., *45, 46,*
Morris. A. S., *192, 205*
Morris, J., *195*
Morris, N., *321*
Mosher, M., *190*
Mosley, J., *306*
Moss, P., *4, 52*
Mrazek, P. J., *152*
Mulligan, G. M., *218*
Mulvey, L., *435*
Munro, B., *3*
Murray, C., *41*
Muthén, B. O., *195, 196, 198, 327*
Muthén, L. K., *196, 198, 327*

N

National Center for Children in Poverty, *390*
National Center for Health Statistics, *229*
National Center on Fathers and Families, *394*
National Survey of Families and Households, *219*
Nederhof, A. J., *194*
Nelson, D. A., *185, 186, 187, 188, 190, 191, 193, 194, 198, 205, 206, 207, 208*
Nelson, L. J., *186, 187, 190, 191, 197, 198*
Newell, L. D., *188, 189, 194*
Newson, E., *47, 48, 130*

Newson, J., *47, 48, 130*
Nix, R. L., *194*
Noam, G. G., *277*
Nock, S. L., *145, 300*
Noller, P., *277*
Nord, C. W., *226, 306*
Nurius, P., *67*
Nurse, A., *74*

O

O'Brien, K. M., *190, 191*
O'Brien, M., *8, 9, 39, 40, 42, 45, 48, 49, 52, 143*
O'Brien, R. M., *195*
O'Connell, E., *221, 222, 224, 226, 228*
O'Connor, T., *49*
O'Connor, T. G., *275, 280*
O'Neil, R., *192, 194, 208*
Oberklaid, F., *191*
Olsen, S. F., 10, *89, 185, 186, 187, 187, 188, 189, 190, 191, 193, 194, 197, 198, 205, 206, 207*
Olson, D., *277*
Olson, D. H., *92*
Olson, M. M., *109, 111, 112, 114, 118, 120, 124*
Olsson, U., *196*
Ong, P. M., *20*
Ortiz, D. R., *21*
Osburn, A., *45, 46*
Osofsky, J. D., *379*
Otto, L. B., *278*
Owen, C., *43*
Oyserman, D., *67*

P

Padilla, A. M., *20, 25*
Palkovitz, R., *21, 43, 64, 72, 91, 109, 188, 218, 219, 226, 274, 322, 336, 421, 444*
Palm, G., *109*
Palmer, G., *192*
Papcosta, A., *51*
Pargament, K. I., *120*
Parke, R., *294, 302*
Parke, R. D., *8, 23, 24, 28, 34, 49, 92, 131, 143, 188, 192, 194, 208, 321, 336, 391, 392*
Partridge, C. R., *158*
Pasley, K., *11, 85, 217, 219, 221, 224, 225, 226, 234*
Paterson, G., *206*

AUTHOR INDEX

461

Patterson, G. R., *28, 191, 194*
Paulsell, D., *430*
Pence, E., *361*
Perez, S., *20*
Perkins, C., *360, 364*
Perry, J., *218*
Perry-Jenkins, M., *321, 397*
Peshkin, A., *166*
Peters, E., *440, 445*
Peters, H., *439*
Peters, H. E., *7, 24, 42, 44, 219*
Peterson, A., *67*
Peterson, J. L., *226*
Peterson, R. R., *143*
Pettit, G. S., *186, 192, 194*
Phares, V., *150, 151, 277, 359*
Pickens, J., *22*
Pickford, R., *51*
Pirog, M. A., *223*
Pitt, E., *322, 387*
Pittinsky, J. J., *35, 63*
Pleck, E. H., *2, 129*
Pleck, J. H., *2, 8, 9, 12, 47, 49, 64, 67, 68, 69, 83, 85, 87, 96, 101, 129, 130, 131, 142, 143, 144, 145, 226, 274, 294, 303, 306, 322, 323, 333, 336, 394, 421, 443*
Plomin, R., *34, 192, 198, 391*
Polkinghorne, D. E., *124*
Pollack, W. S., *321*
Pollock, S., *41, 51*
Popenoe, D., *4, 110*
Porter, C. L., *185, 186, 187, 189, 192, 193, 198, 205*
Power, T. G., *34*
Powers, S., *277*
Presser, H. B., *145*
Pringle, K., *52*
Prior, M., *191*
Prout, A., *42*

Q

Quinlan, D. M., *207*
Quinton, D., *41, 51*

R

Radin, N., *130, 142, 294*
Radke-Yarrow, M., *194*

Rah, Y., *188*
Raikes, H., *435*
Rand, M. R., *360, 364*
Rane, T. R., *85, 321*
Ranged, N., *439*
Ranjit, H., *44*
Ray, A., *386, 395*
Redmond, C., *152, 153, 154, 155, 156, 157, 162, 218*
Reid, J. B., *191*
Reilly, J., *446*
Reise, S. P., *29*
Reiss, D., *34, 391*
Reissman, C. K., *61, 62, 109*
Reitzes, D. C., *85, 92*
Rendall, M. S., *44, 439*
Renk, K., *277*
Rennison, C. M., *360*
Repetti, R. L., *397*
Rethemeyer, R. K., *387*
Rettig, K. D., *221*
Rhine, E. E., *158*
Richards, M., *43, 277*
Rigdon, E. E., *196*
Rigsby, D., *361*
Ritchie, K. L., *194, 359*
Rivera, F., *218, 219*
Roberts, C., *40*
Robinson, C. C., *185, 186, 187, 188, 189, 190, 191, 192, 193, 194, 197, 198, 205, 206, 207*
Rodriguez, M. D., *19, 21*
Rohrer, V., *227*
Rommel, J. I., *110*
Romney, D. M., *192*
Roopnarine, J. L., *143, 189*
Roosa, M. W., *29, 150, 154, 155*
Roschelle, A., *20*
Rosen, K. H., *362*
Rosenberg, H. J., *87*
Rosenberg, S. D., *87*
Ross, C. M., *430*
Ross, J. M., *85*
Ross, M., *227*
Rothbart, M., *191, 192, 193, 206*
Rothbaum, F., *195, 206*
Rubin, R., *85*
Rushe, R. H., *360*
Russell, A., *188, 190, 191, 192, 194, 206*
Russell, G., *130*
Ruxton, S., *41*

Ryan, M., *52*
Ryan, S., *11*

S

Saebel, J., *192*
Saenz, D. S., *19, 21*
Salazar, D., *20*
Sampson, R. J., *275, 365*
Sandberg, J. F., *23*
Sandelowski, M., *62*
Sandler, I. N., *219*
Sanson, A., *191, 192, 193, 206*
Sarbin, T. R., *109, 124*
Saris, W. E., *195, 196*
Satorra, A., *196*
Saunders, D., *359*
Sawin, D. B., *321*
Sayers, J., *379*
Schaeffer, N. C., *228*
Schmidt, J., *234*
Schochet, P., *430*
Schumacker, R. E., *337*
Schupak-Neuberg, E., *150, 154, 155*
Schutz, A., *71*
Schwalbe, M. L., *62, 76, 77*
Schwartz, D., *186, 193, 207*
Segal, L., *51*
Seidel, J., *89*
Seidler, V., *51*
Seltzer, J. A., *228, 276, 294, 300, 301*
Servis, L. J., *321*
Sessa, F. M., *192, 205*
Shaw, C., *52*
Sheeber, L., *151*
Shelton, B. A., *23*
Shemilt, I., *42, 45*
Sheridan, S., *158*
Shin, C., *153, 154, 155, 156, 157, 162*
Shock, A., *10, 149*
Short, S., *47*
Shortt, J. W., *360*
Sicoly, F., *227*
Siegel, P., *444*
Silk, J. S., *192, 205*
Silverstein, L., *2, 25, 359, 361*
Simeonsson, R. J., *119*
Simpkins, S. D., *188*
Simpson, B., *51*
Sirolli, A., *19, 21*

Skinner, C., *40*
Skinner, M. L., *234*
Slattery, S. C., *143*
Slaughter, C., *48*
Slife, B. D., *111*
Small, S. A., *91*
Smart, D., *191*
Smith, E., *45*
Smith, H. L., *143*
Smith, J. R., *219*
Smollar, J., *277*
Snarey, J., *65, 321*
Snijders, T. A. B., *195*
Snyder, A. R., *294*
Snyder, J. R., *192*
Soldano, K. W., *72, 152*
Solomon, Y., *48*
Sonenstein, F. L., *96, 228*
Sorenson, E., *397, 444*
Speak, S., *41*
Spoth, R. L., *152, 153, 154, 155, 156, 157, 162*
Stafford, F., *323*
Staines, G., *145*
Stanley-Hagan, M., *219, 226*
Stanton, L. M., *221*
Steele, H., *49*
Steele, M., *49*
Stein, A., *51*
Stein, J. D., *359*
Steinberg, L., *192, 205, 395*
Stern, P. N., *163*
Sternberg, K. J., *232, 359, 361*
Steuve, J. L., *8, 47, 67, 68, 69, 83, 87, 144, 323*
Stevens, S. S., *195*
Stevenson, H. W., *189*
Steward, R. R., *145*
Stewart, S. D., *224*
Stimson, C., *40*
Stith, S. M., *362*
Stolz, H., *207*
Stolz, L. M., *5*
Stone, G., *6*
Stoneman, Z., *153*
Stouthamer-Loeber, M., *151*
Straus, M., *359*
Strauss, A., *65, 67, 75, 125, 162, 163, 165, 166*
Stryker, S., *85, 96*
Stuart, G. L., *360, 362*
Sue, S., *189*
Sugarman, D. B., *360*
Summerfield, C., *55*

AUTHOR INDEX

Summers, J., *435*
Swain, S. O., *96*
Sweet, J. A., *229, 362*
Sylva, K., *51*
Szinovacz, M. E., *232, 362*

T

Tait, C. M., *152*
Takeuchi, D., *19*
Tamis-LeMonda, C. S., *151, 163, 294, 321,
    322, 336, 419, 441, 443, 444*
Teachman, J. D., *218*
Teng, G., *196*
Thivierge, J., *191*
Thomas, A., *192*
Thomas, N. G., *321*
Thompson, B., *337*
Thomson, E., *306*
Thornton, *275*
Tiedje, L. B., *321*
Tift, N., *387*
Tinsley, B. R., *34*
Tompson, M. C., *152*
Toth, J. F., Jr., *23*
Triandis, H. C., *208*
Trinder, L., *51*
Tseng, V., *185, 189*
Tulananda, O., *143*
Tully, J. C., *85*
Turbiville, V. P., *111, 120*
Turner, C., *446*
Turner, M., *397*

U

U. S. Census Bureau, *18, 20, 21, 217, 224*
Udry, J. R., *223, 304*

V

Vadasy, P. F., *119, 122*
Valdez, E., *20, 23, 24*
Valencia, R. R., *20*
Valle, C., *22*
van den Hoonard, W. C., *62, 69*
van Kammen, W., *435*
VanWyk, J., *365*

Vega, W. A., *19, 20, 21*
Vélez-Ibáñez, C., *19*
Venohr, J. C., *223*
Verropoulou, G., *44, 439*
Vidal, C., *28*
Virdee, S., *53*
Virdin, L. M., *29*
Vogel, C., *430*
Volling, B. L., *322*

W

Waite, L. J., *131*
Wale, C., *43*
Walker, A. J., *222*
Walker, J., *51*
Walzer, S., *62, 72*
Wang, L., *186, 191, 192, 193, 205, 206, 207*
Warchol, G., *360, 364*
Ward, T., *156*
Warin, J., *48, 49, 51*
Warshak, R. A., *228*
Wasserman, D., *158*
Webb-Mitchell, B., *109, 120, 124*
Weisman, S. H., *92*
Weiss-Perry, B., *277*
Weisz, J. R., *195, 206*
Welchans, S., *360*
Weller, R. A., *151*
Wells, B., *18, 19, 20*
Wells, E. A., *120*
Wenk, D., *294, 295, 299, 306*
Werner, N. E., *190, 191*
Weschler, L. F, *150, 154, 155*
West, J., *306*
Wetherell, M., *51*
Wheaton, B., *276*
White, M. B., *109, 111, 114*
Widaman, K. F., *29*
Wilcox, B., *435*
Wild, M., *188*
Williams, J., *40, 234*
Williams, N., *20*
Williams, R. G., *223*
Wilmott, P., *48, 49*
Wilson, L., *19*
Wilson, R. J., *321*
Wilson, T. P., *195*
Wilson, W. J., *365*
Wo, J., *186, 187, 189, 191, 198, 205*

Wolchik, S. A., *219, 222, 225, 227*
Wolkomir, M., *62, 76, 77*
Woodin, E., *2*
Woodworth, S. J., *322*
Wozniak, P., *188*
Wright, B. D., *195*
Wu, H., *186, 187, 189, 205, 206, 207*
Wu, P., *186, 187, 189, 190, 191, 193, 198, 205*

X

Xu, X., *23*

Y

Yang, C., *10, 11, 189, 185, 186, 187, 190, 191, 192, 193, 198, 205*
Yarchek, C., *158*

Ye, R., *192*
Yeatts, D. E., *145*
Yeung, P. P. W., *10, 23, 34, 185, 189*
Yeung, W. J., *323*
Young, D. M., *143*
Young, M., *48*
Youniss, J., *277*

Z

Zao, K., *192*
Zavella, P., *20*
Zeng, Q., *189, 192, 193, 198, 205*
Zhang, Y., *192*
Zhou, H., *186, 192, 205, 206*
Zill, N., *226*
Zinn, M. B., *18, 19, 20*
Zottarelli, L. K., *145*
Zvetina, D., *219*

Subject Index

A

Abusive fathers, *13, 359–382*
Accessibility, *130, 137, 138, 143, 217, 302*
  divorce and, *220, 226*
Adolescence
  aggression during, *10*
  alcohol use during, *154*
  depression during, *152*
  disruptive behaviors during, *152*
  drug use during, *154*
  father involvement during, *48–49, 273, 277,*
    296–300
  offenders programs, *158*
  perception of family life and, *11, 48*
  perception of fathers, *274*
  problematic functioning during, *151*
  substance abuse during, *152, 154*
  well-being during, *150, 274*
Adolescents Surviving and Thriving Program,
  158
Adoption, *5*
Adoptive fathers, *298–299*
African Americans. *See* Black
Afro-Caribbean fathers, *53*
Age
  father's and of child, *306*
  father involvement and child's, *273*
  father involvement and, father's, *263*
American fathers, comparison of, *130*
Australian fathers, *130*
Availability, *130, 222*
Asian families, *9, 10, 53, 185–208,*
  306
Attachment theory, *33*

B

Batters, *360*
Biological-familial issues, *11, 284, 287*
Biological fathers
  age of, *306*
  in American families, *287*
  non-, *295*
  parenting by, *284, 287*
  residential, *293, 307*
  versus stepfather involvement, *295, 312*
Black (African American)
  Families, *241, 324*
  Fathers
    age of fathers coresident with children, 306
    family demography, 306
    fathers not coresident with children, 307
    monitoring children, *23, 278, 284*
  Statistics about, *241, 306*
Boundaries in families,
  divorce and, *221*
Brief Symptom Inventory (BSI), *160*
Britain,
  family researchers in, *39*
British Cohort Study, 45
British Household Panel Study (BHPS), *44*

C

Caribbean families, *9*
Child Support legislation, *40, 223*
Child,
  aggression, *360*
  centered activities, *329*
  competence, *188*

Child (*Continued*)
  custody support, *223*
  poverty, *41*
  temperament, *192*
    measurement of, *198*
Child Development Supplement of the Panel
    Study of Income Dynamics (PSID), *324,*
    345, 334–335
Child care, 42, 45, *129*
  divorce and, *220*
  father and, *133, 361, 393*
  measurement of, *133*
  types of in father involvement, *142*
Children,
  abandonment, *6*
  academic achievement, *395*
  age of father and age of, *329*
  aggression in, *186, 192*
    measures of, *197, 200*
  characteristics of, *244–245*
  Chinese, *185,*
    physical force and use of coercion among,
      187, 201
  coercive control of, *186, 201*
  conflict of parents on, *221–222, 245, 360–361*
  consequences of visitation, custody, and child
    support on, *223*
  control of, *189*
  cooperation in Latino families of, *19*
    measurement of, *200*
  custody support and, *223*
  daily care of, *341–342*
  developmental appropriateness of activities
    with, *226–227*
  disabled, *110, 112, 153–154,*
  divorce statistics and, *217*
  gender of children outcomes, *330, 343*
  internal control, influences upon, *186*
  Mexican American families,
    academic success, *21*
    delinquency, *21*
    depression rates, *21*
    problem behavior, *21*
    suicide rates, *21*
  monitoring of, *23, 278, 284, 329*
  negative emotionality in, *200–204*
  perception of father involvement, *30–31*
  psychological control and, *187*
  psychological well-being, *5*
  ratio of father to mother time, *23, 312, 341,*
    344, 355

Russian, *187, 191*
sex-role development, *5*
social competence, *395*
special needs, *109*
unmarried birth of, *241*
violence and, *361, 378–380*
with coresident father, *307*
Child and Adolescent Services Assessment
  (CASA), *160*
Childhood aggression, *186, 192*
Chinese families, *10, 185–208*
Circumplex Model of Marital and Family
  Systems, 93
Compadrazgo, *20*
Commitment, *110*
Crime and Disorder Bill, *41*
Cuban American families, *8*
Cultural variations, *389*
Custody,
  joint, *220*
  legal, *220*
  payments, *223*
  physical, *220*

D

Dads,
  bad, *359*
  deadbeat, *42*
  deadbroke, *42*
Data analysis
  across measures comparability, *13,*
  longitudinal data sets, *7*
  qualitative data gathering, *22* Data
    management, *29*
Deficit perspective, *6, 43, 111–112, 217, 224*
Developing a Dads Survey (DADS), *13, 418*
Depression, *6*
Demographics,
  family programming and family, *154*
  low income family, *154*
Discourse theory, *51*
Divorce
  and boundaries in families, *221*
  changes in family structure and, *220, 222,*
    307, 322
  child custody support, *223*
  child well-being, *6, 273*
  economic distress and, *6, 222*
  father identity and, *51, 243, 257*

SUBJECT INDEX 467

father involvement following, *225*
mobility, *222*
mothers and, *222*
proximity, *222*
rates, *2*, *217*
relocation, *222*
staffing problem and, *6*
Doing fathering, *9*, *68*
Dual earner households, *45*

E

Early Childhood Longitudinal Study-Birth
  Cohort (ECLS-B), *13*, *294*, *418*
Early Childhood Longitudinal Study,
  Kindergarten Class of 1998–99, *294*
Early Head Start National Research and
  Evaluation Project Father Studies
  (EHS), *13*, *151*, *418*
Economic(s), *2*
  Black families and, *241*
  British families and, *41*
  divorce and, *222*
  Latino families and, *20–21*, *241*
  low income families and, *154*, *241*
  Mexican American families and, *21*
  status, *242–243*, *307*
  stress and, *23*
Ecological model, *64*
Emotional distress, *6*
Epistemological considerations, *61*
Ericksonian theory or perspective, *85*
Essex Economic and Social Research Council
  (ESRC), *46*
European American fathers,
  time spent monitoring, *23*
European Union Working Time Directive 2000,
  42

F

Familism
  definition of, *19*
  Latino families and, *18–20*
Family Assessment Device, *160*
Family,
  boundaries, *221*
  capital, *110*
  diversity of forms, *296–297*

participation in program, *167*, *176*
processes, *275–276*, *300–302*, *315*
routines, *221*, *280*
services, *165–167*
size, *334*
structure, *167*, *217*, *220*, *222*, *245*, *296–297*,
  307
support to father, *51*
type, *281*
violence, *359–361*, *378–381*
Family systems theory, *21*, *50*
  boundaries, *221*
Father(s)
  absence, *387*, *389*
  absence of, *5*, *6*, *40*
  abuse by, *13*, *52*
  adolescence view of, *274–280*
  adoptive, *5*
  agency in, *75*
  attachment of children to, *5*
  authoritarian, *22*
  authority figures, as, *189*
  availability, *130*
  behavior and identity linked in, *85*, *95*, *243*,
    257
  characteristics and program participation,
    154, *162*, *176*
  character self-portrayals of, *65*, *73–74*
  child care by, *42*, *45*, *129*, *133*, *142*, *343–344*
  child visions, *65*, *72*
  Chinese, *187*
  coercion, use of by, *201*
  communion, *75*
  comparative appraisals of, *66*, *74*
  competence, *154*
  confidence, *12*
  consciousness, *66*
  construction of what it means to be a, *62*
  crime and, *41*
  defining, *21*, *388*
  developmental appropriateness and, *226*
  disengaged, *42*, *63*, *217*, *226*
  divorce and, *217*
    mobility, *222*
    motives of divorced, *219*
    proximity, *222*
    relocation, *222*
  economic provisioning by, *5*, *49*, *222*, *262*,
    393
  egalitarian attitudes and, *48*
  employment and, *46*, *257*

Father(s) (*Continued*)
  engagement, *385*
  family services and, *51*
  gatekeepers and, *22, 47, 221, 243*
  health of, *252, 393, 396*
  homeless, *51*
  identity of, *51, 63, 83–84, 257*
  ideological orientation of, *51, 74*
  imagoes, *62, 86*
  incarcerated, *51, 76*
  infants and. *See* Father-infant attachments
  influence on adolescent problem behavior, *151*
  life course trajectory and, *65*
  low-income, *385*
  masculine self and, *77*
  meaning of being a, *42, 62, 115*
  military, *52*
  motivation to become a, *12, 331*
    measurement of, *325*
  mother and father conjointness, *95, 386*
  moral and ethical guidance, *64, 274*
  non-custodial, *385*
  non-residential, *40, 44, 171, 289, 293, 307*
  participation in programming, *149–178, 153,*
    162, 167, 176, 398
  play, *12, 50, 98*
  power issues when, *3*
  procreative beings, as, *63–72*
  protectors, *274*
  providers, provisioning or breadwinning and,
    29, 49, 64, 88, 98, 222–223, 242, 262,
    274, 341, 393, 397
  readiness to be a, *66, 71–72, 75*
  religion and, *109, 243, 252*
  residential, *168, 307*
  residential biological father, *305, 307*
  residential non-biological father, *305, 307*
  role definition of, *48*
  role identity, *84, 85, 389*
    importance or intensity of, *85*
    salience or commitment, *85, 243, 257*
  role-inadequacy perspective and, *111*
  role performance and, *6, 48, 243*
  roles of, *4, 48, 50*
  self-narratives of, *75–76*
  single, *168*
  special needs and, *111*
  step-, *64, 68, 293, 310*
  stepfathers who invest in teens, *299–300, 312*
  surrogate, *298–299, 304, 312*
  themes of, *62, 86*

  transformation of, *48*
  transition to becoming, *63, 342*
  turning points for, *66, 74–75*
  unemployed, *243*
  unwed, *242*
  urban vs. rural, *153*
  vision of, *66*
  visitation of mother in hospital, *260*
  vulnerable, *41, 241–246*
  work hours of, *41, 130*
  work-life balance and, *42, 45, 130*
Father figures,
  conflict over father role, *221*
Fathers Direct, *41*
Father involvement,
  accessibility, *64, 130, 138, 143, 217, 302*
    divorce and, *220, 226*
  adolescent well-being, and, *152, 273–290,*
    277–278
  antecedents of, *322*
  availability, *64, 130*
  barriers to, *152*
  children's gender and, *244–245, 343*
  children's mental health problems, and, *153*
  Chinese families, in, *187–188*
  cohabitation and, *51, 245, 250*
  commitment and, *110*
  competence and, *323*
  composite assessment of, *137*
  correlates of, *140–142, 145*
  daily caring by, *342–344, 348*
  determinants of, *23*
  disengagement of, *63–65, 217, 226*
  divorce and, *217, 225*
  effects on teen development, *41*
  engagement in, *64, 130, 217, 302, 385–388*
  factors that affect, *242*
  family-based programming and, *150, 398*
  family income and, *23*
  family structure and, *245, 307*
  gender role division and, *23*
  institutional factors and, *323*
  Latino families and, *23*
  levels of, *250–251*
  marital relationships and, *23, 245*
  measurement of, *49, 246, 278, 302, 305, 325,*
    344, 348, 363, 387
  mother template and, *42, 111, 151, 386*
  motivation for, *323, 325, 331*
  motives that influence, *219*
  play, *50, 98*

SUBJECT INDEX   469

presence of men and, *49, 393*
provisioning or breadwinning and, *49, 64, 88,*
    98, 222–223, 242, 262, 393
public policy and, *387*
quality of, *293*
quantity of, *293, 390*
responsibility, *64, 130, 137, 143, 302*
role perception about, *152, 330–333*
skills and self-confidence and, *323, 327, 331*
social support and stresses and, *323, 327,*
    331–332
stability of, *130, 138*
time and, *349–351, 355, 366*
transcendent bonds, *116*
work hours and, *41, 45, 130*
Fathering,
as facilitated by mothers, *47*
competence, *154*
conceptualization of, *322*
disabled children and, 110, *112, 153–154*
ideals, *66*
indicators, *385–414, 393*
functional, *110*
monitoring children as, *23, 275, 284, 329*
    accessibility, *64, 130, 138, 143, 217, 302*
    divorce and, *220, 226*
    coparental, *62, 66, 83*
    engagement, *64, 130, 217*
    father-child, *62, 66*
    kinds or types of, *50*
    responsibility, *64, 129, 137, 143, 302*
    self-as-father, *62, 65, 66–67, 92*
    solo parent, *83*
motives and, *219*
practitioners, *400–401*
psychological control and, *191*
responsible, *114, 129, 137, 143*
seeking intimacy and, *75*
time spent in, *22, 130, 344, 366*
visions, *73*
violence and, *341–344, 366*
Fathering Indicators Framework (FIF), *13, 386,*
    392
Fathering research,
conceptualization, *322*
demography and, *44*
mixed methods, *48, 149*
mother-focus and, *42*
self-narratives in, *75, 83–90, 109–119*
Fatherhood,
commitment, *50, 67, 83*

conceptualizing, *4,5*
deficit perspective of, *6, 43, 217, 224*
defining, *49*
definitions, *2, 21*
dimensions of,
    emotional quality, *30–31*
    investment, *30–31*
    responsiveness, *30–31*
essential, *2*
feminism and, *43*
holistic nature of, *43*
image of, *48, 65*
meaning of, *2, 29, 42, 48, 115*
political views of, *40–42*
self-identities within, *86*
self-meanings of, *86, 115*
work and, *49, 90, 130*
Fatherwork, *21, 114*
Federal Interagency Forum on Child and Family
    Statistics, 23, 219, 418
Feminism, *43*
Fragile Families and Child Wellbeing Study, 7,
    11, 151, 418, 420

G

Gatekeepers, *22, 47, 92, 221, 243, 298*
Gender
child gender and father involvement,
    244–245, 343
contexts that promote father distance, *217*
differences in child and view of parents, *286*
differences in parental identity conjointness,
    102, 286
division in child care and, *47, 133*
egalitarian attitudes and, *48*
equity and, *42, 45, 224*
equity during divorce and, *224*
socially scripted patterns of parenting and, *50*
Generative growth, *117*
Generative ingenuity, *118*
Generativity script, *86*
Generativity, theory of, *65, 86, 114*
Growing up FAST(GFAST), *158–159, 163*

H

Head Start, *385*
Hispanic
families, *241*

Historical changes
economics, *2–3, 222*
family structure, *322*
Home Office, *41*

I

Identity theory, *51, 83*
behavior and identity salience linked to, *85, 95*
commitment and, *85*
imagoes, *63, 86*
parent identity in, *92, 95, 257*
role identity and, *83–86, 152*
role salience and, *85, 92*
self-meaning and, *85, 92, 115*
Imagoes, *62,86*
Income,
and father involvement, *23*
differences in male-female, *23*
Incarceration, *6, 51, 76, 158*
Intervention programs, *10, 13, 149–178, 154, 398–400*
experimental, *34*
Immigrant status and Latino families, *18*

J

Juvenile offenders programs, *158*

L

Labor government, *39, 40*
Latino families, *8, 17–38,*
authoritarian, *22, 26*
cooperation with others in, *19*
deferential relationships in, *26*
demographics Latino of ethnic group, *17–18, 306*
economic status of, *20–21, 222–223*
Euro-centric measurement bias, *24*
extended kinship network, *20*
family support of, *19*
fathers
as providers in, *26, 222–223, 242*
familism, *18*
family ritual, 20
monitoring children, *23*
immigrant status of, *18*

machismo (manliness), *19*
obligation to, *20*
parenting, *25*
qualitative data gathering, *22, 162*
religion in, *26*
sex difference emphasis in, *19*
unique assessment of, *18*
Latter-day Saint fathers, *109, 113*
Life course,
changes in, *51, 64–65*
diversity, *294–295*
trajectory and the, *65, 67–70*
transitions, *158, 342*

M

Maternal,
employment, 103, *129, 257, 341*
support during pregnancy, *257*
Mexican American families *See also*, Latino
families, *17–38*
economics, *21*
family themes in, *25–26*
parents in, *25*
religion in, *26*
Measures, general,
Brief Symptom Inventory (BSI), *160*
coordinating measures of father involvement, *420, 422–446*
Family Assessment Device(FAD), *160*
Longitudinal surveys and of father
involvement, *294*
*The Child and Adolescent Services
Assessment* (CASA), *160*
Measures (measuring),
adolescent who live with bio and non-bio
fathers, *297–299*
affective domain, *219*
biased reporting when developing, *227*
biases in, *391*
binary approach to, *5, 217*
children's aggression, of, *197*
clock-time vs. process time used in, *47, 341*
closeness, *306*
coding and, *30–31*
cognitive domain, *218*
composite assessment of father involvement, *137*
continuous vs. categorical data, *195–196*
demographic factors, *325*

SUBJECT INDEX

divorced fathers and, *219, 221, 224*
divorce, during/after, *218, 231*
domain experiences when, *83*
Euro-centric bias in, *24*
experimental studies in, *34*
family structure, *304, 307*
father characteristics, *246*
fatherhood and, *4*
fathering definitions and, *388*
father involvement, *294, 325, 344, 424*
   coordinated across several studies, *422–446*
focus groups in, *25*
identity theory when assessing, *83–86*
institutional factors, *325*
interdisciplinary approaches to, *34*
intimate violence, *363*
item response theory (IRT) in, *29*
marker experiences in, *83*
missing data in, *44*
motivation, *325, 331*
multi-ethnic populations in, *53,131, 193, 306*
multiple self-trajectories over time used in, *69*
multi-stage sampling in, *34*
non-residential father, *305, 307*
objective data when, *228*
parent-adolescent relationship, *305–306*
Parental Responsibility Questionnaire (PRQ), *132, 139*
Parenting Narrative Interview (PIN), use of in, *83, 90–91*
parents behavior and, *90*
parents relationship, *249*
parent identity conjointness, *96, 102*
parenting voice coding, *93, 95*
paternal involvement, *132, 244–245 273–275*
perceived shared caregiving, *346, 347, 389*
play-companionship scale, *90*
positive outcomes and, *387*
problems with, *219*
proximity, *222*
proxy-subjects approaches and, *194*
quantity vs. quality, *303, 390*
referent clarity and, *221*
reporting accuracy, *227*
residential father, *305, 307*
scalar equivalence in, *29*
self-report approaches and, *194*
skills and self-confidence, *325, 327*
social-contextual, of, *246*
social supports and stresses, *325, 327*
teen view of parents, *280*

time-diary studies used in, *47, 130, 134–136, 341*
Men's roles
   adolescent problem behavior and, *152*
   household division of labor and, *43, 45*
   performance, 11
   shifting economics, *2, 222–223*
   transition of, *48*
Mental health problems, *153*
Methods
   inductive, *62, 90*
      longitudinal analysis, *130, 131–132, 278*
   large scale studies, *11, 13, 273–290, 278–281, 293–317, 294, 362, 417*
   limitations of, *157*
   mixed, *48, 50*
   multi-, *149, 390*
   narrative approach, *9–10, 30–33, 83–90, 111–112*
   non-participation issues and, *164, 167, 176*
   open-ended interview questions, *62*
   parenting strategies, *310*
   parenting voice measures, *93*
   privacy issues in research, *153*
   qualitative, *9–10, 22, 29, 61–66, 83–88, 162*
      reliability of, *31, 109–124, 153*
   quantitative, *150, 362, 390*
   recruitment issues, *26, 152*
   retention, *28*
   sample issues and, *157, 186, 229*
      college students as respondents, *229*
   self-narratives, *75–76*
   small-scale study, *10, 159, 186–200*
   strategies and, *159*
   survey, *131*
   time diary, *47, 130, 134, 136, 347*
Millennium Cohort Study, 46, 52
Multiethnic populations, *53, 306*
Multinational Time-Use Study (MTUS) *45*
Mormon father, *109*
Mother(hood)
   biological, *300*
   centered research, *43, 68, 111, 386*
   childcare by, *45, 300*
   coercion used by, *200–206*
   cooperation between stepfathers and, *312*
   divorce and, *222*
   employment, *103, 129, 341*

Mother(hood) (*Continued*)
fathers visiting in hospital, *260*
gatekeepers and, *47, 68, 92, 221, 243, 298*
identity theory and, *85*
images of self, *87*
labor force participation of, *43*
moral transformation or reform, *87*
mother blaming for adolescent problems, *151*
parental identity conjointness, *103–104*
relationship to fathers, *298, 353*
single, *300*
teens and, *49*
template and father research, *42, 45, 51, 68, 151*
we-voice of, *101, 103*
Muslim families, *9, 53*

N

Narrative analysis, *61–63, 75–76, 86–88, 109–125, 163*
development of, *888–89*
life story as, *86*
nuclear episodes, *62, 86, 88*
parents in, *92*
paternal identity and, *86–88, 92–93*
problems with, *77, 111*
program participation, *163, 167, 176*
progressive, *76*
reflexive reconstruction, *86*
regressive, *76*
special needs children and, *109–124*
stability of, *76*
types of in father's stories, *87*
National Center on Fathers and Families (NCOFF), 386, 392
Child and Family Well-being Network, 275, 294
Early Child Care Research Network, 51, 294
National Evaluation of Sure Start, 52
National Family Violence Survey, 359
National Family and Parenting Institute (NFPI), *41*
National Institute of Child Health and Development
National Longitudinal Study of Adolescent Health (Add Health), *11, 293–317, 294*
National Longitudinal Survey of Youth-1979 (NLSY-79), *7*

National Longitudinal Survey of Youth-1997 (NLSY-97), *11, 273–290, 278–281, 420*
National Study of Health and Development (NSHD), *44*
National Survey of Adolescent Males, 323
National Survey of Children (NSC), 294
National Survey of Family Growth (NSG), 420
National Survey of Families and Households (NSFH), *13, 294, 362*
Nuturing Fatherhood, 24, 418, 420

O

Office of National Statistics (ONS), *46*

P

Panel Study of Income Dynamics (PSID), *7, 12, 294, 324, 334–335, 345*
Parent(s),
alliance, *92*
attachment, *5*
behavior, measures of, *90*
cohabiting, *51, 250*
competence, *154*
conflict, *6, 221, 264*
deprivation, *6*
involvement, *45, 275*
monitoring, *11, 278, 284, 329*
narrative, *92*
roles, *322*
shared caregiving, *12, 25, 343–345, 389, 393*
teen view of, *279*
unmarried, *241*
Parenthood, *342*
transition to, *342–343*
Parental Leave directive or policies, *41, 145*
Parental identity, *83–84*
conjointness in, *83, 95, 102, 301*
fathers and, *85*
Parental Responsibility Questionnaire (PRQ), *132, 139, 143–144*
Parenting,
child competence, and, *188*
coercive, *10, 185*

SUBJECT INDEX

defining, *186*
physical force and use of coercion,
186–187, 201
control of children and, *189*
cooperative, *301, 393, 395*
divorce and coparenting or, *217*
hostile, *192*
involvement, *300*
joint strategies, *301, 307*
psychological control and, *191, 196*
self-appraisal of, *85*
skills programs, *155*
socially scripted patterns of, *50*
strategies, *293, 300–301, 307, 372*
violence and, *372–373, 368–381*
styles, measurement of, *198*
time spent, *353*
violence, *361, 366, 378–381*
voice, *83, 91*
Parenting Narrative Interview (PIN), *83, 89,
90–91*
Partner(s),
identity conjointness, *92, 96*
parenting, *91*
multiple, *68*
support, *64*
violence, *359–360*
Paternal
competence, *154*
consciousness, *65, 70–71*
involvement in family-based programming,
150–151, 154
involvement over time, *130, 341*
pathology, *110*
support, *274*
Perceived shared caregiving, *345–346, 389,
393*
Play-companionship scale, *90*
Poverty, *41*
Power,
resources and, *3, 23*
Procreative being, *63, 66*
Program development issues, *398–400*
Public policy, *8, 387*
Psychoanalytic theory, *9, 84*

Q

Qualitative data
fatherhood information using, *52*

gathering and analyzing, *22*
grounded theory, *61, 163*
in-depth interviewing and story telling to
obtain, *61, 86*
life story narrative as, *86*
mixed methods research and, *48*
multiple meaning of, *22*
program participation and, *162, 167, 176*
reflexive reconstruction, *87*

R

Race, *286, 306, 360, 389*
Religion
faith in, *109, 120*
in family life, *26, 53, 109, 243, 252*
Russian children, *181, 191*

S

Self-as-father, *9*
Self-meaning, *9, 115*
Sensitizing concepts, *69*
Shared caregiving, *344–345, 389, 393*
Social Capital, *64, 274, 275–276*
Social learning theory, *190*
Social Support, *12, 327*
Strength in families, *119*
*Study of Marital Instability over the Life Course,
360*
Sweden, *40*
Swedish families, *130, 131*
Symbolic interaction theory, *9, 22, 62, 85,
92*

T

Theory,
attachment, *33, 50*
discourse, *51*
Ericksonian, *85*
family systems, *21–22, 50*
generativity, *65, 114*
identity, *51, 83, 243*
psychoanalytical, *5, 50, 84*
social capital, *64, 274, 275–276*
social learning, *190*
symbolic interaction, *9, 22, 62, 85, 92*

Time-use data collection, *9, 22, 341*
  comparison of Latino, African American,
    Euro American, *22*
  Latino father, *22*
Transcendent bonds, *116*

U

United Kingdom (research about men and
    families), *8*
  public policy in, *40–42*
Unmarried birth of children, *241*
Unique contributions of fathers, *119*

V

Violence, *12–13, 359–361, 378–381*

W

War, *2*
We vs. I voice, *83–84, 94–95, 101,
    102–105*
Women's roles
  shifting economics, *2*
Work place practices, *12, 130–131*